Productive Management of Leisure Service Organizations

PRODUCTIVE MANAGEMENT OF LEISURE SERVICE ORGANIZATIONS:
A Behavioral Approach

Christopher R. Edginton

North Texas State University
Denton, Texas

John G. Williams

City of Sunnyvale
Sunnyvale, California

JOHN WILEY & SONS

New York • Chichester • Brisbane • Toronto • Singapore

Library of Congress Cataloging in Publication Data:

Edginton, Christopher R.
    Productive management of leisure service organizations.

    Bibliography: p.
    Includes index.
    1. Recreation—Administration.   2. Recreation
leadership.   3. Leisure—Management.   I. Williams,
John Griffith, 1932–   joint author.   II. Title.

GV181.5.E33   658′.91′790068   78-5621
ISBN 0-471-01574-1

Printed in the United States of America

10 9 8

To our families

Preface

The application of contemporary techniques to the delivery of leisure services is long overdue. In this book we incorporate many of the management practices and principles developed and successfully used in business, industry, and public agencies. Although we cover a broad range of topics that are important in the management of leisure service organizations, we pay particular attention to the management of human resources.

Obviously, the most vital resources within any organization are its human ones. People make organizations go. They are the catalyst that enables organizations to function. Organizations that are made up of energetic, enthusiastic, dedicated individuals, whose needs are consistent or complementary with the organization's goals, are by and large successful organizations. Organizations whose members dissipate their energies through dissidence, disorganization, interpersonal conflict, and poor management are usually unsuccessful organizations or, at the outset, are considerably less productive than they could be.

In this book we utilize and emphasize a behavioral approach to the understanding of individuals within organizations; that is, we focus on the importance of understanding the needs of people, how they are motivated, and the importance of managerial leadership. We have long advocated that the successful managers in the leisure field are those who understand the needs, interests, and aspirations of their clients. This maxim also applies to the management of employees within leisure service organizations.

Today, in every community across the country, recreation and leisure services are competing with other governmental services for tax as well as other support. In the future, leisure services will have to find ways to deliver more services for less dollars. To do this, leisure service managers must become more proficient in all aspects of managing. They must learn how to get the most out of all resources and how to manage physical and fiscal as well as human resources.

Leisure service organizations do not operate in a vacuum. They are tied to and affected by a host of elements within the environment. Therefore, in this text, we also emphasize the need for managers to understand the relationship between the organization and the environmental subcomponents. Furthermore, we examine the organization itself in terms of its internal components and the relationship of these components to each other and to the external environment.

The scope of this book is broader than that of most textbooks in the parks and recreation field. We have expanded the concept of the management of leisure services to include both public and private organizations. We have moved away from the traditional emphasis on municipal parks and recreation and have incorporated examples from other organizations that are involved in the delivery of leisure services in North America. The bias, however, is in the area of municipal parks and recreation.

Chapter 1 is an overview of the management of leisure service organizations. In it, we discuss the role of the manager and introduce the concept of holistic management. Holistic management emphasizes understanding and identification of the environmental factors that can affect a leisure service organization.

The progression of management theory and practice is the subject of Chapter 2. Four areas are discussed: scientific management, human relations management, management science, and contemporary management. This chapter sets forth relevant management principles through the use of examples from the park and recreation field.

Chapter 3 deals with the importance of understanding the needs of employees and how to meet these needs while accomplishing the goals and objectives of the organization. We point out that work is accomplished through employees by meeting their needs.

Chapter 4 is concerned with motivation. We suggest that the issue is not really one of motivating employees, but of providing an environment in which they are self-motivated. The idea is not to try to make people work, but to try to create an environment in which they want to work and have a job they want to do. A history of some of the more important studies and theories of motivation is given. Several motivation models are also presented to help the reader thoroughly understand the dynamics of motivation and how the leisure service manager can help motivate his employees.

Chapter 5 is devoted to understanding the role of the formal organization in the delivery of leisure services. A number of organizational designs are given. Four organizational designs—bureaucracy, systems theory, decentralization, and the federation concept of organization—are discussed. The relationship of the formal organization to the various environmental subfactors is included. In addition, a procedure for structuring leisure service organizations is described.

Leadership and communications are the subjects of Chapter 6. To accomplish organizational goals and objectives, the manager must communicate with and lead his employees. We present various studies and theories of leadership and communication and integrate them into a system that enables the leisure service manager to be effective, efficient, and productive.

Chapter 7 delineates the methods and techniques that the leisure service manager can use in dealing with his or her boss, co-workers, and the community. A comparison between leadership and management is made. Methods for dealing with employee problems, employee corrective actions, and methods of assuring good teamwork are noted and a new concept, Total Performance Measurement, is described. Decision-making technique and methods for providing controls are presented. Finally, suggestions as to how the manager can create a supportive climate is made.

Marketing leisure services is the topic covered in Chapter 8. Marketing is a management concept that heretofore has had little application in the public sector in the provision of leisure services. The marketing concept applied to the delivery of leisure services has the potential for revolutionizing the manner in which services are provided. The process of marketing involves, in general, the identification of target markets (e.g., senior citizens, youths) and the mixing of components to satisfy the needs of a given target market.

Chapter 9 examines the budget and financial processes used in leisure service agencies. Various types of budgets, types of expenditures and revenues, budget procedures, and methods of implementation and control are discussed. The purpose of this chapter is to prepare the leisure service manager to deal with budget and finances in a positive, well-managed, and acceptable way.

Policymaking and the legal basis for leisure service delivery systems are considered in Chapter 10. The policy process and various policy structures are discussed in the first half of the chapter. In addition, the relationship of policy components to environmental subunits is examined. In the second half of the chapter, we focus on the legal bases that provide leisure service organizations with certain rights, privileges, power, and authority.

The last chapter of the book, Chapter 11, deals with personnel management and training for leisure service organizations. We include a discussion of mechanisms used in the operation of personnel functions such as manpower planning, recruitment, wage and salary administration, labor unions, and training. The latter part of the chapter is directed toward the importance of personnel training.

We gratefully acknowledge the efforts of several individuals who were instrumental in the implementation and completion of this endeavor. Nearly 10 years ago Jim Murphy, of San Jose State University, California, brought us together. We extend our appreciation to him for his continued support. We also thank John Schultz of the University of Minnesota and Robert Toalson of the Champaign (Illinois) Park District for their thoughtful and direct critique of the manuscript, which helped us polish and hone our material. We are grateful to Sally Hellman, Dee Hultman, Susan Edginton, and Maureen Dowhaniuk for their gracious assistance in the preparation of the final manuscript. Finally, we are appreciative of the efforts of Wayne Anderson our editor at John Wiley and extend our thanks.

CHRISTOPHER R. EDGINTON
JOHN G. WILLIAMS

Contents

7 Managing for Organizational Effectiveness   212

Management vs. Leadership • Managers and Their Relationships • Total Performance Measurement • The Leisure Service Manager as a Decision-Maker • Creating a Supportive Climate • Summary

8 Marketing Leisure Services   254

Types of Markets • Developing a Marketing Strategy • Creating Services • Pricing • Distribution of Services • Promotion • Summary

9 Budget/Fiscal Practices for Leisure Service Organizations   279

Information Needed by the Manager • What Is a Budget? • Revenues and Expenditures • Types of Budgets • Budget Procedures • Summary

10 Policymaking and the Legal Basis for Leisure Service Organizations   334

Policymaking • Policy Units • What Policy Boards Do • Consumers and the Policymaking Process • Legal Aspects of Leisure Services • Types of Laws • Powers of Government • Summary

11 Personnel Management and Training for Leisure Service Organizations   371

Personnel Management • Personnel Planning and Job Analysis • Recruitment and Hiring Procedures • Promotions and Discharges • Wage and Salary Administration • Fringe Benefits • Performance Appraisal • Labor Unions • Civil Service Systems • Affirmative Action Programs • Training • Summary

Selected Bibliography   419

Appendixes   424

A A Systems Design for Park Maintenance (Marshalltown, Iowa Parks and Recreation Department)

B City of Sunnyvale Park and Recreation Department Performance Measurement Appraisal Memorandum

C City of Sunnyvale Total Performance Measurement Case Study (1974 to 1976)

D Organizing a Leisure Service: "Art in the Park," a Case Study

Index   523

Productive Management of
Leisure Service Organizations

The Manager and the Management System

Movement into the postindustrial era has brought profound changes in the quality of life available to members of our society. The fabric of our culture has been altered by social, political, economic, and technological changes. Among the factors that have contributed to social change are the formulation of new social organizations, the progression and diffusion of knowledge, population growth, and the changing values of work and leisure.

Leisure has become a dominant force in society and it is projected that its influence will increase. During the past century, discretionary time has been greatly expanded because of cybernetics, a shortened workweek, increased mobility, and a longer life span. These changes have increased access to leisure for a broader cross section of the population. The economic and technological makeup of society has enabled many citizens to accumulate wealth and resources heretofore unattainable by the masses. Increases in productivity have resulted in the provision of goods and services that not only sustain life, but also serve to enrich it. The rate at which goods and services are consumed may be traced directly to the amount of leisure people have available. Today individuals are clamoring for still more leisure, in which to enjoy the social, cultural and material bounty.

Organizations and individuals involved in the delivery of leisure services have affected and have been affected by these changes. The function and structure of many delivery systems have evolved to accommodate the movement of society from a work orientation to a leisure orientation. Obviously, it is important that leisure service delivery organizations recognize changing trends and grow with them. The development of programs, policies, and management practices consistent with emerging trends is vital to their well-being. However, it is not sufficient that a leisure organization recognize and respond to current societal needs and trends; it must do so effectively and efficiently. Directed toward that end, this book has been written to assist leisure service managers and students entering the leisure field in becoming professionally productive.

LEISURE AND DELIVERY SERVICE ORGANIZATIONS

Leisure may be analyzed in a number of ways, depending on an individual's perspective. Within this text, leisure is considered to be an opportunity that can potentially enrich the individual. Leisure activities represent opportunities for human involvement and interaction that can be converted into various forms of behavior. Normally, a leisure experience is thought to be a form of activity, one that allows individuals to meet their needs and express their creative, physical, social and intellectual drives.

The term "leisure" is used in preference to recreation since leisure connotes a broader dimension. Recreation is frequently viewed from a value orientation that may be narrowly defined, and this philosophical framework has often limited the scope of services. Certainly, opportunities for leisure are much broader than those offered by municipal parks and recreation departments. The imposition of a limited set of values restricts the ability of organizations to meet the varying interests, needs, and life-styles of the individuals they serve. By defining leisure in a broader sense, one is able to conceptualize the delivery of services as all-inclusive, recognizing the vast potential for human expression.

Historically, the playground and recreation movement in North America evolved from a concern for children living in depressed urban areas of the United States and Canada. The impetus of the movement in the early 1900's centered around the identification of deprived areas in which recreation activities could be used to offset some of the conditions which produced undesireable behavior (i.e. juvenile delinquency). As such, recreation activities were established as social devices that were aimed toward alleviating or lessening certain social ills. Today, organized recreation and leisure programs are an integral part of North American society and are not necessarily created to solve isolated social problems. Consequently, there is generally a need for a different type of response from the profession today—a different philosophical approach to provision of services, due to our current leisure oriented society.

The phrase "leisure" may apply to *any* activity that is entered into by an individual. It is a state of being. "Recreation," by traditional definition, in the profession, is considered to be *wholesome* activity. But, the question arises "who is to define what is wholesome?" Should the parks and recreation professional be the sole determiner of an organization's program offerings, or should this be a collaborative process? Traditionally parks and recreation services have been dependent upon the *manager's* concept of recreation and what it (recreation) should entail. For example, the dominance of male managers over the last thirty years in the parks and recreation field has brought to bear an emphasis on male dominated, competitively organized, sports and games. Leisure, on the other hand, is dependent upon an individual's personal interpretation and values in regard to what constitutes a leisure experience. In other words, what constitutes a lesiure experience to one person, may not be so to another individual and what constitutes a wholesome leisure experience to one person may be viewed differently by another person. Leisure, thus is more individualized and specific to the person engaging in it.

This view of leisure evolves from a humanistic philosophy that places human values ahead of organizational expectations. Concern for the "whole" person, whether a participant or employee, is a dominant theme of this approach. Recognizing that attention should be given to an individual's emotional, spiritual, social, and physical well-being will enable an organization to operate from a humanistic philosophy. Conventional parks and recreation systems, which operate from a narrow philosophical framework, have a tendency to emphasize behavioral conformity. As such, program offerings tend to be prescribed, managers authoritarian, and participants dependent on the organization for reward. Humanistic organizations utilize the process of collaborative involvement directed toward the creation of self-determined or cooperatively determined experiences. They emphasize the development of individual worth, dignity, and identity. Managers in humanistic organizations act as alternators, facilitators, helpers, and resource persons; participants act as sharers, activators, decision-makers, and planners.

Organizations and Leisure Services

A leisure service organization is a unit whose functions, primary and/or secondary, include the creation and distribution of services that are consumed by individuals during their leisure. This book is concerned with the organization and implementation of services, rather than the production of leisure goods. As such, it will explore private, public, and commercial agencies that interact with persons during their leisure; more fully, it will embrace all of the various organizations that may provide leisure services. In regard to governmental services, Myron E. Weiner writes:

> We need not belabor the point that concern with the use of leisure will be a fundamental function of government in the twenty-first century. It will not be limited to those who operate in agencies or professions that today are identified as government recreation; it will include all public officials or employees who engage with human beings in one form or another—educators; police; juvenile and old age specialists; corrections, fire, and welfare officials; planners, librarians; arts and cultural specialists; and many others.[1]

Commercial agencies that provide leisure services are numerous. The leisure market in the United States has been estimated at $250 billion by the stockbrokerage firm of Merrill Lynch, Pierce, Fenner and Smith.[2] Richard Kraus estimates that the annual consumer spending on recreation in the late 1960s was

[1] Myron E. Weiner, "A Systems Approach to Leisure Services," in Sydney G. Lutzin and Edward H. Storey, *Managing Municipal Leisure Services* (Washington, D.C.: International City Management Association, 1973), pp. 3–4.

[2] *Leisure: Investment Opportunities in $150 Billion Market* (New York: Securities Research Division, Merrill Lynch, Pierce, Fenner and Smith, 1968), p. 4.

$125.9 billion.[3] Commercial enterprises, by far, cater to the largest number of consumers. Golf courses, bowling alleys, movies, bars, nightclubs, amusement parks, and racetracks provide major opportunities for commercial leisure-time participation.

Leisure service organizations are formed to meet the individual and collective leisure needs of society. They provide a framework that allows individuals to collectively do things they would not be able to do alone, thus serving as devices that overcome the limitations of individual action. Leisure service delivery systems are organized specifically to meet the objectives of those they serve. Goals will vary accordingly to meet the needs, desires, and expectations of the organization's constituents. Organizations providing leisure services can be classified according to their goals as follows:

1. Service Organizations. These assist persons by providing leisure services on a non-profit basis. Some require payment from each recipient of services.
2. Economic Organizations. These organizations provide leisure goods and services on a profit-making basis.
3. Religious Organizations. In addition to meeting the spiritual needs of its members, this type of organization provides leisure services as a by-product.
4. Governmental Organizations. Here the organization satisfies the need for order and continuity in the delivery of leisure services.
5. Social Organizations. This type of organization serves the social needs of persons for contact with others, identification, and mutual support. An example of this is a club.[4]

A key element in any leisure service organization is the interaction that takes place between the organization, as it produces services, and those who consume the services—people. Leisure services are people oriented; they foster active citizen participation and involvement, promote social interaction, and serve as a catalytic factor for many forms of expression. John G. Williams compared municipal services with Frederick Herzberg's motivation/hygiene theory. (Motivation factors are those that provide satisfaction to the participant; hygiene factors cause dissatisfaction when they are not maintained, but do not necessarily create satisfaction when they provided.) a detailed discussion of this theory is presented in Chapter 4. Williams writes:

> Recreation programs, park facilities, and library services relate to motivation, by providing individuals with opportunities for growth and development, whereas police, fire, public works, and waste elimination services are relating to the hygiene factors, and when provided keep people healthy. Dissatisfaction results when hygiene factors

[3] Richard Kraus, *Recreation and Leisure in a Modern Society* (New York: Appleton-Century-Crofts, 1971), pp. 3, 17.
[4] Adapted from Herbert G. Hicks, *The Management of Organizations* (New York: McGraw-Hill Book Co., 1967), p. 12.

Table 1.1. Leisure Services and the Motivation-Hygiene Theory

Citizen Dissatisfaction When Not Provided	Citizen Satisfaction When Provided
1. Police and fire protection	1. Recreation programs
2. Street and road maintenance	2. Library programs
3. Waste elimination	3. Parks facilities
4. Environmental protection	4. Social programs
5. Attractive community	
6. Governing body	
Passive—Guaranteed Taken for Granted	Active-Citizen Participation

Source: John G. Williams, "Motivation in Relationship to Executive Leadership" (paper presented at an administrative institute, Asilomar, Calif., November 1974), p. 26.

such as police, fire, etc., are not provided. Alternately, recreation programs, park facilities, and library services promote citizen satisfaction when provided. Active citizen participation is increased when citizens are satisfied. In comparing motivation factors to other services such as police protection, street and road maintenance, waste elimination, environmental projects, etc., the feeling concerning these services becomes passive and is taken for granted.[5]

THE LEISURE SERVICE MANAGER

Leisure service managers are individuals who have the responsibility and authority for providing direction to a leisure service organization and have the ability to move it toward goals and objectives. They are directly responsible for much of the success or failure of an organization. Indeed, the manager's competence, as reflected in his or her skills, knowledge, and ability to move an organization forward, meeting the needs of those served, will be echoed in the growth and achievement of the organization (or operation). Successful managers are able to identify trends, recognize problems, resolve conflict, utilize opportunities, audit poor performance, reward excellent efforts, and lead an organization to its goals.

Management and Productive Management Defined

Two key elements exist within most definitions of management: managers work with people, and they are involved in the achievement of organizational goals.

[5] John G. Williams, "Motivation in Relationship to Executive Leadership" (paper presented at an administrative institute, Asilomar, Calif., November 1974), p. 25.

Therefore leisure service management may be defined as the process whereby an individual works with resources, especially human, to achieve the goals and objectives of the leisure service organization. Managers must have knowledge of the task to be achieved and the ability to motivate people toward the attainment of the task. They must understand the objectives that are to be accomplished and be able to focus on the processes that can be utilized to achieve them. When an individual becomes a leisure service manager, his or her function is to help people and/or groups to fulfill their leisure aspirations. He or she does this by working with and through other people.

It is not enough that the manager direct the organization; the organization must be operated in a productive manner. Productive management can be defined as the relative effectiveness and efficiency of a leisure service organization. Effectiveness is measured by the degree to which an organization achieves its goals and objectives. Efficiency refers to the amount of resources consumed in the achievement of the organization's goals and objectives. A productive organization is effective and efficient; conversely, an unproductive organization lacks these elements. Productivity can be measured by assessing the relationship of inputs to outputs and comparing these to the organization's standards for effectiveness and efficiency.

Productive management is of high concern to the leisure service manager, whose job is to operate the leisure service organization in such a way that its resources benefit those it serves. By integrating the goals and objectives of the organization with the personal needs of those working within the organization, effectiveness may be achieved. An efficient organization achieves its goals and objectives at the lowest possible cost in terms of expenditure of human resources or fiscal resources, or both. Efficiency is sometimes tempered for humanistic considerations, however. It is quite possible that an organization achieve a great deal of effectiveness without being efficient and vice versa.

Roles and Purposes

There are three broad classifications in which persons involved in the management of leisure services can be categorized: the supervisor, the bureaucrat, and the manager.

The Supervisor—The primary function of the supervisor is to motivate the subordinates responsible to him.

The Bureaucrat—The responsibility of the bureaucrat is to manage an organization, adhering to its policies, procedures, and rules.

The Manager—A manager is differentiated from the supervisor or bureaucrat in that he or she is selected for intellectual capacity, not technical knowledge. Because they deal with the future, managers need behavioral flexibility.[6]

[6] Adapted from W. J. Reddin, "Management Effectiveness in the 1980's," *Business Horizons*, August Vol. XVII, No. 4 1974, p. 9.

All these individuals are involved in management and, therefore, are all viewed as leisure service managers. Their individual roles or purposes may vary, but the goals sought are similar.

Henry Mintzberg has developed a set of roles to portray what, specifically, managers do. He suggests that managerial activities may be categorized into three areas. Within the first area are interpersonal roles, which encompass the development of a set of interpersonal relationships between the manager, his subordinates, and his superiors. Specific roles assumed by the manager in this area are figurehead, liason, and leader. The second area includes informational roles, within which the manager receives and sends information. Within this role, the manager acts as a monitor, disseminator, and spokesman. Lastly, the area of the decision-making role, finds the manager performing as an entrepreneur, disturbance handler, resource allocator, and negotiator. In his discussion of management roles, Mintzberg writes:

The Manager as a Figurehead—The most basic and most simple of all managerial roles is that of figurehead. Because of his formal authority, the manager is a symbol, obliged to perform a number of duties. Some of these are trite, others are of an inspirational nature; all involve interpersonal activity.

The Manager as a Leader—The organization looks to its formal head for guidance and motivation. In his leader role, the manager defines the atmosphere in which the organization will work. . . . Leadership involves interpersonal relationships between the leader and the led. In the informal group, the leader is usually followed because of his physical or charismatic power. In informal organizations, where he is most often appointed from above, the manager must frequently rely on powers vested in his office.

The Manager as a Liason—The liason role deals with the significant web of relationships that the manager maintains with numerous individuals and groups outside the organization that he has. These [relationships] are referred to as "exchange" relationships—the manager gives something in order to get something in return.

The Manager as a Monitor—The manager as a monitor is continually seeking, being bombarded with information that enables him to understand what is taking place within his organization and its environment. He seeks information in order to detect changes, to identify problems and opportunities, to build up knowledge about his milieu, to be informed when information must be disseminated and decisions made.

The Manager as a Disseminator—Access to information allows the manager to play the important role of disseminating, sending external information into his organization and internal information from one subordinate to another.

The Manager as a Spokesman—In the spokesman role, the manager transmits information out to his organization's environment. As formal authority, the manager is called upon to speak on behalf of his organization; as nerve center, he has the information to do so effectively. The manager may lobby for his organization, he may serve as its public relations head, or may be viewed as an expert in the trade in which his organization operates.

The Manager as an Entrepreneur—In the entrepreneur role, the manager acts as initiator and designer of much of the controlled change in his organization. . . . This role encompasses all activities where the manager makes changes of his own free will—exploiting opportunities, solving nonpressing problems.

The Manager as a Disturbance Handler—The disturbance handler role deals with involuntary situations and change that is partially beyond the manager's control. . . . The manager acts because he must, because the pressures brought to bear on his organization are too great to ignore.

The Manager as a Resource Allocator—Resource allocation is the heart of the organization's strategy-making system. For it is in the making of choices involving significant organizational resources that strategies are determined. As formal authority, the manager must oversee the system by which organizational resources are allocated.

The Manager as a Negotiator—The manager is responsible for representing the organization in major non-routine negotiations with other organizations and/or individuals.[7]

Mintzberg also delineates six reasons that justify the need for managers in the organizational structure:

1. The prime purpose of the manager is to insure that his organization serves its basic purpose—the efficient production of specific goods and services.
2. The manager must design and maintain the stability of his organization's operations.
3. The manager must take charge of his organization's strategy-making system, and therein adapt his organization in a controlled way to its changing environment.
4. The manager must insure that his organization serves the ends of those persons who control it.
5. The manager must serve as the key informational link between his organization and its environment.
6. As formal authority, the manager is responsible for the operating of his organization's status system.[8]

Skills of the Leisure Service Manager

A leisure service manager must possess certain skills, knowledge, and ability to be successful. Robert L. Katz identifies three areas of skill that are necessary in the management process— technical, human, and conceptual:

Technical Skills—This involves the ability to use one's knowledge in the performance of specific work tasks. Skill in the management of aquatic facilities,

---

[7] Abridged from pp. 58–90 in *The Nature of Managerial Work* by Henry Mintzberg. Copyright © 1973 by Henry Mintzberg. By permission of Harper and Row, Publishers, Inc.
[8] Ibid., pp. 95–96.

MANAGEMENT
LEVELS   SKILLS NEEDED

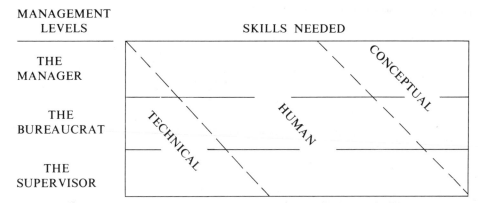

THE
MANAGER

THE
BUREAUCRAT

THE
SUPERVISOR

Figure 1.1. Management skills. (Adapted from Paul Hersey, Kenneth H. Blanchard, *Management of Organizational Behavior: Utilizing Human Resources,* 2nd Edition, copyright © 1972, p. 6. Reprinted by permission of Prentice-Hall, Inc., Englewood Cliffs, New Jersey.

such as pH and chlorine residuals, are examples of skills that can be learned from experience or through the formal education process.

Human Skill—Here the leisure services manager applies his ability to motivate people by working with and through them to achieve organizational goals.

Conceptual Skills—This involves an understanding on the part of the manager as to the manner in which each of the organization's components fit together, in order to meet its goals and objectives. It further implies that an individual has an understanding of how his organization is affected by, and relates to, broader environmental factors.[9]

According to Katz, individual management styles vary in regard to the type of management position one holds. This phenomenon is indicated in Figure 1.1.

As one advances from supervisor to bureaucrat to manager, the mixture of skills needed to be productive changes. A park foreman must have technical knowledge relating to construction, turf care, and vehicle and equipment repair. He is usually responsible for the accomplishment of specific tasks and must train and develop others to complete these tasks. On the other hand, the manager must understand how all the components of the organization fit together. He must have the ability to interrelate various organizational functions in order to meet the overall goals of the organization. While the technical and conceptual skills needed at each level may vary, all positions require equal ability in dealing with human beings. The ability to deal with people is vital and the key to productive management because it is primarily through others that work is accomplished.

[9] These descriptions were adapted from a classification developed by Robert L. Katz, "Skills of an Effective Administrator," *Harvard Business Review,* January–February 1955, pp. 33–42.

LEISURE DELIVERY SERVICE AS A SYSTEM

A complex and diversified environment affects the management and organization of leisure services. Consisting of a number of systems (i.e., social, political, economic, and physical), environmental forces present a challenge to leisure service managers. Their work is greatly influenced by the interrelationships that exist among the various factors in the environment. Each system interacts with each of the other systems, influencing one another and the total environment. A leisure service organization is one of the environmental systems, and as such it affects and is affected by other systems within the total environment. In discussing the interrelationships of the environment, Murphy, Williams, Niepoth, and Brown write:

> The ecology of leisure service delivery systems is concerned with the interrelationships among people in their physical and social environment, and the ways these relationships influence, or are influenced by particular social processes. It is therefore understood that the relationships of each component of the delivery system within any community are viewed as an ecological unit. It is holistic in the sense that any change in the population being served will affect the nature of programming and vice versa. Each component is an integral part of the overall delivery system and each influences another segment of the unit. All elements mutually modify one another.[10]

A dynamic leisure service organization is in constant interaction with the environment. The interaction that takes place between systems in the environment may be defined as an *interface*. When the leisure service organization contacts a participant in the delivery of services, such as when providing face-to-face leadership for an activity, an interface occurs. It also exists at a party or during a coffee break, when members of a leisure service organization discuss their activities.

An important function of the leisure service manager is the recognition of the various systems that affect the delivery of leisure services. Further, it is extremely important that the leisure service manager identify and manage *critical interfaces* (where two or more systems interact with each other) that exist between and within systems of the total environment. This calls for a holistic approach to the management of leisure services.

Holistic Management

The holistic approach to the management of leisure service organizations involves the identification of all the environmental factors that affect the organization and implementation of services. It has two basic components—the *external*, or *macro*, environment and the *internal*, or *micro*, environment—which relate to the

---

[10] James F. Murphy, John G. Williams, E. William Niepoth, and Paul D. Brown, *Leisure Service Delivery System: A Modern Perspective* (Philadelphia: Lea and Febiger, 1973), p. 1.

delivery of leisure services. The macro environment includes those constraints that surround, interact with, and influence a leisure delivery service organization. These constraints, including the economic, social, physical, and political systems, impose various sanctions and affect the delivery of leisure services. The micro environment includes the goals, processes, organizational structure (both formal and informal), and individual behavior of managers and employees in the leisure service organization.

Figure 1.2 delineates the interacting components that have a bearing on the delivery of services. The role of the manager, using this approach to management, is to integrate these components by identifying and managing the critical interfaces to insure the delivery of services in a productive manner. The manager

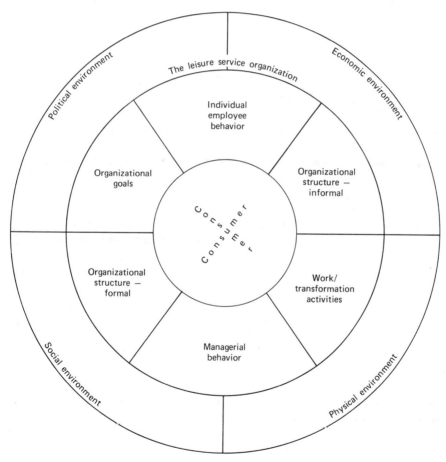

Figure 1.2. The leisure service organization holistic management model.

is responsible for receiving such inputs as money, manpower (professional, skilled, semiskilled, and unskilled), fixed capital resources, equipment, and land and transforming these into outputs in the form of leisure services. A discussion of each of the interacting components of the environment that influence the delivery of leisure services follows.

THE LEISURE SERVICE ORGANIZATION

The Manager and the Employee

The individual behavior of leisure service managers and their employees is perhaps the most important element in the holistic management model. Human beings possess physiological and psychological variables that affect their behavior. One's physiological makeup includes inherited characteristics, such as the nervous system, organs, muscles, and glands. Psychological processes, including perception of others, self-image, ability to learn, and motivation, also affect behavior. Generally speaking, the manager potentially has greater impact on the psychological processes of his or her employees; therefore this duscussion will focus on the psychological, rather than physiological, processes that influence behavior.

Human beings interpret their environment in different ways; this is known as the process of perception. The way one perceives individuals and/or situations has a great impact on his behavior toward others. For example, one leisure manager may perceive an individual employee as a deviant, capable of antisocial behavior; another manager may view the same individual as possessing worth. Individual perception influences sensitivity to the individual and, in turn, affects interpretation and action. This will affect the manager's decision-making role, in that all information which he receives will be modified by the perceptual process.

A person's self-image will also have a bearing on her behavior, and in turn, the manner in which she deals with various environmental components. An individual who has a security-oriented self-image may behave differently than a person who conceives herself to be independent and confident (e.g., a security-oriented individual may be a very authoritarian leader). Consequently, because all components of the system interact, the organization will ultimately be influenced by the individual leisure manager's self-concept.

Learning is another psychological factor that affects individual behavior. An individual's ability to learn has a direct bearing on his ability to understand concepts and absorb knowledge. Attitudes, skills, knowledge, and other forms of behavior are all learned within three domains: the cognitive, the affective, and psychomotor. To illustrate, knowledge of an organization's goals is gained through cognitive processes; loyalty between a manager and his subordinates is learned within the affective domain; and the learning of physical abilities used in the performance of tasks falls within the psychomotor domain. An individual's inability to understand and integrate such concepts and/or knowledge may seriously inhibit his ability to achieve organizational goals.

Motivation is the last element to be discussed that affects individual behavior. Motivation consists of three interacting factors—needs, drives, and goals. Needs may be defined as physiological or phychological deficiencies. Drives are directed toward initiating action to meet needs. Goals are the ends that drives and needs are directed toward. People are motivated by a host of needs, such as security, status, power, and achievement. For example, a leisure service manager may exhibit a need for increased status by striving toward the attainment of higher levels within the organization.

Discussing the interaction that exists between an individual and the institution that employs her, Jacob R. Getzels and E. G. Guba suggest that there are two classes within a social system which affect the processes of management—the institutional, or nomothetic dimension and the individual, or idiographic dimension. They write:

> There are, first, the institutions with certain roles and expectations that will fulfill the goals of the system. Second, inhabiting the system there are the individuals with certain personalities and needs dispositions, whose interactions compromise what we generally call "social behavior." Social behavior may be apprehended as a function of the following elements: institution, role and expectation (nomothetic dimension) . . . individual, personality and need dispositions (ideographic dimension).[11]

Figure 1.3 diagrams the interactive relationships that exist within a social system. Conflicts between individual needs and values on the one hand and organizational goals and role expectation on the other can create friction. Conversely, the role prescribed by the institution for an individual may be well suited to her. The point is that persons bring different characteristics and personal needs to the organization, and these affect their ability to function within a prescribed role. When a conflict occurs within a management system because of an individual's behavior, one of two things can happen: The individual can change her behavior or the organization can change its role expectations of the individual. The leisure manager's role is to find common ground between institutional expectations and individual behavior.

Organizational Goals

The goals (ends, aims, and purposes) of an organization represent the desired outcome toward which a leisure service system is directed. In the public sector, these

---

[11] Jacob R. Getzels and E. G. Guba, "Social Behavior and the Administrative Process," *School Review 65* (Winter Quarter 1957), p. 425.

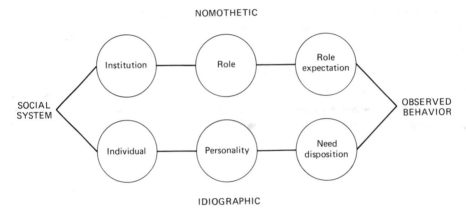

Figure 1.3. Interacting individual and institutional components. (Jacob B. Getzels and E. G. Guba, "Social Behavior and the Administrative Process," *School Review, 65,* Winter Quarter 1957. Used by permission of *School Review.*)

goals are usually established and adopted by a legislative body. They provide criteria for decision-making and assist the leisure services manager in relating to the environment. The resolution of conflict in goals, between and within the external and internal environmental constraints, is a constant activity of the leisure service manager. The goals of a leisure service organization may be categorized into five areas: output, adaptation, management, motivation, and positional goals.[12]

Output goals of the leisure service organization are reflected in the production or creation of services, which usually institute or facilitate behavior change in the participant. There are three types of output goals: direct service goals, participant expressive goals, and participant instrumental goals. *Direct service goals* are those goals that result in the provision of services directly to participants outside the leisure services organization. These include the creation and provision of (1) leisure activities; (2) facilities, such as parks, recreation centers, and swimming pools; and (3) information services, including leisure counseling.

These services are used by the manager as tools to change or modify an individual's behavior in some way. They result in the instrumental and expressive types of behaviors. Instrumental behaviors can be thought of as being linked to a person's needs for basic biological and psychological elements, such as skill development, security, and social affiliation. Therefore *participant instrumental* goals result in services that are directed toward the attainment of some skill and/or the reduction of basic needs, such as food and security. Expressive types of behaviors relate to a person's needs for recognition, self-esteem, and self-

[12] Information for the discussion of goals was adapted from Edward Gross, "Universities as Organizations: A Study of Goals," *American Sociological Review* 33 (August 1968), pp. 518–544.

realization. *Participant expressive* goals are, therefore, services that result in the acquisition of behavior directed ultimately toward self-actualization.

Adaptation goals reflect the interaction of the organization with environmental systems. Stated simply, an organization's ability to relate to and/or adapt to the various environmental subgroupings (which constantly change) will affect its ability to obtain resources that are necessary for its survival and stability. This may entail securing resources, such as finances, staff, capital fixtures, and equipment. Insuring confidence and hence support of those who contribute to the organization (e.g., taxpayers, consumers) is accomplished by making efficient utilization of resources and meeting the needs, interests, and values of the participants served.

Management goals deal with decision-making in such matters as who should run the organization, how conflicts should be handled, and how resources should be distributed and accounted for. Management goals may involve both staff and participants in the governance of the organization, aligning the reward system (salaries, benefits, privileges) with the level of responsibility and maintaining harmony between individuals and/or functions within the organization.

Motivation goals endeavor to insure satisfaction of the participants and the staff and to inspire loyalty to the organization as a whole. This is accomplished, in part, by developing pride in the organization and the ideals for which it stands. Protecting and facilitating staff and participant rights, and insuring that an individual has maximum opportunity to pursue his or her interests, also exemplify this type of goal.

Positional goals maintain the position of the organization as related and compared to other leisure service organizations. Such goals strive to maintain or increase the prestige of the leisure service organization. They are achieved by high-quality programs and services, responsiveness to changing trends, and preservation of characteristics unique to the organization. Leisure service organizations are subject to influences that are directed toward reducing or changing their position and/or status in the community. This challenge to an organization's position may come from other departments competing for the tax dollar in the governmental sector and/or from those commercial organizations that strive for a greater percentage of the leisure market.

Organizational Structure—Formal and Informal

The goals of an organization are achieved in large part through its structure. Although organizational structure will be discussed fully in Chapter 5, there are two aspects of this subject that are relevant to the productive management of leisure service organizations and to this discussion on formal and informal organizations.

The formal organization of a leisure delivery service system is established specifically to accomplish the system's goals. This type of organizational structure requires the collective effort of the entire membership of the organization. According to Herbert G. Hicks:

> A formal organization has a well defined structure that may describe its authority, power, accountability, and responsibility relationships. The structure can also define the channels through which communications flow. Formal organizations have clearly specified jobs for every member. The hierarchy of objectives of formal organizations is explicitly stated. Status, prestige, pay, rank, and other prerequisites are well ordered and controlled. Formal organizations are durable and planned; because of their emphasis on order they are relatively stable.[13]

Formal organizations are structured to increase productivity. But, because of specialization, rules, and a hierarchy that at times stifles communication, formal structures may impede the attainment of the organization's goals. Rules and procedures can become ends in themselves, thus blocking individual initiative; specialization can lead to fragmentation within the organization. On the other hand, formal organizations are a means for orderly and controlled interaction among people. They provide clearly defined lines of authority and responsibility and may positively influence the achievement of an organization's goals and objectives. The nature and complexity of the goals that are to be achieved by a leisure service organization will dictate the degree to which a formal structure is necessary. To function, large systems must depend on extensive formal organization.

The goals of a leisure service organization may also be influenced by informal organization within the system.

> The informal organization plays a significant role in the dynamics of organizational behavior. The major difference between the formal and informal organization is that the formal organization . . . has officially prescribed goals and relationships, while the informal one does not. Yet, it is a mistake to think of the formal and informal groups as two distinctly separate organizational entities. The two coexist and are inseparable. Every formal organization has an informal organization and every informal organization eventually evolves into some degree of formal organization.[14]

Formal and informal systems exist side by side and should complement one another. An informal organization may contribute to the formal organization in the following ways:

1. It blends with the formal organization to make a workable system for getting work done.
2. It lightens the workload of the formal manager and fills in some of the gaps of his abilities.
3. It gives satisfaction and stability to work groups.

[13] Hicks, *The Management of Organizations*, p. 10.
[14] Fred Luthans, *Organizational Behavior* (New York: McGraw-Hill Book Co., 1973), p. 453.

4. It is a very useful channel of communication in the organization.
5. Its presence encourages a manager to plan and act more carefully than he would otherwise.[15]

Because they may have conflicting sets of values, informal organizations can hinder the achievement of the goals of a formal organization. A group of individuals can organize around a concern, on an informal basis, and bring a great deal of pressure to bear on an organization. This can result in considerable expenditure of the organization's resources and may detract from its productivity.

The influence of organizational structure, formal and informal, on a leisure service system as a whole is very important. Relationships that exist between and within an organization continually interact with each other. Individual behavior is modified by the formal and the informal organization and vice versa. The leisure service manager should be aware of the potential and consequences of both formal and informal organizations and be able to take advantage, when possible, of these types of organizations. Goal achievement can be enhanced or diminished by organizational design.

Work/Transformation Activities

Work/transformation activities are the actual functions performed by the manager. They involve the actual effort put into procuring inputs and transforming these inputs into outputs (such as leisure-time activities) by the leisure service manager. Basic work functions of a leisure service manager include financial activity and the creation and distribution of leisure services. The management of fiscal resources (finance) is handled through the process known as "budgeting." There are three stages in the budgeting process: preparation, authorization, and execution. Two tasks, budget preparation and implementation, consume a great deal of a leisure manager's attention. (Financial management is discussed in Chapter 9.)

Creation and distribution of a service includes four activities: the organization, the pricing, the distribution, and the promotion of a service. Essentially, this involves getting the right service to the consumer when she wants it, at the price she is willing to pay, and in the place that is most convenient for her participation. These processes are discussed in Chapter 8. The work functions are accomplished through the processes of planning, organizing, staffing, directing, and controlling.

Planning
Planning is a process that involves the identification of goals and development of the methods necessary to achieve them. It also entails decision-making responsi-

---

[15] Keith Davis, *Human Behavior at Work* (New York: McGraw-Hill Book Co., 1972), pp. 257–259.

bility in the allocation of an organization's resources. Once an organization has set its goals and has determined the direction in which it wants to go, it must ask itself what its priorities are, with the resources available. In addition, it must assess the future and determine how the organization may meet its potential needs.

Organizing

Organizing involves the establishment of specific roles, and the blending of resources into a coherent organizational structure. The determination of roles provides for the delegation of management authority, responsibility, and accountability. Further, a well-defined organization provides for the coordination of activities among workers and of the purposes of the organization and takes into account the resources available in determining relationships among individuals. Ultimately, organizing produces a structure that enables individuals to work collectively toward the achievement of leisure service goals. Tasks and/or roles that take into account the individual abilities and skills of the members of a leisure service organization contribute to increased effectiveness and efficiency. Organizing is, however, a dynamic process and should constantly take place as individual competency within the leisure service organization changes and as the environment outside the organization evolves.

Staffing

Staffing is a process whereby an organization's needs for manpower are met. The process endeavors to meet both present and future personnel needs of the organization and, according to Ernest Dale, includes several specific functions:

1. Recruitment, or getting applicants for the jobs as they open up.
2. Selection of the best qualified from those who seek the jobs.
3. Transfers and promotions.
4. Training of those who need further instruction to perform their work effectively or to quality for promotion.[16]

Directing

Directing is accomplished by encouraging, leading, motivating, and communicating with employees to achieve organizational goals. In general, the role of the leisure service manager is to work with subordinates, communicating to them the procedures necessary to carry out the plans of the organization. In other words, ". . . telling people what to do and seeing that they do it.[17] The manager works to help each subordinate use his or her skills and abilities to maximum potential, and to motivate employees toward the achievement of organizational goals.

[16] Ernest Dale, *Management: Theory and Practice,* second edition (New York: McGraw-Hill Book Co., 1969), p. 370.
[17] Ibid., p. 424.

Controlling

In verifying the extent to which an organization conforms to its plans, a manager is involved in the processes of control. Control concerns the establishment of standards to guide performance. Standards serve as the criteria against which performance is measured. Following the establishment of performance standards, the controlling process proceeds to measure and evaluate performance. This can be accomplished through personal observation, financial accounting, or appraisal of the results achieved by an individual and/or organization.

The final factor involved in the control process is that of corrective action. Corrective action may require decisions to adjust and change and/or integrate individuals in the organization. It also may entail the development of new standards and/or managerial methods that increase employee motivation toward achievement of an organization's plan of action. Controlling depends on feedback from the various units that make up an organization. Without adequate management information systems to provide data on performance, the process of control is ineffective.

ENVIRONMENTAL CONSTRAINTS

The Consumer

The needs, interests, values, and life-styles of individuals served by a leisure service organization are a central concern of the leisure services manager. Age, sex, education, income, cultural traits, occupation, and biological and psychological factors give insight into the elements that affect leisure behavioral patterns.

Leisure activity interests vary with age. For example, younger persons are inclined to find strenuous physical activity, especially team sports, desirable. On the other hand, middle-aged adults are likely to prefer individual and dual sports, which are less demanding physically.

Cultural traits and norms also affect individual behavior. Individual convictions and/or sentiments can serve as a basis for making decisions that affect leisure behavior. The drive for success within our competitive society and the view that activity is a worthwhile end in itself are two examples of value orientations that affect the leisure behavior of North Americans.

Whether a function of biological or cultural factors, the sex of an individual will affect leisure interests. The development of roles through the process of socialization may well determine the type of activity in which males or females may engage. Although cultural values have changed recently regarding the involvement of women in strenuous physical activity, heretofore it was assumed that this type of activity was exclusively within the domain of men.

Education, income, and occupation are all interrelated and are often linked to one's social status. Activity preferences will vary according to one's status. A discussion of the economic factor as it affects leisure patterns is discussed later in this chapter. In addition, it has been traditionally hypothesized that leisure behavior is modified by a number of biological and psychological factors.

The integration of these factors with social, economic, physical, and political systems provides the basis for increased awareness of leisure behavioral patterns. Efforts by leisure service organizations, aimed at the provision of adequate programs, activities, and facilities, are made challenging by variance in leisure life-styles among the individuals they serve. They must deal with differing needs, interests, and values, which are affected by a host of environmental systems. The insensitivity of some managers to these factors has greatly diminished the effectiveness of leisure services. In many cases, this problem has been compounded by individual prejudice (racial, political, religious, or otherwise) and by the delivery of services based on limited understanding and knowledge gained from one's individual perception. The need for interpretive efforts is paramount, whether oriented toward research tools and/or techniques or toward employment of individuals who can relate directly to varying leisure life-styles. Productive delivery of services depends greatly on development of a conscious effort to understand the needs of the consumer, especially as shaped by the systems of the environment.

The Social Environment

The social environment consists of the sum total of interaction that takes place among individuals or groups of individuals and results in the development of formal and/or informal organizations. This interaction produces many forms of human and societal behavior. A leisure service organization is affected by and can affect the activities that take place among individuals and/or groups having opportunities for interaction.

Social behavior can be shaped greatly by leisure. Perhaps the most pronounced change in individual and group behavior affecting the social environment is that of changing attitudes toward work and leisure. Moving from a work-oriented to a leisure-oriented society has produced new individual and group social patterns. For example, new forms of social behavior have resulted in a host of organizations dedicated to leisure pursuits. Television, professional sports, movies, and fast-food chains are all leisure-oriented agents that are contributing to the change in our social environment. Such institutions carry a distinct set of norms or roles that influence consumer values and hence behavior.

Increased participation in outdoor recreation activities is another example of changing leisure behavior patterns. Seymour M. Gold suggests that the need for participation in "outdoor recreation is directly proportional to the degree of urbanization."[18] He suggests that man is driven by both biological and psychological needs to maintain contact with the out-of-doors. The phenomenal

[18] Seymour M. Gold, *Urban Recreation Planning* (Philadelphia: Lea and Febiger, 1973), p. 47.

growth of camping in the last 20 years in the United States has occurred because of changes in our social environment. Attitudes with regard to the preservation of natural resources have come to the forefront of national attention. The camping experience itself is an interesting sociological phenomenon. An entire set of social values have evolved around the weekend camper who jumps in his camping van and scurries off to the nearest campground, where he is able to develop new associations that are temporary in nature.

The structure and nature of the family as a sociological unit have been greatly affected by increases in affluence, mobility, and leisure. Families traditionally have spent most of their leisure together; however, today families seemingly spend less time with each other. Whether such a change in behavior will seriously affect the nature of the family as an institution is yet to be determined.

The misuse of leisure may give rise to antisocial behavior. Gold, noting a number of currently popular assumptions concerning the misuse of leisure, identifies the following themes:

1. Unstructured free time for the masses is the cause of social disorders.
2. There is a definite relationship between the number and type of recreation opportunities and social disorders such as crime, violence, and mental disease.[19]

Further, the National Advisory Commission on Civil Disorders, reporting on the urban disorders that took place in 1968–69, said that the lack of recreation facilities and leadership was a major cause of the riots.[20] The search for the cause–effect relationship that links the use of leisure with forms of socially acceptable behavior and/or antisocial behavior is an important function of those who study the sociology of leisure.

Another important component of our social environment that affects the delivery of leisure services is formal organizations. The leisure service manager is constantly interacting with governmental, social, political, and economic organizations, such as businesses and corporations. Surrounded by formal and informal organizations and groups, it is important for one to remember that the leisure service organization does not operate in a vaccuum and that it is dependent on its relationships with other bodies. The relative success or failure of an organization may depend on its ability to properly manage its affairs with other organizations and groups.

Responsiveness to changes in the social environment is best achieved by recognizing that human behavior is not static, but dynamic. Activities, facilities, and services should be directed toward providing positive and enriching opportunities that satisfy individual and group needs for growth. Further, the values of an

[19] Ibid., p. 41.
[20] *Report of the National Advisory Commission on Civil Disorder* (New York: Bantam Books, 1968), pp. 7–8.

organization are reflected in the types of goods and services it offers. In creating and distributing selected goods and services, the leisure service organization affects the social environment and plays a role in shaping culture and society.

The Political Environment

The leisure service manager is directly affected by both the formal structure of government and the informal process that affects political decision-making. Formal governmental structures exist at the federal, state or provincial, and local levels. Their primary function is to establish laws and policies that enable, inhibit, or regulate the behavior of people in some way. In addition, governments, especially at the local level, have been traditional providers of leisure services. An understanding of the laws formulated by legislative and judicial institutions, is obviously vital to the leisure service manager; this subject is discussed in Chapter 10.

Perhaps of equal importance is the leisure service manager's knowledge of the informal, or de facto, political processes that directly affect or influence the initiation and implementation of policy. Theoretically, a representative form of government provides opportunity for the interests of all to be recognized. It rests on the belief that selfish interests are subservient to the common good. The democratic process, however, is often thwarted by a number of factors that do not contribute to the welfare of all. One of the most important political forces facing the leisure service manager today is that of special-interest, or pressure, groups. Such groups have a profound impact on the functioning of the democratic process.

A special-interest group exists when a group of people band together around a mutual concern. There are many groups in our society today that affect the delivery of leisure services. Examples include swim clubs, hobby clubs, athletic teams, conservation and ecology organizations, and service and political organizations. These types of organizations allow individuals having common interests to share values and develop camaraderie and loyalty. There are few value-free or altruistic groups. Because our society contains many special-interest groups, having varying values and needs, the probability that these groups will interact and perhaps conflict with other groups and organizations is great. These conflicting organizational values give rise to pressure groups.

A pressure group is a special-interest group that actively promotes its own interests. A political party can be defined as a pressure group. In many cases pressure groups attempt to influence the distribution of organizational resources to reflect their interests rather than what is traditionally thought of as the common good. It is with this type of group that the leisure service manager must contend.

A public leisure service delivery system is not a value-free organization. It is initiated to provide a variety of activities, facilities, and services that provide opportunities for use of one's leisure. Existing to serve the leisure needs of the citizens within their legal jurisdictions, they do not cater solely to the specific interests or values of a particular group. This does not imply that this type of leisure service organization does not meet individual and group needs; rather, it implies that such organizations try to promote the concept of the greatest good for the greatest number.

Conflict may develop between a pressure group and a public leisure service delivery system when, in distributing resources to meet community needs, the specific requests of a pressure group are subservient to the welfare of the entire community. When this occurs, pressure groups exert their influence to affect the distribution of resources through the political process. A number of tactics can be used by pressure groups to influence organizations and the political process. They may try to influence the passage of legislation, sway public officials, and/or attempt to mold public opinion. By representing the values of the leisure service organization to the public at large, the manager attempts to counter the impact of pressure groups on the distribution of resources.

An example of the type of confrontation that can exist between a pressure group and a public leisure service organization involves the distribution of swimming-pool time. It is consistant with the aims of many public leisure service organizations to provide a variety of aquatic activities that meet the varying interests and needs of a community. But in many communities, the formulation of a parents' swim club to support the activities of the competitive swim program provides a focal point for conflict between the values of the swim club and the public leisure service organization. The club may demand that the community's aquatic program be organized to serve *its* needs rather than the broad interests of all. Agitating for increased access to the swimming pool, and demanding increased amounts of the leisure delivery system's time to organize their activities are types of pressure group conflict that must be dealt with. It may be that the representatives of the swim club are among the more powerful political leaders of the community, and they may use their positions of authority and influence to affect the distribution of resources.

Special-interest groups need not *necessarily* be thought of as operating in conflict with the aims and values of the leisure service organization. In fact, there are numerous special-interest groups whose values are complementary to those of a leisure service organization. In many cases the leisure service organization and a given special-interest group work together to the mutual benefit of each other. Service clubs with a strong commitment to meeting community needs are often deeply involved with public leisure service organizations. Providing financial support as well as assistance in the form of voluntary manpower, service clubs are engaged in activities such as Halloween parades, Easter-egg hunts, park clean-up activities, and support of capital improvements. They are an important resource to a public leisure service organization. To achieve its aims, a public service organization has the responsibility to use its community resources wisely and to provide opportunities for community service. It is thus able to effectively meet the needs of both the special-interest group and itself.

The Physical Environment

The planning of activities, facilities, and services depends greatly on a community's physical features. Climate, terrain, resources, spatial arrangements, and population density are components of the physical environment that affect the delivery of services. Regional variances in the physical environment provide conditions that foster differing life-styles and hence promote the development of a broad range of leisure-time activities that suit the particular location in which an individual lives.

Climate affects leisure programming as much as any other component of the physical environment. In the San Francisco Bay Area, for example, the Mediterranean climate allows for a host of year-round outdoor recreation activities. Playground programs are operated out-of-doors during the school year, as well as during the summer months. In contrast, communities located in the Toronto metropolitan area traditionally operate their playground programs only during the summer months. As the seasons change in various locations, programming efforts take on new dimensions, reflecting the particular leisure needs that have been created as a result of differing climatic conditions.

The topography or terrain of a given location may also affect leisure tastes. Persons living in mountain areas of the United States and Canada have available unique opportunities for particular types of leisure activities, such as hiking, mountain climbing, and orienteering. Individual's who reside close to large bodies of water are able to enjoy such activities as sailing and waterskiing. Modern technology has overcome some geographic limitations with the use of such innovations as wave machines for pools and artificial snow and ice. Another alternative may involve the transportation of participants from one geographic area to another in order to involve them in seasonal or regional leisure activities.

Individual participation in leisure activities is affected by both man-made and natural resources. Natural wilderness areas, forests, lakes, and rivers all provide abundant opportunities for participation. The preservation of outdoor recreation resources has been a growing concern for the past several years. To insure that future generations have continued access to our natural areas, massive efforts have been undertaken to set aside some areas and to regulate the use of others.

Man-made facilities, such as artificial lakes, picnic areas, swimming pools, parks, and recreation centers also provide opportunities for participation. Communities lacking in both natural and man-made resources are unable to provide adequate leisure services.

Spatial arrangements and population density are interrelated. Urban living characterizes a way of life for our society and presents opportunities for social interaction. Urban life provides a variety of individual choices that can lead to personal fulfillment. On the other hand, the conditions that are created as a result of crowding and overpopulation can initiate antisocial behavior. The leisure service manager plays an important role in improving the quality of the urban environment. The creation of certain environmental conditions promotes positive forms of interaction among people, and by preserving a community's natural beauty, life is enhanced.

The Economic Environment

The economic environment has a profound impact on the provision and consumption of leisure services. Between absolute poverty and complete affluence exists a variety of leisure life-styles. Some individuals enslaved by their economic circumstances are denied opportunities for a fully enriched leisure life-style; others, born within the cult of affluence, are able to fully explore the potential of a leisure-oriented life.

A study conducted by Edgington of the leisure behavior, attitudes, and opinions of a midwestern community (population 20,000) serves to illustrate that income is a factor influencing leisure behavior.[21] A survey of the community indicated that there were three economic areas within the physical boundaries of the community. The first area was racially mixed, had a lower achieved level of education than the other two areas, and was primarily composed of semiskilled and unskilled blue-collar workers. The second area was inhabited by teachers, clerks, and middle managers, and the level of education achieved was higher than that of the first area but lower than that of the third. Predominantly inhabited by professional people (doctors, lawyers, and businessmen), the third area was predominantly white and had the highest educational achievement level.

Factors regarding leisure behavior, such as time use (amount of vacation time, working hours, free periods, etc.), activity participation and interest, facility usage, and ownership of equipment that could be used for leisure-time pursuits were highly correlated with the prevailing economic conditions noted in the three specified areas.

Respondents in the first area spent most of their vacation within the city, whereas those in the higher-economic areas vacationed outside the city. Indi-

[21] Christopher R. Edginton, "Leisure Behavior, Attitudes, and Opinion Study of the Residents of Wooster, Ohio," (Iowa City: Recreation Education Program, University of Iowa, 1973).

viduals in the lower-economic area spent most of their free time with friends and family; conversely, those in higher-economic areas spent more time with organized groups.

The factors of ownership and participation could have a two-pronged effect on the efforts that this community could undertake in regard to program services based on life-styles. First, efforts could be directed toward increasing programs aimed at the specific leisure interests of the respondents. Second, because income seems to affect the quantity and/or variety of leisure experiences of the various groupings, efforts could be directed toward providing services that are ordinarily financially unattainable.

Not only does individual income affect individual participation in various leisure activities, but it also determines the collective wealth of a community and/ or the economic climate of a nation. Perhaps the greatest need for public leisure services is found in poor urban areas of North America. Although there has been a redistribution of financial resources through federal, state, and provincial agencies, the pressing economic conditions that exist in the inner-city areas of the United States and Canada adversely affect opportunities for leisure behavior. Conversely, the more affluent suburbs are able to finance the development and operation of some of the nation's finest public leisure delivery systems.

The economic status of the nation also affects leisure life-styles. One of the most dramatic upsurges in the consumption and participation of leisure activities took place during the Great Depression. During this period, vast amounts of money were provided for the creation of recreation facilities and services. In more contemporary times, high levels of affluence—particularly in the 1960s—resulted in the creation of a multimillion-dollar leisure market.

Interpreting the economic environment involves (1) understanding the effects that different levels of income have on participation in leisure activities and (2) providing increased opportunities for participation in activities that are unattainable because of the economic circumstances of many would-be participants. In the latter role, the leisure service organization acts to fulfill its traditional function of providing collectively the services that are individually unattainable.

SUMMARY

The growth of leisure in North America has resulted in the creation of a vast number of organizations that deliver leisure services. Working with and through human resources, leisure service managers are charged with the effective and efficient, hence productive, management of these organizations. Acting in a number of roles, it is important for the manager to be aware of the various environmental systems that can affect the delivery of leisure services. Environmental constraints include the participant and social, political, physical, and economic factors; organizational elements include an individual's behavior, organizational goals, organizational structure, and work/transformation activities. An awareness of the patterns of interaction, or interfaces, that take place between and within these systems is crucial to the leisure service manager. The productive management of any leisure delivery service organization is dependent on the ability of the manager to work with these constraints and to move the organization toward its goals.

An Overview of Management Theory and Practice

There is a great deal of literature regarding the practice and theory of management. The study of management techniques and thought can provide the leisure service manager with a foundation of theory that can be used to formulate a personal management philosophy. Although management principles can be traced to ancient times, this chapter focuses on management theory beginning in the twentieth century.

The notion that management can be viewed as an exact science based on mathematical calculations is known as "scientific management." It is based largely on the work of Frederick W. Taylor and his associates during the late 1800s. Although stressing the need for cooperation between management and subordinates, scientific management operationally dehumanizes the worker and makes work itself specialized in nature.

Another approach to management known as "human relations," emerged in the 1930s. Pioneered by Elton Mayo and his associates, the human relations theory suggests that workers can be motivated by nonfinancial aspects of the work environment. It further implies that the work situation can be viewed in behavioral terms and that the role of the manager is to create satisfactory interpersonal relationships.

"Management science," the third dimension to be discussed, is an outgrowth and extension of scientific management. Based largely on the application of mathematical equations and use of the computer, the study of management science is an important element influencing organizational and management decision-making today.

The "contemporary management approach," endeavors to draw together a number of management theories that have a bearing on current management practice. These four approaches are by no means all-inclusive; however, they represent the "in vogue" thinking of management theorists.

SCIENTIFIC MANAGEMENT

The rise of industry gave impetus to the development of the scientific management movement. Stimulated by the need to create an increase in goods, the

28

industrial revolution of the late nineteenth and early twentieth centuries called for improved methods of production. As initiated by Taylor, the scientific management movement was directed toward improving techniques of work and, ultimately, increasing worker efficiency.

Taylor was concerned with developing incentive plans for employees that would reward them for extra effort above and beyond a normal day's output. The assumption of this theory was that in a work situation, individuals are motivated by the desire for financial rewards. Scientific management theory further incorporated the premise that once a work task had been analyzed objectively, a specific course of procedures could be determined to complete the task. Once the most effective and efficient way to complete a tast was determined, a worker was trained in the procedure. Workers were expected to contribute a fair day's work and were rewarded financially for output above the minimum standards of expectation.

Taylor's principles of scientific management include the following:

> First, the development of the science, i.e., the gathering in on the part of those on the management's side of all knowledge which in the past has been kept in the heads of the workmen; second, the scientific selection and progressive development of the workmen; third, the bringing of the science and the scientifically selected and trained men together; and fourth, the constant and intimate co-operation which always occurs between the men on the management's side and the worker.[1]

It was assumed that once a worker understood the principle of increased financial incentives, his work output would increase. Enhancing an individual's opportunity for increased economic gains was assumed to be a prime motivating factor.

Fayol's Management Principles

Another individual who contributed to the scientific management movement was Henri Fayol. Fayol defined the management process as including five primary functions: planning, organization, command, coordination, and control. These management functions have come to serve as the foundation of the administrative process found in management literature. Believing that the process of management could be applied universally, Fayol developed 14 principles that he felt could be used by managers to solve problems in a number of situations:

1. Division of work. The principle of specialization of labor in order to concentrate activities for more efficiency.
2. Authority and Responsibility. Authority is the right to give orders and the power to exact obedience.

---

[1] Frederick W. Taylor, *The Principles of Scientific Management* (W. W. Norton and Co., 1967), pp. 36–37.

3. Discipline. Discipline is absolutely essential for the smooth running of business, and without discipline no enterprise could prosper.
4. Unity of Command. An employee should receive orders from one superior only.
5. Unity of Direction. One head and one plan for a group of activities having the same objectives.
6. Subordination of individual interests to general interests. The interests of one employee or a group should not prevail over that of the organization.
7. Renumeration. Personnel compensation should be fair and, as far as possible, afford satisfaction both to personnel and the firm.
8. Centralization. Centralization is essential to the organization and is a natural consequence of organizing.
9. Scalar Chain. The scalar chain is the chain of superiors ranging from the ultimate authority to the lowest rank.
10. Order. The organization should provide an orderly place for every individual. A place for everyone and everyone in his place.
11. Equity. Equity and a sense of justice pervades the organization.
12. Stability of Tenure of Personnel. Time is needed for the employee to adapt to his work and to perform it effectively.
13. Initiative. At all levels of the organizational ladder, zeal and energy are augmented by initiative.
14. Esprit de corps. This principle emphasizes the need for teamwork and the maintenance of interpersonal relationships.[2]

Fayol's perception of management functions and principles provides a means for analyzing the management process. His conceptual framework allows management methodology to be widely applied in industry and government. Emphasizing that management principles are not static, he stressed that managers should use their experience and insight in decision-making.

Scientific management's contribution to management theory is felt today throughout industry and government. By establishing a concern for effectiveness and efficiency, the scientific management movement drew attention to the need for the development of management and organizational theory. Toward that end, the scientific management movement contributed a number of important theoretical concepts. Fremont E. Kast and James E. Rosenzweig write:

> The scientific management movement provided many of the ideas for the conceptual framework later adopted by administrative management theorists, including clear delineation of authority and responsibility, separation of planning from operations, the functional organization, the use of standards in control, the development of

[2] Fremont E. Kast and James E. Rosenzweig, *Organization and Management: A Systems Approach* (New York: McGraw-Hill Book Co., 1974), pp. 58–59.

incentive systems for workers, the principle of management by exception, and task specialization.[3]

Further, the concept of cooperation between management and workers was another important by-product of the scientific management movement. (A fixture of contemporary management theory, employer–employee cooperation, will be discussed in chapters that follow.)

However, scientific management can be criticized from a number of different perspectives. Most notably, scientific management dehumanized the role of the worker and did not allow for such motivating factors as recognition, sense of achievement, and the need for self-esteem.

> By the end of the scientific-management period the worker had been reduced to the role of an impersonal cog in the machine of production. His job became more and more narrowly specialized until he had little appreciation for his contribution to the total product. Naturally, the worker had very little, if any, involvement and pride in his job. Although very significant technological advances were made in ... [this period], the serious weakness of the scientific approach to management was that it dehumanized the organizational member. He was assumed to be without emotion and capable of being scientifically manipulated, just like machines.[4]

HUMAN RELATIONS MANAGEMENT

The behavioral science approach to the study of management embraces a number of disciplines, such as psychology, sociology, and anthropology. The field of behavioral science is directed toward establishing

> ... evidence collected in an impersonal and objective way. ... The ultimate end is to understand, explain, and predict human behavior in the same sense in which scientists understand, explain, and predict the behavior of physical forces or biological factors or closer to home, the behavior of goods and services in the economic market.[5]

Several important studies have contributed greatly to the development of a body of knowledge for the behavioral sciences as they relate to organizational management.

The Hawthorne Studies

The Hawthorne research studies, headed by Elton Mayo, are generally considered to represent the beginning of the human relations approach to management. The

[3] Ibid., p. 57.

[4] Herbert G. Hicks, *The Management of Organizations: A Systems and Human Resources Approach* (New York: McGraw-Hill Book Co., 1972), pp. 373–374.

[5] Bernard Berelson, ed., *The Behavioral Sciences Today* Publishers, (New York: Basic Books, Inc., 1963), p. 3.

Hawthorne research effort consisted of a series of experiments designed to study the relationship between employee conditions and productivity. The first study was organized to determine the effects of illumination on worker production. A sample of workers was selected and divided into two groups, one for control and the other for experimental changes. The experimental group was subject to increases and decreases in the amount of illumination. On the other hand, the control group had illumination held constant. Contrary to the hypothesis tested, both groups showed increases in productivity.

Following the illumination studies another project, known as the "relay room experiments," was undertaken. This experiment was initiated to determine the effects of a number of working conditions on production. Selected variables, such as the number of hours worked per day and the number of days worked per week, were manipulated. After reaching a conclusion similar to that of the illumination studies, it was suggested that the independent variables tested were not the only influences on worker productivity.

Two additional studies, a second relay room experiment and a bank wiring room experiment were undertaken. The second relay room study was undertaken to determine the impact of wage incentives on production. Supervision, general working conditions, and the setting were held constant for both the experimental and control groups. The experimental group, which received wage incentives, showed a 12 percent increase in production at the conclusion of the study.

The bank wiring room studies resulted in findings opposite to those obtained in the second relay room study. Studying the production of workers assembling bank wires, it was determined that output was restricted for a number of reasons, including fear of unemployment, fear of raising the job standard, and protection of slower co-workers.

Obviously, in both experimental situations discussed above some factor was not being held constant or controlled: "This something of course was the complex human variable."[6]

The Hawthorne studies marked the first time that an intensive systematic analysis had uncovered, by accident, the *human variable* in management and organizational behavior. Mayo and others concluded from the experience that there were two factors that affected work and productivity. The first was the importance of group dynamics in the work situation. Behavior exhibited in work groups was by and large a by-product of individual and small-group interaction among workers. Second, it was suggested that the quantity and quality of job supervision affected employee job satisfaction and production.

The Hawthorne studies undermined the theory of scientific management, that is, that higher productivity could be achieved by financial reward alone. They further suggested that an understanding of the behavioral sciences could increase

[6] Fred Iuthans, *Organizational Behavior: A Modern Approach to Management* (New York: McGraw-Hill Book Co., 1973), p. 24.

organization and management effectiveness and efficiency. The Hawthorne studies have been criticized because they did not directly relate employee satisfaction and employee performance. It has also been suggested that early behaviorists, such as Mayo, widely applied their theories to management without due consideration to actual worker productivity.

Leadership Studies

Of historical significance to the development of management and organizational theory are a number of leadership studies. At the University of Iowa in the late 1930s, Ronald Lippitt and Ralph K. White, under the direction of Kurt Lewin, conducted an experiment to determine the effects of leadership style on a number of variables, including frustration and aggression.[7] Three different types of leadership styles—authoritarian, democratic, and laissez-faire—were tested on members of hobby clubs for young boys. It was concluded from the results of these studies that the majority of boys involved preferred leaders who utilized a democratic style of leadership. Further, it was observed that the boys reacted either aggressively or in an apathetic manner to autocratic leadership. Unfortunately, there was no effort to determine the effect of leadership on productivity.

Ohio State University, in the mid 1940s, initiated a number of leadership studies. These studies focused on situational variables affecting leadership, rather than the trait theory approach to leadership. Further, the studies focused on leadership effectiveness. The results showed evidence of two dimensions of leadership behavior: consideration and initiating structure. The consideration factor was the type of relationship that existed between a leader and the group members. The initiating structure was the ability of the leader to organize and direct people toward the accomplishment of a task. These studies pointed out ". . . the importance of [observing] both task direction and consideration of individual needs in assessing leadership behavior."[8] Further, they represented the first efforts to experimentally determine leadership effects on group behavior.

The University of Michigan Survey Research Center also conducted a study in the late 1940s to determine which leadership factors contribute to group productivity and individual satisfaction.[9] The results indicated that employee satisfaction is not necessarily related to productivity and that, in general, the employee centered supervisor is the crucial variable in worker productivity.

The historical significance of these early studies is that they provided new insights into leadership styles, which were empirically verifiable. The behavioral approach to the study of management has allowed for a certain amount of

[7] Kurt Lewin, Ronald Lippitt, and Ralph K. White, "Patterns of Aggressive Behavior in Experimentally Created 'Social Climates,'" *Journal of Social Psychology,* May 1939, pp. 271–276.

[8] Fred Luthans, *Organizational Behavior,* p. 36.

[9] Daniel Katz, Nathan Maccoby, and Nancy C. Morse, "Productivity, Supervision and Morale in an Office Situation" (Ann Arbor: University of Michigan, Survey Research Center, 1950).

generalization; that is, it has been widely applied to the practice and theory of management.

MANAGEMENT SCIENCE (OPERATIONS RESEARCH)

Management science is another major area that affects management and organizational theory and practice. A number of new techniques, such as Program Evaluation Review Technique–Critical Path Method (PERT–CPM), Total Performance Management, and Planning-Programming-Budgeting System (PPBS) are examples of management science techniques. These concepts are applied widely in the delivery of leisure services by both commercial organizations and governmental institutions. Related to an outgrowth of Taylor's scientific management, they involve application of ". . . the scientific method as a framework for problem solving with emphasis on objective rather than subjective judgment."[10]

Management science and/or operations research is geared to provide quantitative information that can be used in management decision-making. Quantitative methods can complement and/or replace subjective methods, such as operating on hunches, operating by rule of thumb, and/or brainstorming. They can help the leisure service manager bypass decision-making based on guesswork. Directed toward solving operational problems, these management techniques have been greatly enhanced by the increased capabilities of electronic data processing.

There are three general areas in which quantitative techniques and tools for management have been developed. The first of these, general systems modeling, involves organizational design, simulation model building, accounting systems and models, and management information systems. The second grouping, scheduling models, includes conventional models, such as milestone charts. Mathematical-statistical models, such as marginal analysis and network analysis, is the last general area in which quantitative techniques exist. Although it is difficult to specifically identify a body of knowledge in the field of management science, management science has a number of key characteristics. These characteristics include:

1. Emphasis upon the scientific method.
2. Systematic approach to problem solving.
3. Mathematical model building.
4. Quantification and utilization of mathematical and statistical procedures.
5. Concern with economic-technical rather than psychosocial aspects.
6. Utilization of electronic computers as tools.
7. Emphasis on total systems approach.

[10] Kast and Rosenzweig, *Organization and Management*, p. 87.

8. Seeking optimal decisions under closed-systems assumptions.
9. Orientation to normative rather than descriptive models.[11]

The successful application of management science first occurred in England during World War II. It was introduced to help the British Royal Air Force intercept invading aircraft. Researchers—with the aid of radar systems—were able to mathematically calculate intercept routes. Following World War II, operations research techniques were applied widely to problems of business and industry in England. During the early 1950s, operations research was applied in the United States. The following steps are widely accepted as operations research techniques that can be used to solve a problem:

1. Formulate the problem.
2. Construct a mathematical model to represent the system under study.
3. Derive a solution from the model.
4. Test the model and the solution derived from it.
5. Establish controls over the situation.
6. Put the solution to work, implementation.[12]

A key concept in management science and operations research is that of modeling. A ". . . model is a simplified representation of the relevant aspects of an actual system or process."[13] It allows the decision-maker the opportunity to simulate reality and, therefore, analyze potential effects with a great deal of predictability.

Models can allow a leisure service manager to experiment by identifying and/or manipulating variables within a system without direct involvement in an actual problem. This provides management with "simulated" information from which decisions can be made without the expenditure of resources. There are two types of models: the descriptive model and the normative model.[14] No inferences are drawn from a descriptive model. It merely describes the manner in which a system functions. It usually displays alternative choices for the decision-maker. On the other hand, normative models are developed to tell "how the system should be, in order to achieve a particular objective."[15]

Managers involved in the delivery of leisure services can benefit from an understanding of quantitative techniques. It is important for the reader to understand that management science models may be complicated and involve a need for

---

[11] Ibid., p. 89.
[12] C. West Churchman, Russell L. Ackoff, and E. Leonard Arnoff, *Introduction to Operations Research* (New York: John Wiley and Sons, 1957), pp. 12–13.
[13] James H. Donnelly, Jr., James L. Gibson, and John M. Ivancevich, *Fundamentals of Management: Functions, Behavior and Model* (Dallas, Tex.: Business Publications, 1971), p. 278.
[14] Ibid., pp. 279–280.
[15] Ibid., p. 280.

detailed and intensive study prior to application. But models can be of aid to the manager of a leisure services system, even if they are utilized in an abbreviated and/or modified form. The following descriptions will provide the reader with a general understanding of a number of techniques that will provide quantitative information for decision-making.

Network Models

The management function of planning, scheduling, and controlling can be enhanced through the graphic means used in network models. These are tools designed specifically to help the leisure service manager determine the relationships that exist between the various tasks associated with any given project or program. Network models allow the leisure service manager to deal with the complexity and uncertainties involved in the organization of projects or programs. These techniques provide the leisure service manager with aids to facilitate decision-making. Network models do not make decisions for managers, but they can serve as a resource to base decisions on.

There are three essential components involved in the utilization of network models. The first phase usually involves identifying and/or planning a project's or program's activities and events and arranging them in a logical sequence. An *event* may be defined as "a specific accomplishment that occurs at a recognizable point in time."[16] *Activities* are "the work required to complete a specific event."[17]

The second phase involved in network modeling is the actual scheduling of the estimated duration of each activity. By proceeding logically through a network and determining the time each activity will take, one is able to estimate the cumulative project or program time. As a program or project progresses, the third major component—controlling—enters the scene. By monitoring the completion of events, changes, and/or modifications in the entire project, an analysis can be undertaken to determine and project future impact on the entire network. By updating the model periodically, a leisure service manager is able to effectively and efficiently control a project program. Figure 2.1 illustrates a network.

Three of the important network models are the Program Evaluation Review Technique (PERT), Critical Path Method (CPM), and Line of Balance (LOB). PERT was developed by the U.S. Navy as "a method of minimizing production delays, interruptions, and conflicts; of co-ordinating and synchronizing the various aspects of the overall job; and expediting the completion of projects."[18] It is directed primarily toward helping an organization complete projects and/or

---

[16] Richard I. Levin and Charles A. Kirkpatrick, *Quantitative Approaches to Management* (New York: McGraw-Hill Book Co., 1971), p. 393.
[17] Ibid.
[18] Ibid.

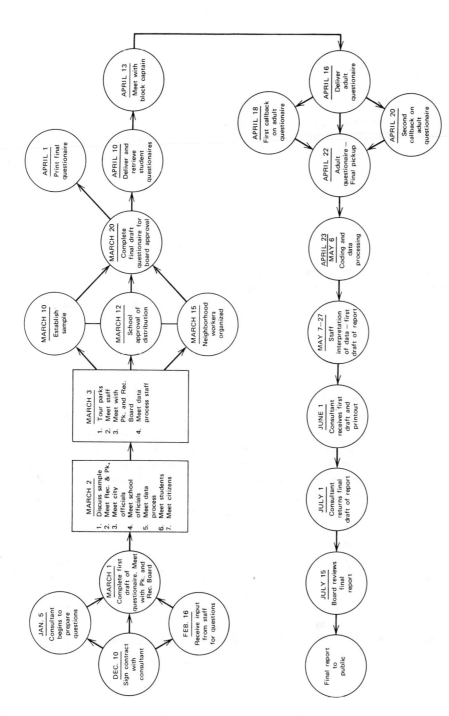

Figure 2.1. A network diagram. (Adapted from Joseph J. Bannon, *Leisure Resources: Its Comprehensive Planning,* © 1976, p. 159. Reprinted by permission of Prentice-Hall, Inc., Englewood Cliffs, N.J.)

programs on time. Events are usually denoted as circles and activities as arrows joining circles in PERT networks.

CPM is a networking model that allows insertion of the concept of cost. It was developed by E. I. du Pont de Nemours and Company to aid in the development and construction of its chemical plants. CPM enables one to determine the earliest anticipated date for completing network ending events. As such, CPM provides for the systematic isolation of tasks (as in PERT) and the identification of the quickest and/or critical path to completing a project or program. Thus determination of the critical path allows for a reduction in program or project cost by identifying the most appropriate and expedient route to complete a given task.

LOB focuses on the key events required for completion of a program or project. The detail in PERT or CPM networks is not required in LOB models.

Planning-Programming-Budgeting System (PPBS)

PPBS is directed toward increasing organizational effectiveness and efficiency by helping the manager to identify specific goals and objectives and to evaluate those objectives based on a review of the cost and benefits of a given program and/or project. A mission-oriented approach to budgeting, PPBS has three important components: establishing measurable and quantifiable goals and objectives, developing an analytical model, and investigating alternatives.

The development of measurable and quantifiable goals and objectives is the first step in the planning process. Defining the ends, aims, or purposes of an organization is the function of goal setting. This is followed by the identification of specific objectives that are attainable and quantifiable. In addition, an organization should attempt to determine specifically how these goals and objectives are to be reached and what organizational arrangements are necessary to achieve them. This process is followed by the development of an analytical model to aid the leisure service manager in assessing the program desired. Analytical models provide information from which predictions can be made, and budget recommendations can also be made. This procedure ties the planning and programming cycle together and affects related budgetary actions. Ultimately, it links an agency's goals and objectives to its financial expenditures.

Finally, a review of the alternatives is essential to the planning process. Choosing among various goals and objectives, with full knowledge of the resources and/or costs necessary to meet these desired ends, promotes rational decision-making. Open and explicit discussion and analysis reduces guesswork and assumptions and permits attention to focus on real political issues.

The sequential establishment and implementation of a program is illustrated by the following cycle (see also Figure 2.2):

1. Analyze the Situation and the Needs. This involves identification of the problem resulting from a close analysis of the situation and the needs resulting from it.
2. Goal Setting. This part of the process involves determination of qualitative philosophical statements denoting ends, aims, or purposes.
3. Developing Objectives. Here the aims or targets are defined in quantifiable, attainable dimensions.

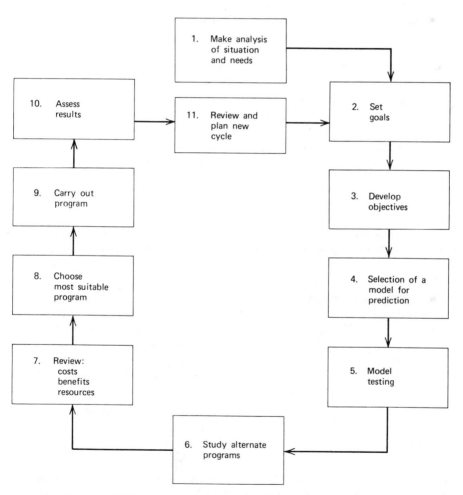

Figure 2.2. The PPBS cycle. (Adapted from *PPBS: For People Who Don't Understand PPBS,* School Management Institute, 1971, p. 9.)

4. Selection of a Model for Prediction. This stage involves the selection of a quantitative model for decision-making.
5. Test the Model. This stage allows the manager to assess and analyze the model's usefulness as a predictive and/or informative tool.
6. Evaluate Alternative Programs. This part of the process provides analytical data regarding cost from which decisions can be made.
7. Review Cost, Benefits, and Resources. This stage allows one to look at the cost and benefits of each alternative based on facts from the model rather than guesswork or assumptions.
8. Choose the Most Suitable Program. Once the alternatives have been analyzed, the manager is ready to make a decision and select a program which may more accurately reflect the goals of the organization.
9. Carry Out the Program. This is the implementation phase of the cycle and involves the transformation of resources into a tangible program.
10. Assessing the Results. This involves evaluating the achievement of goals and objectives and also carefully analyzing the amount of resources used to attain them.
11. Review and Plan a New Cycle. This last step in the cycle feeds new information into the process, thereby allowing for a continual progression and updating of all the factors affecting programming and budgeting.[19]

Simulation

Although simulation is a broad term, it essentially involves the manipulation or reproduction of an organization's potential operations as it moves through time. Simply, one may use simulation to model and represent a number of situations for the purpose of aiding decision-making.

A decision-making tree can help the manager deal with the potential alternatives involved in a decision-making situation (see Figure 2.3). It "is no more than a pictorial diagram that captures the uncertainty of the situation and enumerates the possible outcomes of making the decision in one way or another."[20] By describing or simulating the various alternatives that face the leisure service manager, the potential consequences of a given decision can be graphically illustrated and identified in advance.

Another method of simulation comes through the use of sampling. It would, of course, be difficult to have a total population represented in every decision that affected the allocation of an organization's resources. As an alternative, one can use methods of sampling that accurately represent the entire population. Sam-

[19] Adapted from *PPBS: (Programming-Planning Budgeting System For People Who Don't Understand PPBS)*. (Worthington, Ohio: School Management Institute, 1971), p. 9.
[20] James A. Peterson and Michael F. Pohlen, "Agency Management," in Sidney G. Lutzin and Edward H. Storey, *Managing Municipal Leisure Services* (Washington, D.C.: International City Management Association, 1973), p. 55.

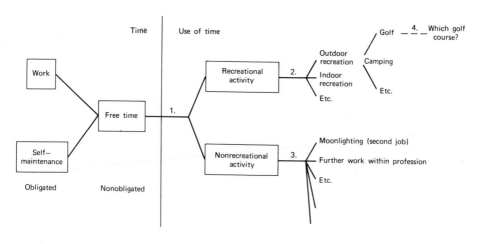

Figure 2.3. Model of free-time activity choice. (Dr. Doug Crapo, Balmer, Crapo, and Associates, Waterloo, Ontario, Canada.)

pling is done with the use of random numbers. A random sample is a method of systematically taking a portion of a given population to insure that each number has an equal chance of being selected. If a sample is randomly selected, it is representative of the total population and is unbiased. By sampling, the leisure service manager is able to simulate accurately the needs, interests, and opinions of those he represents without calling on each person individually. Sampling provides answers to questions and reduces the uncertainty facing the decision-maker. It helps the planner of leisure services to more accurately predict the impact that decisions regarding allocation of resources will have on a given constituency. Although this method does not entirely reduce uncertainty, it does allow for more effective and efficient operations.

Systems Analysis

Systems analysis is a technique that allows the leisure service manager to identify the variables which may be involved in the operation of an organization. It "is a method that reduces a total system into increasingly smaller components until the smallest unit making up the entire system is defined."[21]

Systems analysis broadly applied, according to Richard G. Kraus and Joseph E. Curtis, seeks to do the following:

[21] George Hjelte and J. S. Shivers, *Public Administration of Recreational Services* (Philadelphia: Lea and Febiger, 1972), p. 290.

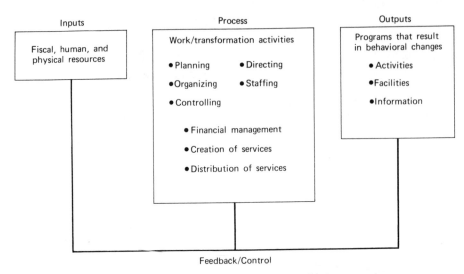

Figure 2.4. A systems approach to the management of leisure services.

1. Establish detailed work objectives that specifically determine what, when, where, and how work is to be accomplished.
2. Develop effective schedules for maintenance and repairing, and group functions together for efficient performance.
3. Develop standardized methods for job performance in which work routines are programmed, with time standards for completion.
4. Provide instruments and techniques for effectively measuring and determining the cost of job performance, to assist in evaluating employee work output and assigning tasks or planning budgets.[22]

There are five components necessary for constructing a system: inputs, process, output, feedback, and control. Output refers to the desired goals or objectives of the system. Inputs are the resources necessary to achieve the desired goals or outputs. Process refers to the procedure, or procedures, that consume resources and allow for the achievement of desired outcomes. Mechanisms for feedback are directed toward evaluation and modification of both the type and amount of resources consumed to produce desired goals or outputs. The function of control is to regulate or change components of the system that can affect the desired outcome. Systems theory suggests that all these components are interrelated and dependent on one another. Figure 2.4 diagrams the systems approach to the management of recreation.

[22] Richard G. Kraus and Joseph E. Curtis, *Creative Administration in Recreation and Parks* (St. Louis: C. V. Mosby Co., 1973), pp. 26–27.

Systems can be viewed in two ways: "(1) closed or (2) open and in interaction with their environment."[23] Closed systems view management and organizational behavior as primarily centered around the internal organization and operation of the agency. Open systems, on the other hand, are in constant interaction with various systems, such as the political, social, and economic environments. Closed systems tend to become static, lacking continual input, feedback, and stimulus from the environment. Open systems maintain a dynamic posture in regard to their environment. They react quickly to changes in the environment and modify the mission and function of the organization to the changing environmental inputs. The management model presented in Chapter 1 suggests that leisure delivery organizations should be open systems responding to the various inputs and constraints which result from continual interaction with the environment.

A systems viewpoint allows a leisure service manager to identify each of these subunits and/or components within a system. In theory, as the components become smaller and more identifiable, they are in effect more manageable. Once a problem affecting a leisure delivery system has been isolated as a subcomponent of the broader environment, a leisure delivery system can be adjusted to contend with the problem. Further, systems that remain in constant interaction with the environment can react to meet the changing leisure-time needs, interests, and behavior of those it serves.

CONTEMPORARY MANAGEMENT

The development of management theory has most recently been characterized by efforts to synthesize and integrate the needs of people with the completion of management tasks. The evolution of management science and the behavioral sciences has influenced the way that management behavior is viewed. In an effort to maximize effectiveness and efficiency, management science and the behavioral sciences have been brought closer together. They are no longer viewed as being opposed to one another; rather, they are viewed as being complementary.

Theory X and Theory Y

Douglas McGregor's Theory X and Theory Y served as a new approach to management behavior. McGregor postulated that there were two basic assumptions of human behavior, Theory X and Theory Y, which, if adopted by a manager, would affect his or her management style. Theory X assumptions concerning the behavior of human beings are characterized by McGregor as follows:

1. The average human being has an inherent dislike of work and will avoid it if he can.

[23] Kast and Rosenzweig, *Organization and Management*, p. 109.

2. Because of this human characteristic of dislike of work, most people must be coerced, controlled, directed, and threatened with punishment to get them to put forth adequate effort toward the achievement of organizational objectives.
3. The average human being prefers to be directed, wishing to avoid responsibility, has relatively little ambition, and wants security above all.[24]

A leisure service manager utilizing Theory X assumptions about the nature of human beings will have essentially an authoritarian, punitive, and controlling approach to management. The theory presumes that people are basically lazy and crave security. Job performance can be achieved only when the manager controls and directs the work environment. Further, Theory X suggests that once a worker is secure in the work environment and free from decision-making responsibility, she or he will be satisfied. Theory X assumptions have guided the practice of many leisure service managers. But these assumptions fail to take into account the findings of behavioral scientists that people are motivated by a number of needs. It is important to recognize that once the basic needs of security and safety are satisfied, a worker will not be motivated solely by offers of financial incentives. For a worker to produce more, a manager must appeal to that person's individual needs for recognition, status, self-esteem, and self-actualization. Certainly every leisure service manager has had an employee who is motivated without threats, or implied threats, of punishment and/or increased financial incentives. This concern is characterized in McGregor's Theory Y.

Theory Y assumptions about the behavior of human beings are basically an outgrowth of the research of behavioral scientists. They include the following:

1. The expenditure of physical and mental effort in work is as natural as play or rest.
2. External control and the threat of punishment are not the only means for bringing about effort toward organizational objectives. Man will exercise self-direction and self-control in the service of objectives to which he is committed.
3. Committment to objectives is a function of the rewards associated with their achievement.
4. The average human being learns, under proper conditions, not only to accept but to seek responsibility.[25]

Theory Y assumptions take into consideration a new set of theories that affect the practice of management based on motivational values. Theory Y indicates that when the goals and objectives of an organization are aligned with an individual's needs, a positive and highly satisfying work environment evolves. Theory X assumptions are based on the belief that people must be controlled and

---

[24] Douglas McGregor, *The Human Side of Enterprise* (New York: McGraw-Hill Book Co., 1960), pp. 33–34.
[25] Ibid., pp. 47–48.

directed. By contrast, Theory Y assumptions note that a manager is most effective when he is able to integrate an organization's goals with the personal needs of his employees. This will be discussed in greater detail in Chapter 4.

Management by Objectives

An approach to the integration of personal needs with organizational goals has been popularly characterized as "Management by Objectives" (MBO). Directed at the management functions of planning and controlling, MBO is a process that can enable the leisure service manager to focus on the achievement of organizational goals while at the same time providing for satisfactory human relationships and experiences.

> It is a systematic approach to management whereby mission statements and job functions—that is, identification of objectives desired, results to be achieved, and courses of action—are mutually agreed upon at the administrative and operational levels. Mutually subscribed objectives and job functions provide for an exchange of information, development of understanding, building of acceptance and belief, and a committment to action between administrative and operational levels within an organization.[26]

Contributing to organizational unity, MBO allows for the identification and development of mutual concerns and interests of an organization's members. Responsive dialogue between manager and subordinates can lead to mutually determined courses of action. A cooperative and satisfying work environment usually can be achieved when a manager makes an effort to include the employee in a discussion of the work objectives to be achieved, rather than merely dictating exactly what the employee is to do. Figure 2.5 illustrates the MBO process. Figure 2.6 is a copy of a form used by the Calgary (Alberta) Parks/Recreation Department in the implementation of its MBO program.

The Managerial Grid

Developed by Robert R. Blake and Jane S. Mouton, the Managerial Grid Theory suggests that successful managers are those who are concerned with both people (human relations) and production (completion of work task).[27] Figure 2.7 shows the Management Grid that they developed. Along the vertical axis, concern for people is rated on a scale of 1 to 9. The horizontal axis measures concern for production.

Blake and Mouton identify five management positions within the Managerial Grid. Position 1,1 represents a low concern for both people and production. High

---

[26] Christoper R. Edginton, "Management by Crisis: There is an Alternative," *Journal of Iowa Parks and Recreation* (February 1974), p. 10.

[27] Robert R. Blake and Jane S. Mouton, *The Managerial Grid* (Houston, Tex.: Gulf Publishing Co., 1965), p. 10.

INFORMATION ON THE USE OF THIS OBJECTIVE FORM

These four functions are suggested for you to group your objectives
It is not necessary to put in a sheet for all four functions
You may put in two sheets for one function
OPERATION__FINANCE__RELATIONSHIPS__PERSONNEL__
INDICATE WITH AN "X" THE FUNCTION RELATED
TO THIS SHEET
TO COVER THE PERIOD From _____ to _____
Suggest six month period: JANUARY to JUNE or JULY
to DECEMBER

P O S I T I O N: _____ of the employee
Date Submitted _____
Date Delivered to immediate Supervisor _____

SHORT TERM GOALS:	COMPLETION DATE:	INDICATORS:	EVALUATION DATE:	IF NOT COMPLETED ADJUSTED DATE:
(1) State your short term objectives for this function of your job	REPORT by DATE	Measurable indicators of achieving the goal set out	Either a July	
(2) Begin with—To achieve —To ensure —To prepare, etc.	or COMPLETED by DATE or	Answer the question "How do we know the goal has been met?"	or January Date	
(3) Ten to Fifteen words try to avoid "and" – "in addition" or double goals in one statement	Progress Report Dates	Time–percentage cost–etc.		

BRIEF DESCRIPTION OF ROUTINE DUTIES INVOLVED:

Responsible for—what are your duties and responsibilities—related to this particular function.

Stress the less obvious.

LONG TERM OBJECTIVE: (Philosophical)

This objective should only require to be revised every two or three years.

It is the long range aim that you wish to achieve in this functional area for your particular section of the Parks & Recreation Service.

Signature of EMPLOYEE	*Signature of* IMMEDIATE SUPERVISOR	*Date of* APPROVAL
SIGNATURE	APPROVED	Date

Figure 2.6   MBO Form, Calgary (Alberta) Parks/Recreation Department

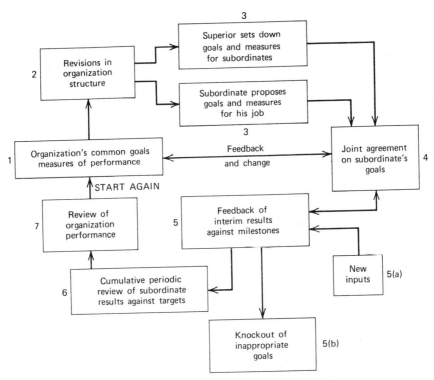

Figure 2.5. The cycle of management by objectives. (From the book *Management by Objectives* by George S. Odiorne. Copyright, ©, 1965 by Pitman Publishing Corporation. Reprinted by permission of Pitman Publishing Corporation.)

concern for both people and production is represented by position 9,9. A low/high score for the completion of tasks and the maintenance of satisfactory human relations would be reflected in position 1,9 or 9,1. the position of 5,5 indicates a managerial style that essentially tries to find a compromise between the concerns of people and the completion of a task.

The 3-D Theory of Management Effectiveness

The 3-D Theory of Management Effectiveness, developed by William Reddin, maintains that a manager's style must remain flexible to be effective. Reddin's theory of management rests on his belief that empirical evidence demonstrates that there is no single appropriate management style. The 3-D Theory of Managerial Effectiveness incorporates the dimensions of concern for completion of a task (TO = task orientation) and the establishment of satisfactory human relations (RO = relationships orientation). These two basic dimensions are similar to the consideration factor and initiating structure identified in Ohio State University leadership studies. They also relate to Blake and Mouton's Managerial Grid's concern for people and production. To these two dimensions, Reddin added a third dimension, which he identified as managerial effectiveness ". . . the extent to which a manager achieves the output requirements of his position.[28] The effectiveness of a manager is found in his ability to change his behavior according to the needs and dictates of the situation.

The basic 3D Theory of Managerial Effectiveness includes four basic types of management: integrated, dedicated, related, and separated.[29] These styles are closely related to the Managerial Grid. The integrated management style is similar to the position of 9,9 on the Managerial Grid; both indicate concern for human relationships and task accomplishment. The dedicated management style correlates to position 9,1, a high concern for task accomplishment and a low concern for establishing satisfying human relationships. The related management style and position 1,9 on the Managerial Grid involves a high consideration of people and a low concern for task accomplishment. Lastly, the position of 1,1 on the Managerial Grid, representing a low concern for task accomplishment and human relations, is related to the separated management style. In analyzing these four basic styles, Reddin notes that managerial effectiveness is determined by appropriate application of one of the four basic styles. Conversely, he notes that inappropriate application of the styles results in ineffectiveness. Reddin expands the four basic styles to eight styles in order to include identification of appropriate, effective management styles and inappropriate, ineffective management styles. He defines them as follows:

Executive. A manager who is using a high Task Orientation and a high Relationships Orientation in a situation where such behavior is appropriate and who is, therefore, more effective; perceived as a good motivating force who sets high standards, treats everyone somewhat differently, and prefers team management.

Compromiser. A manager who is using a high Task Orientation and a high Relations Orientation in a situation that requires a high orientation to only one or neither and who is, therefore, less effective; perceived as being a poor decision-maker, as one who allows various pressures in the situation to influence him too much, and is avoiding or minimizing pressures and problems rather than maximizing long-term production.

Benevolent Autocrat. A manager who is using a high Task Orientation and a low Relationships Orientation in a situation where such behavior is appropriate and who is, therefore, more effective; perceived as knowing what he wants and how to get it without creating resentment.

[28] William S. Reddin, *Managerial Effectiveness* (New York: McGraw-Hill Book Co., 1970), p. 39.
[29] Ibid., p. 41.

Autocrat. A manager who is using a high Task Orientation and a low Relationships Orientation in a situation where such behavior is inappropriate and who is, therefore, less effective; perceived as having no confidence in others, as unpleasant, and as interested only in the immediate task.

Developer. A manager who is using a high Relationships Orientation and a low Task Orientation in a situation where such behavior is appropriate and who is, therefore, more effective; perceived as having implicit trust in people and as being primarily concerned with developing them as individuals.

Missionary. A manager who is using a high Relationships Orientation and a low Task Orientation in a situation where such behavior is inappropriate and who is, therefore, less effective; perceived as being primarily interested in harmony.

Bureaucrat. A manager who is using a low Task Orientation and a low Relationships Orientation in a situation where such behavior is appropriate and who is, therefore, more effective; perceived as being primarily interested in rules and procedures for their own sake, and wanting to control the situation by their use, and as conscientious.

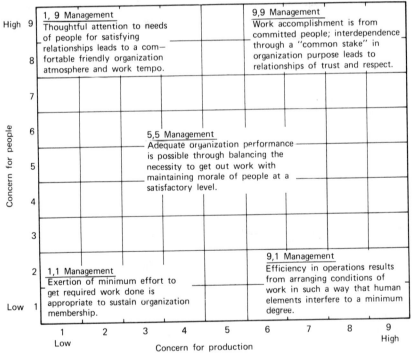

Figure 2.7.   The management grid. (The Managerial Grid figure from *The Managerial Grid,* by Robert R. Blake and Jane Srygley Mouton. Houston: Gulf Publishing Company, Copyright © 1964, p. 10. Reproduced with permission.)

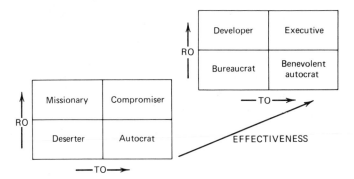

Figure 2.8. The 3-D style model. (From *Managerial Effectiveness,* by William S. Reddin. Copyright © 1970 by William Reddin. Used with permission of McGraw-Hill Book Co.)

Deserter. A manager who is using a low Task Orientation and a low Relationships Orientation in a situation where such behavior is inappropriate and who is, therefore, less effective; perceived as uninvolved and passive or negative.[30] (See Figure 2.8)

The 3-D Theory recognizes that different management situations require the application of complementary management skills. The manager of leisure services must be sensitive to the varying situational demands on the administration of a leisure service organization. Working with professional as well as quasi-professional personnel and the public at large presents a variety of management challenges. Individuals who are involved in the creation of activities must be motivated in a different manner than the park maintenance personnel, who are essentially involved in carrying out routinized tasks. Management behavior should be modified to meet the situational needs found in an organization.

SUMMARY

Management theory and practice may be viewed from a number of perspectives. Four approaches—scientific management, human relations management, management science, and contemporary management—provide a theoretical base for the leisure service manager. Each approach strongly influences the management of leisure service organizations. Scientific management provides a conceptual and historical view of the management process. Human relations management modified scientific management thinking by introducing an increased concern for the human variable. Management science can provide the leisure service manager with a number of specific tools and techniques with which to aid

[30] From pp. 41–43 of *Managerial Effectiveness* by William S. Reddin. Copyright © 1970 by William Reddin. Used with permission of McGraw-Hill Book Company.

decision-making. A brief overview of recent management theories provides the leisure service manager with an opportunity to analyze his own behavior and style. It also provides a basis of theory on which practice can be based. This theoretical base can serve to help managers evaluate their skills, ability, and style and perhaps modify, change, or enhance their management behavior. This is an important step in the productive management of leisure delivery service.

Integrating Individual Needs with Organizational Goals 3

Understanding organizational goals as well as individual needs is the responsibility of every manager. A manager is charged with meeting the goals and objectives of the organization and accomplishes this through the employees that work for him/her. To initiate work among his employees, the manager must provide a motivating environment. He does this by being aware of employees' individual needs and making it possible for them to meet these needs. As employees move to meet their needs, the result is action or behavior that is work activity. The manager who is able to align the individual's goals with the organization's goals will be successful in the accomplishment of both.

INDIVIDUAL NEEDS

Every individual has needs; young or old, rich or poor, employed or unemployed, and regardless of race. Needs must be met in one fashion or another. Every waking hour of every individual's day is directed toward meeting personal needs. An individual has conscious and unconscious needs. Needs are met in different places and during different time periods. Some needs are met at work, some are met during leisure, and some are met in daily maintenance (eating, sleeping, bathing, etc.). In the case of a child, needs are met at school or during play. An adult has another form of play, known as recreation, and oftentimes needs are met within this context. It is important for the manager to understand what the individual needs of his employees are and how to go about meeting them. When an individual's needs are not met, it may result in frustration, anxiety, and other problems.

The Manager's Role in Understanding Needs

Leisure service managers should be aware that employees come to work to meet their own needs. Individuals do not come to work only as employees to help meet organizational goals. They are individuals first and come to work to meet needs that can best be met through employment. The dual function of a leisure service manager is to help employees meet their work oriented needs and to help consumers meet their leisure needs. To plan services that meet the needs of people, managers must be able to recognize participants' needs and their level of development. Only if managers understand this concept can they truly offer meaningful leisure services.

Leisure, work, and daily maintenance all relate to each other and result in activity and behavior designed to meet personal needs. Leisure service managers, as professionals in the field of leisure as well as managers of employees, (1) help individuals meet their needs through leisure services and (2) help their employees meet their needs through their work experiences. Managers who understand the needs of people and help employees meet their needs through work, will release the work capacity of employees that will provide leisure services for the community.

Needs

A need can best be defined as a form of deficiency. A need exists when there is either a psychological or a physiological imbalance. Needs can be complicated or simple. One of the simplest forms of need results when the body is deprived of food or water; there is a deficiency existing. Another need may occur when an individual is deprived of friends or companions.[1]

When there is a need or a deficiency, this usually results in a drive to alleviate the deficiency or meet the need. Drives are action oriented, usually resulting in some form of behavior. For example, if an individual experiences a deficiency of water or food, he attempts to meet that need by searching for food and water. Hunger and thirst needs are translated into hunger or thirst drives. Goals, likewise, are ends at which drives are directed. Thus obtaining a goal, or meeting a particular need, restores the psychological and physiological balance and ends the drive. This process is demonstrated more clearly in the next chapter dealing with motivation; a series of diagrams depict a step-by-step process showing how needs are met through the motivation of an individual.

Classification of Needs

Needs have been classified and explained in many ways. Many theories have been offered to describe how the human being goes about meeting needs. We will examine some of the theories as they relate to meeting needs through work and leisure.

Psychoanalytic Theory.
Sigmund Freud was one of the first individuals to devote a lifetime to understanding human needs. Freud classified people's needs into three types of categories: two

---

[1] Fred Luthans, *Organizational Behavior: A Modern Behavioral Approach to Management* (New York: McGraw-Hill Book Co. 1973), p. 392.

conscious states and one unconscious state. These three states resulted in a system known as "personality." The three states are interrelated and interdependent, working together in an attempt to help humans satisfy basic needs.[2] Freud called these the id, the ego, and the superego. He indicated that behavior is the result of the interaction of these three factors.

The Id. The id is the core of the unconscious. The id consists of the psychological aspects of the person, including instincts, that are present from the moment of birth. The id is always struggling for satisfaction and pleasure, striving to meet the sexual, hunger, and comfort needs. Sometimes the id is extremely aggressive, and in many instances destructive, as it strives to meet an individual's basic needs. During childhood, the id is uncontrolled. It dominates the activities of a child in its constant search for food, warmth, and love. As a child matures into adulthood, she or he learns to control the id, but it is still a strong force throughout life. It constantly affects behavior and activities.

The Ego. The ego represents the conscious part of a human being's behavior. In most cases, the ego keeps the id tendencies in balance and in check when dealing with the realities of life and the external environment. The ego can interpret realities for the id through the reasoning process. For example, to cope with the hunger need (id), the ego might initiate such constructive behavior as growing, preparing, and cooking food.

On the other hand, there are many conflicts between the id and the ego. These conflicts are a direct result of the id's demand for immediate pleasure and satisfaction while the ego tries to deny the demand and put the id in a proper time perspective or place for the satisfaction of a need. This can be exemplified by the desire of the id for food immediately when the only option is to steal it. The ego would attempt to rationalize the hunger need and to follow a logical sequence of getting food by waiting until the individual could get home to prepare it or could go to a restaurant, both being rational responses and more acceptable to society. To resolve the situation, the superego comes into play in support of the ego.

The Superego. The superego is the third element of the Freudian concept. It is best defined by the term "conscience." The superego is represented by the values and ideals of society as interpreted by parents, community, and the society in which a person lives and is reinforced by reward and punishment. The superego is represented by the moral values of the personality. It represents the ideal rather than the real and strives for perfection rather than immediate satisfaction and pleasure. It is constantly discriminating between right and wrong and directing the total individual toward the ideal. The individual is not always aware that the superego is working in his or her behalf. The superego is constantly reminding the

---

[2] Calvin S. Hall and Gardner Lindzey, *Theories of Personality*, second edition (New York: John Wiley and Sons, 1970), pp. 29–72.

individual to play down the impulses which satisfy immediate pleasures of the id. In some cases the superego is in direct conflict with ego.

In summarizing the psychoanalytic theory: The id represents an individual's unconscious desires to satisfy basic needs for gratification and pleasure. Contrary to the id, the ego is conscious. It deals with the reality of the world. The ego is constantly attempting to deal with the id in an intelligent and realistic manner, causing an individual to act more civilized, socialized, and unselfish in dealing with others. The superego represents the conscience of a human being. It provides the norms for the ego and determines what is right and wrong. The superego aids the individual in combating the impulses of the id.

There is a constant and inevitable struggle among id, ego, and superego; a person may act rationally in one situation and just the opposite in another situation, or even in a similar situation. The psychoanalytic theory helps us understand why individuals act and respond in the variety of ways they do.

Maslow's Theory of Needs

Abraham Maslow's theory of needs indicates that an individual will always respond to his or her strongest need. He helped explain his theory by depicting needs in a hierarchical structure, with the more basic needs at the bottom of the model and the higher, or more refined, needs at the top, as seen in Figure 3.1. These needs are classified into five distinct categories: (1) physiological, (2) security, (3) social or belonging, (4) esteem, and (5) self-actualization.[3]

Maslow theorized that there are five principles which affect people's behavior in the attempt to meet their needs. The first principle is that *all human behavior has a purpose*. The individual who is hungry seeks, prepares, and eats food. This involves a certain purposeful behavior; to satisfy the hunger need or deficiency which exists because of the physiological imbalance and the feeling of hunger.

The same approaches to understanding needs of individuals have application to the leisure setting and the planning of services. The recreation leader who is able to recognize a deficiency in the needs of individuals attending a particular leisure program can plan the service accordingly. Recognizing the need for companionship among a group of elderly persons in a particular neighborhood, the astute recreation leader can start an activity for seniors whereby they can meet potential friends. Likewise, a manager who recognizes in an employee a need for praise can meet that deficiency by complimenting the employee for a job well done. A manager might meet the need of an employee who is creative by giving the employee a job that calls for creativity.

Maslow's second principle is that *all human wants and needs are identifiable and can be classified in a hierarchy in which people seek satisfaction of lower needs first*. Again referring to Figure 3.1, this principle indicates that the physiological

[3] Abraham H. Maslow, *Motivation and the Personality* (New York: Harper and Row, 1954).

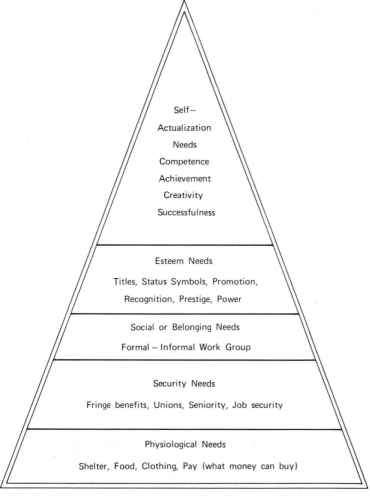

Figure 3.1. Maslow's hierarchy of needs.

needs are the most basic. They must be satisfied first. An individual who is hungry and thirsty is going to seek to satisfy these needs first. After these needs have been satisfied, the individual tends to seek satisfaction of the next level of needs, safety, followed by satisfaction of the social, then esteem, and finally self-actualization needs. The employer or recreation leader who recognizes this hierarchy should determine what level the employee or participant has reached and provide jobs or leisure experiences that will meet and challenge the individual. More insight will be given to this principle when we discuss motivation, particularly the Herzberg theory of motivation, in Chapter 4.

The recreation leader, in trying to plan a program for her participants, must recognize the level of development of the participants. If she is dealing with an inner-city group of children who are still striving to satisfy their safety and social needs, her program should be built around activities that tend to satisfy these needs. It would be impractical for this leader to plan activities that would provide for self-fulfillment and self-actualization needs when the youths have safety and social needs. Obviously environmental factors such as the economic level of the community, affect these needs. In contemporary North American society, many of the basic, lower-level needs are more or less guaranteed by social programs, thus eliminating the lower-level need as motivation factors.

The third principle is that *individual differences exist in respect to these wants and needs. People put a different (1) time priority and (2) intensity priority on their needs.* An individual may experience both an intensity priority and a time priority when he has the needs for exercise and food. Because he is extremely hungry, he puts off his need for exercise until he has eaten. Likewise, an employee might very much want a job promotion that requires her to move to a different city or a different work location. She may not be willing to do this because she places a higher priority on security at that time. The many friendships she has made in her present job and the fact that she has seniority causes her to change her time priorities.

People are constantly placing different priorities on needs. Some needs influence and take precedent over other needs. This balance is constantly changing both in work and in leisure. An individual is constantly having to make a choice about which need to pursue first, provided he or she recognizes the need. A good employer, being aware of time and intensity priorities, can affect the job environment so as to help employees meet their needs in accordance with their priorities. This is not done in an attempt to manipulate employees; rather, it is done in an attempt to meet their needs while meeting organizational goals.

The fourth principle is that *human wants and needs are insatiable.* It is obvious that you can never eat enough so that you never want to eat again. You eat and satisfy the deficiency for a time: but sooner or later you are going to become hungry again. Our needs increase and then decrease as they are met. For example, the mother telling her child once that she loves him does not suffice for the rest of the child's life. He needs constant reinforcement, he needs to hear over and over again that his mother loves him. Likewise, in a job situation, the employee's needs must be reinforced. His need for compliments is insatiable, he needs to hear praise over and over again to reinforce him and motivate him in his job. In a leisure setting, the leader should be aware that participant needs are insatiable and that it is necessary to provide new programs to meet individuals' changing needs. Playing one basketball game does not satisfy a participant's need for exercise forever: nor does participating in one crafts class satisfy her need for creativity for the rest of her life. An individual returns to the activity again because, as the need becomes deficient, she or he knows the activity will provide satisfaction.

The last principle is that *dissatisfaction causes people to change.* When individuals are no longer challenged by a particular activity because their deficiency has been met, they will turn to a new activity or challenge. When a deficiency has been filled, individuals tend to move on to something else. The employee who is dissatisfied with his job because he is no longer challenged by his particular task will want to move on to another task. The employer who is aware of this principle will attempt to find a rewarding task for the employee to do. Likewise, in a leisure program, the leader recognizes that the participant who has acquired a skill may need something new to strive for. Perhaps a change of pace, scene, or a new challenge would stimulate her interest.

The employer or the recreation leader who is aware of these five principles is better equipped to provide a leisure program or job that is meaningful and motivating. All human activity is directed toward a purpose. Every individual's waking hours are filled with attempts to meet needs. By being aware of individuals' needs and by providing the right incentives and opportunities for employees on the job and during leisure, the manager or leader can affect behavior in a positive manner; he or she can meet individuals' needs as well as accomplish organizational goals.

Immaturity-Maturity Theory

Chris Argyris's immaturity-maturity theory indicates that individuals require a management style appropriate to their particular maturity level (see Figure 3.2).[4] Argyris has determined that several changes take place in an individual's personality as he matures; these changes are based on his experience in the environment, and his mental and physical growth. The first of these changes finds *the individual moving from a passive state as an infant to a state of increasing activity as*

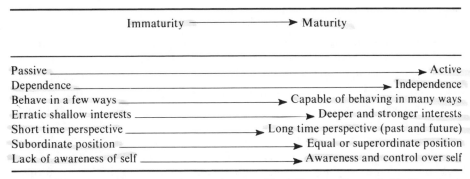

Immaturity ⟶	Maturity

Passive ⟶ Active
Dependence ⟶ Independence
Behave in a few ways ⟶ Capable of behaving in many ways
Erratic shallow interests ⟶ Deeper and stronger interests
Short time perspective ⟶ Long time perspective (past and future)
Subordinate position ⟶ Equal or superordinate position
Lack of awareness of self ⟶ Awareness and control over self

Figure 3.2. Immaturity-maturity continuum. (Paul Hersey, Kenneth H. Blanchard, *Management of Organizational Behavior: Utilizing Human Resources,* 2nd Edition, copyright © 1972, p. 51. Reprinted by permission of Prentice-Hall, Inc., Englewood Cliffs, N.J.)

[4] Chris Argyris, *Personality and the Organization* (New York: Harper and Row, 1957).

an adult. The child is passive in that the number and types of behavioral responses she has are limited. As the individual grows older and matures, she is capable of a variety of new behaviors. She increases her strength, intelligence, coordination, versatility, and so on. The recreation leader who is aware that the mature adult is capable of more diversified forms of behavior should plan activities accordingly. Likewise, the manager can provide a job having more variety, challenge, and responsibility for the mature employee.

The second change that takes place as the person matures is *that he or she moves from a dependent state to an independent state.* A child is dependent on his parents for food, security, care, and many other things. As he grows older, he becomes much more independent. In planning leisure, activities, the leader should be careful to include more activities in which the participant is given freedom of choice in terms of the types of experiences made available to him. He should not be dependent on the leader for exact details on how to do everything; the independent functioning of the participant should be encouraged. In the work situation, the employer should recognize her employees' need for independence as they mature, in terms of the types of jobs she assigns to them. Their jobs should give them a chance to express and meet their level of independent functioning. The employer who does not take these principles into consideration and who keeps employees in a dependent state will not release maximum work capacity because she is not meeting their needs.

A third change that occurs as the individual matures is that *she or he moves from behaving in a few ways to being capable of behaving in many ways.* A child is capable of responding only with immature attitudes and responses. As an individual matures into adulthood he learns to control his behavior and is capable of behaving in more sophisticated ways. These factors can be taken into consideration when planning leisure programs and job responsibilities so they meet the needs of employees.

The fourth factor is that an *immature person has erratic, shallow interests whereas the mature person has deeper and stronger interests.* As people mature the depth with which they perceive various thoughts, concepts and principles increases. They tend to think through things in much greater detail and with greater perception. They are also able to analyze, synthesize and understand a number of ideas and see the relationships between them. Obviously a child or immature person's interest in a recreation leisure service would be much different than that of a mature person in terms of the types of programs that would appeal to him. Likewise an employee that is more mature would be affected similarly in terms of the type of job with which he or she will be satisfied.

Fifth, Argyris states that an *immature person has a short time perspective whereas the mature person has a long time perspective for both past and future activities.* Thus the recreation leader should plan activities for children of a short term nature realizing that the child's interest will wane. If the activity continues too long the child may possibly become a discipline problem because of his lack of attentiveness. Likewise when dealing with an employee, the manager should realize that the more mature an individual is the longer he will be able to stick with an activity without becoming frustrated. He will also need less supervision and direction.

The next factor is that the *immature person is willing to assume a subordinate position whereas the mature person requires an equal or superordinate position.* The immature individual involved in a leisure program, or an employee who is immature, is willing to participate in activities as a subordinate. But as they mature, they become interested in being equal or superordinate. Oftentimes the more mature individual is interested in becoming the leader.

Finally, *the immature individual lacks awareness of self whereas the mature individual has awareness and control of self at all times.* The child engaged in leisure activities may lose his temper, go into a fit of rage, or break down and cry. Likewise, adults who are immature in a work situation do not have control over their emotions. The adult who is in charge of himself learns to control his emotions, feelings and behavior, even when things are not going his way. These various types of behavior may determine the type of leadership style the manager uses to influence the employee as well as the type of responsibilities that the employee is given in a particular job.

Employers and recreation leaders should take into account each of these seven principles when planning assignments. Work tasks should give individuals the opportunity to develop to their maximum potential. Argyris states that individual actions can be found anywhere along this continuum of maturity. As the human personality develops in a healthy manner, the manager must adjust activities accordingly so that individuals are capable of meeting their needs while being challenged in their leisure or work.

To some extent Argyris's theory is analogous to McGregor's Theory X and Theory Y, as described in Chapter 2.[5] McGregor's Theory X indicates that employees believe work is distasteful, that most people are lazy, and that employees are noncreative and need and want to be told what to do. On the other hand, Theory Y indicates that work is as natural as play, that employees want to perform well in their jobs, that they are creative, and that most employees are self-motivated. Thus, the manager using Theory X assumptions of the behavior of man views the employee as existing in an immature state. The reverse is the case when the manager uses Theory Y assumptions.

Argyris states that many individuals are employed in companies or organizations in which they are kept from maturing by the management practices used. In a particular job, they often are given minimum control over their environment and are encouraged to be passive, dependent, and subordinate; therefore they behave

[5] Douglas McGregor, *The Human Side of Enterprise* (New York: McGraw-Hill Book Co. 1960).

immaturely. If an employer wants employees to behave maturely, he must treat them in that manner.

S↔O──→B Model

Norman Maier, in his book *Psychiatry in Industry*, discusses the S↔O──→B model, which is a theory for understanding human behavior.[6] The S stands for and incorporates all aspects of the environment: the stimulus—energy, heat, light, sound; the physical environment—terrain, climate, ecosystems, resources, population; and the sociocultural environment—culture, groups, institutions, organizations, society (see Figure 3.3).

SITUATION ◄────────► HUMAN ORGANISM ────────► BEHAVIOR		
Stimulus	Physiological Being	Overt Response
Energy	Heredity	Movement
Heat	Nervous system	Talking
Light	Sense organs	
Sound	Muscles and glands	
Physical Environment	Psychological Being	Covert Response
Climate	Perception	Thinking
Terrain	Learning	Listening
Resources	Motivation	
Population	Personality	
Ecosystems		
Sociocultural Environment		
Culture		
Groups		
Institutions		
Organizations		
Society		

Figure 3.3. The S ◄──► O ──► B model for behavior. (From *Organizational Behavior: A Modern Behavioral Approach to Management* by Fred Luthans. Copyright © 1973, McGraw-Hill Book Company. Used with permission of McGraw-Hill Book Company.) p. 328.

The O stands for the human organism, being (1) the physiological being—heredity, nervous system, sense organs, muscles and glands and (2) the psychological being—perception, learning, motivation, personality. Finally, the B stands for behavior: overt response—movement, talking—and covert response—thinking, listening.

[6] Norman Maier, *Psychology in Industry*, third edition (Boston: Houghton Mifflin Co., 1965), Chapter 2.

The S in the model includes everything in the work situation: the heat, light, sound, etc. and other complexities of the institution in which one works such as the people, the organizational structure, the cultural effects, and other factors that affect an individual in one way or another. In other words, people work in an environment or a situation that is constantly affecting them as human beings, and, in turn, affects their behavior.

The O, or the human organism, plays an important part in the sequence of events that take place in everyday situations. A person's physiological being and psychological being are constantly affecting what he does according to needs that he is constantly striving to meet.

The S, or situation, and, the O, the physiological and psychological being, results in B, or behavior that affects what people do as they seek to meet their needs. The constant interaction that takes place among each of these elements results in people's behavior. If the environmental situation changes, it affects the individual psychologically as well as physiologically, which in turn affects his or her behavior. As managers and leaders affect or influence the environmental situation, they in turn affect the human organism and behavior. Likewise, as they influence the psychological or physiological parts of the organism, they affect behavior. Another way of stating this is that as S (situation) and O (human organism) affect each other, it causes an interaction that results in B (behavior). Figure 3.4 demonstrates this.

In each of the theories presented—the Freudian theory, Maslow's theory, Argyris's theory, and the S$\leftrightarrow$O$\longrightarrow$B model—it has been shown that human beings are complicated organisms who are affected by their conscious and unconscious states and are constantly attempting to meet their needs in the environment in which they live, all of which affects and results in behavior. Awareness of these theories and interdependent relationships will help in supervising and managing employees as well as planning better leisure services.

Presentation of these theories does not imply that leisure service managers must try to be amateur psychiatrists or psychologists; this is not their role. Nor should the manager try to make individuals over or change their personalities. The manager's aim should be to help each individual utilize her strengths fully so that she may perform in a way that is best for her, rather than the way the manager thinks she should perform or ought to be. As Peter F. Drucker writes:

> An employer has no business with a man's personality. Employment is a specific contract calling for specific performance and nothing else. Any attempt of an employer to go beyond this is usurpation. It is immoral as well as illegal intrusion upon privacy. It is abuse of a power. An employee owes no "loyalty," he owes no "love" and no "attitude." He owes performance and nothing else.[7]

[7] Peter F. Drucker, *Management: Tasks, Responsibilities, Practices* (New York: Harper and Row, 1974), pp. 424–425.

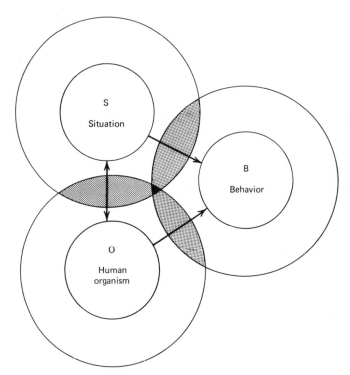

Figure 3.4. The relationships between the situation, human organism, and behavior as it effects the individual.

Although leisure service managers should not try to change a person's personality, we do know how to make the individual more effective, and this is what we should attempt to do. We can assist the person by providing him or her with training for the necessary job skills. We can affect the situation or job environment in which the individual works. We can change the job to make it more creative, interesting, and challenging. Any attempt on the part of the manager to play psychiatrist or psychologist is bound to fail. An individual who comes into a manager's employment brings a personality that is probably well set, and a manager is not trained to change it. That is not the goal. A manager's role and responsibility is to insure performance and the accomplishment of the organization's goals. In short, the manager's only function in dealing with an employee is to deal with him or her as it relates to job performance and nothing else.

INTEGRATING PERSONAL NEEDS WITH ORGANIZATIONAL GOALS

The purpose of any organization is to accomplish goals and objectives through the efforts of its employees working jointly and cooperatively. The board of directors or other governing authority sets goals and objectives for the organization, and the manager—working through the employees attempts to implement them.

The individuals who make up the organization should be viewed as more than just employees, they should be viewed as resources; resources that carry out the goals and objectives of the organization. It is the job and function of the organization, whenever possible, to match employees' needs, values, and aspirations with those of the organization. In the future, organizations will have to find ways to meet its goals and objectives that are complementary with the needs and aspirations of employees. They will have to find ways to help employees be productive on the job and at the same time provide an opportunity for those employees to find self-satisfaction and a sense of achievement in their work. Organizations will have to do this while operating within the confines of society and the communities in which they exist. Today the tax dollar is having more and more demands placed on it, and society is looking more and more critically at government in terms of the types of work it performs. Managers are going to have to find ways to make work more productive and to achieve more effectiveness and efficiency.

Public leisure service organizations exist for one purpose only: to meet the leisure needs of as many citizens as possible in the communities they serve. It is difficult for an organization made up of individuals not to reflect personal choices when planning and implementing programs. When this happens, program decisions are being made for employees rather than the community, and the service will not be effective.

No organization likes to abandon programs or activities that it has had for a long period of time. But sooner or later many programs become ineffective. Either they do not produce intended results in terms of their principles or practices or they do not attract enough participants to justify themselves. Private enterprise has the same problem. But in private enterprise, where profit is a motive, unproductive efforts have to be cut out because they do not produce profit and they no longer can be supported and justified.

Governmental agencies, because they are financed by taxes and have no built-in profit-motivated self-discipline that eliminates unproductive programs, have to be careful to evaluate and make adjustments in programs that are no longer productive. But government tends to double its efforts when programs are failing in an attempt to save them.

Leisure service organizations need to learn to take action to change programs based on performance. This will tend to direct efforts toward the most effective programs and to take advantage of every tax dollar and every resource available. Leisure service organizations need to direct their resources away from areas of low productivity and diminishing results to areas of high productivity and increased results. As indicated, the purpose of any leisure service program is to meet the leisure needs of the participants it serves. As such, participants should help determine what services are to be offered. Likewise, employees within the organization should have some involvement in determining the direction of the organization. There should, however, be an interface between the needs of the employee and the needs of the participant when determining organizational goals. Both employees and participants influence the effectiveness of an organization. As long as the leisure service organization continues to meet the needs of the people it serves, the programs will have support. Obviously the major task of the organization, and the employees within it, is to determine what the needs and programs of the community are. As mentioned earlier, high productivity, that is giving the greatest output of service for the smallest effort of input, should be a main concern. The organization should focus on serving the leisure needs of the community in the most productive way possible. The one way to determine what services should be offerred is to ask the participants what services they want and would be willing to support.

Today's organizations face many problems. The expectations of employees have increased to the point that they are often impossible to meet. Inflation is causing many organizations to go into bankruptcy. In government, inflation has increased to a point that many services can no longer be supported because the public is not willing to support tax increases. Bond issues are failing, and citizens are demanding that services be cut back rather than pay a higher price for these services. People in organizations want more responsibility, more freedom of choice, and more creative opportunities in which to express themselves.

Additionally, it is difficult for organizations to meet the needs of their employees. As a result, organizations have to find new ways to motivate people or make them want to work. In the past employees could be motivated by salaries and other incentives. Today people are overloaded both psychologically and physiologically by the demands that society, work, and the community place on them. The lifestyle and work that people perform have changed and have to be taken into account in terms of dealing with employees in relation to meeting their needs.

As a result of these changes in the need levels of society and employees it will be necessary to adjust organizational goals and structures. In some instances this will result in a different organizational structure, and in other cases it will be necessary to find new ways to motivate people to work.

Changing organizational structure may not guarantee results. For years people have argued whether it is better to design an ideal organization and fit the people into it or to utilize people's needs and personalities as a basis for organizational structure. Obviously, both organizational concepts have value, and both approaches should be used in parallel. The simplest organizational structure that will do the job is obviously the best one. The organization that meets the needs of individuals while meeting organizational goals and objectives is obviously best.

The Effects of Formal and Informal Structure on the Organization

Within any organization, both an informal and a formal organization are at work. Luther Gulick devoted much time to the study of formal organizations. He set forth principles and characteristics of the formal organization that, from his point of view, were necessary for an organization to function properly and smoothly in carrying out its goals and objectives.[8] Gulick's principles have begun to lose their effectiveness because of changes in employee needs. Many organizations continued to hold on to these principles to their disadvantage, and it is important for the manager to realize which ones are no longer effective.

The first characteristic of formal organization is that *authority is from the top down*, the "A–B" concept. This principle is paramount in the formal organization structure. "A" is the boss, "B" is the employee. A tells B what to do, and B does it without question. This concept indicates that power is always from the top down. A has the power and authority to tell B what to do, and B has the responsibility to carry out A's directions. It is believed that without this principle there would be chaos and disorder and the organization could not function.

A second aspect of formal organizations is that of *role playing*. When an individual joins an organization, she or he is expected to play types of roles. The boss has one role to play, and the subordinate has another role. When hired as a secretary you act as a secretary; you type, take dictation, file and do all the other things a secretary is supposed to do. You are not supposed to question your role: you are to play your role as prescribed within the organization.

The third principle provides for *preentry training* so that when a person joins an organization she is trained for her job and knows how she is supposed to perform it. No matter what an individual's intellect or background, preentry training is supposed to gear her for the job at hand. Preentry training is essential in the formal organization because it defines the role of the employee in carrying out specific job assignments.

The fourth principle in the formal organization concept is that *subordinates are dependent*. Each employee is dependent on a higher authority for direction, planning, and goals and objectives. Employees need direction from the top to carry out their work. This follows in line with the "A–B" concept, whereby authority comes from the top down. But this fourth principle goes further by saying that employees are totally dependent on a higher authority to tell them what to do, how to do it, and when to do it; they should not be independent in any way. According to this principle employees should be dependent in order to carry out the functions and purpose of the organization efficiently.

The fifth principle is that of *obedience*. In the formal organization, employees are to be obedient in responding to requests. They do not ask questions or exercise independent judgment, and they do what they are told to do. If they do not obey, they will be disciplined. In the formal organization, this concept is essential.

The sixth principle is that of *predictability*. The formal organization knows that it can predict what the employees are going to do because they are dependent and

[8] Luther Gulick, "Notes on the Theory of Organization," in Luther Gulick and Lyndall Urwick, eds. *Papers on the Science of Administration* (New York: Institute of Public Administration, 1937).

obedient to a higher level of command. Predictability is necessary in terms of knowing just what is going to take place and when. Employees do not use discretion and judgment, but do exactly what they are told to do in a predictable manner.

The seventh principle states that the formal organization *needs rules and regulations to carry out its objectives and goals.* The rules stipulate what employees can and cannot do and the regulations direct their work on a day to day basis. These two premises are extremely important in the formal organization because they provide for predictability, obedience, dependence, and authority from the top down.

The last two principles of the formal organization are *unity of command* and *chain of command.* The unity of command principle states that an employee will have one and only one boss from whom he or she gets direction. It is implied that if an individual is getting direction from two managers, there will be chaos and disorder and the employee will be confused as to which direction to follow and might end up doing nothing.

The chain of command supports the same principle in that the employee knows exactly who to report to and who everybody else reports to, thus minimizing confusion. The chain of command clarifies communication networks, responsibility networks, and many other networks that are necessary to carry out the goals and objectives of the formal organization. Gulick theorized that all these organizational principles must exist if the organization is to function smoothly and effectively. These principles very much support the McGregor's Theory X concept (see Chapter 2).

Are Gulick's nine principles still valid? Many things have changed within society since they were formulated that effect how we now meet employee's needs. Changing life-styles have affected the needs of employees so that today the physiological and security needs no longer motivate individuals to the same degree. The nine principles of the formal organization seem more appropriate for individuals whose needs fall into the physiological and security category.

Between McGregor's Theory X and Theory Y, Theory X more closely identifies with the formal organization principles of Gulick. In the discussion of immaturity-maturity theory earlier in this chapter, it was indicated that an immature person seems to respond passively and dependently, behaves in few ways, shows erratic shallow interests, has a short time-span perspective, is subordinate in position, and lacks awareness of self. If the principles of the formal organization are adhered to, then employees are treated basically as immature people. The formal organization assumes that employees' need levels are at the lower levels, as described by Maslow. They fall in the area of the physical and security level. If this is the approach of the formal organization, it does not give much opportunity to people for development and maturity.

Because of the growth and advancement of society, many employees are no longer passive, dependent and subordinate and lacking awareness of self. On the contrary, most employees want to be treated as being independent, and most are capable of behaving in many ways. They want to be equal and or superordinate, and they tend to be aware and in control of themselves. Employees with these characteristics are more likely to search for the higher-level needs of esteem and self-actualization. They do not want to be managed according to the principles of Gulick's formal organization. This type of supervision can result in a conflict between the employee and the formal organization. A low-motivation work environment can also occur under this type of structure.

If organizations hope to meet the needs of employees they are going to have to change many of the outdated principles of formal organization. Management is going to have to find ways to motivate people in a new way or provide work environments where people want to work, where they are self-motivated. This will be discussed in greater detail in the next chapter.

Organizational Goals

In any organization, be it private enterprise or a government organization, goals and objectives must be geared to gain results. The organization has specific goals and objectives toward which its work is actively aimed. These goals and objectives are expressed in various types of plans, such as budgets and schedules of activities. All these plans, goals, and objectives are aimed at accomplishing specific activities of that organization.

Very broadly stated, an output goal of a leisure service agency is designed to meet the leisure needs of people in a community. These goals may be met by various activities, such as sports, aquatics, arts and crafts, music, and dramatics, and are designed to meet the needs of the community and specific participants of specific programs. These specific programs are carried out by various employees: supervisors, administrators, and recreation center directors and leaders. These individuals work together to meet the goals of the organization. At the same time, however, it is the job of the manager of the organization (a motivation goal) to try to meet the needs of employees.

Figure 3.5 is an example of the direction of the organization's goal in relation to the goal of the employee. As can be seen, the goal of the organization is not in the same direction as that of the employee, resulting in low productivity. The manager should strive to bring the employee goals into line as much as he can with those of the organization. This will result in a much higher productivity, as shown in Figure 3.6.

Figure 3.5 shows a case in which the organizational goal and the employee's goal are different. This results in a less productive employee. The manager who is able to bring the organizational goal into line with the needs of the individual is much more likely to accomplish the goals of the organization and meet employee needs. Although this appears to be a rather simple procedure, it is not simple in actual

Figure 3.5. Organization and employee goals not similar, resulting in the employee headed in a direction not consistant with organization goals. This will result in low organizational productivity. The arrows represent the direction of the effort.

practice in the organization. But the manager who is aware of both organizational goals and employee needs is able to better align them with each other.

In examining Figure 3.6, it becomes apparent that the manager is a third factor affecting the accomplishment of organizational goals. The manager has specific needs. Sometimes the manager's needs are not in line with the goals of employees or the organization. This may adversely affect the meeting of the goals and objectives of the organization. It becomes necessary to align the manager's *and* the employees' needs with those of the organization.

In the next chapter, more detail is given in terms the manager's attempts to align employees' needs with the goals of the organization. Additional attention will be given to the factors that underlie the motivating situation.

THE ROLE OF MANAGERS

The role of the manager is to meet the goals and objectives of the organization that employs her. She does this through one primary resource—the employees that work under her. Her success is determined by how capably she provides motivation to employees and directs their efforts and energies toward meeting the goals and objectives of the organization. The manager does this by using many leadership techniques, being aware of the needs of his employees, and taking advantage of available resources.

Figure 3.6. Organization and employee goals similar, resulting in more consistant direction and higher productivity. The figure also shows that the manager's goals do not totally coinside with that of the organization.

As already mentioned, the manager should know a great deal about human needs. The manager also needs to know a great deal about himself, what his shortcomings are and how they affect his actions. There has to be a mutual respect between the employee, the organization, and the manager. A manager who utilizes Theory Y rather than Theory X gives credit to employees as being mature individuals capable of working and determining their own outcomes. Managers who attempt use to psychology in the manipulation of employees will undermine their own authority. There is obviously a need for psychology and other forms of professional help; but this should be performed by professionals, not by managers. Employees having personal and deep-seated problems should be referred for professional help when the need arises. The role of the manager is that of managing people, working with them in a relationahip that is mutually beneficial to the employee and organization. This must be done with integrity.

Blocking of Employees' Needs

The manager recognizes that employee needs are not always met. Many conditions and factors prohibit individuals from meeting their specific needs. Some of these are self-imposed; others are imposed by the organization, the manager, or other factors in the work situation. The manager, to be effective, learns to deal with individuals when they are successful as well as when they fail. Some blocks are caused by shortcomings of the employees—their attitudes and individual differences—and the manager should be aware of them. Managers are often in a position to help remove the block so that the employee might meet his or her needs. No matter how confident and clever the manager may be in determining what the needs of employees are, if he cannot help them achieve these needs by providing the right motivating situations or removing the blocks, he will not succeed.

It is important to discuss some of the reasons individuals do not meet their needs. The remaining part of this chapter deals with some of the blocks and other elements in the organization that inhibit and prevent individuals from meeting their needs.

Employees and Their Differences.

We have been talking about recognizing the needs of individuals. The first thing we must understand is that every individual is different. People have different needs, which will vary according to levels of intensity and time priorities (refer to the five principles described by Maslow).

Not all individuals are able or willing to perform the same work. Coping with individuals in given work situations is the challenge of management. The manager must attempt to minimize individual differences but utilize these differences to the benefit of the individual and the organization. It would be impossible to manage an organization in which each employee was headed in a different direction in an attempt to meet her or his own needs. The manager must recognize the potential of each individual and find a way to utilize individual differences in a cooperative teamwork fashion.

People differ for various reasons. One's family, education, cultural heritage, and life-style all have an effect on behavior. Employees have different psychological and physiological make-ups, and that is why they respond to work situations differently. It is important to know why employees differ; but it is more important to know how they differ and to be able to take advantage of individual differences while trying to direct efforts in a unified direction.

Again referring to Maslow's theory, people have different physical, security, social, esteem, and self-actualization needs. Individual differences affect what a person can do in terms of performing her job based on her physical, mental and intellectual capacity. If a person is not physically strong enough to perform a particular job or task, no matter how much she may be motivated or inspired to do the job, she cannot perform it. In like manner, an individual who does not have a given intellectual or mental capacity may be limited in terms of certain jobs. The manager must be aware of an employee's limitations and strengths. No matter how strong the motivation, an employee cannot perform if he or she is incapable of doing the task. To push the employee will only cause frustration and anxiety.

Employee limitations may be analyzed by watching him perform his job, testing him, or questioning him. To protect the individual as well as preserve the interests of the organization, the manager should not ask an employee to do something he cannot do. In some situations the manager can provide specific help or training that will improve the employee's skills. But in some instances, regardless of how much the employee wants to improve he or she may not be able to.

Once the manager is aware of the employee's capabilities, the next logical concern is the employee's willingness to perform. What are the elements that affect one's willingness to perform in a given situation? No matter how capable the employee may be, if she is not willing to perform there may be little the manager can do about it. The old saying "You can lead a horse to water but you can't make him drink" is true. You can place an employee in a job, but there is no assurance that just because she is there she is working productively. Many factors affect the employee's willingness to work and perform in a given situation. Several of these will be discussed.

Attitudes.   An attitude is a predisposition to evaluating a given object, person, idea, or situation in a certain way. This evaluation may be favorable, unfavorable, or neutral. When it is favorable or unfavorable it may be of varying degrees.[9]

An employee's attitude obviously affects his work. There are many misconceptions about attitudes and what effect they have on a worker's job performance. The

[9] Norman Kantor and Stanley Powers *The Importance of Attitudes* (Chicago: Industrial Relations Center, University of Chicago, 1968).

manager is often overheard saying, "If I could only instill the proper attitude in him I am sure I could get more work out of him." This is a false belief. It is based on the assumption that attitude will produce behavior or activity. It is just the opposite: A person's value system justifies his behavior. Behavior precedes values. If you believe what you do, behavior is determined by the geography of your life space. Your environment, family, community, and what you have done all the years of your life affect your attitudes.

An attitude is not easily changed. In Figure 3.7, it is seen that attitudes are the second most difficult thing to change in terms of the four behavioral elements of knowledge, attitudes, individual behavior, and group behavior. It takes a long time to change attitudes, if they can be changed at all. Attitudes are affected by many factors. If an attitude change that will affect the work situation is to take place, it must come from within the individual and cannot be imposed by management or the organization.

Although an attitude does not produce behavior, it does affect behavior. For example, suppose an employee is asked to perform a particular task by his boss. If the employee respects and admires his boss, it most likely will affect the enthusiasm and dedication with which he will perform the job. Contrarily, if he dislikes his boss and has little respect for her, it may inhibit him from performing well. If an employee is asked to implement a particular recreation program that he thinks is useless, the employee's enthusiasm for accomplishing the program will certainly be affected. Lack of enthusiasm for a particular project can affect production. A manager, by observing an individual's action, can tell a great deal about the attitude he has about a specific area, subject, or job. A manager making assignments should be aware of cases in which attitudes are in opposition to the assignment. Likewise, a positive attitude toward an assignment would reinforce the employee's behavior in that assignment.

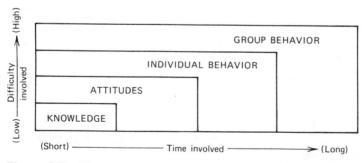

Figure 3.7. Time and difficulty involved in changing characteristics of individuals. (Paul Hersey, Kenneth H. Blanchard, *Management of Organizational Behavior: Utilizing Human Resources*, 2nd Edition, copyright © 1972, p. 2. Reprinted by permission of Prentice-Hall, Inc., Englewood Cliffs, N.J.)

From a manager's point of view, understanding employee attitudes may be critical to understanding job performances. Attitudes affect the way an individual thinks about a certain idea, thing, person, or place. For example, in a given parks and recreation department, an older supervisor who has many years of experience but is not a university graduate may have an unfavorable attitude toward graduates. She may resent that the personnel department requires new recreation leaders to have four years of university education before they may gain employment, since a degree is no substitute for experience. She may express the opinion that, "University graduates try to cover up what they do not know with a lot of fancy language out of books." Such attitudes may affect how this particular supervisor approaches new employees and how she may deal with them in specific work assignments. One's attitudes are usually deep-seated, based on some specific need. In the case of the old-time supervisor and her attitudes about university graduates, it may be a feeling of insecurity causing her to feel indequate about the new young university graduate recreation leader. She may want to protect herself against these feelings: therefore she deludes herself that the university graduate is not competent and just will not work out. Her attitude toward the graduate defends her against the painful feelings of lack of education on her own part.

The attitudes that people have say a lot about them. They sometimes give insight into why a person does not perform on the job. If an employee's attitudes motivate him to cooperate, it probably will result in constructive behavior—the accomplishment of the goals and objectives of the organization. The manager will want to encourage these particular attitudes. But if the attitudes interfere with a particular result the manager wants to obtain, he will have to make adjustments in the work assignment.

Shortsighted snap judgments on the part of an employee may result in attitudes based on a faulty premise and affect job performance. An example of a shortsighted attitude is a *misperception.* Suppose a particular center director feels that attendance reports are a waste of time; they are never used, just filed in the department headquarters, and require a lot of time for no specific purpose. As a result of this misperception, he is not careful or accurate in filling out attendance reports. If the director realized that attendance figures justify and support the budget requests for the following year, he would probably have a different attitude. If he perceived the attendance reports as useful, he would fill them out more accurately and conscientiously.

Another perception that can affect an employee's work performance adversely is *misunderstanding.* Misunderstandings are often a result of individuals perceiving and interpreting things differently. For example, a maintenance staff, after refinishing the gym, may have asked the program staff to stay off the gym for 48 hours. One recreation leader arriving at the gym 24 hours after the floor was refinished, not knowing it had only been 24 hours, may let in a group of boys to play basketball. The next day the maintenance staff observes that the floor has been used. They have the opinion and attitude that the recreation staff is thoughtless and is interfering with maintenance operations. The situation is really a misunderstanding between the two employee groups as to when the 48 hours was up.

Prejudices are negative attitudes toward a particular group. Essentially this results in hostile mistrust. A prejudiced individual fails to evaluate others on their own merit and forms predetermined judgments. Prejudices detrimentally affect how individuals in an organization cooperate and work effectively with each other.

Stereotypes are special examples of prejudice. They involve rigid, biased ways of viewing other persons or objects. A recreation leader may see his recreation supervisor as being stubborn and resistant to change, as a result, he may generalize this attitude to all supervisors. He is stereotyping all supervisors into one category. Stereotypes can also be positive. A supervisor may feel that all college graduates make good recreation leaders. Another may feel that a person with 10 years of experience will do a better job. Although these are cases of positive stereotyping, the individual is still making prejudgments rather than basing judgments on fact.

Misperceptions, misunderstandings, prejudices, and stereotypes all tend to affect the attitudes of individuals. The supervisor must recognize that the various attitudes an individual has serve some specific and important need. An individual who strongly resists change may be protecting his need for security. Change is a threat, and he will avoid it if he can. Many times an individual's job attitudes center around important needs for prestige, recognition, or social approval. When a manager attempts to deal with an attitude of an employee, she must not overlook the need that the attitude may serve. If the attitude does serve a particular need, it will not be changed easily. It might be easier to find another work assignment that will serve the employee's need just as well. By approaching attitudes this way, the supervisor is much more likely to be successful in helping employees meet their needs while meeting organizational goals.

Frustration.   When an individual's needs are blocked, it usually results in frustration. As stated earlier in this chapter, an individual's time is devoted to trying to meet his or her needs. The ways individuals meet their needs can be classified in three ways:

1. The direct approach, whereby the employee's work activity results in meeting his needs and accomplishing his goal.
2. Problem solving, whereby the employee, with or without help from his supervisor, takes steps in his work activities to solve problems that stand in his way in order to meet his needs and reach his goals.
3. Substitute goals, whereby the original goals cannot be reached and substitute goals are accepted.

When an individual, in perceiving or pursuing her goals, attempts to solve the various situations that stand in her way, she engages in problem solving. At times, however, there are cases when a person cannot solve the situation to meet her need, and this results in a block. The alternative in this case is to substitute another goal or a different goal to meet the particular need. If neither problem solving nor substitute goals works, the result will usually be frustration. Frustration results in nonconstructive behavior in an attempt to obtain a goal.[10]

Frustration can be defined as a particular kind of stress an individual experiences when obstacles prevent him from moving toward his goal. It occurs when an individual is blocked from reaching his goal, cannot overcome the barrier that blocks him, and will not give up striving to achieve the goal. Frustration can be real or imaginary. A recreation leader may be frustrated because he feels his boss is holding him back from a promotion. It may be imaginary, but if that is what the employee believes, it is still as frustrating to him as if the boss were really holding him back.

Frustrations can also be caused by habits. A leader who is used to doing things in a certain way may become frustrated when she is prevented from doing them her way. The importance of the need or the strength of the motivation affects the degree of frustration or how quickly one becomes frustrated. The strength or size of the barrier also affects frustration level.

Finally, the pressure from internal/external sources also can affect frustration level. To illustrate, let's say a boy is determined to make the basketball team (strong motivation). Because there is a great deal of pressure and desire on his part to make the team, if he does not make the team he will become very frustrated. Also, the strength of the barriers to making the team could also frustrate the boy; if the team is extremely good and has a number of excellent players, this would tend to frustrate the boy even more because he is a rather good player himself. Pressure from his father to make the team (external pressure) could cause further frustration. Also the stronger the need, the less likely the individual will accept a substitute goal.

One question a supervisor can ask himself when trying to understand the frustration of an employee is, "Is the frustration the result of some habit that has been interrupted or some routine that has been disturbed?" If this is the case, the supervisor may be able to do something to relieve the frustration by either providing substitute goals or alleviating the block. Frustration might also be caused by something in the environment that is new, unusual, or unexpected that an employee is unable to cope with.

The type of pressures that are operating within an individual, external or internal, affect her in her motivation toward a particular goal and result in frustra-

---

[10] *The Meaning of Frustration* (Chicago: Industrial Relations Center, University of Chicago, 1968).

tion when the goal is not reached. The supervisor who is aware of the conditions causing frustration can better deal with the employee in helping her meet her particular needs and goals, helping her find substitute goals, or helping her remove the blocks that stand in her way.

The supervisor must also be aware of the various personality differences that exist among individuals. An individual's attitudes often affect work performance. Some of these attitudes result in frustration because of various factors mentioned earlier—prejudice, stereotypes, misunderstanding. Supervisors who can deal with such factors can help the individual develop attitudes that make it possible to reach his goals, thereby alleviating the frustration. The emotional-maturity level of an individual can also affect frustration level and how the individual deals with it. The supervisor may also be able to help alleviate frustrations that exist when an employee is constantly striving for things he or she can never reach or obtain.

The more alternatives an employee has the less the possibility of frustration. Also, the ease with which a block can be removed affects the frustration level. In each of these cases, the supervisor who is aware of the conditions causing frustration is more likely to be able to help the individual meet her goals and alleviate her frustration. Frustration results in nonproductive behavior both for the individual and the organization in terms of reaching its goals and objectives.

A frustration situation is diagrammed in Figure 3.8. Referring to the diagram, the following is a step-by-step example of a frustration situation and the behaviors that can result:

1. The employee attempts to direct his energies toward his goals. In this example the employee wants to be promoted into the new job of park foreman. He strives for this by working extra hard at his job, coming in early, forsaking coffee breaks, and so on.
2. In this example, the boss is the block. He does not feel that the employee is ready for promotion and that there are other employees more qualified.
3. *Aggression* is the attack on the barrier itself. The employee who is trying for the promotion and feels that he is being blocked by his boss may begin to verbally attack his boss. He feels that the boss is holding him down, has it in for him, or whatever. Aggression is taken out on the boss because he is seen to represent the block or the barrier prohibiting the individual from reaching his goal or objective.
4. *Fixation* is another form of behavior that can result from frustration. Fixation is a behavior that is repeated over and over even though it has already proved unsuccessful. The would-be foreman may perceive that the boss is standing in his way and constantly battle with him, fixed on the situation and the block (the boss) that he believes is holding him down.
5. Another behavior resulting from frustration is *regression*. In this case an indi-

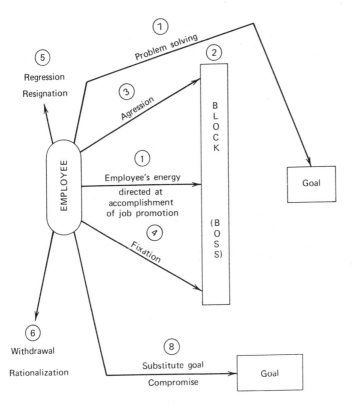

Figure 3.8. Frustration situation.

vidual returns to immature behavior and feelings. The individual who feels that the boss is blocking him begins to act childish. He may not respond to some requests that the boss makes of him.

Resignation is accepting and giving up and not trying to change or substitute a goal. In our example, it may result in the individual changing his job because he is resigned to the fact that in this particular department, because of the boss, he is not going to get ahead.

6. *Withdrawal* is retreat from the conflict. The individual feels he is never going to get the promotion, so he withdraws and becomes resigned to that fact.

Rationalization is finding an excuse for failure. The individual did not want the job anyway, and it is probably just as well because he was not cut out for that particular job.

7. The manager who is in touch with his employees will recognize that this particular employee is frustrated and will help him solve his problem. He might

do this by sitting down with him and outlining how he can prepare for a future job promotion, or he can help him obtain some special training. One way or another, the employee and employer work to meet the employee's goal by problem solving.

8. The manager who recognizes frustration or nonproductive behavior is better equipped to help the individual remove the block or find a substitute goal or some form of compromise that will put him back on a productive tract. A substitute goal might involve giving the employee more responsibility in his present job so he will be more challenged and better equipped for future job promotions. The supervisor can help the employee by watching for signs in his behavior that indicate frustration. The manager who can relieve frustration and divert energies back to normal or acceptable goals of the organization will benefit both the employee and the organization. Frustration can be eliminated if managers help employees achieve their goals or find acceptable substitute goals. The job of the manager is to make work rewarding, satisfying, and as motivating as possible. The more he can understand the employees' problems from *their* point of view, the better the manager's chances are of helping them meet their goals and thus eliminate frustration.

SUMMARY

This chapter is devoted to an analysis of employees' needs, how they affect the organization in the accomplishment of organizational goals and how these needs and goals affect each other. The individual is the basic unit in every organization. The employee is the most important resource by which an organization accomplishes its goals and objectives, without the employee, the organization could not function.

The manager is charged with the responsibility of accomplishing the goals and objectives of the organization. He is responsible for motivating the employees to work and for creating a work environment that will lead to the accomplishment of the goals and objectives of the organization. He does this by meeting the needs of the employees which, in turn, releases work capacity directed toward the goals and objectives of the organization.

The manager must understand what the needs of the employees are. He must realize that employees are constantly seeking to meet their needs. If he can capture the energy of the employees as they are reaching for their goals and objectives, he will also accomplish the organizational goals. The manager must be aware of employee needs, need levels, the factors that may frustrate individuals, the attitudes individuals have toward their job, and the affect that attitudes may have upon the organization. To provide a motivating work situation for the employee, each of these elements should be considered.

Somehow, somewhere, employees are going to meet their needs. Needs may be met in the formal organization or the informal organization. Employees may meet their needs during recreation after work or may turn to a union for recognition and acceptance. The employer or supervisor who is aware of these basic aspects of human behavior, and human nature in general, can meet employee's needs and aid them in their ability to achieve and work productively while acceomplishing the goals and objectives of the organization.

Motivation 4

Motivation is a complex process, and since the beginning of the century much research and writing have been devoted to it. There is still a great deal to be learned about motivation and how one person goes about motivating another person. In a work situation, motivation is at the center of the management process and is the basis for productivity. Several theories on motivation have been put forth. They vary from a simple analysis of a person at work to a complex process involving determination of the needs of an individual, relating these needs to his or her goals, and matching these needs with those of the organization. Some experts theorize that you can motivate employees while others indicate that you cannot. This chapter examines the motivational theories and develops a motivational model to help readers visualize motivation and the various factors that affect it. The intent is to guide managers of leisure services in creating the most motivating environment possible for employees.

The motivation theory presented by the authors stresses that a manager should not attempt to motivate employees per se, but instead should create an environment in which employees are self-motivated. Managers can do little to make people work, but they control and have at their disposal a number of factors that can create an environment in which employees will want to work.

An analogy to the motivation process would be the planting of an acorn to grow an oak tree. The individual wanting to grow the oak tree is similar to the individual wanting to motivate an employee. The oak tree can be likened to the employee who the manager wants to motivate. The individual who plants the acorn does not actually cause it to grow. He or she cannot get inside the acorn and force it to grow, if the acorn itself is not viable, no matter how much the person who planted it wants it to grow, it will not. The same situation exists in the case of an employer wanting to motivate an employee. If an employee does not have the skill or desire to accomplish a particular task, no matter how much the employer wants her to, she will not; if the acorn is not viable, no matter how much the planter wants it to grow, it will not. You do not get inside the employee, nor do you get inside the acorn and force it to grow. You create an environment in which the acorn grows. You plant it in good soil, water it, fertilize it, place it where it will gain a certain amount of sunlight, and as a result the acorn grows itself. It has inside itself all the necessary properties to grow, provided the environment in which it was planted is conducive to growing. The same can be said of an employee. The employee must have the necessary skills, attitude, knowledge, and intelligence to perform a given task. If the employee does not have the capacity for a given task, no matter how much incentive you offer, he cannot be motivated to do it. On the other hand, if an individual does have the right skills, aptitude, and so on, and if his employer creates the right environment, he can be motivated. The employer or manager can create an environment in which an individual is self-motivated.

The last chapter emphasized the importance of being aware of individual needs. It was stated that individuals' efforts and energies are directed primarily at meeting their own needs. If the theory that you do not motivate people but that you provide an environment in which people are self-motivated is valid, then people are more likely to be self-motivated when trying to meet their needs. If this is the case, the basis for motivation in a work situation can be defined simply as *the provision of work opportunity whereby employees can meet their individual needs*.

If the organization can align its goals with those of the individual, it is more likely to achieve them. Contrarily, if the organization has goals that are in direct opposition with those of the employee, the organization's goals may be accomplished only at high costs.

FALLACIES OF MOTIVATION

There are many fallacies about motivation. To help the reader achieve a clearer understanding of the dynamics of motivation, some of the fallacies will be discussed. For example, many individuals feel that if they could instill the proper attitude in the employee, that he or she would show an increase in performance, as mentioned in Chapter 3. It is based on the assumption that attitudes produce behavior, when in actuality behavior develops attitudes. Therefore an individual's attitudes are always appropriate in that they are part of his or her value system. Behavior produces values; People essentially believe in what they do because it justifies their behavior. Behavior is determined by people's experiences and environment.

Another false assumption is that work is something done to the worker, be it positive or negative in terms of a reward or punishment. Over the years this has been described as the carrot-and-stick, or "reward," theory. The basic problem with this theory is that an employee will work only as long as the carrot is dangling in front of him. The minute the reward is taken away he may stop working. Another problem is that maybe the person is full of carrots (particular rewards) or does not like them and is not going to be motivated by them. On the other hand, the individual may run out of carrots. This type of problem is very apparent

Figure 4.1. The carrot approach to motivation.

today. In our society, people's expectations have increased to a point that is difficult to meet. A striking union wanting more wages may price itself right out of the market to the point that the product involved can no longer be made and sold in the public market. There is a limit to how far an organization can go in motivating people purely by some sort of monetary reward (see Figure 4.1).

The "stick," or "punishment," or "negative motivation" theory also has many shortcomings. It is based on the premise that an individual moves, works, or is motivated as long as fear or threat is hanging over her head. However when the threat is removed or the employer turns his back, the employee, because she is not

Figure 4.2. The punitive approach to motivation leading to employee resentment.

self-motivated, will tend to slow down or stop movement altogether. In addition, use of the punishment theory creates frustration within the employee, which in turn breeds aggression. The aggression can be covert, but it nonetheless will affect production and the work environment. Building a fire under someone to get her moving is good only for initial movement; ultimately it backfires in the attempt to create motivation. Figure 4.2 shows a fire that was built under a donkey to get him to move the cart. The problem is that the donkey moves forward only enough to stop the pain and pulls the cart, or the work load, right over the fire. Although the man got the donkey to move, the donkey did not keep moving far enough to make it worthwhile; the idea backfired and the work load was lost.

Employees who fear their supervisors or dislike them may engage in spiteful, vengeful activities. They may deliberately sabotage or slow down work when the supervisors are not around. They may break tools, break rules, and/or gold brick. Negative motivation leads to movement, but not for long and not necessarily in the right direction.

FACTORS BEHIND MOTIVATION

Motivation is the function of four distinct factors.[1] *First, it is a function of our needs, and we all have needs. We move to meet these needs.* We are directed first toward the accomplishment of the need that is most outstanding. (In Chapter 3 a need was defined as a deficiency, either a psychological or a physiological imbalance.) In an attempt to meet this need, we are moved to action; that is, we are self-motivated. The strongest impact or influence on motivation is the need that an individual has at a particular point in time.

Suppose an employee has needs of (1) less harassment from his boss, (2) more independence, and (3) more salary. The desire to get away from his boss, who he cannot stand is the most pressing need at the time. So he makes a lateral move, even though it does not involve more salary or more independence.

Second, motivation is a function of opportunity. No matter how strong an individual's need may be, if the opportunity to satisfy that need is not present the motivation is decreased considerably, if not lost. The more available the goal or opportunity to meet the need, the stronger the motivation. If an employee knows there will be new jobs open in the next three months at a higher rank and salary, she is apt to be motivated toward working hard for one of them if she feels she stands a good chance of getting a promotion.

Third, motivation is a function of ability. This involves the individual's capabilities in terms of the skills, training, and knowledge he has to perform a particular task. No matter how much an individual may have the desire to do something, if physically or intellectually he does not have the ability to do it, his

---

[1] This discussion is based on a lecture given by Frederick Herzberg, May 26, 1976, San Mateo, Calif.

motivation is hindered significantly. No matter how much a person wants to become a great singer, if he does not have a good voice he will never be a great singer. Training and practice may help, but not necessarily.

Fourth, motivation is a function of reinforcement. Suppose an individual who has a need strives to meet that need and gets reinforcement in the way of praise or reward of some sort. This reinforcement will cause her to be similarly motivated again at another time.

Thus the four factors behind motivation are need, opportunity, ability, and reinforcement. It might be stated differently: motivation is a function of potential; the potential of an individual to meet his needs, utilize his abilities fully, have opportunities to meet his needs, and receive reinforcement. These factors are interrelated, and we will discuss them in more detail later.

The manager's job is to find ways to organize both the work and the abilities of employees to maximize their work capacity. This is done by humanizing work, making it more interesting and challenging, and by creating an environment in which employees want to work. The manager has two choices: *to make people work* or to try to *make people want to work.* Trying to maximize efficiency in work, using Taylor's principles of scientific management, is dehumanizing; it is seen as making people work, not making them want to work.

CREATING A MOTIVATING ENVIRONMENT

A motivating environment has three characteristics:

1. A harmonious worker/management view of what a good job consists of and to what it contributes. These goals are determined mutually by the employer on the one hand and the supervisor and employee on the other. For these goals to be met, there must be supportive management and reinforcement of individual needs.
2. Supportive rather than coercive management. Rather than simply pushing workers to perform, the supportive management assists them in finding ways to meet their goals and objectives by helping them remove the obstacles.
3. Reinforcement of employees' needs for feeling worthwhile. This involves giving employees recognition in a way that reinforces their efforts to work and move toward the accomplishment of the goals and objectives of the organization. The most influential recognition will come from an employer's immediate supervisor, who should regularly reinforce him or her on a job well done.

In a work environment where there is mutual agreement and trust, the worker/management view of good work contributes to the goals of the organization and of the individual. There is real and sincere concern with work that contributes to organizational as well as to individual goals. There is concern for the approach to work and the work results. The key to a harmonious worker/management view of what is good work, and what it contributes, is mutual determination. Therefore *both* the supervisor and the employee should participate in developing goals for the employee's job and how to accomplish them. The supportive manager or supervisor removes unnecessary obstacles and provides resources to help employees do what they want to do. Therefore the supervisor will ask, "How can we help you do your job more productively?"

To understand motivation, it might be helpful to give some definitions. Motivation comes from the word *motive*, the Latin word *movere*, "to move." Therefore motivation is anything that moves people to perform. If employees are trying to perform, it is because they are motivated to one extent or another. Motivation is usually connected with some desire. Desire means "to express a wish to." But desire, or wanting to do, does not qualify as the sole prerequisite to motivation. Motivation is that which actually moves a person toward a goal (doing a job), not that which just makes him want, or desire, to move. Motivation is not to be measured or considered in terms of desire, interest, attitude, or morale, but in terms of actual effort to perform. If the individual is not trying to perform, she is not motivated.

In any work situation, there are various methods for achieving movement. One of these, "protective movement," is when the individual performs just well enough to keep out of trouble. He tries to protect his tenure, salary, or certain gains he may have made by temporary spurts in performance, by just putting in time. A merely safe level of performance results from this method.

"Achievement motivation" occurs when the employee gives of herself. She tries to accomplish beyond just a safe level of work. She makes an effort to produce at a high level and extends herself for lengthy periods of time. Therefore sustained effort to perform is the result of achievement motivation.

The employer must realize that there are many barriers to achievement motivation. Most employees really want to do a good job, but are often discouraged from turning this desire into achievement motivation because obstacles keep them from their goal of a job well done. There are conditions that block an employee's performance and make it impossible or difficult to work at a high level of performance. Some of the common obstacles to performance are red tape, organizational policies and procedures, bottlenecks in the work load, lack of money, lack of manpower, improper instructions, faulty job descriptions, sudden change in the goal of a supervisor, lack of communication, too many programs for the number of employees, and lack of authority.

Another obstacle to achievement motivation occurs when an individual can perform but is deprived of work gratification. Obstacles to work gratification are those factors that prevent the employee from attaining the feeling of reward which comes from work itself or which should come directly from having performed in a superior fashion. Some of the common obstacles to work gratification are lack of recognition, unchallenging work, the purpose of the job not being understood, unequal treatment of employees, wrongly defined responsibilities, oversupervision or undersupervision, inconsistent rewards, or lack of goals.

In any case, whether it be obstacles to performance or obstacles to work gratification, the employee is not motivated to the extent possible because of the limitations discussed. The application of these concepts to create a motivating environment will be expanded later in this chapter.

THEORIES OF MOTIVATION

During the past 75 years, various theories of motivation have gained recognition. Frederick W. Taylor's scientific management theory was developed in the early 1900s. This theory of motivation seems to be the most simplistic in its approach and was discussed in Chapter 2. In the 1920s, the human relations approach gained recognition through the Hawthorne studies directed and led by Elton Mayo. In the 1940s the theory of motivation came about as a result of Abraham Mazlow's work, in which he stated that everybody has needs, that they are in a hierarchy, and that they serve the purposes described in Chapter 3. Following Mazlow, Frederick Herzberg developed in the early 1950s a theory of motivation which indicates that motivation is increased by job enrichment (i.e., creating jobs that are interesting and challenging to people so they are self-motivated). The most recent motivation theories are more complex and indicate that motivation is not easily explained. Some of the latest theorists are by Victor Vroom, Lyman Porter, Edward Lawer, Patricia Smith, and C. J. Cranny.

Scientific Management Theory

Taylor's theory maintains that if you totally understand a job, break it down into parts and improve on the skills and the method of performing the job, and then pay an individual according to her or his ability to produce work, you can motivate.[2] Taylor spent many years analyzing small tasks that workers perform, breaking them down into component parts, and improving on each part. Based on this job analysis and improved training, the individual could learn to perform a task at a rapid speed. The employee was paid for faster work on a piecemeal basis, resulting in an ability to make more money through increased productivity. This theory of motivation was popular for a number of years, and many industries picked up on the Taylor approach to improve work productivity.

One of the greatest shortcomings in this method was that it was contingent on the incentive approach to work: If you paid an individual enough, he or she would

---

[2] Frederick Taylor, *The Principles of Scientific Management* (New York: W. W. Norton and Company, 1967).

work at a rapid rate. It did not take into consideration any of the individual's personal needs; it took into account only the need for financial reward. Although this method, or theory, of motivation produced good results in a number of situations, in many other situations it did not. It was found that individuals who were paid on a piecemeal basis increased productivity only when they were paid for greater work rates; never did they increase work rates because of self-motivation. Only external or extrinsic reward encouraged them to work at a higher rate.

Hawthorne Studies

As a result of the Hawthorne studies, organizations began to move away from the scientific approach and toward the human relations approach to management (see discussion of the studies in Chapter 2).[3] But the human relations approach to management generally failed to recognize the importance of underlying psychological processes. This approach was based on three simple adaptive assumptions:

1. Personnel are primarily economically motivated and, secondarily, desire security and good working conditions.
2. Provision of the above rewards to personnel will have a positive effect on their morale.
3. There is a positive correlation between morale and productivity.[4]

Based on these three assumptions, the motivational problems facing management were relatively clear-cut and easy to solve. Theoretically, all management had to do was devise monetary incentive plans, insure security, and provide good working conditions. Morale would be high and maximum productivity would result. Unfortunately, these human relations approaches to motivation did not work out in practice. Although no harm was done and some good actually resulted in these early stages of human relations management, it soon became evident that such a simplistic approach fell far short of providing a meaningful solution to the complex motivational problems facing management. It became clear that motivation is more complex than simply trying to meet employees' needs for certain economical, security, and working conditions.

Maslow's Theory of Needs

In Chapter 3 we discussed individual needs as they related to Maslow's theory. We did not, however, relate it specifically to its application as a motivation

[3] For a detailed description of this research, see F. J. Roethlisberger and W. J. Dickson, *Management and the Worker* (Cambridge, Mass.: Harvard University Press, 1939), and Elton Mayo, *The Human Problems of an Industrial Civilization* (New York: MacMillan Co., 1933).

[4] Fred Luthans, *Organizational Behavior: A Modern Behavioral Approach to Management* (New York: McGraw-Hill Book Co., 1973), p. 482.

theory. Maslow indicated that people's motivational needs could be arranged in a hierarchy. He indicated that it was essential to assure that lower-level needs were met first. Then, once those lower-level needs were met, the individual would begin to strive for higher-level needs. To motivate an individual using this approach, an attempt is made to determine the level of need for which the individual is reaching. Once the proper level of need is determined, the manager or employer attempts to use that level of need to release the work capacity of the employee.

Maslow's original writing was about human behavior as it related to social and personality development, and he did not intend that his hierarchy of needs should directly relate to motivation on the job. In 1954 he wrote a book entitled *Motivation and Personality,* and in 1965 he authored a book entitled *Eupsychian Management,* which described the interrelationships between psychological theory and modern management. This latter book examined principals of psychological, industrial and business management, hence, the word eupsychian, or good psychological management. This book is one of the first attempts to understand how people are motivated on the job.

Other authors began to popularize Maslow's theory in management literature about this time. There is no question that Maslow's hierarchy theory had tremendous impact on various management approaches to motivation. By using Maslow's hierarchy in pyramid form, as shown in Figure 3.1 (p. 57), the needs that are described can be associated with various motivational terms. Psychological, or basic, needs can be associated with salary. Security needs can be associated with seniority, union subsidy, severance pay, and so on. Social or belonging needs can be associated with the formal and informal groups at work. Esteem needs can be associated with title, status symbols, and promotion. Finally, the highest level, self-actualization, is associated with employee achievement wherein the employee gets satisfaction out of the work itself.

In applying Maslow's theory to an organization, it would be relatively simple to meet the first two levels of needs. The challenge comes in trying to meet the higher-level needs of belonging, esteem, and self-actualization. Employees' lower-level needs are being met, so they are striving for the higher levels of needs. Management's task becomes one of finding ways to meet these higher-level needs within the work situation to maintain a high level of motivation.

Although Maslow's theory does not provide all the answers to work motivation, it does give us a great deal of insight into what some of the factors are that affect motivation. The number and names of the levels that Maslow identified are not important. As Maslow himself pointed out, the needs may not always occur in the order indicated and there may not always be a clear distinction between the various levels of the hierarchy. His major contribution lies in the hierarchy concept, the fact that an individual is always reaching for something he or she does not have. Maslow was the first to emphasize that once a need is met or satisfied, it no longer serves as a motivator. This pointed out to management that one must constantly be searching for ways to motivate employees by providing new challenges. The employer must try to be aware of what is likely to be the next need an employee will pursue, one that will excite her or him enough to do an outstanding piece of work in whatever the endeavor is.

Frederick Herzberg's Theory of Motivation

Herzberg built on Maslow's theory of motivation and in 1950 conducted a motivation study with about 200 accountants and engineers employed by a firm in the Pittsburgh, Pennsylvania area. Each of the individuals that participated in the study were interviewed by a professional interviewer. They were asked the following question: "Think of a time when you felt exceptionally good or exceptionally bad about your job. Either your present job or any job that you have ever had. This can be either the long range or short range kind of situation as I have just described it. Tell me what happened."[5] The responses were interesting and generally consistent. Those that involved good feelings about work were associated with job experience and job content. Contrarily, bad feelings were associated with things that surrounded the job, more appropriately called "job context." Herzberg concluded that employees have two different categories of needs that are met in the work situation and that these are essentially independent of each other and affect behavior in different ways.

Those elements that caused job dissatisfaction were associated with environmental factors and came to be called "hygienic factors." When employees felt good about their jobs, this feeling generally had to do with the work itself; these Herzberg called the "motivators." Thus his theory became the "motivation/hygiene theory."

Hygiene Factors
The policies and type of administration that a company puts forth, the type of supervision, the working conditions, the interpersonal relationships among individuals (superiors, co-workers, and subordinates), and employees' salary, status, and security are hygiene factors. These factors are not an integral part of the job, but they affect the conditions under which the job is performed. Herzberg related these to hygiene in the sense that they are preventative and environmental. He found that hygiene factors produced no motivation from workers, but prevented loss in work performance because of work slowdown. If they were not provided for, they became dissatisfied and their work was affected. When the hygiene factors are provided for, it does not necessarily move employees to outstanding performance; these factors just kept them working at a steady capacity. See Figure 4.3.

[5] Frederick Herzberg, Bernard Mausner, and Barbara Snyderman, *The Motivation to Work,* second edition (New York: John Wiley and Sons, 1959), p. 141.

I. Hygiene factors	Motivators
Job dissatisfaction	Job satisfaction

| II. Provide for job dissatisfaction when not maintained | Motivate employees |

III. 1. Supervision	1. Achievement
2. Company policy and administration	2. Recognition for achievement
3. Working conditions	3. Work itself
4. Interpersonal relationships with	4. Responsibility
(a) Peers	5. Advancement
(b) Subordinates	6. Possibility of growth
(c) Superiors	
5. Status	
6. Job security	
7. Salary	
8. Personal life	

Figure 4.3. Motivation-hygiene theory of Frederick Herzberg.

Motivators

The motivators, on the other hand, are satisfying factors that involve a sense of achievement, professional growth, and recognition. They offer a challenge and therefore were referred to as "motivators" by Herzberg. He called these factors motivators also because they seemed capable of having a positive effect on job satisfaction, often resulting in increased work capacity and total output.

Herzberg's theory appears to have a close relationship with Maslow's theory of the hierarchy of needs. The hygiene factors—company policy, administration, supervision, salary, interpersonal relationships, and working conditions—all seem to be affected by the first three levels of Maslow's needs: physiological, security, and social needs. The hygiene factors prevent dissatisfaction, but they do not lead to satisfaction; they tend to bring motivation up to a theoretical zero level. On the other hand, the motivators seem to be aligned with esteem and self-actualizing needs. Herzberg's theory indicates that to motivate employees, the top two levels of Maslow's needs have to be dealt with. An individual must have a job that is challenging in content to be truly motivated.

The Herzberg theory brought new interest to the area of motivation. Prior to this time, in both the scientific management and the human relations approach, attempts to improve motivation dealt with hygiene factors and the environment; but Herzberg's theory indicated that if one truly wants to motivate an employee, one has to deal with the higher-level needs. The management approach prior to this point indicated that if you had a morale problem or were not attaining high production, you should initiate higher wages or more fringe benefits or provide better working conditions. This solution did not work. Oftentimes, management found that they were already paying higher wages than their competition and had a better fringe benefit package, and yet the organization still suffered from lack of motivation. For the first time, Herzberg's theory offered an explanation for this dilemma. By considering only the hygiene factors, management was not really motivating its personnel; it was just keeping them from being "job dissatisfied."

The Herzberg theory does not indicate that hygiene factors are not important; indeed, they are very important. But also important are the motivators contained in the job itself, making it interesting and challenging to the employee. Are employees turned on by their jobs? Are they getting the praise, recognition, and the status they need? Are they provided with opportunities for advancement, achievement, and responsibility? These are the motivators that keep employees working harder and striving for bigger and better things.

In analying the Herzberg theory of motivation, one can also draw many other insights into its value. For example, in the United States and Canada today we have, generally speaking, guaranteed the first two levels of needs, as described by Maslow. Everyone is pretty much guaranteed the physiological and security needs. Hopefully no one is going to go hungry or without shelter of some sort. Some have better pay and security than others; but for the most part these two levels of needs are guaranteed. At one time, when security and income were not guaranteed, they could have been motivators insofar as people were striving to reach these needs. But now that they are guaranteed, they no longer are motivators. Figure 4.4 indicates the effect of the development of our society toward the assurance of lower-level needs, showing the relationship of the Herzberg and Maslow theories.

In trying to analyze how Herzberg's theory affects work in a leisure setting, let's use the example of a park maintenance man who is happy with his job and likes his supervisor. He is performing at a rather high level of work. Suddenly his supervisor is temporarily transferred and is replaced by a supervisor who uses supervisory techniques that the employee does not like. As a result, the hygiene factors of the job are affected and the employee begins to deliberately or unconsciously slow down in his work or take less initiative because of the treatment he receives from the new supervisor. When his original supervisor returns, his work level is brought up to the acceptable level it once was; but it probably will not go up beyond that point. According to Herzberg's theory, the only way the employee's motivation could be increased would be to change his work, to give him a job that is more stimulating and satisfying.

As another example, an employee who suddenly finds that another employee in the same work classification is making more money than she, becomes dissatisfied and begins to slow down in her work because she feels she is not fairly paid.

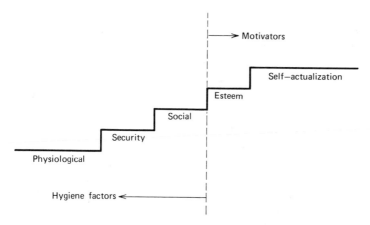

Figure 4.4. Relationship between Herzberg's and Maslow's theories. (Paul Hersey, Kenneth Blanchard, *Management of Organizational Behavior: Utilizing Human Resources,* 2nd Edition, copyright © 1972, p. 56. Reprinted by permission of Prentice-Hall, Inc., Englewood Cliffs, N.J.)

If the employee's salary is brought up to the level of her co-worker, her productivity will probably increase only to the original level.

These two examples deal with the hygiene factors. Again, the hygiene factors are important and must be kept at a good level, but they do not stimulate motivation in the employee. If they are not provided for, the employee will have job dissatisfaction. But if they are improved, it will not improve productivity. If they are not kept high, on the other hand, productivity may fall below what is acceptable or normal for a particular employee.

Now let's consider the potential of motivators in a work situation. Say that an employee gets a new supervisor who begins to give the employee more opportunity for exercising initiative and creativity in his work. She permits him to make decisions, handle problems on his own, and take on more responsibility. In effect, this will stimulate the employee to do bigger and better things. He is motivated. He becomes capable of successfully fulfilling his supervisor's expectations. He not only does his job, but he begins to look at ways to improve his work and please his boss. Giving him an opportunity to exercise responsibility and provide for creativity, the job itself is more interesting to the employee and he is now motivated. He is now producing more work. He is job satisfied, and the supervisor has affected his motivation by changing and enriching his work.

In summarizing these conditions, we might say that the hygiene needs, when satisfied, tend to eliminate dissatisfaction and work restriction but do little to motivate an individual to superior performance or to increase his or her capacity. On the other hand, satisfaction of the motivators will permit an individual to grow and develop in a mature way, often implementing and increasing his or her ability. Herzberg's theory encouraged management to design into work environments an opportunity to satisfy the motivators.

One of the common misconceptions about the Herzberg theory revolves around his concept of job enlargement; that if you enlarged the job and made it more interesting, you would get more productivity out of a worker. In other words, the number of operations in which the employee was engaged should be increased. Herzberg's actual observation regarding this phenomena indicated that changing a person's job by enlarging it does not enrich the job at all and does not provide more motivation for the employee. The example he used was of an employee who washes dishes. If his job is enlarged to washing silverware, pots, and pans, it does not make the job more satisfying. Herzberg indicated that work should be enriched by a deliberate upgrading of the responsibilities, scope, and challenge of work. The term he used is to "vertically load," rather than "horizontally load," the job. Horizontally loading the job means assigning more tasks at the same level. Vertically loading the job means increasing the scope, capacity, and challenge of the job.

Suppose that in a leisure service agency, a crew of maintenance men have a supervisor who is specific and direct in assignments he makes. Little is left to the discretion of the crew, even though they have a variety of things to do. They are told how, when, and where to do everything, leaving little to the imagination. They tend to do only what they are told to do, and when they are done they sit and wait for their supervisor to tell them what to do next. Although they are paid well, and have job security and good hygiene factors, they have little motivation.

Another supervisor has a different approach. He brings the crew together and outlines the overall assignment in broad terms, asking the men what they feel is the best way to carry out the job. He offers suggestions, but relies on input from the men because they express interest and concern. Soon the group of maintenance men begin to see things that need to be done and find new ways to do the job. They begin to find better ways to do what has been done more routinely before. By regrouping jobs and by experimenting with new ways to perform the job, they are turned on. The job has been enriched because there is opportunity for responsibility, creativity, and achievement. As Peter F. Drucker states, "You have made work productive and the worker achieving."[6]

The supervisor can further motivate the outstanding members of the crew by informing them if a new supervisor's position is coming up. Opportunity for advancement into a more responsible job should be highly motivating. Even at the lower levels of an organization one can increase productivity and provide employees with an opportunity to grow and mature. When responsible employees

[6] Peter F. Drucker, *Management: Tasks, Responsibilities, Practices* (New York: Harper and Row, 1974), p. 169.

are given a chance to participate in planning and carrying out their own work, they will more than likely do a better job. According to Herzberg, motivation is in the job itself. Job enrichment prevents a job from becoming obsolescent, it provides for creativity and it provides for maximum performance.

Morale is affected by two opposite conditions, satisfaction and dissatisfaction. Thus, in any job, both the motivators and the hygiene factors can affect morale, and both must be maintained at the highest level possible to assure peak employee morale. If the manager is not willing to change a job to make it more motivating, three conditions will result: (1) the manager will have in her employ a person who is not motivated, (2) she may have to eliminate the job itself and, (3) she will have a morale problem.

Boredom is often the cause of "no job satisfaction." As indicated earlier, the hygiene factors take care of the first few levels of people's needs; motivators take care of the higher-level needs. In other words, there are two sets of needs: (1) those that avoid pains and (2) those that permit an employee to grow psychologically. The opposite of job satisfaction would not be job dissatisfaction, but rather, "no job satisfaction." The motivators and the hygiene factors are not opposite each other; they complement each other. Both must be maintained at the highest level possible. To neglect either one will result in an employee who is not operating at full proficiency.

Using the hygiene factors as motivators is impractical because we cannot bribe people into working forever. We have already reached the level of inflation that cannot be surpassed, without total bankruptcy. Such management, in any case, results in movement that takes place only when the supervisor is present; once she or he is not present, the movement usually stops.

Herzberg, in a lecture in San Mateo, California, presented several concepts that should be considered when dealing with motivation. These concepts generally revolve around fairness in terms of making jobs more interesting and providing for motivation to employees.[7]

The first point supports Herzberg's theory that to make work more satisfying, more motivators must be provided in the work that people perform.

His second point deals with educating people in a broad sense, as well as providing technical training, so that individuals can do more things and indulge in more types of potentially satisfying work. If people are educated conceptually as well as technically, they are assured of more potentially motivating job situations.

The third point encourages the teaching of ethics in education. People should understand that treating one another fairly is important because it creates better relationships, both working and personal, between individuals. A good yardstick to follow is the Golden Rule of "Do unto others as you would have them do unto you." In a work situation this kind of attitude and understanding creates a mutual

[7] Taken from Herzberg's lecture on May 26, 1976.

trust between employees to the extent that they are ready and willing to cooperate at all times instead of being suspicious of each and every request for cooperation. Moreover, an opportunity is needed for people within our educational system to understand the values of fairness in practice rather than learning a code of ethics that is given only lip service.

The fourth point encourages working with the strengths of people, not their weaknesses. Capitalize on what employees do well, not on what they do poorly, and encourage them in their areas of strength. Provide jobs that capitalize on their strengths in the work situation rather than hound them on their weaknesses and incapabilities. If they need training to improve skills, provide training so they can increase their work capabilities.

The fifth point is that one should be decent just for the sake of being decent. Managers should not always calculate everything they do in a job situation. They should treat employees fairly, and they should treat other managers fairly. This tends to provide a work environment of trust, respect, and integrity.

The sixth point stresses that the manager should integrate the job tasks and the abilities of the workers to maximize and humanize their work. This should enable workers to achieve both high productivity and feelings of personal achievement.

Latest Theories of Motivation

Vroom's Theory

Vroom developed one of the most recently accepted theories of motivation. His theory is built around the concept that motivation is a direct result of three factors: valence, expectancy, and force. His assumption is that choices made by an individual among alternative courses of action are related to psychological events occurring simultaneously with the behavior.[8] Figure 4.5 summarizes the Vroom theory of work and motiviation. Vroom indicates that force and motivation are basically the same; they are shown to be the algebraic sum of the products of valence multiplied by expectancy.

Motivation or Force	=	Valance	×	Expectancy
Employee Motivation	=	Valance	×	Expectancy

Figure 4.5.   Vroom's theory of motivation

The definition that Vroom gives *valence* is the strength of the individual's preference for a particular choice (ranging from 1 to 10). Other words that might be substituted for valence include incentive, attitude, or desire. For valence to be positive for the individual, he or she must prefer obtaining the outcome to not obtaining it.

[8] Victor H. Vroom, *Work and Motivation* (New York: John Wiley and Sons, 1964), p. 14–15.

Expectancy is the other variable in Vroom's theory. Expectancy is the probability (ranging from 1 to 10) that an individual might achieve a particular outcome.

The strength of motivation to perform a certain act will depend on the algebraic sum of the products of valence and expectancy. To use an example that might better explain the Vroom theory, let's assume that an employee has a desire for promotion. This desire can be strong, medium, or weak. Obviously the stronger the employee's desire for promotion, the stronger her preference. The same goes for expectancy; the possibility that she will gain the promotion can vary from a good chance to a very poor chance. Therefore, if a numerical value is placed on her valence (her preference for promotion, on a scale from 1 to 10) at 5 and a value is placed on her expectancy for promotion (also on a scale from 1 to 10) at 2, we find the product of 5 times 2, or 10. This reflects a relatively low level of motivation.

If another employee with more confidence in herself has the same desire for promotion (has a valence indicator of 5) but an expectancy indicator of 5, her motivation would be 25, which is considerably higher and would result in a higher level of motivation. Likewise, as either of the variables of valence or expectancy increases or decreases, the product of force, or the motivation, increases or decreases proportionately, indicating that more or less work would be released as shown in the above Figure.

Vroom, in *Work and Motivation,* indicates five properties of work roles. They (1) provide financial renumeration, (2) require the expenditure of energy, (3) involve the production of goods and services, (4) permit or require social interaction, and (5) affect the social status of the worker.[9] Vroom indicates that there is no judgment as to the priority of these different work roles as they affect the employee's strength of preference for working; but they are contributing factors as to why people work.

Vroom also maintains that employees who are involved in the decision-making process and have opportunities to interact on the job have lower rates of absenteeism and turnover. His research indicates that there is a positive correlation between the employee's receptiveness of a job (how she or he perceives and accepts the job in its entirety) and the rate of turnover among job occupants. There is a negative relationship between supervisory consideration (concern for the employee) and absenteeism; that is, the greater the amount of supervisory concern, the fewer the number of incidences of absenteeism.[10]

In general, Vroom found that there are three assumptions about motivation as it relates to ability: (1) People prefer tasks and jobs that require the use of their abilities. (2) People prefer consistent information about their abilities (consistent standards and evaluation) to inconsistent information. (3) People prefer receiving

[9] Ibid., p. 43.
[10] Ibid, pp. 279–280.

information to the effect that they possess valuable abilities to information that they do not possess valuable abilities.[11]

Vroom's theory indicates that motivation is related directly to what a person wants in terms of a particular outcome multiplied by his expectancy that he can achieve that outcome. The stronger his wants, and the greater the possibility of achieving them, the greater will be his motivation.

Porter and Lawler's Theory

Another theory of motivation was advanced by Porter and Lawler. Their theory is multivariable, stressing that there are many relationships that exist between motivation and job effectiveness. Their theory counters some of the simplistic, traditional assumptions made about the positive relationships between satisfaction and performance. They deal with effort, performance, reward, and satisfaction, all of which are interrelated and have an effect on motivation.[12]

Smith and Cranny's Theory

A motivation model forumulated by Smith and Cranny presents a more simplistic, three-way relationship among effort, satisfaction, and reward.[13] Their model is triangular; each variable is in a corner of the triangle, and each has a causal effect on the other (see Figure 4.6).

Figure 4.6. Smith and Cranny motivation model. (Patricia Smith and C. J. Cranny, "Psychology of Men at Work," *Annual Review of Psychology,* Vol. 19, 1968, p. 469.

A new benefit package (reward) may lead to an increase in satisfaction. In turn, a satisfied, cooperative worker may become eligible for promotion. Performance is affected only by effort, not by reward or satisfaction, as shown in the model. Performance is in the center of the model and can influence reward and

---

[11] Ibid, p. 286.

[12] Lyman Porter and Edward Lawler, *Managerial Attitudes and Performance* (Homewood, Ill.: Richard D. Irwin, 1968).

[13] Patricia Smith and C. J. Cranny, "Psychology of Men at Work," *Annual Review of Psychology* 19 (1968), pp. 469–477.

satisfaction, but can itself be influenced only by the effort of intention. The Smith and Cranny model is a simplistic model. It stresses that management's job is to administer reward. But this alone does not have direct impact on performance and falls short as a way for management to motivate employees.

Needs and Motivation

Earlier in the chapter it was mentioned that management's choice is *to try to make people work* or *to try to make people want to work*. The question arises, Can we really make people work? And if we do, How long will they work and with what commitment? It becomes obvious that the most rational choice is to make people want to work, in other words, to create an environment in which employees choose to work because they are excited and challenged by their work.

In Chapter 3 we spent a great deal of time discussing needs of individuals and how these needs should be fused with organizational goals. The manager must remember that people have many needs, all of which are continually competing for the behavior of the individual. No employee has exactly the same combination of needs. Some individuals are concerned with salary, others with status, and still others with responsibility. One of the first things the manager must do is to try to determine what the needs of his employees are. The question he might ask is, "What do workers really want from their jobs?"

A number of researchers have investigated the apparent difference between the employee's perception of her or his job and the supervisor's perception of the employee's job. In a study by U. M. Gluskinos and B. J. Kestelman of Temple University, management was asked to try to put themselves in the workers' shoes by ranking in order of importance a series of items that described things the workers wanted from their jobs.[14] The managers were told not to think in terms of how they themselves would rank the items. The idea was to rank "1" as the item they felt the employees wanted most, "2" the second most, and so on. The workers also ranked the same items.

Figure 4.7 indicates the results of this experiment, which are interesting. The managers ranked high wages as the item they felt the employees felt was most important; they ranked steady work second and pension benefits third. The point to be made in this study is that although the manager is supposed to understand and know employees' needs if she is to motivate them, she may be misguided in her appraisal of their needs. The manager perceived that the incentives directed toward satisfying the psychological and safety motives were most important to workers when actually the workers felt other things were more important. A manager should not act on the basis of what she thinks employees want from

[14] U. M. Gluskinos and B. J. Kestelman, "Management and Labor Leaders' Perception of Worker Needs as Compared with Self-Reported Needs," *Personnel Psychology, 24,* Summer 1971, pp. 239–246.

Job Factors	Factory Employees' Self-ranking	Office Employees' Self-ranking	Management's Ranking of Employees Needs
Steady work	1	1	2
Pensions, etc.	2	8	3
High wages	3	10	1
Getting along with co-workers	4	4	11
Getting along with supervisors	5	3	12.5
Good working hours	6	9	4
Chance to do quality work	7	5	12.5
Not . . . work too hard	8	14	14
Chance to do interesting work	10.5	2	6
Good working conditions	10.5	6	9
Paid vacations	10.5	12	10
Chance for promotions	12	7	7.5
Good unions	13	13	7.5
Chance for raise	14	11	5

Figure 4.7. Employees' self-ranking and management's perception of employee needs. From U. M. Gluskinos and B. J. Kestelman, "Management and Labor Leaders' Perception of Worker Needs as Compared with Self-Reported Needs," *Personnel Psychology*, Summer 1971, Table 1, p. 242.

their jobs; she should act on the basis of what employees actually want. The only way she can determine this is by asking the employees themselves and communicating with them in terms of what they are looking for in their jobs.

Research done by William James of Harvard University found that hourly employees could maintain their jobs, that is, not be fired, by working at approximately 20 to 30 percent of their ability.[15] On the other hand, the study also indicated that individuals who were highly motivated often worked at 80 to 90 percent of their ability. Thus there is a considerable range within which a manager can conceivably increase employees' work capacity. By understanding motivation and the needs of employees, and by meeting these needs, the manager can increase employee work capacity anywhere from 20 to 80 percent above what might normally be expected of unmotivated employees. All in all, this points out that work capacity can be increased with the proper motivation.

In Chapter 3 we found that as much as 70 percent of a manager's time is spent in the area of human skills. An understanding of human skills should enable the manager to recognize the needs of employees and provide the proper motivation

[15] Paul Hersey and Kenneth H. Blanchard, *Management of Organizational Behavior: Utilizing Human Resources*, second edition (Englewood Cliffs, N.J.: Prentice-Hall, 1972), p. 5.

system which will release work capacity and accomplish organizational goals and objectives. By understanding employees' needs and aligning these needs with the organization's goals, he could increase productivity from 20 to 80 percent. However there is more than just one level of employee motivation. Some employees are top achievers. They always seem motivated and work hard at accomplishing goals and objectives. These individuals are self-starters, and in many cases the manager does not have to spend time trying to motivate them. In dealing with self-achievers, the manager may only have to keep frustrations or other anxieties that might hinder motivation out of their way. Herzberg's theory indicated that motivation is inherent in the work itself. The best way to turn workers on to their jobs is to provide jobs that they are enthused about and interested in.

Why is it that a worker who doesn't like his job and "goofs off" all day long may go home at night and put forth a great deal of effort and energy in coaching a little league team for a few hours? Obviously, there are factors that are motivating to the individual in the coaching situation. He may find the work with young people rewarding and challenging, whereas the conditions present in the work situation do not provide this same type of satisfaction. The point is, if the work situation could provide the same elements of satisfaction, the individual would be more productive.

The word *motivation* has many synonyms, such as drive, want, wish, aim, goal, desire, and incentive. Bernard Berelson and Gary A. Steiner define motivation as "an inner state that energizes activities or moves (hence "motivation"), and that directs or channels behavior towards goals."[16] Fillmore H. Stanford and Lawrence S. Wrightsman, Jr., describes motive as "a restlessness, a lack, a yen, a force. Once in the grip of a motive, the organism does something. It most generally does something to relieve the restlessness, to remedy the lack, to alleviate the yen, to mitigate the force".[17] Fred Luthans, in *Organizational Behavior,* shows the motivation process in simple diagram.

$$Need \rightarrow Drive \rightarrow Goal$$

He gives the following definitions for need, drive, and goal:

1. *Need.* The best one-word definition of a need is deficiency. In the homostatic sense, needs are created whenever there is a physiological or psychological imbalance.
2. *Drive.* With a few exceptions, drives or motives (the two terms will be used interchangeably) are set up to alleviate needs. A drive can be simply defined as

[16] Bernard Berelson and Gary A. Steiner, *Human Behavior* (New York: Harcourt, Brace and World, 1964), p. 240.
[17] Fillmore H. Stanford and Lawrence S. Wrightsman, Jr., *Psychology,* third edition (Belmont, Calif.: Brooks, Cold Publishing Co., 1970), p. 189.

a deficiency with direction. Drives are action oriented and provide an energizing thrust towards goal accomplishment. They are the very heart of the motivational process.

3. *Goal.* At the end of the motivation cycle is the goal. The goal in the motivation cycle can be defined as anything which will alleviate a need and reduce a drive. Thus attaining a goal will tend to restore psychological and physiological balance and will reduce or cut off the drive.[18]

In a work situation, the work of the organization is accomplished through people, the employees. In the leisure setting this may involve the recreation leader, the maintenance workers, and the supervisor, all working together to accomplish certain objectives. In a park construction project, the activities may consist of digging, laying blocks, doing various plumbing and electrical activities, and so on. In a recreation setting, the activities may consist of leading games, showing children how to paint a picture and/or supervising a game room. These activities blend together ultimately to accomplish work. Behavior is basically goal oriented. As indicated in Chapter 3, every individual attempts to meet his or her needs. The attempt to meet needs results in behavior. Managers should constantly be trying to understand human behavior, not only to determine the whys of past behavior but to anticipate change and influence future behavior. Behavior directed toward a goal is the unit of activity that results in organizational accomplishments.

Individuals have different needs. They also have different abilities in what they can do and what they will do, based on their capabilities, training desire, and ambition. The motivation of an individual depends on her desire for a particular outcome and the strength of her motive at the particular time. Motives are defined as needs, wants, drives, impulses—depending on the individual. Generally, motives are directed at some goal, which may be conscious or subconscious. Motives lead to behavior as persons attempt to reach goals. A goal, on the other hand, is outside the individual. It sometimes may be referred to as a reward, hope, something at which a motive is directed. The manager who understands motives or the needs of an individual, recognizing that they will be directed at some goal, is on his way toward understanding the motivational process.

A MOTIVATION MODEL

We have developed the following series of diagrams to illustrate the motivation process. These diagrams have been synthesized and created from a number of motivation theories. Although Figure 4.13 combines Figures 4.8 to 4.13, each separate diagram is presented to show each step of the motivation process. The final diagram, Figure 4.13, is referred to as the management model in this section.

[18] Fred Luthans, *Organizational Behavior* pp. 392–393.

Figure 4.8. A need directed at a goal.

Figure 4.8 shows a need, or a motive, and an arrow indicating that it is directed toward a goal. The strength of motives may vary from time to time. Generally, individuals at any one time have several motives moving them to different behavior. Whichever motive is the strongest takes over their activity for that particular time. For example, an individual who feels a need for exercise but a greater need for food, will eat first. Several needs are constantly pulling and tugging at us but, generally, the strongest motive is the one that takes over and dictates the particular activity we will engage in at a particular time. In Chapter 3 we indicated that, as individuals attempt to meet needs, these needs are sometimes blocked. This prevents individuals from meeting these needs, and hence their effort and energy are directed at some other need. As individuals are motivated, their efforts and energies are directed toward a goal that results in behavior. This behavior results in activity. For example, in Figure 4.9, assume that the motive, or need, is hunger. This results in a behavior directed at securing food. The activity that results is *goal-directed activity* consisting of hunting, finding, preparing, and, finally, eating food. Another example would be a person in search of companionship. This behavior could result in the activity of joining a club. The goal itself is a friend or a group of friends. The motive results in behavior that becomes goal-directed activity: finding a group in which to participate and searching for a friend; the activity itself results when the individual has found a group of friends as he or she participates in a recreation program. We can understand the motivation process if we recognize that employees have

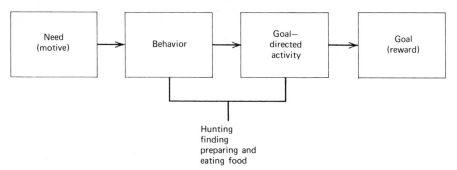

Figure 4.9. Needs directed at a goal that results in behavior and goal-directed activity.

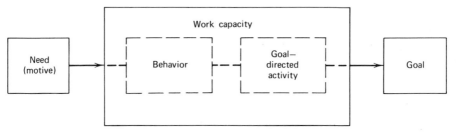

Figure 4.10. This diagram shows that behavior and goal-directed activity are seen as work capacity in an organization.

motives directed at goals that will result in certain behavior, which releases work capacity. We can capitalize on this work capacity by directing it toward the goals of the organization while the individual is meeting his or her needs.

Managers who are aware of the motivation process are constantly seeking ways to provide goals that are of interest to employees, in order to release their work capacity. Managers must recognize what the needs of the individuals are before they can set the goals. Figure 4.10 shows an expansion of the motivation diagram. In it, behavior and goal-directed activity are encompassed in a larger square called "work capacity." The goal of the employer is also a part of the larger goal of the organization. The goal of the organization is made up of the goals of its employees, who are each working toward their goals, which fit together to accomplish the organizational goal. This is shown in Figure 4.11. It is the job of a manager to coordinate the behavior or work of the employees to accomplish the organizational goal.

The motivation process is affected and influenced by many other factors that are outside the individual. Two of these factors are *expectancy* and *availability*.

Figure 4.11. Diagram shows how individual employee needs are coordinated and directed to meet organizational goals.

Managers have influence on and can affect expectancy and availability in a work situation.

Expectancy is the individual's *perceived probability* of satisfying a particular need, based on that individual's past experiences. Expectancy tends to affect motives; it is influenced by past experiences. The individual who expects to find food pursues it. If she expects that she cannot find food, this would certainly hinder her motivation. In the same way, if an individual does not expect to find friendship, his motivational process is slowed down, based on his past experiences. Managers, recognizing that expectancy influences the motivational process, can use this knowledge to set realistic goals. If goals are set that employees do not believe they can achieve (because of lack of ability or lack of training), they are not likely to pursue those particular goals. Thus, one can readily see that expectancy has a great deal of influence on the motivational process.

Availability is related to the *perceived limitations/opportunities* of the environment. It is determined by how accessible a goal is and whether it can be satisfied. If food is not available and an individual realizes this, she is not going to try to find food. Likewise, if an employee realizes that there is no advancement available, he is not apt to work toward it. Contrarily, if he realizes that advancement is possible, he is apt to perceive and pursue the goal with a great deal of enthusiasm and interest, working more vigorously. See Figure 4.12.

Availability, expectancy, goals, and needs all influence the behavior of employees in a work situation. If managers understand these relationships, their

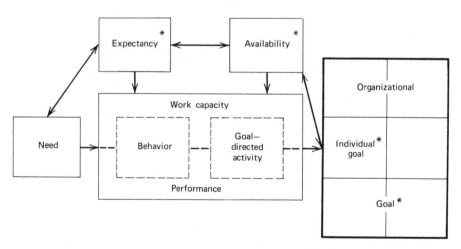

Figure 4.12. Added to the diagram are expectancy and availability showing the effect that they have on motivation. The asterisks indicate those factors over which the manager has some control in a work situation.

chances of providing for the motivation of their employees is much greater. If an employer misjudges the needs, desires, and goals of employees, she is not going to stand much of a chance of motivating them. Employers who understand and perceive the real needs of their employees, are more likely to provide a motivating job.

The combination of behavior and goal-directed activity, enclosed in a larger square called "performance," or "work capacity" is shown in Figure 4.12. Managers, in trying to meet the goals and objectives of the organization as well as the goals of individuals, realize that this is accomplished as individuals strive for the goals that result in behavior and goal-directed activity, that is, "work capacity" or "performance." A manager's objective is to affect the performance of the employee by directing it toward the goal of the organization in the most effective way possible. To do this, the manager affects the various rewards, or goals, that employees strive for. He can affect performance by providing a job that is creative. He influences advancement, and he recommends employees for additional salary increases. Figure 4.12 shows the ways in which the manager can affect goals in a positive way.

If there is a promotion open, availability is a factor in that employees will strive for the promotion by doing a better job or demonstrating new skills. Availability obviously affects expectancy; if employees can reasonably hope to get a promotion, a raise, or a job with more responsibility, this in turn can affect their behavior in that they will work harder for the particular goal. Managers can affect availability insofar as they may have influence as to who is promoted and who is not. Also, they can increase the expectancy of employees by telling them that if they work harder, they can get the promotion. Notice that the arrows in Figure 4.12 point in two directions. This is because expectancy and availability are affected by each other. Expectancy also affects performance and need.

Another factor that managers can affect is the ability of the employee. Managers can do this by providing training, as shown in the lower portion of the diagram in Figure 4.13. The manager can help the employee develop new skills or improve old skills. The manager can give him or her assistance in technical areas, providing training programs, send employees to school, or have employees teach new job skills to other employees. In any case, an employee's performance is affected by ability. If he does not have the ability to reach a given goal, he obviously cannot attain it, be it his own goal or the goal of the organization.

Managers also have control over feedback. They can praise an employee for a job well done and thus affect the strength of behavior toward the goal. Likewise, satisfaction affects ability by providing encouragement to do a job. It is a fact that reinforcement is one of the most positive influences in the motivational process, yet in many instances the supervisor tends to dwell more on providing negative feedback to his employees than he does in giving positive feedback to them. Listed

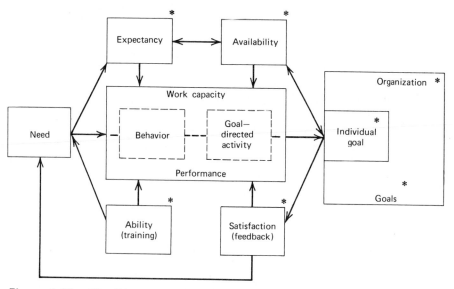

Figure 4.13. The Edginton and Williams motivation model. This model shows the various factors the manager can influence which indirectly affect the work capacity or performance of an employee. The factors that the manager controls are indicated by an asterisk.

below are 8 simple addition problems. Look at each one and let your mind react to them.

$$
\begin{array}{cccccccc}
8 & 9 & 7 & 6 & 9 & 9 & 7 & 9 \\
+\,8 & +\,5 & +\,8 & +\,5 & +\,9 & +\,8 & +\,7 & +\,2 \\
\hline
16 & 14 & 13 & 11 & 18 & 16 & 14 & 11
\end{array}
$$

Following this simple mental exercise, think how you would respond to an employee who had submitted this to you for approval. The most common response would be "Lee, you got 2 wrong" rather than "Lee, you got 6 out of 8 right." Our tendency is to point out people's faults rather than point out what they have done right and giving them positive reinforcement. Obviously we must deal with errors and work that is not acceptable, but we will find we will be able to motivate individuals and employees much more positively and effectively by reinforcement of what they are doing right rather than what they have done wrong.

Appropriate feedback to the situation above would be "Lee, you have done very well. You have 6 right. There are 2 that I would like you to look over again and see if you can improve upon them." In this feedback you have reinforced Lee's good work yet brought it to the employee's attention that improvement is needed in some areas. As a manager or supervisor working with employees, the greatest motivation will come by positive reinforcement of a job well done rather than always dwelling on errors that an employee may make. See Figure 4.13.

In summary, by being aware of the factors we have discussed above and recognizing the needs of employees, managers can indirectly influence the work "capacity" or "performance" of employees.

The above model should help the reader to understand the motivation process. It illustrates the four factors that affect motivation, which are described earlier in this chapter. There we stated that motivation is a function of: (1) our needs; managers can establish appropriate goals to meet employee needs; (2) opportunity; managers can make opportunities available to employees and increase their expectancy; (3) ability; managers can provide employees with proper training and supervision; and (4) reinforcement; managers can make certain that employees get positive feedback and satisfaction from their jobs.

MAKING MOTIVATION WORK

Now that we have looked at some of the motivation theories and have discussed the various elements that affect motivation, we are ready to put our knowledge to work. This will come about by (1) creating a job and an environment that will be most conducive to employee motivation, (2) creating jobs that are directed toward meeting individuals' needs, and (3) creating an environment that permits employees to perform their jobs while working toward the goals of the organization.

In a work situation, individual needs and organizational goals are dependent on each other, and if either one is compromised it will affect efficiency and productivity. The idea is "to make work productive and the worker achieving."[19] Accomplishing this task is not a simple matter and requires the managerial skills of good leadership and communication (which will be discussed in the next chapter).

Employees' needs must always remain central in the thoughts of the manager. (It must be remembered that as the employee strives to meet his or her needs it may result in behavior that, in a work situation, is released work capacity.) The work capacity of a group of employees channeled in the right direction by the manager accomplishes the goals of the organization. If employees' needs are not being met, there is a good possibility they will not be motivated and thus one's work capacity will be used in a nonproductive manner. As stressed, the manager has to find a way to meet employees' needs while also meeting organizational goals. The most successful manager accomplishes organizational goals by meeting individual employee needs first. Trying to fit employees into jobs that do not meet their individual needs results in a waste of time, energy, and other resources.

Let us assume that a manager, or supervisor, is assigned a particular task and consequently directs a park foreman to construct a small building. The manager's

---

[19] Drucker, *Management: Tasks, Responsibilities, Practices,* p. 169.

goal is to complete the building. He could, if he has the skills and the time, complete the building himself. The job can be done better and accomplished more quickly by a group of employees, however. The manager should first analyze the tasks necessary to construct the building. It takes digging and forming for a foundation, pouring cement, bringing water and electricity to the building, laying cement blocks, installing doors and windows, placing the roof, installing shelves and cabinets, as well as other tasks. These tasks would be accomplished by employees.

The park foreman, in assigning the various employees to the various tasks, does not assign them arbitrarily. He assigns the tasks to the employees based on their skills. The carpenter will construct the forms, the mason will lay the blocks, and so on. To do otherwise would be a waste, and the job might be done poorly and unproductively. Likewise, it would be unproductive to assign an engineer with 20 years' experience to dig the foundation, even though he could do the job. If he is not motivated, he might do it slowly and poorly, and he would be overpaid for the job. Although this is an oversimplified example, it makes the point that the abilities of the employee should be matched with the abilities needed for the task at hand to maximize effectiveness, efficiency, and employee satisfaction.

To release work capacity in the employee, the manager has to design a job that will be conducive to employee motivation. The first step in job design is to find out what the employee wants from her job. To determine this, (1) the employee herself can be asked to list a number of things she wants from her job in terms of priority, (2) the manager and the employee can outline what the goals and objectives of the organization are, and (3) the manager and the employee can outline or reaffirm the specific tasks of the job for which the individual was hired. The employee should be asked what she wants from the job, what her goals are, what her ambitions are, and what she hopes to accomplish in the job. By determining and understanding the answers to these questions, the manager can begin to design a job that will motivate the employee.

After the employee has been on the job for a period of time and the manager has formed a working relationship with the employee, the manager will begin to recognize certain factors that motivate the employee. It might be a pat on the back, a word of encouragement, or some other form of recognition. Some employees are motivated by added responsibility. In this case, the manager should attempt to design more responsibility and more independence into the job. Whatever the need may be, the manager should begin to design into the job the things that meet the employees' needs in order to, in turn, meet organizational goals. In other words, the manager must manage both work and the employee at the same time. The manager integrates work and the worker into the accomplishment of both individual and organizational goals.

In today's society, "working" is no longer just a matter of earning a salary to provide security. No longer can management motivate employees by salary, security, and fringe benefits alone. It must provide work that is meaningful, satisfying, and worthwhile by making the work productive and giving the worker the opportunity to achieve. The employee may not necessarily expect work to be enjoyable; but he does expect work to be worthwhile and to accomplish something he feels is of value. On the other hand, to have the employee feel a sense of personal achievement while the goals and objectives of the organization go unaccomplished is futile and unprofitable. If this situation exists, ultimately there will be no job for the employee. The manager must recognize that individuals' needs change and that the factors which motivate them also should be changed. In terms of job design, the manager must constantly change the job to make it motivating and must also provide an environment that is motivating to employees.

Peter F. Drucker, in his book *Management: Tasks, Responsibilities, Practices,* says that there are four separate activities that are necessary to make work productive.[20] First, work requires analysis. The manager should know the specific operations needed for work, their sequence, and their requirements. Second, we need to synthesize the individual operations into a process of production. Third, we need to build into the process the control of direction in order to maintain and encourage quality, quantity, and standards of exceptions. Fourth, the appropriate tools have to be provided. To make work productive, one must start with the end product or service desired. Skills, information, and knowledge, are tools of the leisure service manager. When they are applied, these tools must always be related to the desired end product or service.

The major emphasis on motivation of employees has been directed toward elements outside the job itself. In our society, it has been through work that the greatest number of people have had access to personal achievement and fulfillment. Of course, one of the major goals of the leisure profession is to help people find fulfillment and satisfaction in their life through leisure especially when their work is empty of satisfaction other than material reward. If this is the case, work and leisure complement each other.

To enable the employee to achieve and find satisfaction in her work, the manager must provide her with an opportunity to take on responsibility in her job. This requires meaningful work, reinforcement of positive growth, and continuous learning because it is ridiculous to ask an employee to take responsibility for a job that is boring, meaningless, and unfulfilling. To facilitate employee responsibility, the employee should be part of the planning process. She should have input into the work design and the work process. The more the manager encourages the employee to take responsibility for her own job, the more responsibility she will take for meeting the goals of quality and quantity.

The role of the manager is not one of making employees work. It is a fact that employees today are more knowledgeable and have better information and more training than their predecessors. The threat of losing the job is no longer an effec-

---

[20] Ibid, p. 199.

tive way to make employees work. Also, job security and income stability are no longer factors that motivate employees to work because society has guaranteed these things. Thus the role of the manager must be to facilitate the positive development of the employee, with organizational well-being as a by-product, so to speak.

SUMMARY

Motivation takes place when an employee has found a task that he is enthused and excited about and by which he is challenged. Work that contributes to the employee's satisfaction, growth, and development while contributing to the accomplishment of organizational goals and objectives is the manager's aim. Motivation of employees takes place when the manager understands the motivation process, recognizes the needs of her employees, and is aware of what behavior will result when the employees go about meeting these needs. To be effective, the manager should know what incentives to include in the job in order to release work capacity from within employees. The manager who is aware that the only way she can accomplish the goals and objectives of the organization is through employees will be productive.

The manager knows that motivation is a function of the employee's needs, the opportunities available to the employee, the employee's ability, and reinforcement of the positive growth of the employee. The manager controls a number of the opportunities for which the employee strives, can affect ability by various training and educational programs, and is the best person to reinforce the employee's positive growth.

The effective manager understands that as an employee strives to meet his needs, it results in behavior that is work capacity. Working with the employee, the effective manager designs a job that will meet the employee's needs while accomplishing, at the same time, the organization's goals.

Designing Organizational Structures 5

In this chapter we will explore the structuring of leisure service organizations and discuss the interrelationships that exist among a number of environmental factors. More specifically, discussion will center around the characteristics of formal organizations, the types of organizations providing leisure services, and the factors involved in structuring leisure service organizations. In addition, four organizational structures—bureaucracy, systems theory, decentralization, and federation—are presented, and examples of their application to leisure service delivery systems are discussed.

THE FORMAL ORGANIZATION

The way that a leisure service organization is formally structured can have great impact on its effectiveness and efficiency. The formal organization can best be thought of as encompassing *the roles that are assigned to individuals* working within the system. This means that each individual within an organization is given a functional responsibility to carry out. Thus, members within the organization can be held accountable for their actions. Further, the manager can identify patterns of communication among individuals and an organizational member's status can be identified. The role of the manager in a formal organization is to staff it, train members of the organization in their various responsibilities, and evaluate members' performance to insure that the goals and objectives of the organization are being achieved.

Obviously, each individual brings to the organization different skills, interests, and personality traits that will affect his perception of organizational goals. Dissatisfaction within organizations commonly occurs when there is a discrepancy between the employees' and the manager's concept of their respective roles. In many cases, the rigidity found in organizational structures is the cause of this dissatisfaction. Can anyone recall when a job description was tailor-made to an individual? The function of the manager is to integrate the goals of the organization and the design chosen to achieve these goals with the individual needs of the members of the organization. When these factors are well integrated and compatible, success is assured.

Leisure service delivery systems, as organizations, are deliberately constructed social units designed to attain a set of goals and objectives.[1] They are made up of individuals and have a unique set of characteristics. These elements are universal and can be indentified in any organization. Identification of these factors allows us to differentiate between an organization and a social grouping, such as a family or church group.

Leisure service organizations are *goal seeking.* Typically, they are involved in the creation of leisure services to satisfy the needs and desires of a given set of consumers. They are constructed to bridge the gap between people's needs and the organizational resources to achieve those needs. They provide the means whereby individuals can collectively unite to create services that are unattainable on an individual basis.

Organizations are also involved in *the assignment of tasks.* To accomplish the goals set forth by an organization, there must be a division of labor whereby the responsibility for completing the various work units of the organization is assigned. This commonly allows for the creation of specialized subunits within the organization to carry out the organization's work efficiently and effectively.

Closely related to the division of labor is the fact that all organizations have *power centers.* Within leisure service systems are positions of authority, responsibility, influence, and status. The positions insure that decision-making is possible since the allocation of the organization's resources can be undertaken by individuals and/or units within the organization that can be held accountable.

The last characteristic found in any organization is its position of dependency in that it is *interlinked with other environmental contingencies.* As indicated in Chapter 1, leisure service organizations have interfaces with a host of environmental subgroupings. These subgroupings affect the decision-making process within the organization. The methods used to determine goals and objectives and the way resources are acquired and distributed are examples of factors that can be strongly influenced or determined by external environmental factors.

Types of Organizations

There are numerous organizations that deliver leisure services. The National Recreation and Park Association (NRPA) identifies five occupational clusters within the field of leisure. According to NRPA, these areas, as occupations, are "pursued by persons engaged in performing those functions, including services, products, and facilities required to satisfactorily meet the needs of the individuals and groups engaged in leisure time pursuits."[2]

[1] Amitai Etzioni, *Modern Organizations* (Englewood Cliffs, N.J.: Prentice-Hall, 1964), p. 3.
[2] David M. Compton, "Overview of the Proposed Leisure Occupations Clusters," Career Evaluation Curriculum Development Project (Washington, D.C.: National Recreation and Parks Association, 1975). (Mimeo.)

The five general areas and/or occupational clusters in which leisure services are organized, and examples of them, are identified in the following paragraphs.

1. *Travel, tourism, and hospitality services.* This area includes the management, operation, and promotion of travel, tourism, and hospitality services. Individuals serving as managers in this area might find employment in hotels, motels, resorts, convention centers, steamship companies, railroads, guesthouses and ranches, airlines, buslines, automobile rental agencies, tour-boat lines, and public and private tourism agencies.

Examples of Travel, Tourism, and Hospitality Services
Flagship Tours.   The tourism division of Oivind Lorentzen Activities, Flagship Tours, specializes in the promotion of vacation tours aboard the M.S. *Kungsholm*. It is in the business of providing leisure services to individuals interested in a luxurious and interesting holiday. It offers its clientele a vacation experience on a luxury ship, with food, service, and entertainment. Headquartered in New York City, this organization employs approximately 50 people in its base office and 12 salesmen in various parts of the country. The cruise ship itself offers indoor and outdoor pools, saunas, stores, gymnasiums, a theater, a library, tennis courts, a golf driving range, an indoor sports room, and 10 lounges.

Canadian Government Office of Tourism.   As part of the Department of Industry, Trade, and Commerce, the Office of Tourism is organized for the promotion of travel to Canada. It focuses on and is concerned with studies and analyses of the travel industry in Canada. Its main aims are to promote travel to and within Canada and to coordinate tourism and promotional efforts outside Canada by working with travel bureaus, tourist associations, and the transport industry. The office of tourism consists of 300 branches involved in travel marketing, travel industry, development, and policymaking, and industrial relations.

Altair Vacations, Ltd.   This small Canadian company wholesales package tours to travel agents. Incorporated in 1971, its purpose is to transport tourists from Canada and vice versa. Altair owns hotels in both Florida and Canada; the company operates on the premise that Canadians will enjoy a Florida vacation and that the ideal vacation spot for Floridians is its hotel in Canada. Altair has a full-time staff of six people. Eighty percent of this company's business comes from southern Ontario, where it deals with over 1000 individual agents.

2. *Commercial leisure services.* This subcluster deals with businesses and industries that sell, market, deliver, or otherwise provide leisure services for a profit. (We have excluded from discussion those organizations that manufacture a good or create a product.) One can find individuals serving as managers in organizations classified as "food and beverages" or "entertainment services" in such facilities as ski resorts, camps, campgrounds, billiard parlors, ticket agencies,

carnivals, raceways, nightclubs, rodeos, movie theaters, entertainment bureaus, circuses, amusement parks, bowling alleys, skating rinks, dance studios, gun clubs, hobby shops, and golf courses and in professional sports, in either the management of facilities or actual participation.

Examples of Commercial Leisure Services

Walt Disney Productions. Entertainment and leisure services provided by Walt Disney Productions include Disneyland, Disneyworld, Celebrity Sports Center, and a soon to be opened amusement park—Disneyland Oriental, in Tokyo, Japan. The organization also, of course, produces and distributes motion pictures, including animated color movies, live-action features, true-life adventure films, and other films, mainly dealing with short subjects. Other activities include the licensing of businesses and commercial organizations for use of the Disney name and characters; the marketing of such products as records, books, and magazines; and the production of television shows. Walt Disney Productions has been described as one of the most fabulous and fascinating business enterprises in the world. As a leisure-oriented enterprise, it marks the pinnacle of achievement in this area and is a guidepost to the potential inherent in commercial leisure services.

Maple Leaf Gardens, Ltd. This organization provides leisure services to people on a commercial basis by programming a facility, Maple Leaf Gardens, with top-caliber entertainment in the area of sports, recreation, and cultural services. The primary focus of the organization is ownership of the Toronto Maple Leaf Hockey Club, although Maple Leaf Gardens is programmed with other professional and amateur sports, concerts, ballet, operas, conventions, and so on. Gross revenues in 1975 were in excess of $12 million, with a net profit in the neighborhood of $1 million. Maple Leaf Gardens employs approximately 140 people, including hockey players, coaches, trainers, facility maintenance people, refreshment and ticket sellers, and organizational executives.

Kampgrounds of America (KOA). KOA is the largest system of privately owned campgrounds, with over 800 franchises, in North America. It was established in 1963 on the premise that there was a need for a chain of campgrounds similar to the motel organizations which had been established across the continent. Sales and operating revenue have exceeded $7 million, and the number of overnight stays at KOA campgrounds has been nearly 6 million. Initially, KOA only provided camping facilities; but it is currently improving its facilities architecturally and has increased the number of recreation facilities and programs to encourage people to lengthen their stays. As is the case with many successful organizations, KOA has created a training institution to serve as an educational resource for its franchise members.

African Lion Safari.   Located in the Golden Horseshoe of Canada (near Toronto), African Lion Safari was established in 1969 with a dual purpose. The initial purpose was to create a game preserve to study and protect animal species from all parts of the world. The second purpose was to create a viable self-sustaining business that would render a modest profit. The facility provides an opportunity for animals to be exhibited in large groups in an open, natural setting. It employs 150 persons in the areas of maintenance and animal care, research, and the breeding of animals. In addition to unique exhibits, camping, picnic areas, and a playground are available. Food services and an African-style souvenir shop are also on the premises. The 620-acre facility has been visited by over 3,000,000 people since its inception. Its special programs include educational tours, a special collection of arts and crafts from around the world, and sponsorship of a photographic tour of Africa during the winter months.

3. *Resources-based services.* Services that involve land, water, or air resources are called "resource-based services." There are four subclusters in this area, including administration and supervision, planning and design, enforcement and preservation, and maintenance. Organizations delivering resource-based services range from county conservation systems to national parks. Most resource-based services are publicly owned and operated, although there are a number of privately owned areas.

Examples of Resource-Based Services
Yellowstone National Park.   Managed under the direction of the National Park Service of the U.S. Department of the Interior, Yellowstone National Park was established in 1872 as the world's first national park. Occupying 3,500 square miles, Yellowstone is endowed with many natural features, including geysers, hot springs, lakes, rivers, falls, mountains, valleys, gorges, and wilderness areas. There are a number of recreation facilities and opportunities available, including camps, picnic areas, lodging, boating, swimming, fishing, nature study, and wilderness experience. The park superintendent oversees a staff that is charged with the protection of the park's natural features including its wildlife.

Niagara Parks Commission.   Niagara Falls annually attracts more than 12 million people and is thought of as one of the greatest natural tourist attractions in North America. Established in 1885, the Niagara Parks Commission is responsible for the care, preservation, and maintenance of public access to the land adjacent to Niagara Falls and the Niagara River. The park system, which is recognized as one of the finest in the world, has over 3000 acres of parkland, extending from Fort Erie, Ontario, to Niagara-on-the-Lake, Ontario. Historical sites, golf courses, a marina, campgrounds, swimming beaches, picnic areas, restaurants, gift shops, horticultural gardens and school, and significant natural areas are found within this system. The commission employs nearly 250 people on a full-time basis and from 100 to 1000 part-time individuals, depending on seasonal fluctuations. The budget annually exceeds $15,000,000.

Calloway Gardens. Located in Pine Mountain, Georgia, Calloway Gardens is owned and operated by the Ida Carson Calloway Foundation, a private nonprofit, scientific, religious, and charitable organization. Calloway Gardens was created and is maintained as an area of beauty conducive to wholesome recreation and individual peace and reflection. Among its main attractions is a 175-acre lake, golf courses, historical sites, trails, bike paths, convention facilities, a children's area, picnic facilities, tennis courts, a boathouse, a beach, a skiing area, circus facilities, and many natural areas. Callaway Gardens exemplifies how a private, nonprofit organization can create and operate a public leisure-oriented facility in extremely good taste, promoting the principles of conservation and constructive use of leisure time. It provides many opportunities for individuals to combine leisure pursuits with other (religious, educational, and/or business oriented) endeavors.

Morton Arboretum. This nature area was founded in 1922 by Joy Morton (Morton Salt Company) as an outdoor museum of living trees, shrubs, and vines. A privately endowed, unaffiliated, educational foundation, the Arboretum, located in Lyle, Illinois, is administered by a self-perpetuating board of trustees. The arboretum collection includes over 4800 species and plant hybrids displayed on a 1425-acre tract of land. Facilities include an information center, library, herbarium, climate and map station, greenhouse, shop, and restaurant. The arboretum has several special features, including a hedge garden, a ground cover collection, a street tree collection, and other related displays and activities.

4. *Cultural services.* This area focuses on the promotion and/or production of cultural services. Employees work in museums, zoos, aquariums, and libraries, at historical sites, and in dance/ballet companies, dramatic productions, theaters, and art centers.

Examples of Cultural Services

Herbert Hoover Historical Site and Presidential Library. The Hoover birthplace and presidential library is an example of an historical site that preserves American cultural heritage. Located in the small Iowa community of West Branch, Hoover's birthplace is operated under the jurisdiction of the National Park Service. In addition to the house where Hoover was born, the park service maintains a Quaker meeting house, his father's blacksmith shop, and several other homes in the area. The site, in many ways, is operated as a living historical museum. Guides dress in clothing of the late 1800's, the blacksmith shop is functional, and many of the buildings in the immediate vacinity of Hoover's birthplace have been authentically restored to their original appearance. The presidential library houses most of Hoover's official papers and is laid out as a pictorial biography of his life.

Toronto Metropolitan Zoo. This outstanding zoological park is set in 710 acres of land and has approximately 400 species of animals, birds, reptiles, and fish. Its uniqueness stems from the fact that the animals are displayed in a natural environment and have been grouped according to their geographical region of origin. The regions represented consist of North America, Eurasia, Africa, South America, and Indo-Malaya. Over 1 million people visited the zoo in 1975. The operating budget for the facility is in excess of $5 million, and the zoo has a full-time staff of nearly 250 persons.

Smithsonian Institution. A federally chartered, nonprofit organization, the Smithsonian Institution is involved in scientific, cultural, and educational endeavors. It operates numerous galleries, including the National Gallery of Art, the National Collection of Fine Arts, and the National Portrait Gallery. In addition, it operates the National Zoological Park, which contains over 3000 animals, birds, and reptiles. Several museums are operated by the institution, including the Museums of Natural History, History and Technology, and Air and Space. In addition, the John F. Kennedy Center for the Performing Arts, a national cultural center, is under the direction of the institution and presents concerts, operas, and so on.

The National Arts Centre. The National Arts Centre was incorporated in 1966 to assist in the development of performing arts in Ottawa (the capital of Canada) and throughout Canada. With a budget of over $10 million, this center for the performing arts employs approximately 500 people. Programs offered vary from ballet to orchestra, opera to folklore, theater to musicals, and special entertainers to choral. The facility itself includes a 2300-seat opera house/concert hall, a 900-seat theater, and an experimental studio. In addition to its facility-related, locally centered activities, the National Arts Centre arranges performances elsewhere in Canada and outside Canada. It provides special assistance in the performing arts through its publications, brochures, and media presentations.

5. *Community-based leisure services.* This occupational cluster includes public, private, or other governmental agencies that provide leisure services to individuals at the local level. Usually of a nonprofit nature, this cluster may include facilities such as community centers, aquatic complexes, playgrounds and play areas, sports and special playground centers, mobile facilities, and rehabilitation centers.

Examples of Community-Based Leisure Services
Activity Therapy Department—Hillside Hospital. A psychiatric facility located in New Hyde Park, New York, this institution employs over 25 therapeutic recrea-

tion workers. Using recreation as a modality in the therapeutic program, recreation specialists work as part of a team to evaluate and determine patient goals for individual growth. This facility is a community-oriented, short-term facility with inpatient, day hospital, and aftercare programs. It operates a unique outreach program for drug and alcohol addicts. Recreation therapists work with individuals in groups and on a one-to-one basis. A typical caseload is between 20 and 30 individuals.

Department of Parks and Recreation—Abington Township, Pennsylvania. Operating on a budget of nearly $1 million, this department administers 317 acres of parkland, including a golf course, two indoor centers (nature and senior citizens facilities), and a swimming pool. One of its key areas, Alverthrope Manor and Park (123 acres), includes a mansion converted for cultural and recreational activities, playgrounds, cookout facilities, ball fields, basketball and tennis courts, lakes, a golf course, and bicycle paths. An extensive year-round recreation program is operated, including opportunities for participation in lifetime sports, arts and crafts, nature, music, and swimming; natural ice rinks and sledding areas are maintained during the winter.

YMCA, Burlington, Ontario. This YMCA center was established in 1965 and employs approximately 23 full-time people. Operating on a $300,000 per year budget, the Burlington Y caters to all age groups and both sexes. There are numerous program offerings, including instructional skills and interest-oriented classes, interest clubs, open competition, and drop-in and outreach activities. The adult program, aimed at persons aged 16 and over, includes bridge lessons, fitness classes, Chinese cooking, guitar lessons, and swimming. The teen program, for ages 13 to 19, includes such activities as floor hockey, judo, scuba diving, leadership training, skin diving, and a course in baby-sitting. Programming for children includes swimming, theater, model building, gymnastics, and a gun club. The Y also has initiated a number of family programs. Support for YMCA activities comes from the United Way, membership fees, program fees, rentals, and other donations. The professional staff consists of an executive director, an adult education and recreation director, a youth and teen director, a community outreach director, community and youth director, and three full-time positions in the area of aquatics.

University City Recreation Centre, Ltd. Located in an apartment and townhouse community of 10,000 residents within metropolitan Toronto, University City Recreation Centre is a fairly recent development in private community recreation service. Operating as a limited company with an annual budget of approximately $200,000 it has a 10-man board of directors, 5 from the condominium tenants corporation and 5 from the developer responsible for building the project. There is a director/manager who is accountable only to the board and has responsibility for two-full time program supervisors, an aquatics supervisor and an office supervisor. In addition, there are maintenance staff and several part-time staff doing program, reception, and clerical work.

The facility is one of the largest of its kind in the Province of Ontario; it contains a gymnasium, squash and handball courts, indoor and outdoor swimming pools, a ceramics room, a photography room, lounges, a billiards room, a wrestling room, saunas, and a day-care center capable of serving 65 preschool children. There is also access to park space containing tennis courts, a football/ soccer field, a baseball diamond, a small ice rink, and playgrounds.

A wide range of programs is offered, including racquet instruction, ladder play, competitive leagues in basketball, badminton, table tennis, curling, ceramics and other crafts programs, jazz dance and ballet, Brownies and Girl Guides, youth groups, and an extensive camping program in the summer. The center is also involved with local community groups and the municipal parks and recreation department.

STRUCTURING LEISURE SERVICE ORGANIZATIONS

The form of any leisure service organization must be related to the goals and objectives it strives to achieve. To carry out tasks and assume responsibility within the leisure service delivery system, people must be organized. The establishment of a formal organizational structure allows the leisure service to integrate and coordinate its resources and direct its activities toward the attainment of goals and objectives. The structuring of an organization may well determine the degree to which it is productive. Certainly, human energy, fiscal resources, and technical resources have been used in an ineffective and inefficient manner because of an inadequate formal organization. For example, consider the plight of a park maintenance worker who is locked into a slot on an organizational chart that involves routinized work and lacks opportunities for recognition and achievement. Further, leisure needs of many people go unmet because some organizations are organized too rigidly to respond to changing behavioral patterns. There are several other factors that should be taken into consideration when determining contingencies. These include goals and objectives, basic work activities, environmental factors, and structural variables.

Goals and Objectives

Goals and objectives are the ends toward which a leisure service organization directs its efforts. Goals are broad statements that provide general direction for an organization. Objectives are specific statements that set forth a reasonable set of expectations which can be achieved; they usually include some dimension of time and, as such, are quantifiable and thus, can be evaluated and assessed. The process of setting goals and objectives is involved in the establishment of a hierarchy. Usually the goals of a system are derived from its basic mission or purpose. Then its objectives, both long-range and short-range, are determined. Any objective within an organization is tied to and dependent on a higher set of goals. Frequently, the relationship between goals and objectives is misunderstood. In many cases, the day-to-day operational aspects of the leisure delivery systems are not related to the broad general goals of the system. This results in confusion because questions of decision-making, responsibility, and accountability do not follow any systematic and consistant framework.

What is the relationship between the goals and objectives of a leisure delivery system and its organizational structure? The structure is dependent on the goals and objectives; however, the goals and objectives are defined, to a degree, by the structure. Therefore it is extremely important that the structure of an organization reflect and take into account its goals and objectives. If a leisure delivery system emphasizes grass-roots participation in the decision-making process, then perhaps a flexible organizational structure that allows for external input would be appropriate. On the other hand, there are instances in which input needs to be focused through one channel within the structure; this may call for a more rigid organizational structure that controls input, allowing it to take place only within certain limitations, to avoid chaos.

Basic Work Activities

As mentioned in Chapter 1, all leisure service organizations are involved in a number of basic work activities. These fundamental work activities are the *management of financial resources, creation of a leisure service,* and *distribution of the services*; they provide a basis upon which leisure delivery service can be formally organized. This approach to structuring leisure services is called the "functional approach" to organization.

Consider the provision of leisure services by private organization. The organization performs a service by creating activities and facilities. A structured activity that provides instruction in macrame and building a swimming pool are illustrations of providing a service. For the consumer, these activities represent something of value that has been brought into existence by this type of organization. For the leisure delivery system, this activity of creating services is its reason for existence. Work resulting in the creation of services is the primary function of the organization.

Once the service has been created, the next important function is to distribute it to those who wish to consume it. The service must be packaged and promoted appropriately if it is to reach those it is intended to serve. Macrame instruction may be organized in a formal classroom setting, at a specific time, with a specific set of dates, and may have structured lessons, all of which allows for the attainment of a specific set of skills. On the other hand, it may be organized as a club to provide opportunities for advanced skill development. Or, a macrame program may be organized in an arts center on a drop-in basis, being informally structured to allow the participant to set his or her own goals. These activities may be offered at different times during the day and at different days of the week or times of the year. Further, they may be promoted through the use of a variety of methods and forms, including newspaper articles, brochures, and fliers. The general idea is that the service will be distributed to the consumer in an appropriate form, at the right time, and at the right place.

Finally, the organization must manage the finances used to create and distribute the service. It charges fees and invests funds as ways of acquiring capital to provide services. In addition, the financial resources accumulated are accounted for properly to insure that they are dispersed in an appropriate manner.

These three activities (also known as line functions) provide a foundation upon which formal organizational structures are developed. They must be performed in some manner if an organization, any organization, is to exist.

Staff functions, on the other hand, are those activities that support the three basic work activities. As an organization increases in complexity, support functions, such as personnel and research, usually increase. The expertise that is necessary to manage these support areas insures the prominence of the three basic work functions. Hiring a specialist to manage the personnel functions of an organization, for example, allows other individuals within the structure to concentrate on performing the basic work activities.

Environmental Factors

One of the most important factors to consider when designing an organization is change in the environment. Change has become a dominant factor influencing institutions, forcing society to re-examine or re-evaluate its attitudes and beliefs. Expanding technology has resulted in a flow of new goods and services and has brought about the creation of new knowledge that affects organizations. Edward C. Ryterband and Bernard M. Bass have identified a number of important trends that may affect the work environment. These include population growth, continuing technological change, rising expectations, a continuation of the so-called generation gap, changing popular culture, and the death and/or decline of traditional institutions.[3]

1. *Population Growth.* The world population is more than 4 billion people and has more than tripled since 1860. In the United States, the population grew from 31 million in 1860 to over 200 million in 1976. Canada's population has also expanded tremendously, from over 3 million people in 1860 to over 21

---

[3] Edward C. Ryterband and Bernard M. Bass, "Work and Nonwork: Perspectives in the Context of Change," in Marvin D. Dunnette, *Work and Nonwork in the Year 2001* (Monterey, Calif.: Brooks/ Cole Publishing Co., 1973), p. 69.

million in 1976. Of extreme importance is the composition of the population. "The appearance of more young people in the work force is pressing management to be prepared to deal with younger, better educated employees who bring with them more personalistic guidance and a militant, impatient posture toward achieving their goals."[4]

2. *Technological Change.* The capability for producing new knowledge has expanded enormously. The number of scientists, engineers, and technicians in the United States doubled between 1960 and 1970. To accommodate this knowledge explosion, many work organizations will create internal structures that will be more flexible—structures around temporary task project teams, rather than fixed departments.[5]

3. *Rising Expectations.* The desire to live a fulfilled life is prevalent among all social classes today. Industrialization has provided an abundance of goods, which in turn has led to desire among individuals to consume more. Bombarded by the mass media, people are less willing to wait patiently to attain the "good" life. Individuals strive for immediate satisfaction and gratification. The life-style of increased expectations transcends all institutions, including the work environment. People want a satisfying work experience, and they want it now.

4. *Generation Gap.* Youths today question the values and norms of society. The development of new ideologies will shape the work environment of the future. Organizations will evolve to accommodate the new generation within its ranks. Organizational structures and working conditions will have to be modified if young people are to be attracted into existing institutions.

5. *Popular Culture.* As cultural opportunities become broadly available to more and more people, moving from an elitist orientation to serving the broad membership of society, people's level of sophistication will increase. Increasingly, individuals will bring their social, political, and ethical concerns to the work environment. Means for creativity, self-expression, and spontaneity will need to be available within work situations. Individuals seek opportunities for self-fulfillment through intrinsic rather than extrinsic rewards. Increased freedom of expression will create demands on the work environment for increased opportunities for self-esteem and fulfillment through work activities.

6. *Change in Traditional Institutions.* The work ethic is changing. Religious beliefs that in the past have affected society's attitudes toward work, leisure, and play are rapidly evolving. Perhaps the most cherished of our traditional institutions is that of the Protestant work ethic. Aligning hard work with righteousness, the Protestant work ethic indirectly glorified material gains. A new ethic, emphasizing "personal responsibility and situational ethics,"[6] has

---

[4] Ibid., pp. 70–71.

[5] Ibid., p. 73.

[6] Ibid., p. 82.

emerged. This is forcing organizations to look at their authority structure and allow individuals to assume more responsibility.

Other institutions that are undergoing change include the family and education. The movement from an extended family structure to a nuclear family structure has produced a certain amount of instability in the structure of the family. This change has produced a reaction to predetermined roles, such as authoritarianism, and has led to a host of new attitudes. This trend in behavior has extended into the work environment. In addition, whereas the family was the center of life in past decades, organizations may have to assume this responsibility. The level of education of people in North America has increased dramatically. In a short span of 35 years, the number of students enrolled in American colleges and universities increased from 1.5 million to 35 million. Consequently, sophisticated, competent, and more highly trained people are entering the work force.

Structural Variables

There are a number of organizational structures that can be used in the delivery of leisure services if the appropriate factors for their use are in evidence. The effectiveness and efficiency of an organization will, in large part, depend on the managers's ability to use an appropriate structure that suits the needs of his or her constituents. The responsibility for organizational failure, in the past, has been directed mainly toward the people in the organization, rather than the organizational design. Park and recreation departments have traditionally relied on one method of organizing services, rather than selecting more appropriate forms. In a society characterized by change, a high rate of mobility, highly educated people, and sophisticated technology, meeting leisure needs requires a flexible and innovative organizational design. The dynamics of leisure are such that organizational responsiveness is tied to the survival of the organization. Organizations that can evolve to meet changing leisure trends and needs will flourish; those that do not will experience diminished productivity.

Mechanistic and Organic Organizations

Organizational designs can be viewed on a continuum. Certain types of organizational structures operate more effectively and efficiently when the environment is stable. Others are better suited to environments in which change is a factor. Those that are capable of dealing with change are known as "organic organizations."[7] "Mechanistic organizations," on the other hand, are more appropriately used in stable situations.

---

[7] Joseph A. Litterer, *The Analysis of Organizations,* second edition (New York: John Wiley and Sons, 1973), pp. 335–336.

Organic structures are best able to deal with rapid and unpredictable changes in the environment within which they operate. When an organization produces a variety of goods and/or services to a large cross-section of individuals, its need for flexibility is great. It demands a structure that is adaptable to "changing conditions where the problems to be faced are not predictable and are usually new, removing the possibility of establishing, in advance, programs for their solutions."[8] Organic structures do not have fixed roles that are defined in a hierarchial form. Litterer describes the characteristics of organic organizations as follows:

1. Special knowledge and experience possessed by organization members is looked at in light of what it can contribute to the common or overall task. That is, expertise is not evaluated in terms of how well a person can meet the requirements of a job, but what he can contribute to the goal to be accomplished.

2. Closely connected with this is that each individual's task is looked at from the point of view of what it contributes to attaining the overall goal in terms of the current situation or problems. The question is, "Is it relevent?" not, "Is it glamorous?" Assignments or methods are not rigidly fixed.

3. There are a limited set of rights, obligations, and methods as defined fields of responsibility diminish or disappear. People tend more to ask "What needs to be done?" rather than, "What am I responsible for?" Individual tasks are less sharply defined and are continually being redefined. People feel a responsibility or commitment to the overall work at hand and not just to their specific job or area of technical expertise.

4. Typically problems are not pushed off upward, downward, or sideways as someone else's problem. The continual redefinition of tasks occurs through interaction with others, most of whom are not superiors.

5. Control, authority, and communication move through a wide network rather than a single hierarchal structure. Sanctions may be applied by many people other than hierarchal superiors and are derived from a community of interest rather than a contractual relationship with a central authority.

6. Omniscience is no longer imputed to the head of the organization. Knowledge of what is appropriate can exist anywhere in the organization, depending more on individual information and skill rather than hierarchal position. The locus of this expertise becomes the ad hoc center of control authority and communication. Authority may be decentralized or polycentralized.

7. Interaction tends to be much more lateral than vertical. Communication between people of different ranks involves more consultation than command.

8. Content of communication consists of information and advice rather than

[8] Ibid, pp. 336.

instructions and decisions. This is in keeping with local units maintaining control by local feedback rather than by instructions or plan.

9. People are committed to the organization's task and "technological ethos" of material or service progress and expansion rather than to loyalty and obedience. They would not say, "my organization, right or wrong," but rather, "my organization, I want it to be right."

10. Prestige is attached to the expertise and affiliations that individuals have in the general or social milieu external to the organization.[9]

Mechanistic organizations operate more successfully in an environment that has stabilized. When an organization produces the same good or service for a defined set of individuals with similar interests and needs, it is said to be operating within a stable environment. The consistency of problems facing an organization allows it to prepare standard responses to those situations. The work of the organization becomes fixed, routine and systematic in nature. The characteristics of a mechanistic organization include the following:

1. The overall goal or problem the organization is working on is broken into tasks differentiated by the function they fill and the specialization is carried as far as possible.

2. Each functional role, each task, has precisely defined rights, obligations, and technical methods, that is, there is a high order of standardization.

3. People in positions carrying out these tasks are concerned with doing their job as defined. Furthermore, they take pride in developing their technical expertise in doing the task as contrasted to having a concern for the overall goal of the endeavor.

4. When problems between positions occur they are settled by referring them to superiors, who reconcile differences in a way that is relevent to their own special part of the overall task.

5. Control, authority, and communication usually follow hierarchal patterns.

6. There is a general assumption throughout the organization that higher-ups are in a better position or are better equipped to make decisions. Hence, they can handle the more difficult decisions, and their decisions should take precedence over decisions made at lower levels because they are more likely to be correct. This reinforces the hierarchal structure and makes things centralized.

7. Interaction tends to follow hierarchal lines, primarily between superior and subordinates.

8. Operations and working behavior tend to be governed by instructions and decisions issued by superiors, which in turn may come from an overall plan.

[9] Joseph A. Litterer, *The Analysis of Organizations,* second edition. Copyright © (1973 and Joseph A. Litterer). Reprinted by permission of John Wiley and Sons, Inc., pp. 337–339.

9. There is a strong insistance of loyalty to superiors and the organization as a condition of membership.

10. Prestige is attached to expertise in the rules and procedures of the organization or hierarchal position in the organization as contrasted to general knowledge about a field or what one can contribute to the overall objective. Prestige attaches to local or internal rather than general or cosmopolitan knowledge, experience, and skill.[10]

Because organizations are viewed as being on a continuum, moving from rigid, mechanistic to flexible, organic types, a number of factors must be taken into consideration when developing the organizational structure. Of importance is the degree to which these factors are applied in the development of an organizational form. For example, certain types of organizational forms require a higher degree of specialization than others.

D. S. Pugh and associates differentiated the dimensions involved in structuring formal organizations.[11] These dimensions are specialization, standardization, formalization, centralization, configuration, and flexibility.

1. *Specialization.* This involves the division of labor in such a way that the tasks performed in an organization are distributed and/or concentrated within a number of positions. The extent to which an organization has specialized may be recognized by the number of positions within the organization relative to its size.

2. *Standardization.* This entails a system of rules and regulations that will allow an organization to maintain consistency within its structure. Adherence to a set of abstract rules insures that an organization will maintain stability, on the one hand; but on the other, it may render an organization inflexible and unable to meet change.

3. *Formalization.* When an organization's philosophy, principles, policies, and procedures are documented carefully, it is said to be a highly formalized organization. Organizations that have not precisely delineated their methods in written form are said to have a lesser degree of formalization.

4. *Centralization.* This dimension can be determined by locating the positions in an organization that have the authority to make decisions. Highly centralized organizations find decision-making concentrated in a few individuals. Decentralized organizations find decision-making authority dispersed throughout the organization. Obviously, this can be placed on a continuum, with certain types of organizations having more highly concentrated decision-making than others and vice versa.

---

[10] Joseph A. Litterer, *The Analysis of Organizations,* second edition. Copyright © (1973 and Joseph A. Litterer). Reprinted by permission of John Wiley and Sons, Inc., pp. 336–337.

[11] D. S. Pugh, D. J. Hickson, C. R. Huntings, and C. Turner, "Dimensions of Organizational Structures," *Administrative Science Quarterly* 13, no. 1 (1968), pp. 65–105.

5. *Configuration.* This term refers to the placement of positions within the organization. Certain organizational structures look like pyramids; others are linear in appearance.
6. *Flexibility.* Flexibility involves the ability to accommodate to change. Certain types of organizations adapt readily to changes in the environment, while others adapt poorly, if at all. Flexibility can be placed on a continuum. Organizations that are rigid are mechanistic; those that adapt to change readily are organic.

Figure 5.1 illustrates how each of the factors of goals and objectives, basic work activities, environmental change, structural variables affects the delivery of leisure services. First, the goals and objectives of the organization are affected by environmental factors. Changing attitudes toward work will force an organization to be more concerned about its management goals. The organization will be forced to become more receptive to employees' needs for creativity, expression, self-esteem, and recognition. As leisure behavioral patterns change, the output goals and objectives will in turn affect not only what is produced in terms of goods and services, but also how they are produced. Variables within the organizational structure will be modified, producing a new structural form that meets its goals. This cycle may be continuous in an environment where change is the

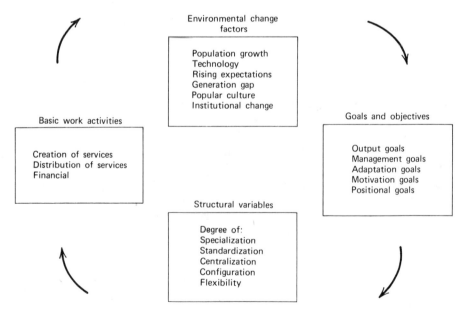

Figure 5.1. Factors influencing the structuring of a leisure service organization's design.

dominant factor. Structures that are rigid and not adaptable to changing traditions are generally not effective. For example, structures that have the inherent ability to modify their form, varying the degree of centralization, will be more effective. However, in an environment where stable conditions are present and change is not a dominant factor, rigid mechanistic structures may be appropriate.

What form of structure should leisure service organization take? Organic or mechanistic? At first it would seem that the answer to this question is obvious. Certainly, we live in a period where change is a dominant factor affecting society. Leisure behavioral patterns change rapidly and are thought to be in a dynamic state. We can, however, point to a number of functions within a leisure service delivery system that are standard and routinized in nature. Parks have become an accepted governmental service. Individuals expect parks to be included among those services provided at the local, state and/or provincial, and federal levels. The procedures used to maintain these facilities have been delineated clearly, and fixed routines have been established. So it would seem that the type of organizational structure to be used would depend on the specific service being offered to the public.

The maintenance of park areas may be better organized in a mechanistic structure, where a set of fixed standards can be applied. For example, the quartz lamps used to light a baseball diamond have a predictable number of burning hours. A maintenance schedule can be established to systematically replace these bulbs based on number of hours of usage. In this case, the maintenance function is predictable and can be organized into a rigid structure. Many park and recreation departments have established work schedules that outline their daily, weekly, monthly, and yearly work operations. Therefore a mechanistic structure that provides for systematic control may be useful in this particular situation.

On the other hand, behavior that results from any one person's involvement in leisure activity is highly individualized. The establishment of predictable norms of behavior, from which standards can be developed, is limited. The relationships that develop between a recreation leader and the persons participating in the activity are highly personalized ones. The ability of the leader to adapt general theories and concepts to the individual needs of each person being served requires a high degree of flexibility.

Because of the highly personalized nature of the recreation and leisure experience and the rapid change taking place in society, especially as it relates to the consumption of leisure services, there is a need to organize services that are highly adaptable. The need for a flexible structure may indicate that the programs and activities offered by a leisure service delivery system might be best structured in an organic organizational manner. Of course, there are exceptions to this suggestion. In programs where participant safety is of prime importance, as in aquatic programs, a more rigid set of rules and procedures must be applied. A mechanistic organizational structure would probably be better in this case.

TYPES OF ORGANIZATIONAL FORMS USED IN THE DELIVERY OF LEISURE SERVICES

Four organizational forms that are used in the delivery of leisure services will be described in the latter part of this chapter: the bureaucratic model of organization, the system approach to organization, decentralization, and the federation method of organization. As shown in Figure 5.2, they can be distributed along a continuum that finds bureaucratic form of organization as the most rigid method of structuring an organization and the federation approach as the most flexible. There are several other organizational methods that can be used in the delivery of leisure services, including the free form model of organization, the collegial model of organization, the egalitarian approach to organization, and still others. Although discussion of the models of organization is not undertaken, this in no way should diminish their importance or potential applicability in the delivery of leisure services. The forms of organization chosen for discussion represent the four most distinguishable forms currently practiced.

Bureaucratic Model of Organization

The bureaucratic model of organization is perhaps the most widely implemented and analyzed form of organization. It is based on the assumption that authority rests at the top of the organization and flows downward throughout the organization. In this way, superior and subordinate relationships are developed among individuals within the organization. As such, each individual is subject to

> . . . an authority system where supreme authority rests somewhere above him, and his responsibility consists, basically, of obeying orders and performing those tasks which are inherent in his particular job.[12]

This division of labor allows for the establishment of an organizational hierarchy. The establishment of superior/subordinate relationships makes the establishment of lines of authority in an organization possible. This arrangement allows each of the organization's work activities to be subdivided into a specific set of tasks. From this arrangement, roles entailing responsibility and authority can be determined.

Max Weber, one of the early pioneers of sociology, formulated many of the founding principles of the bureaucratic form of organization. He viewed bureaucracies as being the most rational method of organization. According to Weber, bureaucracies have five characteristics:

1. *Division of Work.* This involves breaking tasks into their smallest components so individuals could perform them with a minimum level of ability.

---

[12] George H. Rice, Jr., and Dean W. Bishoprick, *Conceptual Models of Organization* (New York: Appleton-Century-Crofts, 1971), p. 20.

Figure 5.2. Organizational forms used in delivery of leisure services.

2. *Centralized Authority.* Weber believed that positions should be arranged in a hierarchy so that a higher position was maintained over each individual in the bureaucracy, that is, to the ultimate source of authority—owner or a policy-making board.
3. *Rules.* Weber suggested that each organization should have a set of abstract rules to guide its internal and external actions. He felt that an organization, to operate rationally, must be bound by a set of rules that promote adherence to a standard.
4. *Rational Personnel Policies.* The application of uniform policies allows each individual to be treated in an equitable manner. Weber believed, for example, that promotions should be based on one's ability rather than social status. This notion supported his feeling that the bureaucratic form of organization was rational.
5. *Records.* Weber believed that bureaucratic organizations should maintain records as a method of increasing their accountability.[13]

Weber believed that bureaucracy was the ideal way to establish an organizational structure. It provided a means whereby organizations could gage their performance with a standard. If an organization was malfunctioning, its component parts could be compared with this standard and corrective action could be taken. Weber's principles, along with those of Henri Fayol and Luther Gulick, provided the foundation for the principles of classic organizational theory. Many of the characteristics of Weber's bureaucratic model are inherent in the organizational principles of unity of command, span of control, authority and responsibility, and scalar and functional processes.

1. *Unity of Command.* Unity of command implies that each individual in the organization is responsible to one single superior. In this way authority is distributed throughout the hierarchy of the organization from the highest to the lowest position. This is known as the "chain of command." It has been suggested by many that individuals work more effectively when they are responsible to only one person. Without adherence to this arrangement in a bureaucratic organization, confusion results.

2. *Span of Control.* This may be defined as the number of individuals who are directed by a manager. It was generally thought that the number of subordinates

---

[13] A. M. Anderson, trans., and Talcott Parsons, ed., *Max Weber: The Theory of Social and Economic Organizations* (New York: Free Press and Oxford University Press, 1947), pp. 330–340.

an individual should oversee should be limited. Although there is not a fixed number of people that can be identified as a "manageable" group, it is generally assumed that supervising more than six individuals will diminish a manager's effectiveness and efficiency. A number of factors may influence the ability of a manager to supervise any given number of people. Lynn S. Rodney writes that these factors include the following:

a. Diversity of services. When division of work is complex or diversified, there is more need for supervision than if the kind of work is repetitive and requires few decisions or personal conferences.
b. Executive skill. The energy, adaptability, and skill of some executives vary from those of others, and hence, the span of supervisory efforts of these people will vary.
c. Skill of employees. Untrained and unskilled employees require more time and effort than those who are more highly competent.
d. Non-supervisory relationships. A person's duties other than those related to a supervisory function will seriously cut down on time spent in supervision.
e. Stability of operation. A highly dynamic work situation in which turnover of employees is high calls for more coordination and control and hence, limits time for supervision.
f. In-service training. Some units require considerable on-the-job training; hence, less time can be spent on supervising others.
g. Type of activities. Supervision of other executives or administrative activities requires different responsibilities from that of supervision of operating employees. Thus, each process requires a different amount of time, and hence, there is a variance in span of control.[14]

3. *Authority and Responsibility.* Once a person is obligated or has the responsibility to perform a task, he must be given commensurate authority to complete the task. It is frustrating to be required to perform a certain function without the proper support in the form of authority. Managers need authority to make decisions, direct subordinates, and expect accountability from their subordinates. In a bureaucratic organization, authority is passed down the hierarchy from one level to the next. For example, an aquatic supervisor receives his authority from his superior, who may be the superintendent of recreation. If authority could not be delegated in bureaucratic organizations, hierarchal structures could not develop. Delegation of authority is a continuous activity of organizations. But in one respect, responsibility cannot be delegated: When a manager delegates authority within an organization, she does not relinquish responsibility for the successful completion of those tasks that she has assigned to the individuals under her direction.

[14] Lynn S. Rodney, *Administration of Public Recreation* (New York: Ronald Press Co., 1964), pp. 36–37.

4. *Scalar and Functional Processes.* Scalar and functional processes deal with the horizontal and vertical growth of the organizational form. What is suggested by this principle is that the functions of the organization will be placed in a coordinated hierarchical structure. This provides for the establishment of lines of authority, from the top of the organization to the bottom. Managers occupy the top level of the organization; supervisors, the middle level; and those individuals providing direct services, the lowest levels (see Figure 5.3). The line of authority in this arrangement runs from the manager at the top through the supervisory level to those at the direct-service level. Communication travels from either end of the hierarchy through these channels of authority.

Figure 5.3 shows how various functions within a bureaucratic structure are arranged in a hierarchical form. Depicted in pyramid form, the authority to develop policy rests at the top of the structure and the primary service of the organization is located at the bottom of the pyramid. The policy level within the structure is responsible for creating legislative guidelines that affect the organization's activities. Individuals working as managers would be responsible for directing and implementing the guidelines as developed by the policy level. Because managers are involved in the formulation of policy and also its implementation, one might say that they straddle the policy making and administrative levels. The next level—the administrative level—is involved in the organization, promotion, and development of services. Administrators provide direction to an organization by enforcing its policy. The third level in the bureaucracy is known as the supervisory level. Although supervisors may directly organize and implement services, their role usually does not entail providing face-to-face leadership. Primarily,

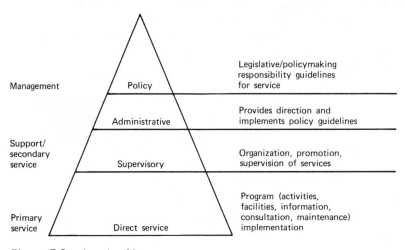

Figure 5.3. Levels of bureaucracy.

they act in a supporting role, providing information, direction, supplies, motiva-tion, inspiration, and control to individuals involved in the creation and/or dis-tribution of a good or service. The last level in the bureaucratic structure is comprised of those people who are actually creating or distributing the product or service. They may be individuals who are operators of machines or recreation leaders engaging in face-to-face leadership.

Types of Ownership in Private Leisure Service Organizations

In profit-oriented organizations, the type of ownership will have great bearing on the way the organization is structured as a bureaucracy. There are three types of business ownership in the United States and Canada: sole proprietorship, partnership, and corporation.

Sole Proprietorship.   When the management and ownership of an organization are one and the same, it is known as sole proprietorship. In this form of ownership, one individual is responsible for the organization's debts and management practices. It allows one individual to claim all the profits of the business, as well as utilize tax benefits available to the individual owner. This method allows a great deal of freedom of action for the individual who owns the company because he or she is able to make decisions without the approval of a board of directors or partner(s). As a result, sole proprietorship allows an individual to react promptly in making decisions that affect the creation and distribution of services. Seventy percent of all businesses in North America are organized in this way, and obviously it is technically the easiest method with which to formulate a profit-oriented enterprise. Sole proprietorship is fundamental to insuring competition in the free market.

Eighty percent of the businesses organized as sole proprietorships fail. Therefore it is important to explore some of the disadvantages of this method of ownership. The primary disadvantage is the unlimited liability of the owner. Unlimited liability refers to the responsibility of the owner for all business debts incurred, even if such financial obligations require his or her *personal* assets (e.g., home, car, savings). Another limitation in the sole proprietorship concerns the restrictions inherent in a business run from only one person's perspective; the talents (managing, marketing, etc.) necessary to successfully operate a business may not all be possessed by one person. It is true that the owner may be able to hire such help. But without the chance for advancement—potential partnership, partial ownership of the business, and so on—as incentive, qualified talent may be difficult to attract and hold. Another significant drawback to this type of ownership is its lack of continuity in the event of the owner's death.

Partnership.   Partnership exists when two or more people decide to form a busi-ness. It is the least popular form of ownership. Although a specific written agreement between the partners is not legally required, most partnerships have a written document that spells out the liabilities and responsibilities of each partner. This prevents misunderstanding and helps individuals avoid problems in the operation of their business.

There are four types of partners found in this type of ownership: (1) At least one partner must assume unlimited liability for the activities of the businness—he or she is known as a "general partner." (2) "Limited partners" are individuals who have assumed a limited role in the business; they do not have the same financial responsibility as a general partner. As a result of this, their authority is usually limited. (3) When a partner keeps his/her identity unknown to the public, he/she is known as a "secret partner." A secret partner can participate in management, but usually has limited financial responsibility. (4) The partner who invests only money is known as a "dormant partner." A dormant partner is not involved in the management of the organization and is liable only for the amount of his or her investment.

A partnership has several advantages, among which are ease of formation, increased availability of financing, diversification of management skills, certain tax advantages, and a high level of personal interest on the part of the partners. In addition, a partnership has a clearly defined legal status. The disadvantages of a partnership concern the mandatory unlimited liability of at least one of the partners, possible discord between partners, and difficulties that arise in conjunction with dissolving a partnership or the withdrawal of one partner. If, for some reason, one partner wishes to withdraw from the business, he/she must find another individual to buy his/her share of the partnership, who must meet the approval of the other partners. This can make it difficult to withdraw one's investments and can be time consuming. When a partnership is dissolved, the entire business must be liquidated, which may represent a loss of the entire investment. A great disadvantage may occur when a partner dies because the partnership may have to be liquidated as part of his or her estate.

Corporation.   Corporations constitute approximately 20 percent of all types of businesses and account for 80 percent of the annual sales of all businesses. The corporation may be defined as a legal entity existing only on paper and in the eyes of the law. A corporation has all the rights and privileges of an individual; it is an artificial being. A corporation can buy, sell, own, manage, and dispose of property. It can sue or be sued. Recognized as the legal owner of the business, a corporation is made up of shareholders who are liable only so far as the amount of their investment.

The structure of a corporation is hierarchical in nature. At the top of any corporation are its shareholders. These shareholders are represented by a board of directors; the board is responsible for representing the rights and interests of the shareholders. The board of directors oversees the day-to-day operation of the organization, formulates its short- and long-term goals and objectives, and hires the corporation's management team.

The major advantage to organizing a business as a corporation is the factor of limited liability, that is, liability only insofar as one's investment; there is no personal liability required by law. Another advantage is the increased ability of a corporation to obtain capital; it may sell shares of stock and borrow money using corporation assets as collateral. Corporations also provide an efficient method for transferring ownership. One's shares may simply be sold in order to rapidly liquidate one's investment in a given corporation. Because a corporation is not dependent on one or more individuals, it has almost unlimited continuity. In other words, if one owner (shareholder) dies, the corporation continues to operate. Corporations may employ a professionally trained management team, which usually results in more effective and efficient management practices.

There are a number of disadvantages to organizing a business as a corporation. For one, not only is the corporation itself responsible for paying taxes, but individual shareholders are also taxed on their investments. Essentially, this results in double taxation. Another disadvantage may be the cost associated with incorporating. At the level of the very small corporation, this cost may not appear great; but the cost increases proportionately with the size of the organization that wishes to incorporate. There is a standard percentage per share issued that the company must pay, in addition to other fees. Corporations must also adhere to a number of governmental regulations, which are policed quite heavily (e.g., equal employment, truth in advertising). Lastly, corporations are essentially public entities. They must publish their financial statements and company activities, which reduces the amount of privacy within the corporation. With the proper court order showing just cause, any shareholder has the right to inspect the corporation's financial accounts.

The Public Administration Model of Bureaucracy

In North America the goals, objectives, and policies of public leisure service delivery systems are determined by the constituents served. The right to influence public institutions is inherent in the democratic way of life. Services important to society's welfare, in many cases, have come under the direct control of the public. The public administration model of bureaucratic organization evolved to accommodate this.

The public administration model of bureaucratic organization provides direct opportunities for participation in the establishment of goals and objectives and the formulation of policy. To control these factors, a group of individuals is elected or appointed to a board or commission to guide the bureaucracy. Their responsibility is in the formulation of policy, and the bureaucracy's function is to carry out and/or implement the policy. Although there is not always a division today between the formulation and implementation of policy, this system affords a rational approach to involving consumers within the rigid framework of a bureaucratic structure. It provides an opportunity for individuals to influence

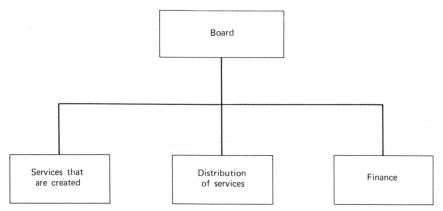

Figure 5.4. The basic work activities of a profit-oriented leisure service organization.

those institutions that affect their lives. Any public leisure service system that uses the bureaucratic form of structure operates, at least in principle, as a public administration model of organization.

There are three types of boards or commissions that are found in public leisure service delivery systems: separate and independent boards, semi-independent boards, and advisory boards.[15] Separate and independent boards are autonomous units that have the authority to develop and enforce policy. Those who serve on this type of board may be elected by the constituents they serve, or they may be appointed by a governmental functionary. They are able to operate independently of other governmental bodies and are usually given jurisdiction to exercise certain rights, including the levying of taxes.

A semi-independent board does not have the full powers that separate and independent boards have. Although this type of board may be charged with the establishment and implementation of policy, ultimate authority may rest with another decision-making body. To control the activities of this group, final financial authority is usually held by another legislative body.

Advisory boards serve as a means for individuals to participate in a bureaucratic structure. They make recommendations to other legislative bodies, however these suggestions have no formal authority.

Development of a Bureaucratic Structure

Public nonprofit and private profit-oriented leisure service organizations do not necessarily follow similar patterns in the establishment of a bureaucratic structure. Figure 5.4 is an illustration of the arrangement of the work activities of a

[15] Robert M. Artz, "Boards, Councils and Citizen Involvement," in Sidney C. Lutzin and Edward H. Storey, ed., *Managing Municipal Leisure Services* (Washington, D.C.: International City Management Association, 1973), p. 61.

private leisure organization governed by a board of directors. In a smaller organization, the board may be able to directly supervise those individuals who are hired on a part-time basis to handle each of each of the basic work activities.

As the organization grows in scope, size, and complexity, the board may employ a manager on a full-time basis to implement the directions of the board. Figure 5.5 shows this new organizational arrangement. The manager supervises those functions that are formally handled by the board. No longer is the board involved in the organization and implementation of services. This responsibility has been delegated to the manager, and the bureaucratic structure has begun to grow vertically. Assuming that the organization continues its growth, the manager may have to hire individuals on a full-time basis to supervise each of the work areas. Thus the organization has again expanded in a vertical fashion.

As the work load continues to increase, the organization will continue to grow taller and taller. The work activities regarding the creation of services might be subdivided into two sections: One section might find an individual in charge of youth services only, and the other might be in charge of adult services only. Not only can a structure be subdivided along functional lines, but activities can be geographically distributed. The work activities relating to the distribution of services in Figure 5.6, might be subdivided into two districts, which represent the

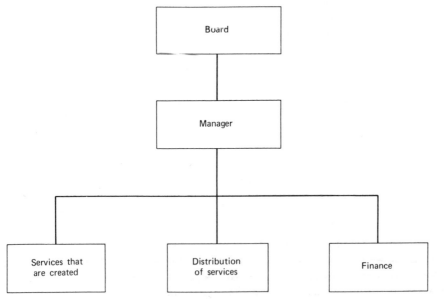

Figure 5.5. An expanded profit-oriented leisure service organization bureaucratic organization.

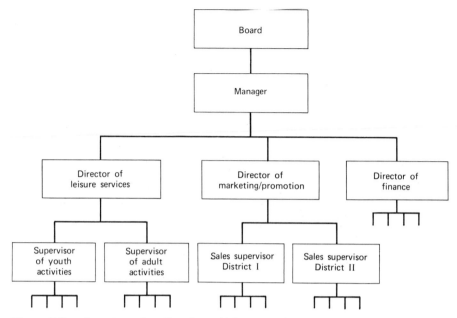

Figure 5.6.   An enlarged profit-oriented leisure service bureaucratic organization.

geographic areas the organization serves. The organization is still growing, even though the tasks have been subdivided; but the growth has been horizontal, as well as vertical.

The organization may grow further by adding other functions to assist the three areas. These new services, which are created to provide support, are known as "staff functions." The three basic activities are known as "line functions" and must be performed for the organization to survive. As previously mentioned, two staff functions are personnel and research. As an organization grows, a full-time personnel manager may be needed to hire and train staff, manage employee benefits, and monitor employee problems.

As public parks, recreation, and leisure services have stabilized, becoming an accepted and permanent fixture of local government, patterns of organization reflecting their functions have emerged. Rodney writes that there are 11 divisions commonly found in parks and recreation departments: special facilities, aquatics, playgrounds and centers, construction and maintenance, special programs and facilities, administration, engineering, horticulture, police, forestry, and botanical gardens and arboretums.[16] Figures 5.7 through 5.12 are organizational charts that show differences in organizing the various tasks found in public park and recrea-

[16] Rodney, *Administration of Public Recreation*, p. 90.

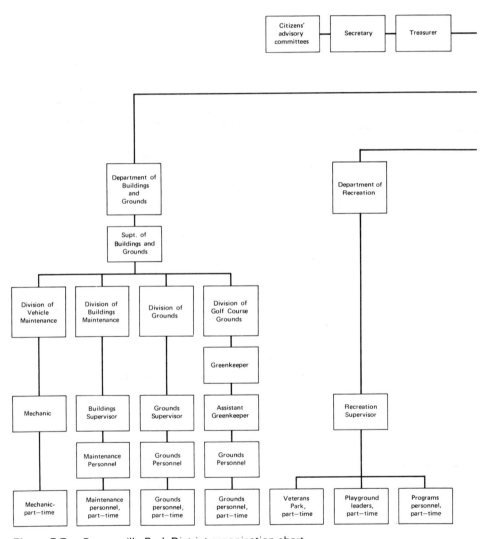

Figure 5.7. Bensenville Park District organization chart.

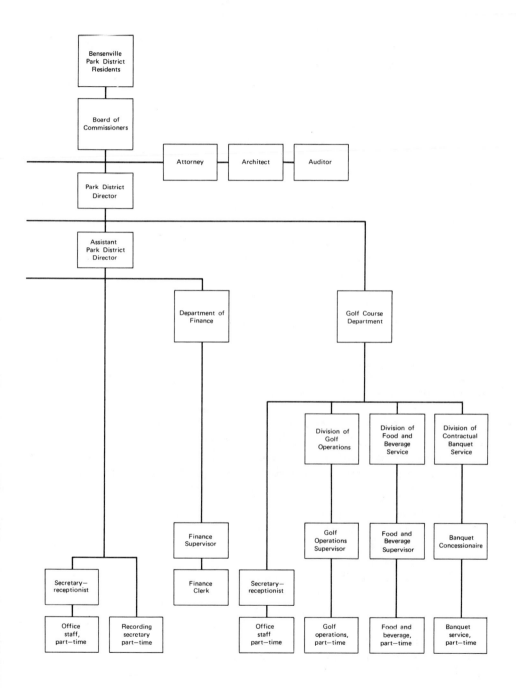

tion departments. These charts represent departments in Bensenville, Illinois; Wooster, Ohio; Kitchener, Ontario; Fort Worth, Texas; Milwaukee, Wisconsin; and Montreal, Quebec.

Bensenville Park District, Illinois.   The organizational chart found in Figure 5.7 is an example of a leisure delivery system that is a separate and independent governmental unit. It has full authority to levy taxes, acquire land, hire personnel, and operate recreation programs. Bensenville is a midwestern community, and the district—founded in 1960—serves a population of 15,000. The park district is organized into four departments: buildings and grounds, recreation, finance, and golf course. It employees 15 persons on a full-time basis.

Wooster, Ohio.   This community has a separate parks board and a separate recreation board that work cooperatively, jointly employing a director of parks and recreation to manage their affairs. Under the director's control are a recreation division and a park division. (see Figure 5.8). In addition, the office staff is directly responsible to the director. Maintenance and minor construction are handled in the division of parks, and the implementation of activities and the operation of facilities comes under the direction of the superintendent of recreation. This operation serves approximately 20,000 people.

Kitchener, Ontario.   Kitchener, Ontario, population 120,000, has a joint parks and recreation department (see Figure 5.9). There are three major divisions within its bureaucratic structure: parks and property, business operations, and recreation and programs. These three divisions are headed by directors who report to the commissioner of parks and recreation. Interestingly, the business manager is responsible for the management of the department's golf courses and major auditorium. The director of the parks and property division manages the horticulture and forestry, design and development, cemetery, and services and works components of the department. The recreation director coordinates the facilities, athletics, senior citizens' programs, and area recreation departments.

Fort Worth, Texas.   The organizational structure of the Fort Worth, Texas (population approximately 400,000) Parks and Recreation Department, as shown in Figure 5.10, has six divisions, which are headed by a park and recreation director. The administrative division handles budgeting, accounting, data processing, and so on. The horticultural division is responsible for the botanic garden and forestry operations. Recreation centers, a recreation program, swimming pools, a tennis center, and athletics are within the recreation division. The zoological division runs the zoo, with its various activities. Parks, street medians, and cemetaries are under the direction of a maintenance and development division. Lastly, the special activities division is responsible for golf-course operations and other specialized facilities and services. (As might be expected, the larger the size of the

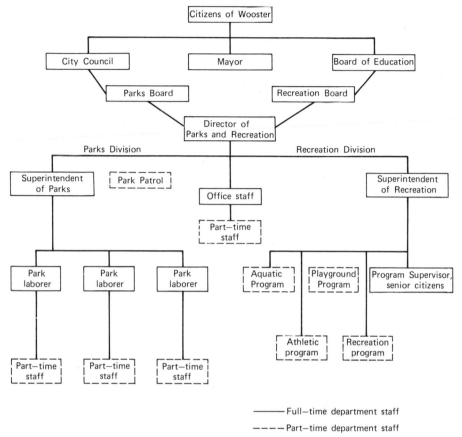

Figure 5.8.   Wooster Parks and Recreation Department organization chart.

community served by various agencies, the more complex is its organizational chart.)

Milwaukee, Wisconsin.   The Milwaukee, Wisconsin (population 717,372), recreation program is organized within the public school system. Since 1912 the school system in Milwaukee has organized recreation activities and has made the schools' facilities available for them. The board of education is allowed to levy a special mill tax for public recreation programs. Figure 5.11 illustrates the organization of the Division of Municipal Recreation and Adult Education under the direction of the Milwaukee Board of School Directors. Within the division itself are three departments: athletics, playgrounds and social centers, and service and

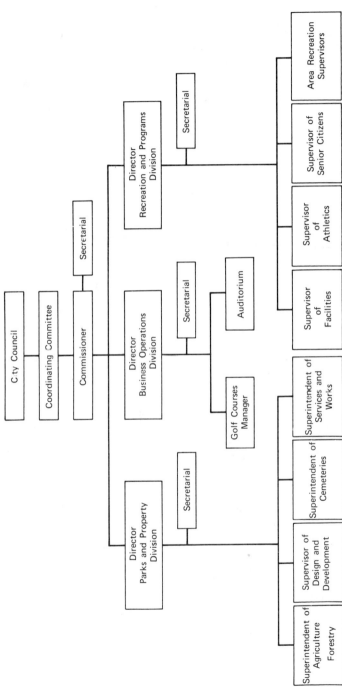

Figure 5.9. Park and Recreation Department, Kitchener, Ontario, Canada organ zation chart.

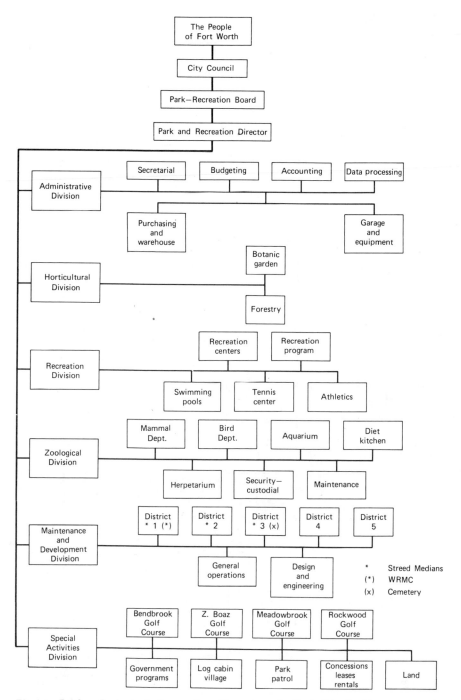

Figure 5.10. Park and Recreation Department, Fort Worth, Texas, organization chart.

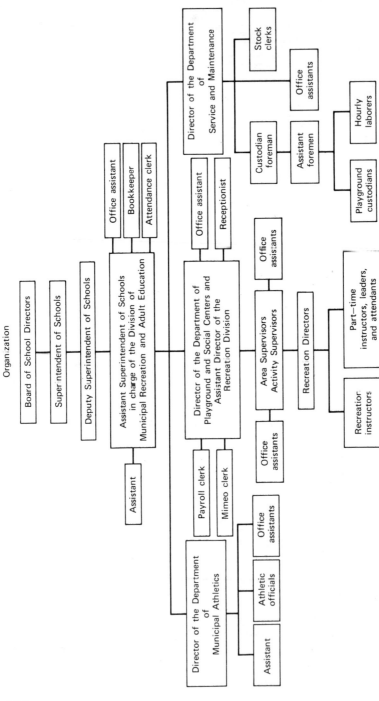

Figure 5.11. Division of Recreation and Adult Education, Milwaukee, Wisconsin organization chart.

maintenance. A key in this approach to providing leisure services is that the school system's facilities are readily made available for leisure-time activities.

Montreal, Quebec.   Le Service des Sports et Loisirs de Montreal [The Sport and Leisure Services Department of the City of Montreal] is responsible for administering sports, recreation, culture, and other services relating to leisure for this city of over 1,200,000 people. This organizational structure is unique in that the management of services is directed by an administrator with the assistance of a cabinet. The director of sports and leisure services, the deputy director, the assistant director of the division of leisure, and two cabinet directors—a technical counselor and a director of research—comprise the cabinet. They are responsible for the coordination and execution of activities relating to the provision of leisure services in Montreal. The organizational structure includes divisions of leisure, sports, administration and planning, libraries, and zoology and astronomy (see Figure 5.12).

Systems Approach

An overview of systems theory was presented in Chapter 2. The purpose of this section of the book will be to show the relationship between theory and its practical application in the delivery of leisure services. A systems analysis allows the manager to look at the interrelationships that exist among the various components in the environment. As indicated in the systems model of the leisure service organization, we can view those constraints that affect the delivery of services on a macroscale and/or a microscale. By viewing the interrelationships that exist among the various systems within the total environment on a macroscale, the manager is able to make more productive decisions. This allows the individual to see the relationships that exist among various subsystems within the environment and to acknowledge and integrate their effects on the leisure service organization. It is with this understanding and information that the leisure service manager is better able to recognize, interpret, and act on those factors that can affect the organization. The manager may position the organization's resources to adapt to constraints based on his or her ability to view the leisure service organization as part of a larger environment.

The leisure service organization itself is also a system. It is a microenvironment operating within a larger system. As such, the activities of the organization can be thought of as being composed of many subsystems. These subsystems, operating internally, are interconnected with one another in a hierarchical form. Each subsystem produces a set of expectations that ultimately result in behavioral outcome. For example, staff behavior may result in the creation of leisure services, may result in the establishment of a supportive work environment, or may breed a nonsupportive work environment. An infinite number of behavioral outcomes can be produced because there are many potential subsystems within an organiza-

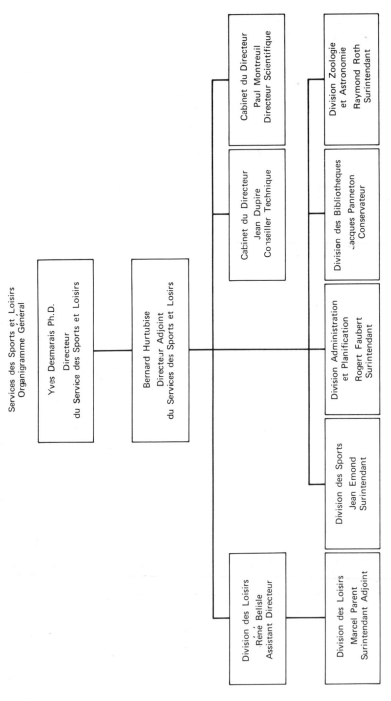

Figure 5.12. Montreal, Quebec, Canada organization chart.

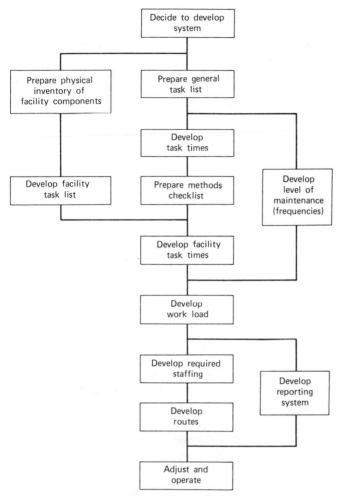

Figure 5.13. Process of developing a maintenance system. (Gerald Bethel, "A Systems Approach to Management of Park Maintenance," *Park Maintenance,* April 1971, p. 12. Used with the permission of *Park Maintenance Magazine,* Box, 1936, Appleton, Wisc.)

tion. The critical factor in using systems theory is to recognize that subsystems can be deliberately constructed to produce a specific set of outcomes, such as the completion of selected tasks or the creation of a supportive work climate.

Applying systems theory to the management of park maintenance, Gerald Bethel outlined a procedure that is illustrated in Figure 5.13. The flow chart indicates the several steps, including:

1. The tasks that need to be accomplished. (Inventorying the maintenance needs of each facility and developing a task list.)
2. How each task is to be accomplished with consideration for materials and equipment to be used.
3. The methods of integration of tasks to be accomplished with organizational standards and available resources.
4. A work schedule based upon the above factors.[17]

The Marshalltown (Iowa) Parks and Recreation Department has utilized the systems method in their park maintenance operation. The approach involves the integration of a general set of maintenance standards with specific work procedures, which in turn yields a routine for each of their facilities. Their approach to the subsystem of maintenance is shown in Appendix A.

Edginton and Eldridge have outlined how systems theory can be applied in creating a more humanistic environment via the utilization of a program of developmental training in park and recreation systems.[18] They suggest that a developmental training program not only can contribute to the output objectives of an organization, but can also provide opportunities to satisfy human needs in an intrinsic and extrinsic manner. Figure 5.14 illustrates the utilization of systems theory in the establishment of this particular component of the leisure service delivery organization.

An extension and refinement of systems theory practiced today is known as "modular organization." In this approach to organizing services, the manager organizes each of the tasks of a specific process or project into functional units. Modular organizations are comprised of a number of units whose activities are coordinated by the use of an established management hierarchy. Functional units may vary in size and composition depending on the project and/or process to be accomplished. The role of the manager is to initially decentralize the work of the organization by placing authority to complete a given unit of work. This specialization allows an increase in flexibility in that it creates opportunity for alternative structures by each project team.

There are five types of modular, or project, structures. The first is "individual project organization," in which the individual project manager completes the assignment by himself without the assistance of other staff members or support teams. The second type of project organization is called a "staff project organization of staff." The individual is involved in leading the project and is given enough support and backup services to complete the task. The third type exists when the manager has the joint responsibility of overseeing line and staff func-

---

[17] Gerald I. Bethal, "A Systems Approach to Management of Park Maintenance," *Park Maintenance*, 24, no. 4 April 1971, p. 12.

[18] Christopher R. Edgington and Robert C. Eldridge, "Developmental Training: Methods and Procedures for Your Department—Part 2," *Park Maintenance* 28, no. 9 (September 1975), p. 8.

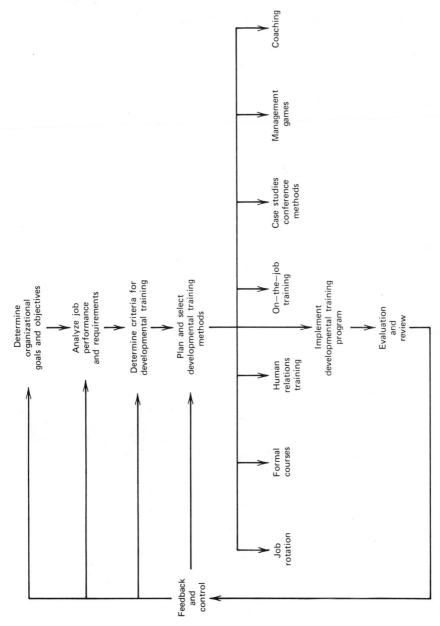

Figure 5.14. A systems approach to developmental training.

tions and selected projects, or modular units, this is known as an "intermix." The fourth type is known as "aggregate project organization." In this arrangement, the project manager is responsible for all the functions necessary to complete a given assignment. The fifth, the "matrix organization," occurs when the project organization exists side by side with the more traditional bureaucratic structure (see Figure 5.15). Individuals operating within this organization may have dual responsibilities. One would be the normal or regularly assigned responsibility, and the other responsibility would be the work of the project team.

In 1975 the Borough of North York (Ontario) Parks and Recreation Department adopted project management as a method of utilizing resources and expanding services. Its method of organization created flexibility and freedom within its structure, which allowed it to develop new ideas and approaches in meeting the leisure needs of the constituents served. By establishing project teams, staff members were not fitted to prescribed jobs; rather, they were assigned to groups of appropriate individuals. This found supervisors directing administrators and park personnel working directly with recreation programmers. Groups were formed to meet shifting leisure patterns brought about by a changing environment. As these groups fulfilled their goals and objectives, they were dissolved. As new challenges came into being, new groups were formed. The information supplied by Frank Burch, Superintendent of Recreation, in the following sections, summarizes the program.

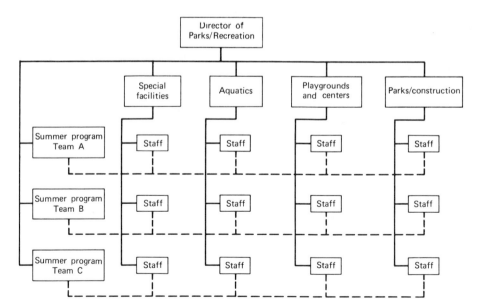

Figure 5.15.   Matrix organizational structure.

Goals and Objectives

To improve the quality and scope of summer services for children and youths.

To provide a system whereby overlap and duplication of services can be rectified on an area or local basis.

To allow staff an opportunity to continue to act in and react to a system and structure that encourages free thinking and team effort.

To investigate as a model the "project management" concept on an operational basis for a specific and limited period of time.

To explore expanding community input into summer services provided by or available through this department.

To expose staff to new and varied leadership and supervisory relations.

To create and apply a structure whereby role and resource interchange among staff or different sections and divisions is paramount to the success of a project.

To immerse staff from different sections and divisions in the philosophies and practices of other staff.

Through ongoing involvement and evaluation by management of each project, to assess staff effectiveness in identifying and implementing recreation services within an identified area.

Teams

Project teams were established as closely as possible to correspond with "families of schools" as defined by the North York Board of Education. For the summer of 1976, seven project districts were established.

Assignments

Staff was assigned to project districts by management personnel. Such assignments considered a combination of (1) current job responsibilities, (2) personal talents or interests, and (3) present district or geographical areas.

Staff Time Commitment

An appropriate balance of staff time was maintained between summer and year-round responsibilities. Minimum time commitments of team members to the summer projects was defined prior to the first meeting of the project team. Involvement in any required cross-borough committees dealing with overall tasks were considered as part of the summer responsibilities (minimum time commitment) for those staff members. Adjustments because of time demands of regular work load were normally negotiated with one's immediate supervisor within the present system. Adjustments because of time demands of project work load were normally begun with the project leader or designate. It was the responsibility of the section supervisor or division coordinator to provide guidelines to each exempt staff regarding their involvement with project team members. In some situations (e.g., aquatics), this involved an associate membership on a team with a definite time commitment and specific objectives in addition to the receipt of all information from team members. In other situations, it involved the sharing of information regarding cross-borough programs (e.g., summer hockey school, tennis).

Project Leaders
Project leadership in each program district was determined by each team of staff. All members of the team, be they recreation assistants, supervisors, coordinators, or a superintendent, were accountable for their team time commitment and team work performance through the project leader. Each team developed a clear understanding of the accountability of each member to the team as well as the team to its members. All job responsibilities within the team were clearly defined, understood, and accepted by the members. Each team member must understand the operational philosophies of each division. Other considerations pinpointed were decision-making in and on behalf of the team, methods for handling discipline problems, and budget control.

Management Roles
At least one recreation supervisor was assigned to each project and was responsible for (1) acting as liaison between each project and establishing methods of communication and interchange between projects, (2) routine supervisory administrative functions, and (3) interpreting guidelines and assuring that such guidelines were applied. The coordinators were each a member of two teams; the superintendent, a member of one. In addition to being a team member, each assumed responsibility for (1) maintaining an equitable balance between staff responsibilities for summer services and year-round duties, (2) assisting in the administrative functions, (3) coordinating various subprojects across the borough, such as supplies, uniforms, training, and publicity, and (4) assuring that other appropriate authorities were informed for all activities of the project teams.

Program
Each project team was encouraged to offer a diversified summer program. This might have included the development of leisure-time opportunities for the entire family. Programs may have had a registration fee or other charges (e.g., materials, transportation, etc.) in order to defray operational expenses, provided same are clearly outlined in preprogram publicity. Fee structure may have been different, depending on the area/communities involved. All revenues that are the property of the borough were to be handled in accord with established revenue-handling procedures. Any program that corresponded closely to or resembled a summer playground as operated in previous years continued to be available on a no-charge basis. However, certain specialized activities within the general playground-like program may have had a fee requirement.

Objectives and Evaluation
Clearly measurable, detailed objectives were set for each project area and team well in advance of summer operations. The evaluation of a summer

project was based on these objectives. Teams looked at both the immediate benefits to the summer operations and at the potential carry-over benefits to the ongoing objectives of each section and division. A detailed report was prepared and presented to the department. A written evaluation of all part-time staff was required.[19]

Decentralization

The drive to make the delivery of leisure services more effective and more efficient has turned the attention of many managers toward the concept of decentralization. As organizations have become more complex, there has been increased concern for finding ways to place individuals in decision-making positions closer to the people who are receiving services. As a bureaucratic structure grows vertically, there is a tendency toward inefficiency. The structure becomes an end in itself rather than a means to an end. Rules and procedures are established and enforced rigidly with no apparent relationship to the output goals of the organization. Communication becomes stifled as layering within the bureaucratic structure increases.

Jack W. Perez has suggested that parks and recreation departments need to develop organizational structures that have the ability to respond quickly to local cultural needs. He suggests that large communities are made up of many cultural groups requiring specialized services. To deal with each of these groups in a meaningful way, parks and recreation departments must focus resources effectively on each group's concerns. He notes that decentralization has proved successful in public leisure delivery systems in the following ways:

1. It provides an instant gauge of local feelings and attitudes through instant communication;
2. it promotes special programs of community interest;
3. it provides a rapport between recreation administration and people who receive recreation service;
4. local business is expedited with dispatch; and
5. each recreation director of the many recreation centers in the area is afforded the opportunity to meet his supervisor regularly, with the knowledge that his boss, so moved, can act on his concern.[20]

Why would a leisure delivery system want to decentralize its operations? Leisure is dynamic and there is a need for organizations to be flexible and have the ability to respond to change quickly. Organizations that have concentrated

---

[19] Information concerning the North York matrix organizational design was supplied to the authors by Frank Burch, Superintendent of Recreation , Borough of North York Parks and Recreation Department, January 1976.

[20] Jack W. Perez, "The Decentralization of Recreation," *California Parks and Recreation,* December 1970, p. 20.

authority at levels within their structure which are closest to those they serve may be more effective. Further, by providing opportunities for individual initiative and responsibility among lower-level staff, job satisfaction is increased. As previously mentioned, people today tend to be more highly educated, thereby having the capability to make decisions. Young people are less willing to accept authoritarian direction. There is a desire for a work environment that is democratic and allows individuals to have responsibility commensurate with their potential. A highly motivated group of individuals, having authority and operating close to the constituents they are serving, should increase the effectiveness and efficiency of a leisure delivery system.

What Is Decentralization?

The concept of centralization/decentralization is tied to the methods used to delegate authority within an organization. In a centralized organization, authority is concentrated among a few individuals. Decentralized organizations are ones in which authority has been dispersed in some way in the structure. Of extreme importance in determining whether an organization is centralized or decentralized is awareness of how much and in what ways authority has been dispersed. As indicated in Chapter 1, organizations are affected by and respond to a variety of environmental constraints. These factors may vary from community to community. Thus, as might be expected, the degree to which organizations decentralize will vary. In addition, the methods used in decentralizing will vary according to the circumstances involved. For example, a public leisure delivery system may organize itself in response to the needs of different geographic areas or cultural groupings.

Fred Luthans writes that there are three types of centralization/decentralization.[21] The first involves the geographic arrangement of a system's operation. The term "centralized," in this case, refers to the placement of all of an organization's operations in one location. A decentralized geographic location would disperse the organization's operations throughout the locale of the constituency it serves.

The second type of centralization/decentralization deals with functional units within an organization. Using the example of the maintenance function in community park and recreation departments, certain departments centralize the maintenance function by locating it administratively under a superintendent of parks. All the maintenance functions within the organization are then directed under his or her authority. Decentralization would occur if the authority and responsibility for handling maintenance functions were assumed by each recreation program area within the department. For example, the custodian at a recreation center would be placed under the supervision of the center director in charge of the facility.

The third type of centralization/decentralization deals with the "retention or

---

[21] Fred Luthans, *Organizational Behavior* (New York: McGraw-Hill Book Co., 1973), pp. 136–137.

delegation of decision-making prerogatives or command."[22] This involves determining the amount of decision-making power that is placed at various levels within an organization. Within certain leisure delivery systems, a great deal of authority, hence decision-making power, is dispersed to various levels within the organization. In others, power is concentrated only in the management positions. This particular concept may not be appraised, according to Luthans, by merely viewing the structure of an organization.

This last factor, the delegation of authority, is perhaps the fundamental concept of decentralization. In many situations, managers are unwilling to delegate authority because they lack self-confidence and/or fear their employees. Many individuals are accustomed to making their own decisions and do not want to give up this power. This conflict makes decentralization difficult. Thus, even if an organization has dispersed on geographic and/or functional bases, if authority to make decisions does not accompany this dispersion, decentralization may really not have occurred. The rate at which decisions are made may in fact have been increased, rather than the efficiency having been increased. To delegate authority and, hence, make decentralization work, according to Harold Koontz and Cyril O'Donnell, managers must be willing to do the following:

1. To give other individuals' ideas a chance to be tried.
2. To give away their right to make decisions to other individuals.
3. To patiently let others learn from their mistakes.
4. To trust those individuals to whom they have delegated authority.
5. To develop methods of control which serve as a basis to judge the effectiveness and efficiency of subordinates.[23]

Ralph J. Cordiner of the General Electric Corporation suggests that there are a number of factors which guide the implementation of his company's decentralization program. These can serve as a guideline for the operation of a program of decentralization in leisure service delivery systems:

1. Decentralization places authority to make decisions at points as near as possible to where the action takes place.
2. Decentralization is likely to get best over-all results by getting greatest and most directly applicable knowledge and most timely understanding actually into play on the greatest number of decisions.
3. Decentralization will work if real authority is delegated and not if details then have to be reported, or worse yet, if they have to be "checked" first.
4. Decentralization requires confidence that associates in decentralized positions will have the capacity to make sound decisions in the majority of cases,

---

[22] Ibid., p. 137.
[23] Harold Koontz and Cyril O'Donnell, *Principles of Management: An Analysis of Managerial Functions* fifth edition (New York: McGraw-Hill Book Co., 1972), pp. 352–353.

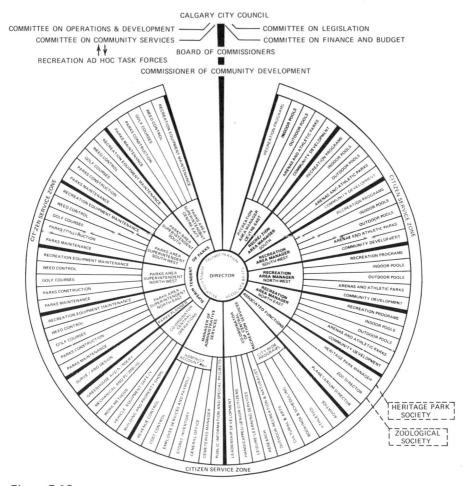

Figure 5.16

and such confidence starts at the executive level. The officers must set an example in the full art of delegation.

5. Decentralization requires understanding that the main role of staff or services is the rendering of assistance and advice to line operators through a relatively few experienced people, so that those making decisions can themselves make them correctly.

6. Decentralization requires realization that the natural aggregate of many individually sound decisions will be better for the business and for the public than centrally planned and controlled decisions.

7. Decentralization rests on the need to have general business objectives, organization structure, relations, policies, and measurements known, understood, and followed, but realizes that definition of policies does not necessarily mean uniformity of methods of executing such policies in decentralized operations.
8. Decentralization can be achieved only when higher executives realize that authority genuinely delegated to lower echelons cannot, in fact, also be retained by them.
9. Decentralization will work only if responsibility commensurate with decision-making authority is truly accepted and exercised at all levels.
10. Decentralization requires personnel policies based on measured performance, enforced standards, rewards for good performance, and removal for incapacity or poor performance.[24]

The plan of decentralization adopted by the Calgary, Alberta, Parks/Recreation Department (see Figure 5.16) is an example of how this concept can be implemented from a philosophical, methodological, and structural perspective. The following information is taken from an interview between the late Harry Boothman, formerly the director of the Parks/Recreation Department for the city of Calgary, and Art Drysdale, editor of *Recreation Canada.*

DRYSDALE: It seems to me that government organizations are always swinging from centralized to decentralized control and back again.

BOOTHMAN: I think the two key words in that statement are: DECENTRALIZED and CONTROL. I find that many people responsible for organizations have the words DECENTRALIZED and DISPERSAL mixed up. They tend to believe that if they place people away from city hall or the central office, out into district or regional offices, that they have achieved decentralization. In fact, all they have done is dispersed their personnel. True decentralization can only come about when responsibility and authority for many management decisions are also distributed.

We in Calgary have just established five area managers for our recreational services. The city has been divided into five geographic regions of approximately 90,000 each and while some city-wide functions had to remain in the central office, the majority of our services have been decentralized and placed under the management direction of the area recreation managers. They are responsible for both facilities and programs in their area of the city. These responsibilities include the financial management of the funds approved and appropriated by council in the budget.

[24] Ralph J. Cordiner, "Decentralized at General Electric: New Frontiers for Professional Managers," in Burt K. Scanlan, *Principles of Management and Organizational Behavior* (New York: John Wiley and Sons, 1973), pp. 217–218.

In other words which seems to give so many of us a problem is that word CONTROL. Old text books on management used to talk about "span of control" and recommended that between three and five supervisors was the maximum number that should report to any one manager. This type of thinking forced our organization into the traditional bureaucratic pyramid. The alternative to this is to think in terms of "span of co-ordination." With this type of philosophy a manager is limited only by the time he has available to co-ordinate various inter-related functions and programs. For example, I have 12 executive personnel reporting to me: the five area recreation managers, parks superintendent who is responsible for the planning functions in the department, zoo director, planetarium director, historical park director, cemetary manager, co-ordinator of central services and financial administrative officer.

DRYSDALE: Two questions come to mind. Can you honestly give enough time to that number of subordinates, and what are the real advantages of such an organization?

BOOTHMAN: The only way that this co-ordination can be implemented effectively is by a system of Management by Objectives, or as some people are now calling it, Performance Evaluation. That is, the manager and the subordinate work out their objectives for the next three or six month period, clearly setting out by what criteria these objectives will be measured at the end of the time period. During the time period the manager performs monitoring and co-ordinating roles and at the end of the time period they share together in a careful evaluation as to whether the objectives (in accordance with the criteria that were agreed upon) were met.

I think that the main advantage of our "flat" organization is the communication system is quicker and compressed. In the traditional pyramid organization, management policies often had to travel through seven to nine layers of supervisors before they reach the action zone. We think in our reorganization we have cut this down to a maximum of four levels of supervision. This not only results in an effective communication of policies but greatly increases the morale of junior personnel.

DRYSDALE: You are critical of the traditional organizations and organizational charts which I know predominate the minds of many of the parks and recreation superintendents whom I visit. Have you got a chart in Calgary?

BOOTHMAN: Well, things usually change so quickly around here that we draw our organizational charts on Kleenex, but we do have a chart which is not intended to really convey lines of authority by a skeleton, with people confined to little coffin-like boxes; but rather to show to the people of this department that are in the action zone how they are really the nerve center or nerve edge of the whole organization. We drew a chart like a circle with the people in the action zone of service on the outside ring touching those who we try to serve. They are the nerve system for the whole department, sending back messages of what the people we are trying to serve really want. We try to explain that the foreman and middle management in our organization circle are the muscle that keeps up our momentum and I see my job in the center as primarily one of co-ordinating to ensure an efficient, effective and united action.

DRYSDALE: How did you bring about the change from an organization based on function; that is some people responsible for swimming pools, some responsible for parks, and some responsible for programs, each with their line of authority; to an organization based on geography in which all of these functions are grouped together?

BOOTHMAN: Well, the total theme behind the reorganization was to "improve service to the citizens." But we were aware that this could only be achieved if we had an enthusiastic staff with high morale. And to achieve this we set about a process of TEAM BUILDING. People working with each area recreation manager included pool and arena supervisors, recreation program workers and parks district foremen. They are now closer together and talking to each other across the lines of their own specialty as members of a team. In particular, I think the approach to team organization is one that is very suited to the outlook of young professional recreation workers. In the 50's and 60's when people graduated from university, they looked for an organization which they could become a part of and tended to become organization men. Today's young graduates are not motivated by permanency and security as much as they were a couple of decades ago. As Alvin Toffler has said in *Future Shock*, we are now becoming more oriented to ad-hocracy rather than bureaucracy. And, young people are more interested in a team with specific tasks to be achieved. We believe that area approach and decentralization tends to meet these modern needs of our staff.[25]

Federation Method of Organization

The federation method of organization allows several specialized groups to associate freely with one another in a flexible organizational framework. It is a method whereby specialized groups having independent modes of operation and interest can combine with each other to pursue a set of common goals. In this way, each group within a federation may contribute the talent, abilities, and skills of its membership to a larger extent. Organized within a loose democratic structure, specialized groups are autonomous units that have very little authority over other specialized groups within the federation. Each group is thought to be an equal partner with other groups. The key features of the federation concept of organization include the following:

1. Specialized groups work cooperatively toward a set of common goals.
2. Specialized groups are autonomous, independent, and self-sufficient.
3. Because of the voluntary nature of involvement, the authority structure of the federation lacks the coercion found in the mechanistic method of organization.

[25] "Calgary Reorganization Aims to Reduce Administrative Levels," *Recreation Canada,* Published by the Canadian Parks/Recreation Association. No. 30/6/1972. pp. 6–7.

Specialized groups in the federation must work in concert with each other to pursue the goals established. The cooperative nature of involvement in a federation is therefore a key factor. The success of each specialized group will contribute to the achievement of the federation's overall goals, so the welfare of each group is important to every other group. If one specialized group fails in some way to successfully fulfill its purpose, its downfall will affect the other groups. Thus it is beneficial for groups within a federation to take an interest in the activities of the other groups. It is not uncommon to find one group advocating the concerns of another group while at the same time pursuing its own interests. This cooperative approach to the delivery of leisure services is perhaps most appropriate in a society characterized by great demands and dwindling resources. In many cases, organizations have operated competitively in the delivery of leisure services. Naturally, this often diminished their effectiveness because it resulted in the diluting of resources and led to confusion on the part of consumers.

Another key feature of this concept of organization is that specialized groups remain autonomous and independent to conduct their own activities. Groups are free to choose any form of organization that best suits their needs. They are free to pursue their own goals and objectives while working toward the overall mission of the federation. In this way, they are allowed to retain their freedom in making decisions that will affect their group's specific activities. This independence allows groups within the federation to react in a manner that is consistent with their own goals and objectives. In addition, each group is responsible for running its own organization, and the federation is freed from the responsibility of internal administrative problems.

The federation method of organization results in a loose democratic structure. Because of this, the authority is not coersive in nature. Groups participate voluntarily. They are involved because they want to be, not because they are forced into the organization. This results in an affiliation of groups that are highly motivated. Individuals and/or groups are more likely to be productive when they participate of their own volition in activities.

What is the role of the manager in a federation? Primarily, he serves as a facilitator, catalyst, and enabler to the group. The manager has no authority to direct any group to do a specific task within the federation. Thus his role becomes that of acting in a coordinating capacity by providing services that help those within the federation. Information and specialized technical resources are the types of services managers are likely to provide. For example, the manager of a federation might identify, collect, and distribute information regarding opportunities for federal funding to each of the groups. He might act as an agent on behalf of the federation, representing its interests to the community. In addition, the manager is in a position to help formulate the general policy of a federation. However, the manager's ability to enforce policy is limited to his ability to inspire the members of the group to work as a cohesive unit in regard to federation activities.

Figure 5.17 delineates a federation of leisure services that involves a number of community institutions which are engaged in the delivery of leisure services. All have an interest, whether it be for altruistic reasons or otherwise, in creating and distributing services. The federation method of organization would allow these institutions to meet or discuss common problems, issues, and concerns. Further, it could act as a clearinghouse for programs, in order to prevent the duplication of activities. It could collectively pool resources to provide services in areas where independent groups are not capable of doing so. The broad goals and objectives of each group could also be promoted through the federation.

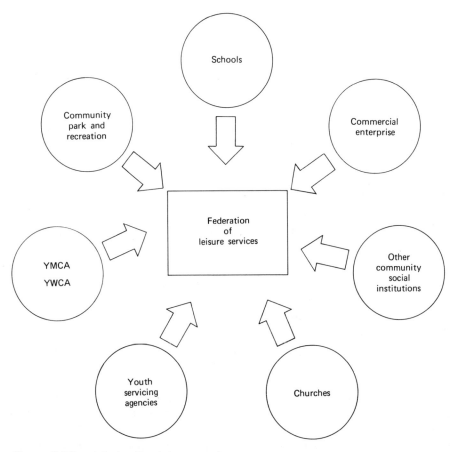

Figure 5.17. A federation leisure service.

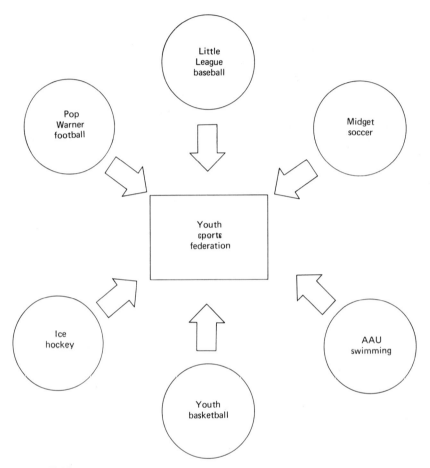

Figure 5.18. A youth sports federation.

Figure 5.18 shows how a specific program area—sports—could be organized into a federation. The activities of this federation would be similar to those in Figure 5.17, but would focus on a different level of concern.

Figure 5.19 illustrates how a community park and recreation department could organize some of its line functions (see page 122 for a definition of line functions) into a federation. The key feature is that each facility can determine its own internal organizational structure. Thus this approach avoids the imposition of a rigid structure where inappropriate, and a flexible structure in facilities that demand flexibility. In the management of a golf course, the tasks to be completed are routine and the structuring of permanent roles is relatively simple; therefore a bureaucratic structure is inappropriate. On the other hand, personnel operating in the community center are subject to a relatively unstable environment. In this situation, it may be appropriate to establish ad hoc groups on a short-term basis to deal with the problem of change. The beauty of this approach, in this case, is that it allows specific functions to develop appropriate organizational structures and at the same time provides a way to coordinate their activities.

The Federation Plan of Community Organization for Leisure adopted by the City of Fremont, California, illustrates how the federation plan can be put into effect in a community park and recreation system.

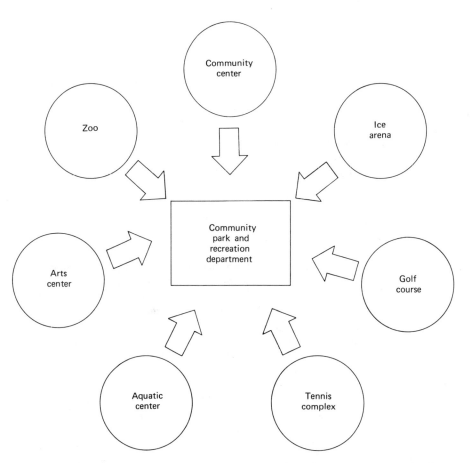

Figure 5.19. A community park and recreation department organized as a federation.

The Federation Plan of Community Organization for Leisure, City of
Fremont, California

In 1964 the citizens of Fremont, California, proposed that the staff develop an
organizational structure pertaining to the delivery of leisure services that would
afford the following:

1. Maximum coordination of facilities.
2. Unlimited participation in planning and implementing programs.
3. Grass-roots view of all activities.
4. A structure to encourage grass-roots participation in an orderly manner.
5. Council and commission with maximum public review, evaluation, and
   coordination.
6. Recognition of the key spokesmen having maximum insights into their fields
   of endeavor.
7. Opportunities and encouragement for people to participate without staff
   dictating the program structure.

As a result, the staff of the Community Recreation Department, as part of its
responsibility to the citizens of Fremont, devised the federation concept of community organization, which would accomplish the following:

1. Provide a means of communication that would give each group equal voice
   in the community, regardless of size.
2. Coordinate all groups for mutual benefit of facilities, funds, and other
   resources not readily available.
3. Act as a clearinghouse and resource center for new groups and rejuvenate
   other groups now inactive or operating at a slower pace.
4. Provide resources and encourage other wholesome leisure activity to grow in
   Fremont.

The concept represented a method that would provide grass-roots
representation; an organized means of communication; and equal
representation on the part of groups, without staff dictating operating
policies. It was recommended in the form of "The Federation Plan of Community Organization for Leisure."

When the people of Fremont isolate a broad area of concern—such as
arts, youths, sports, camping, and so on—in the leisure field, they may form
a federation having representatives of various groups around the common
areas of need, with accompanying opportunity for individual participation.
Most federations, after organizing, see the advantage of incorporation as a
nonprofit institution, which guarantees tax-exempt status for money-raising
events and donations.

The federation concept is, in its essential genius, a group of citizens
organized around a concern—such as sports. The concept offers a link in the
communication chain between citizenry, public, private and voluntary enterprise. It is important to the city government that it has been acknowledged
by a resoltuion establishing the plan.

The federation policy of the city of Fremont states that when groups of like interest organize into a federation and request recognition by the commission as the key spokesman organization in all matters pertaining to public leisure resources in the special-interest area of their federation, and meets all the policy requirements for recognition spelled out in council Resolution no. 1448, then the commission can officially designate (by resolution) the federation as the chief spokesman group for advice and recommendations in all matters of the federation's special interest.

A federation can request staff services and, if authorized by the city council, the city becomes involved through the Community Recreation Department by assigning a supervisor in that general area to act as executive secretary to the federation. As the executive secretary, he provides clerical, research, background, and expediter services, thereby freeing the federation to function in the area of policy decisions. The executive secretary concerns himself with the administration of the program desired by the federation.

Organizationally, the federation may operate through a board of directors elected at large from member groups, or representatives of their respective groups will elect officers and the membership will act as a board in total. In the latter case, representative membership will be involved in the policymaking decisions, thereby operating in a truly democratic fashion.

The primary function of the federation is to develop a work program yearly and recommend to the recreation Commission any policy decisions reached at the federation level. Should these decisions conflict with staff interpretations, then the commission would have two recommendations in consideration, which again will provide maximum public review. Should an individual member group disagree with either recommendation, it may appeal to the commission, citing any circumstances felt conducive to its cause. It should be duly noted that the council has the final prerogative in all appeals and recommendations from federation, commission, staff, or member groups.

The federation is autonomous, being a state-incorporated body, and does not need city-provided staff to function as an organization. Council recognizes the worth of public review provided by this body and has provided for staff assistance if the federation so desires.

The federation, within the boundaries of its autonomy, is not restricted to jurisdiction of the Recreation Commission. It may work closely on projects with the Chamber of Commerce, Fremont Unified School District, civic organizations, and any other individuals or groups needing to utilize the resources of the federation.

The federation may involve itself in many functions, such as fund raising, membership drives, cosponsoring community activities, surveys, research, and so on. Any program and/or monetary groups should be presented to the commission as a "package" compiled and edited by the federation and listed in the order of priority need. The commission will then evaluate all requests and establish priority recommendations to the council.

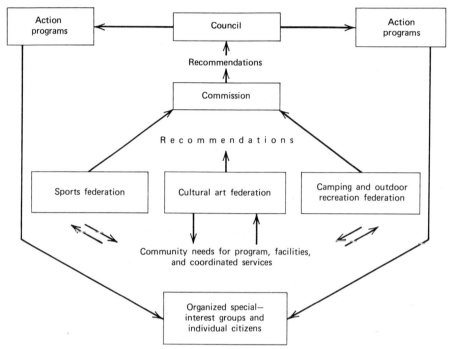

Figure 5.20. Federation plan for community organization of recreation and leisure services, Fremont, California

The federation concept provides the community a democratic organization for the intake and output of policies, recommendations, plans, and programs for the advantage of all its citizens, and as such is the best example of the social process in democracy.

Essentially, each federation will (1) provide the commission with a clear, total picture of the current and anticipated programs in the federation's field of specialty and (2) provide the commission with a clear, total picture of community needs, with recommended priorities and action programs geared to implement the identified needs.

Figure 5.20 is a diagram of the process of community group or individual action made orderly and possible by the federation plan. Essentially, the structure makes it possible for the commission and council to receive action program requests from the community after they have been thoroughly studied and evaluated in terms of the total community leisure needs by all concerned parties. The process would work as follows:

1. The group or individual expresses a need in the form of a request to the federation.

2. The federation, having the total picture of current community programs and needs in its area of special interest, would recommend the best type of action to the group or individual.
3. Those requests determined to be a responsibility of the municipality would be evaluated and passed on to the commission, with recommendations by the federation.
4. The commission would then evaluate the requests in terms of the total leisure needs of the community and pass them on to the city council, with Commission recommendations.[26]

SUMMARY

In this chapter, we have presented a discussion of organizational designs. It is important for a manager to recognize that the structuring of any leisure service organization will be affected by its goals and objectives, basic work activities, and environmental factors. These elements will affect the amount of specialization, standardization, centralization, formalization, flexibility, and type of configuration chosen within a given organizational structure. It is important for the reader to remember that organizational structure may be viewed as existing on a continuum that runs from mechanistic (rigid) organization on one end to organic (flexible) organization on the other. In addition to the goals and objectives of an organization, it appears that a critical factor in the choice of a design is the relative stability of the environment. When the environment is thought to be stable, mechanistic designs are appropriate; conversely, when it is unstable, organic structures should be used. Each manager must evaluate those factors that influence his or her particular situation and apply the principles to determine the most appropriate structure.

It is critically important that the human element in organizations be acknowledged. Managers who take into consideration the unique interests and needs of their organization's membership, while at the same time focusing on the organization's goals, will be successful.

[26] "The Federation Plan of Community Organization for Leisure." (Mimeo.) This information was used with the permission of R. Allan Box, Director of Recreation and Leisure Services, City of Fremont, California.

Organizational Leadership and Communications 6

In this chapter, organizational leadership and communications will be discussed. Leadership can be thought of as the process of influencing group behavior. Thus, a manager's leadership style will have an enormous impact on the organization's effectiveness. Likewise, the manager's ability to communicate with others is essential to the productive management of his organization. Communications involves the transferring of information between individuals and/or groups. It is through the process of communication that a manager is able to understand his employee's needs and translate the goals of the organization to them.

LEADERSHIP

Leadership involves the same components, whether in a leisure service organization or some other public or private institution. Unfortunately, there has not been a great deal of research or writing about leadership styles in regard to leisure services. To examine leadership and give the prospective manager insight into the whole field of leadership, it is necessary to draw on research, studies, and writings from many other disciplines. The first part of this chapter will present a case study of a leadership situation and will analyze its component parts. The literature and research will then be reviewed to determine if there is a style of leadership that is best and the needs for leadership in the leisure service professions.

Following is a brief case study designed to highlight the components that affect management leadership:

Assume that you are a park foreman in a medium-sized park and recreation department. You have been into the office of the director of the Parks and Recreation Department on Thursday afternoon, and he describes a work assignment he wants you to accomplish. Bill Johns, a park foreman from another district, has been sick for the past five weeks. It has just been brought to the director's attention that Bill was responsible for setting up an extensive exhibit at the community's annual garden show, which is to start on Monday. Because Bill has been off work and did not mention this to anyone, the project has slipped by the department and there is only Friday, Saturday, and Sunday to prepare for the exhibit. The director has asked you to take over the responsibilities for setting up the exhibit by Monday, utilizing Bill's crew, who are familiar with the setup procedures as they have done this for the past several years. The director ends the meeting by saying he knows you can get the job done and has the utmost confidence in you. He will be glad to help with anything you need to complete the project by 9:00 A.M. Monday.

You return to your office to analyze the situation and get your thoughts together to determine what is involved. Obviously, it is going to take a great deal of leadership on your part, as the foreman, to accomplish the task.

In analyzing this example, as well as any other in which leadership plays a part, there are three components, or elements, to contend with: the leader, the employees, and the situation. Each of these elements affect the outcome and are interdependent on one another. This can best be explained by examining Figure 6.1.

First, you have the *leader* who, with proper skills, sets clear objectives and directs the work group to accomplish the mission. Second, there are the *employees* who perform the work and carry out the plans to achieve the desired results. Finally, you have the *situation*, the existing environmental conditions that must be considered in the accomplishment of the mission.

The traditional approach to accomplishing the task of setting up the exhibit would be through strong and forceful leadership—directing the employees in the work crew by telling them what to do, how to do it, and when to do it. But in today's work world it is not as easy as that. Many things have changed in the last several years relative to employee's needs, unions, social conditions, and so on that affect the way employees accept leadership. Just because you have been appointed

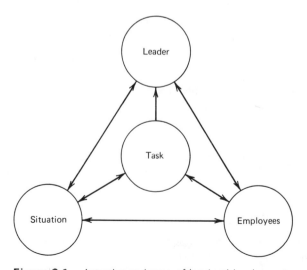

Figure 6.1. Interdependence of leadership elements.

leader and are responsible for the task does not mean that those assigned to work with you will automatically follow your leadership or be particularly enthused about the assignment. Keep in mind the material we have covered in the past chapters (particularly the information concerninng motivation and meeting individual needs) and let's examine how we might use what we have learned to accomplish this particular assignment.

Paul Hersey and Kenneth Blanchard, in their book *Management of Organizational Behavior*, define leadership as "the process of influencing the activities of individuals or a group, in efforts toward goal achievement in a given situation."[1] The leader, to accomplish the goals, is involved in working with and through people. It is obvious that most tasks cannot be accomplished by the leader alone. In our example, the leader must be concerned with task: but to accomplish it, he or she must also be concerned with the various aspects of leadership relationships. This involves communicating, motivating, and directing employees to accomplish the organizational and group goals. In analyzing the example further, we need to determine more detail about each element of the triangle and how it will affect the outcome. By closely scrutinizing the situation, we find that the following factors affect meeting the goal:

1. There are three days in which to set up the exhibit.
2. It is an outdoor exhibit.
3. The weather is predicted to be cold and rainy.
4. Friday is payday.
5. The exhibit must be set up in time.

Obviously, there are other conditions that could affect the situation, but these five are the factors that will affect this triangular relationship.

The next set of factors concern the employees—the crew members who are to accomplish the work.

1. There is a natural leader in the group.
2. The group wants to work all three days because they can make more money working time and a half on Saturday and double time on Sunday.
3. Several employees have been known to come in with hangovers on Saturdays, after Friday paydays.
4. Although the group has a reputation for being productive, they also have a reputation of kidding and joking while carrying out their assignments.

Again, it can be stated that these are just a few of the factors that depict the characteristics of the crew.

---

[1] Paul Hersey and Kenneth H. Blanchard, *Management of Organizational Behavior: Utilizing Human Resources,* second edition (Englewood Cliff, N.J.: Prentice-Hall, 1972), p. 69.

The last aspect of the triangle involves you, the leader:

1. You do not want to work on Sunday because you have other plans.
2. You prefer to work 12 hours on both Friday and Saturday to allow a leeway should there be problems, rather than cutting it so closely.
3. You are a serious-minded foreman and do not like a crew that jokes and kids while performing their job.
4. You do not approve of drinking alcoholic beverages and it makes you angry to see anyone drink too much, particularly when it affects their work the next day.

Which of the three elements of the triangle will be easiest to change: the manager's leadership style, the employees, or the situation. Traditionally, the manager would have taken charge and carried out the assignment and the employees would have followed his leadership and directions. Rationally analyzing this example, it becomes apparent that the element easiest to change is your, the manager's, behavior, or style. Briefly: You have no control over the fact that you have only three days to get the exhibit set up, and you cannot change the fact that the weather prediction is bad and the exhibit will be outside. Friday is payday and although you could hold back the distribution of paychecks so the employees would not come in with hangovers the next day, this could affect their morale and impair their motivation.

In analyzing the crew, or employees: A natural leader in the group can be an advantage or a disadvantage. Certainly it would make little sense to announce to the crew, "Look, I am the boss over this project and I want everyone to know that unless things are done my way there will be trouble." This could create a real morale problem and inhibit the completion of the task. Also, the crew wants to work all three days; although you may have some influence over this, asking them to work two days rather than three days may cause them to slow down in their work. The fact that some of the crew may come in with a hangover on Saturday is also something beyond your control, and you will have to contend with it. Finally, the fact that the crew jokes and kids while working is something that you, as the leader, should not try to change. To state that during the assignment you will not tolerate any joking or kidding may impair their production and motivation.

So, in analyzing this example, it becomes apparent that you as leader have little ability to change the employees or the situation, and it will be easier to change your leadership approach (see Figure 6.2). This will be discussed in more detail later in the chapter.

As foreman, your main objective is to get the exhibit set up by 9:00 A.M. Monday. This means that the way the task is accomplished is secondary, provided the method used is in the interest of the employees and is moral and ethical. In this example, it is a fact that it is easier for you, as leader, to change your leadership approach to capitalize on the strength of the group, even though you do not want to

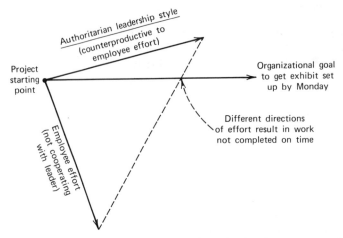

Figure 6.2. The effect of leadership style that is not appropriate for work group and situation.

work on Sunday. You will have to give up your plans, adjust your schedule and thinking, to accomplish the project. Attempting to change the work group's behavior of joking and kidding while working may slow down productivity, and lecturing the group on Friday not to come in with hangovers on Saturday may do more harm than good.

The easiest element of the triangular model to change is the leader's behavior and style of leadership. Traditionally, this has not been the approach. We have been inclined to think of the leader as the one who controls the other factors, the one in control of the situation and the crews. A few years ago, when the needs of employees were at a different level and when security, salary, and other environmental factors were more important to the employee, this approach may have worked. But today it probably will not work at all.

Another way to visualize leadership is to express it in the form of an equation: leadership is a function of the leader's style, the employees, and the situation.

$$L = l \times e \times s$$

If any one of these factors change, it has an effect on outcome, or results. To accomplish a task, the leader must consider each of these three elements and understand that if one changes he will have to adjust his approach accordingly. In most work tasks assigned to him, he will have more control over *his* behavior and leadership style and will get the best results by changing these factors rather than trying to change the group or the situation, which he may not be able to change at all.

Leadership Studies

Great Man or Trait Theory of Leadership

Many of the initial attempts to study leadership involved analyzation of some of the great leaders of the world to determine the characteristics that were indicative of a good leader. Some of the first studies analyzed Greek and Roman leaders; these studies concluded that leaders were born, not made. It was felt that individuals were born with the traits for leadership, and famous figures in history were used to support this theory.

From the late 1930s to the 1950s, additional attempts were made to study the characteristics found in individuals who had great leadership ability. Keith Davis, in *Human Behavior at Work*, listed the following four traits, which he indicated had impact on successful organizational leadership:

1. Intelligence. Research generally showed that the leader has higher intelligence than the average intelligence of his followers.
2. Social maturity and breadth. Leaders tend to be emotionally stable and mature and have broad interests in activities. They have an assured, respectful self-image.
3. Inner motivation and achievement drives. Leaders have relatively intense motivation drives of the achievement type. They strive for intrinsic rather than extrinsic rewards.
4. Human relations. A successful leader recognizes the worth and dignity of his followers and is able to empathize with them. He is employee centered rather than production centered.[2]

Attempts to research leadership involved physical, mental, and personal characteristic analysis. It was found that characteristics, or personal traits, of leaders were not indicative of whether an individual was a good leader. Examples indicated that although an individual may lack one or two personality characteristics, he or she can make up for it with strength in another. So it does not seem practical to analyze leadership on the basis of characteristics or traits.

The theory that leaders are born has been questioned on the basis that many individuals have been found able to improve their leadership capabilities by acquiring certain techniques and skills that are required of a leader. This will be discussed in much greater detail later in this chapter.

Situational Theory of Leadership

After many failures in attempting to analyze leadership from a trait or characteristic point of view, attempts were made to analyze the situations that influence

[2] Keith Davis, *Human Behavior at Work*, fourth edition (New York: McGraw-Hill Book Co., 1972), pp. 103–104.

leadership. These investigations were inspired by the Hawthorne studies, wherein the environment was changed to determine its effect on employees' work production. It became apparent, in approaching leadership from a situational point of view, that situations had many effects on leadership and leadership styles.

Alan C. Filley and Robert J. House, in *Managerial Process and Organizational Behavior*, come to the conclusion that the following situation variables might have an impact on leadership effectiveness:

1. The previous history of the organization, the age of the previous incumbent in the leader's position, the age of the leader, and his previous experiences;
2. The community in which the organization operates;
3. The particular work requirements of the group;
4. The psychological climate of the group being led;
5. The kind of job the leader holds;
6. The size of the group led;
7. The degree to which group members' cooperation is required;
8. The cultural expectations of subordinates;
9. Group member personalities;
10. The time required and allowed for decision making.[3]

This list indicates a variety of situations that may have an effect on leadership. One of the shortcomings of this type of list is that activities or situations have not been researched sufficiently to allow definite conclusions concerning their effect on leadership. Further, it is uncertain whether or not there are other activities or conditions that could also have an effect on leadership.

Lippitt and White Leadership Studies

One of the earliest leadership studies was conducted in the 1930s by Ronald Lippitt and Ralph K. White at the University of Iowa under the direction of Kurt Lewin.[4] In this research project 4 groups of 20 ten-year-old boys were studied as they participated in various hobby-club activities. Each group of 5 boys was exposed to authoritarian, democratic, and laissez-faire leadership. They were studied under controlled conditions in an attempt to show the effect of the various styles of leadership on the boys while measuring the degree of frustration, aggression, and satisfaction among them. Group characteristics were controlled to assure that the boys in each group were basically of the same intelligence and social behavior. Each of the boys' hobby groups engaged in similar projects, involving

---

[3] Alan C. Filley and Robert J. House, *Managerial Process and Organizational Behavior* (Glenview, Ill.: Scott, Foresman and Co., 1969), p. 409.

[4] For specific details refer to Kurt Lewin, Ronald Lippitt, and Ralph K. White, "Patterns of Aggressive Behavior in Experimentally Created 'Social Climates,'" *Journal of Social Psychology*, May 1939, pp. 271–276.

model airplanes, murals, and soap carvings. The physical setting was kept as constant as possible, utilizing the same rooms, identical equipment, and so on.

The physical characteristics and personalities of the leaders were kept as similar as possible. The leaders assumed a different style as they shifted from one group to another every six weeks. The experiments were controlled so the same degree and style of leadership was constant while measuring the variables of satisfaction, frustration, and aggression activity of each of the boys.

One of the conclusive findings from the studies was that the boys overwhelmingly preferred the democratic style of leadership. The boys also chose the laissez-faire style of leadership over the authoritarian style, even though confusion and disorder was an outcome of the laissez-faire style of leadership. One of the shortcomings of the study was that the boys' productivity was not directly examined as part of the study. The research indicated that the boys objected and reacted to the authoritarian style of leadership by either aggressive or apathetic behavior. Also, hostility was much more frequent when authoritarian leadership was exercised. This study was one of the first attempts to analyze leadership utilizing scientific methods of research. The research study indicated that different styles of leadership can produce different types of reactions from similar groups.

Ohio State Leadership Studies

Ohio State University initiated a series of studies in 1945 to identify various dimensions of leadership behavior.[5] The study attempted to analyze situational variables that affect leader behavior, rather than using the trait classification approach. The study attempted to determine what behavior the leader exhibited when directing the activities of the group toward a goal. The investigation eventually narrowed to two dimensions of leader behavior: initiating structure and consideration. "Initiating structure" referred to the leader's behavior in establishing relationships between himself and the members of his work group while endeavoring to create well-defined patterns of organization, channels of communication, and methods and procedures. "Consideration" referred to behavior indicative of friendship. mutual trust, respect, and warmth in the relationship between the leader and members of his work group.

The Ohio State studies found that initiating structure and consideration were two separate and distinct dimensions. Initiating structure is task and goal oriented, whereas consideration is concerned with relationships. Task behavior concerns the extent to which the leader is likely to organize and define rules to the members of the group. In other words, what activities each is to do and when, where, and how the tasks are to be accomplished through well-defined patterns of organization,

[5] Ralph M. Stogdill and Alvin E. Cooms, eds., "Leader Behavior: Its Description and Measurements," Research Monograph No. 88 (Columbus: Ohio State University, Bureau of Business Research, 1957).

channels of communication, and procedures. Consideration behavior is the extent to which the leader is likely to maintain personal relationships between himself and the members of the group. He does this by opening up channels of communications, delegating authority, giving subordinates an opportunity to use their own potential, and encouraging a professional atmosphere of social and emotional support, friendship, and mutual trust.

During these studies, the leadership behavior of individuals was plotted on a matrix on two separate axes rather than a single continuum. Four quadrants resulted to show the various relationships between initiating structure behavior (task) and consideration behavior (relationship), as illustrated in Figure 6.3.

The two-dimensional approach to leadership tended to bridge the gap between the scientific management, concern for task, and the human relations approach, with emphasis on relationships.

Michigan Leadership Studies

The University of Michigan Survey Research Center conducted a series of leadership studies, with a grant from the U.S. Navy, to determine the principles that contribute to both the productivity of a group and the satisfaction group

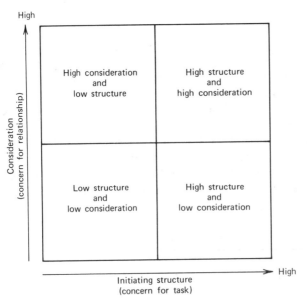

Figure 6.3.   The Ohio State leadership quadrants. (Paul Hersey, Kenneth H. Blanchard, *Management of Organizational Behavior: Utilization of Human Resources,* 2nd Edition, copyright © 1972, p. 74. Reprinted by permission of Prentice-Hall, Inc., Englewood Cliffs, N.J.

members derive from their participation.[6] The study was initiated in 1947 at the home offices of the Prudential Insurance Company in Newark, New Jersey. The Michigan studies attempted to measure the perceptions and attitudes of supervisors and workers. These variables were then related to the measurements of performance; 419 clerical workers were divided into 24 sections, each with a supervisor.

Various factors, such as type of work, working conditions, and working methods, were carefully controlled. The various groups were then evaluated based on their degree of high or low productivity. Interviews were administered to the various work groups. The results showed that the following was significantly more likely to be true of supervisors of the high-producing sections:

1. To receive general rather than close supervision from their supervisors;
2. To like the amount of authority and responsibility they had in their jobs;
3. To spend more time in supervising;
4. To give general rather than close supervision to the employees; and
5. To be more employee oriented rather than production oriented.[7]

Low-producing section supervisors basically had the opposite characteristics and techniques. They were found to supervise closely, to be production oriented, and to be opposite in many other characteristics.

After the Michigan studies, similar studies were initiated in a variety of organizations. The results of those studies were essentially the same as those obtained in Michigan studies.

Coch and French Study

Lester Coch and John French conducted a survey in the 1940s to determine and examine the process of overcoming resistance to change.[8] Their research took place at the Harwood Manufacturing Company in Marion, Virginia. The company produced pajamas and employed approximately 500 women and 100 men. These workers showed a strong resistance to change, and there was an attempt to find methods to initiate change in the various jobs they performed. Experience proved that when change was initiated by management, the workers became ineffective and less productive. Employee receptiveness was negative toward management and oftentimes, when changes were made, a great number of employees left the company.

The study was designed to test the effect of the degree of participation in work

---

[6] For specific details, refer to Daniel Katz, Nathan Maccoby, and Nancy C. Morse, "Productivity, Supervision and Morale in an Office Situation" (Ann Arbor: University of Michigan Survey Research Center, 1950).

[7] Ibid, p. 62.

[8] Lester Coch and John French, "Overcoming Resistance to Change," *Human Relations* 1, no. 4. (1948), pp. 512 532.

groups. Variables to be measured were production, turnover, and attitude of workers. Three groups were established in the experiment. The control group consisted of 18 handpressers, who were not allowed to participate in planning the new method of stacking their work. They were given details, and management explained how they wanted their work to be performed. This group represented the way changes normally were initiated in the plant prior to the experiment.

The second group was a representative participation group in which 13 workers were given a demonstration of improved methods of folding pajamas. The group was then allowed to participate in approval of the method and to select "special operators" from their group to improve and implement the new technique. The special operators were also allowed to make constructive suggestions to management, and they trained the rest of the group on-the-job.

The last group in the experiment was given full participation. After the need for change was demonstrated to the group, the entire group participated in trying to determine the best method of initiating the change, and then they initiated their process.

The results of the Coch-French experiment were very clear. The experiment demonstrated that the control group resisted change and that productivity was below the level maintained before technologically sound change was initiated. In the representative participation group, when the change was first introduced, productivity dropped off lower than the controlled group, but quickly recovered and exceeded the level of productivity before the change. The full-participation group had the best record by far. There was a small drop-off following the first part of the experiment, but it was followed by a sharp climb in productivity; this group outperformed the other two groups by a wide margin.

Employee attitude was highest in the full-participation group and lowest in the controlled group. The controlled group showed the greatest hostility toward management and filed the most grievances. A similar experiment by French and another group of researchers studied the effects of participation in a Norwegian factory. The purpose was to see if participation would affect production, turnover, and attitude of the employees in a different country having different values. The results of the study indicated that participation was not as desirable a factor in the Norwegian factory as it was in the American factory and therefore was not a desirable element in the whole employee-employer relationship.

Other studies have been conducted to determine what the basic factors are that affect leadership. In most cases, leadership behavior studies have found that the critical elements are task behavior and relationship behavior. An individual's leadership style is the result of the various behavior patterns he or she develops while in the leadership role. The leader who exhibits more concern for task behavior tends to be authoritarian in leadership style. Contrarily, a leader who tends to exhibit more concern for relationships with employees tends to be more

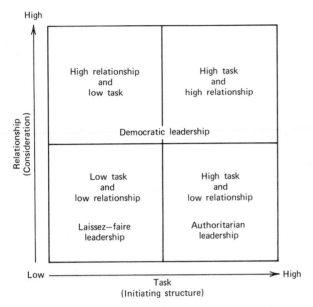

High

High relationship
and
low task

High task
and
high relationship

Relationship
(Consideration)

Democratic leadership

Low task
and
low relationship

High task
and
low relationship

Laissez–faire
leadership

Authoritarian
leadership

Low ⟶ High

Task
(Initiating structure)

Figure 6.4. The relationship of task and relationship behavior as it relates to leadership styles.

democratic in leadership style. Figure 6.4 shows the kinship of task and relationship behavior as it relates to authoritarian, democratic, and laissez-faire leadership styles.

By placing concern for task, or initiating structure, on the horizontal axis of the matrix and concern for relationship, or consideration, on the vertical axis of the matrix, we end up with a matrix that has four quadrants. An individual who is high in task and low in relationship would tend to be authoritarian in leadership style. A person who is low in both task and relationship would tend to be laissez-faire in leadership style. The leader high in relationhip and low in task, as well as one high in task and high in relationship, would tend to be democratic in leadership style.

Another attempt to study and improve leadership styles was made by Robert Blake and Jane Mouton,[9] who developed the managerial grid system (see Chapter 2). Basically, the same approach is used in the managerial grid except that the task is expressed as a concern for production and the relationship is expressed as a concern for people. The grid is numbered from one to nine on both axis. The managerial grid approach to leadership indicates that the most desirable leadership style

[9] Robert R. Blake and Jane Srygley Mouton, *The Managerial Grid* (Houston, Tex.: Gulf Publishing Co., 1965.

has equal concern for people and product, which would be a nine-nine leadership style. The managerial grid system has been highly developed, and Blake and Mouton offer training courses that vary in duration. The thrust of this approach is to redirect the leader's leadership style from a high concern for production or a high concern for people to a combination of equal concern for both production and people.

Is there a best style of leadership?

The greatest failure on the part of any organization is its inability to secure cooperation and understanding from its employees.[10] The success or failure of organizations can be attributed to a lack of or poor leadership more than any other single factor. The successful organization has one major attribute that sets it apart from unsuccessful organizations: dynamic and effective leadership.[11]

The obvious question to be asked is, "Is there a best style of leadership?" The research that we have just reviewed indicates that in any leadership situation, the two central concerns are for the task behavior and the relationship behavior exhibited by the leader. On the other hand, a solution of equal concern for both people and product does not appear to be the answer in every case. In the Norwegian factory, employees did not seem to have a high concern for participation; thus, in that situation, it was not a particularly desirable characteristic in leaders. It appears that every work situation is different. Although employees have some of the same characteristics in common, they are different and require different types of leadership.

It would appear that the next step would be to try to determine what effective leadership is. What must a leader do to be effective? As Drucker puts it "How do we make work productive and the worker achieving?"[12]

Rensis Likert, using the Michigan studies as a base, did additional research to discover the patterns leaders used in high-producing work situations.[13] He found that supervisors with the best record of performance focused their primary emphasis on human aspects of their subordinates' problems and endeavored to build effective work groups with high performance goals. These supervisors were employee-centered, or relationship-centered, in their leadership style. Likert found that supervisors who were job-centered, versus those who are employee-centered, had one—out of six groups—that were high-producing. In other words, five groups that were high-producing had employee-centered supervision, whereas only one had job-centered supervision. Contrarily, out of ten groups that were low-produc-

[10] Hersey and Blanchard, *Management of Organizational Behavior*, p. 1.

[11] Peter F. Drucker, *The Practice of Management* (New York: Harper and Row, 1954), p. 3.

[12] Peter F. Drucker, *Management: Tasks, Responsiblities, Practices* (New York: Harper and Row, 1974), p. 146.

[13] Rensis Likert, *New Patterns of Management* (New York, McGraw-Hill Book Co. 1961), pp. 7–9.

ing, seven had job-centered supervision whereas only three had employee-centered supervision. The results from this survey indicate that the employee-centered supervisors tended to get more production out of their work groups.

Another part of Likert's experiment attempted to determine whether close supervision versus general supervision produced better results in terms of productivity. Out of ten work groups that were high-producing, only one had close supervision whereas nine had general supervision. Contrarily eight of the low-producing groups had close supervision, whereas only four of the low-producing groups had general supervision. The findings from this part of Likert's research indicate that general supervision tended to produce higher production than close supervision.

A similar study in Nigeria showed almost exactly the opposite findings.[14] In Nigeria, the job-centered supervisors who provided close supervision got the best results in terms of production. This indicates that the cultural differences or customs of a different country might affect the style of leadership necessary for good production.

Other factors that might affect leadership styles are standard of living, educational level, and customs of the employees, reinforcing the concept that leadership is a function of the *leader*, the *employees*, and the *work situation*. If one element changes, most likely the leadership style will need to adjust accordingly. A foreman leading a work group digging trenches or doing some other form of manual labor would use a different style of leadership than the recreation superintendent working on a project with five recreation supervisors. It is obvious that the expectations, needs, personalities, and job situations are different in the two groups, thus resulting in the need for a different style of leadership. The studies and research done to date indicate that leadership style must change based on the people that are being led, the work being done, and the environment in which the leadership takes place.

Leadership Flexibility

A desire common to every leisure service manager, whatever level his or her work, is to know what the best leadership style is in given situations. Although examples can be offered that would indicate appropriate styles in given situations, it would be impossible to develop a formula or equation that would be appropriate for all occasions or circumstances. The leader must learn to analyze a situation, understand the needs, expectations, and desires of his employees, then modify his or her leadership style according to the particular circumstances.

The leadership style that a center director might exhibit in planning a program for a group of participants at a recreation center, while working with staff and leading them, might be very participative, with low emphasis on task and high concern for relationship. On the other hand, the same center director, in a situation concerning an emergency in the center (e.g., a fire or threat of a bombing), would

[14] Hersey and Blanchard, *Management of Organizational Behavior*, p. 79.

certainly exercise a different style of leadership. In the latter situation, the director would be very authoritarian. Obviously she doesn't have time to take a vote on whether the group feels it should exit from the building or not. A leader has to be able to change leadership style based on the circumstances and individuals she is leading. The greater the ability of the leader to change leadership style or behavior in a given situation, the more effective she will be in terms of reaching her own goals, organizational goals, and the employees' goals.

But if a leader keeps changing leadership style from day to day, those she leads will be confused. The leader needs to be consistent with employees so they know what to expect and how to deal with her. In terms of changing leadership style, it should be done only when the circumstances change or if the leader's current approach is not working.

Fred Fiedler devoted 15 years to researching leadership effectiveness.[15] His experiments were conducted on all sorts of work groups and individuals: basketball teams, fraternal groups, bomber crews, infantry squadrons, as well as many others. Fiedler felt that the leadership style, in combination with the situation, determines group performance. His model contained relationships between leadership style and the favorableness of the situation. He describes favorableness of the situation in terms of three factors:

1. The leader-member relationship, which is the most critical variable in determining the situation favorableness;
2. The degree of task structure, which is the second most important input into the favorableness of the situation; and
3. The leader's position power obtained through formal authority, which is the third most critical dimension in the situation.[16]

The situation would be favorable to the leader if all three dimensions were high; that is, if the leader is generally accepted by the followers, if the task is very structured, and if there is a great deal of authority and power formally attributed to the leader's position. At the opposite end of the spectrum, if the three dimensions are low, the situation is very unfavorable for the leader. Fiedler felt that the favorableness of the situation in combination with the leadership style determines the leader's effectiveness. Through his research efforts, Fiedler was able to discover that in very unfavorable as well as very favorable situations, task-directed or authoritarian leadership style is most effective. When the situation is only moderately favorable or moderately unfavorable, however, the human relations approach or the more democratic style of leadership is effective (see Figure 6.5).

The very favorable situation occurs when the leader has power, the task is well structured, and the group is ready to take directions and be told what to do. The

[15] Fred E. Fiedler, *A Theory of Leadership Effectiveness* (New York: McGraw-Hill Book Co., 1967).
[16] *Ibid.*, pp. 143–144.

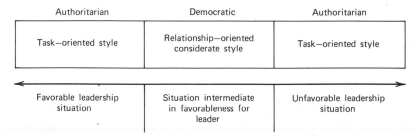

Figure 6.5. Leadership effectiveness based upon situation. (Paul Hersey, Kenneth H. Blanchard, *Management of Organizational Behavior: Utilizing Human Resources,* 2nd Edition, copyright © 1972, p. 81. Reprinted by permission of Prentice-Hall, Inc., Englewood Cliffs, N.J.)

example that Fiedler gives to make this point is as follows: "Consider the captain of an airliner in its final landing approach. We would hardly want him to turn to his crew for a discussion of how to land the airplane."[17] The example that Fiedler gives for an unfavorable situation concerns a disliked chairman of a volunteer committee which is asked to plan an office picnic on a beautiful Sunday. If the leader asks too many questions about what the group ought to do or how he should proceed, he is likely to be told "we ought to all go home."[18] Figure 6.5 shows the outcome of Fiedler's favorableness of the situation model, which should help the student of leadership better understand that the style of leadership she uses is based on a number of factors: situations or circumstances in which she finds herself, the task at hand, and the group of individuals she must lead.

William J. Reddin devoted an entire book to describing managerial effectiveness.[19] His theory is that there is no single management style which is effective in all situations. Reddin's theory deals with task orientation and relationship orientation of employees, but he adds a third dimension: effectiveness. Effectiveness as described by Reddin is the extent to which the manager achieves the output requirements of his position. Effectiveness of the manager is found in his ability to change his behavior or management leadership style according to the needs and dictates of the situation and the employees that he supervises. Reddin combines into the situational elements both the followers and the situation itself; accordingly, there are five standard elements:

1. The organization;
2. The technology that the leader has to deal with (in the case of leisure services it would be the processes used in the creation and distribution of services, one

---

[17] *Ibid.,* p. 147.

[18] *Ibid.,* p. 147.

[19] William J. Reddin, *Managerial Effectiveness* (McGraw-Hill Book Co., 1970).

approach would be the prescriptive approach to program development, and the other would be the cafeteria approach to program development);
3. One's superior;
4. One's co-workers; and
5. One's subordinates.[20]

Reddin believes that an individual can increase his effectiveness by changing his management or leadership style to meet the demands of the given situation. He indicates that there are three basic skills which a leader must possess to be effective:

1. His sensitivity to the situation, which involves the manager's ability to accurately perceive a given situation;
2. His leadership flexibility, which involves the leader's ability to change his style based on a given situation; and
3. His situational management skill, which is his ability to overcome resistance to change.[21]

The greater the manager's ability to deal with these three elements and to change or stylize leadership appropriately, the more effective he will be. (See page 46 for a description of Reddin's model.)

Leadership Effectiveness for Leisure Services

In trying to determine the elements of leadership effectiveness, as well as trying to give the prospective leisure service manager insight into how she or he might become more effective, many theories have been presented. It becomes obvious that no leader can be all things in every situation. Obviously, some leaders are going to be more effective in one situation than another, and even though they can change their leadership style they may not be effective all the time.

Drucker describes four distinct leadership roles. He says, "Top management tasks require at least four different kinds of human beings: the 'thought man,' the 'action man,' the 'people man,' and the 'front man.' Yet these four temperaments are almost never found in one person." "The failure to understand these characteristics is the main reason why top management tasks are so often done poorly or not done at all."[22]

The leader, whether a member of top management or at a lower level, has to have certain skills besides those of leadership, for example planning skills. It is often her responsibility to determine the goals for her work unit as well as to apply creative thinking in order to find better ways to accomplish her work. She has to be

---

[20] *Ibid.*, p. 61.
[21] *Ibid.*, p. 135.
[22] Drucker, *Management: Tasks, Responsibilities, Practices*, pp. 616–617.

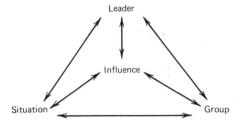

Leader

Influence

Situation   Group

Figure 6.6. The influence system model of leadership. (Edwin P. Hollander and James W. Julian, "Contemporary Trends in the Analysis of Leadership Processes," *Psychological Bulletin,* Vol. 19, May, 1969, p. 390.)

able to communicate with fellow employees. She has to have ability in the area of decision-making and problem-solving, which will be dealt with in the next chapter. She has to have the ability to delegate work and authority for the jobs that must be carried out when she is not present. She has to have the ability to motivate individuals who work for her to accomplish the goals and objectives of the organization. She has to have the ability to evaluate and appraise the work that has been done in terms of whether the goals and objectives were accomplished effectively and efficiently within the organization. All these qualities are not found in any one individual. The manager has to decide what her strengths and weaknesses are and capitalize on her strengths. She needs to find subordinates who can complement her where she is weak to insure an organization that is efficient and productive.

One of the factors that affect leadership is the power of the manager. Basically, there are two sources of power that a manager may have in carrying out his responsibilities. The first is "position power," which can be described as the authority that the manager receives from the organization by virtue of his position. The second is "personal power," which can be called "influence; the manager derives personal power from his followers and it is given to him. The power concept can be described as the leader's ability to influence or initiate the behavior in others. The leader can have full position power or authority from the organization, as well as personal power or influence, because of his acceptance by, and admiration of, the people he leads. In some instances, it is desirable to have both position power and personal power. Most people would prefer to have personal power and would consider it the more important.

The best one-word definition of leadership is "influence." The influence system model of leadership developed by Edwin Hollander and James Julian, is shown in Figure 6.6. This approach reinforces to some extent the theory that influence, or ability of the leader to get the job done, is also affected by the situation and the group who gives the leader personal power.[23]

Each element affects every other element, and all affect influence. In today's organization, there is a great shift away from position power and greater increase

---

[23] Edwin P. Hollander and James W. Julian, "Contemporary Trends in the Analysis of Leadership Processes," *Psychological Bulletin*, Vol 71, No. 5, May 1969, p. 390.

in personal power. The manager of today has to be able to influence his employees and has less and less opportunity to control them by his position power. This shift is a result of many circumstances: the effects of unions, civil rights, legislation, and changes in emphasis in government to more power to the citizenry. Because more employees today are more intelligent and their needs have changed, the possibility of loss of job or other disciplinary action are no longer motivating.

Fiedler's example of the airline pilot landing the airplane and the volunteer chairman also demonstrate a manager's influence. The pilot has a great deal of personal and position power because the passengers have faith in him and the airline has commissioned him as a pilot; the passengers respect and look to the pilot for leadership ability in landing the airplane. A chairman of a volunteer committee, however, has little personal power and absolutely no position power. If the group does not accept her decisions or leadership, there is not much she can do about it.

Power in organizations is shifting, and in organizations of the future, power will come from the bottom of the organization; it will be based on a manager's ability to lead and generate influence. There are examples where leadership shifts from time to time, based on the influence, technical knowledge, or skill that individuals have which best fit the situation at a particular time. Illustrating this is the example of a group of people who are lost in the middle of the desert. At one point, leadership is placed in a military man who has skills in desert training. The group would place leadership in him because they know he has the skills to get them out of the desert safely. Later, when most of the individuals become sick and need medical attention, the leadership may shift to a doctor in the group. Leadership might shift a third time, when all hope is gone and the group is unable to go any further; the leadership may shift to an individual who is trained in the ministry. In this example, the leadership shifted based on the groups' needs.

Determining the Right Style of Leadership

Hersey and Blanchard in *Management of Organizational Behavior*, attempted to integrate a number of theories of leadership with what is known about the needs of employees in an effort to help the student of leadership determine a style of leadership appropriate for a given situation. They called this "the life-cycle theory of leadership."[24] The idea was to determine the right blend of task behavior and relationship behavior on the part of the leader in a given situation with a given group of employees. To help the leader determine the right blend of behavior, Hersey and Blanchard overlayed different motivation, growth, and personality development characteristics on The Ohio State Leadership Quadrant matrix, like the one shown in Figure 6.7.

Fillmore H. Sanford, in *Authoritarianism and Leadership*, indicated that there is some justification for regarding the followers as the most critical factor in any

---

[24] Hersey and Blanchard, *Management of Organizational Behavior*, pp. 134–135.

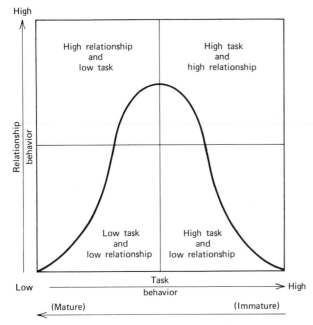

Figure 6.7. Life-cycle theory of leadership. (Paul Hersey, Kenneth H. Blanchard, *Management of Organizational Behavior: Utilizing Human Resources,* 2nd Edition, copyright © 1972, p. 135. Reprinted by permission of Prentice-Hall, Inc., Englewood Cliffs, N.J.)

leadership event. The people who carry out the various tasks in an organization are vital because, individually or as a group, they either accept or reject the leadership that is given to them or actually determine whatever personal power the leader may have.[25]

Hersey and Blanchard felt that a curvilinear relationship would best indicate the style of leadership appropriate for the level of maturity of the followers. If Sanford's theory—that the followers are the most vital factor in any leadership event—is correct, then the style of leadership will be determined by the maturity and motivational level of the followers.

Argyris's immaturity-maturity continuum can be overlaid on the matrix to help the leader determine proper leadership style based on the maturity level of the followers (see Figure 6.8). Argyris' theory indicates that as a person matures, she moves from a passive state to an increasingly active state; from dependency on

[25] Fillmore H. Sanford, *Authoritarianism and Leadership* (Philadelphia: Institute for Research in Human Relations, 1950).

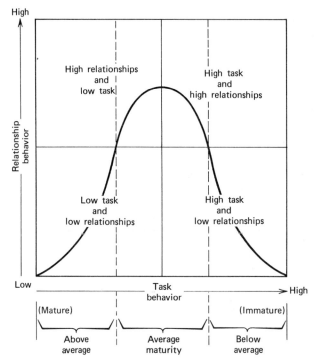

Figure 6.8. Life-cycle theory with Argyris' maturity continuum theories added. (Paul Hersey, Kenneth H. Blanchard, *Management of Organizational Behavior: Utilizing Human Resources,* 2nd Edition, copyright © 1972, p. 142. Reprinted by permission of Prentice-Hall, Inc., Englewood Cliffs, N.J.)

others to relative independence; from behaving in a few ways to being capable of behaving in many ways; from a short time perspective to a long time perspective; and from a subordinate position to an equal or superordinate position (see Chapter 3 for discussion of the Argyris theory.)

The life cycle theory suggests that, as an employee progresses from a state of immaturity to a state of maturity, the leader's behavior should move:

1. through high task, low relationship behavior;
2. to high task, high relationship behavior;
3. to high relationship, low task behavior; and
4. to low task, low relationship behavior.

The more mature a follower or employee may be, the less task behavior needed by the leader. In fact, the extremely mature person may need no leadership at all.

Further expanding the life cycle model, Maslow's hierarchy of needs was superimposed on the matrix. By placing physiological, safety, social, esteem, and self-actualization needs on the life-cycle curvilinear line, Maslow's theory tends to follow the maturity theory. The leader who can determine what level the employee is at, in the hierarchy of need, as it relates to Maslow's theory, can determine—by looking at the matrix—the proper blend of task and relationship behavior when leading the employee (see Figure 6.9).

The most appropriate leadership style for an employee whose primary needs are in the physiological or safety area would be one of high task, low relationship. An example of such an employee in the leisure service field might be an individual who has only a grade-school education and is doing manual labor; his needs are basically in the safety and physiological area, he would look for direction from his supervisor, and he would tend to be very dependent. An individual of average maturity who is approaching the social and esteem level of need development would probably respond best to leadership in the area of high task and high relationship, or high relationship and low task, depending on the maturity and develop-

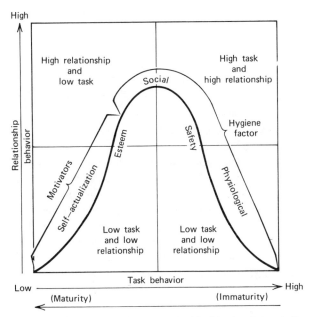

Figure 6.9. Life-cycle theory with Maslow's and Herzberg's theories added. (Paul Hersey, Kenneth H. Blanchard, *Management of Organizational Behavior: Utilizing Human Resources,* 2nd Edition, copyright © 1972, p. 174. Reprinted by permission of Prentice-Hall, Inc., Englewood Cliffs, N.J.)

ment level of her needs. Examples of such individuals working in the leisure service field might be center directors, recreation supervisors, or mid-management park and recreaction professionals. Progressing to an even higher maturity level, an individual whose needs are in the area of self-actualization would function best with low relationship and low task leadership, or no leadership at all. An individual at this level of maturity might be a scientist, researcher, or someone who works independently, is highly creative, and needs no direction. An employee of this type prefers to come and go as he wants and needs little external motivation to perform his task.

Herzberg's theory of motivation was overlayed on the matrix and seemed to further support the life-cycle theory of leadership. As Figure 6.9 shows, an employee who is immature and whose needs are in the physiological and/or safety area, and who is concerned with hygiene factors, would probably respond best to authoritarian leadership—high task and low relationship. An employee who is of average maturity, whose needs are mostly social, who is little concerned with hygiene factors, and who becomes more concerned with the motivators would probably respond best to democratic leadership—high relationship, medium task. An employee of above average maturity, whose needs are mostly esteem and self-actualization, who has little if no concern for hygiene factors, and who is self-motivated will probably respond best to very little leadership—low task, low relationship.

The life-cycle theory of leadership is not an absolute panacea for determining leadership style, but it does give the manager a starting point. The other factor that affects leadership style is the specific situation: The task to be accomplished, the time available, whether it is an emergency or not, as well as other environmental factors, affect leadership style.

Although the life-cycle approach to determining leadership style is not foolproof, it does give the leader some assistance in knowing where to start. After an initial attempt at one leadership style, if it is not appropriate, the leader may adjust his or her task or relationship as needed until the desired results are achieved. As the group being led matures and shows responsibility, the leadership style also changes. As Reddin indicated, the leader must have the sensitivity to perceive the situation, leadership flexibility, and leadership skill to overcome resistance to change. All of this requires good judgment and intelligence on the part of the leader.

COMMUNICATIONS

In previous chapters, a number of characteristics of individuals have been discussed to help managers understand their employees better. It has been pointed out that, to make an employee want to work, there is certain information about him or her that a manager needs to know. In Chapter 3, we dealt with understanding individual and human needs, the idea being that if we recognized and understood the needs of an individual we stood a better chance of providing an environment in which he or she could meet those needs. In Chapter 4, we looked into the various components of motivation; again the attempt was made to understand the various incentives and other motivational elements that would release work capacity to accomplish the goals and objectives of the organization. So far, in this chapter, we have dealt with leadership. We earlier defined leadership as the process of influencing the activities of an individual or a group in an effort toward common goal achievement in any given situation.

With these concepts in mind—understanding the employees' needs, the process of motivation, and the techniques of leadership—we are now armed with the skills necessary to put the employees to work; this will be accomplished through a process known as "communications." Communication is the means by which organized activity is unified. It is the process by which people are linked together in the organization to achieve a central purpose. Group activity would be impossible without information transfer because without it, coordination and change cannot be effected.[26]

In the past 30 years, a great deal of attention has been given to the subject of communications from the standpoint of what it is, how it takes place, what some of the barriers are, and how one is assured of good communications. It would seem obvious that the manager or leader would have the greatest responsibility for good communication. But no matter how well he may communicate with his employees, if for any reason they do not communicate back to him, the effectiveness of the organization is hampered. The purpose of communication in any organization is to affect the behavior of the employees in order to influence action in the accomplishment of organizational goals and objectives.

In a public leisure service organization, the director of the Parks and Recreation Department communicates the goals of the organization to the various employees who, in turn, transform these goals into programs. But it is equally important that the employees communicate back to the director, if the desired goals and programs are to be achieved. In addition, the employee has to relay information to the director from participants or consumers regarding the types of activities they are interested in, in order to meet their leisure needs. To accomplish this, there must be a great deal of exchange of information through the process of communication. Obviously, the larger the organization, the more complex communication becomes due to the various levels of organization and the greater number of people involved in the communication process.

Communication takes many forms: It can be written or verbal; it can be in the form of memorandums, notices on bulletin boards, computer printouts, and so on.

[26] Harold Koontz and Cyril O'Donnell, *Principles of Management*, fifth edition (New York: McGraw-Hill Book Co., 1972), pp. 536–537.

Communication exchanges information upward, downward, and laterally through the organization. Probably more than any other single factor, communication (or a failure to communicate) creates the greatest problems for the leisure service agency. Luthans, in *Organizational Behavior*, states that about 70 percent of an active human being's life, and a higher proportion (about 90%) of a typical manager's time, is spent communicating.[27]

The first step in the process of communications is to determine what information is needed, who it needs to be shared with, and what the best process of exchanging this information is. The manager of the leisure service agency must start with, "What is it that I need to know to perform my job well? What information do I need to make the decisions that are necessary to put the organization into operation? What do I need to know from the policy-making board in terms of the policies they formulate?" There must be a communications system and a network to acquire this information.

Second, there must be an information system to transmit the information, interpret it, retain it, and recall it as needed. To assure good communication, the manager has to provide telephones, a filing system, a computer program when appropriate, and various other techniques. Communications must be worked on constantly to be improved and to assure that it is meeting the needs of the organization. In addition, it must be adjusted according to the scope, size, and other peculiarities of the organization, to meet its needs effectively.

Communication Flow

There are three directions in which communications flow: downward, laterally, and upward. The formal organizational structure generally concerns itself with downward communications.

Downward Communications

Daniel Katz and Robert Kahn, in *The Social Psychology of Organizations*, describe five points, or goals, of downward communications:

1. To give specific task direction about job instructions;
2. To give information about organizational procedures and practices;
3. To provide information about the rationale of the job;
4. To give subordinates feedback regarding their performance; and
5. To provide ideological-type information to facilitate the indoctrination of goals.[28]

---

[27] Fred Luthans, *Organizational Behavior* (New York: McGraw-Hill Book Co., 1973), p. 234.

[28] Daniel Katz and Robert L. Kahn, *The Social Psychology of Organizations* (New York: John Wiley and Sons, 1966), p. 239.

In most organizations, more emphasis has been placed on the first two goals and the last three have been neglected. If we are to move away from the authoritarian type of leadership to a more participative type of leadership, we will have to give more attention to the last three goals. For example, if employees know the reasons for their assignments, this will often stimulate them to carry out their jobs more effectively. If they understand how their jobs relate to other jobs in the organization, they are more likely to identify with organizational goals.

In some organizations, there is not enough downward communication, but more often it is the case that there is too much downward communication. Communications should be accurate and easily understood by the individuals who carry out the assignments, so they can meet their goals and the organization's goals. Not only can there be a problem with too much or too little downward communication, but other factors—such as misinterpretation, distortion, and mistrust—enter the picture. Ralph Nichols in "Listening Is Good Business," indicates that there is a tremendous loss of information. In a study he conducted, 37 percent of the communication was lost between the board of directors and the vice president. General supervisors accurately received 56 percent, plant managers received 40 percent, and the general foreman received only 30 percent of what had been transmitted downward to them. An average of only 20 percent of the communications sent downward through five levels of management finally reached the workers.[29]

Lateral Communications

In every organization a need exists for lateral communication—communications among various work units that depend on and cooperate with each other in the carrying out of the goals and objectives of the organization. The primary purpose of lateral communications is for cooperation and coordination of effort, which becomes extremely important the larger an organization becomes. If it were not for lateral communications, the whole process would be slowed down to a point where the modern organization would not be able to function effectively. Without lateral communication, communication could come only through the chain of command; it would have to start with the top manager in the organization and trickle down (see Figure 6.10).

Lateral communications can be facilitated or impaired depending on the relationships of the individuals communicating. In most instances, communication takes place among employees of equal status or on the same level. In many cases, communications at a lateral level are more comfortable because the individuals communicating feel they are equal and have mutual trust in each other. On the other hand, individuals who do not trust each other slow down or totally fail to use

[29] Ralph G. Nichols, "Listening Is Good Business," *Management of Personnel Quarterly*, Vol 2, No. 2, Winter, 1962, p. 4.

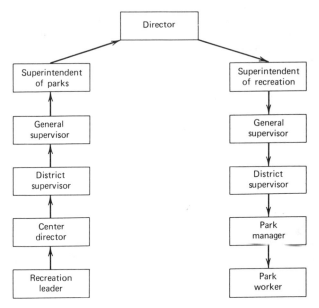

Figure 6.10. The need for lateral communication. This request for the ball field to be prepared by the recreation leader for a softball game at 7:00 P.M. instead of 9:00 P.M. would have to go through 11 individuals before the park worker who will do the work gets the message, if the chain of command were followed.

lateral communication. In many instances, lateral communications are outside the formal structure of the organization and take place in the informal structure. In any case, the competent manager is aware of the need for lateral communication and encourages this process wherever possible, particularly where it increases the effectiveness of the organization. As indicated earlier, in larger organizations, lateral communications are necessary in carrying out the functions of the organizations.

Upward Communications

Of the three types of communication, upward communication is probably the most neglected and abused. In most organizations, downward communications overwhelms upward communications. It was indicated earlier that downward communications are directive, order-giving, and instructional; upward communications are generally nondirective. Upward communications enable top management to find out what is going on in the organization and the effect of its leadership. In the example listed in Chapter 4, employees were asked to rank which of 14 items concerning their work was most important to them. The managers were also asked to rank in priority what they felt the employees wanted out of their work. There was a great deal of difference between what the employees wanted and what the manager thought these employees wanted; this indicates a real lack of upward communication. Likewise, in many other instances in any organization (particularly in a leisure service organization, where the services delivered to the public should be geared to the needs and desires of the participants), there is no way to obtain this information except through upward communication. The recreation leader or instructor at the lowest level of the organization is the person who is in contact with the participant and who is in the best position to know their needs and desires.

There are various methods by which the manager can encourage and facilitate communication upward. One is for the manager to visit facilities, programs, and activities to talk with the various participants and recreation leaders. He can give the employees an opportunity to express their concerns and verbalize the problems they are facing in carrying out their assignment. Although this can be done by the immediate supervisor, oftentimes she refuses or forgets to share information with the director of the department. In other cases, a supervisor may block information that she feels her superior does not want to know.

Another method which encourages upward communication is that of public hearings with citizen groups related to planning new facilities or programs prior to the final decisions being made. This gives the manager an opportunity to get feedback in an upward way and to improve the effectiveness of the organization. The director of parks and recreation and the superintendent of parks can also meet with various work crews on a rotating basis, having lunch or coffee with them, and informally discussing concerns they may have or sharing information of an organizational nature. If done regularly, this type of informal meeting is the greatest opportunity for upward communications on a firsthand basis. It gives the manager an opportunity to share with employees information about the organization in general or information that is relevant to them in carrying out their assignments.

The "open door" policy provides employees with the opportunity to discuss concerns and ideas they have about the organization with their superior. It is a continuous invitation for them to visit and talk with the manager, thus providing an opportunity for upward communications. In actual practice, however, not many individuals take advantage of an open-door policy, and in many instances it is not a particularly valid method to achieve upward communications.

Interviewing or utilizing questionnaires to gain information about participants or employees relative to a number of issues, procedures, programs, and activities within the department is another way for a manager to get upward communications. Obviously, to get accurate information, the questionnaires or interviews must provide for confidentiality as well as assure a good cross section of individuals and questions to obtain accuracy. This method of obtaining information probably assures more accuracy than any other of the methods of upward communication and will be discussed further in the next chapter.

Another way to get upward communications is to provide individuals at all levels of the organization an opportunity to share in decision-making relative to matters that affect them. This can be accomplished on either a formal or an informal basis. Individuals can also be represented and express their feelings through committees or other group processes. Other opportunities, such as a suggestion box, employee suggestion award programs (where employees are given awards for submitting good ideas in writing) and anonymous questions to the management also provide for upward communications.

But more than anything else, a desire for upward communications has to be sincere. Employees who are willing to provide information, thoughts, suggestions, and ideas have to be convinced that this input is really wanted and that ideas which are not popular, are contrary, or are in opposition to higher-level personnel will not result in retaliatory action. Upward communications supplies various types of information of a personal nature about ideas, attitudes, and performance. It provides top management with a better opportunity to make decisions and evaluate effectiveness of the organization. For upward communications to be effective, those receiving the information have to become good listeners and learn how to deal with the information confidentially and effectively so that those who have given the information fell their efforts and energies have been well spent.

As stated earlier, communications downward are generally commands, instructions and directions. A manager cannot communicate downward effectively unless she understands her employees, their ideas, thoughts, and what will motivate them. This can be accomplished only by upward communications from employees who believe that top management is interested and willing to listen.

Katz and Kahn list seven types of information a manager can obtain from employees through upward communication:

1. What the person has done;
2. What those under him have done;
3. What his peers have done;
4. What he thinks needs to be done;
5. What his problems are;
6. What the problems of the unit are; and
7. What matters of organizational practice and policy need to be reviewed.[30]

Communication Is Perception

Drucker, in *Management Tasks, Responsibilities, Practices*, presents a unique concept about the communication process.[31] He indicates that it is the recipient who communicates. The communicator, the person who talks, does not communicate;

---

[30] Kats and Kahn, *Social Psychology*, p. 245.
[31] Peter F. Drucker, Management: Tasks, Responsibilities and Practices (New York: Harper and Row, 1973).

he makes sounds. Unless there is someone who hears and understands, there is no communication; there is only noise. The communicator speaks or writes, but does not communicate. He cannot communicate; he can only make it possible or impossible for a receiver to perceive. Drucker indicates that perception of communication does not necessarily deal with logic, but, rather, experiences, and this is what gives the receiver the ability to *understand* a communication. The way something is said, the facial expressions of the sender, the environment—all these affect how a person perceives a message. An individual can perceive only what he is capable of perceiving, what he is capable of comprehending and understanding. It is impossible for an individual to understand a complicated mathematical formula if he has not had algebra or a mathematical background, even though the words and the explanation may be extremely thorough, precise, and fitting. In communicating with another individual, whether employee or participant, the first concern should be that the communication is within the recipient's range of perception. Can he really perceive it?

The second observation Drucker makes about communications is that *communications involve expectations*. He indicates that we generally perceive what we expect to perceive. Individuals tend to make presented thoughts and ideas fit into frames of reference with which they are familiar. They tend to resist change when the situation is not comfortable to them. Before managers communicate they should try to understand the individual with whom they are going to communicate. They should understand his or her attitudes, prejudices, and feelings. Once they understand these things about the individual in terms of what he or she expects, they are in a better position to communicate effectively.

Drucker's third point is that *communication makes demands*. Communication generally asks for some form of change—changes in behavior, attitude, feelings, and so on. People generally resist and do not like change. Therefore communications themselves are suspect. People tend to block out communications in many instances because of these reasonings. If the communication does make demands that require change or action, it will be more effective if it meets the receiver's needs, values, and attitudes. If the communication meets the needs of the receiver, it is effective; but if it doesn't fit, it may not be received at all.

Drucker, in presenting these concepts, was attempting to indicate that downward communication will work only after upward communication has successfully been established. Upward communication focuses on matters and details that both the receiver and the person communicating have in common. Upward communication tends to encourage confidence, respect, and trust.

Communication Model

The communication model shown in Figure 6.11 will help the reader visualize the process of communication as it takes place. At the left side of the diagram is an

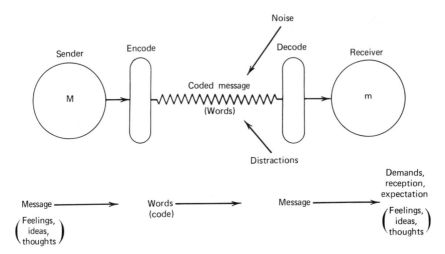

Figure 6.11. Communication model.

individual ("M") sending a message to another person. The sender has some message she wants to send to another person, the receiver ("m"). The message is some feeling, idea, or thought she has about something or someone. The sender has no way of communicating this idea, feeling, or thought directly; therefore, she must encode these feelings, ideas, and thoughts into words. The encoding takes place as the sender transforms these feelings ideas, or thoughts into words, while she then speaks. They are transmitted in the form of sound waves directed toward the receiver; or, in the case of a written message, the thoughts are encoded onto a piece of paper. The coded message then travels toward the receiver. The effectiveness of the sender of the message is determined by her choice of words, vocabulary, clarity of speech, facial expressions, as well as other factors.

In the process of the transmission, the message has interference in the form of noise and other distractions, which affects clarity. The receiver then decodes the message as it enters his ears and is transmitted to his brain in terms of feelings, thoughts, and ideas. Unfortunately, in the process, many things can go wrong. The sender may not accurately encode her feelings, thoughts, or ideas into proper words, thus conveying the wrong message. The noise level in transmission may distort the message to the point that it cannot be received adequately. Or, the decoding by the receiver can be incorrect as it is translated in his mind in the communication process. The receiver's perception and expectations as well as the demand that the message will make on him will affect the communication.

The point of the diagram is to depict visually the problems in the act of communicating, to point out the various elements that affect the communication process. At any step—the thought process of the sender, encoding, noise, the decoding and the thought process that takes place when entering the mind of the receiver—something can go wrong to the extent that the message sent may not be received accurately, if received at all.

Problems in Communicating

To this point, we have discussed some of the reasons for communications within an organization. Now let us examine some of the problems of communication. To communicate, the first thing that must be done is to prepare or *get ready to communicate*. Too often, this facet of communication is taken for granted. One has only to stop and listen to a few people talk or communicate and it becomes evident that they have not thought much about what they were going to say before they started talking. To communicate, a person must have a clear objective in mind. He should think through what he wants to say and select the proper words before beginning to communicate. Only after this has been done is a person really ready to communicate.

Another problem with communicating is the various *barriers that affect the communications process.*[32] There is probably no such thing as a perfect communication. On the other hand, if the sender of the message is to communicate, he must be aware of the perception and expectations of the person receiving the message; he must also be aware that a communication makes demands on the receiver. One of the first problems in terms of barriers to communications is that of a poorly expressed message. Poorly chosen words and phrases, omissions, poor organization of thoughts and ideas, bad sentence structure, vocabulary problems, slang words, words with double meanings—all contribute to misunderstanding and poor communication. Not only can there be a problem in choosing proper words when communicating, there is also the *problem when translating a message* to supervisors, peers, and subordinates in an organization into language they will understand. The person originating the message may know very well in her mind what it is she wants to say and may choose proper words and communicate the message properly. But if the receiver translates the message improperly, the message is incorrectly passed on.

The *loss of meaning of a message in the transmission* also affects the communication process. In large organizations that have three or four levels of management, communications problems can develop as the message is transmitted from one level to the next. A simple matter of a word being changed, left out, or added can drastically change the intent of the original message. Reflecting on Nichols' findings, 37 percent of the message was lost in the first transmission and 30 percent was lost in the last level of transmission; only 20 percent of the original communication was received at the level where a worker was to implement a particular

[32] Koontz and O'Donnell, *Principles of Management*, pp. 543–546.

program. In a larger organization with even more levels, the problem is complicated even further.

Lack of attention by the person receiving the message can also create a problem in communications. The individual may have his mind on something else, be it a personal problem or a golf game planned for that afternoon. Whatever the case, if the receiver is not listening attentively, much communication can be lost. Personal problems of the receiver certainly affect the communication. A person who is sick, or experiencing emotional stress would not be in a position to receive a communication as clearly as might be necessary. The person sending the message must be aware of what the receiver's problems are before he can communicate with him adequately.

Another problem area is *distrust of the communicator.* Employees who distrust their manager, who are suspicious or have reason to question her integrity, would possibly question her communications.

Last, and probably the largest barrier to communications is a *failure to com municate at all.* Often in an organization, communicaitons from a top-level manager to the next level are clear and distinct. However, if the next-level manager fails to relay the communication, for whatever reason, the communication chain is broken and no communication takes place. On the other hand, there would seem to be times in an organization when it would be appropriate not to communicate certain information, particularly if the information is not meaningful or useful to the organization or is a form of gossip or exaggeration. In any case, the person doing the communicating has to be aware of the various barriers of communication and the problems with communicating so he or she can communicate as effectively as possible.

Nonverbal Communication

Nonverbal communication also plays an important part in the whole process of communicating. Commonly referred to as "body talk" or "body language," a great deal of the communication process is affected by it. How an individual raises and lowers his voice could indicate to the receiver how he may feel about a given subject. The communicator's emotion or facial expressions often conveys as much meaning as the words themselves. Other clues, such as tone, vocal quality, or becoming angry and having her face turn red, indicate some form of emotion on the part of the sender even more strongly than the words.

One's eye attention in the communication process tells how a person may feel about a particular item or matter. The hand, either trembling or shaking, may indicate a person's concern or fear. Nervous twitches can indicate how a person is relating to a given subject. All in all, as receivers, we learn to detect the meaning of various clues given in nonverbal communications.

Effective Communication

The concepts we will discuss now can be useful in establishing good communications. They direct the communicator's or sender's attention to those factors that will enable the receiver to comprehend the information correctly in a manner that will permit him to carry out and meet the goals and objectives of the organization.

Communication Clarity

The sender's first concern in the communication process is that the words he uses to express his thoughts, ideas, and feelings truly represent what he wants to convey as he translates them into words. It is equally important that the message be expressed and transmitted so that the receiver will comprehend those thoughts, feelings and ideas in a like manner. One method of testing this is for the sender to ask the person who receives the message to repeat it back so the sender can determine if anything was lost in the communication process. But if the sender asks the receiver to repeat the message after every communication, there will be a question of confidence and trust between the sender and receiver. What the sender can do is to test his communications from time to time to make sure he is putting them in terms (words and expressions) that are understood by the receiver.

It is the responsibility of the person sending the message to be accurate, honest, and sincere in his message. He must choose the proper words and transmit his message accurately while being aware of the perceptions, emotions, and feelings of the receiver. No matter how much the sender intends his message to be clear, its effectiveness is determined by the receiver and how he perceives it. The communicator who is constantly aware of the clarity principle is taking a step in the right direction by constantly checking out whether his messages are being received as he intended them.

Communication Integrity

The purpose of communication within an organization is to gain understanding and support of employees who carry out organizational work to attain goals and objectives. The integrity of the organization depends on the support given it by its various employees and managers. Although it is extremely important that the employees at the lowest level of the organization receive communications clearly and accurately, it is equally important that the individuals and managers in between the top and the bottom not be left out of the communication process. In order to maintain organizational integrity, the communication process should extend throughout the organization without bypassing or neglecting anyone.

Communication by the Informal Organization

Although many of the communications that are carried through the organization are carried through the formal organization, the effective manager also uses the informal organization to supplement communications channels. The informal organization meets many employee needs and is a strong force in most organizations; it exists because the formal organization is not meeting the needs of individuals. The competent manager, although utilizing the formal organization, also utilizes the informal organization to transmit communications whenever possible.

Congruent Communications

Congruent communication involves a sender's attempt to transmit an effectively received message. The sender also attempts to determine in every way possible whether her message has been received as she intended it. This involves taking risks, but it can result in building real bridges between people as they communicate. Some of the principles of congruent communications are the following:

1. For the sender, a desire to make a statement; for the receiver, a willingness to hear the message. The words you send in your message must be in agreement with your feelings, thoughts, and ideas. To send a congruent message, it is necessary that you have an adequate vocabulary to express your feelings, thoughts, and ideas. Many times we do not really communicate in terms of how we actually feel because we have learned to communicate how we think people want us to feel. We tend to communicate what we think people want to hear rather than being honest with our feelings as we communicate. How long has it been since you said to one of your subordinates, "I am frustrated, confused, embarrassed, pleased, thrilled, excited, delighted, eager, enthusiastic, touched, uninspired, worried, depressed, disgusted, afraid, or even nervous"? Too often, we do not really know what our true feelings are. As you practice sending congruent messages, you will learn more about yourself and your relationships with others.
2. For the sender, the selection of words that express his intent and the use of nonverbal clues—such as posture, facial expression, tone of voice—that complement the words; for the receiver, comprehension of the words and awareness of the nonverbal communications being received. As mentioned earlier, body talk (or body language) often does not express the same meaning as the words. Frequently, body language is more honest and sincere, thus confusing the receiver. An attempt should be made to make both the expressed words and the nonverbal communication the same.
3. For the receiver, the responsibility for acknowledging and checking out the messages received; for the sender, the responsibility for checking out whether the receiver is receiving the message the way it is intended. The sender can ask the receiver to repeat what he thought he heard; the receiver can periodically indicate that he understands so the sender is aware that the message is being received the way it was intended.

4. For the sender, the use of "I" statements in sending messages; for the receiver, the use of "I" statements in reacting to the messages heard. The intent is to make sure that the feelings or ideas expressed by the sender are her own and that she is not hiding behind a group, a boss, or someone else. When we pass along orders or instructions to subordinates that we want carried out, we tend to use expressions like "Well, we have to get this done" or "The boss said. . . ." The "I" statement would be "I would like to get this done," thereby not conveying a feeling that the direction may not really be your own. Every attempt should be made to make statements in terms of "I" so the receiver can really know that these are your honest, sincere feelings. Likewise, the receiver should respond how he feels in terms of "I" statements.[33]

Congruent message-sending tends to bring more honesty and sincerity to communications and can be developed with practice. The more trust and confidence one can convey in her communications, the more effective and productive she will be as a manager.

Listening

One of the hardest parts of communication is that of listening; many organizations have problems with upward communications, which indicates that people are not listening. Most managers are more anxious to give directions downward than they are to hear from their subordinates the concerns, problems, and information they have. A good communicator is also a good listener. A good manager is just as concerned about integrity, honesty, and clarity in the listening process as he is in the sending process. The same procedures and guidelines should be followed when listening as when communicating. The listener needs to check out that what he heard is what the sender intended to say. He has to be attentive, listen enthusiastically, and concentrate on listening—not trying to determine what he himself is going to say next.

Instead of listening, a lot of people begin thinking ahead about how they are going to respond, what they are going to say. Egotistical communicators are more concerned with their communicating than with their listening. This definitely interferes with the listening process. To listen properly, the listener must give her undivided attention to what the other person is saying. She must try to keep her mind clear of all other thoughts, really concentrating on the listening process. An employee who comes to a manager or supervisor with a problem wants the manager or supervisor to listen to her and can quickly tell how sincere the listener is. Body language is also a factor in listening. If, in listening, you show great expression of concern, dismay, or disapproval, you will inhibit the person convey-

---

[33] Based on a presentation by Martin Rogers at the Parks and Recreation Administrators Institute (Asilomar Conference Grounds, Pacific Grove, Calif., November 10–15, 1974.

ing the information. As important as it is to be a good sender of messages, the good communicator should also practice being a good listener.

Feedback

Feedback is communication with a person (or group) which gives that person (or group) information about how he is affecting others. As in a guided missile system, feedback helps an individual keep her behavior on target and, thus, better achieve her goals and objectives. Some of the criteria for the use of feedback are the following:

1. It should be descriptive rather than evaluative. In dealing with an employee, the supervisor might use a statement such as, "Bob, that was a dumb thing to do." That is being evaluative. The supervisor is telling Bob he is dumb; more appropriately, the supervisor could say, "Bob, by being more careful in digging, you would not have cut the telephone line." Being descriptive, the supervisor has indicated to Bob what he has done or should not have done. He is giving Bob his reaction, which leaves Bob free to use the information he gets from the supervisor as he sees fit. The supervisor has avoided evaluative language, reducing the need for the individual to be defensive.

2. It is specific rather than general. To tell a supervisor that he is "dominating" probably will not be as useful as it would be to tell him how he was dominating in a given instance. You could tell Jim that when he conducted his staff meeting he did not give his staff a chance to contribute and that you felt his domination inhibited the group from participating and, that does not encourage imagination and creativity. In this way, you are suggesting a correction that Jim can make.

3. It takes into account both the needs of the receiver and the giver of the feedback. Feedback can be destructive when it serves the needs of only the giver and fails to consider the needs of the person on the receiving end. In giving feedback as a supervisor, for example, you will hopefully inform the employee of the reasons corrective action is needed and how corrective action would let him do a better, and maybe faster, job. You would be helping to improve his work skills.

4. It is directed toward behavior the receiver can do something about. Frustration is only increased when a person is reminded of a shortcoming over which he has no control. To tell Bev she is too short to do a good job only puts her down and frustrates her. She cannot help or do anything about being short. To tell Bev that if she were to take a course in supervisory skills, she would stand a better chance in getting a promotion is something she can take action on.

5. It is solicited rather than imposed. Feedback is most useful when it is requested by the receiver. When it is welcomed or invited there is a much better chance that the feedback, if it is constructive, will be utilized. Feedback is most useful when the receiver himself has initiated and formulated the kinds of information he is seeking through the feedback process. Feedback

is more apt to be solicited in an environment where criticism, faultfinding and reprimanding of individuals is minimized. To help individuals, employers would do well to remember that more positive growth, improvement and development are achieved when emphasis is placed on what people do right rather than what they do wrong. Faultfinding generally causes people to cover up and not admit mistakes. When a supervisor accepts mistakes as a part of the growth process, feedback and support for correction is more often solicited.

6. Feedback is well timed. Generally feedback is most useful at the earliest opportunity after a given behavior and while the event is fresh in the minds of all concerned. Feedback is obviously dependent on the person's willingness and readiness to receive feedback. An overwhelming amount of critical feedback at one time might be more than one could accept and utilize and could be harmful rather than good. The other 6 points regarding the use of feedback are important when considering the timing of feedback. An employee who has recently faced a number of personal problems as well as just having been passed over for promotion, would not find constructive criticism regarding part of his work particularly beneficial and well timed. Feedback that is positive and reinforces positive growth is much more beneficial than negative feedback. If constructive criticism is to be beneficial it should be best balanced with positive reinforcement and offered at an appropriate time.

7. Feedback should be checked to insure clear communications. One way of doing this is to have the receiver try to rephrase the feedback she has received to see if it corresponds to what the sender had in mind. (Examples of this have been given.) Feedback is a way of giving help. It is a control mechanism for the individual who wants to learn how well her behavior matches her intentions, it is a means for establishing one's identity. Feedback can be a positive form of communications but, used improperly, can be destructive.[34]

Communication, like leadership, can take on various styles, depending on the situation, circumstances, and those being led. Appropriate changes in communication style can make communication much more effective. The style of communication, like the style of leadership, should be determined by what is appropriate for a given time and circumstance.

Forms of Communication

Figure 6.12 presents a model that can be useful in understanding different forms of communication. The circle is divided into four quadrants—control, defend, develop, and relinquish—indicating the four approaches to communication.

---

[34] Based on a presentation by Louis McCoy at the Parks Recreation Administrators Institute (Asilomar Conference Grounds, Pacific Grove, Calif., November 10–15, 1974.

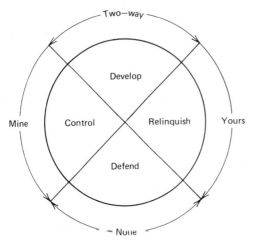

Figure 6.12. Model showing influence of communication. (*Building Team Effectiveness* Educational Systems and Designs, Inc., Westport, Conn., 1970, p. 39.)

Control

In the control situation, the leader wants the most influence. It would be best represented by downward communication where direction, procedures, and process are defined distinctly and exactly. Authoritarian types of leadership would be most associated with this type of communication.

Defend

Defense is used when the manager wants to stay uninvolved, neither exerting nor responding to any influence. This would be associated by the laissez-faire type of leadership. The communication process does not involve any influence on the part of the leader; the group decides for themselves what should take place. In this situation, there is little communication from the leader.

Develop

Developmental communication would be expressed by "I want to use my ability and yours to solve the problem." This is a two-way approach to communication, providing an opportunity for giving direction as well as for a great deal of feedback. This would be associated mostly with a democratic style of leadership in which a mutual give-and-take approach by the leader and the group is used. In this situation, there is a need for a great deal of communication by both leader and subordinates.

Relinquish

The last approach to communications involves relinquishing influence: "I want you to make the decision." This approach would fall somewhere between laissez-faire and the democratic leadership style and is used in situations in which subordinates have a great deal of knowledge and require a minimal amount of communication from, or to, their superior. In determining the best approach to communication, the individual in the leadership role must match the appropriate form of communication to the particular time and circumstance.

Whenever we deal with people, employees or participants, our communications fall into a pattern. When speed is important and we have the knowledge and experience to make decisions, the controlling pattern of communication is often effective. But we have to recognize that when we control, we often cut off the other person's ideas. We also run the risk that the person will cover up any resistance he or she has. Resistance has a way of bouncing back if the other person feels pressured. So, the best time to control is when we are sure we are right and when the other person is not resistant.

On the other hand, when the other person has most of the facts and knows what's required, we may relinquish influence. Rarely is it desirable for an employee to withdraw, but we should appreciate that fight (when an employee tends to oppose an idea, thought or suggestion) flight (when an employee tends to escape dealing with the reality of an idea, thought or action), are normal reactions and should be responded to with understanding. Finally, the developmental approach is often useful in identifying causes of resistance to change or in working out joint solutions to problems.

Written Versus Oral Communications

As has been stated, the purpose of communication is to achieve change. Whether it is achieved formally or informally is not important. The type of communication to be used is more a matter of whether the communication requires moderate speed and is to be retained for further clarification and reference, or whether the communication is to be fast and not too explicit. More than anything else, the situation will determine whether communications are put in writing or given orally. Oral communication is obviously faster and permits interchange. Questions can be asked, and the sender can interpret what the reactions to his or her message are and how it has been received. Oral communications are generally less costly in terms of the time it takes to complete them. On the other hand, if the message is not clear, there is nothing to refer to at a later time.

Written communications have certain advantages. They can be retained as records to be used at a later date for additional consideration. They generally cost more in terms of the time it takes to think through the message, write it down or dictate it, have a secretary type it and send it out, and it usually takes more time to deliver this type of communication. In each situation, the communicator must decide what is the best type of communication to deliver—written or oral.

The Effect the Manager Has on the Communication Process

It is sometimes difficult for the manager to exercise the right amount of control over the communication process within an organization. On the other hand, it is in the best interests of the manager to assure that communication within the organization is as effective as possible. As expressed earlier, communication is the process by which the organization is linked together to achieve a central purpose. The best way for the manager to facilitate a good communication system is to communicate well himself. He should assure that there is downward, upward, and lateral communication taking place within the organization, that everyone is as fully informed as possible, and that he is using informal lines of communication within the organization to the advantage of that organization. He should assure that there is a proper balance between written and oral communication, both being used in the right situations.

Downward communication will work only after upward communication has been successfully established. To be good communicators, we also have to learn to be good listeners. We must remember that to communicate, we also have to be aware that those who are receiving the message are able to perceive what we are saying, and we have to be aware of their expectations.

We must also be aware that communications make demands on people insofar as they may require change. We have to be aware of whether people are ready for any changes we are asking them to make; whether their beliefs, prejudices, or personal needs will be confronted or reinforced by the communication. Communication should start with an employee or subordinate's concerns, perceptions, and expectations. These make communication a tool he can use rather than a demand being placed on him.

SUMMARY

In this chapter we have explored two important components involved in the management of leisure service organizations. First, we looked at the process of leadership. It is important to recognize that there is not one "best" leadership style for a manager. But, rather, that the manager must be cognizant of the various environmental factors that call for a specific style of leadership. Two factors that may affect the selection of one leadership style over another include the task to be accomplished and the psychological and/or physiological needs of the people in the group being led. Most contemporary research studies focus on the degree to which a leader satisfies the human relations requirements of the group with the desired objectives or task to be accomplished. Ultimately, the leadership style selected by a manager for a given situation will be a blend of these two factors. In certain situations, one will be emphasized more heavily than the other. It is vital that the manager be able to diagnose the environment and select an appropriate leadership style for the particular situation he or she is involved with.

In the last half of this chapter we discussed the importance of communication. The ability of the manager to communicate effectively with subordinates is perhaps one of the most vital skills that she or he can possess. Communications can be thought of as a process in which information is transferred from one party to another. This transfer may occur in many forms—written, verbal, nonverbal, and so on. The flow of communication can be thought of as a current running downward, upward, and laterally. Upward communication is perhaps the most neglected area of communication. Problems usually associated with communication deal with the distortion that can occur between the sender and the receiver. The development of good listening and direct and articulate presentation of ideas are key skills that the leisure service manager should possess.

Managing for Organizational Effectiveness

7

In this chapter we will explore a number of concepts that can contribute to the productive management of leisure service oganizations. Concepts based upon the authors' practical professional experience as well as management literature are presented. The ultimate success of any organization depends upon the ability of the manager to motivate, communicate with, and lead his employees. These are the primary skills needed by the manager to effectively deal with the human resources of an organization. The ideas presented in this chapter can serve as guidelines to help the manager use the above mentioned primary skills to operate more effectively. Discussed is the relationship of management to leadership, management skills and traits, the relationship of the manager to his superiors, subordinates and co-workers, and Total Performance Measurement. In addition, we will cover the role of the manager as a decision-maker, as an evaluator, and as a facilitator in creating a supportive climate.

MANAGEMENT AND LEADERSHIP

The manager of a leisure service agency, in addition to having management skills, must possess leadership skills—and the two terms are not synonymous. The effective manager, however, is usually an effective leader. Let's examine some of the differences between management and leadership.

Management is concerned with the accomplishment of organizational goals and is sequentially characterized by the following:[1]

1. A formal organization must be created to carry out the functions of planning, organizing, staffing, directing, and controlling. Authority in management is from the top down.
2. The manager is responsible for assisting in the establishment of goals that are clear and can be operationalized.

---

[1] Based on a presentation by Patrick M. Williams, member of the faculty of School of Business, California State University, San Jose, at a city of Sunnyvale Management Training Session, August 10 1972, Sunnyvale Calif.

3. To accomplish organizational goals, information is needed about resources, personnel, equipment, and facilities.
4. Resources have to be provided for the creation of a service, as does a method for distributing the services.
5. Motivation has to take place. In order to move, there has to be cognizance as to the direction the organization should take.
6. After the organization decides where it wants to go, management must make decisions, the organization is then ready to move into action.
7. The plan is put into action by the manager who give directions via orders and communications.

Although this may be an oversimplification of the management process, these are the basic steps the manager must follow to put the organization into operation.

Let's examine leadership and what is involved in the leadership process. Leadership involves working with and through people to help them accomplish their goals. These goals may not necessarily be organizational goals. Leadership involves the following:

1. The leader is concerned with the individual and his or her needs.
2. The leader is interested in helping the individual meet his or her goals.
3. Meeting the individuals's needs results in behavior or activity that accomplishes work.
4. The leader determines needs through a feedback process, one of the most important parts of leadership.
5. Finally, the leader assumes a role and works through and with the individuals she or he leads to meet these needs.

Now let's examine the relationship between leadership and management. To be an effective manager, one must also be a leader. The manager-leader must utilize elements of both leadership and management to the benefit of the individual and the organization.

1. The basic factor that the manager and leader have in common is that they both work with and through people: *employees as individuals* and *employees as members of the organization.*
2. The manager-leader can tie together the *goals of the organization* and the *needs of the individual* if he can identify what they have in common. The manager-leader identifies the common purposes and tries to satisfy both at the same time. (This point has been stressed in preceding chapters.)
3. The manager-leader makes functional use of the *behavior* of the individuals. Does the behavior of the individual accomplish the work of the organization?
4. How available are the *resources* of the organization to satisfy the *needs of the individual?* If the resources are available and can be matched with the needs of

the individual, there is a good chance that work capacity will be released to accomplish the organizational goals.

5. It is necessary for the manager-leader to make employees aware of *dissidence* in order to provide *motivation* for change in behavior. The purpose of feedback in terms of leadership is to provide motivation by creating an awareness of dissidence in terms of where the person is now and where he would like to be. For change to occur, the individual must recognize dissidence: I am here; I want to be there. This is what moves individuals toward the accomplishment of goals and objectives. This supports Maslow's principle that dissatisfaction causes people to change.

6. Once there is a desire for change, the organization and the individual are ready to move into action. You cannot make a *decision* for change until you have *awareness*. Decision, whether made by the organization or by the individual, results in action—and this is where change begins. Decision points are really change points.

7. Action takes place, ultimately culminating in the stimulation of both leadership and management process. The manager gives *orders and directs* the organization. However, None of the processes of need, identification, behavior, desires, feedback, or awareness can be translated into action until someone is *playing a leadership role*. The leader *has* to be playing some kind of role within the organization in order to initiate action in employees. Thus, the manager who is also in the role of a leader is in the best position to accomplish the missions of the employee and the organization. The roles of manager and leader can be different, but they are not incompatible. They can be integrated for the greatest effectiveness.

Another difference between the manager and the leader is that the manager has a position of authority in the organization. The leader need not have position authority and may not even function in the chain of command. The manager possesses formal authority over subordinates, whereas the leader possesses acceptance authority or influence. The manager can delegate authority to subordinates. The leader can never delegate authority because it resides in him, not in his position. The manager is held accountable to the organization, whereas the leader is held accountable to fellow employees. The manager who wants to be productive and effective has to learn to blend the skills of management and leadership. To rely on one without the other will lessen effectiveness.

Management Skills and Traits

The manager of a leisure service organization must have competence in two distinct areas: technical and managerial. *Technical competence* deals with having knowledge or expertise in a given area of specialization. Typical areas of expertise are recreation programming, park maintenance, landscape design and building maintenance. The park manager supervises gardeners and other landscape technicians. It is desirable for him to have some technical knowledge of their jobs, however it is far more important for the people doing the work to have the most technical competence. For example, it is more important for the gardener who actually does the pruning to know the proper techniques and procedures for pruning than it is for the supervisor to have a high level of competence in this area. But the supervisor has to be sufficiently knowledgeable to know when someone is not pruning properly. He has to be able to take corrective action or be sure the gardener takes training to become expert in this area.

Figure 1.1 (page 9) shows the skills the manager needs to carry out his job. The diagram indicates that greater technical skills are needed by lower-level managers than by top-level managers. To carry this concept a step further, the person actually doing the work needs the greatest technical skill. (Technical skills are beyond the scope of this book, which is designed to deal with the management skills necessary to carry out the work.)

In Chapter 6, it was pointed out that any attempt to identify traits that assure leaders or managers of success is futile. Research into the traits possessed by leaders has shown that there are no certain attributes that all have in common. However, the authors of this book feel there are some traits that are essential to good managerial leadership. These traits are not necessarily discussed in order of importance.

The first of these is *integrity*. Integrity is something a person cannot acquire: "If he does not bring it to the job, he'll never have it. . . . A man's subordinates will know in a very short period of time whether a man has integrity or not. They may forgive him for a great deal of incompetence, ignorance and bad manners, but they'll never forgive him for a lack of integrity. . . . A man who concentrates on an individual's weaknesses, rather than his strengths, shows lack of integrity. . . . The person who questions who is right, rather than what is right also shows lack of integrity."[2] Integrity is something a manager builds upon over a long period of time. It is not something that comes and goes; it is something an individual must have to be an outstanding manager.

Another trait an effective manager possesses is *honesty*. Honesty involves a sense of honor, being upright and fair when dealing with people, and being decent to them without hidden motives or forethought. Honesty assumes truthfulness at all times regardless of the circumstances, the pressure, or the consequences.

The next characteristic is *sincerity*. Sincerity, like honesty, conveys openness and trust. It conveys a feeling of being interested in and concerned for others and should result in a mutual trust between individuals.

Empathy is the ability to place oneself in the position of another individual and understand that person's feelings and values. The manager who has empathy has

[2] Peter F. Drucker, *Management: Tasks, Responsibilities, Practices* (New York: Harper and Row, 1974), p. 462.

the ability to better understand her subordinates. She can appreciate their problems, concerns, anxieties. She is less likely to jump to conclusions or take actions that would not be in the best interest of all concerned. A manager who has empathy conveys this to her employees, and enables her to work with her employees in a way she otherwise could not.

Another characteristic essential to the manager is *objectivity*. The manager should strive to examine events and situations as unemotionally as possible. Even though the manager depends heavily on his subordinates, he needs to do this without becoming too emotionally involved with them. It is important for the manager to be able to evaluate them accurately and intelligently to make the decisions he must make as their superior. The ability of the manager to be empathic with his employees, and at the same time be objective about them, requires delicate skill.

Of the five characteristics that have been described so far, objectivity is one that the leader can acquire, practice, and strengthen more than the other four. With practice and determination, she can overcome quick judgments, anger, and other emotions that would tend to make her less objective. But, generally, a manager who has integrity, honesty, sincerity, and empathy will be able to deal with individuals objectively.

The final characteristic to be discussed here is *self-knowledge*. One of Shakespeare's often quoted sayings is "To thine own self be true." This is a valuable characteristic for any manager to have. How can a manager deal with other individuals, employees, and co-workers if he doesn't reveal himself to others and is not honest with himself? It is impossible to be honest and sincere, to have integrity, and to convey empathy and objectivity if one is not aware of one's own personality and characteristics. The manager should be aware of his own strengths as well as his weaknesses and be willing to build on the strengths and minimize the weaknesses. The manager who knows himself is in the best position to capitalize on his strengths and assist others in developing theirs. He is also capable of admitting his shortcomings and errors and of taking corrective action to improve his leadership abilities.

Managers and Their Relationships

The manager of an organization, at any level, does not operate in a vacuum but is forced to deal with many individuals. He is forced to have relationships with his boss, subordinates, co-workers, and individuals in other organizations and in the community.

Dealing with the Boss

In most organizations, whether the individual realizes it or not, she is apt to feel more frustration and anxiety as a result of her relationships with her boss than any other single relationship. How well a manager operates is determined by her ability to get support and cooperation from her boss. Drucker states: "I have yet to sit down with a manager, whatever his level or job, who is not primarily concerned with upward relationships and upward communications. Every vice-president feels that the relationships with the president are a real problem. And so it is on down to the first line of supervisors, the production foreman or chief clerk who is quite certain that he could get along with his men if only the "boss" and the personnel department left him alone."[3]

Upward relationships are probably a manager's first concern. One of the reasons for the anxiety and frustration that exists in dealing with the boss is that you have limited control, if any, over your boss, whereas you sometimes have a great deal of control over your relationships with co-workers and subordinates. If you are faced with a problem as it relates to your subordinates, you can put it aside for a while. You can turn it off or you can take action to settle the situation even though it may not be to the liking of your subordinates. But in the case of dealing with your boss, you often do not have those alternatives. You have to deal with the situations with your boss as he prescribes them, even though you may have quite a good relationship with him.

The competent manager knows his boss. The best way to succeed is to work for a very effective, efficient boss. No matter who we are or what position we are in, we all work for somebody, be it a board, commission, or city manager. The best way to assure that you will have a good working relationship with your boss is to try to reach an agreement and understanding before you accept a job. When accepting a job, you have as much at stake as the employing agency has in accepting you. It behooves you to find out as much about the person that you are going to work for as you possibly can. It is a fact that after you accept the job, the chances of changing your boss are slim. The best way to find out about the person you will be working for is to ask others who are already working for that individual. Ask about such things as his style of leadership. Is he the kind of individual you can be open and honest with and who will be easy to work with? Does he evaluate employees on their results or performance? Is he fair and honest and does he have integrity? Does he permit employees to disagree with him? Each of these items are important issues and may determine how effectively you can work for that person.

Many times the answers to your questions are not going to be answered by asking the boss himself. If you ask the boss if he is the type of person you can disagree with, obviously there is only one answer: "Certainly I'm that kind of boss. Everyone thinks of me as being extremely fair, honest, and open-minded." You are more apt to get a realistic answer from some of the people who are presently working for the individual or who have worked for him in the past. Although individuals do change from time to time, the likelihood of your boss changing is minimal.

[3] Ibid., p. 380.

Assume that you have accepted the job because he is the type of person you could work for without too much difficulty. The next step is to try to find out the techniques and methods that will assure the greatest amount of success in your relationship and will assure that you get approval of your recommendations and support for the various things you want to do in your job.

Just as it is important to determine the needs of employees, it is important to find out what your boss's needs and peculiarities are in order to work better with him. To do this, we will discuss four distinct areas:

1. How to deal with his leadership style.
2. How he likes information presented.
3. The method he uses for decision-making.
4. The personal quirks he may have.

Leadership Style.   If there is a particular leadership style that you as an employee cannot work under, you should not accept a job with a boss who uses that style. On the other hand, you may have to work with someone who employs a leadership style that may not be totally compatible with yours. There are some important observations and techniques you can utilize to facilitate relations with such a person and gain her support. If she is the type of boss who does not like you to disagree with her, try to minimize those areas in which you would disagree. Some bosses tend to show their strength by being firm and uncompromising in most decisions they make. With this in mind, try to minimize contact with your boss when disagreement is likely and capitalize on those areas you know he will be in agreement with.

A boss may also expect you to emulate her management style. If she makes decisions quickly, is firm and uncompromising, then she may tend to judge democratic or participative management as weaknesses on your part. Therefore you should make her aware of incidences in which you have taken strong, firm action to gain her support and favor, even if that is not the way you are most comfortable managing. The most important thing to remember is that you should work for her and with her, not against her. This may sometimes require you to change *your* ways in order to get a decision made or the job done.

Information.   Another important area when dealing with your boss may regard how he likes his information, when he likes it, and how much of it he likes. Does he like simple, to-the-point reports, or does he like reports with a great deal of documentation and background? Does he like reports with the conclusion at the beginning and supportive data following it or the supportive data with the conclusion? Does he like the report to indicate your opinions or does he like them to indicate only the facts, without opinions? Does he like the reports several weeks in advance or does he like them just prior to his having to make a decision? Some bosses like verbal rather than written reports.

Some bosses are not concerned about these matters, while others consider them important. In either case, when working for someone else, it is best that you find out how he likes information presented so you can deal with him in the most effective, efficient way possible to encourage a favorable response.

Decision-Making.   How does your boss make decisions? Some individuals try to make every decision, whereas others are willing to share decisions and like to delegate authority for decision-making to lower members of the organization. An effective way to deal with your boss in the decision making process may be to approach her with your plan or idea several days/weeks before the decision making deadline. This technique has two advantages:

1. It permits the boss to think about your proposal well in advance and she doesn't feel rushed and pressured to make a decision.
2. This oftentimes permits the boss to have some inputs and encourages her to think that the idea was more her own than if she was forced to make a decision on the spot.

Some individuals like to make decisions through a group process, utilizing a committee or management group; other bosses sometimes dislike such participation in decision making. Being aware of this, you can either utilize this process or minimize it, whichever is to your advantage. Another technique to encourage a favorable response to your ideas is to work through someone else, someone you have confidence in, who sees eye to eye with you and has the respect and attention of the boss. Although *you* may not be able to get certain decisions directly through your boss by going through a third party, decisions you favor may gain approval that otherwise would not. Whatever the case, it behooves you as a manager to know your boss and her decision-making proclivities so you can approach decision situations in the most effective way possible.

Personal Quirks.   Just about every individual has personal characteristics or quirks that affect the way he or she approaches management. Although there are a great number of quirks that could be mentioned, only a few will be discussed to give the reader an indication of the types of things that he or she might have to deal with.

Some bosses like to make decisions in the morning, when they are fresh. Some may have certain other times when they read reports, study, or indulge in various planning activities. If the boss does not like to be interrupted during certain periods of time, it would behoove the manager to know when the most appropriate time would be to approach the boss for information or action.

Some individuals like to be "in the know" about everything that happens. So by simply keeping the boss informed on many matters, even though you may feel some are insignificant, may keep you in good stead with him. Other items that might represent minor irritations to the boss are talking business when he is on his coffee break, being called at home unless it's an extreme emergency, or not being called by his last name. Whatever the case, if you are aware of any pet peeves or idiosyncracies he may have, and can accomodate them, you may improve your working relationship with the boss.

Another important item to consider in dealing with your boss is the size of his ego. If he has a rather large ego, he may require a great deal of praise and personal attention. He may like to be the center of attention in the meetings he attends. He may like to be invited to most of the functions that your department sponsors and offers. The shrewd and smart manager learns to evaluate and size up the needs of the boss so he can meet these needs in a way that gains favorable decisions and the greatest amount of support for his programs.

Subordinate Relationships

The majority of this book has dealt with managing subordinate relationships within an organization. In addition to the factors that have already been discussed, there are additional areas that should be given special mention.

Equitable Treatment of All Employees. It has been stressed over and over that the way to motivate employees is to provide them with an opportunity to meet their individual needs. But because every employee has a different set of needs, there would seem to be a contradiction in treating all employees similarly or fairly. Equal treatment means assuring that all employees have an equal chance for job promotions (provided they meet the requirements and specifications for a particular job), that the system for promotion and the criteria used are fair, above-board, and understood by all employees.

Nothing affects the morale in an organization more than the "people decisions" it makes in terms of placement, promotion, pay, and various disciplinary actions. People decisions indicate to every member of the organization what the organization really stands for, wants, and values. Personnel decisions should always be based on factual records of performance measured against the specific goals and objectives the organization has established, rather than on the basis of management's opinions or a person's potential. Nothing will destroy morale and motivation in an organization faster than for employees to see a particular candidate promoted if he doesn't deserve it, or receive special attention because of "who he knows" rather than the kind of performance he has given. Equal treatment of employees is also important in terms of disciplinary action taken by a company or organization. Poor morale may result if employees detect an imbalance in disciplinary action. Nothing will assure better morale than equal treatment of all employees in all circumstances and in all situations.

Employees Personal Problems. It is a well-known fact that when an organization hires an individual, it hires the whole person. The individual doesn't come to work and leave her personal problems at home. She comes to work as a total individual. She is concerned about house payments, her family, her religion, and her political interests. The competent supervisor or manager recognizes this and is prepared to deal with it. Although as her supervisor you may not be able to solve her personal problems, you must be aware of them and how they affect her productivity. As a supervisor, you have the responsibility to meet her needs as they affect the performance of her job. You can adjust her work to meet certain needs, but there may be cases where her personal problems are incompatable with her job assignment. In some instances it is possible to change the employee's job, work location, or work group or take other corrective action to help her solve some of her personal problems and upgrade her job performance to an acceptable level.

There may be other personal problems that are beyond the supervisor's capacity to deal with. Most organizations take into consideration certain personal problems that individuals will have on the job. Such things as sick leave, workmen's compensation, death leave, and health and medical insurance are provided for to help an employee deal with personal problems that everyone expects to have at one time or another during their working career. On the other hand, some employees have other personal problems that cannot be dealt with by the supervisor in a normal working situation. These include such things as alcoholism, deep-seated emotional problems, and other problems that affect an individuals' personality, ability to get along with other employees, and job performance. However, many organizations provide for psychiatrists to help employees with these types of problems at private clinics. As Drucker says, ". . . an employer has no business with a man's personality. Employment is a specific contract calling for specific performance, and for nothing else. Any attempt of an employer to go beyond this is usurpation. It is immoral as well as illegal intrusion of privacy. It is abuse of power. An employee owes no loyalty," he owes no love and no attitude—he owes performances, and nothing else."[4]

An employee who has a personal problem that begins to detract from his job performance is obviously of concern to the supervisor as well as the organization. The individual's personal problem should be dealt with solely on the basis that his job performance is not up to standard. A supervisor has to recognize personal problems that are affecting job performance and be concerned about them. Although the employee may or may not discuss personal problems as they relate to work, it is the supervisor's job to find a solution to problems that affect job performance either by working with the employee or referring him to professional help.

Managers are not equipped, trained, or competent to deal with personal problems in most cases. As has been stated before, they are not psychiatrists or psychologists; and furthermore, they have no right to practice psychotherapy. Figure 7.1 may help the reader to distinguish between behavior that supervisors have or have not a right to deal with. Extracting certain parts from the motivational model in Chapter 4, we see employees' needs characterized in the square to

---

[4] Ibid., pp. 424–425.

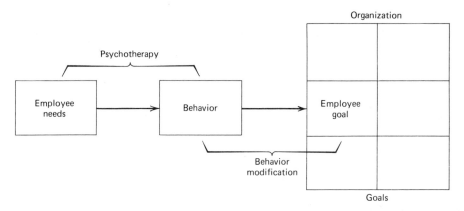

Figure 7.1. The difference between psychotherapy and behavior modification.

the left. As the employee goes about meeting her needs, this results in behavior directed towards reaching her goal, which is also part of the organizational goals that supervisors are responsible for accomplishing. Supervisors have a right to deal with behavior modification to obtain compliance and cooperation from the employee in the accomplishment of organizational goals and objectives. But they have no right to deal with the employee's *personality* as it relates to her needs and affects her behavior. Psychotherapy is based on an assumption that to change behavior, one first has to understand the feelings and attitudes within an individual. Supervisors are not equipped professionally to do this.

Figure 7.1 shows the distinction between psychotherapy and behavior alteration. When you as supervisor observe poor work performance, you should bring it to the attention of the employee. You should indicate that something is affecting her work and, as her supervisor, you expect her to correct it and will be glad to help her in any way you can to bring her work performance up to an acceptable level. If she is late for work, you expect her to be on time; why she is late is none of your business. If she is having accidents because she can't keep her mind on her work, you should indicate that you will be glad to help her find a solution to her problem by arranging for professional help.

A supervisor's only rationale for dealing with an employee's problem, as stated before, is within the context of job performance. Personal problems as well as behavioral problems can generally be referred to the personnel department, which has access to medical assistance which the employee can use in problem solving. It is our responsibility as supervisors to solve the work performance problem. If it is something we can do, something over which we have control or influence, we should take appropriate action. If it is something of a personal nature over which we have no control, we need to bring it to the attention of the employee and encourage her to correct it herself or with professional help.

Performance Appraisal.   Although personal appraisal will be presented in greater detail in Chapter 10, it is important to discuss this subject as it relates to subordinate-manager relationships. Most organizations use an employee evaluation system of one form or another. The system usually consists of an annual or semiannual review of the employee by the supervisor, rating a number of characteristics that relate to his job. The supervisor generally ranks, or rates, individual characteristics from one to ten, comparing the employee to a standard or to other employees. Although this method of evaluation informs the employee as to where he ranks and provides him with some feedback, it serves little value in helping him improve his job performance.

Attempts to improve the evaluation procedure have led to programs such as Management By Objectives (MBO), discussed in Chapter 2. Although MBO is superior to the more traditional employee evaluation and goal-setting procedures, it concentrates almost entirely on results. New attempts to improve on employee evaluation as well as mutual goal-setting have resulted in a new system called "performance appraisal." Harry Levinson outlined the functions of performance appraisal as follows:

1. To provide adequate feedback to each person on his or her performance;
2. To serve as a basis for modifying or changing behavior towards more effective working habits; and
3. To provide data to managers with which they will judge future job assignments and compensation.[5]

The performance appraisal concept is central to effective management. One of the drawbacks of MBO is that evaluation is entirely geared to results; although the results may be very good, the basis on which the results were achieved may be poor and unsatisfactory. Examples can be given in which managers have achieved great results but in doing so have destroyed employees and other resources of the organization. Without evaluation of performance, sometimes results can be misleading. Some of the problems incurred in performance appraisal are as follows:

1. Judgments of performance are usually subjective and impressionistic.
2. Appraisals may provide inadequate information, and managers using them to compare employees for the purpose of determining salary increases often make arbitrary judgments.
3. Ratings by different managers in different units are not comparable.
4. In comparisons made on the basis of a curve of normal distribution, which is in turn based on rating of results rather than behavior, competent employees may not only be denied salary increases, but may also become demotivated.
5. Trying to base promotions and layoff decisions on appraisals of performance data leaves decisions open to debate.

[5] Harry Levinson, "Thinking Ahead," *Harvard Business Review,* July/August 1976, pp. 30–46.

6. Although managers are urged to give feedback freely and often, there are no built-in mechanisms for assuring they will do so.
7. There are few effective established mechanics to cope with either the sense of inadequacy managers have about appraising subordinates, or the paralysis and procrastination that results from guilt about playing God.[6]

One of the main sources of trouble with performance appraisals systems is that frequently the outcome of behavior rather than the behavior itself is evaluated. Levinson says that there are four objectives of good performance appraisals:

1. To provide good feedback data. When there is an appraisal made, be it semiannually, annually, or more often, the employee will have no surprises. There will be an on-going method provided to let the employee know how he is doing on a regular basis. This can be done by placing reports of critical incidents into the employee's folder on a regular basis.
2. To provide for good coaching data. When the employee receives feedback information at the time of an incident he will be more able to adapt his behavior and take corrective action. If the employee does not or cannot change his behavior the facts will become evident to him through repetitive reports. If the employee feels unfairly judged or criticized he may appeal immediately. In any event, both manager and employee will know which behavior is being appraised.
3. To provide promotional data. With such an accumulation of critical incidents the manager is in a position to evaluate repeatedly how the employee is dealing with his behavior, particularly if that behavior needs to be changed. If an employee is passed over for promotion there is a better record of why. The employee has been made aware of it on a regular basis. But more important, the employee has information and feedback that offers him an opportunity for change and success. It gives him an opportunity to change his behavior.
4. To provide for long-term data. Frequently new managers do not know their employees and all too often have little information about them. The critical incident performance appraisal provides the manager with a great deal of information about the employee, both positive and negative.[7]

An example of an appraisal system that attempts to combine some MBO techniques with performance appraisal is being used in the city of Sunnyvale, California. Although this example may not be appropriate in all situations, it shows how one organization has attempted to integrate employees' daily performance with the evaluation of end results. This will provide the manager and the employee with better feedback and a basis for changing and modifying behavior, as well as information for the manager to use in making future judgments regarding the employee (see Appendix B).

[6] Ibid., p. 31.
[7] Ibid., p. 36.

Employee Corrective Action.   A time comes in all organizations when all attempts at positive action have failed to motivate a particular employee or change her behavior. When an employee becomes disruptive to the organization or if her action is detrimental to the accomplishment of goals and objectives, something has to be done. When this becomes the case, the manager has no alternative but to take some corrective action to move or eliminate the individual who is creating the problem. Before such disciplinary action is taken, every attempt should be made to try to modify the employee's behavior to bring it back into line with the accomplishment of organizational goals and objectives. But when all else fails, some sort of discipline may be the only course of action.

Disciplinary action should be administered fairly and in the best interest of all concerned. Employees who are conscientious and work hard will become quite upset and disheartened if they see other employees abusing privileges, goofing off, and being unproductive. Unless there is fair and quick corrective action, good employees may tend to lose interest in their work and be demotivated themselves. It is often unpleasant to take corrective or disciplinary action, but when the time and situation calls for it the manager is obligated to take such action. Unless he learns to do it fairly, precisely, and quickly, the effectiveness of the organization can be adversely affected and ultimately totally destroyed. The manager has a responsibility to accurately assess every problem situation, making sure he understands the situation thoroughly before taking any corrective or disciplinary action. The manager must be sure that he knows which individual(s) is at the root of the problem and that he is not taking action against the wrong person(s).

In every organization, from time to time, there are individuals who have personality problems or there are situations that create friction and poor working conditions. Sometimes the problem can be corrected by simply moving an employee to another work location. Care should be taken to follow the transferred employee closely to see that a similar problem doesn't begin to erupt and get out of hand in the new work assignment. If this is the case, it would be a good indication that the employee who was transferred is the cause of the problem.

On the other hand, the manager has a responsibility to support the employee who is trying to do an outstanding job but is being pressured by other employees to slow down her work because she may be showing the others up. He has a responsibility to provide an environment in which an employee who is willing to put forth extra effort can do so and at the same time make an effort to find out why other employees are not being motivated properly.

When an employee is incompetent or incapable of performing a particular task, it is unfair to him as well as the organization to permit him to remain in the position. To do so is to slow down productivity, and interfere with the overall goals of the organization. An employee in this situation should be removed from his position and placed in another position where he can perform adequately or, as a last resort, fired. Employees who are found to be dishonest or constant troublemakers or are disruptive in other ways need to be removed from their particular jobs or, if necessary, fired. But releasing an employee should be done only after a thorough investigation of the circumstances, so the manager can be assured that the right employee has been singled out.

If an individual has been promoted beyond his capabilities, he should not be permitted to stay in the job. The manager will do the employee, as well as the organization, a favor by taking corrective action, counseling the employee, or referring him to an appropriate counseling service to help him find a job that he is capable of doing and that will give him greater job satisfaction.

Whatever the situation, if it requires corrective or disciplinary action, the manager has a responsibility to take such action.

Socializing with Employees.   An area seldom mentioned or given much attention from a manager's point of view is that of socializing with employees. Although there are no hard and fast rules about socializing with employees, a general discussion of the topic is valuable and may save a manager a great number of problems. In every organization, employees are conscious of relationships that develop, particularly relationships with superiors. In many organizations, you hear such comments as "I know why Linda got the job" or "Linda got a favorable decision because she is a good friend of the boss." Whether this was the basis for the decision or not, socializing with employees can create problems. The good manager is careful concerning his relationships with subordinates. Although he should always be friendly, interested, and concerned toward them, it is unfair for him to give special attention to one employee and neglect another. Such relationships are bound to breed contempt and resentment.

Fair and equitable treatment to all employees is the best policy. If the boss is going to socialize on an informal basis, it is best done with all employees in the work group rather than with individual employees. No matter how careful the boss may be, employees will tend to criticize him if they feel that one individual is getting special attention. The manager should make every attempt to avoid the possibility of any one employee becoming his "fair-haired boy." This can best be done by treating all employees fairly and equally both in the work situation and off the job.

Relationships with Co-workers
In every organization you will have relationships with co-workers. These relationships may be informal or formal, but whatever the case they will have an effect on your ability to perform your job. In many instances, you are dependent on your co-workers to carry out your assignment. A good principle of organizational structure is to arrange jobs so that individuals have total control for decision-making and allocation of resources and can perform independently. But there are still times when you are dependent on other employees to assist you in your work.

As the director of parks and recreation in a city government, you are dependent on the personnel, finance, public works, and police departments, as well as many other departments headed up by department directors with equal status, to assist in carrying out a program of leisure services. There is a constant need for cooperation from other departments. Likewise, on many occasions these other departments are dependent on you and your department. So the key word seems to be cooperation.

At a lower level of the organization, supervisors are often dependent on each other for cooperation in carrying out the programs between various divisions and sections. In all relationships, either lateral or vertical, the golden rule would seem to apply; that is, we should treat others as we would have them treat us. Being fair, honest, and sincere in these relationships usually insures the manager of the same kind of treatment in return.

On the other hand, not all individuals necessarily respond to the same type of treatment. One departmant director may want all correspondence and requests for action to come directly through her; another department director may permit direct contact with subordinates for action and requests for assistance. Many of the same concepts can be applied in dealing with co-workers that are applied when dealing with the boss. The shrewd and competent manager learns quickly that she is more effective in dealing with co-workers when dealing with them on their terms rather than always insisting on her own. Nothing aggravates, angers, and makes co-workers more uncooperative than an individual who is rigid and inflexible, always right, and appears to know it all.

Cooperation between coworkers is also contingent upon good interpersonal skills. The co-worker who is always trying to impress everybody with her cleverness and intelligence, or the co-worker who flaunts the fact that he has the boss's ear more than anyone else, may win some favors and decisions from the boss; but such co-workers may lack cooperation when it comes to dealing with other departments.

An astute manager is also aware of how his subordinates handle their relationships with co-workers. The manager should attempt to encourage employees to co-operate with each other in every way possible and to minimize rumors that any given co-worker has more influence and admiration from the boss. If the manager can convey to each of his subordinates, as well as co-workers, that he respects each of them for their strengths and abilities, it is more likely they will cooperate with one another in accomplishing the overall mission of the department. The manager who permits one employee to become the favorite, to get special privileges and special attention, invites contempt, jealousy, and inhibits motivation. Every attempt should be made by the manager, when supervising subordinates and co-workers and when dealing with other department heads or managers, to assure equality, fairness, sincerity, and integrity.

Teamwork and Team-Building

Most leisure service organizations consist of a number of departments or sections that work together to carry out the goals of the organization. Usually each of these sections or divisions is headed up by a member of the management team. Under each manager is a group of employees through which the manager carries out the goals and objectives of that particular unit or division. Within the recreation division of a community recreation and park department, there are usually such components as playground sections, special programs, aquatics, and sports. In the parks division, there are usually such sections as park maintenance, special facilities maintenance, construction division, and so on. In order to carry out the overall mission of the organization, the component parts need to cooperate with their respective managers and function as a team. It is essential that this team work together cooperatively and constructively. Should one manager be uncooperative due to personality conflicts or whatever, it is detrimental to the whole organization and affects productivity.

Drucker offers some valuable advice with respect to six team-building concepts that should be followed to assure teamwork among top management: "A top management team has to satisfy stringent requirements to be effective. It is not a simple structure. It will not work just because its members like each other. Indeed, whether the members like each other or dislike each other is beside the point. Top management teams must function no matter what the personal relationship between its members is."[8]

The first of Drucker's six concepts is as follows:

1. Whoever has the primary responsibility in a given area has in effect the final say. To have a functioning top management, subordinates should not be allowed to appeal a decision by one member of the team to another. Every member speaks with full authority of top management. To deviate from this and to allow an appeal from one member of the top management group to another level invites politicing. [Politicing, in this context, means that an employee who works under one supervisor goes to another supervisor of another unit to solicit support of his ideas, actions or behavior.] It undermines the authority of the entire top management group.[9]

Within a leisure service organization, under the recreation division (as was mentioned earlier), there might be four or five subsections, such as playgrounds, sports, special recreation, and aquatics. The manager, of the sports section in the recreation division has a primary responsibility for that section and the final say. No recreation leader or program specialist in that section can appeal a decision made by the supervisor of the sports section to any of the other section supervisors. Oftentimes, a member of one of the sections (e.g., a member of the sports section) does not like a decision that has been made by her supervisor and, if she has contacts with another supervisor, she may appeal or discuss the decision with a

[8] From pp. 622–623 in *Management: Tasks, Responsibilities, Practices* by Peter F. Drucker, Copyright 1973, 1974 by Peter F. Drucker. By permission of Harper and Row, Publishers, Inc.

[9] Ibid., p. 622.

supervisor from another section. To do so violates the concept of primary responsibility and invites dissension. It tends to undermine the authority of the supervisor in charge of the sports section.

If the supervisor from the other section permits the employee to discuss the matter of the sports section, he is undermining the effectiveness and authority of the supervisor in charge of the sports section. Encouraging or permitting the employee to discuss the situation undermines the effectiveness of the entire organization. The correct action for the supervisor of the other section is to indicate that this is not within his realm of responsibility, that he doesn't feel it is fair to discuss it with the employee, and that the employee should go back to her supervisor and discuss the matter.

On the other hand, if an employee within a given division (again assuming it's the sports section) feels that a decision has been made poorly or not in the best interests of the section, he can always appeal it to the manager who is in charge of the overall recreation program, the superintendent of recreation. If such an appeal is made, the superintendent must be very careful that he does not undermine the effectiveness of the sports section manager. Only in a rare situation, or in a case where a great deal is at stake, would the superintendent reverse a decision made by a lower-level manager, but still this option should be available and open.

The second of Drucker's six concepts is as follows:

2. No member will make a decision with regard to a matter for which he does not have primary responsibility. Should such a matter be brought to him he would refer it to his colleague whose prime responsibility it is. Indeed, it is a wise precaution for a member of top management team not even to have an opinion on matters that are not within his own area of prime responsibility.[10]

This concept very much follows the first concept. For example, any matter coming to the attention of a manager regarding one of her supervisors is referred directly to that supervisor and, generally, the manager would do well not even to comment or express an opinion on what she thinks, feels, or believes about the matter. The same approach should be taken by a superintendent when matters are referred to him that are the responsibility of a subunit or section under his direction. The superintendent should, however, contact the appropriate supervisor or individual of responsibility and inquire as to the decision that was arrived at. But again the superintendent's first responsibility is to refer the matter to the appropriate program manager.

The third concept is as follows:

3. Members of the top management team need not like each other. They need not even respect each other. But they must not agitate each other. In public, outside top management's conference room, they should not express opinions of each

[10] Ibid., p. 622.

other, they should not criticize each other, they should not belittle each other. Preferably, they should not even praise each other.[11]

Although this concept may seem a bit harsh and shocking at first reading, the more one thinks it through, the more practical it becomes. This concept does not indicate that members of the management team cannot or should not like each other. Instead, it is not necessary for them to like each other to accomplish the mission of the organization; more important, if they do not like each other, they should not aggravate or undermine each other in any way. Anything that one manager does to destroy, undermine, or tear down another manager affects the entire organization, making it less effective and productive. The enforcement of this rule is the responsibility of the team captain, or in the case of the example we have been using, the superintendent of recreation. The superintendent must assure that no individual of the organization who is a member of the top management team be allowed to express public criticism, dislike, or contempt for any other member of the top management team.

Drucker's fourth concept is as follows:

4. A top management team is not a committee, it is a team. A team needs a captain; the team captain is not the boss. He is a leader. In many instances the team captain of an organization is appointed by his position within the formal organization. Although the team captain has the legal power to overrule his colleagues on the management team, if he is really going to operate with a team concept, he very seldom will use his authority. He will listen carefully to all that is said and make a final decision only after he knows exactly where every one of his colleagues of the top management team stands on a particular item.[12]

In some situations the team captain will designate a member of the team who is to make a particular decision in a particular situation, which then must be accepted by everybody. But in every situation there must be a team captain, and at times of crisis he has to be willing to take over.

The fifth concept is as follows:

5. Within his assigned sphere a member of top management is expected to make decisions, but certain decisions should be reserved. There only the team itself can make the decision. At least the decision has to be discussed with the team before it can be made. It is desirable to think though in advance what these areas are or should be.[13]

In leisure service organizations, there are many decisions that should be made by the management team itself, as a group. One of these might be: What is the pur-

---

[11] Ibid., p. 622.
[12] Ibid., p. 622.
[13] Ibid., p. 623.

pose and function of the recreation division? The abandonment of certain services or the addition of new services should also be discussed by the entire management team. Also, certain key personnel decisions should be left to the entire group, particularly if the positions in question affect and serve the entire management team.

There are matters that the entire management team need to consider as a group, even though the final decision may be made by only one of the members of the group. Within a public recreation department, decisions of this type would involve facilities that need to be built, the scheduling of facilities that are shared by members of the group, and policies and procedures related to personnel and other program matters that affect the entire membership of the group.

In general, any decisions that, when made, cut across or affect several sections within the recreation division, should be discussed by the entire team. On the other hand, decisions that affect only the operations of one section should be referred to that section for decision in compliance with the previously discussed concepts.

The sixth concept is as follows:

6. The top management task requires systematic and intensive work on communications among the members of the top management team. It requires this precisely because there are so many different top-management tasks, each, however, with decisive impact on the welfare of the entire organization. It requires it, above all, because each member of the top management should be able to operate with a maximum of autonomy within his own sphere—and that can be granted him only if he makes every effort to keep his colleagues fully informed.[14]

Communications within a top management team should be open, honest, and forthright. It is important for the members of the top management team to be aware of what is going on in the entire division or section. This can take place only with open communications. Although one member of the top management team may have no effect over certain decisions made by another member, she should still be fully informed about what is going on.

The public, in general, is not aware of the distinctions between the various responsibilities and functions of the recreation division. It may make an inquiry of any one of these sections. It is important, therefore, for the members of the top management to speak with assurance about what's taking place in the organization to keep the public well informed. This can be done only if communication is open and shared among all the members of the top management team.

However, if a team captain does not insist on the previous stated concepts and, for example, permits members to criticize and undermine each other, communication is going to be affected drastically and nothing will be shared for fear that it will

[14] Ibid., p. 623.

be used to someone's detriment. So, for communication to take place and be effective, the team captain has to ensure that all six concepts are adhered to throughout the organization. Teamwork within an organization can have a tremendous impact on the organization's effectiveness, and it behooves the manager of an entire department, as well as each individual submanager, to assure that these interrelated concepts are all adhered to.

What the manager needs to know. If a manager of an organization is to effectively manage the work and the workers, he needs to have a great deal of information about all of the component parts of the organization, the service it renders, and the people who use the service. He can only accomplish this by getting accurate, up-to-date, factual information. We will give examples of how the manager can get this information, evaluate it, and, in some instances, store it for future use. The areas that the manager needs information about are the community, what the community's needs are, and what the needs of the individual members in the community are. He also should determine how needs differ from one part of the community to another, and what services should be provided?

In addition to knowledge about the community and the people within that community, the manager needs to know what the needs of employees are. An example is given of an employee survey technique, which can assure the organization of accurate information about employees' needs in the next section. First, an example will be given of Total Performance Measurement, a program developed in Sunnyvale, California, that will show the relationship of citizen interest and employee attitude to performance measurement.

TOTAL PERFORMANCE MEASUREMENT

Total Performance Measurement is a management tool designed to increase an organization's productivity by utilizing traditional methods of management science and newer techniques drawn from various behavioral sciences. It is designed to: (1) provide data on current employee and consumer needs with interpretation and recommendations; (2) give a bottom-up approach of feedback to make certain that consumers and employees understand the relationship of organizational inputs to outputs; and (3) provide a method of continuous performance evaluation. The TPM process provides an organization with the opportunity to identify, collect and integrate three basic types of information. These deal with productivity measurements, measurements of consumer satisfaction and need and measurements of employee attitudes. The TPM system is predicated on the notion that an organization wants and needs to increase its effectiveness and efficiency.

For the past few years, government agencies have stressed the importance of using productivity measures in conjunction with other measures of performance. Performance has two dimensions. One is the dimension of efficiency, which involves the organization of employees and equipment to perform certain jobs or carry on certain functions, it is measured by such techniques as productivity rates, work measurement systems, and standards. The other is an effectiveness dimension, which deals with the impact of those jobs or functions on the accomplishment of objectives, the contributions of the jobs and functions to public needs, and the levels of quality and service. Reliance on productivity measures alone can, of course, result in misinterpretation and misconceptions about total organizational performance.

During the past few years there have been experiments with a supplementary approach to performance measurement—employee and consumer attitude measurement. An attempt has been made to develop a model that would consist of four interrelated aspects of management: productivity, effectiveness, employee attitude, and consumer attitude. The integration of attitudinal data with hard measurement data provides a powerful data base for assigning performance. Figure 7.2 depicts this integration model. As can be seen from the model, employee attitudinal data relate to both productivity and effectiveness, while consumer attitudes relate only to effectiveness. For example, employee attitudes will affect

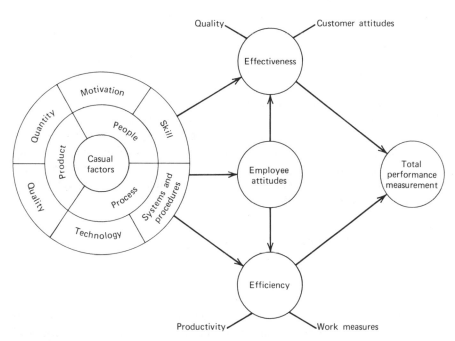

Figure 7.2. Total performance measurement system. (*Source.* Joint Financial Management Improvement Program, General Accounting Office, Washington, D.C. 20584.)

the final output in terms of quality and efficiency, while consumer attitudes will reflect the quality of the output or service provided. Attitude measurement, properly administered and used, gives an added dimension to performance assessment and problem diagnosis that is powerful in identifying significant targets of opportunity for performance improvement.

Employee Attitude Measurement

The major objective of employee attitude measurement is to provide top management with the information needed to improve the human side of productivity and effectiveness. It is *people* who produce well or poorly, turn out good or poor quality products and services, stay or leave, communicate or hold back information; it is they who take actions based on their views of their work and the work environment. An attitude questionnaire attempts to measure what employees think, why they feel the way they do, and what they plan to do about it. Employee attitudes toward work itself, barriers to performance, communications, competence of supervision, and workload factors are major determinants of employee motivation and behavior and, therefore, contributors to organizational productivity and effectiveness.

Recent experience, however, has demonstrated that, for employee attitudes measurement to be useful in assessing performance, it must differ from the usual employee or opinion surveys in the following respects:

1. The focus of the survey should be on issues directly related to performance, not on the usual personnel- or morale-oriented questions.
2. The questionnaire should not be prepackaged, but should include questions about the specific organization, its programs and policies.
3. To assure the involvement and interest of the entire organization in making needed changes, all levels of the organization must be involved in the feedback process. A "bottom–up" approach, whereby unit supervisors feed the results to their employees and then report to higher management on the changes they are prepared to make, has proved highly effective.

See Appendix C for a case study of a new concept of governmental performance management called "total performance measurement," used in the city of Sunnyvale, California.

Consumer Attitude Measurement

A promising and relatively untapped measurement tool is the use of surveys to obtain direct feedback from consumers concerning the effectiveness of products, programs, and services. Many quality aspects of services cannot be measured in any practical way other than through direct consumer surveys. Especially in the area of governmental services, consumer perceptions represent a major aspect of delivery effectiveness. It has been found that if surveys are undertaken periodically, with several questions repeated each time, the resulting trend can show whether consumers perceive improvement or deterioration in the quality of services. Questions that identify the reasons for dislike or nonuse of the product, program, or service should also be included to help identify performance deficiencies; they should be repeated to detect trends. Other uses of consumer surveys include pretesting consumer demands for new programs or services and seeking consumer opinion about the overall policies and practices of an organization. By relating this information to quantitative measures of performance, management will have comprehensive data on quality, reasons for dislike or non-use of service, potential demands for new programs or services, and indicators of the impact on overall program management.

Knowing how well a product, program, or service meets the expectations and needs of consumers is extremely important. In the private sector, the market forces quality control because the survival of a commercial organization depends on having satisfied consumers which, in turn, depends on having a satisfactory product. Unfortunately, in the public setting, the same built-in disciplines may not be present. Often the public agency is the only source of the service so, being a monopoly, it can vary the quality and timeliness of the service, without feedback as to its impact. The consumer survey can provide valuable information in helping to assess performance. (See Appendix C for a case study done by the city of Sunnyvale to determine citizen interests.)

Data Integration

All four measures are integrated to highlight "targets of opportunity" for performance improvement. It is at this point that management must be completely involved in data analysis. The process of integration can be thought of as a total system, as illustrated in Figure 7.3. The three basic steps involved are:

1. Diagnosis of the problems and needs of the organization through the four aspects of performance measurement. Determination of the structural factors that can be used in solving the problems identified by the diagnosis. Identification of the human-factor solutions required and how these should be combined with and related to the structural factors.
2. Implementation of approved solutions.
3. Repetition of all four measurements after implementation of the solutions to determine whether the problems initially identified have been overcome. The feedback process should be concerned with how the performance of the organization and the attitudes of the employees and customers may have changed.

Governmental agencies need to continue to test this approach in selected agencies. Initial results from ongoing tests indicate that this integration of data provides valuable insight into causes of performance problems.

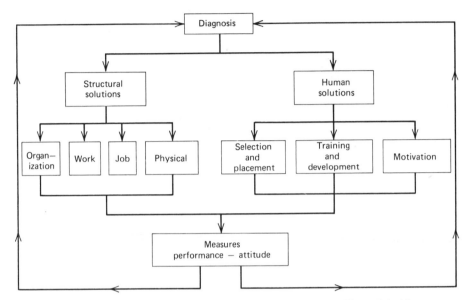

Figure 7.3. A total systems approach. (*Source.* Joint Financial Management Improvement Program, General Accounting Office, Washington, D.C. 20584.)

THE LEISURE SERVICE MANAGER AS DECISION-MAKER

In the preceding chapters, as well as part of this chapter, a number of practices, concepts, and techniques have been discussed to assist the manager in acquiring information that would permit him to make a good decision. Decision-making is a matter of choosing among various alternatives. There are basically four phases of the decision-making process, as outlined by William Newman, Charles Summer, and E. Kirby Warren:

1. Making a diagnosis;
2. Finding alternative solutions;
3. Analyzing and comparing alternatives; and
4. Selecting a plan to follow.[15]

Although other steps have been offered as being necessary to decision-making, they are generally an expansion or contraction of these four steps. Although the process may seem relatively simple when broken down into four steps, in reality decision-making can become quite complicated and difficult because of various

[15] William H. Newman, Charles E. Summer, and E. Kirby Warren, *The Process of Management*, second edition (Englewood Cliffs, N.J.: Prentice-Hall, 1967), p. 317.

distractions, pressures, prejudices, attitudes, and other factors. Decision-making is also affected by the people around us—boss, co-workers, and subordinates. But a good rule of thumb in decision-making is to determine *what is right rather than who is right* and *what is in the best interest of the organization, which is made up of individuals.*

Let us take each of the steps and analyze them in detail to gain better insight into the decision-making process. We will look at the various tools, methods, and techniques that can be employed to assure that decision-making is done effectively, efficiently and in the best interest of the organization.

Making a Diagnosis

The first phase of decision-making is making a diagnosis. The fact that something needs to be done may become apparent from different sources—personal observation, verbal or written reports, complaints, etc. Some action is called for: it may be subtle or it can be rather dramatic. But in any case, it becomes apparent that some sort of action is necessary.

There are various types of decisions that have to be made. In everyday life people have many personal decisions to make that are almost automatic, not requiring a great deal of thinking or forethought. In other cases decisions sometimes become much more complicated. A decision may affect individuals, a work group, or an entire organization. The larger the decision in terms of the number of people it will affect and its consequences, the more difficult it is to make. Within organizations, however, there are many basic decisions that are made every day which are routine and require little forethought. However, whether it is a big decision or a small decision, there is some risk involved.

Drucker, in *Management: Task, Responsibility, Practices*, describes in great detail the difference between how the Japanese make decisions and decision-making by Americans: "The Japanese, we are told, debate a proposal throughout the organization until there is agreement and only then do they make a decision."[16] He describes the frustration of many American firms when dealing with Japanese firms that keep sending new groups of individuals every few months to investigate a matter before a decision is made. Each time, the new group appears not to have heard of the situation before; that group returns to Japan and then, six weeks later, another team of people from a different area of the company show up to investigate the matter just as if they had never heard of it, taking copius notes and then going home.

What the Japanese are trying to do is involve the people who will actually have to carry out the decision when it is made in order to obtain consensus before the deci-

---

[16] Drucker, *Management: Tasks, Responsibilities, Practices*, p. 466.

sion is made. Only when all the people who have to carry out the decision have come together will the decision be made to go ahead, and only then do negotiations really start, and then the Japanese usually move with great speed. What the Japanese are trying to do is not to give answers; they are trying to determine what the question really is and if a decision is really necessary.

North Americans tend to make decisions very quickly, possibly without all the facts and input from the various levels of the organization that will have to implement the decision. Even though the North Americans arrive at their decisions more quickly, once a decision has been made, because many people have not been involved in the decision-making process, a great deal more time and energy have to be spent, selling the decision to those who have to it carry out. In some cases the decision is never actually initiated because some people are not willing to accept it. The Japanese, on the other hand, are ready to move into action very quickly because everyone has had so much involvement.

All in all, the Japanese spend a great deal more time on diagnosis of the problem so they are sure they really understand the problem rather than having to attack the symptoms of the problem. This can be compared to a doctor attempting a diagnosis. It may be easy to diagnose that the patient has a fever, but the fever is not the real cause or the problem. It is a symptom of the problem, and the real problem may be something much more serious. In decision-making, a great deal of time should be utilized to make sure the problem is really understood and that not just symptoms are being dealt with. Again, the Japanese do not focus on giving an answer; they focus on determining the question.

Finding Alternative Solutions

The second aspect of decision-making involves finding alternative solutions to the problems. Various methods of creative thinking have been advised to help the manager find alternatives in the decision-making process. One of these, brainstorming, was developed by Alex Osborn to stimulate ideas in the advertising field. The process was developed to try to come up with the greatest number of ideas possible, from which the best ideas would be selected, in an effort to maximize creativity by the group doing the brainstorming. Four basic rules were set forth:

1. Judicial judgment is ruled out. Criticism of ideas is withheld until later.
2. Free-wheeling is welcomed, the wilder the idea the better. It is better to tame the ideas down than to broaden them.
3. Quantity is the ideal; the greater the number of ideas, the more likelihood of winners.
4. Combinations and improvements are sought. In addition to contributing ideas of their own, participants should suggest how the ideas of others can be turned

into better ideas or how the two or more ideas can be joined together to form still another idea.[17]

Osborn also suggested that five additional rules would lead to the most efficient brainstorming process:

1. The session should last 40 minutes to an hour, although brief 10 to 15 minute sessions can be effective if time is limited.
2. Generally the problem to be discussed should not be revealed before the session.
3. The problem should be clearly stated and not too broad.
4. A small conference table, which allows people to communicate easily, should be used.
5. If a product is being discussed, actual samples are useful as a point of reference.[18]

The brainstorming process has been found to be a valuable tool in creating alternatives in the decision-making process, particularly to problems and decisions of a significant nature. Although traditionally brainstorming is thought of as a group process, the individual manager can utilize some of the principles in arriving at alternatives herself. She can list the alternatives on a piece of paper, adding to them from time until she has a number of solutions to the problem.

Another method of finding alternatives is to utilize experts in the given problem area. Ask various experts to offer suggestions in terms of alternatives and solutions to the problem. This can be done independently or in a group, which would tend to simulate brainstorming. Such inquiries of experts can be made in person, by letter, or by questionnaires. But whatever the method used, it is important that the expert be given enough background information as to the problem, relevent conditions, and any other pertinent information so that the alternatives he offers will be practical and have application to the problem.

Another method for determining alternatives is to use the people who will ultimately be affected by the decisions. Oftentimes the workers, the people who implement decisions, are not given consideration in terms of input prior to decision-making. Not only do they tend to implement the action more quickly if they have been a part of the decision-making process, but they often have ideas from a practical point of view in terms of alternatives that may aid in the decision-making process. Although these individuals may not be a part of the management group of an organization, they often have good ideas and should be utilized whenever possible.

The Japanese decision-making process essentially involves four steps:

---

[17] Alex Osborn, *Applied Imagination* (New York: Charles Scribner's Sons, 1953), p. 297.
[18] Ibid., pp. 300–301.

1. Focus on deciding what the decision is all about. Do not focus on giving answers or finding solutions; focus on defining the question.
2. Bring out dissenting opinions; because there is no discussion of the answer till there is consensus—a wide variety of opinions and approaches is being explored.
3. The focus is on alternatives rather than "right solutions." This process further brings out at what level and by whom a certain decision should be made.
4. The above three steps eliminate the need to sell a decision; they build effective execution into the decision making process. Finding alternative solutions to problems and decisions is one of the most essential parts of the decision making process.[19]

It is a fact that a decision is going to be no better than the alternatives from which the decision-maker can choose. The more alternatives there are, the more alternatives that have been explored and thought through, the better is the chance that the decision made will be a good one.

Analyzing and Comparing Alternatives

The next step in the decision-making process is that of analyzing and comparing alternatives. A decision is a judgment, a choice between alternatives. There are three ways to evaluate alternatives. The first of these is on the basis of past experiences. These can be the experiences of the decision-maker himself, or they can be tested against the judgment of others who have experience or expertise in a given area. Past experiences generally tell us what has worked well before, and the assumption is made that if it has worked well in the past, it will probably work well in the future. In many cases, past experiences do help us in decision making. Obviously, they are self-limiting; but the more experiences an individual has had, the more apt she is to choose the proper decision in the future.

Another method of selecting from alternatives is by experimentation. In many cases, however, experimentation can be extremely costly. The more costly the decision in terms of resources and staff, the less likely we are to experiment and try things out. On the other hand, with decisions where little will be lost, the experiment is worth trying.

The last method of selecting from alternatives is research. Obviously, certain decisions lend themselves to the research method much more than others. To date, in the leisure service field there has been limited application of the research technique in decision-making. The solution to some problems can be found by developing a model to analyze various alternatives to a particular decision. An example of this might be in developing a small-scale model of a building or some other recreation facility before trying it on an actual-size basis. Various mathematical calculations can be used to determine whether certain factors are valid. Reducing some-

[19] Drucker, *Management: Tasks, Responsibilities, Practices*, p. 470.

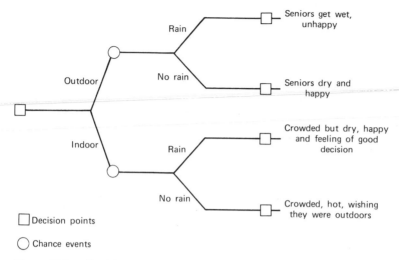

Figure 7.4. Decision tree of a recreation event of a senior citizens party.

thing to paper in terms of diagrams, schematics, and hypotheses, and testing them from a theoretical point of view or even testing them in reality can be cost saving in the long run.

The PERT analysis, is a method which may give the decision-maker insight into the various steps in a particular decision. In Chapter 2, a PERT chart was developed to test the timing of the various activities that were necessary to administer an attitude and interest survey in a community.

Another method of selecting alternatives utilizes a decision tree, such as the one given in Figure 7.4. The decision tree is a graphic representation of a decision and the various alternatives. It is one of the best ways to analyze a decision by seeing the various possible directions of action that might be taken. The branches of the tree show the various outcomes and what will be accomplished if a particular branch is followed. The decision tree allows the decision-maker to examine various solutions in an attempt to determine the outcome of each course of action.

In both the decision tree and a PERT diagram, the decision process is reduced to a geographic representation. The detailed steps of the decision are laid out in a time-sequential order, which helps in analyzing each of the activities that go into the decision-making.

Another method to assist the manager in a decision-making process is the flow-chart. A flowchart is similar to the PERT chart and the decision tree and, like them, graphically lays out the alternatives and decision points to assist the manager in thinking systematically through the decision process. Figure 7.5 depicts, in flowchart form, the decision process in the scheduling for a community

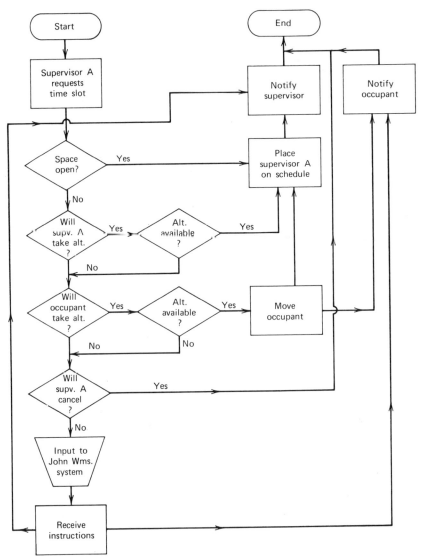

Figure 7.5. Community center. Scheduling process for Sunnyvale Parks and Recreation Department requests, current as of April 1975.

center. The chart shows the various alternatives when a requested facility is vacant and when it is in use by another group. As the circumstances change, they affect the decision process in the scheduling of the facility. Whatever process is followed, an attempt to analytically think through a decision will help the manager make better decisions.

Decisions are not made well by acclamation. Decisions are made well only when there are conflicting views and dialogue between different points of view that force the choices between different alternatives. The first rule in decision-making is that one does not make a decision unless there is a disagreement.[20] There are three reasons why dissent is necessary:

1. It safeguards the decision maker against becoming a prisoner of his own organization. Everybody always wants something from the decision maker. The only way to break out of the prison and special pleading and pre-conceived notions, is to make sure of argued, documented, thought-through disagreement.
2. Disagreement alone can provide alternatives to decisions. In a decision without alternatives, it is a desparate gambler's throw, no matter how carefully thought through it might be.
3. Dissent stimulates the imagination. Dissent converts the plausible into right and the right into good decisions. In analyzing and comparing alternatives, every possible action should be taken to make sure that the alternatives have been examined thoroughly and carefully before the decision is made.[21]

Another method of analyzing alternatives is to take each alternative and list its advantages on one side of a piece of paper and its disadvantages on the other. A similar method of accomplishing the same results is to list driving forces that would tend to support the decision and restraining forces that would tend to block the decision. In either case, after listing all the advantages or driving forces and all the restraining forces or disadvantages, a comparison is made and each is analyzed to see what advantages are really not advantages and what disadvantages can be turned into advantages. An attempt is made to thoroughly analyze each alternative and to pick the one that stands the best chance of being put into action with the least amount of restraint and will accomplish the goals and objectives of the organization.

Selecting a Plan to Follow

The final process of decision-making is that of selecting a plan of action. When an alternative has been selected, if it is to be an effective decision, it is necessary to have commitment to the plan. Hopefully, everyone who will implement the decision is in total agreement with the decision, which is likely to occur only if they have commitment to the plan. The effectiveness of any action is influenced by two factors: the appropriateness of the decision and the commitment that the employees make in carrying out the decision. *Result* is the product of the relative appropriateness of the decision times the relative commitment made to carry out that decision. Utilizing a value between 1 and 10 for appropriateness of the decision and the strength of the commitment, it can be seen that the greater the value of

[20] Ibid., pp. 472–474.
[21] Ibid., p. 473.

the variables, the more productive the result. Utilizing "D" for decision, "C" for commitment, and "R" for result, assume that the appropriateness of the decision in a situation is placed at 8. The commitment to the decision, because of non-support, is 2. $D \times C = R$, or $8 \times 2 = 16$. Because the commitment is low, although the decision was appropriate, the end result was low, a value of 16. In another example the decision was appropriate, the end result was low, a value of 16. In another example the decision is less appropriate to the solution of the problem, a value of 6, but the commitment is greater, placed at 8 because of involvement and belief in the decision, the end result is 48. It can be seen that the end result in terms of outcome is three times higher even though the decision is less appropriate. Hopefully, everyone who will implement the decision will be in agreement with it, but this is likely to occur only if they have participated in the decision-making process. Participation is not just a matter of being democratic; rather, it is a matter of involving the individuals who will implement the plan in advance of the decision so that once it is made, it is implemented with expediency and precision. If a decision has to be sold after it is made, there is little chance that any action will result. It is extremely important that we build action commitments into decisions. Until action takes place, decisions are only good intentions. To convert decisions into action requires answers to the following questions:

1. Who has to know of the decision?
2. What action has to be taken?
3. Who is to take the action?
4. What does the action have to be so the people who have to take the action can do so?[22]

The first and last steps in the decision-making process are often overlooked. No matter how good the diagnosis, how good the generation of alternatives, or how good the analysis of alternatives, unless the final step—implementing the decision with the expectation of achieving the end result—is made, all the steps that go before it are worthless. Decision-making is not a simple process, and it requires practice and hard work to make good decisions. By following the steps outlined in this discussion, it is certain that decisions will be made better in the future.

The Manager as Evaluator

In every field of endeavor, and the leisure service field is no exception, control and evaluation are needed. Without these, one cannot determine if goals have been reached. As planning starts the management process, controls and evaluation complete the process. Without controls and evaluations, the management process is ineffectual: "Controlling is a process by which the manager measures and evaluates the accomplishments of the organization against its predetermined goals,

[22] Ibid., p. 477.

objectives, budgets or schedules and makes any necessary changes that will assure more accomplishment in the future."[23]

The control and evaluation process permits the manager to see if he is on target and if he stands a chance to reach his goals and objectives as planned. Controls permit the manager to take corrective action when necessary and to determine the status of the organization at any point in time. Most controls are accomplished through people and are a measure of the effectiveness of the organization. "The best control is to prevent things from going wrong before they actually go wrong. Controls should be forward looking, probing, and enabling prediction at every stage, for possibility of error."[24]

Misconceptions About Controls

When the word "control" or "evaluation" is mentioned within most organizations, there are usually sighs, groans, and complaints from the employees because, over the years, controls have had a negative connotation for employees. The North American system has always valued individual freedom and the negative reaction to controls is, possibly, a result of that ideology.[25] Generally, though, without some control there is chaos and freedom itself is then threatened. Control is often thought of as a management tool of the entire organization, giving it a negative connotation.

Controlling the work process means control of the work, not control of the worker. Control is a tool of the worker and must never be her or his master. It must also never be an impediment to working. It should always be remembered that control is a principle of economy, not of morality. The purpose of control is to make the process go smoothly, properly, and according to high standards. To spend a dollar to protect 99 cents is not control; it is waste. The right question to ask is, What is the minimum amount of control that will maintain the process.[26] If controls are to become effective, the manager should do everything possible to eliminate their negative connotation and make the workers feel that controls can help meet their goals and objectives and give them an indication of whether they are on course.

What are controls? Controls need to focus on results—what is wanted, what is desirable, what is best. Controls should attempt to make work productive and the worker achieving. If they interfere either with production or the achievement of the worker, they defeat their purpose. They are for economy, not morality. They

[23] Dalton E. McFarland, *Management Principles and Practices* (New York: McGraw-Hill Book Co., 1958), p. 299.

[24] Harold Koontz and Cyril O'Donnell, *Principles of Management*, fifth edition (New York: McGraw-Hill Book Co., 1972), p. 587.

[25] Fred Luthans, *Organizational Behavior: A Modern Behavioral Approach* (New York: McGraw-Hill Book Co., 1973), p. 256.

[26] Drucker, *Management: Tasks, Responsibility, Practices*, pp. 217–218.

should bring order to work and accomplishment of organizational goals and objectives. For controls to be effective, it is necessary to have goals and standards stated in quantifiable terms. It is difficult to measure anything that is stated in vague or immeasurable terms. One of the best assurances of good controls is good management.

Elements of Controls

The first step in creating a good control system is to establish meaningful standards. Standards are criteria against which end results can be measured. The second step of a good control system is to design it well. It should be able to detect any deviation from standard at a very early stage so corrections can be made as quickly as possible. Obviously, the earlier the deviation can be detected, the easier it is to correct. The third step is to design measures that will restore control as quickly as possible.[27]

Figure 7.6 is a model showing the control process with feedback. Circle 1 indicates the planning process; determining the goal and stating it in measurable standards. Circle 2 indicates that the plan is put into action and the project is implemented to attain the target in circle 4. As action toward the desired project continues, something goes wrong, as indicated by the distorted circle 3. But the error is detected, fed back, and compared to the original goal; corrective action is instituted to place the agency back on course (circle 5). (Also, a change in the original goal can be made. In any case, some type of corrective action is taken and the project is under way again toward its target.) Circle 6 shows the evaluation procedure as a two-way process that functions to insure that the agency will obtain its goals or the alternative goals formulated later.[28]

Qualities of good controls include:

1. Control is a principle of economy; the less effort needed to gain control, the better the control design. The fewer controls needed, the more effective they will be. Indeed, adding more controls does not give better control; all it does is create confusion.
2. Controls must be meaningful. This means that the events to be measured must be significant either in themselves or they must be symptoms of at least potentially significant developments; that is, a sharp rise in labor turnover or absenteeism. Trivia should never be measured.
3. Controls have to be appropriate to the character and nature of the phenomenon measured. This may well be the most important aspect of controls and yet it is the least observed in the actual design of controls.

[27] McFarland, *Management Principles*, p. 311.
[28] James F. Murphy, John G. Williams, E. William Niepoth, and Paul D. Brown, *Leisure Services Delivery System: A Modern Perspective* (Philadelphia: Lea and Febiger, 1973), p. 192.

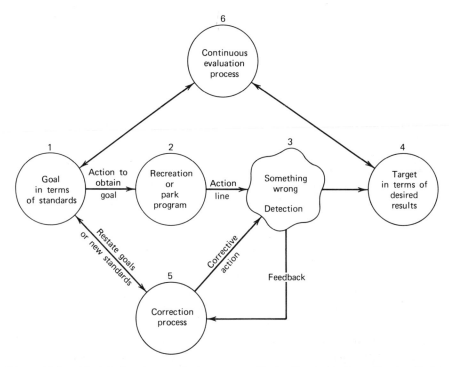

Figure 7.6. Model showing control process with feedback. (*Leisure Service Delivery System: A Modern Perspective*, by James F. Murphy, John G. Williams, E. William Niepoth, and Paul D. Brown, 1973, Lea and Febiger, publishers.)

4. The control measurements have to be congruent with the events measured. The manager has to be able to determine when it is appropriate to require more accurate controls because the more control, the more costly the service or product.

5. Controls have to be timely. Time dimension of controls is very similar to congruency, but control that comes too late or too early is no control at all.

6. Controls need to be simple. Oftentimes, complicated controls require more work than they are worth, are too difficult to understand, and will never be used. Controls that are easy to understand, for the purpose for which they were intended, stand a much better chance to be implemented.

7. Controls must be operational. They must focus on action and must help the manager make decisions quickly and promptly.[29]

[29] Drucker, *Management: Tasks, Responsibility, Practices*, pp. 499–504.

The following are examples of controls that can be used in the leisure service profession:

1. Work-hour projection report
2. Revenue report
3. Operating statement
4. Performance report
5. Achievement record
6. Payroll check register
7. Payroll analysis and distribution
8. Report on active temporary employees
9. General ledger activity report
10. Capital equipment outlay
11. Capital project operating statement
12. PERT

There are many misconceptions about controls and, generally, in most organizations, the word control or evaluation has a negative connotation. As a result, controls may be used improperly or not used at all. The control process should include standards and objectives in the measurement process that will determine if the organization is on course and headed in the right direction. Finally, controls provide indications of where, when, and how corrective action can take place. Without a proper and good control and evaluation system, the organization can never reach its goals and objectives or may never know if they have accomplished what they set out to accomplish.

OTHER MANAGEMENT JOBS

The head of a leisure service organization and other top management personnel do a great deal to set the tone of the agency with respect to its *effectiveness*, *efficiency*, and *productivity*. This book has attempted to give the leisure service manager insight into ways she can accomplish these three objectives. There are many other techniques and methods by which the manager can create an environment conducive to the achievement of these goals. The remainder of this chapter will be devoted to discussing a few of them. Although the ones that will be discussed are by no means all-inclusive, they are some of the more important ones.

Creating a Supportive Climate

It is the responsibility of every manager to do all he can to create a supportive, wholesome, and happy climate within his organization, as well as a good public image in the community in which it operates. The tone set for this supportive climate is determined by the head of the agency more than any other single person within the organization. It behooves the top manager to become aware of this and to do all he can to encourage this tone. There are several ways this can be done.

Convey a Feeling of Happiness, Friendliness, and Sincerity

In most organizations, the employees look up to the boss and, whether he realizes it or not, he sets a tone for the entire organization. Hopefully, as the top manager or head of an agency, you are happy in your work and in your personal life, and you convey this feeling of happiness. Although no individual has everything going his way, to do a good job you should be reasonably happy. This happiness can be conveyed to others in the organization by being friendly, by saying hello to people at all levels of the organization when you meet them in the hall, in a meeting, or on a project. Whether you are preoccupied or have a lot on your mind is not known to the employees you meet. Being friendly and going out of your way to say hello with a smile conveys a great deal of meaning for most employees. Knowing them by name, which sometimes can be difficult in a large organization, is still important. Asking about a sick wife, a birthday, or congratulating an employee for a job well done goes a long way in helping the morale of an organization.

Any attempt by top management to convey a feeling of happiness and friendliness in the organization will assist the organization in many ways. It goes without saying that this friendliness and happiness should be conveyed with sincerity; employees generally will see through insincerity very quickly. Although the qualities just mentioned are, hopefully, ones that a manager brings to a job, they are not automatic. The manager should keep them in mind and should constantly work on them.

Get Out and See the Organization in Operation and Get to Know the Employees Better

No manager can effectively run her organization from her office. It is important for the manager to get out into the field as often as possible to see what is going on, to learn firsthand what is taking place. Dwight Eisenhower and many other military people learned long ago that you can't always take at face value the information being passed up the chain of command. The only way you can find out for sure what is happening is to get out and see for yourself and make inquiries.

Not only do you learn what's happening within the organization, but your presence and interest convey to the people who work within the organization that you are interested and do care. It also gives you an opportunity to talk with employees and find out their concerns and problems, although you can't expect this type of response the first time you visit a facility. In fact, unless you get out often, your employees may never feel free enough to ask questions and convey their concerns to you. On the other hand, you have to make sure that your attempt to meet with employees in their environment is not taken as mistrust of them or of middle-level managers. To destroy middle-level managers' effectiveness by visiting would destroy the value of your getting out in the first place.

On some occasions, you as a top-level manager should schedule visits to facilities, programs, and special operations so that employees know you are coming and will be ready to show you specific work activities. In either case, whether an impromptu visit or a scheduled visit, you should not convey that your visit is a "spying" visit or an attempt to "find fault"; if that is the case, it will destroy the value of the visit.

Have an Open-Door Policy

Although most managers who consider themselves fair and interested in their employees indicate that they have an open-door policy, it is questionable whether they do and whether it is even possible. The idea of an open-door policy is to convey to the employees that if they have concerns, questions, or ideas, they should feel free to come and talk to top management. But with an open-door policy, in many cases, employees might be bypassing their immediate supervisors. It is questionable whether many individuals feel comfortable in bypassing their immediate supervisors, and it would probably be a rare situation for someone to take advantage of the open-door policy. The open-door policy is valid, though, because it shows good intention.

Be Interested in All Personnel

In many organizations, managers tend to be interested in select personnel only, be it their own work unit, another work unit with which they deal on a regular basis, or a group that may be part of the informal organization. It behooves the manager to be interested in all personnel, at all levels, be it the chairman of the board, the public at large, or an employee at the lowest level of the organization. Managers who convey the attitude that they are better than others do harm to the organization. As mentioned before, managers should be friendly, happy, and sincere and should convey this feeling to everyone—not just to management or to individuals at their own level or higher than themselves. Creating a class-conscious organization that segregates management from the work force creates many problems, destroys morale, and lessens productivity in the organization.

Keep the Organization Informed

Nothing is more embarrassing and detrimental to the morale of an employee than to have some member of the public ask him when the new tennis courts are going to be built and for him to be totally unaware that there are any new tennis courts planned for his park. The public expects the employees who work in an organization to know what is happening in that organization, even though it may be happening outside their own work unit. There are many ways to keep the organization informed of what is going on as well as what is planned for the future. One of these is through weekly, bi-weekly, or monthly bulletins to all employees, in which important happenings, plans, or projects can be listed (e.g., capital improvements, changes of personnel).

Another method is to have "state of the department" messages delivered by the top manager within the organization on a regular basis at a meeting of all personnel. Items such as budget information, capital improvement programs for the next several years, changes in policy, and changes in the direction of programs and activities and departmental philosophy can be discussed. These are of interest to the personnel and will help them perform better and understand their jobs, as well as be informed so they can answer questions of the general public.

It is human nature for employees to feel that they are "in the know," that they know what is going on and what is planned for the future. As indicated earlier, nothing is more embarrassing than for an employee to feel that others know more about her department, organizaton, and work group than she does.

Participate in the Community

It is important for the manager, at whatever level he operates, to know not only what is going on in his organization—above as well as below him—but also to know what is going on in the community. The best way to do this is by participating in community activities and affairs external to his his own organization. Managers of leisure service agencies spend a great deal of time in serving the general public, but during their own leisure they may not become actively involved in the community. However, if he is to do his job well, a manager needs to be aware of what is happening in the community. This can be done by participating in various social organizations (e.g., luncheon clubs, church organizations, community fund-raising drives) and by participating with his children and family in various forms of recreation activities, be they part of his own organization or operated by a private group (e.g., Young Men's Christian Association, Boys' Club, Girl Scouts). In any case, the manager should participate in community affairs so he will have a feel of the community, knowing what is going on in it and knowing the people that he serves.

Be Honest and Fair, Be a Good Example

The old adage "Don't do as I do, do as I say" isn't a good practice for a manager to follow. As mentioned earlier, the manager should set the tone and be an example for the organization. The best way managers can do this is to be honest and fair. They should be honest with their employees at all times and treat them fairly, whether passing out privileges or administering discipline. As the director of the agency, a manager should not expect special privileges or exceptions to the policies and procedures that other employees are expected to follow. The more the manager lives the example he expects of his employees, the more apt the employees will be to live up to his expectations.

Settle Conflicts

When two or more people are brought together in a work situation, a recreation program, or in any other place, there are bound to be times when conflicts arise. Most conflicts should be dealt with and handled through normal channels and by the immediate supervisor. There are, however, occasions when conflicts do occur that are not settled by a supervisor because she may not be aware of the seriousness of the conflict or may not possess the skills to solve it. Whatever the case, the director of the department, as well as other top management, need to be aware of conflict situations and to find solutions to them before they get out of control. Conflicts that occur might be the result of poor management practices. This could include poor leadership, organizational problems, or improper handling of personnel. In any case, it is in the best interest of the organization that these conflicts be settled quickly, fairly, and, hopefully, permanently.

Oftentimes compromise is the easiest solution to conflict, but in the long run compromises may only temporarily eliminate the problem. When an organizational conflict arises, the first attempts to solve it should be made by the immediate supervisor of that work group. Only after all such attempts at a lower level have failed should the manager at a higher level become involved.

The first step in settling conflict is the same as in the decision-making process: determining the problem. Often it is easier to determine some of the symptoms and sub-problems and difficult to get at the real problem. Unless the real problem is dealt with and solved, it may not be settled. Although the problem may submerge temporarily, it is bound to crop up again if it is not corrected properly.

The second step in settling a conflict is to approach the problem to determine what is wrong, rather than who is wrong. Following procedures and steps similar to decision-making the manager should be sure he understands the problem and has analyzed all the alternatives; then he is ready to select the solution he feels will solve the conflict. The corrective action should be taken quickly and promptly. However, every precaution should be taken to assure the problem will not develop again. All parties involved should understand the need for the action and, hopefully, accept the solution to the problem. The chances of the problem recurring are greater if the individuals involved do not agree or accept the solution.

In conflicts that exist between two individuals or two groups, usually the opposing sides expect the other side to change or give in. When a conflict arises it is usually not totally the fault of one individual or one group, and the solution to the conflict generally requires each side to make some concessions. It is up to the manager to develop a positive attitude toward change on the part of both sides. As mentioned in the chapter on leadership, the leader is the only one who has control over her own behavior. Likewise, in a conflict situation, each individual should consider the fact that he has control over his own behavior and very little control over the other person's behavior, and that if he initiates change then possibly they can be on their way to settling their differences.

Before change can take place, the individual or parties have to admit to themselves that change needs to take place and that they are willing to take the first step to bring about some change. Any organizational conflict—between two individuals, two work groups, management and labor, union and management, whatever the case—should be approached from the standpoint of *what is right rather than who is right*.

SUMMARY

This chapter offers the leisure service manager some insight and ideas on how he can make his organization more effective. The successful organization has one major attribute that sets it apart from the unsuccessful organization: dynamic and effective leadership. To be effective, the manager must be a good leader; he must also have technical knowledge, the necessary managerial skills, and an understanding of managerial practices in order to implement them throughout the organization. He must know how to deal with his boss, be it the city manager, the park and recreation board, or the city council. He must be able to get along with his co-workers, securing cooperation and support from them.

The manager needs to know and understand community needs and employees' needs to make decisions in the best interest of the organization and the community. He assures that the organization accomplishes its goals and objectives by the implementation of a good system for control and evaluation. The manager accomplishes this sizable task by being a good manager and leader and by setting a good example, and exhibiting sincerity, honesty, and integrity.

Marketing Leisure Services

8

Just as it is important to understand the principles of management, motivation, communication, leadership, and financing, it is also essential to understand the concept of *marketing* as it applys to the delivery of leisure services.[1] Marketing is a method of directing the activities that take place in an organization toward the satisfaction of consumer needs and demands. Although there is no universal agreement on how to define marketing, it is generally agreed that marketing involves an exchange of values between two parties. In a profit-oriented organization, a service is provided by one party to obtain revenue from another. In this case, marketing is based on the assumption that satisfaction of customers will insure profitability. In a nonprofit organization, such as a tax-supported park and recreation department wherein tax revenues and/or fees and charges are exchanged for services, the marketing motive is directed toward insuring the survival and stability of the organization (without necessarily turning a profit). Application of the marketing concept allows an organization to maximize its impact by constantly adjusting its output in terms of the projected needs of the consumer.

---

[1] We recognize that the concept of marketing leisure services is not completely philosophically consistent with the delivery of public leisure services. Further, we recognize that use of the word "consumers" implies that recreation and leisure personnel are involved in what can be termed a non-professional occupation. A profession usually defines those who participate in its activities as clients. One of the key distinctions between a professional and a nonprofessional is that the former dictates to the individual what is good or bad in terms of value judgments. The premise of professional action presupposes that an individual does not have an appropriate background to make decisions in that he or she isn't experienced or knowledgeable in the particular field.

Contrary to this notion of professionalism is the voluntary nature of involvement by individuals in the consumption of leisure services. People do have the ability to discriminate and choose among a variety of resources in fulfilling their leisure needs. Further, if they so choose, they may organize their own leisure services without the aid of the leisure service expert. We have tried to bring a dual perspective to this book; that is, we have tried to incorporate management practices that can be applied in either public or private leisure delivery systems. Marketing, in the authors' opinion, is one of these techniques.

TYPES OF MARKETS

What is a market? Markets are people. They consist of individuals who have certain needs and are willing to exchange something of value to satisfy those needs. Markets may be differentiated from one another by identifying subclusters of individuals who consume a specific type of service. Thus persons consuming leisure services may be referred to as existing within the subcluster known as the "leisure market." Individuals within a subcluster may be described, according to Jack Z. Sissors in a number of ways:

1. SIZE OF MARKET. The market may be understood by simply viewing its size. Size may be measured in terms of total dollar sales and/or the number of individual units of potential consumers. In public parks and recreation, the number of households in a community is typically used as a yardstick when planning family-oriented recreation programs.
2. GEOGRAPHIC LOCATION OF CONSUMERS. The geographic distribution of consumers within a local community, region, or state can have tremendous impact on the planning of leisure services. The density of population in a given area can serve as a guideline for location of facilities, services, and programs. On the other hand, the location of consumers in a given area might necessitate transportation to facilities. Geography, obviously, is also influenced by climate and physical characteristics.
3. DEMOGRAPHIC CHARACTERISTICS OF CONSUMERS. Consumers are grouped and classified according to sex, age, income, marital status, ethnic origin, race, religion, and occupation. As indicated in Chapter 1, for example, a person's income level will affect the type of leisure products he or she owns. This, in turn, will influence participation in certain leisure-time activities.
4. SOCIOPSYCHOLOGICAL CHARACTERISTICS OF CONSUMERS. This allows the manager to gain some insight into consumer needs based on social class, human values, degrees of introversion-extroversion, degrees of submissiveness-aggressiveness, risk-taking propensity, and other factors. For example, until recently, tennis was pursued and had high-status appeal among the affluent. Activities such as hang gliding, skin diving, and auto racing have become increasingly popular, presumably among individuals who have a high propensity for risk taking. Their psychological needs for adventure are on a higher plane than most people's and are satisfied through such activities.
5. IDENTIFICATION OF THE PURCHASER OF THE SERVICE AND THOSE INFLUENCING THE PURCHASER. The purchaser of the service may or may not be the participant in the service involved. For example, a mother might purchase swimming lessons for her children. Thus it is important to identify the purchaser of the service to better determine the market that one is directing one's effort toward. Obviously, this becomes important when selecting various promotional activities. The question becomes, "Who does the manager try to com-

municate with?" It can be the individual purchasing the service, the individual possibly influencing the purchaser, or both.

6. WHEN SERVICES ARE PURCHASED. People have leisure at differerent times. This can be viewed in two ways. First, daily leisure time may vary depending on one's working hours, vocation, and age. For example, school-age children will not ordinarily be free until after school, whereas preschoolers are free during the day. Some adults may be home during the day, some may be free only in the evening, and for many, weekends represent a wide time frame for leisure activities. Second, looking at when leisure services are purchased on a broader scale, it is reasonable to consider seasonal fluctuations and the affect they have on consumer behavior. Within the parks and recreation field, the summer months reflect a tremendous increase in services purchased; it is the most active season of the year. Not only are certain seasons busier than others, but specific seasons will entail the consumer purchase of services relative to that season only. In other words, ice skating may be at a premium in the winter months, whereas baseball leagues may be one of the services most in demand during the spring and summer months.

7. HOW SERVICES ARE PURCHASED. There are two important factors that should be considered when determining how services are purchased. The first is to determine whether buying is done on an impulse basis or whether it is done with a good deal of forethought. This might integrate with income— demonstrating the synergism that exists between all of these factors. Recreation theorists have traditionally hypothesized that anticipation prior to engaging in an activity is an integral part of the leisure experience. Although this may be true, there is also a case to be made for spontaneous leisure happenings. These two elements will influence the type of services that are created and the methods used to promote them. The second factor of importance is the frequency of consumption of a given service. The number and frequency of consumer visits to a given region will affect its hours of operation, hence its availability.[2]

In determining a market, one must be mindful of the interrelationships among these seven factors. Although segmenting the market is extremely helpful in understanding and dealing with the consumers to be served in a logical manner, we are dealing with people in a holistic sense. All the facets used in differentiating among consumers are interrelated. For example, how services are purchased will be related to income level, hence demographic characteristics.

Differentiating allows the leisure service manager to more accurately identify the needs of her or his constituency. To assume that there is an eagerly awaiting mass of individuals ready to consume a given organization's leisure services results in unproductive management. In the public sector, this approach to pro-

[2] Jack Z. Sissors, "What Is a Market?" *Journal of Marketing, 30* (July 1966), pp. 18–19.

viding services has yielded mediocrity and has contributed to waste in bureaucratic organizations; in business, it has led to failure. Differentiation also allows the manager to pinpoint consumer needs that are already being met through other agencies. This is critically important in the public sector, where funds are limited and duplication of services is a waste of resources. It also allows managers to identify new services that can be created where there is a vacuum.

There are a number of sources that can be used to help determine market needs. Census data can provide information describing such things as age, sex, and marital status and are readily available at any library. Information concerning attitudes and behavior can be obtained by reviewing trends in participation, as exemplified by attendance at activities. Still another method available is that of surveying through the use of questionnaires. Use of the survey format can provide information on leisure behavior and attitudes. Many public parks and recreation departments have advisory or policy making boards to help determine consumer needs and interests. In many cases, an individual will represent a select group of consumers, voicing their needs and concerns. Citizen participation has been a cornerstone in the formulation of leisure services. The process of involving people in decisions that affect their leisure life-style should be encouraged as a method of gaining market information.

DEVELOPING A MARKETING STRATEGY

Planning a strategy utilizing the marketing concept involves two interrelated tasks:

1. Selecting a target market.
2. Developing the most appropriate mix for the target market.[3]

A target market consists of a homogeneous group of consumers toward which an organization may direct its services. The market mix consists of four basic variables: *creation, pricing, distribution,* and *promotion* of the service. There are three basic types of services created by leisure service organizations: activities, facilities, and information and consultation. The promotion of activities involves publicity, advertising, use of the media, and public relations. The distribution of a service essentially involves finding appropriate locations and times to provide the service to the consumer. Pricing is the method used to determine the charge to be made for a service. These are discussed in detail later in the chapter.

Jerome McCarthy and Stanley Shapiro emphasize the interrelatedness of these factors. They suggest that one cannot be accomplished without the other and that they must be done concurrently. When attempting to meet the needs of a target

[3] Jerome E. McCarthy and Stanley J. Shapiro, *Basic Marketing* (Georgetown, Ontario: Irwin-Dorsey, 1975), p. 69.

market, the types of services to be offered, as well as the cost of these services and their location, must be taken into consideration.

The marketing process involves close examination of the target population. An analytical tool used in this process is known as the "market grid." Market gridding involves identification of the relevant characteristics of the group the organization is trying to serve and plotting them on a grid to facilitate analysis. Figure 8.1 represents a market grid concerned with providing leisure activities to a variety of age groups. Each box represents an individual target market, for example, hobbies for senior citizens. Once the target has been identified, it is again segmented to determine the potential that exists in this area. The process continues until a precise target has been determined.

By adopting a market strategy, an organization makes more effective and efficient use of its resources for two reasons. First, it more carefully aligns itself with consumer expectations, and therefore its resources are concentrated in areas where they will most benefit the consumer. Second, by understanding the marketing process and the interrelatedness of these functions, the control an organization has of its basic work activities is increased. Use of the marketing strategy forces an organization to develop a solid foundation of knowledge for making decisions. An increased exchange of information within an organization will allow individuals within the organization to look at different marketing components in relation to his or her own assignment.

Marketing is a process that can be thought of as an orderly method of carrying out the objectives of an organization. The alternative is to haphazardly deliver services without due consideration of the controllable factors that exist within the domain of an organization. Marketing allows managers to take calculated risks, rather than perform administration tasks purely by guesswork. In the remainder of this chapter, discussion is centered on the four activities in the marketing process: creating, pricing, distributing, and promoting services.

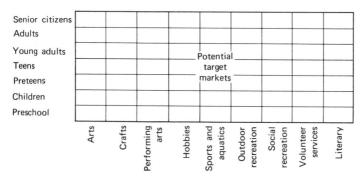

Figure 8.1. Targeting need areas for leisure service activities.

Creating Services

This process attempts to develop a service that can be offered to the consumer to satisfy his/her needs. Three types of services are discussed: activities, facilities, and information and counseling. It is important to remember that services are created to meet the needs of a specific target market. A large portion of any leisure service organization's resources are consumed by the services created. Consequently, it is vital that the leisure service manager be exact in identifying the relationship between the needs of the target market and the services that are created.

Activities
Activities are carefully designed, purposeful, plans of action directed toward producing behavioral changes in people. They are structured, although the program form chosen may result in a flexible or rigid format. Leadership is the key element in the successful implementation of any activity. Functions carried out by a leader may range from giving instruction to providing general supervision. There is an array of activity *areas* within the domain of leisure delivery styems, and they can be used to meet the varying needs, interests, and capabilities of the individuals being served. These include the following:

1. *The Arts.* Programs in the arts may include both graphic and plastic forms. Among the art activities that could be incorporated into a leisure service delivery organization are oil painting; pen-and-ink drawing; photography; stone, metal, and clay sculpturing; tapestry making; block printing; and wood carving.
2. *Crafts.* A craft may be distinguished from an art as producing a product that serves a utilitarian purpose. Some examples might be leather craft, sewing, embroidery, tie-dyeing, candle making, snow and ice sculpturing, ceramics, fly tying, furniture refinishing, and macrame.
3. *Performing Arts.* This term involves artistic expression in which the participant is the mode of expression (e.g., acting, singing, and dancing). The important determinant is that the participant is actually involved in doing the activity. Whether an audience is present is of no consequence, although viewing performing arts (e.g., the theatre) is an extemely popular leisure pursuit. Modern dance, pantomime, puppetry, opera, barbershop quartets, symphony orchestras, and dramatizations are all examples.
4. *Hobbies.* A hobby is a recreation activity pursued over an extended period with immense interest. Two classifications of hobbies are "collecting" and "creating." Examples of collecting hobbies might be stamps, coins, guns, books, antiques, nature objects, dolls, and models. Creative hobbies could include writing, composing, cooking, and gardening.
5. *Sports, Games, and Athletics.* Any physical activity that requires gross and/

or fine motor muscle control may be categorized herein. Swimming, track and field, rifle shooting, archery, golf, weight lifting, handball, badminton, volleyball, softball, and water polo are all examples.

6. *Outdoor Recreation.* Outdoor recreation activities are oriented toward natural resources. Among those recreation activities that strongly depend on natural resources are sailing, fishing, camping, hiking, and hunting.

7. *Social Recreation.* Social recreation involves activities that are created with the purpose of bringing about interaction among individuals. Generally speaking, the setting in which the event is carried out is most important. Consumers attending parties, drop-in programs and dances are participating in social recreation activities.

8. *Volunteer Services.* Volunteer programs involve the use of one's skills and abilities during one's leisure time, with the purpose of giving to others. Whereas other individuals may receive satisfaction from directly participating in an activity, the volunteer receives his or her satisfaction from the services rendered to others.

9. *Travel.* This is perhaps one of the most frequent leisure activities in which individuals indulge. It can range from visiting a friend or relative to extensive sight-seeing tours to exotic locales. The travel and tourism industry is a vast network that can plan comprehensively for its clients; services rendered include lodging, transportation, eating facilities, guided tours, and so on.

10. *Literary.* Literary activities provide recreation and leisure opportunities that emphasize mental and linguistic activities. An example would be a group of individuals meeting to discuss current events, politics, religion, or books of interest.

Although the activity areas mentioned emphasize participant involvement, this is not intended to de-emphasize the fact that many individuals use their leisure time to enjoy activities through observation. Certainly, an individual can become deeply involved in and derive personal satisfaction and pleasure from attending a play, concert, or athletic event. These are all activities that could be part of a leisure service organization's program.

In addition to offering leisure programs in a variety of activity areas, the method, or form, used to deliver the service is important. Activity *form* refers to the way an activity is organized. In many cases, the method used to deliver an activity will dictate its success or failure. Again, if diverse needs are to be met, programs and services must be organized and structured so they appeal to the appropriate target market. Activity forms that might be utilized in organizing leisure services include the following:

1. *Competitive.* Many recreation and leisure activities, especially sports, games, and athletics, can be competitive in nature. Competition can stimulate interest and provide motivation among participants. This is not true only for sports

enthusiasts; it is also true in other program areas. Recreation and leisure activities that focus on competition should take into consideration the relative skills and ability of the participants involved and correspondingly adapt the level or intensity of competition. Common methods used to organize program areas into competition include leagues, tournaments, and contests.

2. *Drop-In Activities.* These provide the participant with an element of freedom as the counterpart to activities that operate on rigidly fixed time schedules. Generally speaking, activities are arranged in a manner that allows them to be either ongoing or capable of producing opportunities for spontaneous involvement. Examples might be utilization of a gymnasium for jogging or a library for reading.

3. *Class.* Another method of organizing recreation and leisure activities is through instructional classes. Classes are generally formal when compared to the drop-in setting. They usually involve the hiring of an instructor to teach within a given subject area. Although the class setting may be formal in comparison to other program forms, the emphasis in this setting is one of individual concern and attention.

4. *Club.* A club consists of a group of people who are associated with each other for a common purpose. The club membership usually provides its own leadership, organization, and perhaps finances. A club is usually a self-contained unit, except that it often needs facilities where it can hold meetings and carry out its purpose.

5. *Special Events.* A special event is a method of organizing an activity in a unique manner. Ranging from simply executed activities to elaborate and lengthy productions, the special event is a method of stimulating interest; it has tremendous potential for any leisure delivery system. Special events might include exhibits, parades, festivals, concerts, trips, demonstrations, and carnivals.

6. *Workshop.* The workshop is a method of organizing activities and people into a format that allows for intense participation in a short period of time. The duration of a given workshop is usually determined by the amount of material to be covered. Workshops are usually no longer than two weeks in length, however, and in many situations they are organized for much shorter periods of time.

7. *Outreach.* Many programs and services are organized around the utilization of facilities rather than around people and their needs. Outreach programs meet people in their own locale. Emphasis is placed on taking the activity to the participant, rather than having the participant come to the facility in which the activity is located. Mobile swimming pools, libraries, nature centers and zoos are examples of outreach programs.

All activities, regardless of the setting in which they are provided, follow a similar organizational pattern. The manager, after identifying the target market, must take into consideration the activity area to be used, the form that will be used to deliver the service, the duration or length of the activity, the type of equipment and/or facilities necessary for implementation of the service, and the type and number of leaders to be employed. Once these factors have been taken into account, the service can be blended with the other variables within the market mix—pricing, distribution, and promotion. If all of these principles and factors are observed, one should be able to organize any activity appropriate to a given setting. Special conditions in certain settings may, however, require modification of the rules of a game or the type of equipment used.

Facilities
Facilities are the areas and/or buildings that are used in the delivery of leisure services. They are central to the effective provision of leisure service activities to the target market. Without an appropriate facility, the organization and implementation of certain activities (basketball, swimming) is virtually impossible. Further, the provision of a certain type of area, such as a park, gives individuals the opportunity to choose self-directed and self-planned activities. A park becomes the vehical for many activities, some of which are chosen spontaneously and some of which involve detailed planning. Almost any area or building has the potential for the provision of leisure services. One's home or residence is undoubtedly the greatest resource for leisure.

A facility can be developed that allows for the incorporation of a leisure experience as a supplement to its primary function. For example, a festive atmosphere exists at Ghirardelli Square, San Francisco, California, which is a private development that includes shops, restaurants, art galleries, and entertainment housed in what was formerly Ghirardelli Chocolate Factory. This square provides the opportunity for individuals to experience leisure in a creative setting.

A number of facilities have been associated with the provision of leisure services. Some of these are the following:

1. *Parks*. The primary function of a park is to provide individuals with an opportunity to participate in outdoor leisure activities. Often, a park is equipped with benches, picnic tables, landscapes, plantings, play equipment, trails, and water areas. It may also include areas that can be utilized for baseball, football, and so on.
2. *Aquatics Complexes*. Complexes used for aquatics may involve the construction and operation of swimming pools, beaches, lakes, and marinas. Aquatic activities associated with these various facilities are popular leisure services. Investment by public and private agencies can be quite substantial in this area.
3. *Playgrounds*. This facility provides space for active recreation, especially for children. Provision for play equipment, paved open space, landscaped areas,

benches, picnic tables, and/or small shelters are usually made. A playground is thought to be distinct from a park in that urban areas may have playgrounds that consist solely of asphalt and playground equipment.

4. *Gymnasiums.* This type of facility accommodates a variety of activities, including basketball, badminton, volleyball, gymnastics, floor hockey, physical fitness programs, square dancing, and shuffleboard. Gymnasiums are usually designed today as multipurpose facilities to accommodate many different types of leisure services.

5. *Tennis, Handball, and Squash Facilities.* Perhaps one of the fastest growing activities in North America is tennis. Simultaneous with an increase in participation has been the construction of indoor and outdoor tennis facilities. With the advent of air-supported structures, many outdoor facilities have been transformed into indoor ones. A well-developed indoor tennis complex may include handball and squash courts, sauna baths, and exercise equipment.

6. *Golf Courses.* This facility not only provides participation in the sport of golf, but also serves as an open-space area. Most golf courses generate enough revenue to produce a profit and can be complemented by such other facilities as restaurants, driving ranges, and shops where equipment and clothing can be purchased. Frequently, golf courses are the primary focus in a complex that includes swimming pools, tennis courts, social meeting facilities, and so on.

7. *Physical Fitness, Judo, and Karate Centers.* Frequently operated on a profit basis, these types of facilities run the gamut from elaborate buildings that include exercise equipment, swimming pool, sauna baths, and a gymnasium to sparse rooms that may include nothing more than exercise mats.

8. *Ice Rinks.* Artificial and natural ice rinks provide opportunities for ice skating, hockey, curling, and speed skating. Ice rinks have been developed by public and private agencies across North America. Their popularity has steadily increased during the past several decades.

9. *Amusement Parks.* Theme parks established by Walt Disney Productions have made the amusement park concept a dynamic leisure enterprise. A variety of activities can be found at an amusement park, depending on its sophistication.

10. *Skiing Facilities.* The ski slope is the primary facility and attraction found in ski resorts. A ski slope is usually supported by a large number of services and other facilities. They may include lodging, food and beverage services, ice rinks, sled runs, and so on.

11. *Theaters.* A theater is a facility used to present an event before an audience. It accommodates people for educational, cultural, and entertainment programs. This may include live stage productions, films, concerts, operas, children's theater, lectures, and dance programs.

12. *Billiard and Bowling Complexes.* The old poolroom has taken a new twist. Billiard facilities that are considered to be respectable establishments, catering to the entire family, have been constructed. Bowling is one of the oldest and most popular sports. Virtually every community in North America has a bowling alley.
13. *Recreation and Community Centers.* Such facilities are usually operated under the direction of a public agency and may include a gymnasium, multipurpose room, stage, locker-room facilities, clubrooms, arts and crafts rooms, lounging areas, photography room, kitchen, swimming pool, archery range, rifle range, music room, wrestling room, and meeting rooms.

It is important that the leisure service manager understand the processes involved in the planning and construction of leisure service facilities. Marvin Gans has developed a sequential process model that can be utilized in the development of a leisure facility. Modified by the authors, the steps in this model are essentially as follows:

1. Realize that the need for future facilities may fluctuate based on the expansion of existing activities or the creation of new ones.
2. Involve and organize all the personnel who will have a role in planning the facility. This might include consultants, financiers, and people that will be operating and using the facility.
3. Select and hire a well-qualified architect.
4. Gather information concerning space needs, programming trends, existing facilities, modern facility innovation, and available equipment.
5. Write a detailed description of the service to be provided, its associated needs, and its manner of functioning.
6. Write the detailed qualitative and quantitative space requirements necessary to accommodate the proposed services.
7. Develop a well-defined and realistic project calendar.
8. Review carefully the architectural drawings and specifications at each stage.
9. Select and hire reputable contractors for the construction of the facility.
10. Complete the facility under the control of a well-qualified project supervisor.
11. Formally accept the facility, install the fixed and movable equipment, and orient the staff.
12. Occupy the facility and initiate the service.[4]

Information and Counseling
Provision of information services is a new function being performed by leisure service delivery systems. A leisure-centered life-style calls for the development of

---

[4] Marvin Gans. "Sequential Steps in Planning Facilities for Health, Physical Education, Recreation and Athletics," (doctorial dissertation, University of Utah, 1972), p. 98.

a host of new attitudes and capabilities on the part of consumers. It also results in the need for the creation of innovative services. Many public leisure service organizations have recognized that they cannot be all things to all people. It is simply not feasible financially. Therefore they have adopted a new role: increasing the public's awareness of services that are provided in both the public and private sectors. Many organizations are identifying, storing, and disseminating leisure and community services information. Recognizing that it is extremely difficult for the consumer to have a comprehensive awareness and understanding of all existing activities, facilities, and other services, these organizations have established a central point that serves as a clearinghouse for compiling and disseminating leisure information.

An example of this service is the Leisure Information Services Bureau operated by the Department of Recreation and Leisure Services, Fremont, California. This bureau disseminates information to the public, primarily via the telephone. Information regarding both public and private leisure services is indexed and passed onto consumers on request. For example, should an individual want to visit a museum in San Francisco, the bureau would be able to inform him or her as to the locations of the museums, their hours of operation and cost, and current activities of interest within these facilities.

This approach to providing information is unique because it recognizes that an integrated, holistic approach in regard to community information best serves the needs of consumers. The lack of information about leisure services seriously restricts consumers' ability to maximize their leisure options. By increasing consumers' awareness of potential leisure services, an organization is in a position to best meet its constituents' leisure needs. In addition, this type of approach provides assistance to all organizations delivering leisure services by publicizing their programs.

Another new service being provided by leisure service organizations is leisure counseling. As Ken Cross states, "The leisure counseling process focuses on the individual and is concerned with: understanding the self concept; self development; interpersonal skills; clarification of values; leisure lifestyle; decision-making; and self evaluation."[5]

Gene Hayes has outlined a process that can be useful in understanding leisure counseling. He suggests that it is essentially a developmental process that allows a professional person with specialized skill in and knowledge of: 1) leisure and recreation; 2) psychomotor, cognitive and affective domains of individual growth and development; and 3) individual and group facilitation techniques. The professional person also helps the client by establishing a framework for communication that will facilitate individual decisions and action through the following:

[5] Ken Cross, "Leisure Counseling, An Overview with a Community Setting Emphasis," *Recreation Review 6*, no. 1 (July 1976), p. 23.

- discussion
- personal encounter
- activity involvement
- observation in activities and discussions
- identification of community leisure resources

This will help the client to acquire the following:

- personal values and attitudes
- individual goals and objectives
- self-confidence and self-esteem
- skills, knowledges, competencies
- successful experiences

This process should enable the client to successfully enjoy his free time, or leisure time, in the manner which he chooses and which is in concert with his own value system. The process would also provide the framework for the individual to pursue his interests on his own volition.[6]

The counseling process can help individuals adjust to a leisure-centered life-style. The leisure explosion is a recent phenomenon, and many people have not yet developed the personal capabilities to deal with the leisure void. Leisure delivery service organizations have long been involved in providing educational activities that allow people to acquire leisure skills. Leisure counseling serves the same function, although it is a process which recognizes not only that people need to acquire cognitive and psychomotor skills and develop leisure-oriented attitudes, but also that a person may require assistance in identifying his/her own abilities, skills, and attitudes prior to sampling an activity. It allows an individual to gain an understanding of the leisure phenomenon, relate the concept to his/her own value system and skills, and thereby maximize his/her own leisure experience.

An example of a leisure counseling program is the Leisure Services Center in the twin communities of Kitchener and Waterloo in Ontario, Canada. The purpose of this center is to help individuals toward a better leisure experience. To do this, the center offers an information system of community leisure opportunities, a counseling service, a somewhat restricted leisure education program, exploratory devices and aids, and a small library.

The center emphasizes counseling, or the personal facilitation process. Individuals are helped to explore and clarify their own needs and interests and then to act on these. The information system, with cross files and categories specific to the twin communities, is used as a counseling aid, providing a wide range of opportunities from which to choose.

---

[6] Gene A. Hayes, "Leisure Education Counseling Model," a monograph, University of Waterloo, Ontario, 1975.

Because this is a demonstration project with limited government funding, an important aspect is the eventual integration with an appropriate community agency. Future plans include establishing a Leisure and Learning Exchange, which may be partly self-supporting through membership fees.

Pricing

Pricing is another one of the variables in the marketing mix that is within the control of the manager. The goals and objectives of profit-oriented organizations will differ from nonprofit organizations in the area of pricing their services. Generally speaking, a business is interested in achieving customer satisfaction and profit. Nonprofit organizations are also interested in customer satisfaction, but success in this area is not necessarily equated with profit. Both types of organizations produce revenues; however, the profit-oriented business expects to have surplus income after expenditures. Even nonprofit organizations that receive tax subsidies are more often assessing fees and charges to their customers in an effort to extend the services they provide. Certainly, both types of organizations are concerned with the concept of pricing, although the extent to which pricing strategies have been utilized is far greater and more sophisticated in the private than in the public sector.

Why is pricing so important? The price of a service is the single most important determinant of its demand, which is why pricing is so vital to the success of the service. Generally, a lower-priced service is going to create more demand than a higher-priced service; however, this does not indicate that the lower price will result in the greatest income for the organization. An organization must select the target market and accordingly adjust the price to reflect it. A higher-priced service may be more effective financially if it is aimed at a high-income target market, although the demand for the service, in numbers of persons, is less. The marketing efforts, in terms of promotion and so on will be greatly influenced by the pricing philosophy adopted. Again, the target market, and the pricing which that market may generate, will determine the slant that promotional efforts will take and the types of services that will be provided.

Three factors have to be taken into consideration when settling on a pricing strategy. First, all organizations need a flow of cash to purchase the resources that are transformed into services. Any organization's minimum expectation is to reach the break-even point, that is, the point at which expenditures equal incoming revenues. In a public parks and recreation department, this minimum expectation can be the goal that guides pricing strategy. In other words, the department does not alter or inflate the prices it charges for services in order to create a surplus of funds. On the other hand, to insure profitability and a reasonable return on investments, businesses must go beyond the break-even point. Their profit margin must exceed their operating costs and must also provide investors with a satisfactory return on their investments.

The second factor that influences the pricing strategy is the amount an individual will pay for a given service. If we accept the concept of marketing, we essentially believe that the role of the manager is to determine the target market—a set of individuals with homogeneous characteristics. Implied in this concept is that various groups will have different needs and interests and a different ability to pay for a service. In the private sector, profit-oriented organizations will establish different types of services priced at different levels. They pick a target population that they hope to attract, and their pricing may not be within the range of accessibility of all people. Governmental agencies, on the other hand, may develop a pricing strategy that is directed toward equalizing economic inequities. One of the main reasons that a given group of people band together collectively (e.g., into organizations) is to create and distribute services that are unattainable on an individual basis. National parks serve as an example of this, as do community swimming pools.

Third, the image that a service has can be affected by its pricing. Many times a high-priced service is viewed as being more valuable than a lower-priced service ("you get what you pay for"). Pricing may also relate to the status or prestige attached to a given type of service. An example of this phenomenon is the preference of swimming at a country club as opposed to the community public pool. Also, people's expectations tend to increase with the price of the service offered. Thus, when a service is offered at a high price, the consumer will be more discerning and critical of the service, becoming dissatisfied if it does not meet her or his expectations. One of the problems that occurs in governmental agencies is that pricing comes under a blanket philosophy of charging a minimal fee for services. Again, this notion, while perhaps well intended, ignores the marketing principle of applying pricing that is relevant to the dictates of the target market. There is a danger of discouraging participation because the price is too low and consumers suspect the quality of the service.

A number of methods are used in pricing and, although they apply primarily to profit-oriented leisure delivery systems, certain of these concepts are applicable to governmental agencies as well.

Multiple-Unit Pricing

This involves providing the consumer with a discount on the regular per capita price, providing he or she buys in quantity. The consumer buys more units, but pays less. Municipal parks and recreation departments have long engaged in multiple-unit pricing by selling family season passes for summer swimming programs. In this case, the family pays less as a group than they would on an individual basis.

Full-Line Pricing

This approach provides for a variance of prices throughout the services offered by an organization. Basically, this is intended to expand the target market to many income levels for a given service. For example, a travel agency may offer a trip to the Bahamas that ranges from an economy, no-frills tour to an expensive and luxurious first-class venture.

Leader Pricing

This form of pricing entices the consumer into a facility or an activity with a low fee, and then inflates the prices of other items associated with the activity (e.g., food or supplies). A manager must be wary of this technique because it may result in consumer dissatisfaction. An example of this method in the public leisure sector might be a knitting class offered at a low fee, but involving the purchase of expensive materials for use in the class from the class instructor. On a larger scale, there are many private, profit-oriented amusement parks that charge one low entry fee, but surprise their consumers with extremely high-priced food items and other expensive extras.

Penetration Pricing

To build up a clientele, sometimes it is desirable to initiate customer participation, even at a loss. This technique is applicable to both profit and nonprofit organizations. It allows one to build a market for a service.

Skimming

Frequently utilized by businesses, this technique establishes a high price for a new service in order to reap the profits from the high-income target market. The price is steadily declined to systematically reach those who are progressively less affluent. For example, a new amusement park may start out with a high admission fee. However, it will lower its price in several increments, covering various income levels, until it finds the appropriate target market.

Distribution of Services

This variable attempts to determine the most effective way to present a service to the consumer. To do this, the manager must select an appropriate location that will have maximum attraction to the target market. She must also identify the correct time to provide the service to the consumer. And, further, she must decide who will be responsible for carrying the service to the consumer, including the delineation of those who will be in charge of its promotion and actual implementation. In other words, this variable involves identification of those responsible for distribution of the service, and where and when it will take place. If there is a maxim to be followed in the distribution of services, it is that the manager should get the services to the consumer where he wants them and when he wants them.

When selecting a location or facility, a number of factors must be taken into consideration. The first and most important is its availability to the consumer. Although we live in a very mobile society, accessibility is an extremely critical factor in the selection of a service. While serving with the Oak Park (Illinois) Recreation Department, one of the authors plotted the residences of consumers who were participating in a lighted schoolhouse program (After-hours use of schools for adult recreation programs), in relation to the location of the facility attended. It was found that most of the participants lived in close geographic proximity to the facility where the activity was held. Very few individuals would travel across the village, which was just one mile by four miles. In this particular situation, to encourage participation in other geographic areas of the village, it might have been appropriate to establish more than one distribution center for the service offered.

Obviously, the selection of a location and/or facility should be determined by its relationship to the community's living patterns. One has to take into consideration both the type of service being provided and its relationship to such factors as transportation networks, population densities, residential dwellings, and industrial areas. Ideally, the best location for a given service is in an area where there is a high concentration of the target population.

Another factor to be taken into consideration when choosing a location and/or facility to provide a service is the compatibility of the distribution point. People, when consuming community-based leisure services, want their services to be located within their range of general activity.

A wide variety of facilities can be used to distribute leisure services. Parks, community centers, schools, stores, shopping center malls, public squares, streets, and private homes are all channels through which leisure services can be distributed. Organizations that have a large and diversified number of services catering to numerous target markets should seek out a wide array of facilities in which to provide services. In this case, it can be an error to become strictly facility oriented, operating only those programs that can be accommodated within a given facility. On the other hand, there are many organizations, especially profit-oriented ones, that market a service involving a unique facility. This type of organization usually has a specific target market, very narrowly defined, and can adequately meet the needs of its consumers by limiting its service functions.

Selecting an appropriate time to distribute a given leisure service seems to be a simple enough task. We have traditionally thought that people's time could be broken up into blocks consisting of subsistence (food, work, etc.), existence (work), and leisure time. In this book, we dispute this notion because we believe that a leisure experience can be integrated in a holistic way with other life functions. The critical factor is determination of the type of service being offered and the behavioral consequences that will occur upon participation in it. It is obvious that certain types of individuals engage in leisure at different times. The factory worker is tied to a rigid, inflexible schedule, whereas the college professor's time is relatively flexible. In addition, people have preferences for specific days on which to engage in leisure pursuits. A person's life-style will therefore influence his preference for the time of day, the day of the week, and the time of the year that he chooses to participate in an activity. Discovery of appropriate times to offer services is critical to the success of the manager in effectively distributing services.

The final element to be considered in the distribution of services is the establishment of a system of accountability and responsibility. Someone has to be responsible for the various components that are involved in providing a service. In some organizations, pricing is handled by one individual, creation of the service by another individual, promotion by others, and implementation by still others. For these functions to be carried out effectively and efficiently, a network must be established among individuals to coordinate the flow of activities that take place to market a service.

Promotion

Promotion may be thought of as a process of communication between the leisure services organization and the consumer. It is an exercise in informing, persuading, and influencing the consumer. Essentially, promotional efforts are directed at the target market to let consumers know that services are available at a certain cost, location, and time.

Why is promotion important? The distance between those providing services and those receiving services is increasing. Barriers that are broken down by promoting a service may be physical, social, or psychological in nature. No longer can one assume that information can be passed by word of mouth and reach the target market. The physical distance between the provider and consumer of services may be great. The transportation network greatly increases the geographic boundaries of the target market; therefore it is necessary to use means other than word of mouth to disseminate information.

The bureaucracy found in governmental agencies creates a psychological and social distance between the provider and the consumer. Many people feel that governmental agencies are inaccessible and do not understand their functions or services. Promotion of services increases the awareness and understanding that people have of their government. It allows them to become more knowledgeable and thus become more discriminatory. The more information a consumer has about the kinds of services that are available in either the public or the private sector, the more effective the provision of services becomes.

A number of promotional methods can be used by the leisure service manager:

1. *Advertising/Publicity.* Advertising and/or publicity is the presentation of information about an organization's services in an impersonal way. It is usually done through newspapers, magazines, television, fliers, and/or radio. Advertising and/or publicity may be directed toward encouraging the consumer to immediately take advantage of a service; this is known as "direct action" advertising. "Indirect action" advertising attempts to create a long-

range demand for a service. This method seeks to instill in the consumer the knowledge that a service is available if and when she is interested in pursuing it. For example, if a YWCA has swimming available on a drop-in basis throughout the year, it would want to engage in indirect advertising to promote this particular service. Advertising may also take on the subtle dimension of institutional advertisement. Promotion in this area may range from sponsorship of a community event to sponsorship of a Little League team. Its focus is directed toward creating goodwill.

2. *Public Relations.* The cultivation of an organization's image is known as public relations. This involves the creation of a positive attitude and feeling of goodwill toward an organization. In addition to using advertising, an organization creates its public image through its community service activities, employee practices, and the way it handles consumers. The image that an organization portrays to the public is vital to its success. The good name of any organization is its greatest asset in dealing with the public it wishes to attract. Conversely, any adverse publicity attached to an organization is difficult, if not impossible, to rectify. The public has a long memory for improprieties. It is important to recognize that public relations activities are a legitimate function of any organization and should not be viewed as necessarily self-serving. It is an important component of an organization's promotional activities.

3. *Sales Promotion.* This includes any activities designed to stimulate consumer involvement in terms of the service the organization wishes to promote. Generally speaking, there are four activities entailed in this type of promotion: sampling, coupons, contests, and demonstration.

Sampling is an attempt to presell the consumer. For example, an organization attempting to promote arts and crafts lessons for children might want to allow the children to participate in one class free of charge. This provides the child with an opportunity to sample the experience, with the idea that he will be influenced to participate in an entire series of lessons.

The *coupon* concept has been greatly utilized in the promotion of products, but has yet to reach its full impact in the area of social services. This simply involves providing the consumer with a coupon that reduces the cost for a service. The one area where this has been effectively used in the delivery of leisure services is senior citizen participation. Many organizations provide reduced rates for senior citizens (often during a given time of day or day of the week) providing they have a special card or coupon. This senior citizens example is actually profitable to the organization in two ways. Not only does the organization attract a group of consumers who are ordinarily unavailable to it, but it also enhances its public image.

Contests have also been used to stimulate consumer interest in a service. Participation in a contest may result in cash prizes, food, and so on for the winner or winners. An example of the constructive use of a contest in the delivery of leisure services is the traditional Easter Egg hunt. (Oftentimes augmented with special prizes for locating certain items). Sometimes a competitive program form is used in the provision of the service. A flower-arranging contest will motivate people to participate in the activity. Using the contest is also a promotional method directed toward creating enthusiasm and interest in the activity.

Demonstrating a service to the target market is still another method used in sales promotion. To create interest for a class in judo instruction, a demonstration might be arranged to take place at an intermission during a sporting activity, at a shopping mall, or at a school assembly. Essentially, this method allows the consumer to see the skills, attitudes, and other benefits that can be derived from participation in the activity.

4. *Personal Selling.* Perhaps the most underutilized method in the delivery of public leisure services is personal selling. Whereas the aforementioned methods are essentially impersonal ways of contacting the consumer, personal selling involves face-to-face contact with the target market. Although people usually think of personal selling in regard to private or profit-oriented enterprise, it is applicable to public, nonprofit organizations as well. Take for example the parks and recreation director who is engaged in speaking to various groups throughout the community. In this capacity, she may suggest that people support a referendum, participate in a summer program, or offer a reminder of the facilities that are available. Although this may represent a high cost in the leisure services area, it is desirable in that it personalizes the relationship between the provider and consumer of services. It is a flexible way of delivering a message that can be tailor-made to the occasion. It provides for immediate feedback to the organization and/or individual providing a service. There is a minimum of wasted effort in this approach in that the customer cannot disregard the message being transmitted. Those successful in personal selling are usually highly creative, resourceful, and dynamic individuals who are knowledgeable about the services their organization provides and how these services can meet a consumer's needs.

Various media can be utilized in a promotional effort. These serve as the vehicle for communication with the target market. Some of the most important are the following:

1. *Annual Reports.* These are usually reports of organizations' activities over a fiscal year. The report may contain financial information, information on services provided, and projections for the future.
2. *Brochures.* These are used to provide information to consumers about an organization's activities, facilities, and other services. There are basically two types of brochures: One type focuses on a specific event and/or facility, and

the other type provides information over an extended period of time as to an organization's program and facilities. The second type is usually distributed on a quarterly or semiannual basis.

3. *Bulletin Boards, Displays, Posters, Outdoor Advertising.* This category is directed toward providing information to a target market by attracting and holding attention for a brief period of time. The message presented is ideally brief and dynamic in composition.

4. *Fliers.* These can be thought of as miniature posters that give the vital details of a service or activity in brief. They are usually designed to be attractive and eye-catching.

5. *Logos/Emblems.* A visual symbol, a logo represents an event, activity, or organization. A logo can become so well known that the appearance of the design itself is interchangeable with the concept it represents, that is, the organization, service, or whatever.

Figure 8.2 is the logo of the Bensenville, Illinois, Park District. This logo is

Figure 8.2.   Bensenville (Illinois) Park District logo.

Figure 8.3.   Wooster (Ohio) Department of Parks and Recreation logo.

somewhat unique in that it does not follow the almost traditional practice of using leaves, trees, and/or people to symbolize a parks and recreation department. It is, however, extremely representative to the people of Bensenville in that the train in this design is located in the district's largest park. The train is one of the most popular pieces of play equipment and is strongly identified with the Bensenville Park District by members of the community. The logo contains the boundaries of the district, and the train represents the founding of Bensenville as a train stop.

The logo represented in Figure 8.3, from the Wooster, Ohio, Department of Parks and Recreation, is a more traditional design. It features a leaf overlaid on a log. This logo was designed to honor one of Wooster's former public

Figure 8.4. Ferguson (Missouri) Parks and Recreation Department logo.

officials (Paul Tilford), by incorporating into the design the leaf of a tree that had been named after him (The Tilford Maple).

Figure 8.4 is a contemporary approach to designing a logo; it is the logo for the Parks and Recreation Service for the city of Ferguson, Missouri. The figure of the man represents the human concept of services, and the tree in the background represents concern for the environment.

6. *Newspapers.* Perhaps the most effective form of nonpersonal communication used by the leisure delivery system is the newspaper. In many cases leisure service managers are required to write their own news releases and/or advertisements. Well-written newspaper articles usually describe what the

Figure 8.5. Press release forms.

activity is, where it will be held, when it will take place, what the cost is, and whom the service is directed toward. Examples of press release forms, which are used to call a newspaper's attention to an organiation's news, are shown in Figure 8.5. Actual news articles concerning a leisure event are represented in Appendix D, pages 511–521.

7. *Radio and Television.* The most dominant forms of media today are radio and television. Many stations will provide time to nonprofit organizations for free public service announcements. A manager can be selective in communicating via these media by broadcasting between different types of programs and at different times of the day (listening and viewing audiences vary during the day).

8. *Public Speaking.* Closely integrated with the concept of personal selling is public speaking. The person making a presentation to a civic club, chamber of commerce, and/or business group is usually there to inform, influence, and stimulate interest in his or her organization. The use of visual aids, (e.g., slide presentations), in addition to the speech itself, has proven successful to many in the leisure services professions.

9. *Telephone.* Use of the telephone can be an effective way of communicating to a market, however it can also be harmful to the goals of the organization. Many individuals dislike telephone solicitation, and consequently it can work to the detriment of an organization's carefully planned public relations program.

10. *Word of Mouth.* This can be a productive way of exchanging information. The goal of any leisure delivery system is to have satisfied consumers. In turn, such satisfied consumers are an excellent source of advertisement to friends.

When planning a promotional effort, it is important to conduct it in a coordinated manner. Advertising, publicity, public relations, sales promotion, and personal selling should be integrated. Effective promotional campaigns are usually based around a single theme. Use of a logo, a phrase, color scheme, or a mascot are all examples of techniques that can be used. Any or all of these techniques may be used; however, consistency is essential to the success of the campaign as a whole. Whenever McDonald's advertises a product, the consumer can identify with the corporation through its logo, the golden arches. In the case study presented in Appendix D, "Art in the Park," an artistic design was used to coordinate the various promotional activities of the event. This same design, or logo, has been retained throughout the years and has become a symbolic representation of the event itself, easily identifiable to the consumer.

SUMMARY

In this chapter, the authors have presented the marketing concept as it applies to the delivery of leisure services. Marketing is a process that is directed toward satisfying consumer needs. It involves two tasks: selecting a target market and developing a marketing mix. Target marketing is a way of segmenting out groups of homogenous consumers. This may be done by looking at demographic characteristics, sociopsychological characteristics, and so on. The market mix (creation, pricing, distribution and promotion) is directed toward the provision of activities, facilities, information, and consultation. Pricing concerns the selection of an appropriate fee or charge for the service provided. Two key elements—finding an available and convenient location and an appropriate time to provide a service—are involved in the distribution of a service. Promotion, the last factor, centers on providing the consumer with information about the service.

Budget/Fiscal Practices for Leisure Service Organizations 9

Leisure service organizations accomplish their work through the utilization of human and material resources. If the leisure service manager is to work effectively and efficiently, he must have information about these resources and whether their use results in the achievement of organizational goals. In other words, organizations need some mechanism to provide a manager with resource information so that he has a reliable basis for decisions. The system that allows a manager to plan and control the use of organizational resources is known as the process of "budgeting."

In terms of budgeting, we can classify leisure service organizations into two basic categories: profit-oriented and nonprofit-oriented. The purpose of a profit-oriented organization is essentially to earn a profit; that is, a profit-oriented organization, to be effective, must insure that its revenues are greater than its expenditures. On the other hand, a nonprofit organization is not primarily concerned with earning a profit; rather, it is concerned with providing a service. But it, too, is concerned with insuring that expenditures do not exceed the revenues which it produces or acquires for its operation. Both profit and nonprofit organizations are concerned with the manner in which their resources (assets) are utilized. Both types of organizations seek to maximize their operating efficiency. The profit-oriented organization does this to increase its profit margin; the nonprofit-oriented organization does this to maximize its impact regarding services. Increased efficiency may result in a reduction of the cost of producing services, enabling an organization to (1) increase the number of services available and (2) reduce the cost of services. Although the process of budgeting is basically the same in profit and nonprofit organizations, we will focus on nonprofit organizations in this text.

INFORMATION NEEDED BY THE MANAGER

Although the specific type of information needed within a given organization will vary depending on the particular needs of the agency, there are a number of common types of information needed by most leisure service organizations. Generally speaking, information needed by a leisure service manager can be categorized into three classifications. The first is *operations information*. To conduct the day-to-day operations of a leisure service organization, a manager needs a considerable amount of information. The manager needs to know the daily status of the organization's resources. For example, he must be aware of whether his organization has the resources it needs to make certain purchases, pay bills, and cover other expenditures. He also needs to know precisely what bills the organization must pay and on what dates, and the income it is likely to have and when.

The second type of information needed by the leisure service manager is *management information*. In the transformation of resources into programs, the manager needs information that allows him to plan, control, and coordinate the work of the organization. For example, as a planning mechanism, the budget allows the manager to establish a program to meet the organization's objectives. In this manner, the manager is able to tie the goals of the organization to the resources available to achieve them. Planning and decision-making go hand in hand. Thus the budget that serves to guide the organization's operations provides a manager with vital information affecting short- and long-term decision-making.

The third type of information needed in the management of leisure service organizations is *financial information*. Financial information about an organization is important primarily so the manager may establish the credibility of the organization to outside appraisers. Most, if not all, organizations are involved in making financial transactions with other organizations. This may range from simply engaging in an agreement, to purchasing a given resource, to borrowing money on a long-term basis to finance the development of a facility. It is in the best interests of an organization to have a reputation for financial integrity. As will be discussed later in this chapter, municipal corporations are appraised and rated in terms of their credit risk. A lower credit rating may restrict an organization's ability to acquire resources, thereby seriously hampering the achievement of its goals.

WHAT IS A BUDGET?

A budget may be thought of as a statement that allows an organization to plan and control its resources for a specific period of time. It may be stated in dollars, works hours, units of production, or any other descriptive or measurable unit. The budget provides information as to what resources the organization will acquire and how they will be acquired, how these resources will be spent, and in what services they will result. The budget allows a manager to estimate or predict how the resources of the organization are to be acquired and/or spent. In making financial estimates, the leisure service manager is able to engage in the development of advanced strategies that allow him to more accurately predict and control actions he might take. In governmental organizations, a budget can be thought of as a legal tool that is used by an appropriately authorized body to finance a stated set of services. The final adoption of a budget by a governmental agency provides the organization with an estimate of the income it is to produce or acquire, how it will expend this income, and usually a method or plan of financial operation.

Budgeting is used by agencies for many important and practical reasons. The advantages of budgeting are numerous but, generally speaking, they can be listed as follows:

1. Budgeting allows the manager to organize the financial operation of the agency in a systematic fashion.
2. Budgeting requires a manager to think ahead to the work that must be accomplished within an organization and the costs that will be incurred in these efforts.
3. Budgeting provides a manager with a basis from which to develop a work schedule and organize the resources within the organization to meet its goals.
4. A budget forces a manager to view resources (both human and material) in quantifiable, measureable terms and to relate these figures to the goals of the organization.
5. Budgeting promotes standardization within financial operations. The desire for efficiency dictates the necessity for a unified approach to the acquisition and expenditure of resources. Standardizing financial operations allows an organization to increase its efficiency.
6. The budget allows the manager to communicate with subordinates and coordinate their activities in monetary terms, which are commonly understood by both management and subordinates.
7. The budget serves as a reference that the manager and his or her subordinates can refer to, to help clarify or support decisions.
8. The budget provides legislative decision-making bodies with information necessary to the evaluation of their organizations' programs and services.
9. The budget in the public sector provides the taxpayer with an explanation as to how resources are produced, acquired and expended.
10. The budget, as a point of reference, serves as a legislative body's mechanism of control. In other words, the budget can serve as a guideline and measuring device that determines the level of effectiveness and efficiency in a given area of the organization.

The budgeting process oftentimes seems overwhelming, mysterious, and complex to the prospective leisure service manager. The budget and financial processes of any organization are extremely important and should be well managed; but the budgeting process does not have to be overwhelming, complicated, or complex, and it should be easily understood. It involves three basic steps:

1. Developing a budget plan expressed in dollars that anticipates results of a future period;

2. Co-ordinating these dollar estimates into a well-balanced program; and
3. Comparing actual performance with the estimated balance programs.[1]

Almost any organization that the new leisure service manager might join, in which he will have responsibility for budgeting and financial matters, will have a section or division that has budgeting and financial matters as its primary function. This division will probably have existing procedures, policies, and a format that it follows in the preparation, execution, and control of the budget.

In many organizations, the budget process and procedures are in writing and spelled out in detail. During budget preparation, a budget manual is usually given to those who are responsible for developing the budget. It gives the manager a format, timetable, and method by which the budget will be submitted. During the year there will be controls and procedures to assure that the budget is adhered to, not overexpended, as well as methods to evaluate what has been accomplished.

The Budget Cycle

Budget planning can be developed for a fixed number of days, weeks, or months. Generally speaking, a budget plan is associated with a period of time or a cycle that covers an entire year's operation within an organization. This yearly cycle is known as a "fiscal year." A fiscal year can start at any time during the year and end with the settling of financial accounts. A fiscal year may run concurrently with the calendar year, starting January 1 and ending December 31, although it would still be called a fiscal year. In the United States, in many governmental organizations, the fiscal year starts on July 1 and runs to June 30 of the following year.

In addition to budgets covering one year, many leisure service organizations project their budgets anywhere from three to eight years in the future, depending on the planning cycle adopted. Budgeting more than one year at a time enables an organization to get an indication of the type of commitments it is going to have in the future so it can anticipate the revenues it needs to meet these commitments. Also, looking into the future helps the manager determine other effects, such as inflation, a shift in program emphasis, the effects of new programs, and what adjustments have to be made as a result of additional revenue or decreasing revenue in the future. On the other hand, it is impractical to try to think too far into the future. As Peter F. Drucker has written:

". . . planning is not forecasting. It is not masterminding the future. Any attempt to do so is foolish. The future is unpredictable. We can only discredit what we are doing by attempting it. No one can forecast what's going to happen ten years from now which is proven by the many surprises that face the world every day. . . .
On the other hand, by analyzing what we do today we certainly have a better idea

---

[1] William H. Newman, Charles E. Summer, and E. Kirby Warren, *The Process of Management*, second edition (Englewood Cliffs, N.J.: Prentice-Hall, 1967), p. 697–698.

Program: 265.08 Parks maintenance
Function: Environmental services
Objective: Keep parks safe, attractive, and usable

Fiscal Year	Work Hours	Total Cost	Production Units (Work-Hour Output)	Cost per Unit	Unit Cost in Constant Dollars 1972–1973
Actual 1972–1973	80,811	807,564	108,634	7.43	7.43
Actual 1973–1974	80,576	819,747	108,634	7.55	7.18
Actual 1974–1975	76,685	869,776	108,634	8.01	6.93
Estimated 1975–1976	81,654*	979,455	116,445	8.41	6.60
Proposed 1976–1977	76,825	1,169,480	124,965	9.36	6.77
Projected 1977–1978	76,825	1,257,680	124,965	10.06	6.80
Projected 1978–1979	76,825	1,349,801	124,965	10.80	6.83
Projected 1979–1980	76,825	1,430,007	124,965	11.44	6.82
Projected 1980–1981	76,825	1,504,078	124,965	12.04	6.83
Projected 1981–1982	76,825	1,578,917	124,965	12.63	6.82
Projected 1982–1983	76,825	1,658,103	124,965	13.27	6.82
Projected 1983–1984	76,825	1,740,618	124,965	13.93	6.82

Figure 9.1. City of Sunnyvale, California, resource allocation analysis. (* Includes 4,781 CETA employee hours for 1975–1976.)

of what effect it might have in the future. If we know that it takes 99 years to grow a Douglas Fir in the Northwest for pulpwood size, planting seedlings today is the only way we can provide for pulp supply for 99 years from now.[2]

So it becomes obvious that we need to look into the future somehow to determine what effects the things we are doing today will have on the future, and

[2] Peter F. Drucker, *Management: Tasks, Responsibilities, Practices* (New York: Harper and Row, 1973), pp. 123, 127.

there is no better example than the budgeting process. Not only is it necessary and valuable to look into the future, it is also helpful to examine what has happened in the past and see what trends have taken place. For this reason, most budgets show two or three years of past history in terms of accomplishment, expenditures in both work hours and other resources, and indications of trends and present needs. Figure 9.1 shows a budget with three years of history, estimate for the present year, the requests for funds of a given year, and seven years of future projections.

REVENUES AND EXPENDITURES

Although the organization of an agency's budget will vary depending on the type of process adopted (line or program budgeting—their differences will be explained later in this chapter), the basic structure of a budget consists of two components. The first of these is the *revenues* that are produced or acquired by the leisure service organization. Types of income include taxes, fees and charges, grants, interest earned on investments, and donations. The other component is *expendi-*

LINE ITEM DETAIL

Program: 265.08 parks maintenance
Function: Environmental services

	1974–75 Actual	1975–76 to 4/3/76	1976–77 Proposed
WORK HOURS			
4111 Regular salaries—work time	59,348	44,270	61,290
4112 Temporary personnel	16,829	12,775	15,160
4113 Overtime	508	310	375
TOTAL WORK HOURS	76,685	57,355	76,825
RESOURCES			
Human Resources			
4111 Regular salaries—work time	$328,671	$277,803	$ 432,707
4112 Temporary personnel	65,558	49,125	78,074
4113 Overtime	4,474	3,010	4,256
Subtotal	398,703	329,938	515,037
4116 Leave time	56,671	47,891	74,642
4117 Retirement/payroll insurance	92,917	94,478	159,104
Total Human Resources	548,291	472,307	748,783

Figure 9.2. City of Sunnyvale, California, resource allocation plan, 1976–77 fiscal year.

	1974–75 Actual	1975–76 to 4/3/76	1976–77 Proposed
Other Resources			
4201 Custodial supplies	5,343	4,990	6,000
4204 Special activity supplies	10,846	9,039	16,275
4215 Clothing	1,397	1,483	2,186
4231 Materials—buildings	3,843	3,758	4,200
4232 Materials—office equipment	196	394	543
4233 Materials—other equipment	1,661	2,105	2,062
4234 Materials—land improvements	52,969	33,927	68,117
4235 Materials—repair facil-vandals	7,359	3,178	10,000
4245 Small tools/implements	2,265	2,143	4,069
4270 Services—mtn buildings	3,737	1.578	5,968
4271 Services—mtn land improvements	30,279	18,317	39,724
4280 Services—mtn other equipment	5,045	3,445	4,557
4282 Services—repair vandalism	7,815	3,658	5,534
4306 Weed abatement contract	425	—	—
4331 Gas/electricity	28,036	30,737	46,000
4332 Telephone	5,761	4,937	5,043
4333 Water	33,832	30,138	54,250
4340 Travel/meeting expenses	77	6	96
4344 Equip rental—private	—	—	100
4372 Laundry	545	523	942
4501 Rent	4,800	5,760	5,760
4504 Taxes/licenses	6,149	6,190	7,000
4505 Fire insurance	5,790	5,668	6,500
4531 Equip rental—city pool	103,315	87,544	125,771
Total Other Resources	321,485	259,518	420,697
TOTAL RESOURCES	$869,776	$731,825	$1,169,480

Figure 9.2. (Continued)

tures. There are two basic types of expenditures made by leisure service organizations: *operating expenditures* and *capital expenditures.* These will be explained in detail in this section.

Expenditures

Operating Expenditures

Operating expenditures are made for personnel, materials, supplies, and services, as well as other regularly occurring costs. Figure 9.2 shows some of the items that would typically be budgeted as operating expenses. Usually the largest single expenditure in the operating budget is personnel services. A large percentage of an organization's operational expenditures goes to pay full-time, temporary, and seasonal personnel and the necessary overhead costs, such as retirement, leaves, social security, and other insurance programs. The remaining percentage of the budget is for all other needs. Some budgets may not reflect these percentages since other needs may run much higher. This usually happens when programs utilize a great deal of equipment or supplies that are extremely costly or the rental of buildings or equipment is extremely high. Remembering percentages is not important; the main point is that the cost of personnel usually is the largest cost incurred year after year. With inflation, personnel costs can easily get out of control. The competent manager will do all she or he can to monitor personnel costs and plan for the future, making sure that revenue to cover personnel costs is provided for.

If revenue begins to drop, it will become necessary to cut operating costs. Although some costs can be cut in materials, supplies, and equipment, if there is a need to cut a great deal it will ultimately be necessary to cut human resources.

Using the statistics in Figure 9.2, 61,290 work hours in the 1976–77 year are equivalaent to 29 full-time employees. Dividing $432,707 (the cost of salaries of the 29 employees) by 29 equals $14,920 annual salary. In addition, the city has to pay for leaves, retirement, and other benefits of $74,642 plus $159,104, which totals $233,746, or an additional 35 percent ($5,222 dollars per employee). This places costs of an average full-time employee at $20,142 per year. The cost for supplies, materials, and equipment that an employee needs to work with is approximately $11,063 per year. The total cost to the city for an employee in salary and benefits and materials, supplies, and equipment is $31,205 per year. Assuming that an employee works 25 years, this would cost $780,125 dollars.

By cutting one employee, you would be able to save approximately $20,142 in salary and benefits and $11,063 in material, supplies, and equipment. To cut supplies alone does not make sense because, first of all, they are not the most expensive item; also, if you don't have the supplies and equipment, the employee probably can't perform the work. It is also apparent that cutting human resources or other resources will affect production and effectiveness to some extent. But when revenues do not match expenses, something has to be done. It is the manager's job to determine what is the proper balance—to cut human or other resources. The other alternative is to increase revenue, which will be discussed later.

. Another item that has to be considered in operating costs is the factor of inflation. Comparing 1974–75 with 1976–77 in Figure 9.2, a two-year period of time, there is an increase of $299,704, or 34.5 percent. This is an increase of a little over 17 percent per year. The total work hours increased only 140 hours.

Certain other resources increased substantially: Fertilizer and chemicals (code 4234) increased 28 percent; gas and electricity (code 4331), 64 percent; and water (code 4333), 66 percent. Some of this increase was due to use, but most was a result of inflation.

An increase in inflation of 6 percent per year on a $868,776 budget equals $52,187 per year, with no increase in service. In other words, it would take approximately $52,000 more per year to deliver the same amount of service. In 10 years, this would be an increase of half a million dollars.

Figure 9.3 shows a program budget summary for the recreational services of the Department of Recreation and Parks for the city of Baltimore, Maryland, and is also an example of operational expenses. This particular budget gives actual expenditures for the year 1967–68, the budgeted figures for 1968–69, and the request for funds for 1969–70. In addition, the total costs of the department's 21 programs are listed. Each of the programs would be further explained as shown in Figure 9.2 in order to provide additional detail and provide for control.

The operating portion of the budget is used to finance the day-to-day operations of the organization on a pay-as-you-go basis.

Agency: Department of Recreation and Parks		Program: Recreational Services			480
PROGRAM BUDGET SUMMARY					
(1)	(2)	(3)	(4)	(5)	(6)
		Actual 1967–68	Budget 1968–69	Requested 1969–70	Recommendation
	Employment Summary Authorized salaried positions	335.0	367.0	465.0	
	Man-years: Salaried positions		348.9		
	Labor				
	Part-time, temp, & overtime				
	Total man-years				
Code	**Summary By Object**				
01–15	Salaries and wages	2,399,800	2,901,435	3,992,820	
16–25	Other personnel costs	219,058	278,165	385,549	
26–50	Contractual services	277,095	238,441	444,110	
51–65	Materials and supplies	168,817	108,991	240,940	
66–75	Equipment—replacement	9,467	—	5,874	
76–85	Equipment—additional	9,520	47,027	95,404	
86–88	Grants and subsidies	2,400		2,000	
89–91	Debt service				
92–94	Land				
95–97	Buildings				
98–99	Improv. excl. bldgs.				
	ANNUAL TOTAL	3,086,157	3,574,059	5,166,697	

Figure 9.3. City of Baltimore, program budget summary.

	Summary By Function			
01	Administration	92,787	78,791	93,208
02	Central office & storeroom serv.	165,387	159,576	215,431
03	Municipal sports	126,864	154,859	160,298
04	Street clubs for problem youth	35,392	267,002	373,649
05	Recreation centers	1,990,394	2,080,430	2,739,521
06	Recreation for handicapped	44,951	29,076	47,947
07	Senior citizens activities	37,260	33,929	48,814
08	Traveling play leaders	6,987	25,624	35,620
09	Swimming instruction	21,125	53,523	221,580
10	Music (group participation)	24,009	27,642	33,994
11	Dramatics	6,397	8,293	13,064
12	Dancing	28,405	18,742	21,650
13	Arts and crafts	34,416	28,290	50,225
14	Nature and gardening	15,968	17,278	18,615
15	Physical fitness	23,299	34,581	44,315
16	Playgrounds	432,516	511,423	564,680
17	Modernization of existing facilities	—	45,000	14,800
18	Operation Champ	—	—	—
19	Accessory enterprises	—	—	264,286
20	Community schools	—	—	264,286
21	Municipal Athletic Association	—	—	15,000
	ANNUAL TOTAL	3,086,157	3,574,059	5,166,697

	Summary By Fund			
01	General	2,929,749	3,394,059	4,976,697
02	Special	156,408	180,000	190,000
03	Motor vehicle revenue Working capital			
	ANNUAL TOTAL	3,086,157	3,574,059	5,166,697

Figure 9.3. (Continued)

Capital Expenditures
These expenditures are made to finance projects that are extremely costly, such as land acquisitions, park and building construction, and other projects that could conceivably utilize all the revenue during any one given year. The capital portion of the budget is sometimes used for such equipment as automobiles, trucks and recreation equipment, which is expensive, nonexpendable, and serviceable for many years. Usually there are policies governing capital equipment and projects which state that anything over $100 or $200 is to be considered capital equipment or a capital project. Anything under those amounts would be paid for out of the operating budget. Figures 9.4 and 9.5 show several examples of capital expenditures and how different agencies account for these types of costs.

Figure 9.4 shows the city of Baltimore's capital improvement program for land acquisition and facility development. A similar program is presented for each year for five years into the future. Before the program or project can be completed, it must be approved by the parks and recreation board, the city planning commission, and the city council, and then approved by the public in a bond election by a majority vote or two thirds vote, depending upon state or provincial law.

Each year the Department of Parks and Recreation submits an update of the capital projects program, which includes an additional year in the future. Projects are placed on the program in accordance with the city's 20-year look into the future, trying to determine needs based on changes in population, the need to replace old facilities, and other sociological and demographic information.

In addition to planning for capital projects, the manager of a leisure service agency also has to plan for the effect these capital projects will have on operating costs. If new facilities are built, they require staffing and maintenance on an ongoing basis, and these costs have to be built into the operating budget. This is one of the reasons why it is necessary to budget for several years into the future. It is also necessary to anticipate revenues in the future so it can be determined if

BUREAU OF PARKS

L	Zoo—Continuation of master plan	$1,000,000
L	Park acquisition & development	500,000
L	Small playgrounds	100,000
G	Security park lighting	100,000
	Sub-total, Parks:	$1,700,000

BUREAU OF RECREATION

L	Rec. center and playfield, Clifton Park	$ 400,000
L	Rec. center, Calloway School	300,000
L	Rec. center, Brehms Lane	300,000
L	Rec. center, Patterson Park	300,000
L	Rec. center, Medfield Heights	300,000
L	Rec. center addition—gym—Curtis Bay Center	200,000
L	Rec. center, Fairmount Ave. and Ann St.	300,000
	Subtotal, Recreation:	$2,100,000

GRAND TOTAL, Department of Recreation and Parks, Fiscal Year 1975:

$3,800,000

BREAKDOWN OF FUNDS

G	$ 100,000
L	3,700,000
TOTAL:	$3,800,000

Figure 9.4. City of Baltimore, capital improvement program, fiscal year 1975. G indicates General Funds, L indicates Loan or Bond Funds.

Project: 710 Serra Park Tennis Courts
Function(s): Environmental Services

Resource/Element	Expended to 6-30-76	PROPOSED 1976-1977	Projected						
			1977-1978	1978-1979	1979-1980	1980-1981	1981-1982	1982-1983	1983-1984
Workhours	-	150	-	-	-	-	-	-	-
Resources (Dollars) .49 Parks	-	40,000	-	-	-	-	-	-	-
Total Resources	-	40,000	-	-	-	-	-	-	-

This project would provide for two tennis courts with lights at the Serra Park addition. City Council authorized project in 1976.

Operating costs this project will incur: $10,000 per year

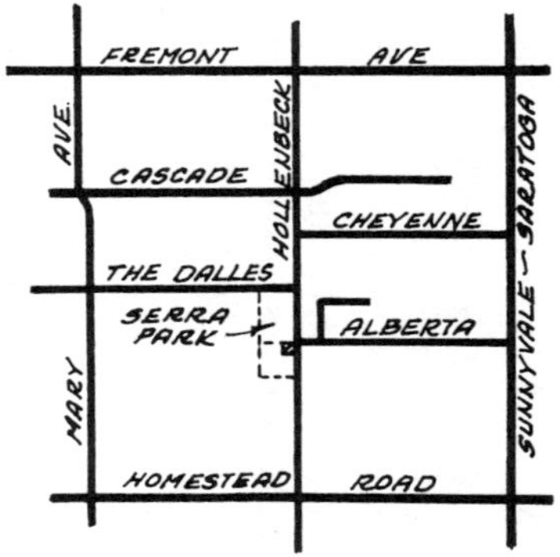

Figure 9.5. City of Sunnyvale, California, projects.

there will be adequate funds to pay off the debt of capital projects as well as pay the operating costs that the capital projects will incur.

Figure 9.5 is an example of a specific project in greater detail. The figure shows when the project will be built and the source of funding for its construction. The example also shows what the operating costs will be on an annual basis.

Different leisure service organizations may handle operating and capital expenditures slightly differently. Operational and capital expenditures can be likened to an individual's financing. An individual usually has a salary and other forms of income, such as investments, rental property, savings accounts, and stocks and bonds. This income during a given year totals a specific amount. For the sake of explanation, let's assume that it is $20,000 a year. The $20,000 a year is the revenue that must be used to pay for all the various items and expenses the person needs or wants. He needs a home, an automobile and life insurance, and possibly such luxuries as a boat and a summer cottage. These items total more than the $20,000 income that he will have for a given year. To purchase such items as a house, a boat, or an automobile, he borrows money for several years: the house, 25 years; the automobile three to five years. Similarly, with *capital expenditures,* it is impossible for any agency to buy all the land or parks or construct all the facilities needed in any one given year. Therefore these items are financed over a period of time. In the case of an individual's house and automobile, he borrows from a bank and pays back the debt over a certain time period. The debt consists of the principal, which pays back the money borrowed, and the interest, which is for the privilege of borrowing money. Likewise, the leisure service organization borrows money from lending firms, banks, and other financial institutions and pays this money back on a time basis—the principal as well as the interest.

The daily expenses of the individual for food, clothing, entertainment and other such items can be compared to the *operating expenditures* and are paid for from the salary. The house, boat, automobile, and summer cottage are paid for with the borrowed money, and the principal and interest are paid back over a period of time out of the salary. The individual has to plan how much of the salary he can afford to spend on capital items and how much of his salary he needs for daily operating expenses.

Be it a personal budget or an agency budget, a determination has to be made as to what percentage of the budget will be expended for the operating versus the capital expenditures. Most cities use as a rule of thumb a bond indebtedness limit of no more than 5 percent of the full assessed value of the city for bonds at any one time. Banks that lend money to individuals for personal use have credit ratings on individuals which indicate how much of a risk that individual is in terms of lending. Likewise, cities and governmental agencies have bond ratings that indicate how well they finance and manage their money and how good a risk they are. Standards and Poor's has a rating criteria that starts with an AAA rating which is the best

Table 9.1. Standard & Poor's Municipal Bond Ratings

Rating Criteria

AAA, prime. These are obligations of the highest quality. They have the strongest capacity for timely payment of debt service.

AA, high grade. The investment characteristics of general obligation and revenue bonds in this group are only slightly less marked than those of the prime quality issues. Bonds rated "AA" have the second strongest capacity for payment of debt service.

A, good grade. Principal and interest payments on bonds in this category are regarded as safe. This rating describes the third strongest capacity for payment of debt service.

BBB, medium grade. This is the lowest investment grade security rating.

BB, speculative grade. Bonds in this group have some investment characteristics, but they no longer predominate. For the most part this rating indicates a speculative, non-investment grade obligation.

B, low grade. Investment characteristics are virtually nonexistent, and default could be imminent.

D, defaults. Payment of interest and/or principal is in arrears.

NCR. No contract rating. No ratings are assigned to new offerings unless a contract is applied for.

Provisional ratings. The letter "p" following a rating indicates the rating is provisional, where payment of debt service requirements will be largely or entirely dependent upon the timely completion of the project.

Source. Pamphlet by Standard and Poor's Corporation, 345 Hudson St., New York, N.Y., p. 5–7.

rating a city can have. An AA is next best, and ratings go all the way down to a NCR rating for poor risks. Table 9.1 shows the various ratings.

The higher the city's or agency's rating, the more easily it can borrow money, usually at a lower interest rate. A one percent difference in interest rate on $1 million for 20 years would amount to a savings of $200,000.

Revenues

Taxes

Most revenues that are used to support governmental leisure service organizations are from taxes. There are a number of different types of taxes, including property tax, income tax, sales tax, and other special taxes. But the majority of income for operating expenses at the local level of government comes from property taxes. There are two types of property tax: *real property tax* and *personal property tax.* Personal property can be divided into two categories: tangible and intangible. Tangible property, which can be taxed, might include equipment, merchandise, and/or supplies; in other words, physical assets. Intangible property includes accounts, stocks, bonds, and other similar assets, which are not taxed.

Much of the income for local government leisure service organizations comes from real property tax. This is a tax assessed against such "real property" as homes, land, industry, as well as commercial enterprises that are within the jurisdiction of the organization. It not only includes land, but also anything that can be permanently attached to it (e.g., buildings and other improvements). Real property tax is assessed by determining the value of the property; this is known as the "assessed valuation" and is evaluated on a regular basis by a local tax assessor. The assessor appraises the property to determine its value based on factors that indicate its worth. In most cases, property is not assessed at its full value, but rather at a percentage of its actual, or real, value. The figure or percentage utilized by the assessor to determine the value of the property is usually set by state or provincial legislative authority. Whether the local legislative authority uses the full percentage allowable under law is usually subject to its discretion.

Once the assessed value of the property is determined, this figure is multiplied times the tax rate. Tax rates are also usually established by state or provincial legislative authority, and application is subject to local government discretion. Local government authorities are not able to set a tax rate higher than the allowable maximum as indicated by law unless approved by the voters of a community. Tax rates are expressed in terms of mills. One dollar would equal 1000 mills. Figure 9.6 presents figures for the conversion of various monetary units into mills. As an example of this concept, a house in Sunnyvale, California, with an actual property value of $50,000, would be assessed at 40 percent of the actual value, giving it an assessed valuation of $20,000. The tax rate in Sunnyvale, in 1976, was $1.13 per $100. Therefore the taxpayer would owe the city $266 in real property taxes.

1.00 = one dollar
0.10 = one dime
0.01 = one cent
0.001 = one mill
0.00150 = one and one half mills
0.01 = one cent (10 mills)
0.05% (of 1%) = 0.0005 mills
0.1% (of 1%) = 1/10 of one percent or 0.001 (1 mill)
0.5% (of 1%) = 1/2 of one percent or 0.005 (5 mills)
1.0% = 0.01 or one cent per dollar (10 mills)

Figure 9.6. Tax rate summary.

Property taxes are usually levied within a community to provide revenues for the general fund from which the local subdivision of government operates its services. The general fund is used to finance all general governmental services. Leisure services, in a local community, would usually finance their operations through this fund. In certain states, special legislation exists to allow for a tax levy to support specific services, including park and recreation services. State statutes usually allow the local subdivision of government some discretionary power in the assessment of such taxes.

Another type of tax that may be used for leisure services is the special tax. This type of tax is levied specifically for park and/or recreation services. Other taxes used to finance local park and recreation services include a sales tax, amusement taxes, and special product or service taxes. These types of taxes are usually collected by a state or provincial government and reimbursed to local subdivisions of government.

Fees and Charges

Another source of income for governmental services are fees and charges. These are used to offset costs of operations. For example an organization might have a fee to enter a swimming pool or to participate in a special class or other type of activity. There are varying philosophies concerning the basis on which charges are made. In many communities, these charges are made only for a specialized or more advanced activity or program; the premise is that the introductory, or beginning, level should be underwritten by the general operating funds of the community and that fees and charges should be made only for specialized activities or more advanced instruction, equipment, or facilities. The user is asked to pay for the costs related to more sophisticated programs, rather than the taxpayer who may not use the specialized facility or program. Generally, such programs as golf courses, special tennis programs, and high-skilled classes in recreation are offset by such charges.

Fees and charges may be classified as follows:

1. Entrance Fees—Fees charged to enter a large park, botanical garden, zoological garden or other developed recreational area. The areas are usually well defined but are not necessarily enclosed. The entrance is the patron's first contact with the park. It may contain additional facilities or activities for which fees are charged.
2. Admission Fees—Charges made to enter a building, structure or natural chamber are designated as admission fees. These locations usually offer an exhibit, show, ceremony, performance, demonstration or special equipment. Entry and exit are normally controlled and attendance is regulated.
3. Rental Fees—Payment made for the priviledge of exclusive use of tangible property of any kind is considered a rental fee. This fee gives the patron the

right to enjoy all the advantages derived from the use of the property without consuming, destroying or injuring it in any way.

4. User Fees—When a charge is made for the use of a facility, participation in an activity, or as a fare for controlled ride, it is referred to as a user fee. The patron usually enjoys the privilege simultaneously with others. It is not the exclusive right as in the case of the rental fee.

5. Sales Revenues—All revenue obtained from the operation of stores, concessions, restaurants, etc., and from the sale of merchandise or other property is included in this category. Unconditional ownership of the item must pass from the seller to the buyer with each sale.

6. License and Permit Fees—License and permit will be considered synonymous. A license is a written acknowledgement of consent to do some lawful thing without command; it grants a liberty or privilege and professes to tolerate all legal actions. It usually involves permission to perform an action. It seldom grants authority to occupy space or use property.

7. Special Service Fees—The charges made for extraordinary articles, commodities or services or accommodation to the public are considered special service fees. Such accommodations must be unusual in character and not normally considered a required governmental service.[3]

Grants

Another method of financing leisure service programs is grants from state or provincial governments. In the past few years, the U.S. government has offered assistance to local agencies through federal revenue sharing, the Land and Water Conservation Fund, block grants, summer recreation programs, and the Comprehensive Employment Training Act (CETA).

In the province of Ontario, an unusual approach to raising money has been established by the Ministry of Culture and Recreation. Monies acquired through a public lottery, known as "Wintario," are used to support physical fitness, sports, recreation, and cultural activities. Individuals, groups, and organizations can apply directly to this provincial agency for grants to support their programs. In general, these grant programs help relieve local agencies of the heavy tax burden and aid in overcoming unemployment and a sagging economy. In many communities, these funds have been used for recreation and park programs and projects.

Some precautions should be given in regard to these funds. Foremost is the fact that grant programs are for a limited time period and will be terminated. When grant funds have been used for programs that cannot be terminated when federal funds stop, the local agency has to be ready to continue them and pick up

---

[3] Thomas I. Hines, *Revenue Source Management in Parks and Recreation* (Arlington, Va.: National Recreation and Park Association, 1974), pp. 101–103.

the funding locally. Many times it is difficult if not impossible to stop a program once it is started, particularly if it is a popular program. One of the intents of a grant program is to help communities that are overburdened by taxes; but to start a federally funded program that ultimately will increase the local tax burden does not indicate a good management decision.

CETA was designed to help communities with high unemployment by providing employment on a short-term basis; but, more importantly, it was designed to help train individuals and retrain the underemployed. Communities and agencies that use the funds to employ individuals to fill regular job vacancies because of lack of funds at the local level will ultimately have to lay off these individuals or provide local funding. This was not the intent of the program and reflects poor management.

In any program that is undertaken with local, state, or provincial funds, the manager responsible for the program must realize in starting it what the commitment is to the future in terms of personnel, dollars, and facilities. For this reason, many communities have used federal and state funds that are of a one-time or short-term nature for capital projects. When these capital projects are complete, it is the end of the commitment, except for the operation and maintenance costs—which can generally be absorbed by the local agency.

Donations

It is not unusual for leisure service organizations to accept donations. Financial arrangements can be made within an organization for it to receive gifts and other donations. Usually this is accomplished by the establishment of a special fund or account. Often an organization will establish a special fund for the purpose of soliciting monies to develop a facility or acquire park acreage. Sometimes an organization may even establish a foundation for this purpose. The operation of the foundation is set up outside the governmental agency and is nonprofit and tax exempt. Donations to such foundations or special funds are ordinarily tax deductible.

Public leisure service organizations also establish special accounts that permit individuals or groups to give donations toward the purchase of special items. This type of fund is often held in a special account and used only for the specific purpose for which the account was established. Many parks and recreation departments have established special funds to accept donations for tree replacement, playground equipment, and the like.

Many youth-serving agencies depend greatly on donations to finance operational activities. In most other organizations, however, donations are ordinarily used to finance capital expenditures. Organizations that must rely primarily on donations for their day-to-day operations spend a great deal of time in fund-raising activities. This can diminish the impact of a leisure service organization because the effort spent in acquiring donations may very well drain the creative energy and time of the staff.

Interest

Progressive organizations may invest unneeded revenues in order to increase their ultimate revenue. During any given period of time, an organization needs only a certain cash balance to maintain its operations. Excess cash revenues can be invested, and the interest paid on these investments can serve as an additional source of revenue for the organization. Organizations can determine what funds can be invested on a long- or short-term basis. Long-term investments are usually made for six months to two years. Short-term investments can be made from one day to one year, but they are typically made for a period of thirty to sixty days.

Bond Programs

The majority of the capital improvements that are made in most public leisure service organizations are funded by bond programs that require referendum by the general public to determine whether it wants to be taxed for such facilities. The procedures for bond programs are usually established by the laws of the state or province as well as local agencies, which govern the requirements for such bond programs in terms of the percentage of the electorate that has to endorse a program before it can be undertaken. As mentioned earlier, most communities have a bond indebtedness limit that they cannot go above. Bonds are the major source of revenue for capital improvement programs and a basis of borrowing money for 15 to 30 years.

Generally, there are two major types of bonds utilized in governmental bonding. The first of these is the *general obligation bond*. This type of bond is one that is guaranteed with full faith and credit by a municipality to insure payment. The municipality guarantees to pay out of its general operating budget a certain amount of money on an annual basis for the privilege of borrowing the money. Such a system permits the municipality to acquire several million dollars at a time to acquire land and construct capital facilities that it could not otherwise acquire or provide for out of its operating budget.

The other form of bond is the *revenue bond*. These bonds are often used to finance such facilities as golf courses, swimming pools, and other facilities that would produce revenue; hence the term "revenue" bond. The revenue produced by the facility is pledged to pay off the bond indebtedness. Golf courses are probably the most common example of facilities that utilize revenue bonds.

Bonds may be also classified according to the method in which they are retired. There are three methods of bond retirement, or types of bonds, used by municipal leisure service organizations: term, callable, and serial bonds. Describing the differences between these types of bonds, Richard Kraus and Joseph Curtis write:

Term Bonds. In this type of bond the government agency promises to pay off the entire principle at the end of a given period of time. Normally, it would use the "sinking fund" method, under which an annual sum is put aside each year, with the amount accumulating each year until the full principle has been set aside at the end of the term of the bonds.

Callable Bonds. This is a special type of bond in which the government has the option of calling in the bond issue for payment at a specified period of time before the end of its term, or any time it chooses. Since bond interest rates tend to fluctuate, it is thus possible for the issuer to call in a bond and reissue it at low interest rates, depending upon market conditions.

Serial Bonds. Under this method of financing capital outlays, the government pays the bond purchaser a specified portion of the principle, plus interest, each year that the bond issue is in effect. Thus, a percentage of the bond is reduced each year through payments of approximately equal sums.[4]

As already stated, bond programs are regulated by laws, and the leisure service manager only has to understand the laws that govern his or her agency to place a bond issue before the public. *The secret of bond programs is getting them approved by the public.*

There is only one reason why bond issues fail: They get more no votes than yes votes. There are many reasons why an individual may vote no, for example:

1. The bond program does not provide anything of interest to that individual.
2. The voter does not want her or his taxes increased.
3. The voter does not have confidence in the agency sponsoring the bond issue.
4. The voter does not understand the issue.
5. The bond program is poorly timed.

Generally, people vote for bond issues for only one reason: *There is something in it for them.* In most cases, it is a waste of time to try to change the mind of a person who is against a bond program. Except in the case of misunderstanding, you will not change his or her opinion.

To pass a bond program, the following procedures should be followed:

1. *Make sure the timing is good.* Depending on the situation, timing is very important. If a large voter turnout will help pass the issue, it would best be presented at a general election. If the taxpayers are overburdened, it is not a good time to put the issue on the ballot. If the image of the parks and recreation agency is poor at the time, it would be bad timing to place the issue on the ballot.
2. *Provide a factual and informative public information document.* This should be provided to all voters. In many states and communities, government agencies themselves cannot take a stand on bond issues. No public funds can be spent

[4] Richard G. Kraus and Joseph E. Curtis, *Creative Administration in Recreation and Parks* (Saint Louis: C. V. Mosby Co., 1973), p. 159.

on trying to sell the issue because of a conflict of interest. The public agency *can* provide the facts about the program, what it will cost the taxpayers, what it will provide, and what its purposes are. Figure 9.7 (on page 300) is an example of such a fact sheet.

3. *Provide for a citizen committee to support the program.* This may sound contradictory to the previous point; however, it is understood that at some point in time there is a decision that the public should be given an opportunity to vote on a particular bond issue. Usually such a proposal is made by the parks and recreation staff. This is presented to the city council or governing board that decides whether to put the proposal before the voters. If it decides to put it to the voters, the council (or board) is the one to appoint a committee to support the bond issue. The committee should raise funds to support the program, publicize it, and engage in any other activities that will promote the program.

4. *Provide a bond program which is of interest to enough citizens that it stands a chance of passing.* As indicated earlier, people are going to vote for an issue only if it offers them something. One or two swimming pools in isolated areas of a large community will not poll enough voters to pass a bond issue. It is a good idea to examine past bond issues and determine how many individuals voted, which areas passed issues and which did not, as well as to try to gain any other information that will help the leisure manager determine how he or she can best present the bond issue so it will stand the best chance of passing. Usually, a proposal for large number of facilities distributed strategically throughout a community stands the best chance of passing.

5. *Do not spend a lot of energy and time trying to convince no voters to vote yes.* Most no voters have their minds made up and you are not going to change them. You may change a few who have been misinformed with a good factual information pamphlet.

6. *Develop a sound park and recreation program.* The best publicity for selling a bond issue is a citizenry that is convinced that the parks and recreation program is the best use of public funds.

Whatever the type of bond issue, be it revenue or general obligation bonds, if it is a "good deal" for the community, it will pass; if if is not, it won't.

TYPES OF BUDGETS

Many types of budgets can be used by leisure service organizations. Basically, they fall into two categories. The first category is *line item budgeting*. Among the types of line item budgets commonly found in leisure service organizations are "functional budgets" and "objective classification budgets." The second category of budgeting is comprised of *program budgeting* and *performance budgeting.*

Orchards and open fields once filled the City of Sunnyvale. The favorable climate and location that produced high quality fruit also proved attractive to some of the most innovative industry in the country.

Over the last 20 years, apple, cherry and apricot orchards have been replaced by sleek, modern industrial complexes and thousands of new homes. Experts now estimate that somewhat over 100 acres of residentially zoned open space remain, and most of this land will be developed within two years at current rates.

Sunnyvale is a community that has a nationwide reputation for good planning and progressive city government. Sunnyvale citizens have made sound decisions in the past and have avoided many of the problems facing other cities today. It is now time for Sunnyvale citizens to decide on the issue of open space. The City Council seeks your decision.

If citizens vote "yes" on Measure C, the City will purchase open space land parcels for public ownership. A "no" vote will allow future development of much of the land. A bond issue has been judged the most equitable means of financing the purchase of land. Its passage requires authorization by two thirds of the voters in the November election.

Open Space Bond Issue: Questions and Answers

Q. *What is the amount and purpose of the proposed bond issue?*

A. $5,000,000—to acquire undeveloped land within the city limits of Sunnyvale for open space purposes.

Q. *How much of the $5 million will be used for land acquisition and how much will be used for impovements to the land?*

A. The bond measure limits the use of bond sale proceeds for improvement of property to 10% or $500,000.

Q. *How much land is available for acquisition?*

A. Parcels identified as priority open space sites total approximately 93 acres plus two school sites of approximately 20 acres.

Q. *Can there be a tax rate increase?*

A. Once the bonds are sold, the City may raise property taxes in an amount sufficient to meet the annual cost. It is estimated that the general tax rate will be increased from its present $1.31 per $100 assessed valuation to $1.39 per $100 assessed valuation or an 8¢ increase. It does not require the City Council to increase taxes if other revenues are adequate.

Q. *What would be the increase in property taxes for the average Sunnyvale homeowner?*

A. Assuming a $10,000 assessed valuation ($40,000 home) this would mean an additional $8.00 per year in property taxes.

Q. *In the event the bond issue fails, will the City still attempt to buy the parcels that are available?*

A. Each year the City Council allocates community resources to various programs. The budgeting of funds to acquire open space or any capital or operating items is subject to the decisions of the City Council each fiscal year. If revenue sharing continues, it

Figure 9.7. "The Open Space Story," City of Sunnyvale Report to Citizens, fall 1974.

may be possible to purchase additional sites from those available at the time.

Q. *Will the City develop the property for parks and other uses in future years?*

A. This determination will be made by city councils at the time each annual budget is adopted.

Q. *What are the maintenance and operating costs?*

A. Maintenance and operating costs are dependent solely upon the level of development and the level of maintenance that is determined as proper by each city council for each fiscal year.

Q. *In view of the unfavorable market conditions, will it be possible to sell the bonds in the event the citizens approve the issue?*

A. The City of Sunnyvale has an "AA" credit rating which is very high and places the City in the preferred customer category with respect to municipal bond issues. The maximum rate that can be paid is 7%. It is unlikely, unless the money market continues to deteriorate, that there will be any problem in marketing the bonds.

Q. *Why does the City have to purchase surplus school sites? Has not the public already paid for them?*

A. The sites were purchased with state bond money or through local school financing. Unless the state loan has been paid off, the schools are required by law to sell surplus sites at an auction to the highest bidder. The money can only be used for school capital improvements or loan re-payments. Schools are paid for by residents of the school district—not residents of the city.

Q. *Must the City pay the highest price for school sites?*

A. No. The City pays only the fair market value as determined by independent appraisals.

Q. *How much land does the City presently have in neighborhood parks and other types of open space?*

A. 153 acres in neighborhood parks
250 acre Mountain park
145 acres, Sunnyvale Municipal Golf Course
30 acres, Sunken Gardens Golf Course
172 acres, Bayland Park (future development)
220 acres, Bayland Park (county ownership)

Figure 9.7. (Continued)

Each of these two categories of budgeting give the manager different types of information. In the second approach, an effort is made to tie the financial information to the outputs or benefits that result from an organization's efforts. The first approach, line item budgeting, does not usually yield this type of information.

Which of the two approaches should the leisure service manager choose? Simply, it depends on the information that is needed. Should a manager find that she needs information beyond the day-to-day operational type, it may be that a program budget would be most appropriate. On the other hand, if a manager in a certain situation needs only operational information, it may be that she should use the line item budget approach. In most organizations, some combination of budgeting types is used because the needs for information vary.

Functional Budgets

When a budget is subdivided and classified according to management units and/ or functions, it is known as a functional budget. In a typical leisure service organization, a budget might be classified by units into three categories: administration, parks, and recreation services. The administration section of the budget would cover the management costs that are incurred to oversee the entire operation. The functional classifications in the recreation unit might be playgrounds, recreation centers, swimming pools, cultural activities, sports programs, and other classifications that describe the type of activity for the purpose of giving individual accountability and control. In the parks unit, one might find general parks maintenance, construction division, street tree services, road and median maintenance, building maintenance, and others. Any number of programs or divisions that the department would like to keep track of separately, for whatever purposes it may have, can be established (See Figure 9.3).

Object Classification Budgets

Another method of classifying a budget is by object classification. Object classification includes such services as the following:

Personnel Services—This classification includes the direct labor of individuals who are employed within the organization on either a regular or a temporary basis and are paid on either an hourly wage basis or a fixed salary.

Contractual Services—This classification includes those services that are performed under an expressed or implied contract. The contractual arrangements of a leisure service organization range from postage, telephone, printing, and repairs to the cost of heat, light, and power. A contractual arrangement between a leisure service agency and another organization would not only involve the use of that organization's equipment, but also the personnel necessary to implement said service.

Supplies—Supplies are commodities that are entirely consumed or show rapid depreciation in a short period of time. Examples would be fuel, office supplies, cleaning supplies, or turf-care products.

Materials—Materials are commodities that have a more permanent and lasting quality than supplies. These may include such things as materials used in construction and repair parts for equipment.

Current Charges—This type of expenditure includes the cost of clothing allowances, insurance, rental of typewriters, dues, and any other charges that are contracted at the option of the organization.

Current Obligations—These consist of fixed charges that have resulted from previous financial transactions entered into by the organization. For example, the payment of the organization's share of social security (United States) or social insurance (Canada) and its contribution to its retirement or pension program would be found in this classification. Also included may be the cost of interest on the organization's debts, which may have resulted from borrowing money for capital improvements.

Properties—This classification includes the cost of improvements that are made to an organization's physical resources. It also includes the direct purchase cost of any new equipment or other physical resources; in other words, anything that is appreciable and has a calculated period of usefulness. This might include such things as playground equipment, machinery, office equipment, the cost of real estate, and any improvements made to existing properties.

Debt Payment—Debt payments may be distinguished from current obligations in that debt payments refer to the organization's payments on the principle of a given debt, rather than the interest.

A system that an organization might follow in laying out an objective classification budget is shown in Table 9.2

Object classification budgeting is traditionally referred to as line item budgeting because each element of the budget has a specific line that describes the type of classification and the amount of money associated with that particular element. One of the shortcomings of line item budget is that often the city council, or governing board, spends too much time in budget hearings arguing over particular line items. Many budget hearings get bogged down in discussion about whether you have two much fertilizer or not enough, whether you really need a new vehicle or a new maintenance person. As a result, the more important issues in terms of what services should be rendered or what activities should be provided are not dealt with in the proper perspective. Although there will probably always be a need to keep track of funds and expenditures on the basis of line items, the line item budget is being de-emphasized as a tool in terms of budget presentation before governing boards and is being used more as a control for the manager.

Performance Budgeting

Performance budgeting is a mechanism whereby an organization breaks down its work activities into detailed subunits for the purpose of determining the specific costs of each of these units. In other words, a manager using a performance approach to budgeting would further subdivide or arrange the functional and/or objective classifications of budgeting to get a detailed cost of given program. It is not unusual for organizations to have a cross-reference system that shows objective classifications on the vertical axis and functional classifications on the horizontal axis. Performance budgeting is often used in organizations where the cost of a given activity is paid by the user. For the organization to have an idea of the

Table 9.2.   Example of Objective Classification System

	1000 Personnel Services
1100	Wages and salaries, regular
1200	Wages and salaries, temporary
1300	Other compensations
	2000 Contractual Services
2100	Communication and transportation
2200	Power, water, and sewage
2300	Printing and advertising
2400	Repairs, janitorial services, and other services
	3000 Supplies
3100	Fuel and lubricants
3200	Office supplies
3300	Cleaning supplies
3400	Food
	4000 Materials
4100	Building materials
4200	Repair parts
	5000 Current Charges
5100	Insurance
5200	Equipment
5300	Clothing allowances
5400	Subscriptions on dues
5500	Taxes
5600	Refunds
	6000 Current Obligations
6100	Pensions and retirement
6300	Interest
	7000 Properties
7100	Building structures and improvements
7200	Equipment
7300	Land
	8000 Debt Payment
8100	Serial bonds

total cost and/or appropriate cost for a given program, all the expenditures for that activity must be calculated. Once this has been accomplished, the organization can suggest a fee or charge to cover the expenses that are incurred. Some of the key features of performance budgeting are the following:

1. Performance budgeting does not preclude budgeting according to a classification of functions, subfunctions and objectives of expenditures.

2. The data supplied by the process of performance budgeting are more valuable to top administrators and to the appropriating body than to administrators of single programs who are close enough to the enterprise to make judgements without performance budget data.
3. Formal procedures used in performance budgeting are more valuable to those who are removed from the operating process than those involved in the operations.
4. The existence of a formal system of performance budgeting tends to encourage thinking of expenditures in relation to unit cost.
5. The need for a performance budget system diminishes as cities decrease in size.[5]

Program Budgeting

Within the last several years, more and more agencies have been moving toward a program-type budget and away from the line item budget in terms of budget presentation and accountability. The idea behind the program budget is to put more emphasis on dealing with programs that are desirable and on associating costs with each of these programs in terms of resources necessary to carry them out; in other words, to determine which programs the policymaking or governing boards want to offer and to permit the manager to determine how to finance these programs and assure accountability.

One of the newest and most popular budget procedures is the Planning Programming Budgeting System, more commonly referred to as PPBS. PPBS budgeting is an analytical tool designed to assist management in the allocation of resources to accomplish stated goals and objectives over a designated time period. Analysis is focused primarily on output and the budget is structured in such a manner that the outputs are related directly to the goals and objectives desired. Although it may sound simple, the determination of measurable output is one of the most difficult aspects of PPBS budgeting, but is entirely essential if it is to be effective. Once the goals and objectives have been determined and the outputs specified, the outputs must be expressed in quantitative terms and a means of measurement to determine an acceptable level of achievement must be developed.

Another feature of PPBS analysis is comparison of the cost of alternative programs with their projected benefits. This budgeting process is designed to assist management as well as the policymaking board in terms of making decisions as to what services they want to include in their program of operation for a given year. The design of the PPBS budget is also meant to give management an operational control, at the lowest level of manager, on a cost-centered basis. PPBS is used to allocate not only fiscal resources but all resources within the jurisdiction of the organization. These include equipment, building space, work hours, inventory, and

[5] Hines, *Revenue Source Management*, p. 3.

all other resources that contribute to the accomplishment of goals and objectives. The resource allocations are directed toward the accomplishment of goals and objectives which requires that the goals and objectives are clearly stated and understood by all individuals who have power to direct and utilize the resources. PPBS budgeting also requires a time frame that is generally five years or more. Long-range considerations are extremely important in the PPBS budgeting system.

Two of the most important documents produced in the PPBS budgeting system are (1) program and financial plans and (2) program statements. To begin the process, program areas, units, or elements must be designated within an organization. These program elements, in turn, produce both types of documents. The plans and statements help each of the units establish and internalize their objectives, alternatives to achieving these objectives, and the costs and benefits of each alternative. These documents, then, when presented to top management, serve to provide information to guide decision-making and, hence, the distribution of an organization's resources.

Program and financial plans have three basic components: identification of outputs, financial costs, and special considerations. Output statements involve the determination of the specific outputs that are produced by a given program within an organization. For example, a swimming pool program may result in the involvement of X number of participants, an indicator of outputs. It should be noted that output statements must be made in nonfinancial, measurable (quantifiable), units. This does not, however, preclude the development of measurements of qualitative factors, as opposed to just quantitative ones (See Figure 9.8).

The next step in the development of programs and financial plans is the tabulation of financial costs for programs. The cost of each program element should be calculated and tied to the organization's accounting system. The total cost of each program should be displayed and should include the cost of support services required to create the particular program. For example, the cost of administrative support services to create a swimming pool program should be reflected in the tabulation of its total cost. The cost of administrative services may be on a reimbursable basis, but nonetheless it contributes to the overall cost of the program. Administrative services provided to the swimming pool program would be one of the program outputs of the administrative service element of the budget.

The last part of program and financial plans is special concerns. This might include such things as the amount of revenue produced from fees and charges. Again, using the illustration of the swimming pool, the special concerns part of the program and financial plan would report an estimate of the amount of money that could be derived from daily admissions, season passes, swimming lessons, rental, and so on. Still further, the special concerns section might also include or show major capital investment. It is desirable to include such information in order to give a comprehensive perspective of the actual costs and benefits of a given program.

Program statements provide the analytical backup information for the programs indicated in the program and financial plan. Generally speaking, program statements should specify the relationship of proposed program offerings to the overall goals of the organization. Further, they should provide information as to the specific objectives of a given program and should detail the probable effectiveness and cost of the proposed actions. Program statements should outline and compare the alternative ways of meeting the objectives stated within the proposal. Lastly, a program statement should include a discussion of the priorities within a given program area within the organization. In addition to the detailed information, a program statement should also carry a set of recommendations and a summary of the proposed activities.

A detailed program statement will serve as the program element's justification for its program and financial plan. As such, it should assess the degree to which a given program is effective in meeting the organization's goals, as well as provide information regarding the efficiency of the proposed activity. As a tool for planning, this component of the PPBS system is far superior to line item types of budget in that it allows an organization to link its financial planning with actual program activities. Because these program statements often reflect long-term trends in terms of the effectiveness of the service provided, the manager is in a position to assess the impact of the budget.

PPBS should be viewed as an ongoing process that enables an organization to reevaluate and update its objectives, performance, and costs. As such, an organization using this procedure should adopt a continuous process of review and revision. This process is usually cyclical, with specific checkpoints established throughout the fiscal year.

The city of Sunnyvale, California, initiated the PPBS budget system in 1967 and today has probably one of the best examples and most thoroughly documented PPBS systems in the country. As a result of the PPBS budget system, the city has been able to increase service levels to the public; at the same time, it dropped property tax from $1.31 to $1.18 to $1.13 and then to $1.04 per $100 of assessed valuation.

The Sunnyvale PPBS budget has grouped all activities into 63 operating programs managed by 50 program managers. These programs are grouped into five functional areas: protective services, environmental services, cultural and community services, support services, and legislative and legal services. Each program contains an overall objective, and quality goals, expressed in terms of effective measurements and production plan.

Figure 9.8 is an example of PPBS budget. Resource allocations are expressed in terms of dollars and work hours. Each program has a table showing actual costs and work hours for four previous years, proposed costs and work hours for the coming year, and the project costs and work hours for the next seven years. Each program identifies a production unit in terms of output, cost per unit as well as unit costs modified by inflation utilizing the San Francisco Bay Area Consumer

Price Index. Each program budget shows graphs depicting productivity trends over a ten-year period, comparing production units output, as well as a cost trend in terms of constant dollars. This approach to resource allocation enables managers and policymakers to focus on what is accomplished with the resources used. They are also able to set goals for the next eight years.

PPBS is a system aimed at helping management make better decisions by allocating proper resources, to the various alternatives presented, in ways that will

Program	301.09 Neighborhood recreation activities	
Function	Community and cultural services	
Objective	Provide recreation at city park sites and facilities	

Fiscal Year	Work Hours	Total Cost	Production Units (Work-hour Output)	Cost per Unit	Unit Cost in Constant Dollars 1972–73
Actual 1972–1973	80,701	2995,552	107,101	2.80	2.80
Actual 1973–1974	83,184	336,790	102,728	3.28	3.12
Actual 1974–1975	85,135	380,254	111,126	3.42	2.96
Estimated 1975–1976	89,692*	413,384	117,965	3.50	2.75
Proposed 1976–1977	70,736	429,875	107,126	4.01	2.90
Projected 1977–1978	70,736	460,530	107,126	4.30	2.91
Projected 1978–1979	70,736	492,408	107,126	4.60	2.91
Projected 1979–1980	70,736	522,288	107,126	4.88	2.91
Projected 1980–1981	70,736	549,300	107,126	5.13	2.91
Projected 1981–1982	70,736	576,399	107,126	5.38	2.90
Projected 1982–1983	70,736	605,365	107,126	5.65	2.90
Projected	70,736	635,715	107,126	5.93	2.90

Figure 9.8.   City of Sunnyvale, California, resource allocation analysis.

Quality Goals
- Improve productivity measurement for neighborhood recreation programs
- Replace 5% of total program with new programs based on population changes
- Train 100% of staff
- Train 100% of part-time staff

Fiscal Year Production Plan
- Provide 1,957,591 participant hours at 12 park sites year-round and 9 summer school sites
- Provide 78,738 participant hours for 6 junior high programs
- Provide 259,440 participant hours for 12 summer teen programs
- Provide 91,303 participant hours for 4 teen centers
- Provide 42,092 hours of assistance through Sunnyvale Voluntary Action Corps

Special Notes
* Includes 3,961 CETA employee hours for 1975–76

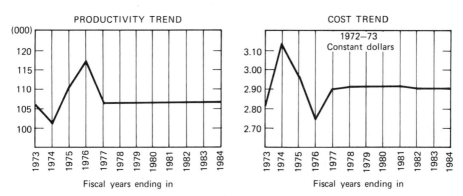

Figure 9.8. (Continued)

obtain organization objectives. The primary distinctive characteristics of the PPBS budgeting are the following:

1. It focuses on identifying the fundamental objectives of the organization and then relating all activities regardless of organizational placement (which department may administer the program) to these.
2. Future years' implications are explicitly considered.
3. All pertinent costs are considered including capital as well as noncapital costs and associated support costs (e.g., employee benefits, vehicles, and building maintenance costs) as well as direct costs.
4. Systematic analysis of alternatives is undertaken. This characteristic is the crux of PPBS. It involves the following:
   a. identification of governmental objectives
   b. explicit, systematic identification of alternatives

    c. estimation of the total cost implications of each alternative

    d. estimation of the expected results of each alternative

    e. presentation of the resulting major costs and benefit tradeoffs among the alternatives, along with the indentification of major assumptions and uncertainties.[6]

Although PPBS is not a panacea to all budgeting problems, it certainly holds many benefits in terms of giving direction to government agencies in budgeting systems.

Zero-Base Budgeting

Zero-base budgeting is a process that has emerged recently and is being adopted by both profit and nonprofit organizations. It was developed in private business in 1969 by Texas Instruments, Inc., and was first adopted for governmental use in 1973 in the state of Georgia by the then governor, Jimmy Carter. Its wide application in a relatively short period of time, in both public and private organizations, makes it appear to be an important budgeting technique that is likely to have an impact on the approach to management of leisure service agencies. It can be thought of also as a program budget.

    The usual process of determining annual budget increases within an organization was accomplished by adding the projected cost of new programs and inflation to the organization's base budget for the previous year. In this way the organization did not have to rejustify its previous year's appropriations. For example, if an organization had a budget of $2 million, and the projected inflation percentage was 6 percent and the projected cost for new programs was 10 percent, its budget would be increased automatically by 16 percent, or $320,000. Such increases have been made traditionally without due consideration of the effectiveness of past programs relative to their cost.

    The zero-base approach to budgeting does not allow an organization to simply request automatic increases because of inflation or as a result of the development of new programs. Rather, using this approach, the organization is required to *justify* its total request for funds from a zero-base. An organization must look at each program or service and its relationship to its cost as if it were considering placing the item on the budget for the first time. In this way, the organization is forced to look at and evaluate its program and service offerings to insure that they are effective in meeting organizational goals and are being operated efficiently.

    The zero-base budgeting method also asks the organization to determine whether a past program is of sufficient impact to retain, or whether it should be replaced by a higher-priority program. The technique forces an organization to

[6] "What Is PPBS?" (Washington, D.C.: George Washington University, January 1967), p.2.

constantly reassess its activities. Not only does this allow an organization a method of budgeting that maximizes the effectiveness of its expenditures, but—on a year in year out basis—it encourages the organization to remain fresh, vigorous, and competitive in its approach to providing services. Many organizations rely on tradition in developing their programs and, as a result, become stale in their approach to meeting the needs of those they serve.

The zero-base technique should be thought of as more than a budgeting process. It is a total thought process that involves the development of organizational goals and objectives, evaluation of programs and services, and, ultimately, managerial decision-making. The process suggests that there is a linkage between many of the management activities within an organization and that, in the end, these will be reflected in the budeting process, and vice versa. In many organizations, the budgeting process is thought of as a separate and distinct activity that takes place some distance from the operational activities of the organization. The zero-base approach, however, ties operational activities directly to the budgeting process.

The zero-base approach to budgeting can serve as an aid to legislative bodies as well as management and operational units within an organization. Each of these units will have unique and special types of informational needs; but, according to Peter Pyhrr, to initiate the zero-base approach to budgeting, each of these decision-making units must focus on two primary concerns:

1. Are the current activities efficient and effective?
2. Should current activities be eliminated or reduced to fund higher priority new programs or to reduce the current budget?[7]

These two concerns are the basic essence of the zero-base approach to budgeting. An organization must ask itself, "Are our programs, activities, and services meeting the stated goals of the organization? And, are the resources that are used to produce these programs being consumed in an appropriate manner?" In addition, the organization must ask itself whether the expenditures it is making are as important as other potential uses for the financial resources of the organization.

The zero-base budgeting process requires four basic steps: identification of decision-making units within an organization, development and analysis of the decision-making packages within designated decision-making units, analysis and evaluation of alternatives within all decision-making packages; and preparation of a detailed operational budget.[8]

Identify decision-making units. Decision-making units are any groupings within an organization that have the authority and responsibility for planning and

---

[7] Peter A. Phyrr, "The Zero-Base Approach to Government Budgeting," *Public Administration Review,* Vol. 37 January/February 1977, p. 1.

[8] Ibid., p. 2.

controlling financial resources and programs. Decision-making units may be lead by division heads (e.g., the superintendent of parks and/or superintendent of recreation) or the coordinator of a set of functions, facilities, or activities. The zero-base approach to budgeting is built around these decision-making units; its purpose is to provide information to the manager or governing board so they can use the data that is generated in making decisions.

Analyze decision-making in a decision-making package. The "decision package" is the building block of the zero-base concept. It is a document that identifies and describes each decision unit in such a manner that management can (a) evaluate it and rank it against other decision units competing for funding, and (b) decide whether to approve it or disapprove it.[9] To comparatively evaluate one decision-making unit with another, a common denominator must be established. Without a criterion that can be used in the measurement and evaluation of the various units in an organization, comparative decision-making is difficult. The purpose of a decision-making package is to provide management with information that is comparable for each decision-making unit, so that management can evaluate one request for funds versus another. In this way, a manager or a legislative body is presented with a number of clear alternatives that can be evaluated in terms of achieving the organization's goals. Decision-making packages can develop the following types of information:

1. Purpose and objective of the decision-making unit.
2. Description of the proposed actions or activities. In other words, what is the unit going to do and how is it going to do it?
3. Cost and benefits of various levels of funding. Simply what is the relationship between input levels and output levels?
4. Work load and performance measures.
5. Alternative means of accomplishing the objectives.[10]

Evaluate and rank all alternatives within decision-making packages. Assuming that all organizations operate on limited resources, they must evaluate proposals from decision-making units and determine what activities should be approved and how much these activities will cost. Essentially, managerial decision-making involves the weighing of alternatives. In determining which courses of action an organization will follow, its funding requirements are developed. Comparing the decision-making packages and alternatives within these packages allows the manager to identify the benefits that can be accrued from the selection of one alternative versus another. In this way, the organization is better able to predict the potential consequences of a given alternative within a package. Further, comparing decision-making packages and alternatives allows an organization to weigh differences in terms of cost. It may be that one decision-making unit within

[9] Ibid., p. 3.
[10] Ibid., p. 3.

an organization can accomplish the same outputs at a lower cost than another unit. Thus it would be possible to reduce the overall cost of providing services.

In prioritizing alternatives, the manager or legislative body of the organization ranks these according to their relative benefit to the organization. This ranking process is the backbone of the zero-base budgeting process because it allows the manager to engage in systematic decision-making. Decision-making in many organizations occurs by default. Without information that can be compared and ranked as to its potential contribution to the goals of the organization, a manager is not in a position to make effective decisions. He or she is simply reacting to the organizational environment as opposed to actively directing the organization by choosing among alternatives in a careful, systematic manner.

Prepare a detailed operational budget for the selected alternatives within decision-making packages. Once the organization has selected alternatives within the decision-making packages, the next step within the zero-base approach to budgeting is to establish a detailed operational budget for the items that have been selected. This budget may reflect traditional approaches to budgeting, including the use of the standard classification type of budget.

The zero-base approach to budgeting should not be viewed as a short-term project that can be implemented without adequate staff development and training. Rather, it is a long-term management process in which an organization can identify alternatives toward achieving stated goals. As such, it insures that an organization will identify in advance the costs and benefits of potential services and that existing programs and/or activities will remain effective. By ranking alternatives, an organization is in a position to justify the elimination of its nonessential or low-priority activities. As a result, an organization may redistribute its resources in such a way that it concentrates on high-impact programs, thus increasing its overall effectiveness.

The process also encourages an increase in an organization's efficiency. This occurs primarily because of the systematic approach—detailing the potential actions of the organization in relation to costs and benefits. Also, costs are reduced as a by-product of the healthy competition that is introduced among decision-making units. The savings that an organization realizes because of increased efficiency can be plowed back into the agency to increase its services, and/or it can be used to reduce the burden of the taxpayers.

Cost/Benefit Analysis

With the advent of program budgeting and zero-base budgeting, an understanding of cost/benefit analysis is extremely important to the leisure service manager. In traditional approaches to budgeting, the manager was concerned primarily with balancing off expenditures with revenues. Little thought was given to the relationship between the expenditures made and the social impact or benefit of programs, services, or activities. The newer methods of budgeting tie finances directly to the impact or effectiveness of a given service. Therefore an understanding of the methods that can be used to determine the qualitative relationship between the benefits and the costs of services must be developed. This qualitative relationship must be measurable in quantitative terms to be useful in decision-making, however.

L. Hale Meserow and associates have noted that cost/benefit analysis can be useful to park and recreation organizations in a number of ways. It can accomplish the following:

1. Foster valid comparisons within and between operational facilities and departments;
2. Permit the assignment of priorities to specific programs and services;
3. Provide targets and guidelines for management decision-making and resource allocation;
4. Assist in continual evaluation of agency objectives and procedures;
5. Provide valuable support data for justifying budget requests;
6. Identify high- and low-cost programs and services as related to maintenance, administrative, and direct leadership costs per participant-hour of service rendered;
7. Provide essential data for policy formulation and revision.[11]

There are essentially two ways to approach cost/benefit analysis. First, it can be viewed simply as an analysis of the economic efficiency within an organization. This approach can be useful should the purpose of the analysis be to compare alternatives primarily on the basis of cost. A manager could compare two similar program proposals that are aimed at achieving common goals, or appear to have the same impact, choosing the alternative that can be accomplished at the lower cost. In this way, the organization is able to increase its efficiency simply on the basis of choosing between alternatives, one of which can be implemented more frugally than the other. But most organizations do not have a single goal (i.e., economic efficiency); rather, most organizations are concerned with the accomplishment of a variety of goals. Therefore the application of cost/benefit analysis should be considered from a nonefficiency standpoint.

Nonefficiency cost/benefit analysis should be used in addition to measurements of financial efficiency. In establishing nonefficiency cost/benefit programs, one is basically concerned with making value judgments as to the impact the agency desires to achieve. A number of faulty assumptions are made when comparing the nonefficiency approach to the efficiency approach, using cost/benefit analysis. The most common faulty assumption is that the cost of individual programs can be equated to one another. Some programs may cost more, but may also have a higher social value. For example, a swimming program for the handi-

---

[11] L. Hale Meserow, David T. Pompel, Jr., and Charles M. Reich, "Benefit-Cost Evaluation," *Parks and Recreation,* Vol. 10 No. 4, February 1975, p. 30.

capped will cost vastly more than a swimming program for the general public. A public agency may, however, charge the same fee for both programs and underwrite the majority of the cost for the former program, having decided that its social value is worth the added investment.

In other words, an organization must look at the potential benefits of a program as it relates to the overall goals of the organization (servicing the community as a whole). Evaluating and choosing among alternative benefit packages or proposals becomes extremely important. The organization should not simply determine the cost of services based on their marginal cost; rather, it should consider the broader effect of its social programs. In fact, one might ask, "*What would the social cost be, if the organization did not provide the service or program?*" This is one of the great differences between profit organizations and nonprofit government organizations. In the case of the former, the task is to maximize the price of the service in relation to its actual cost in order to earn a profit. The nonprofit organization provides services that are prioritized on the basis of social need, even though the organization may have to underwrite the entire cost of the program.

Of the two types of cost/benefit analyses, efficiency analysis is more fully developed in terms of methodology in the leisure service field. One such system— efficiency cost/benefit analysis—has been developed for the Surrey, British Columbia, Park and Recreation Department. Discussing the procedure, William Webster and Charles Reich write that cost/benefit data are based on the number of user hours of service rendered per dollar cost.[12] Further, they suggest that specific application to the leisure service field depends on an understanding of the following key concepts:

> *Participants* may be either active (i.e. taking part in a sponsored recreation activity, or otherwise utilizing the department's facilities), or passive (i.e. spectators).
> *Participant-Hours or User-Hours* includes both spectators and participants and is a term which refers to the number of participants multiplied by the duration of their stay at the facility or program (e.g. ten participants in a ceramics program for two hours a week over two weeks equals 200 participant-hours).
> *Net Cost* refers to the total expenditures, minus all revenue collected.[13]

As indicated in Figure 9.9, the participant hours are combined with spectator hours to determine the total user hours for the programs indicated. The next step is to calculate the net cost of the program. This is accomplished by subtracting income produced by programs from their gross costs. The total user hours are then divided by the net cost to determine the net cost per hour of service rendered.

---

[12] William D. Webster and Charles M. Reich, "Benefit/Cost Analysis—Its Uses in Parks and Recreation," *Recreation Canada,* No. 35/1/1977, p. 25.
[13] Ibid., p. 25.

	Participant Hours	+ Spectator Hours	= Total User Hours	Gross Cost	- Income	= Net Cost	Net Cost per Hour of Service Rendered
Public Swims	8,126	642	8,768	4,312	2,681	1,631	$0.19
Lessons	3,041	2,770	5,811	4,521	2,299	2,222	.38
School bookings	0	0	0	0	0	0	.00
Rentals	345	0	345	436	35	401	1.16
Club programs	77	50	127	258	117	141	1.11
General nonassigned	0	0	0	2,401	578	1,823	—
TOTAL OPERATIONS	11,589	3,462	15,051	$11,928	$5,710	$6,218	$0.41
For Cloverdale Town Center for January through March Quarter 1975							
Cultural programs	2,421	0	2,421	$ 2,623	$1,320	$1,303	$0.54
Sports and Fitness	2,579	0	2,579	2,766	1,421	1.345	.52
Outdoor programs	849	0	849	757	608	149	.18
Social programs	4,067	0	4,067	1,883	795	1,088	.27
Meetings	450	0	450	215	150	65	.14
Special events	0	0	0	0	0	0	.00
Miscellaneous nonassigned	0	0	0	1,852	0	1,852	—
TOTAL CENTER OPERATIONS	10,366	0	10,366	$10,096	$4,294	$5,802	$0.56

Figure 9.9. Summary of benefit and cost evidence collected and analyzed for North Surrey indoor pool during July 1975. *Source:* William D. Webster and Charles M. Reich, "Benefit/Cost Analysis—Its Uses in Parks and Recreation." *Recreation Canada,* No. 35, January 1977. p. 25.

BUDGET PROCEDURES

The budget process basically consists of four activities:

1. Budget preparation
2. Budget design
3. Budget presentation
4. Budget implementation and accountability

Budget Preparation

Budget preparation is the first phase of the process. Most agencies have a budget manual that gives a timetable of the budget process: when it is to be submitted, in what form, and various other procedures that are part of the budget process. The budget procedure is usually developed by the finance agency in accordance with a timetable that will meet the requirements of the governing authority. The budget manual gives general instructions, a timetable for submission, examples of forms to be used, as well as other instructions to aid the manager in submitting the budget.

The budget process is ongoing throughout the year. One of the best ways to assure that the budget is an ongoing process is for the leisure service manager and other top-level personnel to establish a budget folder in which ideas and suggestions can be accumulated throughout the year. When needs become apparent, the manager can write a memo covering the subject area and include it in the budget folder for consideration at budget time. To try to remember all the ideas and submit them at one time during the year is impractical, if not impossible. Establishing some procedure whereby ideas are accumulated on a year-round basis gives much greater assurance that everything will be included when the budget is submitted. In addition, other ideas, changes, corrections, deletions, and additions can be included in the budget folder; these will help the manager at the time of preparing the budget to modify and make necessary changes. The budget folder is more or less an ongoing tickler file that helps the manager to do a better job.

Another procedure that is helpful in budget preparation is the initiation of public hearings to get citizen input prior to submission of the budget. Such meetings should be public and held in various parts of the community, obtaining ideas as well as support from residents. At such public hearings, the manager can review past programs and activities and present ideas she or he may have for the future, then open the meeting to the public for general discussion. Such public meetings impart to the community the feeling that the agency is concerned with its needs and interests. To have public support at the time the budget goes before the governing board is important. Recreation and parks programs are for the public, not the professional staff, and, when supported by the public, are given more credibility.

Budget Design

Budget design or technique will vary from one agency to another depending on the type of budget process adopted. In most instances, the budget consists of a number of parts. The first of these is usually a *budget message*, a description of a budget in terms of the highlights, changes, or new programs that are being suggested. It gives the reader, whether a city council member or member of the general public, an overview and basis for understanding what is included in the budget in capsule form.

After the budget message, there is usually a one-page *budget summary*. The summary sheet would report the major categories within the budget. For example, in an objective classification budget, under expenditures, this sheet would summarize estimates for personnel services, supplies, materials, and so on; under revenues, it would indicate tax figures, fees and charges, grants, and the like.

In addition to the budget message and summary, there is sometimes a *budget narrative* that accompanies each subprogram or activity, such as sports, special services, aquatics, and playgrounds. The narrative, similar to a budget message, describes the highlights of each activity. Its purpose is to center on each activity in a more descriptive fashion rather than just in terms of dollars and cents.

Following the budget narrative, or sometimes in concert with the budget narrative, is the *budget detail*. Again depending on the type of budgeting process utilized, the budget detail will include a specific accounting of all the proposed expenditures and/or program elements within the budget design. It is this portion of the budget that takes the most time to develop, and serves as the primary guide for organizational finances and/or program operation. The budget detail may be so specific that it may indicate the number of pencils and basketballs needed, and their cost. It also lists such costs as personnel in terms of the specific number of people to be employed, how many hours they are to work per day, and how much they will be paid per hour. In a line item budget, such proposed expenditures would be detailed by classification or function. In a program budget, they would be detailed according to units designated within an organization.

Various graphs also can be utilized as part of the design of the budget to visually help the reader understand trends or what the budget is trying to accomplish. Using graphs and charts to show productivity trends or unit cost increases or decreases can be more helpful than just presenting dollar figures. Graphs can help justify budget changes of one form or another (see Figure 9.10).

Another method of showing trends in a budget is to provide indications of productivity, which show measurements of work accomplished. In the case of recreation programs, these might be the number of participants served or, in the case of a park division, the number of acres maintained. Productivity within a golf program might be the number of rounds of golf played during a given year. Productivity can be shown in other forms by utilizing the total costs of the

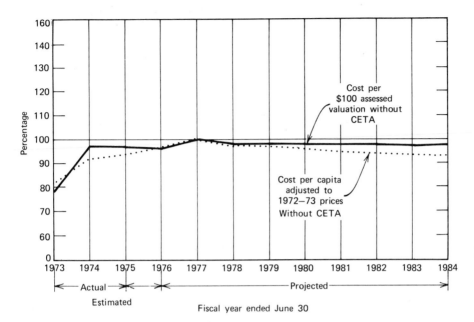

Figure 9.10. Community and cultural services operating costs related to population and assessed valuation, percentage of 1976-1977, 1972-73 tp 1983-84 fiscal years.

activity divided by the work hours or participant hours served to give an indication of the unit costs of activity.

Figure 9.11 shows a system developed in Sunnyvale, California, to indicate productivity in various programs. The leisure service manager compares one year to the next to see if productivity is increasing or decreasing and to try to determine why. A new piece of equipment that cuts down work hours may cause an increase in productivity, whereas a decrease in productivity might be caused by a serious morale problem in the organization. It is the manager's job to be constantly aware of changes in productivity, to determine why they occur, and to take corrective action when necessary.

Budget Presentation

The next aspect of the budget process is the *budget presentation*, which is usually made to the governing board that has to approve it, in terms of budget appropriations. Prior to the presentation to the governing board, the budget is usually presented to the city manager or other administrative officers who have administrative control over the funds. In either case, the budget presentation is generally the same. Although budget presentation is extremely important, more important

EXPLANATION OF TERMS

Base Year

The year selected to determine the relationship between raw count and work hours.

Raw Count

The actual count of production units measured.

Work Hours

The number of work hours required to produce the raw count.

Units per Work Hour

Raw count divided by work hours.

Standard Dividend

The number into which all other units per work hour are divided. It was developed as follows:

Item Measured	Raw Count	Work Hours	Units per Work Hour	Multiplied by .1
Accounting Transactions	85,325	6,428	13.2740	1.3274

The number 13.2740 was multiplied by .1 in order to keep the size of numbers manageable.

Weight Factor

The value obtained by dividing the standard dividend by units per work hour. The resultant weight factor is a productivity relationship between all of the citywide items selected for measurement. For example, production units of 1,000 in the Accounting Program and 1,000 in the Street Maintenance Program represent an equivalent amount of work (productivity).

Production Units

Raw count times weight factor. These data are displayed on each resource allocation analysis under the heading "Production Units (Workhour Output)."

Productivity Trend Chart

A graphic display of production units (work-hour output).

Cost Trend Chart

A graphic display of unit cost in constant dollars, 1972–73 (1972–73 = 100).

Calculation of Weight Factor

	Base Year	Raw Count	Work Hours	Units per Work Hour	Standard Dividend	Weight Factor	Raw Count	Production Units
							1976–77	1976–77
251.07 *Neighborhood Center*	1975–76 (Est)							
Recreation participant hours		20,000	1,880	10.6383	1.32740	.1248	20,000	2,496
Library items circulated		8,000	7,488	1.0684	1.32740	1.2424	8,900	11,057
Neighborhood resource officer:								
Responses		274	872	.3142	1.32740	4.2247	300	1,267
Community outreach projects		790	1,308	.6040	1.32740	2.1977	800	1,758
								16,578
261.08 *Parks and Recreation Management*								
Production units coordinated (all programs with Summary Codes .08 and .09 and programs 806.60 and 813.60)								544,039
262.08 *Parks Management*								
Production units coordinated (all programs with Summary Code .08 and programs 806.60 and 813.60)								266,660
265.08 *Parks Maintenance*	1971–72							
Square feet maintained		6,664,680	81,621	81.6540	1.3274	.0163	7,666,553	124,965
268.08 *Public Bldg Landsc Maintenance*	1971–72							
Square feet maintained		710,028	7,405	95.8849	1.3274	.0138	710,028	9,798

Figure 9.11. Productivity units of various programs, Sunnyvale, California.

321

Calculation of Weight Factor

1976-77

	Base Year	Raw Count	Work Hours	Units per Work Hour	Standard Dividend	Weight Factor	Raw Count	Production Units
275.08 *Parking District Landsc Maint* Square feet maintained	1971-72	82,764	2,598	31.8568	1.3274	.0417	108,900	4,541
276.08 *Community Center Landsc maint* Square feet maintained	1971-72	827,640	5,251	157.6157	1.3274	.0084	827,640	6,952
277.08 *Street Landscaping Maintenance* Square feet maintained	1971-72	609,840	5,257	116.0053	1.3274	.0114	925,650	10,552
278.08 *Street Tree Services* Trees serviced	1971-72	32,389	14,930	2.1694	1.3274	.6119	36,710	22,463
281.08 *Golf Course Maintenance* Square feet maintained	1971-72	4,573,800	15,985	286.1307	1.3274	.0046	5,619,240	25,849
293.08 *Swim Centers Maintenance* Cubic feet maintained	1971-72	81,334	4,608	17.6506	1.3274	.0752	104,000	7,821
300.09 *Recreation Management* Production units coordinated (all programs with Summary Code .09)								277,379
301.09 *Neighborhood Rec Activities* Participant hours	1971-72	2,428,604	80,701	30.0939	1.3274	.0441	2,429,164	107,126
305.09 *Special Recreation Services* Participant hours	1971-72	257,887	11,562	22.3047	1.3274	.0595	472,270	28,100

310.09 Sports, Parks and Recreation								
Participant hours	1971–72	193,750	11,419	16.9673	1.3274	.0782	423,300	33,102
311.09 Tennis Activities								
Number of court hours						1.0000	41,800	41,800
312.09 Aquatics								
Participant hours	1971–72	173,400	14,389	12.0509	1.3274	.1101	381,600	42,014
313.09 Golf Discount								
Rounds of golf discounted						1.0000	8,000	8,000
314.09 Special Groups Recreation								
Participant hours	1971–72	42,678	578	73.8374	1.3274	.0180	62,086	1,118
317.09 Community Center Management								
Activity hours of use	1975–76	45,929	9,403	4.8845	1.3274	.2718	59,303	16,119

Figure 9.11. (Continued)

is the reputation that the agency develops on a year-round basis. Few agencies receive large appropriations based on the kind of presentations they make. More importantly, they receive appropriations based on the quality of services they offer throughout the year.

In terms of selling a budget, the type of service offered on a year-round basis, the competence with which programs are operated, and the thoroughness and follow-up provided to assure the public of a worthwhile, well-run service goes a great deal further than a flashy presentation once a year. The purpose of a budget presentation is to summarize, in narrative form, what the budget includes, particularly any new programs or changes made. Prior to the presentation, the governing body has usually studied the budget; the budget presentation is meant to summarize and highlight specific programs and answer questions about the budget.

Various methods are used in making the presentation. They may include slide presentations, verbal presentations, and/or tours of facilities. During the formal presentation, it is wise to try to avoid talking about dollars and cents and to concentrate more on program accomplishments and goals and objectives of the department. To spend a great deal of time talking about how many baseball bats are needed for the sports program is a waste of time. Again, if the governing board has confidence in the administrator and in the agency, the budget is generally accepted much more readily than if there is a lack of confidence. As indicated earlier, budgeting is a year-round process. Although the budget presentation is important, it is only a small part of the total budget process.

Budget Implementation and Accountability

The last aspect of the budgeting process is implementation and accountability of the fund once approved by the governing board. Usually, after the budget presentation, the governing board formally adopts the budget through a budget resolution. A budget resolution is a legal document that provides the funds with which the agency operates for a given year. Once the budget is approved, it is necessary to provide the necessary controls and procedures to see that it is administered properly and that carelessness, waste, and misappropriation are not permitted. There are various forms of control that can be utilized to assure good management of the budget once it is approved.

It is important to budgetary control to have a system whereby an organization records the collection of its revenues and expenditure of its funds. The procedure or system utilized to insure that an organization has information regarding these transactions is known as *accounting*. Accounting may be defined as the classifying and recording of financial transactions that take place within an organization and between it and other agencies. The concepts of accounting and budgeting are often confused. For the purposes of this text, accounting is thought of as a tool that enables the manager to collect, summarize, and report certain types of information, primarily for the purposes of controlling the budget.

There are a number of approaches to accounting, each providing different types or combinations of information to the manager. Two types of accounting methods commonly used are *cost accounting* and *accrual accounting*. Cost accounting has evolved as a result of the growth of program and performance budgets. In this approach to accounting, the report of expenditures is broken down into the functions, programs, or specific activities that the agency has designated in its budget. In this way, the manager is able to view the expenditure in each of the units and thus maintain control over their activities. Cost accounting is also used as a mechanism to compare cost and benefits.

Accrual accounting is a standard method used in most leisure service organizations. Discussing the accounting procedures used in this method, Thomas Hines writes:

> Unpaid bills are obviously shown and charged against the proper account items; thus a current and accurate appraisal of the department's financial condition is evident. The department executive should receive each month a statement of the agency's financial status, and this statement should not require any additional computations on his part. Certainly, the statement should provide current information as it relates directly to the original budget, and it should be designed so that it will point to and suggest the procedures that should be taken to expedite the department's program development and services.[14]

A system of monthly or regularly scheduled statements of expenditures can assist the control procedure. With the assistance of computers, expenditures can be kept track of accurately and paid promptly. Figure 9.12 is an example of the city of Sunnyvale's operating statement, which is produced by a computer every 28 days. It is basically a line item budget in which cost and expenditures are input on a daily basis, the manager can at any time recall exact expenditures to be informed as to how much money has been spent or how much is left. It is important for the manager to review the expenditures on an ongoing basis so as not to overexpend or underexpend the budget.

Also shown on the operating statement are work hours planned and used, unit costs, and production units planned and actually accumulated. This report gives total expenditures in personnel services, other resources, and a grand total. By evaluating this report on a regular basis, the manager can see where he or she stands at all times so as not to overexpend or underexpend the budget. Although this type of report can be done with the computer, it can also be done manually, but it then becomes more cumbersome and difficult to produce. Other reports that also give the manager control can be produced by computer quickly and on a regular basis.

[14] Hines, *Revenue Source Management,* p. 78.

10 GENERAL OPERATING FUND   09 DEPT RECREATION   305 SPECIAL RECREATION SERVICE

ACCOUNT	DESCRIPTION		APPROPRIATION	ENCUMBRANCE	EXPENDITURE	PRIOR MO. ADJ	VARIANCE	HRS PLANNED & USED	
4111	REGULAR SALARIES-WT	CUR			3,218.97		3,218.97-	3,760.0	632.5
		YTD	22,710.00		26,661.34		3,951.34-	25,081.0	5,380.4
4112	TEMPORARY PERSONNEL	CUR			8,711.88		8,711.88-	1,532.1	
		YTD	135,187.00		104,144.10		31,042.90	19,721.4	
4113	OVERTIME	CUR			50.60		50.60-	4.0	
		YTD							
4116	LEAVE TIME-APPLIED %	CUR			554.77		554.77-		
		YTD	3,917.00		4,596.13		679.13-		
4117	RETRE & INS-APPLIED %	CUR			1,218.37		1,218.37-		
		YTD	10,823.00		11,050.46		227.46-		
	TOTAL AMOUNTS PERSONAL SERV	CUR			13,703.99		13,703.99-	2,164.6	
		YTD	172,637.00		146,502.63		26,134.37	28,841.0	25,109.8
4203	OFFICE SUPPLIES	CUR							
		YTD	400.00		151.04		248.96		
4204	SPECIAL ACTIV SUPPLIES	CUR			1,347.63		1,347.63-		
		YTD	18,864.00		12,572.04		6,291.96		
4210	BOOKS & PUBLICATIONS	CUR			79.48		79.48-		
		YTD	240.00		514.91		274.91-		
4215	CLOTHING	CUR							
		YTD	90.00				90.00		
4245	SMALL TOOLS & IMPLEMTS	CUR			299.16		299.16-		
		YTD	700.00		516.90		183.10		
4252	PHOTOGRAPHY & BLUEPRNT	CUR			164.46		164.46-		
		YTD	800.00		701.27		98.73		
4280	SERV MAINTAIN OTHER EQ	CUR			16.00		16.00-		
		YTD	500.00		42.10		457.90		
4305	STAFF DEVELOPMENT	CUR							
		YTD	580.00		238.00		342.00		

10 GENERAL OPERATING FUND   09 DEPT RECREATION   305 SPECIAL RECREATION SERVICE

ACCOUNT	DESCRIPTION		APPROPRIATION	ENCUMBRANCE	EXPENDITURE	PRIOR MO. ADJ	VARIANCE	HRS PLANNED & USED
4334	HYDRANT RENTAL	CUR			162.00		162.00-	
		YTD						
4380	TRAVEL & MEETING EXP	CUR						
		YTD	144.00		94.00		50.00	
4342	MILEAGE	CUR			94.67		94.67-	
		YTD	200.00		531.03		331.03-	
4344	EQUIP RENTAL-PRIVATE	CUR			136.00		136.00-	
		YTD	4,500.00		802.87		3,697.13	
4345	POSTAGE	CUR			31.99		31.99-	
		YTD	1,302.00		179.60		1,122.40	
4346	REC EXCURSIONS	CUR			59.50-		59.50	
		YTD						
4375	DANCE BAND SERVICES	CUR			644.00		644.00-	
		YTD	5,600.00		2,785.98		2,814.02	
4383	SPECIAL SERVICES	CUR			765.00		765.00-	
		YTD	7,600.00		5,186.50		2,413.50	
4391	REC INSTRUCTIONAL SRV	CUR			510.00		510.00-	
		YTD	6,100.00		3,286.00		2,814.00	
4500	PROF TECH SERV FEE	CUR			35.00		35.00-	
		YTD	70.00		76.00		6.00-	
4530	PRINT SHOP CHARGES	CUR			871.59		871.59-	
		YTD	8,240.00		9,847.50		1,607.50-	
4531	EQUIP RENTAL-CITY	CUR			174.60		174.60-	
		YTD	1,343.00		3,883.14		2,540.14-	
4538	RENTAL SERV-COMM CTR	CUR			6,895.71		6,895.71-	
		YTD	74,274.00		69,486.17		4,787.83	
	TOTAL AMT OTHER OPER COST	CUR			12,065.29		12,065.29-	
		YTD	131,547.00		110,997.55		20,549.45	
	TOTAL AMT THIS ACTIVITY	CUR			25,769.28		25,769.28-	2,164.6
		YTD	304,184.00		257,500.18		46,683.82	25,109.8
	PRODUCTION UNITS PLANNED/USED	CUR		2,995			2,995-	28,841.0
		YTD	28,100	28,726			626-	
	COST PER UNIT	CUR		8.60				
		YTD	10.83	8.96				

A general ledger of all funds or money transactions gives the manager good control over the budget. This report shows from what account a transaction was made, the date, amount, check number, to whom it was paid, a description of the item, and a voucher number. Figure 9.13 is an example of the general ledger.

As indicated earlier, the largest expenditure in a budget is the cost of salaries. Full-time salaries usually have good controls. On the other hand, part-time salaries can easily get out of hand, and an agency can overexpend its budget if it is not carefully governed. Sunnyvale has developed a *work-hour part-time control report* accounting system to help with this concern (see Figure 9.14). An attempt is made to plan how the hours are going to be used throughout the year on the basis of a reporting period, which is usually monthly. In the example, every 28 days is the reporting period. This turns out to be 13 equal reporting periods per year. In each of the reporting periods, the number of work hours that are going to be utilized are shown and indicated as *hours by period*. The *hours to date* are indicated in the second column and is the accumulation of all the preceding workhours used to date. This process is followed for each program activity, 300.09, 302.09, etc. Once the entire plan is prepared, it becomes a guide for the entire year and should be adhered to. If adjustments are to be made, the entire plan should be revised. Figure 9.15 is an example of the projection report completed every 28 days. Each program activity is reported indicating *hours planned for period* taken from the master plan (Figure 9.14) *hours used for period* taken from the operating statement (Figure 9.12), *hours planned to date,* and *hours used to date* are then calculated.

A *year to date variance* is then shown, which tells the manager if the plan is being followed. By doing this report every 28 days, the manager of each program—as well as the director of parks and recreation—can keep track of what is happening and take corrective action before any program gets out of control.

If halfway through the year the manager finds that he has overexpended in a given area, it can be caught and slowed down before it is too late. On the other hand, if a surplus of hours builds up, additional programs can be planned. Whatever the case, a close watch needs to be kept on part-time hours.

Budget Transfers
Once the budget is approved by the governing board, the manager is expected to stay within the limitations set relative to the amount of money within the given program. To add or transfer funds, a request has to be made of the governing board. Within a given program account, however, transfers can usually be made between activities, such as moving money from one line item to another. To move money from the sports account to the neighborhood recreation programs account needs action by the governing board, in the form of a resolution. This assures that

ACCOUNT NUMBER	DATE	TRANSACTION DESCR.	DEBITS	CREDITS	CHECK	VENDOR NAME	ITEM DESCRIPTION	VOUCHER
10-4346-304-09	05/14/77	CASH DISBURSEMENT	307.75		13820	MARINE WORLD	REC TRIP	CD536
			323.75 ::	.00 ::				
10-4531-304-09	05/13/77	0	2.40-					ER03057
			2.40-::	.00 ::				
10-4204-305-09	05/11/77	CASH DISBURSEMENT	10.99		13555	TERRY SHIMUZU	REIMBURSE INST	CD527
10-4204-305-09	05/12/77	CASH DISBURSEMENT	11.12		13605	J C PENNY CO	SG	CD529
10-4204-305-09	05/14/77	CASH DISBURSEMENT	31.81		13727	ALPHA BETA CO	SG	CD532
10-4204-305-09	05/14/77	CASH DISBURSEMENT	26.97		13726	BAYSHORE CERAMIC	SG	CD532
10-4204-305-09	05/14/77	CASH DISBURSEMENT	7.36		13731	CRAFTSMAN	SUP	CD532
10-4204-305-09	05/14/77	CASH DISBURSEMENT	11.52		13780	SAFEWAY STORES	REC SUP	CD534
			99.77 ::	.00 ::				
10-4210-305-09	05/11/77	CASH DISBURSEMENT	15.98		13551	BALA	PA	CD527
10-4210-305-09	05/12/77	CASH DISBURSEMENT	7.50		13673	SUBURBAN NEWSPAPER	SUBSCRIP	CD530
			23.48 ::	.00 ::				
10-4245-305-09	05/12/77	CASH DISBURSEMENT	299.16		13650	CYNDY GOLDSBOROUGH	SERV-REC	CD530
			299.16 ::	.00 ::				
10-4342-305-09	05/11/77	CASH DISBURSEMENT	9.84		13528	LINDA PEDRONCELLI	STATEMENT OF EXP	CD526
10-4342-305-09	05/11/77	CASH DISBURSEMENT	28.88		13588	PATRICIA L PLANT	STATEMENT OF EXP	CD528
10-4342-305-09	05/11/77	CASH DISBURSEMENT	11.55		13589	RAE DICKSON	STATEMENT OF EXP	CD528
10-4342-305-09	05/14/77	CASH DISBURSEMENT	11.40		13717	DEE VOLZ	MILEAGE	CD532
10-4342-305-09	05/14/77	CASH DISBURSEMENT	8.85		13865	SYLVIA BUSTAMANTE	STATEMENT OF EXP	CD537
			70.52 ::	.00 ::				
10-4345-305-09	05/11/77	CASH DISBURSEMENT	19.50		13537	POSTMASTER	POSTAGE EXPENSE	CD526
			19.50 ::	.00 ::				
10-4375-305-09	05/11/77	CASH DISBURSEMENT	200.00		13536	TOM TAYLOR	PA	CD526
10-4375-305-09	05/11/77	CASH DISBURSEMENT	200.00		13536	JACK JOHNSTONE	PA	CD526
10-4375-305-09	05/12/77	CASH DISBURSEMENT	200.00		13711	DAVID ADAMS	PA	CD531
			600.00 ::	.00 ::				
10-4383-305-09	05/11/77	CASH DISBURSEMENT	300.00		13533	DAVID WAYNE	PA	CD526
10-4383-305-09	05/11/77	CASH DISBURSEMENT	300.00		13535	JOE LEON	PA	CD526
			600.00 ::	.00 ::				
10-4391-305-09	05/11/77	CASH DISBURSEMENT	50.00		13534	ELIZABETH LUCE	PA	CD526
10-4391-305-09	05/11/77	CASH DISBURSEMENT	200.00		13577	ANGELA DEWREE	PA	CD528
10-4391-305-09	05/12/77	CASH DISBURSEMENT	10.00		13662	DWIGHT WRENCH	AWARD	CD530
10-4391-305-09	05/12/77	CASH DISBURSEMENT	10.00		13657	ONEIDA HAMMOND	AWARDS-PARK & REC	CD530
10-4391-305-09	05/12/77	CASH DISBURSEMENT	50.00		13664	GREG REUTER	AWARD	CD530
10-4391-305-09	05/12/77	CASH DISBURSEMENT	10.00		13658	GUIN RASMUSSEN	AWARD	CD530
10-4391-305-09	05/12/77	CASH DISBURSEMENT	10.00		13661	JAMES DALY	AWARD	CD530
10-4391-305-09	05/12/77	CASH DISBURSEMENT	10.00		13659	NANCY CROWLEY	AWARD	CD530
10-4391-305-09	05/12/77	CASH DISBURSEMENT	10.00		13660	ALBERT SENZATIMORE	AWARD	CD530
10-4391-305-09	05/12/77	CASH DISBURSEMENT	10.00		13663	JOHN MARTINEZ	AWARD	CD530
			370.00 ::	.00 ::				
10-4530-305-09	05/11/77	CASH DISBURSEMENT	197.68		13594	XEROX CORP	MAR RENT	CD528
			197.68 ::	.00 ::				

Figure 9.13. General ledger activity report by account.

	300.09		302.09		303.09		304.09		305.09	
Period Covered	Hours By Period	Hours To Date	Hours By Period	Hours To Date	Hours By Period	Hours To Date	Hours By Period	Hours To Date	Hours By Period	Hours To Date
7/1–7/24	320	320	3,958	3,958	3,040	3,040	2,402	2,402	2,024	2,024
7/25–8/21	320	640	4,692	8,650	3,588	6,628	2,576	4,978	2,144	4,168
8/22–9/18	—	640	—	8,650	24	6,652	480	5,458	1,289	5,457
9/19–10/16	·72	712	1,448	10,098	1,152	7,804	1,224	6,682	1,993	7,450
10/17–11/13	72	784	1,448	11,546	1,152	8,956	1,224	7,906	2,113	9,563
11/14–12/11	72	856	1,448	12,994	1,152	10,108	858	8,764	1,910	11,473
12/12–1/8	72	928	1,448	14,442	1,152	11,260	1,098	0,862	1,358	12,831
1/9–2/5	72	1,000	1,448	15,890	1,152	12,412	1,170	11,032	1,949	14,780
2/6–3/5	72	1,072	1,232	17,122	972	13,384	1.152	12,184	1,949	16,729
3/6–4/2	72	1,144	1,288	18,410	992	14,376	690	12,874	1,914	18,643
4/3–4/30	72	1,216	1,072	19,482	812	15,188	1,152	14,026	1,930	20,573
5/1–5/28	72	1,288	1,448	20,930	1,152	16,340	984	15,010	2,184	22,757
5/29–6/30	196	1,484	3,006	23,936	2,342	18,682	2,118	17,128	2,324	25,081
TOTAL	1,484		23,936		18,682		17,128		25,081	

Figure 9.14.   City of Sunnyvale, work-hour part-time control report.

the money is spent according to the plans set by the governing board and does not leave this type of activity to the discretion of the administrator.

Methods of Expending Funds

The last aspect of the budget and financing activities of an agency are the various methods of expending funds once approved by the governing board. There are various methods for initiating action to pay for the services, supplies, equipment, and salaries provided for in the budget.

The payment of salaries is usually handled by the submission of some sort of document that indicates the number of hours an employee has worked in a day, week, or month, and it is signed by the employee's supervisor. Without such a control, individuals could be paid for more time than they have worked. Some agencies utilize daily time cards; other agencies utilize payroll forms submitted to the finance department or payroll division once a month or every two weeks.

Most materials and supplies purchased are handled by a purchasing division, established by the city charter, that governs how monies are to be expended. Controls are usually set on making purchases. For example, the amount of petty cash that can be expended may have a set limit of $5.00 or less; anything above that would have to be submitted to the purchasing department on a standard purchase requisition. The requisition usually states the item wanted, the quantity, and a

Period Covered	306.09 Hours By Period	Hours To Date	310.09 Hours By Period	Hours To Date	312.09 Hours By Period	Hours To Date	317.09 Hours By Period	Hours To Date
7/1–7/24	1,349	1,349	2,777	2,777	5,000	5,000	515	515
7/25–8/21	1,580	2,929	1,370	4,147	5,600	10,600	515	1,030
8/22–9/18	100	3.020	572	4,719	1,800	12,400	473	1,503
9/19–10/16	388	3,417	1,570	6,289	1,100	13,500	458	1,961
10/17–11/13	388	3,805	1,939	8,228	500	14,000	497	2,458
11/14–12/11	162	3,967	1,421	9,649	100	14,100	497	2,955
12/12–1/8	262	4,229	1,269	10,918	300	14,400	352	3,307
1/9–2/5	334	4,563	2,670	13,588	500	14,900	515	3,822
2/6–3/5	316	4,879	2,733	16,321	500	15,400	544	4,366
3/6–4/2	334	5,213	2,017	18,338	550	15,950	540	4,906
4/3–4/30	216	5,429	2,329	10,667	600	16,550	529	5,435
5/1–5/28	414	5,843	3,823	24,490	1,200	17,750	492	5,927
5/29–6/30	993	6,836	2,897	27,387	3,650	21,400	469	6,396
TOTAL	6,836		27,387		21,400		6,396	

Figure 9.14. (Continued)

description of the item. Depending on the procedures of the given agency, the item may require advertising for a formal bid on a competitive basis or, under a certain amount, may be acquired on an informal basis by calling three vendors to get the lowest price. But, again, in most agencies, there are policies and procedures established by the governing board that indicate how purchases will be made and the controls set to make these purchases. Most public agencies require bidding for purchases over $1000 or $2000, or they are advertised on a formal basis and people submit sealed bids to secure the best price, thus eliminating dishonesty and corruption on the part of any employee.

Whatever the procedure, steps should be taken to insure that controls are provided to eliminate dishonesty and that the agency gets the greatest value for the least cost. In most agencies, procedures are set by the governing board, in some cases, the state sets procedures that must be adhered to to insure honesty and to insure that the public the agency gets the most service possible for the least amount of money.

Budget Audit

At the end of the budget year, an audit is done by an outside firm to determine and assure that honesty and integrity have been adhered to in the handling of public funds. The audit is usually done by an outside private firm of good reputation to give credibility to the audit.

Sunnyvale Parks and Recreation Department (.09)
Report No. 3
Period Covered: August 22–September 18, 1977

	Activity	Hours Planned for Period	Hours Used for Period	Hours Planned to Date	Hours Used to Date	Year to Date Variance	Comments
300	Recreation management	0	143.0	640	469.5	+170.5	Carry-over from previous cycle
302	Neighborhood rec. activities Parks and playgrounds—north	0	149.0	8,650	9,022.1	−372.1	Adjustments due to summer program
303	Neighborhood rec. activities Parks and playgrounds—south	24	73.5	6,652	6,188.7	+463.3	Carry-over from previous cycle
304	Neighborhood rec. activities Teens—north	480	490.0	5,458	4,401.5	+1,056.5	Carry-over from previous cycle
305	Special recreation services	1,289	1,532.1	5,457	4,808.1	648.9	Carry-over from previous cycle
306	Neighborhood rec. activities teens—south	100	77.0	3,020	3,454.2	−434.2	Adjustments due to summer program
310	Sports	572	601.7	4,719	5,024.7	−305.7	Carry-over from previous cycle
312	Aquatics	1,800	2,049.0	12,400	11,168.0	+1,232.0	Carry-over from previous cycle
317	Community center management	473	420.8	1,503	1,239.6	+263.4	Carry-over from previous cycle

Figure 9.15. City of Sunnyvale, work-hour part-time projection report.

SUMMARY

The entire budget and financial process is intended to give the manager a financial plan to follow and a system to insure that it *is* followed. The best assurance of a good plan, procedures, and controls is a good manager. The budget is a financial plan and consists of an operating and a capital budget. To support the plan, there have to be revenues. The budget process consists of budget preparation, budget design, budget presentation, and budget implementation and control. However, an agency's budget and financial system is only as good as the services it renders to the public, because the final determination of how much financial support an agency will receive is in the hands of the taxpayers.

Policymaking and the Legal Basis for Leisure Service Organizations

10

Leisure service managers need an understanding of the concepts involved in the process of policymaking. They should be able to conceptualize the many facets involved in this process and integrate these as they pertain to the organization. Managers must understand the nature of policies, the process of policymaking, the different types of policy structures, factors affecting the policy process, and their role in the policy process. A policy, like a budget, is a plan. It is a way for an organization to delineate a course of action that guides the behavior of both employees and consumers.

Policies provide leisure service organizations with guidelines that delineate such factors as the types of services to be offered, acceptable forms of employee behavior, the relationship between the employees and the consumers, and standards for consumer behavior (e.g., acceptable forms of consumer behavior in public park facilities). Policies are made by people; they are not organizational monoliths. In the first section of this chapter, we will discuss policy, the process of policy formulation, and the environmental factors of which managers must be aware.

In the second half of this chapter, we will discuss the legal basis for leisure service organizations. Any group of individuals has a set of rights, privileges, power, and authority that allows it to operate within society. This is also the case with leisure service organizations. In many cases, these rights and so on are derived from formal legal codes. Legal considerations fall within the political environmental subsystem. Knowledge of the legal parameters will enable the leisure service managers to concentrate their efforts on areas that they know will serve their clients most productively.

POLICYMAKING

What is Policy?

Policy is usually thought of as the formal guidelines an organization has established for itself; but there may also be a set of informal policies within an organization. The definition used in this book maintains that a policy is a course of action that guides human behavior. For our purposes, this suggests that a policy, as a course of action, will govern the behavior of individuals within an organization. Formal policies, usually expressed as written documents, delineate the purposes, aims, goals, objectives, principles, procedures, and rules that provide direction to individuals within an organization. Informal policies consist of norms, mores, and customs present within an organization that affect individual and collective behavior. Informal policies may have great impact on the organization because they have the potential to displace formal policies. Essentially, policies—formal and informal—may be thought of as the plan or plans that organizations follow.

There are three ways in which policy affects behavior in organizations:

1. Enabling behavior to occur that would be difficult or even impossible without policy.
2. Regulating behavior into routine matters.
3. Inhibiting behavior that would be widespread or easy without policy.[1]

An example of a policy that would enable behavior to occur is the adoption of a rule which sets forth the hours and days of operation of a community swimming pool by a park and recreation board. Adoption of this policy *enables* the park and recreation director to open the facility at a certain time and utilize the resources of the organization to operate and promote the activity. It also *inhibits* certain types of behavior in that it restricts the hours the pool can be used. When formulating a policy, the manager must be cognizant of the complementary nature of inhibiting and enabling behavior; the adoption of a policy that enables certain kinds of behaviors can in fact inhibit other behaviors.

Policies also serve the function of *regulating* certain types of behaviors. By routinizing certain patterns of activity, an organization is able to concentrate more of its resources on major issues. It reduces the need for repetitive decision-making in areas that can be delegated to subordinates by a manager. If a manager were confronted with the task of having to make decisions on each matter of concern to the organization, his or her time and energy would be misused. A park manager can routinize maintenance procedures so that the maintenance staff knows what jobs have to be done and during what time period, rather than having to decide on a daily basis. On the other hand, routine can be equated with rigidity. Organizations must be extremely careful in this regard because ruts can be created within an organization. People can easily become creatures of habit, inflexible and unable to respond to changing expectations. The manager must periodically review the tasks that have been routinized in the organization to insure that they are in fact consistent with organizational goals and objectives.

---

[1] John N. Warfield, *Improving Behavior in Policymaking* (Columbus, Ohio Battelle Institute and Academy for Contemporary Problems, 1975). p. 4.

Policies are useful to organizations for several other reasons too. They help clarify relationships and patterns of communication by establishing networks of communication and levels of authority and responsibility. They can help an organization evaluate its goals and objectives by presenting a clear picture of the methods and procedures utilized to achieve them. Policies also provide for consistency. The resources of an organization, especially its human ones, can uniformly be directed toward the goals of the organization. If all employees know the direction in which the organization is moving, they can contribute their work effort toward this end.

Once an organization has developed a documented set of policies and has set forth its philosophy, goals and objectives, and rules and procedures, its actions become somewhat predictable. If an organization says that its purpose is to provide leisure services by organizing activities, it can be assumed with a relatively high degree of assurance that it won't be publishing books. Predictability can lead to the reduction of criticism both from within and without the organization because individuals understand what to expect from it. The establishment of policies allows individuals to develop a set of expectations that are likely to be realized in regard to the organization and its activities.

There are a number of characteristics that well-written policies incorporate. Raymond Ziegler maintains that there are five important characteristics in the creation of productive policies:

1. Flexibility. A policy can be seen as existing on a continuum between rigidity and flexibility. Ones that are flexibly written can change as environmental conditions change. This is not to imply that policies do not have some degree of stability, only that they can be adapted. A manager's judgment in determining the amount of flexibility needed in a given policy is the primary method used to determine this factor.
2. Comprehensiveness. The comprehensiveness of a policy is the extent to which it covers the actions that are necessary to implement a program. The degree of comprehensiveness will be directly related to the course of action pursued. For example, if a policy is directed toward the use of an organization's automobiles, it will not be as comprehensive as a policy covering an organization's marketing functions.
3. Coordinative. A policy must be interrelated and coordinated with other types of policies. The test of any well-written policy is whether or not it can be linked to the other policies within the organization. Procedures, rules, and plans of operation do not stand alone, but are tied to policies that set forth the mission and objectives of an organization.
4. Ethical. Policies must be written to insure that ethical practices are maintained. They should be be formulated to provide for fair play and equality in their implementation. A policy should be discharged impartially and comprehensively. The ethical concepts that are incorporated into a policy

usually are written to conform with the norms and mores that exist within society. The leisure service manager has an important responsibility in maintaining the ethics of a given policy.

5. Clarity. A policy should be written in a manner that can be readily understood by the individual/group that it is intended to affect. A well-written policy will simplify the manager's task in communicating with his subordinates. This will save time and energy and lead to better relationships between a manager and his subordinates, in that both parties will know what to expect from the other.[2]

The ultimate effectiveness of any policy can be determined by the extent to which it fulfills its intended purpose. Policies that do not produce the type of behavior which is expected should be reevaluated. Thus the process of policymaking can be viewed as an ongoing effort in which policies are continually reviewed and revamped.

Policy Structure

The policies of an organization can be viewed as existing in a hierarchy that finds general statements, which deal with broad concerns, at the top. As policies increase in specificity, they are placed lower on the hierarchy until the most detailed are reached at the base. Lower-order policies are derived from the policies that appear directly above them in the hierarchy. For example, a general policy advocating safety may be the catalyst for a series of specific safety rules relating to smoking on the premises, necessity of a hard hat, and so on.

R. M. Hodgetts and M. S. Wortman, Jr., have outlined a series of policy statements that range from the general to the specific.[3] They identify them as major policies, secondary policies, functional policies, minor policies, procedures and standard operating plans, and rules. They suggest that a manager's effectiveness can be strengthened by developing policies based on knowledge of their relationship to each other within the policy hierarchy.

1. Major Policies. This type of policy is a broad statement that reflects the aims of the organization. It delineates the type of services to be provided and their general purpose (e.g., the purpose of a leisure service organization is to enhance the quality of life by providing leisure services).
2. Secondary Policies. These are derived from the broader major policies. They delineate the target market (e.g., the leisure service organization will serve all ages and races by providing activities, facilities, and information).
3. Functional Policies. The management operations of an organization are spelled out in its functional policies. This may include the major services to be provided (e.g., activities, facilities, information, consultation), marketing

[2] Raymond Ziegler, *Business Policies and Decision-making* (New York: Appleton-Century-Crofts, 1966).

(pricing and promotional factors), finance (how funds are to be appropriated and accounted for), and personnel (job specifications, hours of work, etc.). These types of policies are derived from secondary policies.

4. Minor Policies. The next level, minor policies, further details operational aspects of the organization. These may specify different activity areas (e.g., arts, sports, etc.), facility standards, and maintenance expectations.

5. Procedures and Standard Operating Plans. This type of policy is drawn from functional and minor policies. Procedures and operating plans detail the step-by-step methods necessary to organize, implement, and evaluate the various functions of an organization (e.g., the standard operating plan and procedures adopted in the management of a swimming pool may detail its hours of operation, program, and staffing requirements.)

6. Rules. In turn, rules are obtained from procedures and standard plans. They govern the day-to-day conduct of individuals within an organization. Rules are rigid and not subject to interpretation (e.g., no smoking).[3]

The Policy Process

The process of policymaking is carried out in three phases: *formulation, implementation,* and *evaluation.* These involve determining where the organization is going, what procedures should be used to get it there, and what corrective measures must be taken to keep it heading toward its primary mission. These three functions are interrelated, and the success of an organization depends on the manager's ability to coordinate them.

When *formulating* a policy, a number of factors must be taken into consideration. The policy must be related to the overall mission or purpose of the organization. It must also be drafted with an understanding of its relationship to environmental subgroupings both within and external to the organization. The resources that are needed must be taken into consideration when formulating a policy. Many policies are written that can never be implemented because their authors have not appraised the availability of resources. Finally, these questions have to be considered: Has the policy been realistically conceived? Can it really work? Will it produce the type of behavioral outcomes expected? Will people accept the policy? After careful analysis of all these factors, an organization will be in a position to formulate a sensible set of policies, that can provide invaluable aid to a manager in the administration of a leisure service organization.

Policy *implementation* occurs when a policy is put into operation. This is done Policy implementation occurs when a policy is put into operation. This is done through the design of an organizational structure from which positions of authority and responsibility are created. Once the assignment of roles within the

---

[3] R. M. Hodgetts and M. S. Wortman, Jr., *Administrative Policy: Text and Cases in the Policy Sciences* (New York: John Wiley and Sons, 1975). pp. 5–6.

organization has taken place, policy implementation is carried out through a system of rewards and penalties. The implementation of a policy, like the formulation phase, must take into account the organization's resources. Many well-conceived policies have failed because they ignored this factor. The extent to which a policy represents the needs of the organization's members will determine its chances of success.

Policy *evaluation* represents the efforts of an organization to determine to what extent its policies have achieved their desired end. Essentially, this is a process of control. Control usually involves the establishment of standards, the measurement of performance against standards, and the correction of deviation from standards.[4] Organizational outputs are measured against a set of standards in policy evaluation. In this sense, standards are an absolute toward which an organization strives and they are usually quantifiable.

The measurement of performance involves comparing the outputs of the unit with the standards to determine whether the policies have been achieved. As policies become stagnant and unproductive, corrective action should be initiated and the policy should be changed or abolished. This last factor suggests that the policy process is one wherein the manager maintains flexibility.

In any organization, there is an element of risk in the formulation and implementation of policies. Effective managers will calculate closely the risks involved in the adoption of one policy versus another. This is done to optimize the allocation of an organization's resources. It is important to note, however, that all organizations will be confronted with a certain amount of failure. We learn and grow by making errors. The lack of failure may be an indication that an organization is not extending itself to meet people's needs and is overly conscious of its security. There is a saying that "if you're not failing, you're not trying anything new."

Koontz and O'Donnell have suggested a number of guidelines that can be followed in the policymaking process.[5] Noting that all organizations have policies, they suggest that it is virtually impossible for any given body to be effective without the existence of written policies. They further suggest that the use of written policy manuals does not guarantee effective management; that this is accomplished through the understanding that the policy process is dynamic and ongoing. All policies represent a form of communication among individuals within the organization. And, like any form of communication, policies are dependent on the intentions of the sender and the receptiveness of the receiver. There must be an openness and willingness to engage in two-way communication. One cannot assume that an organization will have effective policies without attention to a number of basic guidelines governing them. Koontz and O'Donnell have

[4] Harold Koontz and Cyril O'Donnell, *Principles of Management*, fifth edition (New York: McGraw-Hill, 1972), p. 583.

[5] Ibid, pp. 217–219.

outlined seven ways in which the policymaking process can be enriched and the management of policies made more productive.

1. The policy process should contribute to the goals and objectives of an organization. There is a need to insure understanding of the relationship that exists between major policies, secondary policies, functional policies, minor policies, procedures and rules. Employees will benefit from understanding the relationships that exist between various types of policies. As each policy is developed and written, it should be linked to higher-order policies to maintain consistency within the organization. The manager should never have to say to subordinates, "There's no good reason why we do it, it is just our policy."[6]

2. The policy process should not be ambiguous. One policy should not conflict with or contradict another policy. It is surprising how many policies within organizations present contradictory information to employees and/or consumers. In addition, many policies are written to give preferential treatment to certain individuals and/or groups. This approach to policy formulation usually places the manager in an untenable position because he or she is forced to justify inhibiting behavior in certain people while condoning it in others. For example, if a parks and recreation board were to approve requests for facility usage on an ad hoc basis without the establishment of a set of guidelines, it might find itself discriminating among groups making requests, without a rationale for doing so.

3. The policy process should be adaptable. We live in a time of relative ethics predicated on rapid change in society. Therefore it is extremely important that policies be formulated and implemented so as to accommodate change. This is not to infer that a policymaking body should vacillate in its decision-making, catering to pressure from individuals and groups; but rather, it should be cognizant of changing trends in society and how they affect the implementation of policy. Whenever there is an opportunity to apply a policy that will result in a positive gain for an individual and/or group, the manager should have the ability to flexibly apply the policy. A certain amount of discretionary power in decision-making should be available to the manager.

4. The policy process should enable one to distinguish among rules, major policies, and procedures. Earlier in the chapter, a hierarchy linking major policies to procedures and rules was presented. Major policies are written within a broad context to provide general direction to an organization. On the other hand, procedures and rules are action programs that are established as specific guidelines for employee behavior.

5. Policies and the policy process should be in writing. By providing written policies, the manager has at his/her command a document that supports his/her authority to enable, regulate, or inhibit certain kinds of behavior. Written

---

[6] Ibid.

policies reduce the confusion that can arise from verbal direction. By writing out a policy, it becomes less (although not completely) open to unwarranted interpretation. It also allows the manager to clearly spell out what is intended in a procedure or rule. This eliminates the confusion that can emerge as a result of word-of-mouth communication.

6. The policy process should be taught. It is a poor assumption to believe that people will take it upon themselves to be knowledgeable about an organization's policies, procedures, and rules. Many policies are subject to broad interpretation. Appropriate discussions should take place between manager and staff as to the proper way to apply certain types of policies. In a training session, where there is a certain amount of give-and-take, many times questions concerning the application of a policy are raised. By openly discussing a particular situation, a manager may be able to impart to subordinates his/her philosophy and method of applying a certain type of policy. In the long run, this will minimize the amount of conflict that will exist within an organization. Essentially, a greater understanding between manager and subordinates will lead to a more productive work environment—not only for the organization, but also for the individuals working in it.

7. The policy process should be controlled. One cannot assume that people will adhere to policy decisions or that a policy will stand the test of time. Therefore policies must be constantly controlled. Frequent checks need to be made to determine whether a policy is being adhered to and if not, why. Policies can become obsolete and it is important to recognize that policies, if they are to be effective, need to be kept up-to-date.[7]

Policy Units

The authority to make policy in public leisure services is usually vested in a board or commission appointed by another legislative body or elected by the public at large. In private leisure delivery systems, policy is formulated either by the owners of the organization or by a board of directors elected or appointed to represent the owners' interests.

Public Policymaking Board

This type of policymaking unit is usually appointed by a legislative body or elected by the public at large to provide direction and control of the public park and recreation services. It receives its legal powers to collect and assess tax levies and to provide certain select services through state or provincial enabling acts, city charters, special legislation, or local ordinances. Some boards have complete authority and independence to make policy in their designated area. Other

[7] Based on Koontz and O'Donnell, *Principles of Management*, pp. 217–219.

boards, known as "semi-independent boards," have partial powers and are usually tied closely to other legislative units within the governmental structure. For example, a semi-independent board may have authority to determine its program policies, but will not have the ability to levy taxes to provide these services.

Public Advisory Board

This type of board has no final power or authority, but it can exert considerable influence over policy decisions by other legislative bodies. Advisory boards are appointed to provide a policymaking unit with an in-depth perspective of the community's leisure-time needs. Basically, they serve a resource function. By providing information and making recommendations, advisory boards affect policymaking at various levels. This type of board allows for citizen participation within the governmental structure.

Sole Proprietorship

This is an arrangement, in a private profit-oriented organization, in which one person assumes the legal responsibility for said organization. As such, the sole proprietorship is a mechanism whereby one person has the authority to make decisions regarding all policy matters. Although subject to applicable governmental laws (e.g., unlimited personal liability), this method of organization gives the sole proprietor the advantages of speed of action, privacy, and freedom in policymaking. A single owner of a business is free to make any decisions she or he feels are appropriate, without waiting for the approval of others. The single owner can decide what services are to be offered, how people are to be hired and fired, and so on.

Partnership

This type of arrangement exists when two or more persons decide to link their efforts together to establish a business for profit. Generally speaking, the more individuals involved in an organization, the greater the range of talent, ability, and viewpoints. In a partnership, each partner contributes his or her expertise in the formulation and implementation of policy. The combined efforts of partners in an organization can be very beneficial, avoiding the problems inherent in decision-making based on a single perspective. There are different types of partnerships, and the extent to which an individual will be involved in the policymaking of the organization will be, to a large extent, determined by this factor.

Corporation

A corporation is a method of organizing profit- and/or nonprofit-oriented enterprises. The corporation has a legal existence of its own. Unlike sole proprietorships and partnerships, whereby the owner or owners are legally responsible for their organization's actions and finances, the corporation itself is the legal entity (an "artificial person," so to speak). In a corporation, the elected or appointed board of directors is responsible for management. Board members are morally responsible to the corporation rather than the shareholders who elected them. The board is given the power to make the rules that will govern the conduct of business. In addition to determining the functions and duties of personnel, board members may also determine the allotment of shares and the payment of dividends to shareholders. Policy established by the board of directors is subject to the approval of the shareholders of the organization. A corporation is required by law to hold a shareholders' meeting annually and to provide each shareholder with an annual report of the company at least three weeks before this meeting.

What Policymaking Boards Do

Policymaking boards perform a number of important functions. Their responsibility varies according to the nature of the organization. Businesses having a prime function of making a profit require slightly different responsibilities of its board members than public nonprofit organizations. Maurice Archer writes that the tasks of the board of directors of a business corporation include the following:

1. Approving and helping to formulate long-term and short-term goals and plans for the company;
2. Appointing the company president and other chief executives;
3. Insuring sufficient funds and approving capital and other important budgetary expenditures;
4. Approving the distribution of profits;
5. Keeping shareholders informed of the progress of their company; and
6. Insuring that all other legal requirements are met.[8]

These examples are very general, and it should be realized that each of these responsibilities may entail more specific action in regard to personnel, finance, public relations, and so on.

A 1974 study of the current practices of boards of directors in voluntary organizations provides an excellent perspective of the activities of board members and their areas of responsibility and concern. This study included a large number of nonprofit recreation organizations. Board members who responded in this study reported that their key functions included policymaking, fund raising, activity on board committees, recruitment of new board members, community relations, evaluating the organization's budget, training new board members, personnel practices, and administration.[9] Problems investigated included those related to

---

[8] Maurice Archer, *Introduction to Canadian Business, 2nd edition (Toronto: McGraw-Hill Ryerson Limited, 1974), p. 158.*

[9] Nelly Hartogs and Joseph Weber, *Boards of Directors* (Dobbs Ferry, N. Y.: Oceana, 1974), p. 60.

board operations, the budget, personnel, administration, and public relations. Among the problems identified by board members, the following were stressed: the need to increase participation of inactive members, recruit younger members, broaden the range of skills in the makeup of the board, and make board membership more representative of the community.

A primary budgetary concern involved the obtaining of funds from a variety of sources, including the government and foundations. Some of the problems relating to programming, identified by board members, were establishing program priorities within available resources, increasing program relevancy to meet changing needs, increasing the number of individuals being served, and undertaking program evaluation. Improving salaries, fringe benefits, and personnel policies were key personnel problems identified by board members. In the areas of public relations and administration, the need to increase operating efficiency and provide more effective methods for fund raising were identified.

Jesse Reynolds and Marion Hormachea, discussing public recreation boards, identified a number of basic functions that all public recreation boards undertake. They note that these functions may vary according to enabling legislation and local laws. The functions they identify include the following:

1. To employ the recreation and park executive and to establish his duties and responsibilities.
2. To establish the purposes, objectives, policies, procedures, and other guidelines for the management of the agency programs and services, refer them to the executive for execution, and give him support.
3. To establish the standards of quality and the scope of the services to be rendered.
4. To serve as liaison between citizens and agency; to interpret citizen needs and interests and provide programs, facilities, and services to serve their needs; to interpret the value of recreation to the public in order to gain their interest, understanding, and assistance.
5. To establish a sound fiscal plan satisfactory to the community; to recommend sources of income and to approve the budget and fiscal matters.
6. To keep the general public and public officials informed concerning the status of the recreation and parks programs.
7. To receive and evaluate reports from the executive, and act as a board of appeal on any action not resolved satisfactorily by the executive. Its actions are final since it is the highest authority related officially to the department.
8. To represent the department at ceremonials and official events including budget matters.
9. To make rules for the conduct of the commission's business and meetings.[10]

[10] Jesse A. Reynolds and Marion N. Hormachea, *Public Recreation Administration* (Englewood Cliffs, N. J.: Prentice-Hall, 1976), pp. 84–85.

Consumers and the Policymaking Process

An important component in the process of policy making in the public sector is the involvement of consumers. This is especially true of public agencies. Historically, the consumer has played a small role and has even been ignored in the formulation and evaluation of policies. Why is this the case? A number of problems arise with regard to consumer involvement in the policy process. The first revolves around the determination of which individuals should be involved in the process. Does a public leisure service organization open its process only to those specifically affected by a given program, or is it necessary to consider the views of the entire political unit that a board represents? If the latter view represents the position of an organization (and this is usually politically safer), the problems created by the scope of this undertaking may prohibit effective policy development. On the other hand, if all individuals are not included in the policymaking process, they may feel that their interests are not effectively represented.

Another concern that occurs as a result of consumers' participation in the policy process is that their presence may make objective and rational planning and evaluation difficult. The average consumer is without expertise in the leisure delivery field and may cloud rather than clarify the issues at hand. Individuals tend to be interested in their own gains, rather than the whole, and therefore program planning becomes adaptive and incremental rather than being accomplished on a holistic basis. As a result, organizations are often unwilling to include the consumers because their subjectivity biases the process of policy development.

Another factor that may prevent consumers from participating in policy processes is that of political expediency. Politicians have often ignored citizen input so that their particular programs or philosophy are not jeopardized or questioned. If a politician wants to push through a program, the quickest way may be to bypass consumer involvement. If the program or a policy is to be evaluated, and it has been endorsed by a politician, he or she may want to avoid the risk of involving dissatisfied individuals. Even though a citizen group may be supportive of a particular policy, its initial involvement may result in the creation of a cohesive unit that is capable of dissention in future policy evaluation.

What can be done to overcome these problems? F. P. Scioli, Jr., and T. J. Cook identified five factors that can help strengthen consumers' involvement in the policymaking process.[11] They suggest that, first, policymaking must include not only the population who will benefit directly from a program, but should also be open to those individuals and/or groups who will not benefit. Second, there must be a method whereby the expected outcomes of the program can be measured. This part of the process should emphasize the reaction of the

[11] F. P. Scioli, Jr., and T. J. Cook, *Methodologies for Analyzing Public Policies* (Lexington, Mass.: D. C. Heath, 1975), pp. 28–30.

consumers served by the program. Third, the future needs of individuals must be taken into consideration in evaluating a program or policy. Fourth, the process should include a step that allows for resolution between the second and third factors (how present needs are being met and what direction an organization plans to take in the future). Fifth, policymaking is a dynamic process; it cannot be conceptualized as taking place within a finite period, but rather should be viewed as a continuous social process.

Some of the mechanisms that can be used to encourage participation in the formulation of policy in public leisure service organizations are the following:

1. Citizen Advisory Groups. Citizen advisory groups have traditionally been used by community parks and recreation departments to encourage participation. Their main function is to assist elected government bodies by serving as consultants. It is not unusual for a citizen advisory group to serve or represent the needs of a geographic area within a community or to provide assistance in the operation of a facility or program area.

2. Task Forces. The task force is an extremely popular way to involve consumers in the formulation of policy. Task forces are usually created to investigate a specific issue or problem. They may produce recommendations that the elected officials of a government agency may find useful in decision-making.

3. Polls and Surveys. Polls are directed toward determining the attitudes of individuals on specific issues, whereas surveys are directed toward the measurement of a broader set of concerns. These mechanisms offer opportunities for participation, although there have been cases in which statistics have been manipulated to suit the ends of the pollster. Nonetheless, if properly used, polls and surveys can be a valuable tool to encourage participation in policy formulation.

4. Public Meetings and Hearings. Opportunities for individuals to voice their opinions at official meetings and hearings also encourage consumer involvement. Although public meetings can be a one-way form of communication, they can also be opened up to establish dialogue in which viewpoints are exchanged, issues made known, and consensus sought.

5. Written Submissions. Petitions and briefs are also useful tools that can be used to promote consumer involvement. A petition carries the signatures of a large number of individuals and reflects their opinion on a specific issue. A brief is a concise statement relating to the concern of an individual or group on a specific issue.

6. Plebiscites. One of the most direct methods for obtaining consumer involvement is via the use of a plebiscite. A plebiscite places the decision of a given issue directly in the hands of the voter. A referendum to secure funds for the development of a community center is an example of a plebiscite.

7. The media. The media, including newspapers, television, and radio, are perhaps underutilized for involving consumers in the policymaking process.

President Jimmy Carter demonstrated the potential of the media format via a call-in question-and-answer program on television in 1977. The media can be an effective tool for disseminating information and receiving consumer feedback.

By involving consumers in the process of policy formulation and evaluation, it is hoped that program offerings and policies will be linked more closely to consumer needs. By increasing an organization's sensitivity to consumer interests and concerns, effectiveness and efficiency may be increased. But one must be cognizant of, and prepared to deal with, the problems that arise from consumer involvement. It is important to remember that the framework that is established for consumer input will dictate the appropriateness and accuracy of the information received. Policymaking can be enhanced if mechanisms that insure validity and viability are utilized.

The Role of the Manager

There are a number of perspectives as to the role that a leisure service manager should take in the formulation of policy. Some spokesmen suggest that managers have no role in policy formulation and serve only in the implementation of policy that has been formed by others. In the case of an organization that has a policy-making board, the manager would simply administer the policy decisions made by it. Others advocate that the leisure service manager should have some involvement in the function of policymaking in that he, because of his training and background, is in a more knowledgeable position than the nonprofessional.

Many people have suggested that because there are numerous types of policies, formulation and implementation might be undertaken by different people at different levels within the two units that make policy within an organization: One unit is the legislative body and the other is the administrative body. Legislative bodies deal with policy decisions regarding values; value judgments are those policies that represent the aims, purposes, and general direction of an organization. Administrative bodies deal with what is known as "factual policies;" factual policies represent the practical means and technical knowledge that is needed to carry out policies which represent values. Within this approach to policymaking, the manager usually makes precise decisions regarding how things are to be run and where and when they are to be done. The legislative body would present policies in the form of guidelines and directions, which would be intended as a general guide for the manager to follow.

Another approach to the role of the manager in policy formulation and implementation has been suggested by Joseph J. Bannon. He maintains that a manager and a policymaking board should develop a cooperative relationship in order to effectively utilize the knowledge available from both parties. If a board member has sufficient knowledge in technical areas, Bannon recommends that this individual be allowed to contribute her expertise. If the manager can better interpret the interests of the target market, he should be allowed to contribute to the process of making value-oriented policy. Bannon writes:

> A close and cooperative relationship should exist between a director and the recreation and park board. A joint policy making relationship does not imply impingement by either party on the other's prime responsibility; rather it implies a sharing of knowledge and experience and a logical overlap of functions for organizational enhancement.
>
> The combination of interesting and concerned board members and a professional astute staff can be a catalyst for achieving quality recreation programs within a community. If properly used, a partnership or a "common market" of skills, expertise, and responsibilities between board and director can be successful.[12]

The area of policy implementation is clearly the major management function carried out by a leisure service manager. The basic work activities—financing and marketing services—are primary areas in which the manager carries out the policies of the organization. These activities are carried out through planning, organizing, directing, staffing, and controlling. The manager plans and organizes the leisure delivery system by determining its long-, middle-, and short-term objectives and by carefully designing its organizational structure to meet the mission of the system. He then staffs the organization by hiring and training the human resources needed to carry out various policy assignments. This then sets the stage for the manager to direct the organization, especially its human resources, toward the achievement of its goals. The final function, control, finds the manager measuring the achievement of policies and taking whatever actions necessary to correct deviations from the policies.

The responsibility that managers assume in the formulation and implementation of policy should not be taken lightly. They must recognize that their actions will influence people and affect their leisure behavior. Leisure service managers, as a result of their position of influence in the community, have to be more cognizant of the impact of their actions. Managers should realize their social responsibility to the individuals, community, and society within which they operate. Managers cannot afford to live in a vacuum, unresponsive to the broad implications of their actions for the total environment. The process of decision-making must incorporate a strategy whereby the manager can take into consideration the above concerns.

Factors Affecting Policy

As noted in Chapter 1, leisure service organizations are affected by four environmental components: the physical environment, the social/cultural environment,

---

[12] Joseph J. Bannon, "Who Really Makes Policy?" *Parks and Recreation*, 8, No. 7, July 1973, pp. 31–32.

the political environment, and the economic environment. Individuals within the organization are concerned with these four environmental subgroups as well as with other components of the organization itself. These elements are in constant interaction with one another and effect policy formulation.

Organizations are made up of individuals. Each individual comes to the organization with a personal set of values. These values can have a tremendous effect on the policies of an organization. As discussed in Chapter 3, one of the most important functions of the manager is to align the personal needs of the members of the organization with the organization's goals. The wider the discrepancy between these two factors, the less likely that the policies of the organization will be effective. Undoubtedly, the most significant factor influencing the creation of policies will be the philosophy and values of an organization's management team. A management philosophy which suggests that the role of the manager is to intervene in people's lives to change their behavior differs significantly from one which suggests that the role of the organization is to react to the expressed desires of the target market. These two beliefs will result in completely different approaches to the provision of services. Further, a manager's personal characteristics—such as risk-taking propensity, introversion-extroversion, and submissiveness-aggressiveness—can affect approaches to policy formulations and implementation. A dynamic risk-taker is more likely to recommend policies that allow the organization to expand its services to the target market.

The political environment affects policy in a number of ways. The legal mandate that empowers the leisure service organization will affect policy. Enabling legislation, which will be discussed later in this chapter, sets forth the guidelines under which an organization operates. Local, state or provincial, and federal government agencies have different functions and political frameworks. This will obviously affect the type of constituents, amount of resources, and types of services offered. Other political factors that affect policymaking include additional laws (regulatory and special) and the influence that one political subdivision has over another. To illustrate the latter, local government agencies must adopt policies of the federal level when accepting grants or other monies. Special-interest and/or pressure groups also can affect the formulation of policies. They are able to exercise influence by gaining access to many parts of government.[13] They can bring intense political pressure on the formulation of policies in public leisure service organizations.

The sociocultural environment influences both formal and informal policies. Expected norms or mores of behavior found in society will also be present in the formulation of policy. When designing a policy concerning the use of parks by consumers, certain codes of behavior will be incorporated into that policy. For example, park policy might not allow people to carry firearms in the park, light

[13] Peter Woll, *Public Policy* (Cambridge, Mass.: Winthrop, 1974), p. 53.

fires, or destroy park property. An example of a rule that has been modified by a change in the normative behavior of people is the use of bathing caps by females in swimming pools; as males grew their hair longer and swam without caps, the rule was negated. Sociocultural changes in the form of trends also affect policy. For example, recent interest in the sport of soccer may affect the programming policies adopted by leisure service organizations in the future. A dynamic cultural change that has profoundly affected the programming policies has been the upsurge of female participation in active sports and coed activities. Policies that prohibited females from participation in Little Leagues, for example, have literally been abolished in the last few years.

The physical environment affects the development of policies in leisure service organizations in a number of ways. The first is that leisure service organizations are tied to an ethic which suggests that the quality of the environment has an affect upon the quality of people's lives. Not only are people concerned with creating a more humane social environment, but they are also concerned with the preservation and/or conservation of the natural environment. Ecological problems posed by "water pollution, air pollution, solid waste disposal, noise pollution, and chemical pollution" are serious threats to lives.[14] The policies of many leisure delivery systems reflect a concern for this problem. Such systems incorporate into their policies their philosophies of conservation, preservation, and quality of life.

As mentioned in Chapter 1, the geographic location of a delivery system will also affect its policy formulation. Climatic conditions, the physcial terrain, and other natural features can have an impact on policy formulation.

The amount and type of resources available to a leisure service organization can be, in large part, determined by economic conditions. The expansion and contraction of the economy can be related to cycles of growth and the provision of leisure services. Historically, when the economy has been either extremely depressed or extremely healthy, there have been booms in leisure services. During the depression of the 1930s, the federal government invested large sums of money in the creation of recreation facilities. During the early 1960s, a period of economic growth, products and services created by the private leisure sector increased greatly; the leisure market was placed at over $150 million. The economic viability of a given community and/or group of people within a community can also affect policy formulation. An individual's ability to pay for a given leisure service will affect the formulation of pricing policies. In depressed urban areas of North America, the policy strategies used differ from those used in affluent suburban areas. In urban areas leisure services may be viewed as a prescriptive tool to allay certain social ills, whereas in other areas the philosophical thrust may be different.

---

[14] Hodgetts and Wortman, *Administrative Policy*, p. 21.

Table 10.1. The Philosophy of the Palo Alto Recreation Division, Palo Alto Community Services Department

---

General Aim

The general aim of the Recreation Division is to provide leisure pursuits that are creative, meaningful, and satisfying; to help individuals discover themselves, maintain their human dignity, and attain their optimum physically, mentally, emotionally, and socially.

Examples of Policy

Palo Alto, California

A statement of the general aim of the Recreation Division of the Palo Alto Community Services Department is shown in Table 10.1. This statement may be considered a major policy reflecting the general direction or purpose of the organization. It is a broad statement that gives direction to the organization.

Kitchener, Ontario

Table 10.2 represents a portion of the resource-oriented goals and objectives of the Kitchener Parks and Recreation Department. This statement reflects three types of policies: major, secondary, and functional. The goals of the organization can be considered its major policies. The objectives listed for each goal statement are examples of policies that are derived from the broader goal statements. The section on physical resource implications spells out a number of functional activities that may affect the management operation of this organization. This document is an excellent example of the manner in which different types of policies are linked within a hierarchical policy structure.

Glenview, Illinois

The policy presented in Table 10.3 (page 354) represents the Glenview Park District's policy concerning standards for community parks. It is a minor policy, which is based on the Park District's functional policy concerning land and facilities. It defines the standards which have been established for this particular type of park.

Marshalltown, Iowa

Table 10.4 (page 354) depicts, in part, operating procedures of the Marshalltown Park and Recreation Department. This type of policy details the procedure that employees are to follow. Included is a discussion of hours of work, attendance requirements, and rest periods. The items presented serve the function of inhibiting, regulating, and enabling certain kinds of behavior.

Table 10.2. Resource-Oriented Goals and Objectives of the Kitchener Parks and Recreation Department

Goal	Objectives	Physical Resource Implications
Goal 1—To coordinate the roles of groups and individuals providing the various forms of park and recreation experiences and resources in the city of Kitchener, so as to maximize the availability and utility of these opportunities for the benefit and overall enjoyment of the citizens of Kitchener.	1-1. To establish and maintain liaison with providers of park and recreation opportunities in Kitchener.	1-1. Must develop coordination mechanisms with board of education, separate school board, YM/YWCA, private golf clubs, ethnic associations, churches, commercial operators, Grand River Conservation Authority, etc. Joint development/operation agreements with other suppliers to optimize return on municipal expenditure.
	1-2. To form ongoing working relationships with community recreation associations and other community-oriented groups providing park and recreation experiences and resources within Kitchener, so as to insure a comprehensive park	1-2. Must encourage the development of and support (financial and advisory) representative community recreation associations in each community. Encourage participation in physical resource planning, development, and operation.

and recreation supply system for the residents and to limit unnecessary duplication of resources.

1-3. To create and continuously update an inventory of all park and recreation resources and opportunities within Kitchener as a base for determining levels of supply and areas of deficiency.

1-4. To provide technical and financial assistance, wherever required and deemed feasible, to insure continuous, high-quality, beneficial park and recreation experiences and resources for all citizens of Kitchener.

1-5. To insure community awareness and to encourage communication from residents on matters related to park and recreation opportunities and resources.

1-3. Work with all "providers" to develop and maintain an inventory classification and reporting system.

1-4. Support other suppliers capable of providing opportunities more efficiently (cost) or effectively (community response).

1-5. Community involvement in all major planning and development decisions, particularly at the neighborhood or community level.

Table 10.3. Policy Concerning Community Parks, Glenview Park District

Definition: A large park area providing broad expanse of natural scenery and capable of accommodating large numbers of people; often includes special features of districtwide interest.

Examples of Provided Features: Picnic areas, bridle paths, nature trails, zoos, band shells, fishing and sports areas.

Principles of Location and Design:

1. Each major section of the community should be within convenient distance of a community park, and it should be easily accessible from a major thoroughfare.

2. The community park should be large enough to take the urban dweller away from the noises and rush of urban environment.

3. The park should be developed for both active and passive use for all ages, but the development of active play areas should not destroy the primary purpose of the park.

Recommended Standard: One community park for at least each 40,000 population or one acre per 400 minimum. Size—100 acres or more where possible, within one to two miles of every home where possible.

Example: Harms Woods Forest Preserve.

Table 10.4. Working Hours, Conditions, and Workweek, Marshalltown Park and Recreation Department

Section 1: Hours of Work

The hours during which the Park and Recreation Department shall be open for business and service shall be determined in the department's best interest by the director.

Section 2: Workweek

The working time per week shall be 40 hours, with special provisions for additional hours uniformly to meet existing conditions or a living wage.

The above rules apply only to hourly people and all salaried people having the result and productivity clause to regulate and determine their hours for continued betterment and growth of the department.

Section 3: Attendance

All employees shall be at their station in accordance with these rules at the appointed time and with regularity. Failure to comply is adequate reason for dismissal.

Section 4: Rest Periods

If authorized by their superintendent, employees may take two 15-minute coffee breaks or rest periods each workday, under provisions and in accordance with the limitations as set by their department heads. Such breaks shall be considered a privilege and not a right, and shall never interfere with proper performance of the work responsibilities and work schedule of the department.

Table 10.5. Arlington Heights Park District Ordinance No. 260

An Ordinance Defining Misdemeanors and Providing Penalties for Such Misdemeanors

BE IT ORDAINED by the Board of Commissioners of the Arlington Heights Park District, Cook County, Illinois:

SECTION 1. For the purpose of this ordinance, the following terms shall have the definitions given herein:

A. "District" is the Arlington Heights Park District, Cook County, Illinois.

B. "Board" is the Board of Commissioners of the Arlington Heights Park District.

C. "Director" is the Director of Parks and Recreation, the chief administrative officer of the District.

D. "Park" is any playfield, playground, swimming pool, ice skating rink, open area, building or parts thereof or other facility and the materials and equipment therein owned, leased or in use by the District.

E. "Person" is an individual, firm, partnership, group, association, corporation, governmental unit, company or organization of any kind, except the District, its employees and Board members while said employees and Board members are engaged in the performance of District duties.

F. "Vehicle" is any conveyance, whether motor powered or self-propelled, except baby carriages, and conveyances in use by the District.

SECTION 2. No person shall engage in any sport, game, amusement or exercise in any Park, except in such parts thereof as are designated for that purpose by the Director.

SECTION 3. No person shall enter a Park or part thereof posted as "Closed to the Public," nor shall any person use or abet the use of any such Park or part thereof in violation of posted notices.

SECTION 4. No person shall hinder, interfere with or cause or threaten to do bodily harm to any employee of the District while such employee is engaged in performing his duties in and on behalf of the District.

SECTION 5. No person shall expose or offer for sale any article or thing, nor shall any person station or place any stand, cart, or vehicle for the transportation, sale, or display of any such article or thing in any Park, except a regularly licensed concessionaire or other person acting under an official permit of the Board; nor shall any person within any Park or on its borders announce, advertise, or call the public attention in any way to any article, or service for sale or hire.

SECTION 6. No person shall paste, glue, tack or otherwise affix or post any sign, placard, advertisement, or inscription, whatever, nor erect or cause to be erected any sign whatever on any structure or thing in a Park, except as authorized by the Director.

Arlington Heights, Illinois

Table 10.5 presents rules that can be found within an organization. This selection was taken from Ordinance 260, which defines misdemeanors in the Arlington Heights Park District. It spells out specifically a rigid set of guidelines that are subject to extremely limited interpretation. For example, Section 9 (not shown) is very explicit, stating that "No person shall throw a stone, brick, or other missile in or upon any park." This rule is designed to inhibit certain types of behavior.

LEGAL ASPECTS OF LEISURE SERVICES

In the last half of this chapter, laws that enable leisure service organizations to exist and operate, as well as other legal concerns that effect the delivery of leisure services will be reviewed. Generally speaking, the law is thought of as a code that governs or regulates people's behavior and lives. It defines, in the simplest sense, what is good or acceptable and what is bad or unacceptable. Laws enable or insure people's rights to engage in activities that society defines as being acceptable; conversely, laws regulate or prohibit those activities that society maintains are unacceptable. The law is a formal code of behavior that exists to maintain the welfare of the culture. Laws enable individuals and organizations to prioritize the needs of organizations in relationship to society as a whole. Thus, by having a uniform set of legal codes, people are able to live together harmoniously, contributing to the general welfare of society as a whole.

Although most societies have judicial and law enforcement systems to control the behavior of individuals and organizations to insure that they conform to the law, these mechanisms in and of themselves are not sufficient to make the application of and compliance with the law successful (at least in North America). Efforts must be made within leisure service orgnizations to educate their members and those they serve as to the importance of the law as it applies to service delivery if they are to operate productively. Thus we will now discuss legal matters as they pertain to the delivery of leisure services.

Types of Law

There are a number of types of law that affect leisure service organizations. Each type governs different relationships and has a different source of power. A few of the more common types of law that affect leisure service organizations, are as follows:

1. *Public law* consists of laws that come into existence by government formulation. They serve to regulate the relationships that exist between government and individuals at the federal, state or provincial, and local levels.
2. *Civil law,* basically, governs relationships between individuals and affects such matters as contracts, personal liability, and transfer of property.

3. *Common law* establishes relationships between individuals. They occur as a result of judicial rulings, which are based on the norms and customs of society.
4. *Statutory law* is derived from legislative bodies. At the federal level, in the United States, senators and representatives establish the law. In Canada, members elected to Parliament make the law. At the state or provincial level, elected individuals are also engaged in the establishment of statutory law.
5. *Administrative law* is that set of laws established by various public agencies to enable or regulate their work activities. These laws may govern such activities as collecting revenues and dispensing licenses and permits.

There are many other types of law, including admiralty, case, citation, martial, probate, penal, military, and international, to name a few. Each of these types of law is written and enacted for a specific purpose and to govern particular relationships. All the types of law mentioned, and still others, may have an impact on leisure service organizations. But public, civil, common, statutory, and administrative laws are those with which the leisure service manager should be familiar. Although it is important for a manager to have an understanding of various types of laws, the actual interpretation and application should be handled by an attorney. Most agencies have a lawyer as part of their staff or contract for a lawyer's services when needed.

Powers of Government

Government at the federal, state or provincial, or local level is endowed with certain powers by virtue of its sovereignty. Sovereignty may be viewed as the legitimacy that a government body maintains in its jurisdiction. A government's sovereignty enables it to exercise certain powers. Among these are the powers to levy and collect taxes; provide services for the general welfare of citizens; establish and enforce certain laws, rules, and regulations; and exercise eminent domain.

Federal Authority

The initial authority for providing leisure services in Canada and the United States rests at the federal level of government. Two important documents, the U.S. Constitution and the British North American Act, serve as instruments that provide for the establishment of sovereignty and serve as the legal basis for government. Both documents spell out the relationship of the federal government to its subdivisions. They provide an orderly division of power, functions, and responsibilities between the federal government and state or provincial government.

The U.S. Constitution establishes a federal system whereby the federal government shares power with state governments. Listed in the Constitution are powers that are delegated to the states and those which are implied and/or explicitly held by the federal government. The expressed powers listed in the

Constitution inlude the right of the federal government to collect taxes, declare war, and regulate trade. The implied powers exist to enable the federal government to be responsible for the welfare of its citizens in an ever changing environment. It is under the jurisdiction of implied powers that the federal government is enabled to address itself to the leisure needs of the nation.

The Constitution provides that certain powers are reserved exclusively for state governments and that, in some cases, the federal and state governments may concurrently provide services. It is under this provision of the Constitution that states have the power to address their efforts to the leisure needs of their constituents. Establishing these relationships between the federal government and individual states has provided a framework whereby the aims of government and the steps in achieving them are facilitated.

Canada was established as a federal state in 1867 by an act of the British Parliament. The British North American Act federally united existing provinces under one dominion. This act provided Canada with internal self-government by establishing a parliamentary system of government modeled after that of Great Britain. The act gives the Canadian Parliament the power to "make laws for peace, order, and good government." It specifically establishes the relationship that is to exist between the provinces and the federal government. The federal government was assigned general powers that were not exclusively assigned to the provinces. The act serves as the legal basis for the Canadian Constitution. In turn, the Canadian Constitution sets forth (in written form and by implication) the framework of government and provides for the orderly exercise of its power. The act and the Canadian Constitution provide the legal and moral basis for the federal government to meet the social needs of Canada's citizenry. It is within this general mandate that the leisure needs of Canadians are officially addressed by government.

State or Provincial Authority

The federal constitutions of both the governments of the United States and Canada reserve certain powers for state or provincial governments. As such, state and provincial governments engage in a variety of activities that result in either the provision or the regulation of leisure services. State or provincial governments maintain law and order, regulate business, and operate a number of public service programs, including state and provincial park and recreation systems. Further, state and provincial governments have direct authority over local governments, including municipalities, townships, and counties. The relationship between state or provincial governments and local forms of government is somewhat similar to that which exists between the federal government and states or provinces; that is, certain activities are reserved by the state or provincial government; and other powers are delegated to local subdivisions of government.

Local Authority

Local authority is granted to local jurisdictions by the state or province and is usually established in the form of city or county charters. These documents, and the authority they grant, form the basis on which the local agency offers leisure services; these documents also establish the laws and ordinances that regulate the use of these leisure services. Profit-making leisure service organizations are also affected by local laws and ordinances. For example, local laws may affect hours of operation, location of facilities, and other factors. Local laws or ordinances must not be in conflict with federal, state, or provincial laws. In many states and provinces, the basis for establishing public leisure services is very specific, whereas in others such legislation is more general, as in "home rule" legislation. According to Reynolds and Hormachea, there are five types of legislation that grant legal powers to local subdivisions of government to provide parks and recreation services: enabling acts; special purpose laws; regulatory laws; special districts; and provisions for home rule.[15]

Enabling Acts.   An enabling act is a statutory law that authorizes a local subdivision of government to establish parks and recreation services within its area of jurisdiction. This type of permissive legislation, does not necessarily *require* local subdivisions of government to establish parks and recreation services. Broad enabling legislation usually provides a local subdivision of government with the power to

> authorize a board or agency or a means of administering, staffing and financing a recreation service; specify the powers, conditions and restrictions; authorize the organization and conducting of recreation activities and programs; permit two or more public agencies or jurisdictions to operate recreation programs jointly; and authorize the acquisition, ownership, development, and maintenance of recreation areas and facilities, and the accepting of gifts.[16]

Table 10.6 serves as an example of enabling legislation; it is for the establishment of public parks in Ontario. This law, the Public Parks Act, enables local municipalities to establish a system of parks, avenues, boulevards, and drives. It provides for the establishment of a board for the general management of the park system, including the development of bylaws and the collection of revenues.

Table 10.7 shows legislation that relates to the establishment of parkland in Missouri. The two statutes listed in the table allow third-class cities and cities of less than 30,000 people to purchase and maintain public parks. These two state statutes provide for the establishment of an appointed board of directors to serve as a governing board, and it also provides for taxing powers and acquisition powers.

[15] Reynolds and Hormachea, *Public Recreation Administration*, p. 42.
[16] Ibid.

Table 10.6. Excerpt from Province of Ontario, The Public Parks Act, R.S.O. 1960, Chapter 329 as Amended by 1961–62 Chapter 119

1.   (1) A park, or a system of parks, avenues, boulevards and drives, or any of them, may be established in any municipality and the same, as well as existing parks and avenues, may be controlled and managed in the manner hereinafter provided.

    (2) Subject to subsection 5, if a petition, praying for the adoption of this Act, is presented to the council of any county or city signed by not less than 500 electors, or to the council of any town or township signed by not less than 200 electors, or to the council of any village signed by not less than 75 electors, the council may pass a bylaw giving effect to the petition, with the assent of the electors qualified to vote at municipal elections, given before the final passing of the bylaw as provided by the Municipal Act.

2.   (1) The parks, avenues, boulevards and drives, and approaches thereto, and streets connecting the same shall be open to the public free of all charge, subject to the bylaws, rules and regulations of the board of park management, and subject also to sections 13 and 14.

    (2) The board of park management may pass bylaws for prescribing fees to be payable for the use of any facilities provided in any park.

    (3) The board of park management, with the approval of the council of the municipality, may pass bylaws for prescribing fees to be payable for entrance to any park.

3.   (1) Where this Act is adopted, the general management, regulation and control of all existing parks and avenues, and of all properties both real and personal applicable to the maintenance of parks belonging to the municipality, and of all parks, avenues, boulevards and drives which may be thereafter acquired and established under this Act, shall be vested in the exercised by a board to be called "The Board of Park Management."

    (4) The board is a corporation and shall be composed of the head of the municipality and of six other persons, who shall be residents or rate-payers of the municipality, but not members of the council, and shall be appointed by the council.

11.   (1) The board may pass bylaws for the use, regulations, protection and government of the parks, avenues, boulevards and drives, the approaches thereto and streets connecting the same, not inconsistent with the provisions of this Act or of any law of Ontario.

12.   (1) Real or personal property may be devised, bequeathed, granted, conveyed or given to the municipal corporation for the establishment or formation of a park, or for the purpose of the improvement or ornamentation of any park of the municipality, and of the avenues, boulevards, and drives and approaches thereto, and of the streets connecting therewith, and for the establishment and maintenance on park property of museums, zoological or other gardens, natural history collections, observatories, monuments or works of art upon such trusts and conditions as may be prescribed by the donor.

13.   (1) The board may acquire by purchase, lease or otherwise the land, rights and privileges required for park purposes under this Act.

Table 10.7. Exerpt from State of Missouri, Legislation Governing Park Purchases and Operations in Third-Class Cities

Statute	**77.140—Parkland Purchases in Third-Class Cities**
Opinions and Cases	The council of cities of the third class may lease, improve, regulate, purchase or sell public parks belonging to the city and may purchase and hold grounds for public parks within the city or within three miles thereof.
	Opinion 43, 1/9/67. A city acting alone may not undertake to construct a park located four miles outside its corporate limits.
Statute	**90.500—90.550—Public Parks—Third-Class Cities and Cities of Less Than 30,000**
For	Cities of less than 30,000 and third-class cities.
Purpose	To establish and maintain free public parks and provide for suitable entertainment therein.
Adoption Procedure	One hundred taxpaying voters shall petition the mayor and common council for an annual tax levy, not to exceed 40¢ on the $100 valuation. Mayor and council shall direct notice to be given of an annual or special election called for the purpose of voting on the question of whether a tax shall be levied for public parks.
Governing Body	The mayor shall appoint, with the approval of the council, a board of nine directors. None of these may be a member of municipal government. Three new members are to be appointed each year to take office June 1.
Taxing Powers	A maximum tax of 40¢ on the $100 valuation may be levied, but such tax must be within the constitutional limits of the city. Funds are allocated from the general fund of the city.
Acquisition Powers	The park board shall have power to buy, sell, lease or rent lands for park purposes. They may also recommend use of eminent domain.

Special Purpose Laws. State governments can also establish special purpose laws, which authorize the establishment of a specific type of leisure service within a specific locality. For example, special legislation may be enacted to allow an individual community to establish park services with a unique type of governing body. Park and recreation services in Clinton, Iowa, were established through a specific act of the state legislature. This act provided a separate, independent government agency to operate the community's park and recreation services. No other community in the state of Iowa has the specific type of governing arrangement that is found within this jurisdiction.

Another example is the "Niagara Parks Act" in the province of Ontario, which was enacted to preserve the beauty surrounding Niagara Falls. This act, legislated by the provincial parliament in Ontario, has enabled this particular system to acquire and maintain a large number of park areas and to operate a number of unique services, including its own educational institution. The important thing to remember about special laws is that they apply only to the specific locality the law is written for.

Regulatory Laws. Regulatory laws are established to inhibit or regulate certain types of behavior for the health, safety, and protection of the public.[17] These state or provincial laws are directed toward insuring that uniform standards and/or codes of behavior are maintained in certain types of operations. Perhaps the best example affecting park and recreation agencies is that law which regulates the operation of aquatic facilities. Throughout Canada and the United States, swimming pool managers are required by law to maintain certain levels of sanitation. Other regulatory laws that affect leisure service managers in both public and private agencies are those governing the handling of food.

There are a number of federal laws that affect both public and private leisure service organizations. Perhaps the most significant are those which deal with civil rights. The federal governments in Canada and the United States prohibit discrimination in the provision of services and the employment of individuals based on race, color, or national origin. The Fourteenth Amendment to the U.S. Constitution prohibits racial discrimination and guarantees equal protection of the law to all citizens of the United States. This amendment also infers that the separate but equal doctrine is not valid in the provision of leisure services. Another example of federal legislation that may affect public and private leisure service organizations is that dealing with employment practices, such as child labor laws minimum-wage standards, safety of employees, and others. Laws governing business activities are usually regulated by state authority and/or jointly regulated by state and federal government.

Another form of governmental regulation occurs when federal agencies establish guidelines that must be adhered to when accepting federal funds. For

[17] Ibid., p. 43.

example, in the United States, state agencies receiving money from the Land and Water Conservation Fund Act must accept the provisions established by the federal government, specifically those of the Department of the Interior. All other applicable federal statutory law and federal administrative regulations must also be adhered to by the grantee. This results in a complementary relationship whereby the federal government uses its vast resources to influence the operation of state and local governments. Still another source of governmental regulations are the rulings made in federal courts.

There are many statutory laws, administrative regulations, and court decisions that have an effect on the provision of leisure services. Still further, there has been a strengthening of the federal government in the past several decades. This has resulted in a lack of clarity as to the boundaries between federal and state/provincial jurisdiction. For example, many states have specific legislation regarding discrimination. It would, however, be difficult to determine what role the federal government has played in the creation and enforcement of this type of law. Obviously, it would be extremely difficult to document all of the federal, state, or provincial laws that affect the provision of leisure services in either the public or the private sector.

Special Districts. Numerous states have established provisions that allow for the establishment of special parks and recreation districts. This type of legislation allows for the provision of a specific type of governmental service having independent and autonomous governing boards with taxing powers. Originally, special districts were established to insure that parks and recreation services had an independent and continuous flow of tax revenues and that individuals on governing boards in their role as board members were dedicated solely to the provision of leisure services. Also, special districts have enabled the establishment of agencies having broader areas of jurisdiction than traditionally defined by a given local subdivision of government.

Thus park districts and other types of special districts, such as water and sanitation, have allowed for a more effective and efficient way of meeting the needs of a given constituency. Perhaps the two states most dominated by this method of organization of public park and recreation services are Illinois and California. Table 10.8 shows the steps that the Park District Code in the state of Illinois outlines for the establishment of a park district. There are numerous reasons why the park district form of organization has been suggested as an excellent mechanism for the provision of community leisure services. On the other hand, many individuals have suggested that the establishment of a separate, independent unit of government leads to chaos, lack of cooperation, and increased governmental fragmentation. Rodney outlines the pro and con sides of the argument:

1. A recreation district provides for fiscal independence and thus, better continuity of services.

2. District boards and their professional staffs are free from political influences.
3. District boards can devote all their time and energy to recreation and park problems.
4. Greater flexibility in establishing and changing programs is possible under an organization pattern that is focused upon one basic function.
5. District operation makes it easier to interpret needs directly to the people.
6. Unified long-range planning for programs and facilities can be given to a

Table 10.8.   Illinois Park District Code

(1) A territory having a population of less than 500,000 legal voters and so lying as to form one connected area, no portion of which lies in an incorporated park district, may be incorporated as a park district.

(2) A petition bearing the signatures of not less than 100 legal voters resident within the limits of the proposed district is filed with the Clerk of the Circuit Court of the county in which the greatest portion of the district lies requesting that the Circuit Judge call an election to submit the proposition of organizing a park district to the voters.

This petition must (a) define the boundaries of the proposed district, (b) set the name of the district, and (c) request the judge, in writing, to set a date and time for a public hearing not less than 30 days nor more than 180 days after the date of filing the petition.

(3) Upon the filing of the petition the Judge is required to set a date, time and place for a hearing upon the subject of the petition.

The Clerk of the Court is then required to give a 20 day notice of the hearing on the petition by publication in one or more daily or weekly newspapers having a general circulation within the proposed district.

(4) If the Circuit Judge finds, upon the hearing, that the petition as filed meets the requirements of The Park District Code, and that the boundaries as set forth in the petition are reasonable boundaries, the Circuit Judge is required to order an election. In the order the Circuit Judge also fixes the time and place or places within the proposed district at which an election may be held to determine the question and to elect five commissioners as the governing body of the park district. The order also names the persons to act as election judges.

The Clerk of the Court is then required to give 20 days notice of the election by publication in one or more newspapers or by posting in five public places if no newspaper of general circulation is published within the district.

(5) The form of ballot is specified in the Code and in addition to the names of nominees must contain five blank lines for write-in votes.

(6) The Park District Code requires the signing of an affidavit in all elections, which affidavit shall contain the following: (a) the name and address of the voter, (b) statement that the voter resides within the particular district and (c) statement that the person desiring to vote is a registered voter.

Table 10.8. (Continued)

(7) Each person desiring to run for commissioner must file his nominating petition, bearing the signatures of at least 25 qualified voters, with the County Clerk not less than 15 days prior to the date of the election.

(8) The return of the election is made to the Circuit Judge who conducts the canvass of the returns and enters an order determining and declaring the results. If the district lies in two or more counties, a copy of the order must be filed with the County Clerk of each county other than that in which the order was entered. The cost of the election on the proposition to organize a park district is paid by the county or counties in which the district is located.

(9) Within 30 days after the declaration by the court of the result of the election, the five commissioners elected are required to meet and determine by lot the term for which each shall hold office. Two shall serve for six years; two shall serve for four years; and one shall serve for two years, respectively, from the date of the next odd year an election would otherwise be held.

(10) At this meeting of the commissioners, the Board also elects one member as President, and one member as Vice-President, who hold their office for a term of one year. The Board also shall then appoint a secretary and a treasurer, who need not be members of the board, and prescribe their duties and fix their compensation.

If the secretary and treasurer are selected from the members of the board, they must serve without compensation.

The board may also appoint an attorney, a director of parks, and recreation superintendent, fix their salaries and define their duties. One person may serve as director of parks and recreation.

(11) At the first meeting of the commissioners of a newly formed park district, or as soon as possible thereafter, the board should adopt (a) an ordinance prescribing the rules for the conduct of the business of the park district; (b) an ordinance setting forth the regulations and restrictions for the use of the park system; and eventually (c) a traffic ordinance. Appropriations and Tax Levy Ordinances will also be needed.

(12) Following the adoption of the administrative ordinance, the following committees from the membership of the board may be appointed by the President: (A) Finance; (B) Buildings and Grounds; (C) Police; (D) Recreation; and (E) such other special committees as may be desired, i.e., concessionaires, etc.

---

geographical area encompassing all the people, rather than being restricted to artificial political boundaries of a city.

7. Larger districts that encompass a number of urban areas make for economy of operation and less duplication of service.

On the other hand, opponents to district organization stress the points that:

1. Establishment of a recreation district only aggravates government problems by adding another overlapping taxing jurisdiction.

2. Independent-district organization fragments government services and creates problems for unified planning.
3. It is more economical to have one governing body provide for all services, rather than have independent boards plan separately for single functions.
4. A multiplicity of small recreation districts can neither plan effectively nor enlarge their services, owing to their limited tax base.[18]

Home Rule. What is home rule legislation? Enabling legislation sets forth specific guidelines that local subdivisions of government follow in the establishment of their services. Enabling legislation covers such items as the type of government the local subdivision may form (e.g., council manager, strong mayor), how much it may levy in taxes, and what specific types of services it may provide. Home rule legislation is permissive legislation in that it allows a local subdivision of government to determine what specific type of government it would like and how that government is to be arranged internally. It further allows local communities to determine at what rate they are to be taxed.

Why is this important for parks and recreation services? We live in a period of time dominated by one factor: change. Even though much enabling legislation has been written in a general manner, it has not met the specific needs of some communities, that have occurred as a result of change. Enabling legislation, for some communities, is restrictive legislation. As government in the United States and Canada has grown, there has been, in general, a need to find mechanisms that allow individual communities to create and group services in ways that are specific to the needs of a particular community. Further, certain communities rely more heavily on their governmental services than others and therefore have need for a broader tax base. In other words, home rule legislation allows individual communities to tailor-make the type of governmental structure that best meets its needs.

Tort Liability

When an individual engages in an act that results in some form of injury to another person, it is known as "tort liability." The act may be a result of carelessness, lack of proper planning, poor judgment, or other unintentional behavior. It may result in personal injury, damage to another person's property, or damage to an individual's reputation. An individual may be allowed to collect for such damages in the form of money, punitive action, or other settlement. For example, if an individual is injured on a piece of park equipment that has not been kept in good repair, the injured individual may be awarded a settlement for injury and loss of work resulting from said accident. If a recreation leader, while supervising a gymnastic activity, permits a child to try a trick beyond his or her ability, resulting in injury, tort liability can also result.

[18] Lynn S. Rodney, *Administration of Public Recreation* (New York: Ronald Press, 1964), p. 82.

There seems to be a real tendency by the public to sue government agencies. Therefore agencies need to take extra precautions to prevent and eliminate accidents. It is important that all employees in an organization, not just managers, be aware of tort liabilities. It is the employee, at the operational level, who usually works with the public and is in the best position to prevent accidents.

Leighton Leighty writes that there are six types of liability, which vary in degree according to the proximity of the offending individual to the tort.[19] They range from the individual whose specific actions result in the actual tort to those sponsoring the action from a more distant vantage point. He notes that each individual is responsible for her/his own conduct in fulfilling the duties of her/his job and that individuals who are in a supervisory, or superior, position are not responsible for the torts of their subordinates.

The doctrine of sovereign immunity has historically provided local units of government with protection from prosecution except in cases of trespassing, nuisance, or functions that may be characterized as proprietary in nature.[20] Today local subdivisions of government are being prosecuted for tort liability more often. The notion of sovereign immunity was derived essentially from English common law, from the notion that the crown could do no wrong and thus could not be sued without its consent.

Torts may be categorized into three areas: intentional torts, unintentional torts, and nuisance. Intentional torts occur as a result of deliberate wrongdoing. These might include trespassing on private property, assault and/or battery, false imprisonment and malicious prosecution. An unintentional tort occurs when an individual within organizations takes unreasonable risks that result in harm to another individual (i.e., negligence that results from a breech of duty). Nuisance may be defined as an annoyance or disturbance that offends an individual and/or organization. The creation of certain conditions within parks, such as the placement of lighting fixtures, may serve as a nuisance to individuals living within close proximity to the park. A lawsuit that results in a multimillion-dollar settlement can be detrimental to any organization.

Eminent Domain

The right of eminent domain means that government has the power to take property it deems necessary for public use. Eminent domain is based on the notion that all property is subject to the control of the state and is under its sovereign power. The right of eminent domain gives government agencies the right to take the property of an individual, if that individual has refused to sell it

---

[19] Leighton L. Leighty, "Legal Considerations," in Sidney G. Lutzin and Edward H. Storey, (eds.) *Managing Municipal Leisure Services* (Washington, D.C.: International City Management Association, 1973), p. 90.

[20] Ibid., pp. 96–97.

to the governmental agency for an equitable sum. The process utilized by government to facilitate this maneuver is known as "condemnation." If an individual refuses to sell her or his property to the government, the government can bring court proceedings to acquire the land.

It is generally thought that the use of eminent domain is the last resort to which a public park and recreation agency should turn in order to acquire land. Government agencies may be required to show the necessity of this action. There are some limitations to the use of eminent domain: in certain cases it is unconstitutional. For example, not all leisure resources are considered within the auspices of eminent domain. As Leighty suggests, public beaches have been regarded as a legitimate resource that can be acquired through the use of eminent domain, but public theaters have not.[21]

Contracts

Many organizations, especially private ones, enter into cooperative arrangements that are mutually beneficial. This exchange, known as a "transaction" or "contract," involves the transferring of goods and services from one party to another.[22] Contracts permit organizations to enter into agreements to provide or receive certain products or services. In the case of the latter, organizations contract for services that they are not equipped to provide for themselves for reasons of practicality, flexibility, or specialization.

Contracts are created by mutual agreement between two or more parties and are enforceable by law. For a contract to exist, there must be mutual agreement between the parties. The contract must be between two parties that are capable of binding themselves to such an agreement. Contracts must also stipulate the consideration (e.g., money) that is to be exchanged between parties. Lastly, a contract must conform to other laws in order to be legal. In other words, an organization cannot sign a legal contract to do something illegal. If an organization cannot meet its contractual obligations, state or provincial laws governing contract performance may be brought into effect. Contracts that are subject to interpretation and are disputed are settled in the courts.

Why is contract law so important? Contract law covers the entire field of business law. Therefore it affects sales, property, partnerships, and other factors that affect private and public leisure service organizations. Some general guidelines relating to the legality of contracts are the following: (1) Illegal contracts are not enforceable; (2) contracts that give one party an unfair advantage over another are not enforceable; (3) incompetent individuals are not responsible for obligations stemming from their involvement in contractual agreements; (4) in general, contracts may be verbal or written, but certain transactions must be made in

---

[21] Ibid., p. 85.

[22] Michael P. Litka, *Business Law* (New York: Harcourt, Brace and World, 1970), p. 76.

writing (e.g., the selling of real estate); (5) once one party has accepted the offer of another, the contract becomes legal; (6) most contracts must guarantee that both parties receive some consideration; and (7) when an organization violates an agreement, the matter may be taken to court and damages may be awarded the wronged party.

Generally speaking, individuals within leisure service organizations are not liable as individuals (in terms of their personal assets) for any damages resulting from a breech of contract. It is important to remember that illegal contracts are not binding contracts. So, if a representative of a leisure service organization has made a contract outside the jurisdictional limitations of the organization, the contract is void. On the other hand, if the disputed contract is within the authority of the organization and resulted simply as an exercise of poor judgment, the contract can be enforced. An individual in an organization or corporation who acts as an agent of the organization/corporation is not personally liable for disputed contracts; that is, an individual is viewed as an agent of the organization and the organization, as the principal, is responsible for the actions of its agents.

Some of the more common contracts entered into by leisure service organizations include those made for construction of facilities; operation of special facilities, such as golf courses, restaurants, and amusement parks; joint use of facilities; and special services, such as custodial and janitorial services. As stated earlier, contractual arrangements permit an organization to acquire help in areas of specialization that they are not equipped to provide because of limited resources or skills.

SUMMARY

In the first part of this chapter, we explored policies and legal forces of which the leisure service manager should be cognizant. A policy is a plan that inhibits, enables, or regulates behavior in some way. A policy may be written so that it enables and inhibits behavior at the same time. Policies can be seen as existing in a hierarchical fashion, which finds major policies at the top and rules at the bottom. Major policies give broad direction to an organization, whereas rules spell out specific rigid regulations that are to be followed. The leisure service manager plays a dual role in the policy process. He or she helps policymaking bodies formulate policies, while at the same time carrying the responsibility for their implementation and enforcement. This dual role requires a high order of ability, as the leisure service manager is placed in the somewhat tenuous position of both setting policy and enforcing it.

In the latter part of this chapter, we discussed the relationship of the law to the delivery of leisure services. There are a number of types of law—public, civil, common, statutory, and administrative law—of which the leisure service manager must be knowledgeable. These bodies of law are derived from a variety of sources, including constitutions, legislative bodies that make statutory laws, administrative rulings, and laws which are derived from the rulings of the judicial system.

The ultimate authority establishing sovereign power in the United States is derived from the U.S. Constitution. In Canada, sovereign power comes from the British North American Act and the Canadian Constitution. These documents set forth the legal powers that are granted to various divisions of government. The power to establish public leisure services is ultimately vested in these documents. State or provincial authority, which is derived from these documents, sets forth the conditions under which businesses may operate and local governments function.

Personnel Management and Training for Leisure Service Organizations

11

Personnel management can be thought of as a staff function within an organization, supporting the primary line functions of creating, distributing and financing services within the leisure delivery system. Every organization is involved in personnel management, and the successful operation of various personnel functions may very well determine the productivity of an organization. Emphasized in this chapter, are the functions of personnel planning and job analysis, recruitment and hiring procedures, promotions and discharges, wage and salary administration, fringe benefits, performance appraisal, labor unions, civil service, affirmative action programs, and training. The latter part of this chapter focuses entirely on the topic of training; it includes a discussion of the various mechanisms that can be used in orientation, in-service, and developmental retraining programs.

PERSONNEL MANAGEMENT

Personnel management is concerned with the human resources of a leisure service organization. Whenever human resources are involved within an organization, the tasks that are carried out under the heading of "personnel services" play an important role in its productivity. The employees of an organization that has developed an awareness of the importance of personnel management services will, generally speaking, have high morale and job satisfaction. Such awareness allows for an organization to interact with its employees in a positive manner, recognizing that people are the most important resource within an organization.

Although large organizations may have separate personnel departments, the personnel functions that are undertaken within any organization, regardless of its size, are fairly uniform. These functions include procurement, development, placement, and remuneration for employees.[1]

---

[1] Herbert J. Chruden and Arthur W. Sherman, Jr., *Personnel Management* (Cincinnati, Ohio: South-Western Publishing Co., 1968), p. 10.

Procurement of Employees

The recruitment of leisure service personnel may range from nationwide selection efforts to a local campaign to hire part-time instructors for activity classes. The recruitment of highly qualified staff plays an important role in the development of an organization's human resources. Without competent staff, a key building block in the success of any leisure delivery system, an organization's efforts will be diminished. The process of selecting employees may be based on the establishment of elaborate criteria or on the individual preferences of managers. In either case, the selection of personnel is a necessary and important function.

Employee Development

The development and training of employees serves two purposes. First, it enables an individual to acquire the skills necessary to successfully fulfill the requirements of a job. Second, it allows an organization to identify and focus upon individuals' needs within the organization and help them develop in such a way that they are personally rewarded and the organization benefits. The development of employees not only refers to the acquisition of job-related skills, but also to the development of job and personal attitudes and values. As such, training and development can involve many dimensions. The latter part of this chapter is devoted fully to the many aspects of an organizational training program.

Placement of Employees

This is a process that involves integrating the individual abilities which people bring to a work setting with the organization's needs. It is naive to think that an organization can tailor-make a job to fit each person's particular skills, knowledge, abilities, and interests. On the other hand, it is also naive for an organization to assume that it can locate individuals with the specific skills, values, and attitudes necessary for particular jobs. Therefore there is a tremendous need within organizations to find the best way to utilize each employee's skills. This may involve changing a job by expanding or making it more flexible to meet a particular individual's interests. It may also mean moving an individual from one position to another one. Generally, an organization should attempt to effectively utilize its human resources by integrating individual abilities and needs with organizational requirements.

Remuneration

Individuals are motivated on the job by both intrinsic and extrinsic factors. Remuneration in the form of financial incentives can play an important part in the overall productivity of employees. For this to be the case, equitable pay programs must be established and administered. This may involve the structuring of objective wage systems and merit programs. Other forms of remuneration may include employee fringe benefits, such as paid vacations, holidays, health insurance, and recreation services. Fringe benefits are usually thought of as supplementary to an individual's basic wage.

Procurement, development, placement, and remuneration constitute the process of personnel management. They may be conducted independently, or they may be integrated with one another. They can be conducted formally, based on a highly structured set of policies, or they may operate on an informal basis. The point is that all four functions operate within an organization to one degree or another and affect an organization's human resources. A poorly conceived personnel program can have disastrous effects on the effectiveness and efficiency of an organization. Employee productivity can be increased or decreased, depending on the manner in which the personnel program is administered and the extent to which an organization recognizes its responsibility for the development of the program.

PERSONNEL PLANNING AND JOB ANALYSIS

There are three important components involved in personnel planning and job analysis. The first is that of identifying and forecasting personnel needs. The second involves a job analysis of the specific work activities to be accomplished and a resulting job description upon which to base recruitment of personnel. And, the third is the development of a sound detailed plan to meet future personnel needs due to expansion, specific future short- or long-term projects, the normal rate of turnover, and so on.

Forecasting an organization's personnel needs can be a difficult and extremely sensitive area. It is difficult to predict fully or accurately changes in the economy that will affect both business and government. Further, it is difficult for organizations to predict changing consumer expectations in an area such as leisure, which is dynamic and fluid. In spite of these problems, however, organizations should attempt to project their future work-force needs and determine the amount and type of employees they will need. In a business, this is done largely by determining the work volume expected in the future. This is accomplished by multiplying the expected growth by the ratio between the amount of work currently done and the number of individuals required to do it.

In the government sector, personnel planning is usually based on two factors. The first factor, which is somewhat stable, is the amount of tax revenues that will be generated over a fixed period of time. A city can determine with a certain degree of accuracy the increase in land values and, hence, the assessed valuation of property. With this figure, government organizations can predict their potential revenues for the future, which allows personnel forecasting to be undertaken. Further, government organizations can predict personnel needs based on projected capital improvement in the leisure services area. This is especially true in the development of revenue-producing facilities that are self-supporting.

The second factor—political changes—is somewhat more difficult to deal with effectively. The political programs of elected officials can have a significant impact on personnel planning. Certain politicians advocate the reduction of governmental services, while others suggest that they should be expanded. This uncertainty in political philosophy makes planning difficult but not entirely impossible. An organization usually will try to forecast its personnel needs over a five-year period.

An important step in personnel analysis is the determination of the specific work required. To adequately plan for future personnel needs and, ultimately, screen and select new employees, an organization must know (1) what specific jobs are to be done and (2) the specific talents and abilities required to do them. The process of integrating these two concerns is known as "job analysis." This is usually undertaken by an organization in an attempt to identify the activities that an individual will engage in while performing a specific task. Once this has been done, and linked to the competencies necessary to complete a given task, a job description is usually written. A job description states the title of the job, spells out the activities or duties that are to be performed in the job, and delineates the skills and abilities required to complete the job (see Figure 11.1). It is from the job description that future personnel recruitment is done. The specifications found in a job description serve as a basis upon which a leisure service manager can fulfill the organization's future personnel requirements.

Once an organization has completed its projection of future personnel needs, its next task is to develop a plan to meet these future needs. This may involve an analysis of the organization's current work force. The amount of expected turnover for a variety of reasons, including retirements, job transfers, and normal attrition, can be determined. Once this task has been completed, a plan that incorporates these findings with the forecasted human resource needs can be completed. This plan should spell out the positions that are necessary to meet the organization's future needs and the mechanisms necessary to secure employees to meet these future demands. This plan should also identify the step-by-step procedures that organization will take to recruit new employees.

RECRUITMENT AND HIRING PROCEDURES

To meet the personnel needs of an organization, a manager must spend considerable energy and time in the recruitment and hiring of new staff. The recruitment and hiring process involves locating qualified individuals to assume positions that have been authorized within the organization. Once sources of employees have been located, the next step is to screen employees by reviewing

GENERAL DESCRIPTION: The Director of Parks and Recreation is the chief executive officer of the Parks and Recreation Department. He is responsible for the supervision, coordination, and leadership required to implement the efficient operation of the department under the policies and guidelines established by the Parks and Recreation Board.

Major Duties:

1. To inform the board on all matters germane to the functioning of the department as requested by the board.
2. To recommend courses of action, plans, and policies required to insure the smooth operation of the department and its purpose.
3. To direct the operations of the department and include the staff, programs, maintenance, financial, and facilities.-
4. To recruit, select, and employ or to recommend employment of department personnel.
5. To administer the budget—directing, controlling, and accounting for the expenditure of department funds in accordance with budget appropriations. Supervising the keeping of complete financial records for the department.
6. The director will assume the perpetual goal of upgrading the staff through in-service training.
7. Improving the public awareness of the department's services through good public relations.
8. To enlighten the department's philosophy and objectives and stimulate the total growth through a planned program of acquisition, planning, design, and construction of recreation and parks facilities.
9. To study and analyze the effectiveness of the department's services, upgrading programs and facilities in keeping with conditions, needs, and trends that affect leisure services in the community.
10. To establish and develop a program for continuing use of volunteers and to act as a consultant on leisure resources with public and quasi-public agencies.
11. To prepare and issue regular and special reports for use by staff, board, community officials, and others, and for the information of the community.
12. To perform other duties as may be assigned by the board.

Desired Qualifications

College graduate in the field of Park and Recreation Administration. A minimum of three (3) years of progressive experience in the park and recreation field. A director must have the ability to organize and supervise a wide range of administrative functions and the ability to develop leadership within the staff and have attributes of personal leadership himself.

Figure 11.1. Wooster (Ohio) Parks and Recreation Department, job description for Director of Parks and Recreation.

their applications and/or résumés. Interviewing prospective employees is the next procedure, and investigation of the backgrounds of potential employees is undertaken. Finally, the candidate selected for the position is hired. This process may vary depending on the level and type of job the manager is recruiting for. Further, the intensity with which organizations pursue each of these steps will vary according to the needs of the organization and its resources.

Locating Qualified Individuals

There are two main sources an organization can utilize to secure individuals for positions within the organization. It can look internally for individuals who can be promoted. Simultaneously, it can cultivate external sources to locate potential employees. Depending on the type of position available within an organization, a variety of resources may be tapped. In the case of professional positions, the National Recreation and Park Association's job referral program is an excellent source. Similarly, state and provincial professional organizations maintain job listings and/or publish journals in which job openings can be advertised. Another source of potential professional employees is the colleges and universities having a recreation education curricula.

For nonprofessional employees, an organization may advertise in a newspaper, receive referrals from state or provincial employment agencies, and/or receive referrals from private employment agencies. Another method for locating qualified individuals is through personal referrals. Often individuals within the organization will know of potential candidates for a given job.

Screening Potential Employees

Obviously, the criteria used to screen future employees will vary from position to position. But there are numerous instruments that can be utilized to aid the manager in selecting and placing potential employees. For example, instruments that test the candidate's personality factors, general level of intelligence, and aptitudes and limitations relative to various types of work are available. When reviewing these data, along with an individual's application and/or résumé, the manager should be able to piece together enough information to know whether that individual should be hired. The manager should also realize that, although he may not currently need a certain candidate, he may in the future; the manager should so stipulate to the potential employee and should have a system for retaining applications.

Interviewing The Employee and Reviewing His Background

Interviews can be conducted in a variety of ways. Certain organizations have a formalized procedure wherein the candidate for employment appears before a panel of people representing the organization. These people ask questions that have been predetermined and follow a strict format in terms of time and length of the interview. On the other hand, less structured interviews can be conducted between a manager and potential employees. Those who advocate this approach suggest that they would rather talk to a person in a relaxed, comfortable environment, where the constraints to open communication are removed.

In either approach, the personnel interview allows an organization to meet certain aims. First, it offers an opportunity for an organization to clarify the employee's background and application. In addition, it provides a format whereby the applicant's background can be pursued, probing areas vital to employee success. Further, the interview allows the organization to sell itself to the candidate. In many cases, an organization will want to discuss its needs with a potential candidate, making her or him aware of the problems in the organization and its expectations.

PROMOTIONS AND DISCHARGES

The advancement of employees from one position to another is a way of rewarding excellence within an organization and recognizing potential for growth. Promotions contribute to the overall morale of individuals by providing examples of opportunity for upward mobility and growth. Generally speaking, all organizations should try to promote individuals within the organization rather than pursue potential candidates from the outside. Obviously, this cannot be adhered to in all cases, but it is a policy that has merit. Rewarding effective employees is a good way to increase organizational morale. Occasionally however, this can create resentment when two employees vie for the same position.

Two factors can be considered in the selection and promotion of an individual. The first is *merit*. When an individual has demonstrated an ability to perform and has proved that she/he has the knowledge, skills, and ability to handle a higher-level job, she/he is promoted on the basis of merit. The second factor is *seniority*. Seniority involves giving preference for promotion to an individual who has a long service record with the organization. When individuals of equal ability are reviewed for potential advancement, usually the one with a longer record of service to an organization will be rewarded. But when seniority is the prime criterion for promotion, it can work to an organization's disadvantage. It prevents aggressive, young, and talented employees from advancing in the organization beyond a certain level. Thus the organization risks losing some of its most talented individuals to other organizations. Using seniority as the sole criterion has the added disadvantage of narrowing the organization's selection process. The senior person may not be the best person for the job. Seniority is used primarily in the promotion of nonprofessional employees, especially in organizations where workers are represented by labor unions.

Occasionally, it becomes necessary to remove an employee from a job on a temporary or permanent basis. When employment is withdrawn on a temporary basis, it is known as a *layoff*. Layoffs occur in business primarily for economic reasons. Sometimes cycles in the economy result in recessions, which interrupt the normal pattern of the creation of services. In this case, organizations reduce their work forces to reduce their costs for human resources. In government organizations, layoffs can occur as a result of a withdrawal of funding.

When an employee is discharged permanently from a position for incompetence or the serious violation of an organization's policy, he or she is *fired* (*terminated*). Occasionally, an organization will have to fire an employee because she or he does not have the knowledge, skills, or attitudes necessary to successfully undertake a specific job. Termination should be viewed as a failure on the parts of both the individual and the organization. It often occurs as a result of poor communication between supervisor and subordinate; usually, expectations are not made clear and the result is employee failure. Sometimes certain employees are extremely difficult to motivate, having personal problems that cannot be overcome through generally accepted management practices. Obviously, when an individual is terminated from an organization, there can be deep personal resentment. There are few amicable separations between individuals and organizations. A manager should strive to help an employee understand why she or he was terminated and what action can be taken so that the individual can correct the difficulties in the future. An organization should also look inward to determine in what way it could have altered and changed its procedures and management practices to retain the employee.

WAGE AND SALARY ADMINISTRATION

Wages and salaries are used by leisure service organizations to attract high-quality employees in order to achieve stated goals and objectives. A well thought out wage and salary plan can serve to meet the extrinsic needs of employees and, as such, contribute to employee motivation and job satisfaction. A wage and salary schedule that is updated periodically can allow an organization to remain competitive with other organizations that are vying for the same professional and nonprofessional individuals. The salary and wage schedule may also compensate employees for changes in the cost of living, longevity of service, and outstanding contributions.

Wages are usually paid to nonprofessional employees who are involved in manual, semiskilled work; payment is generally made on a weekly basis and is based on the number of hours an individual worked during that period of time. A *salary* is usually paid to professional employees who are involved in tasks in which the work is not routinized and the work hours are not fixed; salaries are dispersed on a biweekly or monthly basis. The interplay of supply and demand may determine the amount paid in either salaries or wages to a given set of employees. For example, there are few skilled carpenters as opposed to individuals who can perform general laborer tasks. As a result, a carpenter is paid a higher wage than a laborer. Further, salaries and wages can serve as an indication of the relative importance of a job within an organization. A director of parks and recreation is paid more than a secretary because he or she has more responsibility and in a relative sense is more important to the organization. The wages and salaries of many organizations will depend on the agreement negotiated between them and the labor unions that represent employees.

To determine what one individual or group of individuals ought to be paid in relation to others in an organization requires an evaluation of the jobs within the organization. Job evaluation is a systematic method of determining the importance of work positions within an organization. Archer identifies four methods commonly used by organizations to determine how jobs should be compared with each other: job ranking, job classification, factor comparison, and the point system.[2]

Job Ranking

Job ranking involves identifying each job within an organization and ranking it hierarchically. Simply, this approach allows a manager to rank jobs in order of their relative importance. Wage and salaries are then based on this ranking. In this approach, there is no effort to accommodate comparable positions on the same level within an organization's hierarchy and, thus, it has limited potential as a method to be employed in anything but small organizations.

Job Classification

In this approach, the manager establishes a number of job categories based on the difficulty of a job or its value to the organization. Within each job classification, allowance is made for an individual with advanced skills to be paid more than a person who is just beginning the job. An employee's pay would be determined by the level within the classification she/he is at depending on her/his skill or length of service to the organization. The value of this approach is that it allows individuals to increase their wage earnings by demonstrating increased knowledge or skill.

Factor Comparison

This method of job evaluation involves identifying the various factors an individual must possess to successfully undertake a given job. Management might

---

[2] Maurice Archer, *An Introduction to Canadian Business* (Toronto: McGraw-Hill Ryerson, Limited, 1974), p. 528.

identify the amount of experience and education, the physical and mental demands involved, and the amount of responsibility an individual must assume in a certain job. Other factors may be the number of employees a person is responsible for supervising, the amount of money within his or her jurisdiction, and the number of facilities and pieces of equipment he or she must operate. All these factors serve as a basis for comparing the various jobs found in an organization. Once this comparison has been undertaken, a standard wage is established for key jobs that represent different wage levels within the organization. The amount of money paid to each individual will vary depending on his or her relationship to these key positions and the input and output requirements of each position.

Point System

This approach consists of the establishment of job classifications based on points, which are determined by identifying the relative importance of a job. For example, a job may be broken down by the input requirements (education, experience, etc.) and points assigned to each of these factors. The total number of points for a given job will determine what class it is to be placed in. Each class is then assigned a certain wage. For example, Class I employees might be paid $2.50 per hour and Class II employees might receive $3.50 per hour. This system clearly delineates the inputs required for a job and relates them equitably with other jobs within an organization. The relative worth of all jobs is then linked to the wage system. The system allows jobs from one classification or category to be compared with those of another. Thus there is an equitable determination of the importance of each job within an organization. This allows the manager to pay individuals equally for work that requires comparable abilities, skills, and knowledge.

FRINGE BENEFITS

Fringe benefits are utilized by an organization to help improve employees' pyschological and social well-being. They compensate employees above and beyond their normal wage or salary. Although fringe benefits cost an organization money, many individuals perceive them as an organizational ploy to distract the worker from the issue of wages or salary. This is certainly not the case; fringe benefits have been long sought by employee and labor groups and can be thought of as contributing to the overall welfare of employees.

Why do organizations have fringe benefits? First, and perhaps most important, fringe benefits contribute to both the mental and physical health of an organization's employees. By providing an insurance program, for example, an organization can relieve the individual employee of the tension that arises from the concern for personal and family health. As another example, employees who are rested as a result of paid vacations or holidays are more fit psychologically for the work environment. Another important reason for fringe benefits is that organizations can purchase such things as insurance in a very large quantity and thus get it at a much lower price than the employees would have to pay individually. Organizations are always in competition with one another for personnel. It is to their advantage to attract and hold employees. Fringe benefits represent a means to instill in employees satisfaction with their situation and an inclination to remain with the organization over many years.

There are a number of different types of fringe benefits, including the following:

1. *Paid Vacations*. It is common practice among many organizations to provide full-time employees with a minimum of two weeks of paid vacation. The length of a vacation period may be increased in direct relationship to the amount of service an individual has given an organization.
2. *Paid Public Holidays*. There are a number of holidays throughout the year that occur as a result of national legislation. Independence Day in the United States and Dominion Day in Canada are examples of holidays that are legislated. In addition, states and provinces celebrate certain events in their history, and employees are granted time off with pay for these occasions. Certain religious days are also declared as holidays (e.g., Christmas, Good Friday).
3. *Employee Breaks*. Many organizations give their employees short periods of time off during the day. Examples are coffee breaks and lunch periods. There is no reduction in salary or wages.
4. *Sick Leave*. Another fringe benefit that many organizations provide is paid sick leave. Individuals are allotted a specific number of days per year that they can take off for medical reasons.
5. *Reduced and Flexible Workweek*. Historically, one of the earliest fringe benefits was the reduction of the work week from 60 to 48 hours. Today the 40-hour week is standard, and some organizations have reduced this still further. An innovation in the hours spent on the job has been the restructuring of the workday from the normal 8:00 A.M. to 5:00 P.M. routine. Many organizations are experimenting with longer workdays and shorter workweeks. Flexible work hours enable individuals to schedule their work pattern to correspond with their life-styles.
6. *Overtime Payment*. Organizations usually give compensation for work in excess of the regular workday. Individuals are either paid time and a half for overtime or given compensatory time off.
7. *Bonuses*. Bonuses have been given by many profit-making organizations for many years. There are two common types. The first, profit-sharing bonuses, allow employees to share in the profits of the organization. Each employee receives a certain percentage of the profits. The second, stock bonuses, allows

individuals to purchase stock at a cost below the current market price. In this way, individual employees can participate in the ownership of the corporation. Bonuses are also being given by government institutions. They usually take the form of merit pay, with which a individual is rewarded for exceptional service. If the bonus becomes part of an individual's salary, it is not considered a fringe benefit. But if it is above and beyond his/her wage and does not become part of his/her annual earnings, it is considered a bonus.

8. *Pension and Insurance Plans.* An organization's retirement plan can be considered a fringe benefit, as can health, accident, and life insurance programs. These types of programs can be subsidized fully or partially by the organization.

9. *Other Benefits.* There are a variety of other fringe benefits that an organization can provide its employees. Among these are recreation and leisure facilities and programs, legal advice and assistance, reduction in the cost of services provided by the organization, payment of educational fees, and on-the-job health care, including counseling services.

PERFORMANCE APPRAISAL

An important role in the management of personnel is the periodic evaluation of staff. Every leisure service organization expends vast sums of their fiscal resources on personnel. To insure that an organization is run effectively, the performance of its personnel must be audited and either corrected or rewarded, depending on the situation. An effective performance appraisal system can provide the leisure service manager with information that can be used to guide decision-making regarding promotions, training, and long-range planning.

Performance appraisal, for many years, has served primarily as a mechanism whereby an organization decides who merits salary increases and/or promotion. This device has been used as a rational method of linking the expectations of an organization with the performance of individual employees. It was thought that by establishing selected criteria, an organization could systematically identify and reward outstanding performance. In addition, it was thought that this approach would reduce the amount of favoritism and bias which occurred in organizations that did not have a systematic approach.

We will discuss a number of performance appraisal procedures that are used in organizations. Our discussion will include traditional methods, such as rating scales, and newer approaches, such as Management by Objectives.

One of the recent shifts in the use of performance appraisal techniques is the movement toward using them to aid in developmental training programs. Many organizations are concerned about the development of their employees. To aid in the task of constructing effective employee-oriented developmental training programs, performance appraisal techniques are being utilized to help employees better understand their own strengths and weaknesses. Rather than simply viewing these mechanisms as tools to evaluate a person's working performance for merit considerations, they are being used to help point out to employees areas in which they can improve.

This added perspective is changing the nature of employee appraisal. In the past an employee's evaluation was viewed strictly in black-and-white terms; her or his work was either good or bad, and depending upon this appraisal, she or he either got an increase or did not. Today organizations are using appraisal systems in a much more positive sense. They are no longer viewed as potentially negative or undesirable by either management or employees; rather, they are seen as opportunities for managers to work with their subordinates, and vice versa, to improve the effectiveness and efficiency of the organization.

Another trend in the use of performance appraisal has been in the area of long-range planning. There are two ways that it contributes to the planning process. First, it allows an organization to identify potential problem areas and take corrective action. If, for example, an organization has a morale problem, or certain of its employees lack the skills to perform certain jobs, resources within the organization can be shifted to counter these concerns. In this way, an organization can determine some of its long-term needs and proceed accordingly.

The second way performance appraisal contributes to an organization's long-range-planning efforts is by identifying individuals within the organization that have promise for the future. Organizational resources can be allocated to help groom likely management prospects. Not only does the organization invest in a long-term training activity, but it is also able to compare and contrast current organizational personnel resources with future needs. If an organization finds that it does not have sufficient internal resources to meet its long-term personnel needs, it can plan long-term recruitment strategies that will enable it to find the needed resources.

Performance Appraisal Techniques

Performance appraisal techniques can be seen as existing on a continuum that runs from those emphasizing an individual's personality traits (inputs rather than outputs) to those which stress result-oriented performance (outputs rather than inputs). The latter is concerned with measuring what an employee produces, and the former focuses on identifying what the employee brings to the job in terms of personality. The trend in performance appraisal is clearly shifting from approaches used to measure personality traits to result-oriented appraisal mechanisms. Five methods—rating scales, forced distribution, forced choice, critical incidents, and Management by Objectives—will be discussed.

Rating Scales
This technique involves the utilization of a form having a list of selected criteria, usually a list of words, that can be used to describe an employee's performance.

These words are placed in checkerboard style with the criteria that have been developed for appraisal. The manager simply checks the appropriate word that, he feels, describes an employee's performance. For example, if the criterion is "leadership," the form may present options ranging from "unsatisfactory" to "exceptional." The manager would check the term that best describes an employee's leadership ability (see Figure 11.2).

There are two types of rating scales. The first is known as the "additive" approach to performance appraisal. In this method, an employee's overall performance score is determined by adding up all the scores given for the criteria established. For example, descriptive terms are given a numerical score; "unsatisfactory" might have the value of 1, and "exceptional" might be given the value of 5. The manager records the number of each of the selected criteria (leadership, loyalty, etc.) and determines a total, or overall, score. Despite the simplicity of this approach, it presents a number of problems in effective performance appraisal. For one, it assumes that all the factors being evaluated are of equal importance. But in certain jobs, loyalty may be more important than leadership; in other jobs, creativity may be more important than loyalty.

The other type of rating scale avoids the problems found in the additive approach. Rather than lumping all the criteria together to achieve an overall score, this approach allows a manager to evaluate an employee's performance on those criteria that relate specifically to an employee's position. In other words, an individual's appraisal is more tailor-made to the specifics of his or her job. The manager can simply ignore the criteria that are not applicable or that she or he is unable to evaluate effectively.

In both approaches to performance appraisal, the stress is placed on the intentions or personality traits of individuals, rather than concrete job accomplishments.

There are numerous problems associated with using the rating-scale approach to performance appraisal. Among the more significant drawbacks, as identified by George Strauss and Leonard Sayles, are the following:

1. *Clarity of standards.* Frequently, individuals using the rating scale approach vary as to their perception of what constitutes unsatisfactory and/or exceptional performance. For one person, exceptional performance may be viewed as theoretically unattainable. Another person may use a comparative approach to determine exceptional performance. The result is that these terms mean different things to different people and present a problem in accurate evaluation of individuals.

2. *Insufficient evidence.* Because this approach is essentially a one-way mechanism that finds the manager rating his subordinates, it is slanted from the manager's viewpoint. That is to say, the manner in which the employee interacts with the manager will be the primary determinant of his rating out-

come, regardless of the way he may interact with co-workers, or indeed his own subordinates.

3. *Differing perceptions.* It is extremely difficult for individuals to be impartial in the evaluation of others. One's own particular prejudice, bias, and values can distort evaluation or make impartial evaluation impossible.

4. *Excessive leniency or strictness.* The perception that a manager has of himself and his job will affect his approach to appraisal. Some individuals see themselves as being hard managers responsible for maintaining discipline within the organization. As a result, their evaluations may be overly harsh. On the other hand are the managers who try to create a country club atmosphere and be one of the "guys." Their evaluations may be very lenient.

5. *Halo effect.* This problem is created when a manager allows himself to be influenced by the success of an employee in one particular dimension of appraisal. What happens is that the manager carries over the success of the individual's performance in one area to all other areas. The reverse of this can also occur.

6. *Influence of a person's job.* There is a tendency to rank individuals operating in higher-level jobs as being more effective. It is important to remember that each job within an organization has specific requirements, and appraisal should consider these factors rather than where one is located in the organizational hierarchy.[3]

Forced Distribution

In this approach to performance appraisal, the manager ranks employees within a given class against one another and places them on a hierarchical scale. It is similar to the procedure of grading on a curve. For example, using the employee's overall performance appraisal score, ten percent of the individuals maybe forced into the top category, 30 percent in the next category, 40 percent in the "average" category, 10 percent in the next category, and 10 percent at the bottom. This mechanism is commonly used to distribute the funds available for merit increases; dividing the funds according to staff ranking on a curve.

This approach allows managers to overcome some of the problems associated with the rating-scale method. It usually assures that the standards found in appraisal systems are applied equally by all managers. Further, it eliminates the possibility that employees in one job classification will be compared with those of another. In addition, it eliminates some of the biasing that occurs as a result of the different perceptions individual managers have of employees by actively making them compare the work of one individual to that of another in the same job class. Further, this system is a relatively straightforward way of evaluating

[3] Based on George Strauss and Leonard R. Sayles, *Personnel: The Human Problems of Management* (Englewood Cliffs, N.J.: Prentice-Hall, 1972), pp. 511–512.

EVALUATION OF PERSONNEL

Recreation
Fool

☐ Rated by:

EMPLOYEE _____

HOME ADDRESS _____ Phone _____

Employment Period: from ___ 19___ to ___ 19___

Date _____ (Title)

Salary $ _____

POSITION HELD _____

Previous Position with Wooster Parks and Recreation Department

	Excellent	Good	Fair	Poor	Not Observed
1. *Personality and Attitude*					
A. Cheerful and friendly with everyone					
B. Alert for new ideas					
C. Cooperative attitude toward fellow workers, supervisors, and patrons					
D. Suitable personality for recreation leadership/swimming instruction					
E. Interest in and loyalty to the district and discretion in discussing it and its policies					
F. Loyalty to superiors					
2. *Administrative Ability*					
A. Plans and carries out suggested programs to full extent of ability and facilities					
B. Shows originality and initiative in program planning and conduct of activities					
C. Receptive to suggestions from superiors					
D. Submits reports promptly					
E. Works with and encourages volunteers					

3. *Leadership*
   A. An example to others
   B. Not content with the status quo; constantly trying to improve both the program and himself
   C. Has an ability to provide leadership
   D. Enthusiastic
   E. Skills and past experience enrich program
   F. Attendance raises or remains constant

4. *Reliability*
   A. Is punctual in meeting all time schedules
   B. Accepts full share of responsibility
   C. Carries out, in cooperative spirit, policies and requirements

5. *Appearance*
   A. Presents a good personal appearance

6. *Facilities*
   A. Keeps facilities and supplies in good condition

REMARKS: _____

REHIRE: _____   NOT REHIRE: _____

Figure 11.2. Example of a rating scale for performance appraisal.

employees and, although it may take considerable time to rank employees, it is a mechanism that is usually understood by those being evaluated.

Obviously, there are also drawbacks to this system. First, and perhaps most important, it may set one employee against another reducing the cooperative efforts necessary for an organization to achieve its goals. This approach also assumes that not everyone within an organization is *capable* of achieving a maximum standard of performance. Because there is no absolute set of criteria with which to measure effectiveness, employee productivity may decline. Within any organization are peer pressures to keep the "rate busters" in line. As a result, this approach to performance appraisal may create considerable tension within an organization.

Forced Choice

This approach to performance appraisal was developed by the United States Army at the conclusion of World War II. It is a procedure that is directed toward eliminating prejudice and bias in the evaluation of individuals. Essentially, the manager is presented with a number of statements that describe the behavior of an employee. He is given a dichotomous choice for each statement and must check one of two items, ". . . one of which is the most and the other least characteristic of the person being rated."[4] Certain choices that are included in the list of statements have no relevance to the performance appraisal. If a manager responds to a statement that does not relate to the task required in a given job, this ranking is disregarded. Conversely, if the manager responds to statements that do relate directly to job effectiveness, they are included in the score determined by the overall appraisal. The manager does not know which statements have bearing on job performance and which are bogus and have no bearing. Thus the bias of the manager is partially eliminated. The manager has no way of knowing in advance which statements will contribute to positive or negative performance appraisal, which also contributes to objective evaluation.

This approach to performance appraisal seems to be one of the more effective mechanisms that can be used. It has not been incorporated in leisure delivery systems with any degree of significance for a number of reasons. For one, it is an extremely costly method of evaluation because it requires an organization to specifically delineate the tasks necessary for a given job. Herein lies one of its strengths and one of its weaknesses. It is very time-consuming for managers to detail the requirements of a given job and therefore very expensive. On the other hand, each set of statements must be custom-developed for each position or set of positions within an organization; this insures that the evaluation criteria utilized will be relevant to the job being performed.

Another reason this approach has not been utilized widely is that it is based on the assumption that managers do not have the capacity to evaluate individuals

[4] Ibid, p. 514.

without injecting their own biases. This naturally makes them leery of using the method because it seems to indicate their inability to operate competently. Another problem is that the manager may not answer honestly, thinking he has figured out which statements will count and which won't. This problem revolves around the fact that it is extremely difficult to discuss the contents of the evaluation form with employees if the manager himself doesn't know what items are meaningful and which are not.

Critical Incidents

As mentioned in Chapter 1, an important function of the leisure service manager is the management of the critical interfaces that exist between the leisure service organization and various environmental subcomponents. The same could be said about any employee's job. There are a number of critical interfaces that each individual must direct her or his efforts toward to insure that the organization operates productively. The identification and evaluation of these critical interfaces is known as the "performance appraisal technique of critical incidents." Each job has a select number of critical job requirements. Once these have been determined, the next step is to analyze to what extent an individual organizational member has fulfilled these requirements. For each individual, the manager maintains a record of how the employee handles the critical requirements found in her or his job. There is no attempt in this approach to qualify the results in any way. The record of successes and failures of an individual serves as a basis for interaction between the manager and his or her subordinates.

   The strength of this approach to performance appraisal is that it allows the manager to utilize objective information. The manager can point out specific instances where an employee dealt with a given situation in a positive or negative manner. It allows the manager to appraise individuals based on actual observed activities rather than personality traits. The weakness of this method is that managers can become overly concerned with recording what people are doing. In a sense, this mechanism can create tension between a manager and his employees because they may perceive his record-taking activities as a way of maintaining a file on each of them.

Management by Objectives (MBO)

MBO is a results-oriented performance appraisal system that has evolved from the need to provide clear and more effective measures of evaluation. It is based on the notion that an employee should be appraised on what he does rather than his personality or position in the organization. MBO is based on the concept that managers and their subordinates can determine the outcomes or goals of a given job in relation to the overall goals of an organization. It involves identifying precisely the objectives to be accomplished by a given staff member during a specific period of time. Objectives are usually developed in such a way that they can be measured. The individual employee is then evaluated on his ability to achieve mutually agreed on objectives. For example, if an aquatic supervisor in a municipal park and recreation department wanted to improve the effectiveness of her operations, she might specifically design an objective that would allow her to increase the number of participants coming to her facility while at the same time stabilizing the cost of operating it. In this case the aquatic director and the manager might fix a specifically targeted increase of participants and stipulate that the cost of operation cannot increase over the previous year. Further, they might specifically delineate the step-by-step procedures necessary to achieve this objective. The acquatics supervisor would be appraised on her ability to achieve this objective.

The essence of MBO is that individual employees participate in the development of an appraisal program that is tailor-made to their specific job requirements and abilities. It is a mechanism that allows for two-way communication between individuals and managers. In this way the appraisal system is meaningful to the individual employee and is also tied to the needs of the organization. In addition, it allows an individual to concentrate on what is required of him or her in the future rather than what he or she has done in the past. A person's prior performance—which cannot be changed—is minimized, and the expectations for his future performance—which he can control—are maximized. The manager in this system changes her role from overseeing individuals to that of helping them, enabling them to achieve their individual objectives. Again, the emphasis of MBO is on performance rather than personality.

There are a number of problems in developing an MBO system. It is an extremely time-consuming and costly program to implement initially. It requires a wholesale change in thinking, moving from nonquantifiable appraisal into highly measurable performance indicators. Individual goal-setting can also be a misleading activity. All organizations have certain needs and goals, and it is folly to think that individuals can be turned loose without an effective way of controlling their activities. Usually, the goal-setting process in MBO starts from the top down and, therefore, reduces individual initiative in setting objectives.

Managers must be extremely careful not to manipulate individual employees involved in the objective-setting process. It must be a mutually subscribed to activity, which takes a lot of time and requires managers to shift their management style. Another problem is that not all factors in organizations can be measured statistically. Creativity is extremely hard to quantify, as is employee morale. Further, because of the heavy emphasis on statistics, organizations often become more concerned with quantity rather than quality.

In spite of its limitations, the MBO process, in the opinion of the authors, is an effective tool that can be used in the delivery of leisure services. It is a procedure that allows individuals to link their activities with the overall goals of an organization. It provides opportunities for people to have input into the activities of an organization and also be evaluated according to their efforts rather than their personality characteristics.

Conducting Evaluation Interviews

Regardless of the technique used in performance appraisal, the manager and subordinate should sit down and openly discuss the employee's evaluation. Appraisal is an opportunity for the employee to receive feedback and identify factors that can potentially improve performance. Evalution interviews, if structured properly, can be extremely useful mechanisms to help individuals improve themselves. On the other hand, if improperly conducted, they can serve to create tension and broaden the gap that exists between manager and employees. Strauss and Sayles developed a standardized procedure which can be utilized in an evaluation interview. The process is as follows:

1. The superior tells the subordinate the purpose of the interview, and that it is designed to help him do a better job.
2. The superior then presents the evaluation, giving the strong points first and then the weak points. (There is no reason why the superior has to show the entire evaluation to the subordinate, nor . . . does he have to be 100 percent frank about the subordinate's prospects.)
3. Next the superior asks for general comments on the evaluation. He anticipates that the subordinate may show some hostility to negative evaluations and allows him to blow off steam.
4. The superior then tries to encourage the subordinate to give his own picture of his progress, the problems he is meeting, and how these can be solved.
5. The interview ends with a discussion of what the subordinate can do by himself to overcome his weak points and what the superior can do to help. The superior tries to accept any criticism or aggression on the part of the subordinate without argument or contradiction. He helps the subordinate save face and does not expose his unjustified alibis.[5]

LABOR UNIONS

In 1976 the National Recreation and Park Association reported that 41 percent of municipal park and recreation departments in cities with populations from 10,000 to 500,000 and more had organized employee bargaining units. Although most of the union activity was concentrated among semiskilled and nonskilled employees, nearly 25 percent of the cities studies in this survey reported that professional employees were unionized.[6] The labor movement in North America is one of the most significant factors in society today. Labor unions have been formed to achieve economic reform wherever individuals are employed, whether in the free enterprise sector or in government. Increasingly, labor unions are playing a significant role in the organization of professional and nonprofessional workers in the leisure service field.

[5] Ibid., p. 517.
[6] Robert A. Lancaster, "Municipal Services," *Parks and Recreation, 2* (July 1976), p. 26.

Aims of Labor

Labor unions represent the collective interest of individuals and address themselves to many issues within the work environment. They exist primarily to improve the general welfare of those they represent. A union may try to improve employee wages, job security, fringe benefits, working conditions, and other related factors. Labor unions have played a key role in improving work conditions, especially in the area of higher wages and shorter work hours; the 40-hour week has its historical roots in the work of labor unions. Labor unions have also directed their attention to removing dangerous work hazards and improving other work conditions to create satisfactory work experiences.

The aims of labor can conflict with those of management. In business, the management role is to make a reasonable profit. In government, the management role is to effectively and efficiently provide services within the limits established by taxpayers. In many cases, the aims of labor can be in conflict with those of management in either businesses or government. A labor union tries to equalize the distribution of funds within an organization in such a way that its members receive a higher share of the organization's resources. Management, on the other hand, tries to minimize its cost by keeping labor costs at a reasonable level. The balance between the needs of labor and management is usually negotiated. It is important to understand these two differing perspectives because they can influence the manager's attitude toward working with labor unions. But this dual perspective can help insure that the best interests of the organization are represented.

Let us now examine some of the specifics regarding points of conflict between labor and management. The first is wages and fringe benefits. From a management point of view, wages are one of the costs incurred in the operation of the organization. As a result, the thrust of management is to hold down labor costs and also the costs of fringe benefits. If employee wages are too high, businesses will not achieve their profit target and government agencies run the risk of cutting into revenues that are necessary for other services. For labor, increased wages and fringe benefits are merely a way of dividing the resources of an organization in an equitable manner. Labor unions suggest that increasing employees' wages helps stimulate the economy as well as improve employee morale and job satisfaction.

Another point of conflict revolves around how jobs are structured. Because of the way that many jobs are organized and/or tasks subdivided within an organization, individuals find them of little challenge or interest. Management seeks to find efficient ways of structuring jobs, especially through specialization. In many cases this results in jobs that are monotonous, routine, and boring. Labor unions seek to have management organize its work in such a way that it is less frustrating to employees.

Another point of conflict is that which relates to hiring practices and job tenure. When management is faced with declining revenues, its first concern is to reduce costs. Labor unions seek to control the retrenchment plans of businesses and government in an effort to protect the security of those they represent. Closely related to the concept of retrenchment due to economic factors is the reduction of personnel due to technological innovation. Again, if management can reduce its costs by using a new technological process, personnel may be cut from the organization. Labor unions try to regulate the effects of technology on employee hiring and retirement policies.

The last point of conflict between management and labor deals with the everyday exchanges that take place between managers and their subordinates. Labor unions are concerned that their employees are treated with respect and dignity and not viewed merely as economic commodities.

Collective Bargaining

Once a group of employees has designated a union as their representative agency, this union may negotiate a contract with an organization. The discussions that take place between a union and an organization are known as "collective bargaining." Typically, the union will make its demands for wages, fringe benefits, and so on, and the organization will then make counteroffers. The two groups will discuss these proposals and try to come to some sort of agreement. If there is no agreement, a union may call for a strike. In this case, union workers refuse to continue to work and attempt to discourage other employees from working. Should labor and management still be unable to reach agreement, they may submit to mediation. In this case, an individual who is agreeable to both parties is appointed to help the sides resolve their problems. Usually, a mediator is called in prior to a strike.

Grievances

An important part of the relationship that exists between an organization and a labor union consists of the mechanisms used to settle disputes. When a labor contract has been violated by an organization—more specifically, when an individual feels he has been wronged—a grievance may be filed. A grievance is simply a method of suggesting that the organization has not lived up to its contractual abilities. In the usual process, an individual discusses the problem with his superior and union representative. If there is no solution to the problem at this point, the individual may ask for a meeting of the union's grievance committee and the organization's representatives. If this meeting does not resolve the issue to the employee's satisfaction, an arbitrator may be called in to settle the matter. An arbitrator's action is legally binding on both parties.

Working with Unions

Many individuals in management positions today view unions in a negative manner. It is the opinion of the authors that managers should work more closely with unions and try to establish a relationship that will benefit both parties. Unions increase an organization's accountability. They make management responsible for the welfare of individual employees, while at the same time insuring that employees are responsible for fulfilling their contractual obligations. Managers should strive for a solution to labor conflicts that allow the organization to maximize its goals while at the same time providing equitable employee work conditions. It is important to recognize that satisfied employees are more productive employees. Without giving away the rights of management, individual administrators can work with labor unions in such a way that they benefit the organization. Managers should strive for a "win-win" solution to labor problems, one that allows the needs of the organization as well as the needs of employees to be met.

CIVIL SERVICE SYSTEMS

Most leisure service organizations that are part of a government agency are under some form of civil service system. These systems were established as a result of the political nature of employment practices in government organizations. It was not uncommon in past years for an elected official to hire friends or relatives for government jobs. In an attempt to eliminate this practice, civil service boards, commissions, and agencies were established. These bodies set forth rules and regulations that govern the employment, administration, and dismissal of government employees. Many of the concepts to be covered in this section were previously discussed in this chapter. However, in civil service systems these concepts have been formalized into rules and regulations approved by a legislative body, thereby making them administratively mandatory. The establishment of civil service systems has minimized the political pressures associated with hiring practices in government organizations. In other words, it has reduced political patronage, cronyism, and nepotism.

The goals and objectives of the Sunnyvale, California, civil service system are as follows:

1. Obtain and retain the best qualified personnel available for service;
2. Assure that appointments and promotions are made according to merit and fitness, to be ascertained, so far as practicable, by competitive examination; and
3. Assure, through formal appeal provisions, that disciplinary actions or separations from service are consistent with the best interests of the city.

Civil Service Boards

Most civil service systems have a board that establishes rules and regulations for the system's operation. In addition, the board may receive appeals from employees who feel that, after following normal grievance procedures, they have been treated unjustly. Some boards do not have policymaking authority, but instead serve in an advisory capacity to the governing body regarding personnel rules and regulations. Boards vary in size, commonly having from three to seven members. These individuals are usually appointed for a fixed term of two to four years by a legislative body.

Many civil service systems establish two categories of employees: classified and unclassified. Unclassified employees include individuals serving as elected officials, members of boards and commissions, top administrators, department heads, and casual or temporary workers. These individuals are not under the jurisdiction of the civil service system, whereas classified employees would be. Classified employees would include individuals actually engaged in the delivery of services, for instance, full-time recreation leaders, program coordinators, park laborers, park foremen, and recreation supervisors.

Recruitment

In the recruitment process, the civil service regulations usually require that general standards be set forth regarding the level of education, experience, ability, and personal and physical characteristics that are required to perform a specific job. Generally, prior to a job being filled, a job description is prepared in accordance with the rules and regulations set by the civil service system. Today most civil service systems have an affirmative action program for hiring that sets forth employment goals which reflect the demographic composition of the community. Additional information relative to affirmative action programs will be given later in this chapter.

Also covered under recruiting procedures are the minimum standards employees have to meet, such as minimum age requirements, ability to pass a medical examination, and legitimate reasons for disqualification of applications. Under disqualification of applications are such factors as failure to meet minimum standards, addiction to intoxicating beverages or narcotics, conviction of a felony, false statements made on the application, and other factors that would designate an employee as a poor risk.

Civil service systems often have other rules, such as nepotism rules that prohibit the agency from employing relatives of employees, city council members, or board or commission members. A civil service system may also have prescribed methods for soliciting applications, indicating how long in advance the organization must advertise a given position before examination(s) and filling of the position.

Examinations

Various types of examinations are given as part of the selection process in filling vacancies in civil service organizations. They consist of the filed applications, written examinations, oral examinations, and interviews, or a combination of these. Various civil service organizations weigh and grade components of the examination procedure differently. Some place more weight on the written examination, others place more weight on the oral interview. Whatever the procedure, the ultimate goal is to establish an eligibility list to provide the best qualified candidates for the position and eliminate favoritism. Some civil service systems also provide credit for veterans who have served in the armed forces, giving them special consideration when filing for examinations.

Eligibility Lists

Once the examination process has been completed, most civil service organizations establish an eligibility list that provides the names of the candidates with the highest qualifications for a position. Different civil service systems have different procedures regarding the number of persons placed on an eligibility list; most have three to five names. The hiring department may then hire anyone on the list of names. Some civil service systems require that the first person on the list be hired, unless it can be shown that a person lower on the eligibility list is more suitable for the job. In any case, the person ranking highest on the eligibility list is supposedly the best qualified person for the position. Usually, eligibility lists are in effect for one year before they expire. Then a new eligibility list is established by the procedures just described if there are vacancies for the position.

Appointments

Once a person is selected from the eligibility list, she or he is appointed to a position for six months to one year, on a probationary basis. During this period of time, the employer has the opportunity to evaluate the capabilities of the employee and determine whether she or he is going to work out satisfactorily in the particular position. During the probationary period, the employee is evaluated carefully so that at the end of the probationary period a determination can be made whether to appoint him or her to a regular position. Once appointed to a regular position, the employee has the protection of the civil service system. Generally, an employee can be terminated during the probationary period without much difficulty. But once the employee obtains a regular appointment, it is difficult to terminate him or her except for serious cause and with a great deal of documentation.

Performance

Most civil service systems prescribe a method for evaluating employees, which is standardized throughout the organization. The system sets forth performance standards, methods of evaluation, a rating system, and other relative guidelines that regulate and standardize the evaluation procedure. Usually the evaluation system is utilized when selecting employees for advancement and laying off employees during slow work periods; it is also used as a basis for termination in the case of poor performance.

Separation

Employees leave positions for many reasons. They may resign after a number of years of service to take an early retirement or to accept a job with another agency. Separation procedures are outlined in a civil service system's rules and regulations. Outlined in detail, they delineate the criteria for laying off employees and for dismissing employees in the classified positions. In most civil service systems, dismissal procedures are quite specific, outlining in great detail procedures that must be followed to dismiss an employee and the basis for dismissal.

Grievance Procedures

Most civil service systems outline a grievance procedure for employees who feel they have been treated unfairly. The procedures set forth indicate what action the employee can take to file a grievance, as well as the responses and time frame the employer must adhere to when responding to an employee's grievance. Usually, the matter will come before a personnel board for final hearing and decision if all the channels of communication within the department in which the employee works have been exhausted. Depending on the particular civil service system, other items may be covered in the grievance procedure in order to protect the employee as well as the governing agency and to guarantee a fair procedure for both.

Other Items Under Civil Service

Such things as military leave procedures, reinstatement of employees, methods for keeping personnel records, and personnel training procedures may also be covered under civil service. Whatever the system, its intent is to bring integrity and consistency into the methods and procedures of personnel administration.

AFFIRMATIVE ACTION PROGRAMS

Within the past ten years there have been attempts in the United States and Canada to eliminate discrimination, which occurs in spite of the principles set forth in the U.S. Constitution and the British North American Act. Equal opportunity employment for minorities, the handicapped, and women has often not been upheld. This failure has resulted in the passage of specific legislation that demands positive action, often referred to as "affirmative action programs." The Equal Employment Opportunity Commission established by the U.S. Congress also sets forth guidelines and laws to assure equal opportunity. Many states, likewise, have established a fair practices commissions to assure equal opportunity of employment.

Although merit-based civil service systems theoretically should be consistent with equal opportunity employment and affirmative action principles, they do not always achieve equality. As a result, some local governments are establishing affirmative action programs to assure positive direction within government agencies, toward an equal-for-all base. Within the last few years, many suits have been brought against government agencies that have not followed fair employment practices. Injunctions and court orders that spell out the actions which government agencies must take to correct inadequacies in their approach to fair employment have been handed down. Some court actions have dictated that all jobs in a particular agency are to be filled by minority persons until a minimum quota has been filled in order to realign the employment ratio to closely approximate the demographic makeup of the community.

In addition, employees who feel they have been discriminated against on the job now have procedures for filing grievances, not only with their agencies, but with state and federal governments as well. Employees filing grievances, in many instances, have won their cases and have been reemployed when fired, reinstated when demoted, and even promoted after being passed over when discrimination has been proved. In some cases, employees have been given back pay for the period of time they were discriminated against. In any event, affirmative action is an integral part of the leisure service movement and will affect its methods of employment and promotion in the present and future.

TRAINING

Training is essentially the responsibility of the employee's immediate superior. Although many managers recognize that training within their organizations is an important component, little time is invested, proportionately, in this area. Training—for one reason or another—has taken on an unfavorable image. For a great number of people, training has been thought of as an unpleasant task to organize and a process to be endured.

Productive leisure service managers recognize that training can be a valuable organizational tool. They are aware that training can increase performance and create opportunities for individual employees' growth. The productive manager will set aside organizational resources that can be invested in the training process. Essentially, organizational inputs in terms of the training process will increase employee output. Training is a process with which organizations can enable their employees to operate more effectively and efficiently. It can, and should, be viewed as a positive force within an organization, a mechanism that can be beneficial in meeting the individual needs of employees as well as the goals of an organization.

What Is Training?

Training should not be viewed as an end in itself. It is a process that enables an organization to reach certain ends or goals. The formal procedures utilized in a training program can facilitate employee development. Training is undertaken to produce behavior that will contribute to the attainment of an organization's goals and objectives. Therefore we define training as *a process that organizations utilize to change employee behavior,* which contributes to the overall mission of the organization and the personal and professional growth of the persons involved.

Training helps organizations in many ways. It reduces organizational costs by reducing the amount of time necessary to orient a new employee to the job environment. Training helps an organization deal with its inexperienced employees by providing them with knowledge and skills that enable them to perform at an optimum level within a short period of time. It also reduces the losses that occur because of waste in the production of services; training helps an organization make better use of its resources by minimizing wasted human energy, materials, and supplies. Training programs are generally viewed by employees as being supportive in nature. Finally, training helps improve the delivery of services to consumers in that many suggestions for improving the creation, management, and distribution of activities, facilities, and information are offered during training sessions. Therefore not only do employees benefit from the training process, but so do those who consume services.

Training programs can fail for a number of reasons. Among the more significant is the refusal of management to accept the responsibility for developing and implementing training activities. The process of training cannot be undertaken on an ad hoc basis. It must be thoroughly planned and well thought out because it represents an investment of an organization's resources. Failure by managers to develop clear guidelines that are well integrated with an organization's goals results in chaos.

Determining Training Needs

To determine what training procedures are required, an organization must undergo an analysis of itself and its subcomponents. First, it must determine what it is trying to do. The content of any training program must be linked to the tasks that are to be completed by an organization. There should be an understanding of the relationship that can potentially exist between a given training program and the tasks or assignments within an organization. Next, the organization must determine exactly what skills, knowledge, or attitudes an individual employee must have in the performance of a given job. In other words, both the operations of an organization (i.e., the tasks that are to be performed) and the individuals within the organization must be analyzed. In this way, the organization is able to fuse together the jobs as it has designed them and the individual skills of employees. Determining needs simply involves fitting these two components together.

Once an organization has analysed its operation and its employee needs, it must determine who within the organization is going to be responsible for a training program. Large organizations have formal training departments. In smaller organizations, the training function is the responsibility of various staff members. In either situation, an organization must assign to someone the authority to carry out training activities. Again, many training efforts fail because there is not a well thought out plan that provides for training activities.

An important factor in the concept of training involves educating employees to recognize the benefit of training. Individuals learn much more effectively if they are motivated toward some goals that they feel are attainable and meaningful. In Chapter 4, we discussed the theoretical concepts involved in motivating people. These concepts obviously apply to the training process. The question centers on how to get individuals moving toward the achievement of training goals and have them recognize the benefits of an organizational training program. A number of positive steps can be taken by the leisure service manager regarding this. First, she or he can spell out the goals of the training program by documenting its specific objectives and identifying the procedures necessary to carry them out. Next, the manager can show employees how they can directly benefit from a training program. It might be demonstrated that jobs are made easier, that employees may grow within the system by taking advanced training which will lead to higher-level jobs, that consumers are better served if employees increase their technological competence, and so on. Finally, the manager can demonstrate to individuals that a training program can contribute to their needs and goals. By developing a new skill or improving an existing one, individuals will feel a sense of achievement and, as a result, increase their job satisfaction.

A number of organizational activities can be taken into consideration when designing a training program. These factors may be considered jointly or addressed singularly. They assist the manager in analyzing the organization's training needs. They include the following:

1. *Identify the process, operation, or task around which a training program is to be developed.* This involves breaking down the activities of a given job. The

task of the manager is to identify these components and analyze the specific activities for which a training program is to be developed. For example, the procedures involved in leading a recreation activity in a social setting can be broken down and placed in a pattern. In this instance, the pattern would probably involve first comer activities, mixers, active games, and end with passive games. The idea is that the social recreation program can be broken into a sequential pattern and training activities developed to deal with each segment. The same can be true for a maintenance procedure or for the operation of a sports activity.

2. *Identify the equipment or facilities necessary in the implementation of a leisure service program.* This process is similar to the first process and in many cases is done concurrently. When an organization buys a new piece of equipment, it cannot be assumed that the staff has all the necessary skills to operate it. When a new facility is developed, it is necessary to identify the equipment within that facility and train people in its uses. Equipment may also be modified, and this calls for training. One of the key elements discussed in earlier sections of this book was the rate of technological change and its impact on organizations. The rate at which new equipment (e.g., swimming pool filtration systems) is being produced in the leisure service field is staggering.

3. *Identify problems within the organization that affect its ability to operate productively.* All organizations are confronted with conflicts. Leisure delivery systems are not free from the day-to-day problems that might emerge as a result of poor management. By isolating these problems, especially operational problems, training programs can be developed to help the manager and his or her staff solve them. For example, the problem of poor public relations in an organization could be traced by analyzing the strategies used. One might consider how the receptionist greets people at the door, how staff members answer the phone, and how information is disseminated to the public. Once the problem areas have been isolated, a training program may be implemented to equip staff with the necessary skills to improve the organization's public image. For example, staff members may be instructed in a procedure for answering the telephone, or it might be stipulated that newspaper articles be written in accord with a specific format and require approval prior to distribution. A training program can be established to help identify problems and correct deficiencies.

4. *Identify individual behaviors that require modification.* Opportunity for growth and development of individual employees is an important concern of all responsible organizations. Training programs can be established to provide individuals with insights into their behavior. Further, training programs can be established to deal with antiorganizational forms of individual behavior. Such behavior can be a serious problem for the organization. It often occurs because

an individual has a poor self-image, a poor understanding of the organization's goals, or a lack of ability to relate well to others. Training programs can be instituted to provide individuals with an opportunity to analyze themselves in relation to other individuals and also to the organization.

5. *Identify organizational problems.* Poor organizational design can weaken the effectiveness and efficiency of a leisure delivery system. In Chapter 5, we discussed numerous ways leisure delivery systems can be organized. A given organizational design is utilized to achieve specific goals. One goal may be to see that employees experience job satisfaction. Absenteeism, high turnover, and uneven distribution of work loads are problems that may occur as a result of poor organizational design and are linked to job satisfaction. Essentially, the manager may ask himself and the organization, "Are there better ways to organize the activities of our department?" Once the problems have been identified, a training program may be developed to explain how the new design may be implemented. Changing from a classical bureaucratic structure to a systems design (e.g., modular organization) may require a good deal of new information for employees; a host of new relationships will be developed, and there will be a need for understanding the significance of these changes.

6. *Identify ways to measure and improve performance.* The appraisal of performance within organizations is an important task. Every organization establishes mechanisms to control its activities. These mechanisms insure that the organization is accountable for the expenditure of resources. Training programs can be developed in two areas of performance measurement. The first is in the utilization of existing mechanisms of control. An organization may use a cost/benefit analysis to measure the relationship between its financial expenditures and its service program. Training in the implementation of this type of approach to measuring performance would insure consistency in its application throughout the entire delivery system. The second area in which training may take place is the development of new and/or more appropriate mechanisms of measuring performance. In many training sessions, the exploration of new ideas has led to more effective and efficient ways of measuring performance. Again, the training of individuals in this area may be done jointly with other types of training.

Types of Training

There are three types of training: orientation, or preservice training; in-service training; and developmental training.

Orientation or Preservice Training

This type of training is directed toward providing a new employee with the necessary knowledge, skills, and attitudes to perform a function with an organization prior to actual placement in the work environment. This may involve instructing a new person in the specific requirements of the job. The training may simulate the actual work experience. A person who will be required to operate a riding lawn mower on the job may be instructed in the operation of a nonrunning mower—a dry run, so to speak.

Orientation training may also involve indoctrination of a new staff member in the philosophy of the organization. A person may be required to discuss the policies of an organization with an appropriate staff member. Discussion may also involve employee benefits, work hours, uniform requirements, payroll distribution, and other related matters. Indoctrination is perhaps one of the most important areas of employee training and also often one of the most neglected.

Finally, orientation usually involves introduction of the new staff member to the work environment and co-workers. Basic to the experience of being a new employee is the element of uncertainty. She or he is faced with unfamiliar surroundings and people. The point of this type of orientation training is to allow the person to become comfortable in the environment. In many cases, this can involve even the trivial elements of a new job (e.g., where to obtain office supplies, how to use the phone). This training takes the edge off the employee's impending uncertainty about his or her new job.

Why is orientation (preservice) training important? Primarily, this type of training represents the employee's first contact, thus his first impression of the organization. This impression will most likely be a lasting one, and it is to an organization's advantage to make it a favorable one. Certainly, the attitudes that are developed during this initial period of time will be pronounced and will affect to a certain extent the long-term success of an individual within an organization. Each new person should be viewed as part of the team of the organization. After all, everyone in an organization was a new staff member at one time. People should be made to feel comfortable and be encouraged to become an active and productive member within the mainstream of the organization. Orientation training facilities this activity.

In-Service Training

Once a person joins an organization, her need for training continues. It cannot be assumed that a person has been given all the information she needs during the initial training period, or that she ceases to grow professionally. There are three types of in-service training. The first type revolves around the mandatory training required with new technological advances, the second type concerns the reinforcement and expansion of the initial training, and the third type is developmental training to enable individuals to expand their knowledge and abilities.

Technological advancements in society have a dramatic effect on the delivery of leisure services. Leisure service organizations are continually being approached by companies with new products and services that change or modify the nature of professional practice. To keep up with these technological advancements, staff members must receive training. When a new product is introduced, corresponding knowledge and skills must be acquired by members of an organization to use it effectively. The new advancement may require proficiency in a technical skill (e.g., conversion from hand shears to an electric hedge trimmer), or it may involve the acquisition of new cognitive information (e.g., the use of network analysis in construction projects).

The second type of in-service training is the reinforcement and expansion of the initial training. It is extremely difficult for a manager to cover all the areas necessary in the orientation of a new employee. As a result, training must be spread out over a period of time. It is shortsighted to think that an individual will have the ability to cover and retain, during the orientation period, all the material relating to his job. Further, the manager may lack sufficiently large blocks of time to give proper orientation training.

Initial training should be reinforced for two reasons. First, individuals will not retain all the information presented during the initial orientation training; it may be necessary to reiterate some of this information. Second, training is undertaken to elicit certain types of behavior or responses. To insure that employees exhibit certain kinds of behavior, the manager uses in-service training to reinforce organizational ideals. In other words, employees can stray from the goals of the organization. By continually discussing the direction of the organization in light of employee's needs, an organization becomes more productive.

Leisure service organizations are dynamic institutions, responding to the changes that occur in society. These changes may be reflected in the adoption of new organizational policies and procedures. In-service training in this area is crucial. As organizations assume new directions, their human resources should be brought in line with the changes. Primarily, this type of training revolves around the discussion of new programs and the mechanisms that are to be used to provide them. For example, one of the more dramatic changes in the provision of public leisure services has been the expansion of sports programs for women. Such a change affects policy within a given leisure organization, necessitating the acquisition of new skills, knowledge, and attitudes on the part of staff.

Developmental Training

Developmental training is a long-range program that helps individuals realize their potential for growth. It is directed toward improving work performance by providing individuals with an opportunity to expand their personal knowledge, skills, and ability. It emphasizes individual growth by allowing individuals to fully realize as much of their own potential as a given learning environment will allow. Edginton and Eldredge write that developmental training allows people to expand their individual abilities and capacities and help them satisfy their needs for growth. They state:

Individuals have a need to satisfy intrinsic and extrinsic values. Intrinsic aspects of work relate to the need for personal fulfillment, recognition, self-enhancement, responsibility, and self-esteem. Extrinsic needs include financial remuneration and work conditions. People are motivated by each of these elements and if they are provided with an opportunity to take advantage of either set, job satisfaction should result. This is especially true when extrinsic needs are met and an individual can move towards satisfying his intrinsic needs. Opportunities for individual growth and development obviously go hand in hand with both sets. A developmental training program which allows an individual to realize potential, will contribute to the growth and development of one's abilities and capabilities, adding to the satisfaction of intrinsic and extrinsic values.

Individuals, in order to be proficient in fulfilling their designated role, should improve and enhance their professional knowledge, skills, and attitudes. The area of knowledge involves acquiring those intellectual concepts and techniques which can enhance their performance. Park and recreation managers are far too often anti-intellectual in their approach to acquiring contemporary management knowledge and information. This deprivation retards the park and recreation movement. Skills involve the "doing" or direct application of conceptual knowledge. Examples of skills important to park and recreation managers could include: communicating, motivating, problem-solving, etc. Application of one's value system to the work environment is reflected in one's attitudes. Affecting an individual's self identity, his ability to accept and share responsibility, and influence other people, the development of an individual's attitudes is an important component of a developmental training program.[7]

Concerning the key concepts of a developmental training program, they also write:

Developmental training is a "long-range" training program whereas orientation and in-service training programs usually satisfy short-term or immediate objectives. Commitment to the development of an individual takes place over an extended period, and should be viewed as a cyclic process which is continuous. Short-term objectives are continuously recycled until the broader goals (maximizing human potential) are realized. As this process essentially has no end, developmental training is a program which, once initiated, continues until organizational goals are achieved rather than the actual ultimate maximization of an individual's potential for growth.

Developmental training rests upon the assumption that management on the whole, is responsible for providing a non-coersive supportive work atmosphere. This involves giving "active support" to employees. Active support and its resulting climate, is distinguishable from acceptance or approval, in that it leads to the development of trust, loyalty and confidence between a manager and his subordinates. This relationship is necessary to allow an individual to expose his or her weaknesses, in order that the growth process can take place.

[7] Christopher R. Edginton and Robert E. Eldredge, Developmental Training: Methods and Procedures for Your Department—Part 1," *Park Maintenanance* 28 (August 1975), pp. 12–13. Used with permission of Park Maintenance Magazine, Box 1936, Appleton, Wisconsin.

A negative environment is one in which individuals spend time attempting to placate one another, rather than actively acknowledging each other's feelings and thoughts. It is important to recognize that each person is an individual with genuine interests and needs. Merely approving or accepting one's point of view usually results in closed communication prior to actually discovering the basis for a person's point of view or need.

As mentioned, developmental training must focus on the needs and concerns of each individual. Since no two people are alike, the same training procedures, methods, and techniques cannot be employed to develop any two individuals.

It is important to recognize that external forces do not necessarily modify behavior. An individual's behavior is internally modified. Developmental training only provides an opportunity which may, or may not, facilitate behavior modification in an individual. As the modification of behavior is an individual matter, the ability of a manager to perceive individual differences and capabilities, and accordingly plan, is essential. Further, when an individual recognizes a need for development, it may be self-induced and self-sustained. Although a program may result from external forces outside an individual, development can be carried through a person's own efforts informally or formally.

Developmental training focuses on an individual's ability to perform a given task or assignment, rather than on his or her personality. Too often, employees . . . [are] . . . provided . . . [with] . . . opportunities for growth because their particular personality traits are complementary to those of their superior. Many competent individuals have been summarily sacrificed because a park and recreation director was more interested in promoting a social relationship, than a professional one.

As all individuals within an organization have the ability to contribute or detract from organizational goals, developmental training should be universal. Staff and line positions, full time and part-time personnel, can all be given the opportunity to achieve their growth potential. It seems critically important that more attention be given by park and recreation departments to the development of those individuals actually delivering services. The essence of any park and recreation department is found in the services which it delivers to the public. Hence, the public's impression of a park and recreation department results, in part, from those individuals actually offering services. The majority of these people are part-time people who are fortunate to have orientation training, let alone developmental training. These individuals who have a major impact on the success or failure of organizational goals, are forgotten when it comes to training. Although many employees are with an organization only a short period of time, it seems essential to create opportunities which allow for individual growth and hence contribute to the achievement of organizational goals.

Developmental training should . . . [enhance] . . . an individual's current work assignment, rather than focusing primarily upon training a person for promotion. The immediate thrust of a developmental program should be directed toward improvement of current work performance. Directing a person's attention away from his present job situation, in many cases, results in an erosion of work performance. It is desirable to continually broaden an individual's horizons, however not at the expense of his present work assignment.[8]

---

[8] Ibid., pp. 13, 16–17.

Training Objectives

Training can be viewed as purposeful activity that is directed toward producing changes in behavior among an organization's employees. As a result, it is extremely desirable to be able to measure the effects of a training program on individuals participating in it. This can be accomplished by establishing training objectives for each training activity.

Objectives are desired ends which when translated into written statements, may be observed and measured. In a training program, they are written in terms of the type of behavior that the participant is to produce or demonstrate at the end of the program. They are not written in terms of what the manager is to do; instead, they are written in terms of how the employee is to act, what he is to know, and what skills he is to demonstrate. This approach allows the manager to separate what she does from what she expects employees to accomplish as a result of a training program. Simply, this allows the manager to emphasize behavioral changes in people and to measure these changes and even predict potential behavioral changes as a result of the intervention of a training activity.

How does the manager write training objectives for employees within an organization? Four factors must be taken into consideration in developing objectives. The objectives should be written for the employee in terms of (1) desired knowledge and actions, (2) the manner in which he/she is expected to demonstrate the specific behavior required of him/her, (3) the special conditions that may affect the acquisition or demonstration of a specific type of behavior, and (4) the minimum level of acceptable achievement for his/her demonstration of a given type of behavior.

The first step in the process of writing objectives is to state the terminal behavior expected. It is usually desirable to use an action verb to describe what is to be done or known. The second step is to identify, for the employee, exactly how the behavior should be demonstrated. It is extremely important to remember that employees must exhibit a type of behavior that can be seen so their performance can be measured. It is difficult, if not impossible, to measure a behavioral change that takes place mentally within an individual. Determining the special conditions that may inhibit or aid an individual in the acquisition of a skill is the third step in the process. Fourth, the process delineates how well the behavior is to be demonstrated, this involves the determination of a minimum level of achievement. Speed, accuracy, quality, and quantity are dimensions that can be measured.

In conclusion, identification of objectives can help the manager to understand the behavioral outcomes that are expected to occur as a result of a training program. Utilizing objectives allows a manager to increase an organization's accountability and, hence, increase its productivity. Objectives emphasize behavioral outcomes in employees (actual achievement) rather than the processes that are utilized by managers.

Training and the Learning Process

Training activities are directed toward helping individuals change themselves. It is important to remember that only individuals themselves can initiate responsiveness to the learning/training process. Training creates the opportunity for people to change themselves by providing certain types of experiences that facilitate growth. As such, training should be viewed as an individualized process that helps an employee acquire the skills, knowledge, and attitudes necessary for her or him to be more productive on the job.

Learning may be defined as a relatively permanent change in behavior. This infers that there will be an observable change in a person's behavior as he gains, acquires, and/or modifies his knowledge, skills, and/or attitudes. A number of factors determine the amount an individual will learn and the rate at which he will learn. The environment is one of these factors. It consists of a variety of stimuli—sounds, objects, people, and so on. There are two types of stimuli within the environment that affect learning: nominal stimuli and functional stimuli. Nominal stimuli are those many factors scattered within the environment that an individual *could* be experiencing (i.e., has the potential to experience) but, because there is a lack of focus toward these stimuli, they are not necessarily attended to. In other words, it is happenstance if the individual notices and/or gains information from these stimuli. Functional stimuli are the stimuli that the individual is *in fact* experiencing.

The role of the manager is to structure the environment to insure that a person focuses on certain stimuli. The training process is used as a method of drawing an individual's attention to a given set of circumstances within the environment in order to bring about a change in that individual's behavior. The manager provides training to insure that an individual focuses on a particular set of information (functional stimuli). Learning, then, occurs within the individual during the training process. Productive training results in individual behavior changes that the process has been structured to achieve.

Learning may be seen as occurring in a cyclical manner, that is, there are certain steps an individual may go through in order to modify her behavior. This does not imply, however, that all individuals experience this same process all the time. Further, it does not mean that training environments cannot be structured in such a way as to modify this cycle to facilitate the learning process. In the process of acquiring a new skill, attitude, and/or knowledge, the following learning cycle takes place:

1. *Concern.* When initially confronted with new stimuli, an individual may express concern with his ability to cope with it. Because this is the first exposure that a person may have with a new idea or concept (or even with the organization as a whole), it is vital for the manager to alleviate this initial concern and create a supportive climate. This allows an individual to express

his curiosity without fear of embarrassment. This initial impression may set the stage for the entire learning procedure and mark the success or failure of same.

2. *Frustration.* Once a concept has been presented to an individual, she may have some difficulty in understanding and/or mastering it. Basically, frustration results from a feeling of being helpless and overwhelmed. This could be caused in part by an unsupportive climate in that the individual has no resources to turn to to help her learn. If an individual receives too much information in rapid succession, unclear information, or information unsuited to her skills and ability to understand, she will likely become frustrated. Sometimes the learning cycle stops at this point and is blocked permanently.

3. *Confusion.* Confusion occurs when a person receives new information that conflicts with information he has learned already, or when he receives two sets of information that conflict with each other. The manager has some amount of control over this factor in that he can screen the information presented for obvious conflicts, clouding, and disorganization. On the other hand, the manager may want to present conflicting statements as a method of stimulating intellectual growth and problem-solving.

4. *Exploration.* Once two conflicting pieces of information have been discovered, the next step in the learning cycle is to explore the structures of the conflicting information. If a manager or an employee is fairly regimented in his or her particular viewpoint, exploration is especially necessary to open up the possibility of alternative propositions. A possibility in this instance might be to say, "we've run this operation the same way for the last 25 years; however, since you presented your new proposal, I think I can visualize it as an alternative to our present method." Thus, the person (manager and/or employee) in this case has mentally explored the possibility of an alternative method of operation. Therefore it might be inferred that this individual has the ability to modify or change his behavior.

5. *Discovery.* This is the process of allowing an individual to find solutions to problems freely. Discovery is the creative part of the learning process or the learning cycle. It occurs when the individual has learned to weigh the alternatives and find a solution, or a new alternative, to a problem. The role of the manager in this portion of the cycle is to guide the individual in the discovery process. Guiding individuals can be seen as existing on a continuum. The more information given a person, the more guidance necessary. The less guidance, the more actual discovery. Obviously, a balance between the two is needed, depending on the individual's experience, level of sophistication within her field, and personality qualities.

6. *Integration.* This is the final step in the learning cycle. It implies that the individual has integrated the new material in such a way that he has modified his behavior. The individual is able to demonstrate the acquisition of new

knowledge, skills, or attitudes by consistently demonstrating them in his behavior. In other words, he has completed the process of learning.

A number of conditions must be present for effective learning to take place. First, the material presented must have some meaning to the individual and the training process; it must be relevant. The content and substance must be concrete and relatively easy to grasp. Second, there must be a supportive social climate surrounding the manager and those being trained. Situations that produce adverse feelings between people are not conducive to good training. It cannot be a we-they type of environment. Third, there must be open and honest, hence effective, two-way communication. Training is essentially the process of developing people and, as such, there must be opportunities for individuals to explore and test their ideas and feelings. Fourth, there must be an understanding of the principles of learning as they apply to the training process.

Calvin Otto and Rollin Glaser, who integrated the concept of learning with the process of training, identify nine principles that can be used as guidelines in the training process. The following is a list of the nine principles, each accompanied by our discussion of it:

1. *People learn by what they do.* This principle suggests that individuals are influenced greatly by their own actions. Therefore it is extremely important for individuals to learn proper methods and procedures. Once an individual has learned an incorrect method and/or procedure, he is likely to retain this skill as taught, even though it may be in error. It is necessary to remember, when establishing a training program, that there are adequate ways to reinforce appropriate skills and knowledge. It is wrong to assume that a person will learn a correct response simply by the process of discovery. It is not effective and efficient to perpetuate the trial & error philosophy of learning over an extended period of time.

2. *People learn more effectively when they are reinforced immediately.* Training sessions often fail because they do not provide adequate mechanisms for feedback from employees. We all have endured unimaginative training activities that were essentially one-way processes of communication. This is not an effective way of having people learn. There must be opportunities for immediate feedback and reinforcement if effective learning is to take place. By rewarding individuals for their ability to learn new concepts and material, a training program can be greatly enhanced. We recommend that positive rewards of reinforcement, rather than negative ones, be utilized. Training programs should be arranged in such a manner that feedback and immediate reinforcement become an integral part of the training process.

3. *People learn more effectively when correct responses are rewarded frequently.* Not only should a reinforcement be immediate, but it should also be frequent. Reinforcement can increase the retention of material. Feedback should

initially be fairly continuous, scaling down to intermittent reinforcement. Eventually, the individual being trained should develop her own internally generated reward system for performance. At this point, the manager need only act as a resource person and provide reinforcement to the individual occasionally, as indicated by her performance.

4. *Training an individual in a variety of settings will increase the range of situations in which the individual may function with the learned skills.* One of the goals of training is the transfer of knowledge from the training session to the work environment. Training programs that provide an opportunity for an individual to experience a range of different settings/experiences are more successful in terms of equipping an individual to cope professionally in a variety of situations. It is hoped that, by equipping individuals with certain skills in the training program, they will be able to apply this general knowledge to unique problems that can occur in their jobs. For example, the authors have served as National Recreation and Park Association (NRPA) interns for approximately a year, respectively. During this period, the training program was structured to provide the intern with an opportunity to see and be involved in nearly all facets of a community recreation department's activities. Some of the opportunities included working with community groups, acting as a leader, supervising a lighted schoolhouse program, attending board meetings, working in maintenance operations, and being involved in various professional activities. This particular internship training program is directed toward equipping individuals with the skills to cope with and operate in many different situations and represents the optimum in training programs, enabling an individual to transfer learning from one situation to another.

5. *The climate created by a manager's motivational efforts will affect the acquisition of desired behaviors.* In this book, we have stressed motivation as a key to managerial responsibility by devoting an entire chapter to it. The training environment represents a setting wherein the principles of motivation outlined in Chapter 4 can be applied. The critical element to recognize is that the type of motivational techniques used by a manager can have a great impact on a person's ability to learn. For example, individuals can be motivated primarily by reward, in the form of approval, from their superiors. This approach can result in a positive motivational climate. On the other hand, individuals can be motivated by threat or punishment. This approach may result in a negative motivational climate. Another way to motivate people includes the creation of a climate that allows for curiosity, stressing the opportunity for individuals to explore their own abilities and the environment. It is important for the manager to recognize that both positive and negative forms of motivation will reinforce learning. Negative motivation, however, will in the long run produce such undesirable side effects as frustration, feelings of aggression, and/or feelings of helplessness. Obviously, such side effects should be avoided because

they will eventually affect the performance of the individual adversely and cause organizational conflict.

6. *Learning with understanding is more permanent and can be transferred more effectively than rote learning.* This suggests that learning has more impact and is more easily retained when an individual understands the broad concepts as opposed to fragmented bits of information. Frequently, maintenance personnel are trained in specific aspects of their job (e.g., tree trimming, grass cutting, etc.) without knowledge of the reasons behind their functions or an apprecia- tion and/or understanding of the relationship of these functions to a depart- ment's entire operations. For example, teaching an individual how to prune a tree can be accomplished in two ways. The first procedure, by rote, is to sug- gest that there are three necessary steps: Make a cut in the limb from the bot- tom six inches from the trunk of the tree; cut the limb from the top two inches from the first cut; finally, cut the limb off. On the other hand, it is more appropriate to explain to a maintenance worker the *reason* that the three cuts are made in a tree: to take the weight off the limb to avoid stripping the bark from other parts of the tree. In addition, it might be important to further explain why a park and recreation department would be involved in tree trim- ming. By explaining the reasons for tree pruning (e.g., to control the shape and beauty of the plant), the maintenance person is in a better position to under- stand why he is doing what he is doing and learning should have greater impact.

7. *An individual's perception of what he is learning will determine how com- pletely and rapidly this information is absorbed.* It is important to remember that the way in which material is received is greatly dependent on individual discrimination. If a person feels that the information being transmitted to her has little value, she will have a more difficult time learning it *unless* the manager is able to change or modify this perception in his presentation of the material. It is extremely important to bear this in mind when selecting a strategy for presenting material.

8. *Individuals learn better at their own pace.* The rate of learning varies as people vary. Although in principle this concept is sound, it is difficult to establish self- paced learning programs. Much of the training that takes place in leisure delivery systems is undertaken within a fixed time frame. This is especially true in the training of part-time personnel in activity leadership positions. It might be appropriate to take into consideration this factor when selecting employees for a job and/or establishing a training program. For example, an organization may desire to screen out individuals who learn at a slower pace because their resources are not equipped to handle them. On the other hand, an organization may choose a number of different training vehicles that cater to the rate at which people learn at several levels. Still other organizations might select and design training programs that allow for self-pacing. For

example, one way to present the rules and regulations of an organization is to have a person lecture to a group of people, responding to questions as they arise during the discourse. Another way would be to provide individuals with the rules and regulations and a question-and-answer study guide for home use. In this way individuals can learn the rules at their own pace.

9. *Different types of learning require different training processes.* As previously indicated, there are three domains of learning—cognitive, affective, and psychomotor. The basic principle in this concept is that the acquisition of certain kinds of knowledge, skills, and attitudes requires different training methods. Learning how to dribble a basketball cannot be accomplished without demonstration by the trainer and active physical participation on the part of the person being trained. Attitudes and values may require an experiential approach to training that allows the person being trained to engage in meaningful discussions and to have an opportunity for value clarification. Again, different types of learning require the manager to select different training processes. But there is a common thread that binds all these approaches together. Trainees must have an opportunity for verbal and/or physical participation for the experience to be meaningful to them. Much like students in the classroom, to learn effectively individuals must have more than just a manual or a book and must have more to do than just sit passively through a lecture. They must have the opportunity to respond, question, and be questioned. In this way the learning environment becomes more productive.[9]

Training Methods

The selection of a particular training technique should be done only after careful consideration of the type of training needed, the information that is to be transmitted, and the abilities of those who are to train and those who are to be trained. Many training programs fail because inappropriate techniques are selected. It is important to remember that not all managers have the ability, for example, to present a meaningful lecture. Further, it is difficult for certain individuals who are being trained to participate in highly structured, formalized types of training exercises. It is only after analysis of a number of variables that the methods to be used in a training program should be determined.

What, then, are the variables that affect the selection of training techniques? Because the abilities of individuals vary, one of the primary concerns in selecting a training method is individual characteristics. Certain individuals have the capacity to receive and synthesize a great deal of information over a short period of time, others learn at a slower pace. This means that the type of training technique utilized will have to vary according to individual learning capabilities.

[9] Based on Calvin P. Otto and Rollin O. Glaser, *The Management of Training* (Reading, Mass.: Addison-Wesley Publishing Co., 1970), pp. 106–111.

Another factor that influences the selection of training methods is the age and experience of the trainees. Training methods may have to be more persuasive to intrigue the more experienced employees, whereas younger or inexperienced employees may be quite eager to receive the training being offered.

The types of behaviors that are to be acquired by the individuals participating in the training program will also influence the selection of the training method. When people are involved in orientation training and are studying the policies and procedures of the organization, it may be best to discuss these informally rather than making a formal presentation. When a new piece of equipment is purchased, it is probably more appropriate to train in the field setting, where the equipment may be demonstrated, rather than simply give an explanation.

Also important in the selection of training methods are the number of people to be trained. Certain types of techniques do not lend themselves to large or, conversely, small groups. The last factor that must be considered is cost. The cost per individual for using certain types of training techniques becomes prohibitive for many organizations. For example, it may be extremely costly to train each employee individually, even though that might be the most desirable method. Technological innovations have great bearing on the cost factor. It is now possible to tape-record or videotape information that is to be presented to large numbers of successive groups. This reduces the number of actual hours necessary in the training process. Because personnel costs are perhaps the highest costs in an organization, time saved by the use of a mechanism such as a tape recorder can improve the organization's effectiveness and efficiency.

A number of methods can be utilized by leisure service organizations in the process of training. Among them are the lecture, coaching, the case method, role playing, the risk technique, human relations training, management games, and the conference method.

1. *Lecture.* This is the most direct form of transmitting information and perhaps the most common method utilized in training programs. A lecture is a means of transmitting knowledge, information, or attitudes. The advantages of the lecture are that it is a direct, clear method of communication; it can be controlled by the manager; and it can be accomplished in a relatively short period of time. The disadvantages of a lecture are that the manager may be a dull or boring speaker and that the lecture is a form of one-way communication, with no group participation. Poor lecture techniques have been responsible for undermining the most well-intended training programs.

   What are the components of a good lecture? Generally speaking good speakers will motivate the people they are addressing. It cannot be assumed that people are eager to listen. In addition, the presentation must be well developed and carefully organized. Points must be stated in a clear and orderly fashion and be presented in such a way that the information which is presented is natural, direct, animated, and enthusiastic. Two maxims regarding speaking are worth noting. The first is, Tell them what you're going to tell them, tell them, and tell them what you've told them. The second is that the role of the speaker is to inform, entertain, and enlighten.

2. *Coaching.* In this procedure, a manager provides guidance and/or instruction to subordinates on a day-to-day basis. Essentially, the manager works with subordinates by guiding them while on the job. In this way, the employee is able to learn the manager's philosophy and values and also derive specific information regarding the technical components of a given job. The constant interaction that takes place allows for a freeflow of ideas and suggestions. Discussion may involve not only job-related tasks, but may focus more specifically on helping employees analyze their strengths and weaknesses. The coaching technique encourages individuals to express their personal needs and concerns. It allows them to develop their self-confidence by having a manager available to respond in a positive manner to their concerns, needs, and work efforts. Although coaching is not thought of as a formal technique, managers should recognize that coaching takes place frequently and thus should be acknowledged as an important training mechanism.

3. *The Case Method.* This involves the analysis of a simulated or real situation relating to events or problems that might occur on the job. There are numerous approaches to the case method. The Harvard method was developed in 1880 to help students learn by themselves by creating opportunities for them to think independently and discover basic principles that affect human behavior. This was accomplished through simulation of real-life situations, in written form, to be solved by the student. This method has been widely utilized throughout North America. Another approach is the Wharton School method. The essence of this approach is that it focuses on an actual case that has just happened or is still occurring. Another approach is known as the Henley Syndicate. The outstanding feature of this approach is that it emphasizes the sharing of experiences in small groups.

Regardless of the type of method, all cases are based around four core elements. The first is the case report. In this part of the case method, a picture of the situation is developed. It may be written, transmitted verbally, presented on film or television, tape-recorded, and/or created through role playing. The second component is discussion of the case. In this part of the case method, attention is given to expanding the original material presented and trying to deduce the problem(s). Case analysis is the third element; it involves analysis of the human, technical, and time dimensions of the problem(s). In this part of the method, the situation is scrutinized and possible solutions identified. The fourth element is to identify the current situation and its relationship to other considerations and/or group process in general.

4. *Role Playing.* This technique provides forms of human interaction that reflect realistic behavior in imaginary situations acted out by group members. Role playing provides an opportunity for individuals to narrow the gap between

thinking about how they would react to a situation and actually reacting. In other words, rather than talking in a group about how one would react to a particular situation, role playing stresses acting out the behavior one might apply in a given management situation.

There are two types of role playing: structured and spontaneous. Structured role playing is usually oriented toward the teaching of a selected principle of management. A situation or behavioral problem is acted out, with group members playing preselected roles. This type of role-playing exercise allows individuals to learn by practicing and to observe how others handle problems; it also provides opportunities for analysis. Spontaneous role playing is similar to the structured approach in that roles are acted out. But spontaneous role playing does not have a preselected format. Opportunities exist for individuals to react in whatever way they feel is appropriate. In this way, people are free to respond to the dictates of a given situation and/or explore alternative behavioral responses to the problems encountered.

5. *Risk Technique.* This is a discussion method that can be used by a manager to explore problems concerning an organization's members. In the risk technique, a situation, hypothetical or real, is presented to the group members. They are then asked to identify what risks the organization and/or individuals within the organization must assume to solve this problem. Each risk identified by group members is explored and examined by the group. This is a way of encouraging an individual in an organization to express his or her underlying job-related fears while at the same time encouraging other individuals in the group to examine and share their concerns. Hopefully, by sharing common concerns, an organization can lessen the risk factors involved in solving certain problems. This technique is especially successful in dealing with issues about which individuals are hostile or negative.

6. *Human Relations Training.* This training technique is directed toward helping individuals explore and understand themselves and others better. There are a number of techniques under this heading, including sensitivity training and management grid training. Sensitivity training focuses on improving the quality of interaction that takes place between people. In sensitivity training, opportunities exist to increase awareness of oneself and sensitivity to others, improve communications skills, understand group dynamics, and develop diagnostic abilities. Management grid training allows individual managers to sensitize themselves to their management-leadership style. This technique usually involves testing individuals to determine their human relations orientation and their task orientation. Generally speaking, management grid training allows individuals to gain perspective of themselves and analyze how their style or behavior relates to the goals of an organization. This technique offers an opportunity for individuals to diagnose their style and change according to the needs of the situation they are working in.

7. *Management Games.* A management game is an exercise that incorporates elements of a situation faced by individuals and/or organizations. There are numerous game packages that organizations can buy which can be utilized in a training program. These games usually provide opportunities for individuals and/or groups to make decisions around simulated real-life problems. The primary benefit derived from management games is that they allow individuals to learn from experience without paying the price that results from faulty decision-making. In addition, they allow individuals to test out hypotheses and experiment to determine how a given course of action will affect the activities of an organization.

8. *Conference Method.* This training technique allows individuals to share their experiences and opinions around a common concern. A conference may be distinguished from a meeting in that the latter tends to be extremely rigid and rule oriented. A conference is held to encourage mutual group thinking. It is characterized by free discussion, which finds group decisions being made by consensus rather than by vote. The conference method allows individuals to contribute their knowledge, experience, and opinions and provides a format whereby problems can be analyzed. A key to the success of this training method is the leader of the group. The leader's chief function is to raise questions, help the group stay on track with regard to the topic, and help summarize the findings of the conference. It is important to allow all individuals to express their viewpoints freely.

SUMMARY

Personnel management is a staff function concerned with the management of human resources. All organizations, to one extent or another, are involved with personnel functions. The procurement of employees refers to the identification and recruitment of individuals who will help an organization attain its goals; employee development refers to the training of individuals in the areas of knowledge, skills, and attitudes; placement of employees involves integrating individual abilities with organizational needs; and remuneration refers to the financial compensation that individuals receive for their work.

There are a number of specific activities in which the leisure service manager may be active, including the development of a personnel plan, recruitment and hiring of staff, promotion and discharge of employees, administration of a wage and salary program, administration of fringe benefits, appraisal of employee performance, work with labor unions, and the training of employees. The development of a personnel plan includes forecasting future employee needs and developing job descriptions for recruitment purposes. Recruiting and hiring involves finding qualified individuals and screening and interviewing potential candidates. Promoting individuals within an organization is based on two factors: merit and seniority.

Merit is based on an employee's work performance, whereas seniority refers to an employee's length of service. Wages and salaries are used to help organizations remain competitive with other systems, while at the same time rewarding excellent performance. Benefits paid beyond an individual's normal wage are known as fringe benefits. Sick leave, holidays, and vacations are examples of these types of employee benefits. Related to employee wage increases, although not the only reason for them, is the concept of performance appraisal. Performance appraisal is used to audit the work of an organization's employees.

There has recently been an upsurge in the number of personnel represented by labor unions. In this chapter, we discussed the impact of labor unions and presented a philosophy which suggests that labor unions and management may work in harmony with one another.

In the latter part of this chapter, we discussed the training of employees. Training is directed toward changing employee behavior; it has been neglected by many leisure service delivery managers. There are three types of training. Orientation, or preservice, training is directed toward providing new employees with the skills they need for successful placement in the working environment. In-service training helps employees learn new job-related skills and reinforces previously learned material. Developmental training attempts to help individuals develop their capabilities while at the same time supporting the work of the organization.

Personnel management, unlike other organizational functions, is concerned with the management of people within the organization. Its primary function is not to produce services for public comsumption, but instead to insure that the individuals working within the organization are dealt with fairly and equitably. In turn, it is assumed that satisfied employees will be productive employees and that the services offered to a given constituency will be optimally delivered.

Selected Bibliography

Aiken, Michael, R. Dewar, N. DiTomaso, J. Hage, and G. Zeitz, *Coordinating Human Services,* Jossey-Bass, San Francisco, 1975.

Archer, Maurice, *An Introduction to Canadian Business,* McGraw-Hill, Ryerson, Toronto, 1974.

Argyris, Chris, *Personality and Organization,* Harper, New York, 1957.

———, *Integrating the Individual and the Organization,* Wiley, New York, 1964.

———, *Organization and Innovation,* Richard D. Irwin, Homewood, Ill., 1965.

Bannon, Joseph J., *Problem Solving in Recreation and Parks,* Prentice-Hall, Englewood Cliffs, N.J., 1972.

———, "Who Really Makes Policy?" *Parks and Recreation,* vol. 8, no. 7, 1973.

———, *Leisure Resources: Its Comprehensive Planning,* Prentice-Hall, Englewood Cliffs, N.J., 1976.

———, ed., *Outreach: Extending Community Service in Urban Areas,* Charles C Thomas, Springfield, Ill., 1973.

Barrett, Jon H., *Individual Goals and Organizational Objectives,* Institute for Social Research, University of Michigan, Ann Arbor, 1970.

Bennis, Warren G., *Changing Organizations,* McGraw-Hill, New York, 1966.

Berelson, Bernard, ed., *The Behavioral Sciences Today,* Basic Books, New York, 1963.

Bethel, Gerald I., "A Systems Approach to Management of Park Maintenance," *Park Maintenance,* vol. 24, no. 4, 1971.

Blake, Robert R., and Jane S. Mouton, *The Managerial Grid,* Gulf, Houston, 1964.

Blau, Peter M., and Richard Scott, *Formal Organizations,* Chadlex, San Francisco, 1962.

Boulding, Kenneth, "General Systems Theory: The Skeleton of Science," *Management Science,* vol. 2, no. 3, 1956, pp. 197–208.

Beuchner, Robert D., ed., *Recreation and Open Space Standards,* National Recreation and Parks Association, Washington, D.C., 1969.

Bureau of Outdoor Recreation, *Outdoor Recreation Space Standards,* Department of the Interior, Washington, D.C., 1976.

Burton, Thomas L., *Making Man's Environment: Leisure,* Van Nostrand Reinhold, Toronto, 1976.

Butler, George O., *Introduction to Community Recreation,* fourth edition, McGraw-Hill, New York, 1967.

"Calgary Reorganization Aims to Reduce Administrative Layers," *Recreation Canada,* no. 30/6/ 1972.

Carlson, Reynold E., Theodore R. Deppe, and Janet R. Maclean, *Recreation in American Life,* Wadsworth, Belmont, Calif., 1963.

Carzo, Rocco, Jr., and John N. Yanouzes, *Formal Organization,* Richard D. Irwin, Homewood, Ill., 1967.

Chruden, Herbert J., and Arthur W. Sherman, Jr., *Personnel Management,* South-Western, Cincinnati, 1968.

Churchman, C. West, Russell L. Ackoff, and E. Leon Arnoff, *Introduction to Operations Research,* Wiley, New York, 1957.

Crowston, Wallace B., "Models for Project Management," *Sloan Management Review,* vol. 12, no. 3, 1971, pp. 25–42.

Dale, Ernest, *Management: Theory and Practise,* second edition, McGraw-Hill, New York, 1969.

Davis, Keith, *Human Behavior at Work,* fourth edition, McGraw-Hill, New York, 1972.

Doell, Charles, *Elements of Park and Recreation Administration,* Burgess, Minn., 1963.

Donnelly, James H., Jr., James L. Gibson, and John M. Ivancevich, *Fundamentals of Management: Functions, Behavior and Model,* Business Publications, Dallas, 1971.

Drucker, Peter F., *The Practice of Management,* Harper, New York, 1954.

———, *Managing for Results,* Harper, New York, 1964.

———, *The Effective Executive,* Harper, New York, 1967.

———, *Management Tasks, Responsibilities and Practices,* Harper, New York, 1973.

Dubin, Robert, *Human Relations in Administration,* third edition, Prentice-Hall, Englewood Cliffs, N.J., 1968.

Dunnette, Marvin D., *Work and Nonwork in the Year 2001,* Brooks/Cole, Monterey, Calif., 1973.

Edginton, Christopher R., "Management by Crisis: There Is an Alternative," *Journal of Iowa Parks and Recreation,* vol. 3, no. 1, 1974.

———, "Bring out the Best with Job Enrichment," *Parks and Recreation,* vol. 9, no. 10, 1974.

Edginton, Christopher R., and Robert E. Eldredge, "Part-1, Developmental Training: Methods and Procedures for your Department." *Park Maintenance,* vol. 28, no. 8, 1975, pp. 12–13, 16–17.

———, "Part-2, Developmental Training: Methods and Procedures for Your Department." *Park Maintenance,* vol. 28, no. 9, 1975, pp. 8–10.

Etzioni, Amitai, *Modern Organizations,* Prentice-Hall, Englewood Cliffs, N.J., 1964.

Evarts, Harry F., *Introduction to PERT,* Allyn and Bacon, Boston, 1964.

Fabun, Don, *The Dynamics of Change,* Prentice-Hall, Englewood Cliffs, N.J., 1972.

Fayol, Henri, *General and Industrial Administration,* Pitman, London, 1949.

Fiedler, Fred E., *A Theory of Leadership Effectiveness,* McGraw-Hill, New York, 1967.

Filley, Alan C., and Robert J. House, *Managerial Process and Organizational Behavior,* Scott, Foresman, Glenview, Ill., 1969.

Fisch, Gerald G., "Modern Management," a paper prepared for the conference on "Productivity Through New Technology," Economic Council of Canada, Toronto, May 1965.

Galbraith, Jay R., "Matrix Organization Designs," *Business Horizons,* vol. 14, no. 2, 1971, pp. 29–40.

Getzels, Jacob R., and E. G. Guba, "Social Behavior and the Administrative Process," *School Review,* vol. 65, winter quarter, 1957, p. 424.

Gibson, James L., John M. Ivancevich, and James H. Donnelly, Jr., *Organizations: Structure, Processes, Behavior,* Business Publications, Dallas, 1973.

Godbey, Geoffrey, and Stanley Parker, *Leisure Studies and Services: An Overview,* Saunders, Philadelphia, 1976.

Gold, Seymour M., *Urban Recreation Planning,* Lea and Febiger, Philadelphia, 1973.

Griffith, C. A., "Management and the Leisure Service Delivery System," *Recreation Canada,* no. 32/2/1974.

Halmos, Paul, *The Personal Service Society,* Schocken Books, New York, 1970.

Hartogs, Nelly, and Joseph Weber, *Boards of Directors,* Oceana, Dobbs Ferry, N.Y., 1970.

Hersey, Paul, and Kenneth H. Blanchard, *Management of Organizational Behavior: Utilizing Human Resources,* Prentice-Hall, Englewood Cliffs, N.J., 1972.

Herzberg, Frederick, *Work and the Nature of Man,* World, Cleveland, 1966.

Hicks, Herbert G., *The Management of Organizations,* second edition, McGraw-Hill, New York, 1972.

Hines, Thomas I., *Revenue Sources Management in Parks and Recreation,* National Recreation and Park Association, Arlington, Va., 1974.

Hjelete, George, and Jay Shivers, *Public Administration of Park and Recreational Services,* Macmillan, New York, 1963.

———, *Public Administration of Recreational Services,* Lea and Febiger, Philadelphia, 1972.

Hodge, Billy J., and Herbert J. Johnson, *Management and Organizational Behavior,* Wiley, New York, 1970.

Hodgetts, Richard M., and M. S. Wortman, Jr., *Administrative Policy: Text and Cases in the Policy Sciences,* Wiley, New York, 1975.

Hormachea, Marion N., and Carroll, R., *Recreation in Modern Society,* Holbrook, Boston, 1972.

Horney, Robert L., "Administration by Motivation," *Parks and Recreation,* vol. 3, no. 8, 1968.

Howard, Dennis, "Flow Chart," *Illinois Parks and Recreation,* vol. 6, no. 4, 1965, pp. 6–7.

Hummel, Ralph P., *The Bureaucratic Experience,* St. Martin, New York, 1977.

Johnson, Richard A., Fremont E. Kast, and James E. Rosenzwieg, *The Theory and Management of Systems,* McGraw-Hill, New York, 1963.

Kahn, Daniel, and Robert L. Katz, *The Social Psychology of Organizations,* Wiley, New York, 1966.

Kast, Fremont E., and James F. Rosenzweig, *Organization and Management: A Systems Approach,* McGraw-Hill, New York, 1970.

Katz, Robert L., "Skills of an Effective Administrator," *Harvard Business Review,* vol. 33, no. 1, 1955, pp. 33–42.

Killian, William P., "Project Management—Future Organizational Concepts," *Marquette Business Review,* vol. 15. no. 2, 1971, pp. 90–107.

King, David, *Training Within the Organization,* Tavistock, London, 1964.

Koontz, Harold, and Cyril O'Donnell, *Management: A Book of Readings,* third edition, McGraw-Hill, New York, 1972.

———, *Principles of Management,* fifth edition, McGraw-Hill, New York, 1972.

Korman, Abraham K., *Industrial and Organizational Psychology,* Englewood Cliffs, N.J., 1971.

Kraus, Richard, *Recreation Today: Program Planning and Leadership,* Appleton, New York, 1966.

———, *Recreation and Leisure in a Modern Society,* Appleton, New York, 1971.

Kraus, Richard, and Joseph E. Curtis, *Creative Administration in Recreation and Parks,* Mosby, St. Louis, 1973.

Laudenslayer, Ralph, "PPBS: An Approach to Recreation and Park Management," *California Parks and Recreation,* vol. 12, no. 5, 1970, p. 6.

Levin, Richard I., and Charles A. Kirkpatrick, *Quantitative Approaches to Management,* McGraw-Hill, New York, 1971.

Levin, Richard I., and Rudolph P. Lamone, *Quantitative Disciplines in Management Decisions,* Dickenson, Belmont, Calif., 1969.

Levinson, Harry, "Management by Whose Objectives?" *Harvard Business Review,* vol. 48, no. 4, 1970, pp. 125–134.

Levy, Ronald B., *Human Relations—A Conceptual Approach,* International Textbook, Scranton, Pa., 1969.

Lewin, Kurt, Ronald Lippitt, and Ralph K. White, "Patterns of Aggressive Behavior in Experimentally Created 'Social Climates,'" *Journal of Social Psychology,* vol. 10,,1939, pp. 271–276.

Likert, Rensis, *New Patterns of Management,* McGraw-Hill, New York, 1961.

———, *The Human Organization,* McGraw-Hill, New York, 1967.

Liske, Craig, William Loehr, and John McCamant, *Comparative Public Policy: Issues, Theories and Methods,* Wiley, New York, 1975.

Litterer, Joseph A., *The Analysis of Organizations,* Wiley, New York, 1965.

Luthans, Fred, *Organizational Behavior: A Modern Behavioral Approach,* McGraw-Hill, New York, 1973.

Lutzin, Sidney G., and Edward H. Storey, *Managing Municipal Leisure Services,* International City Management Association, Washington, D.C., 1973.

Lyden, Fremont J., and Ernest G. Miller, *Planning, Programming, Budgeting: A Systems Approach to Management,* Markham, Chicago, 1967.

McCarthy, Jerome E., and S. J. Shapiro, *Basic Marketing,* Irwin, Georgetown, Ontario, 1975.

McGregor, Douglas, *The Human Side of Enterprise,* McGraw-Hill, New York, 1960.

————, *The Professional Manager,* McGraw-Hill, New York, 1967.

McFarland, Dalton E., *Management: Principles and Practices,* third edition, Macmillan, New York, 1970.

Magee, John F., "Decision Trees for Decision Making," *Harvard Business Review,* vol. 42, no. 4, 1964, pp. 126–138.

Mansell, Richard, "Fiscal Program Evaluation," *Illinois Parks and Recreation,* vol. 6, no. 4, 1975, pp. 16–17.

March, James G., and Herbert Simon, *Organizations,* Wiley, New York, 1958.

Maslow, Abraham H., "A Theory of Human Motivation," *Psychological Review,* vol. 50, no. 4, 1943, pp. 370–396.

————, *Motivation and Personality,* Harper, New York, 1954.

————, *Eupsychian Management,* Irwin and Dorsey, Homewood, Ill., 1965.

Meserow, L. Hale, David T. Pompel, Jr., and Charles M. Reich, "Benefit-Cost Evaluation," *Parks and Recreation,* vol. 10, no. 2, 1975, p. 29.

Mittelstaedt Arthur H., Jr., and Henry A. Berger, "The Critical Path Method: A Management Tool for Recreation," *Parks and Recreation,* vol. 7, no. 7, 1972, p. 14.

Mintzberg, Henry, *The Nature of Managerial Work,* Harper, New York, 1973.

Mitcheltree, Wallace A., "How To Get Acceptable Job Performance from Your Employees," *Park Maintenance,* vol. 27, no. 12, 1974.

Morriscy, George, *Management by Objectives and Results,* Addison-Wesley, London, Ontario, 1970.

Murphy, James F., John G. Williams, E. William Niepoth, and Paul D. Brown, *Leisure Service Delivery System: A Modern Perspective,* Lea and Febiger, Philadelphia, 1973.

Newman, William H., Charles Summer, and E. Kirby Warren, *The Process of Management,* second edition, Prentice-Hall, Englewood Cliffs, N.J., 1967.

Novick, David ed., *Program Budgeting: Program Analysis and the Federal Budget,* second editions, Harvard University Press, Cambridge, Mass., 1967.

Odiorne, George S., *Management by Objectives,* Pitman, New York, 1965.

Otto, Calvin P., and Roland O. Glaser, *The Management of Training,* Addison-Wesley, Reading, Mass., 1970.

Perez, Jack W., "The Decentralization of Recreation," *California Parks and Recreation,* vol. 11, no. 6, 1969.

————, "An Argument for Decentralized Administration," *California Parks and Recreation,* vol. 12, no. 6, 1970.

Perrow, Charles, *Organizational Analysis: A Sociological View,* Wadsworth, Belmont, Calif., 1970.

————, *Complex Organizations: A Critical Essay,* Scott, Foresman, Glenview, Ill., 1972.

Petit, Thomas A., *Fundamentals of Management Coordination: Supervisors, Middle Managers, and Executives,* Wiley, New York, 1975.

Pies, Ronald A., "Tempe, Arizona Uses Computer for Maintenance Statistics," *Park Maintenance,* vol. 24, April 1971, p. 8.

Porter, Lyman W., and Edward E. Lawler, III, *Managerial Attitudes and Performance,* Irwin, Homewood, Ill., 1968.

Price, James L., *Organizational Effectiveness,* Irwin, Homewood, Ill., 1968.

Pugh, Derek S., *Organization Theory,* Penquin, Harmondsworth, Middlesex, England, 1973.

Pyhrr, Peter A., "The Zero-Base Approach to Government Budgeting," *Public Administration Review,* vol. 37, no. 1, 1977.

Reddin, William J., *Managerial Effectiveness,* McGraw-Hill, New York, 1970.

————, "Management Effectiveness in the 1980's," *Business Horizons,* vol. 17, no. 8, 1974, p. 9.

Reeser, Clayton, *Management: Functions and Modern Concepts,* Scott, Foresman, Glenview, Ill., 1973.

Reynolds, Jesse A., and Marion N. Hormachea, *Public Recreation Administration,* Prentice-Hall, Englewood Cliffs, N.J., 1976.

Rice, George H., Jr., and Dean W. Bishoprick, *Conceptual Models of Organization,* Appleton, New York, 1971.

Richards, Max D., and Paul S. Greenlaw, *Management Decision Making,* Irwin, Homewood, Ill., 1966.

Robbins, Stephen P., *Managing Organizational Conflict,* Prentice-Hall, Englewood Cliffs, N.J., 1974.

Rodney, Lynn S., *Administration of Public Recreation,* Ronald, New York, 1964.

Scanlan, Burt K., *Principles of Management and Organizational Behavior,* Wiley, New York, 1973.

Schaefer, Theodore H., Jr., "You Can Analyze Operation and Maintenance Costs by Using the Data Collection Method," *Park Maintenance,* vol. 26, no. 11, 1973.

Schein, Edgar H., *Organizational Psychology,* Prentice-Hall, Englewood Cliffs, N.J., 1965.

Schleh, Edward C., *Management by Results,* McGraw-Hill, New York, 1961.

Scioli, F. P., Jr., and T. J. Cook, *Methodologies for Analyzing Public Policies,* Heath, Lexington, Mass., 1975.

Scott, William G., *Organization Theory: A Behavioral Analysis for Management,* Irwin, Homewood, Ill., 1967.

Sessoms, H. Douglas, Harold D. Meyer, and Charles K. Brightbill, *Leisure Services: The Organized Recreation and Park System,* fifth edition, Prentice-Hall, Englewood Cliffs, N.J., 1975.

Shivers, Jay S., *Principles and Practices of Recreational Service,* Macmillan, New York, 1967.

Simon, Herbert A., *The New Science of Management Decision,* Harper, New York, 1960.

———, *Administrative Behavior,* Free Press, New York, 1965.

Strauss, George, and Leonard R. Sayles, *Personnel: The Human Problems of Management,* Prentice-Hall, Englewood Cliffs, N.J., 1972.

Tannebaum, Arnold, *Control in an Organization,* McGraw-Hill, New York, 1968.

Taylor, Frederick W., *Principles of Scientific Management,* Harper, New York, 1947.

Teague, Michael L., "How to Control Judgemental Conservatism," *Parks and Recreation,* vol. 11, no. 8, 1976.

Thompson, Gerald E., *Linear Programming,* Macmillan, New York, 1971.

Tilman, Albert, *The Program Book for Recreation Professionals,* National Press, Palo Alto, Calif., 1973.

Twardzik, Louis F., *The Recreation and Parks Commissioner,* Madisen, Appleton, Wis., 1966.

Van der Smissen, Betty, *Legal Liability of Cities and Schools for Injuries in Recreation and Parks,* W. H. Anderson, Cincinnati, Ohio, 1968.

———, *Evaluation and Self-Study of Public Recreation and Park Agencies: A Guide with Standards and Evaluative Criteria,* National Recreation and Park Association, Arlington, Va., 1972.

Vroom, Victor, H., *Work and Motivation,* Wiley, New York, 1964.

Webber, Ross A., *Management: Basic Elements of Managing Organizations,* Irwin, Homewood, Ill., 1975.

Webster, William D., and Charles M. Reich "Benefit/Cost Analysis—Its Uses in Parks and Recreation," *Recreation Canada,* no. 35/1/1977.

Weissman, Harold H., *Overcoming Mismanagement in the Human Service Professions,* Jossey-Bass, San Francisco, 1974.

Wiest, J. D., and F. Levy, *A Management Guide to PERT/CPM,* Prentice-Hall, Englewood Cliffs, N.J., 1962.

Williams, John G., "Try PERT for Meeting Deadlines," *Park Maintenance,* vol. 25, no. 9, 1972.

Woll, Peter, *Public Policy,* Winthrop, Cambridge, Mass., 1974.

Appendix A
A Systems Design for Park Maintenance Marshalltown, Iowa Parks and Recreation Department

This appendix illustrates the application of systems design to the park maintenance function. Presented below is a sample from the Park Maintenance Manual of the Marshalltown Parks and Recreation Department. As such, it is not an entire systems design but is rather an example of several of the components found in this organization's park maintenance program.

GENERAL MAINTENANCE STANDARDS

PERSONNEL

    A. ONE PARK CARETAKER SHOULD BE ASSIGNED FULL-TIME TO EACH THIRTY-FIVE (35) ACRES OF PARKLAND.

BUILDINGS

    A. OVERALL APPEARANCE: IMMEDIATE GROUNDS NEATLY KEPT; LANDSCAPE ELEMENTS ADEQUATE; HOUSEKEEPING IMMACULATE.

    B. PAINTED SURFACES SHALL BE MAINTAINED WITHOUT CHIPPING, CRACKING, FLAKING, SCALING, OR WRINKLING.

    C. NATURAL WOOD SURFACES SHALL BE MAINTAINED IN NATURAL COLOR AND TEXTURE, WITH NO ROT, FUNGUS, OR LOOSE PARTS.

    D. PLASTER WALLBOARD SHALL BE KEPT CLEAN AND WITHOUT CRACKS.

    E. ALL DOORS SHALL REMAIN UNOBSTRUCTED, AND IN GOOD OPERATING CONDITION.

    F. WINDOWS AND GLASS AREAS SHALL BE CLEAN, WITHOUT CRACKS OR BREAKAGE.

    G. FURNITURE AND FURNISHINGS SHALL BE KEPT IN GOOD CONDITION.

PLUMBING

    A. ALL FIXTURES SHALL BE KEPT INTACT, FUNCTIONING CORRECTLY, SECURELY ANCHORED, WITHOUT LEAKS, CLEAN AND POLISHED, AND FREE OF CORROSION.

    B. ADEQUATE ACCESSORY SUPPLIES WILL BE PROVIDED.

PAVED AREAS

   A. PAVED AREAS SHALL BE MAINTAINED REASONABLY SMOOTH, SUCH
       THAT NO HOLES, NO VEGITATION, NO CRACKING, SHIFTING, OR
       SETTLING OCCURS, AND EDGES DO NOT ROLL.

FENCES

   A. ALL FENCES SHALL BE MAINTAINED IN A TIGHT, VERTICAL
       ALIGNED POSITION.

   B. GATES AND HINGES SHALL BE SECURE AND OPERABLE.

LANDSCAPE

   A. ALL PLANT MATERIAL MUST BE APPROPRIATE AND IN A HEALTHY
       CONDITION.

   B. IRRIGATION AND DRAINAGE FACILITIES MUST FUNCTION PROP-
       ERLY AND EFFECTIVELY.

   C. TREES SHALL BE NEATLY PRUNED AND CONTROLLED.

   D. LAWN AREAS SHALL BE KEPT NEATLY TRIMMED AND FREE OF WEEDS.

   E. ALL LANDSCAPE SHALL BE KEPT FREE OF LITTER.

PLAY EQUIPMENT

   A. ALL PLAY EQUIPMENT SHALL BE MAINTAINED IN GOOD CONDITION,
       FREE FROM HAZARDOUS CONDITIONS, WITH MINIMUM WEAR.

   B. ALL PAINTED SURFACES SHALL BE NEAT AND IN GOOD REPAIR.

   C. ALL CUSHIONING GROUND COVER, E.G. SAND OR TANBARK, SHALL
       BE MAINTAINED AT AN ADEQUATE DEPTH AND CLEANLINESS TO
       INSURE SAFE USE OF EQUIPMENT.

DRINKING FOUNTAINS

A. FOUNTAINS SHALL BE CLEAN AND FREE OF OBSTRUCTIONS.

B. NOZZLES SHALL BE IN GOOD OPERATING CONDITION.

PICNIC AREAS

A. PICNIC TABLES AND BENCHES SHALL BE MAINTAINED IN A CLEAN, SMOOTH CONDITION.

B. BARBEQUE UNITS SHALL BE STRUCTURALLY SOLID AND CLEAN.

C. NO FIRE HAZZARD SHALL BE PERMITTED TO EXIST.

CUSTODIAL

A. ALL MAINTENANCE EQUIPMENT SHALL BE KEPT CLEAN, IN GOOD WORKING ORDER, AND NEATLY STORED IN THE FACILITY DESIGNATED FOR STORAGE OF MAINTENANCE EQUIPMENT.

B. AN INVENTORY OF ALL MAINTENANCE EQUIPMENT SHALL BE MAINTAINED. A COPY OF THE FACILITY INVENTORY SHALL BE IN A PROMINENT LOCATION IN THE STORAGE AREA, AS WELL AS A PERMANENT PART OF THIS MANUAL.

GENERAL

A. ALL GROUNDS AND FACILITIES SHALL BE NEATLY KEPT IN A SAFE AND OPERABLE CONDITION.

B. TRASH AND LITTER CONTAINERS SHALL BE PROVIDED THROUGHOUT THE PARK FACILITY, AND SHALL BE EMPTIED REGULARLY.

WORK PROCEDURES

1. GENERAL DAILY RESPONSIBILITY
   A. MAINTAIN HIGH QUALITY APPEARANCE OF ALL FIXTURES, PLANTS, AND APPARATUS.
   B. INSPECT LIGHTING.
   C. REPORT IMMEDIATELY ALL REPAIRS WHICH CANNOT BE PERFORMED AT THE SITE WITHOUT INTERRUPTING NORMALLY SCHEDULED WORK AND/OR REQUIRE SPECIAL SKILLS OR TOOLS.
   D. ALLOW NO UNSAFE CONDITION TO EXIST.
2. TURF AND PLANTING AREAS
   A. DAILY
      1. PICK UP LITTER.
      2. TRIM, PRUNE, AND REPAIR PLANTS AS REQUIRED.
   B. WEEKLY
      1. MOW LAWN AREAS.
      2. EVERY EFFORT SHALL BE MADE TO MOW TURF ONLY WHEN DRY TO OBTAIN MAXIMUM EFFICIENCY.
      3. EDGE LAWNS AS REQUIRED.
   C. QUARTERLY
      1. PRE-EMERGENCE SPRAYS ON ALL SHRUB WEEDS.
   D. THREE TIMES YEARLY
      1. AERIFY TURF AREAS.
      2. FERTILIZE TURF AREAS.

E. SEMI-ANNUALLY

    1. PRE-EMERGENCE SPRAYS FOR ALL TURF WEEDS.

F. YEARLY (AUTUMN)

    1. PRUNE ALL TREES AS REQUIRED.

    2. PRUNE ALL SHRUBS AS REQUIRED.

3. RESTROOM FACILITIES

    A. RESTROOM AREAS SHALL BE CLEANED AS DESIGNATED AT THE BEGINNING OF EACH WORKING DAY. AT THE COMPLETION OF EACH WORKING DAY, AN INSPECTION OF THE RESTROOM BUILDING WILL BE MADE, AND SHALL BE CLEANED AS NECESSARY TO PROVIDE A CLEAN AND SANITARY FACILITY.

        1. SANITIZE W/C.

        2. WASH MIRROR.

        3. WASH BASIN AND ALL FIXTURES.

        4. REPLENISH ALL SUPPLIES, E.G. TOWELS AND PAPER.

        5. INSPECT LIGHTS AND REPLACE BULBS AS NECESSARY.

        6. INSPECT FLUSHING AND PROPER FUNCTIONING OF ALL DRAINS.

        7. EMPTY TRASH.

        8. WASH FLOORS

    B. THE FOLLOWING SHALL BE PERFORMED WEEKLY IN THE MAINTENANCE OF RESTROOMS FACILITIES.

        1. WASH WALLS.

        2. POLISH BRIGHTWORK.

4. CAMPGROUNDS
   A. DAILY
      1. CHECK FUSES.
      2. EMPTY TRASH.
      3. REPLACE FIREWOOD.
      4. PICK UP LITTER.
5. PICNIC SHELTERS
   A. PICNIC SHELTERS SHALL BE CLEANED AND INSPECTED ON A
      DAILY BASIS FOR CLEANLINESS AND SAFETY.
      1. CLEAN TABLES AND BENCHES.
      2. PICK UP ALL LITTER.
      3. EMPTY TRASH CANS.
      4. CLEAN AND MOP FLOORS.
      5. REPLENISH FIREWOOD.
      6. INSPECT FOR DAMAGE.
   B. WEEKLY
      1. CLEAN FIREPLACE.
   C. INDEPENDENT PICNIC TABLES SHALL BE CLEANED AS REQUIRED
      IN ACCORDANCE WITH ITEMS 1, 2, 3, AND 6 ABOVE.
6. RECREATION BUILDINGS
   A. RECREATION BUILDINGS SHALL BE CLEANED AS DESIGNATED,
      FOLLOWING USAGE BY ANY PERSON AND PRIOR TO USE BY
      ANOTHER PERSON.

1. DUST ALL FURNITURE AND FIXTURES.
2. INSPECT LIGHTS AND REPLACE BULBS AS NECESSARY.
3. INSPECT FOR DAMAGE.
4. SWEEP OR DUST MOP FLOORS OR WASH AS REQUIRED.
5. EMPTY TRASH.

B. WEEKLY
  1. WASH FLOORS.
  2. CLEAN FIREPLACE.

C. PERFORM THE FOLLOWING MAINTENANCE TASKS ON A MONTHLY BASIS, OR MORE FREQUENTLY IF REQUIRED.
  1. WASH AND WAX FLOORS.
  2. WASH WINDOWS, INSIDE AND OUT.
  3. CLEAN KITCHEN FACILITIES.

D. OUTSIDE BUILDING AREA, ON A DAILY BASIS, PERFORM THE FOLLOWING MAINTENANCE TASKS.
  1. SWEEP ALL PAVED WALKWAYS OR HOSE IF NECESSARY.
  2. PICK UP ALL LITTER.
  3. EMPTY ALL TRASH CANS.

7. PLAYGROUND APPARATUS AREAS

A. PLAYGROUND APPARATUS SHALL BE INSPECTED AND CLEANED DAILY.
  1. PICK UP LITTER AND GLASS.
  2. INSPECT SWING CHAIN LINKS FOR WEAR AND REPLACE AS REQUIRED.

3. EMPTY TRASH CANS.

   B. THE FOLLOWING SHALL BE PERFORMED ON A YEARLY BASIS, OR MORE FREQUENTLY AS REQUIRED.

      1. REPAINT ALL PAINTED PLAY EQUIPMENT.

      2. REPLENISH SAND.

8. FERTILIZER AND AERATION

   A. TURF AREAS SHALL BE FERTILIZED AND AERIFIED TWICE YEARLY.

9. WEEDING

   A. TURF: PRE-EMERGENCE SPRAYS SHALL BE APPLIED TWICE YEARLY.

   B. SHRUBS: PRE-EMERGENCE SPRAYS SHALL BE APPLIED TO ALL SHRUBS QUARTERLY

10. ADMINISTRATIVE OFFICES

   A. WEEKLY TASKS

      1. EMPTY LITTER AND ASHTRAYS.

      2. CLEAN TOILETS.

      3. POLISH FURNITURE.

      4. VACUUM.

11. SWIMMING POOLS

   A. WINTERIZING PROCEDURE TO BEGIN THE DAY FOLLOWING THE CLOSING DAY OF THE SEASON.

   B. OPENING PROCEDURE SHOULD COMMENCE SIXTY (60) DAYS BEFORE THE OPENING OF THE SEASON.

INVENTORY AND SPECIFIC WORK PROCEDURES

ADMINISTRATIVE OFFICES
SEVEN EAST STATE STREET
   FACILITIES AND EQUIPMENT INVENTORY
   1. OFFICE FURNITURE
   2. OFFICE EQUIPMENT
   WORK PROCEDURES TO BE FOLLOWED (SEE WORK PROCEDURES)
   ITEM: 10
ANSON PARK (17.19 ACRES)
THIRD AVENUE AND ANSON STREET
   FACILITY AND EQUIPMENT INVENTORY
   1. PLAYGROUND
       A. SWINGS
       B. SLIDES
       C. TEETER TOTTERS
       D. MERRY-GO-ROUND
       E. CLIMBING BARS
       F. TURNING SWINGS
   2. ALL PURPOSE CONCRETE COURT
   3. RECREATION BUILDING
   4. PICNIC SHELTER AND TABLES
   5. LIGHTED SOFTBALL DIAMOND

6. TENNIS COURTS

7. RESTROOMS

WORK PROCEDURES TO BE FOLLOWED (SEE WORK PROCEDURES)

ITEMS: 1, 2, 3, 5, 6, 7, 8, AND 9

ARNOLD PARK (1.06 ACRES)

SEVENTH STREET AND LINN STREET

FACILITY AND EQUIPMENT INVENTORY

1. PLAYGROUND

A. SLIDES

B. SWINGS

C. CLIMBER LADDER

D. BARREL OF FUN

E. CYCLONE SLIDE

F. GEODESIC CLIMBER

G. TWIRLING SWING

H. HORSE SWINGS

I. CLIMBING APPARATUS

2. BICYCLE RACKS

WORK PROCEDURES TO BE FOLLOWED (SEE WORK PROCEDURES)

ITEMS 1, 2, 7, 8, AND 9

ASSISTANCE LEAGUE PARK (1.26 ACRES)

HIGH STREET AND TENTH AVENUE

FACILITY AND EQUIPMENT INVENTORY

1. PLAYGROUND

    A. CEMENT TURTLE

    B. SWINGS

    C. SLIDES

    D. TEETER TOTTERS

    E. MERRY-GO-ROUND

    F. SWINGING GATES

2. PICNIC SHELTER

WORK PROCEDURES TO BE FOLLOWED (SEE WORK PROCEDURES)

ITEMS: 1, 2, 5, 7, 8, AND 9

BUSINESS AND PROFESSIONAL WOMEN'S PARK (.76 ACRES)

FIFTH AVENUE AND MARION STREET

FACILITY AND EQUIPMENT INVENTORY

1. PLAYGROUND

    A. SANDBOX

    B. SWINGS

    C. MERRY-GO-ROUND

    D. TEETER TOTTER

    E. JUNGLE JIM

    F. CLIMBING LADDERS

    G. BASKETBALL COURT

WORK PROCEDURES TO BE FOLLOWED (SEE WORK PROCEDURES)

ITEMS: 1, 2, 7, 8, AND 9

CROSBY MEMORIAL POOL AND MINI-ARBORETUM

SIXTH STREET AT INGLEDUE STREET

FACILITY AND EQUIPMENT INVENTORY

1. SWIMMING POOL

2. MINI-ARBORETUM

WORK PROCEDURES TO BE FOLLOWED (SEE WORK PROCEDURES)

ITEMS: 1, 2, 3, 8, 9, AND 11

ELKS PARK (.88 ACRES)

500 NORTH THIRD STREET

FACILITY AND EQUIPMENT INVENTORY

1. PLAYGROUND

    A. SANDBOX

    B. TEETER TOTTERS

    C. SWINGS

    D. MERRY-GO-ROUND

    E. SLIDE

    F. JUNGLE JIM

2. RESTROOMS

3. BASKETBALL COURT

4. BADMINTON COURT

5. BACKSTOP

WORK PROCEDURES TO BE FOLLOWED (SEE WORK PROCEDURES)

ITEMS: 1, 2, 3, 7, 8, AND 9

FRENCH PARK (3.25 ACRES)

NINTH AVENUE AND BROMLEY STREET

    FACILITY AND EQUIPMENT INVENTORY

      1. PLAYGROUND

          A. SWINGS

          B. MERRY-GO-ROUND

          C. TEETER TOTTER

          D. SLIDE

          E. JUNGLE JIM

          F. CLIMBING LADDERS

          G. TIRE

      2. BICYCLE RACKS

      3. RECREATION BUILDING

      4. BASKETBALL COURTS

      5. TENNIS COURTS

      6. BALL DIAMONDS AND BLEACHERS

      7. ICE RINK

    WORK PROCEDURES TO BE FOLLOWED (SEE WORK PROCEDURES)

    ITEMS: 1, 2, 3, 5, 6, 7, 8, AND 9

KIWANIS PARK (15 ACRES)

THIRD AVENUE AND NEW CASTLE ROAD

    FACILITY AND EQUIPMENT INVENTORY

1. PLAYGROUND

    A. BARREL OF FUN

    B. CEMENT TILES

    C. SWINGS

    D. MERRY-GO-ROUND

    E. JUNGLE JIM

    F. SWING BRIDGE

2. BASKETBALL COURT

3. BACKSTOP

WORK PROCEDURES TO BE FOLLOWED (SEE WORK PROCEDURES)

ITEMS: 1, 2, 7, 8, AND 9

MARSHALLTOWN LITTLE LEAGUE PARK (33.41 ACRES)

SOUTH TWELFTH STREET

1. BALL DIAMONDS

2. RESTROOMS

WORK PROCEDURES TO BE FOLLOWED (SEE WORK PROCEDURES)

ITEMS: 1, 2, 3, 8, AND 9

SUZIE SOWER PARK (.25 ACRES)

SECOND AVENUE AND STATE STREET

WORK PROCEDURES TO BE FOLLOWED (SEE WORK PROCEDURES)

ITEMS: 1, 2, 8, AND 9

TANKERSLEY PARK (6.16 ACRES)

TWELFTH AND STATE STREET

WEST END PARK
THIRTEENTH STREET AND SUMMIT STREET
   FACILITY AND EQUIPMENT INVENTORY
      1. PLAYGROUND
          A. GEODESIC DOME
          B. SWINGS
          C. SLIDES
          D. JUNGLE JIM
          E. MERRY-GO-ROUND
          F. TIRE
      2. ARCHERY RANGE
      3. PICNIC SHELTER
      4. BALL DIAMONDS
      5. TENNIS COURTS
      6. RESTROOMS
   WORK PROCEDURES TO BE FOLLOWED (SEE WORK PROCEDURES)
   ITEMS: 1, 2, 3, 5, 7, 8, AND 9
RIVERVIEW PARK (133.0 ACRES)
NORTH THIRD AVENUE AND WOODLAND
   FACILITY AND EQUIPMENT INVENTORY
      1. PLAYGROUND
          A. AIRPLANE
          B. MERRY-GO-ROUND

C. SWINGS

      D. SEESAWS

      E. CLIMBING APPARATUS

      F. CONCRETE TUNNEL

      G. TIRES

      H. FIRE ENGINES

      I. TWIST SWING

      J. SLIDES

      K. INFANT SWINGS

      L. MINIATURE TRAIN

      M. CANNON

      N. COVERED WAGON

   2. RESTROOMS

   3. SHELTERS

      A. PICNIC

      B. COMMUNITY (SEMI-ENCLOSED)

      C. HISTORICAL SOCIETY LOG CABIN

      D. SWIMMING POOL

      E. CAMPING AREA - 65 UNITS

      F. SNOWMOBILE TRAIL

      G. ATHLETIC FIELDS

         1. FLAG FOOTBALL

         2. SOFTBALL

H. MISCELLANEOUS

    1. HISTORICAL MARKER - FIRE BELL

    2. PICNIC TABLES

WORK PROCEDURES TO BE FOLLOWED (SEE WORK PROCEDURES)

ITEMS: 1 THROUGH 9 AND 11

Appendix B
City of Sunnyvale
Parks and Recreation
Department MBO Process

Appendix B presents a technique used by the City of Sunnyvale Parks and Recreation Department to combine the traditional MBO approach to goal setting with a means of evaluating the methods by which goals are achieved. This contrasts with the traditional MBO approach, which has placed heavy emphasis on goal accomplishment and sometimes has minimized how managers have achieved these goals. This appendix is in support of the discussion of performance appraisal in Chapter 7 and in Chapter 11.

CITY OF SUNNYVALE
CALIFORNIA
August 4, 1976

To:	Parks and Facilities Superintendent Recreation Supervisors
From:	Director of Parks and Recreation
Subject:	Performance Measurement Appraisal

Last year we attempted to develop a Management Achievement Program whereby you would be evaluated annually on a more objective basis. On several occasions we had discussions relative to the program insofar as it really hasn't gone far enough to accurately assess performance and accomplishment of objectives.

In any undertaking there are basically two aspects of evaluation of the accomplishment of one's job. One is the evaluation of the end result and the other is an evaluation of the method, or means of accomplishment. Generally the evaluation has been more on results rather than the means. Within certain limitations and certain conditions this makes sense from a management point of view. On the other hand, from a potential growth, promotional and advancement point of view the means by which accomplishment is achieved becomes important. Even though an individual may accomplish a task or even exceed the accomplishment of productivity, if by accomplishing it he has destroyed individuals in terms of relationships or abused other resources, in the long run this would have effect on his overall performance.

To carry the Management Achievement Program further, I would like to develop with each of you a Performance Management Appraisal system that would help me evaluate you as a manager in relationship to the accomplishment of your organizational objectives as well as an evaluation of your managerial relationships. In order to do this it would be necessary for us to jointly arrive at mutually agreed upon objectives and relationship standards.

Attached to this memo is a set of preliminary objectives I have developed for each of you. I would like each of you to review these, adding, deleting or changing them based on your perception of your assignment and responsibilities. Following your reviewing these I would like to sit down with you and review them and mutually agree upon them with you. This would be done with the fiscal year just started in mind, particularly for certain aspects of the appraisal. In addition to an annual review it would be my intent to review on a semi-monthly basis, the status and accomplishment of these objectives. Periodically appropriate comments, in memo form, would be added to the appraisal file indicating performance as it relates to accomplishment of objectives. The idea would be to not wait until the completion of a task to comment on performance but to comment on it periodically to assist each of you in growth and development. By combining appraisal of end results as well as means in accomplishing end results, I feel it would benefit your development.

Performance Measurement Appraisal, continued   Page 2

Following are the categories that we will mutually agree upon and objectives and standards that would be developed, tailoring each appraisal to each manager.

1. ACHIEVEMENT RELATED OBJECTIVES

   Under this category, in a reasonable amount of detail, list objectives as quantifiable and as specific as possible. Examples are:

   A. Prepare for, carry out and analyze class registration 3 times annually.

   B. Supervise reservation system for all facilities for departmental, public and private use.

   C. Prepare activity guide for public distribution.

   D. Supervise a plan to administer and evaluate 20 classes in Creative Arts, area, 30 in the Performing Arts area, 40 in the Home Arts area and in the Special Interest area.

   E. Plan and supervise activities in special groups, outdoor recreation, senior citizens.

   F. Provide for 12 departmental training programs per year.

Any other specific assignments related to the task would be related under this area wherever possible quantifiable objectives would be listed. In the evaluation of each of these objectives a narrative comment would be given relative to the degree of accomplishment of the objectives as well as any other comments relative to the method of accomplishment that would assist the individual in taking any corrective action in the future, if necessary. In addition, comments relative to outstanding performance would be indicated.

2. SPECIAL PROJECT OBJECTIVES

   Any projects that are more or less one-time assignments or are in addition to the on-going program assignments would be listed in this category. This list would be arrived at at the beginning of the fiscal year as well as added to during the year, when appropriate. Such special projects might be:

   A. The formation of a library for the work units.

   B. Establishing a part-time evaluation system.

   C. The work of the Bicentennial Committee to hold two picnics on the 4th of July.

   D. Work for the City Manager on special project of in-service training.

   These special projects would have a starting time, a completion time and any other significant information that would describe the project at the completion of the project as well as an evaluation, comment or memo placed in the file.

3. MANAGEMENT RELATIONSHIP OBJECTIVES

   Under this category there would be several managerial traits listed that all supervisors would have in common. Comments would be made relative to the person's ability or lack of ability in each of these areas. I would assume that many of the leadership characteristics would be common to the standard evaluation forms.

Performance Measurement Appraisal, continued   Page 3

Each of you might suggest specific characteristics that are appropriate to Recreation and Parks personnel.

A. Communication abilities

B. Relationship with co-workers.

C. Initiative and resourcefulness

D. Adaptability

E. Job knowledge

F. Effectiveness in planning and organizing of work

G. Amount of work accomplished

H. Directing and motivating subordinates

4. PERSONAL GROWTH OBJECTIVES

Under this category I would attempt to outline, with mutual agreement by you, some personal growth areas that you need to work on. These might include areas of behavioral improvement as well as educational improvement or other professional growth. Examples are:

A. Applying for a Superintendent of Recreation position.

B. Work on ability to delegate more of one's tasks to subordinates.

C. Following through on activities better.

D. Completing a course in Supervisory Practices.

Enough detail would be given about the personal growth or behavioral improvement so as to be specific in terms of what improvement is desired. It would be very important during the entire year of the evaluation process to comment on these areas regularly. This would be one of the main areas where an attempt would be made to evaluate performance rather than necessarily end results.

5. OBJECTIVES FOR SUPERVISORS TO WORK ON TO IMPROVE WORKING RELATIONSHIPS

Under this category I would request each of you spell out an area that I might improve upon that would assist you in your carrying out your job. Specific items might be listed of things I am doing or not doing that interfere with your accomplishing your assignment. This would be an opportunity for you to give me some feedback in ways I can better assist you so that I might grow and improve upon my relationship with you.

A. Keeping supervisors more informed on what the Commission is doing.

Performance Measurement Appraisal, continued   Page 4

B. Keeping supervisors informed of what's happening in the Parks Division.

C. Meeting weekly for one hour with the supervisors.

D. Visiting facilities with supervisors on a regular basis

All in all I feel some real assistance could be provided to each of you as well as to myself with this type of performance appraisal. It would provide a mechanism for more feedback that would assist us in our growing and maturing into better management leaders. Some general guidelines of utilizing the appraisal would be to try to be specific in activity description rather than general, to take into account the needs of both the receiver and the giver of the feedback, that it be directed at behavior the receiver can do something about, that it is solicited rather than imposed and that it is not the attempt to totally be critically evaluative but an attempt to be helpful.

In addition it would be very valuable that there be mutual agreement to the items that are placed on the appraisal rather than it being one-sided.

During the next week or two I will be developing the specific plan for each of you and as I accomplish this I will give them to you for your review and consideration. Please review it carefully and then we will discuss it.

John G. Williams
Director of Parks and Recreation

JGW/dh

Appendix C
City of Sunnyvale
Total Performance
Measurement

Appendix C presents a case study of a new concept of government performance management, Total Performance Measurement (TPM), that was recently tried in the city of Sunnyvale, California. TPM grew out of a need to improve government productivity and was conceived by Brian Usilander and Jay Meyer, Industrial Engineers with the U.S. General Accounting Office, and Dr. David Sirota, a behavioral scientist with David Sirota and Associates, Inc. Camille Cates coordinated the TPM project for Sunnyvale and recorded the process in several city documents. A brief description of this project was given in Chapter 7. This case study goes into great detail on how the project was conducted and offers reactions to various phases of the project. It is felt the case study could be valuable, in total or in part, to other communities that might be interested in establishing a similar project. Additional information and questions are welcomed by either of the authors, John G. Williams or Christopher Edginton.

BACKGROUND AND ORGANIZATIONAL CLIMATE

Sunnyvale was the first city in the nation to apply TPM, which analyzes the relationships among the quality of management, productivity, employee attitudes, and citizen satisfaction. This city of 105,000 people is located 40 miles south of San Francisco in the Santa Clara Valley of California. Sunnyvale has a diversified industrial base, with aerospace, electronics, computer software and hardware firms, and food processing plants dominant. The population is relatively homogeneous (5.4% are nonwhite) and relatively affluent but not wealthy (having a median family income of $12,000 compared with a national median of $10,196, based on the 1970 Census). During the period of its rapid growth (1945–70), the main concern of Sunnyvale's city government was to provide the physical facilities necessary to support and encourage further growth (e.g., streets, sewers, parks, water supply). By 1974 most of these physical facilities had been built, so the city's focus began to change.

There are 500 regular civil service employees and up to 500 temporary and Comprehensive Educational Training Act (CETA) employees. According to the

1976 TPM employee survey, the regular employees are mostly male (72%), white, and of various ages; 66% had been employed from 3 to 15 years. Managers are predominantly male, white, highly educated, and of varied ages; 52 percent had been employed from 6 to 15 years. Temporary employees are predominantly female, white, young, and employed 5 years or less.

Since 1968, the city has implemented a Planning, Programming, Budgeting System (PPBS), supported by a computerized management information system. In each year, the Resource Allocation Plan (budget) shows actual costs for 4 previous years, the proposed cost for the coming year, and the projected cost for the next 7 years. Each program has an identified overall objective, quality goals (effectiveness measures), production plan (work program), production units, unit costs, total costs, and productivity trends. The budget shows a history of expenditures for 4 years and projections for the 8 years into the future, and the city services are grouped into 63 operational programs, managed by 50 program managers and 8 department directors. The computerized information system provides on-line reporting of expenditures and production. Computerized modules include personnel/payroll, utility billing, accounting, purchasing/inventory, equipment rental, public safety, library, and environmental information. The city has also instituted a performance auditing system for public safety to evaluate the use of resources in relation to the service provided. Private accountants conducted the first performance audit in conjunction with the regular financial audit in 1975.

In addition to changes in budgeting and information systems, Sunnyvale has also experienced changes in management training, employee participation, and citizen involvement. Since 1971 the management group has been involved in organizational development training, including annual retreats and bimonthly workshops. Training also includes a management rotation program, whereby department directors and program managers rotate assignments for two months.

In the past three years, additional channels for employee participation have also been implemented. Standing employee advisory committees are the Safety Training Committee, the Employee Development Committee, and the Manager's Advisory Council (MAC).

These changes in budgeting, information systems, management training, employee involvement, and citizen participation have enabled Sunnyvale to increase services, even though the per capita general revenue available to the city is 20 percent less than for other cities in the state. Over the past three years, the city's productivity has increased at an average annual rate of 4.3 percent, for productivity savings of almost $3 million. Sunnyvale's organizational climate was receptive to the TPM project. The employee survey portion of the project confirmed that most of those who work for Sunnyvale (93% of the managers, 62% of other employees) think it is an effectively managed, well-run organization. Most employee's organizational effectiveness is improving (76% of managers, 54% of employees), and they are proud to work for Sunnyvale (96% of managers, 75% of other employees). TPM was a reasonable addition to the work of the organization and part of the innovative style familiar to it.

APPLICATION

In the application of the TPM concept, Sunnyvale developed a workable system for measuring performance that incorporates three types of data: (1) productivity information, (2) citizen perceptions of effectiveness, and (3) employee attitudes. Sunnyvale has had extensive experience with the first two types of information through its PPBS and citizen participation programs.

ANTECEDENT CONDITIONS

Although the TPM concept was a new process for the city, there were several antecedent conditions that contributed to its success. The management group, consisting of 50 program managers—including department directors and first-line supervisors—had experienced related processes through training programs, the budget process, and the performance auditing project.

City employees had experienced related processes through the budgeting process, the employee information program, and employee committees.

The city council had experienced related processes in the budget process, the information programs, and neighborhood council meetings.

Citizens in general had experienced related processes in the information programs, other citizen surveys, and neighborhood council meetings.

Management Training

Management training is an ongoing process in the city that facilitated the TPM project. In the past ten years (1968–77), training for the management group has concentrated on the Sunnyvale data processing system, management by objectives, performance evaluation, and organizational development, including courses on organizational awareness and team building. Each fall for the past six years (1971–77), there has been a three-day retreat for the management group. One-day management workshops are held every two months during the rest of each year. The workshops are designed to give the management group an identity, distribute information on new management concepts, and generate ideas for improving the existing management system.

Recently, the continuing education program of the management staff has included a management rotation program. During the fall of 1973, each of the 8 department directors rotated to a different department for three months. In the next two years, 40 of the 50 managers rotated jobs to gain new experience and recommend improvements. These training programs facilitated management's involvement in the TPM project.

Budgeting Process

Each manager is also involved with the budgeting process. Sunnyvale has an operational PPBS supported by a computerized management information system. The management staff prepares the program budget on an eight-year allocation cycle. There are 63 operational programs in the city. Each program has an overall objective, a proposed work program, and quality goals (effectiveness measures). A sample budget page is shown in Figure C.1. City employees and the city council are also familiar with the goal-oriented budgeting process.

Performance Auditing

The TPM project began as an expansion of a performance auditing project sponsored by the United States General Accounting Office and the International City Management Association in 1973–74. The performance auditing project was limited to the public safety (police and fire) function. Its purpose was to develop measures for the effectiveness of the nine public safety programs.

The performance auditing project refined these effectiveness measures (quality goals) and the information system that monitors their progress throughout the year. The project quickly illustrated the importance of setting meaningful goals. The TPM project began as a way of incorporating citizen opinion and evaluation of effectiveness of city services into the goal-setting process.

Employee Involvement

The employee information program consists of a regular information bulletin delivered every two weeks with the paychecks. The bulletin describes city programs. In the past four years (1973–77), the city manager has also developed employee groups to involve employees in the city, its management system, and their own career development. The Manager's Advisory council (MAC) reviews city policies and proposed city projects. The Employee Development Committee recommends career development programs, and the Safety Training Committee recommends safety improvements.

MAC reviewed the TPM project durings its various phases. All employee committees illustrate a commitment to more employee involvement, such as that incorporated in the TPM project.

City Council and Citizens

The community relations information program is the ongoing method for communication between the city council and the citizens. Brochures describing city

CITY OF SUNNYVALE

RESOURCE ALLOCATION ANALYSIS

PROGRAM	—	312.09 Aquatics
FUNCTION	—	Community and Cultural Services
OBJECTIVE	—	Offer recreation and physical development through swimming activities

FISCAL YEAR	WORK HOURS	TOTAL COST	PRODUCTION UNITS (WORKHOUR OUTPUT)	COST PER UNIT	UNIT COST IN CONSTANT DOLLARS 1972-73
ACTUAL 1972-1973	16,178	54,437	19,091	2.85	2.85
ACTUAL 1973-1974	18,587	62,729	24,057	2.61	2.48
ACTUAL 1974-1975	22,306	77,804	37,798	2.06	1.78
ESTIMATED 1975-1976	21,000	75,813	39,592	1.91	1.50
PROPOSED 1976-1977	21,400	91,024	42,014	2.17	1.57
PROJECTED 1977-1978	21,400	97,390	42,014	2.32	1.57
PROJECTED 1978-1979	21,400	104,221	42,014	2.48	1.57
PROJECTED 1979-1980	21,400	110,359	42,014	2.63	1.57
PROJECTED 1980-1981	21,400	116,024	42,014	2.76	1.56
PROJECTED 1981-1982	21,400	121,913	42,014	2.90	1.57
PROJECTED 1982-1983	21,400	128,042	42,014	3.05	1.57
PROJECTED 1983-1984	21,400	134,412	42,014	3.20	1.57

QUALITY GOALS —
. Provide 50% of the population supervised swimming
. Instruct 15% of the population in water safety and aquatic skill
. Provide aquatic programs corresponding to population, skill and interest levels
. Offer an Open-Age Group, AAU sanctioned swim team

FISCAL YEAR PRODUCTION PLAN —
. Offer the following number of participant hours for each activity: 305,000 recreation swimming; 19,000 youth and tadpole instructional programs; 2,000 adult instructional programs; 1,600 life saving instructional programs; 21,500 varied special instructional programs; 4,500 SCUBA instructional programs; 28,000 swim team programming.

SPECIAL NOTES —

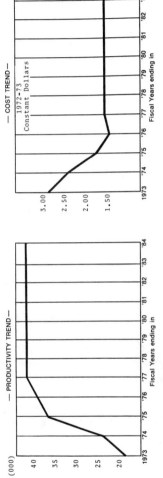

— PRODUCTIVITY TREND —

— COST TREND —

Figure C.1. City of Sunnyvale resource allocation analysis.

programs are mailed to households in Sunnyvale every month. In addition, five neighborhood council meetings are held each year. At these neighborhood sessions, city council meets informally to discuss citizen problems and city programs.

There has also been limited experience with citizen surveys. The city sponsored a citizen survey in 1969 to gather information for use in a Community Renewal Plan. The survey was a written questionnaire (no interviews) administered to 3200 people. A second citizen survey was conducted in 1970 as part of an evaluation of a mobile community services van, a federally funded project to improve police-community relations. Conducted in two phases, it was a written survey of 238 van users. Each of the two surveys was designed for a specific, limited use. Neither was widely publicized nor used in the city's budget process.

SUMMARY

Sunnyvale is a medium-sized city in a metropolitan area that has experienced rapid growth. That growth has created demands for physical facilities and services, some of which have been met and some of which need to be met. The purpose of Sunnyvale's TPM project was to involve various groups in identifying those needs and ways to meet them.

Although the TPM project was a new process for the city, the antecedent conditions, as discussed, contributed to its success. The project was built upon the experience of the budgeting process, management training programs, the performance audit project, employee information and involvement programs, and community relations programs.

The TPM project consisted of and is an attempt to analyze the relationships between citizen satisfaction, employee attitudes, and management productivity data.

CITIZEN SURVEY ("NEW DIRECTIONS")

The first part of the Total Performance Measurement (TPM) process was the citizen survey, which the city called "New Directions."

PART I: THE PROCESS

Scope and Cost

The "New Directions" project lasted one year, from May 1974 to June 1975, and consisted of department meetings, a citizen survey, briefing sessions, informational reports, a town workshop, and citizen task forces. Groups involved in the process included city employees, the city council, and citizens. The project explored the major services of the city: public safety (police and fire), public works (streets and utilities), community development (planning, zoning, code enforcement), parks and recreation, library, and information. It also explored some noncity services (e.g., public transportation, cable television) and possible new city services (e.g., child care, low-income housing).

The cost for the consultant who administered the citizen survey was $15,927.50. All other costs (approximately $40,000) were absorbed through existing city programs.

Assumptions

A major assumption of the project was that the participation of various groups would (1) inform more people, (2) get more information and opinions into the process, and (3) increase the probability that the information would lead to action. A second, related, assumption was that the project would be most effective if linked to the ongoing processes of the city, particularly the antecedent conditions described earlier.

Timetable

Figure C.2 depicts the basic timetable of the "New Directions" project from May 1974 to June 1975. The chart also depicts the four major phases of the project: (1) issue research, (2) issue definition, (3) issue testing, and (4) issue action.

Phase 1: Issue Research

In the initial phase of the project, four groups analyzed city issues: (1) management staff (departmental groups), (2) city council, (3) community groups, and (4) individual citizens. Figure C.3 depicts the involvement of these groups during this phase.

The first public mention of the citizen survey was in an oral report to the city council on March 12, 1974. The survey was linked to the performance audit process as a way of improving the goal-setting process. More detailed plans for a citizen survey were presented to the department directors the second week in May and to the city council the following week. The purpose of the survey was to gather information regarding changing community conditions and needs.

Department Research. With the council's endorsement, the project began. During May and June, program managers met in departmental groups to begin the research of issues facing the city. These sessions began with a briefing on the survey process. The managers then reviewed the service goals stated in the Resource Allocation Plan (budget) and related them to their assumptions about community needs. The purpose of this process was to examine the basic purpose

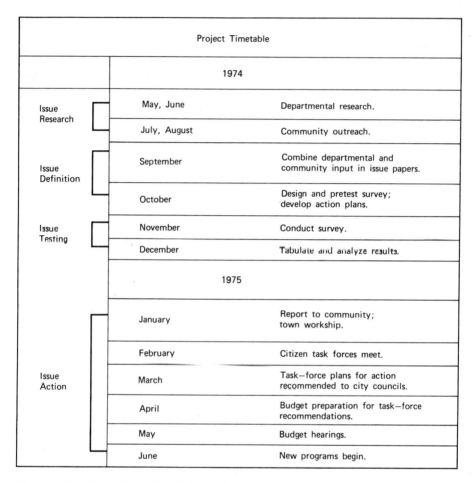

Figure C.2. "New Directions" timetable.

for providing government service and to think broadly about the mission of the department.

Departmental groups then identified clienteles for their services. For example, teens were a clientele population in both the Park and Recreation Department and in the Public Safety Department. Thinking about specific client populations enabled managers to focus on specific needs met by existing services. It also illustrated the lack of information regarding who was being served by a particular service. The clientele for more open space programs, for example, was not clear. The focus on clientele also helped make explicit the assumptions managers had about the community. "The citizen survey indicated that citizens were particu-

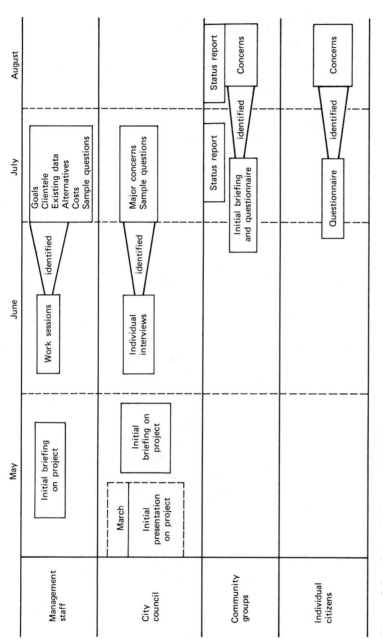

Figure C.3. Phase 1: Issue research.

larly interested in saving dollars and having the city perform the desired services in an efficient, economical manner."

After identifying the clienteles, departmental groups discussed groups whose needs were not being met. For example, parents with children aged two to six could use the weekly preschool program at parks in the summer, but parents needing year-round, day-long care for their children had no programs and were a potential clientele. Departments used demographic and other planning data to identify potential clienteles and needs of the community.

The next step in the departmental research portion of the issue research phase of the project was to develop alternative programs to provide the needed services. The new or modified services were examined in terms of (1) a general description, (2) clientele served, (3) yearly costs, and (4) impact. From these descriptions, departments formed initial questions for a citizen survey. An example from recreation concerned Little League fields:

The Little League program is presently operated by five Little League organizations throughout the city. Each league utilizes its closest neighborhood park to carry out its programs. In an attempt to give better service, would you like the city to consolidate its services into one or two centralized Little League complexes? Circle the number 1, 2, or 3 that best expresses how you feel about the type of complexes the city should provide. By circling 1 it would indicate that service should be left as they are. Circling 3 would indicate a desire to move toward centralizing facilities on a shared basis. Circling 2 would indicate a combination of both.

$$1 \qquad 2 \qquad 3$$

1. *Description:* 10 neighborhood ball fields used in neighborhood parks.	1. *Description:* 1 or 2 centralized ball field complexes (approximately 6–8 fields in a complex).
2. *Clientele:* Boys and girls, aged 8–13.	2. *Clientele:* Same.
3. *Cost:* Same as now.	3. *Cost:* 20% reduction.
4. *Impact:* Independent scheduling and ground rules.	4. *Impact:* Little Leagues would need to change scheduling to share facilities. Would require acquisition of additional land, higher-quality maintenance.

The questions were too complicated to use in the actual survey, but they captured the issues of greatest concern to the departments. Identifying issues and thinking in terms of alternatives were the major products of the departmental research.

Community Outreach.   During the summer, questions similar to those discussed in the departmental sessions were answered by the citizen council, community groups, and individual citizens. In individual interviews in June, the city council discussed the project, city priorities, new services, and issues about which it wanted more information. Council members asked questions about the citizen survey and gave specific areas to be covered in it. Examples were citizens' opinions on new bike paths and taxes.

Individual citizens also had the opportunity to respond to similar open-ended questions. The July issue of the city newsletter (*Sunnyvale Action*), which is mailed to every household, contained a questionnaire (see Figure C.4). This questionnaire asked people what they liked and did not like about the city, what they felt the city's major problem was, and what new services they wanted. Citizen survey exhibits were set up in city hall, the library, and the community center. These displays explained the purpose of the survey and had questionnaires to fill out.

During July and August, meetings were held with community groups to explain the project and get their perceptions and concerns about Sunnyvale. Types of groups contacted included the following:

service clubs	cosponsored clubs
business and professional organizations	churches
Chamber of Commerce	historical society
senior citizens	PTA
boards and commissions	schools
county officials	Girl Scouts
referral organizations	sports groups
political organizations	homeowners' organizations
women's groups	cultural and entertainment groups
special-interest groups	agricultural groups

A speaker went out to each group having regularly scheduled meetings to discuss the project. After the discussion, group members filled out the same questionnaire that had been mailed to the homes and used in the displays. A total of 1000 questionnaires were completed, half from mailings and displays and half from the group meetings.

Groups varied in their expressions of concern, generally along the organizing interest of the group. For example, dance clubs were interested in more covered recreation facilities; business organizations and the Chamber of Commerce were interested in downtown redevelopment; and senior citizens were interested in transportation.

General concerns of most groups were their continuing involvement in the project and use of the survey results. One group wanted to take more control in the process and review and approve all questions before they were included in the

CITIZEN SURVEY

The City of Sunnyvale is planning to conduct a city-wide scientific citizen survey this fall. To help us design that survey we need various opinions and perceptions from people in the community about what kind of service the city is giving and what goals people have for their city. You can help by answering these questions.

1. What concerns you about Sunnyvale's future? (Mark all that apply)
_____ crowding
_____ traffic
_____ public safety and order
_____ pollution
_____ real estate prices
_____ housing opportunities
_____ employment opportunities
_____ community identity
_____ recreation opportunities
_____ cultural-entertainment opportunities
_____ citizen participation in gov't
_____ social services
_____ public transportation
_____ library facilities
_____ race relations
_____ others (please specify)

2. What kinds of services would you like to see the city provide that the city is not now providing?

3. What, in your opinion, is the biggest problem facing Sunnyvale today that the city can do something about?

4. What city services do you think are especially important? Should we be doing more of these types of things?

Return the form to City Hall. Use additional sheets, if necessary.

Figure C.4. Preliminary citizen questionnaire.

458

final questionnaire. Several meetings were held with this group to insure adequate input without jeopardizing the objectivity of the final questionnaire. It was at this point that monthly status reports were instituted to inform the community groups, the press, and interested citizens of the past and upcoming month's project activities. The status reports continued throughout the project.

Phase 2: Issue Definition

The second phase of the "New Directions" project was issue definition. Figure C.5 represents this two-month phase, which combined the data collected in the issue research phase into clear issues. Each of the responses to the open-ended questions on the 1000 preliminary questionnaires was coded and tabulated. In addition, comments relating to specific city services were grouped by the department providing that service.

The departmental groups met again to review the results from citizens, community groups, and the city council. The groups were also given the sample questions and lists of concerns they had developed in the issue research phase. Groups made comparisons between their original perceptions and the direct input of the other groups. Examples of the type of new information were (1) the feeling of the majority of citizens responding that Sunnyvale was too crowded and (2) public transportation being viewed as a major concern.

The preliminary questionnaire was not designed as a specific tool to precisely reflect citizen needs or evaluations of effectiveness. It was designed to institute citizen input into the formulative stages of the process. That involvement (1) informed citizens of the process, (2) insured consideration of major concerns, and (3) was the basis for increased citizen involvement later in the process.

Once the results of the preliminary questionnaire were tabulated and compared with initial departmental information, the city manager directed each department director to prepare issue papers. The topics of the issue papers were as follows:

Administration	Employer-employee relations
	Citizen participation and information
	Affirmative action
	Child care
Finance	Financial posture
General Services	County transit service
Park and Recreation	Open space
	Park services
	Bicycle system
	Recreation services
Library	Library service and facilities

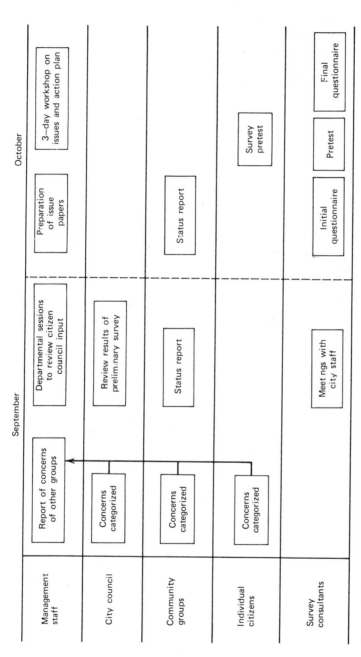

Figure C.5. Phase 2: Issue definition.

Public Safety	Organization and planning
	Emergency medical service
	Neighborhood center
	Fire protection service
Public Works	Street maintenance
	Traffic conditions
	Water pollution centrol
	Potable water system
	Solid waste collection and disposal
Community Development	Downtown renewal
	Housing
	Industrial development

The manager directed that each issue paper be a comprehensive exploration of the topic, including: (1) history and background, (2) current status, and (3) options for the future.

These issue papers were the basis of a three-day management workshop at the Asilomar conference grounds at Pacific Grove, California. Before the workshop, each of the 50 program managers received a booklet containing one-page summaries of all the issue papers, grouped into six issue areas: environment, city appearance, traffic and transit, recreation and cultural, new services, and upgrading existing services. Twelve facilitators were chosen from the management group to lead small-group sessions at Asilomar. Each facilitators was either new to the city or had had no previous experience as a group leader. The consultant for the workshop met with the facilitators prior to the workshop for an afternoon training session on how to run the groups.

At the workshop sessions, the small groups identified issues and developed action options, revising the ones expressed in the issue papers and creating new ones. The small groups were composed of managers from different departments to encourage varied perspectives on problems and to familiarize the entire group with the many issues facing the city. Once issues and action options were identified, the small groups conducted a force field analysis on the options, a force field analysis is a technique for identifying forces that encourage and those that restrain the execution of action options.

On the last day of the workshop, the manager presented plans for using citizen task forces to work with the survey results. The results of the workshop were distributed after the workshop for inclusion in the issue papers. The city council, in three small-group meetings, also received the results of the preliminary questionnaire and discussed plans for using the results. The only involvement citizens had during Phase 2 was to receive status reports and participate in the survey pretest. A copy of the status report to groups that had participated in the initial formation of the survey is presented in Figure C.6.

Department of Parks and Recreation

SUNNYVALE CITIZEN SURVEY

STATUS REPORT
July, 1974

Community Outreach

The Report

This is the first in a series of monthly status reports on the
citizen survey. Many people in the city who have become involved
in the survey process want to stay involved and up to date on
what's happening with the survey. These status reports will keep
you informed as things happen.

The report is sent to each of the groups contacted and to the news
media. Other groups or individuals may also request to be on the
mailing list.

If anyone has any questions or comments on the report, please call
or drop by city hall. If there's something your entire group is
interested in hearing about, let me know and we'll arrange a discussion meeting.

Timetable

May, June	1974	Departmental Research
July	1974	Community Outreach
August	1974	Design Survey
		Contract with Consultant
September	1974	Pretest survey
October	1974	Redesign survey based on pretest
November	1974	Conduct survey
December	1974	Tabulate results
January	1975	Initial analysis and report
February	1975	In depth reporting and plans for action

What's Been Done

1. During July contact was made with 78 separate groups to talk to
them about the survey and to get their perceptions and concerns
about Sunnyvale. Types of groups contacted include:

Figure C.6. Status report to participating groups.

service clubs
business and
    professional organizations
Chamber of Commerce
senior citizens
boards and commissions
county officials
referral organizations
political organizations
women's groups
special interest groups

co-sponsored clubs
churches
historical society
PTA
schools
girl scouts
sports groups
homeowners
cultural and entertainment groups
agricultural groups
community schools

These are groups of both professionals and other citizens interested in Sunnyvale.

People in each group met with filled out questionnaires and talked about their concerns and opinions. These responses will be fully considered in designing the survey.

2. The July issue of the city newsletter "Sunnyvale Action" took the questionnaire form to each household in Sunnyvale. Response for this type of questionnaire was good. 316 people so far have taken the time to write responses (many wrote several additional pages of comments), cut out the survey, stamp it and mail it in. These responses will also be fully considered in designing the survey.

What's Next

During the next month we will:

1. Begin the process of hiring a professional polling firm to conduct the survey.

2. Tabulate all returned questionnaires.

3. Meet with representatives of three other cities who have conducted surveys.

4. Begin design of survey questionnaire.

Observations

The response from the community has been positive: people are interested in what happens in Sunnyvale and many want to be involved. We are off to a good start and thank you all. You'll be hearing from us.

Camille Cates
Administrative Assistant

Field Research Corporation, a public opinion research consulting firm, was hired by the city to administer the questionnaire and aid in defining the issues. In September, consultants met with department directors to hear their concerns. The directors reviewed the initial draft of the questionnaire before it was pretested with a small sample (20–30) of citizens.

The city manager and department directors, working as a project committee, reviewed eight drafts of questionnaires during October. They reviewed in-house drafts compiled from the questions and concerns raised during the issue research phase. The purpose of these reviews was to prioritize the many concerns and familiarize directors with the questionnaire content. Directors also reviewed two questionnaire drafts developed by the survey consulting firm. The purpose of these reviews was to check the language of the questions for possible bias and to shorten the questionnaire so it would take only 30 minutes to complete.

To decrease the possibility of bias, the manager and the department directors did not review the final questionnaire. The city council did not see any of the drafts of the questionnaires. The project manager gave approval of the final questionnaire that was used during the survey.

While working with city staff on the questionnaire, the survey consultants also drew a random sample of households and trained 20 interviewers to conduct the survey. With the issues defined, the questionnaire completed, background papers prepared, the sample selected, and the interviewers ready, the project moved into the next phase.

Phase 3: Issue Testing
The third phase of the project was testing the issues through a citywide survey with a scientific sample of 653 residents. About 80 percent of the survey was completed in the first two weeks of November, with callbacks to those who were not home the first time, to complete the administration of the questionnaire the third week. The consultant firm was completely in charge of the survey administration, including verification, coding, and tabulating responses.

On December 6, the city received the initial responses to the questionnaire. Answers were expressed in percentages of the sample; they were not broken down by the demographic characteristics of the population. For example, the city knew that 35 percent of the people answering felt very safe walking alone in their neighborhood at night, 45 percent felt reasonably safe, and 18 percent did not feel safe at all. But the city did not know how many women, as opposed to men, felt safe or where in the city those who felt unsafe lived. The cross-tabulations providing these kinds of answers were not available until later in December. These cross-tabulations showed a breakdown of demographic characteristics by census tract. This information was helpful in assessing needs in specific neighborhoods.

Figure C.7 illustrated the involvement of various groups in the two-month testing phase. Citizen involvement during this phase was through the actual survey.

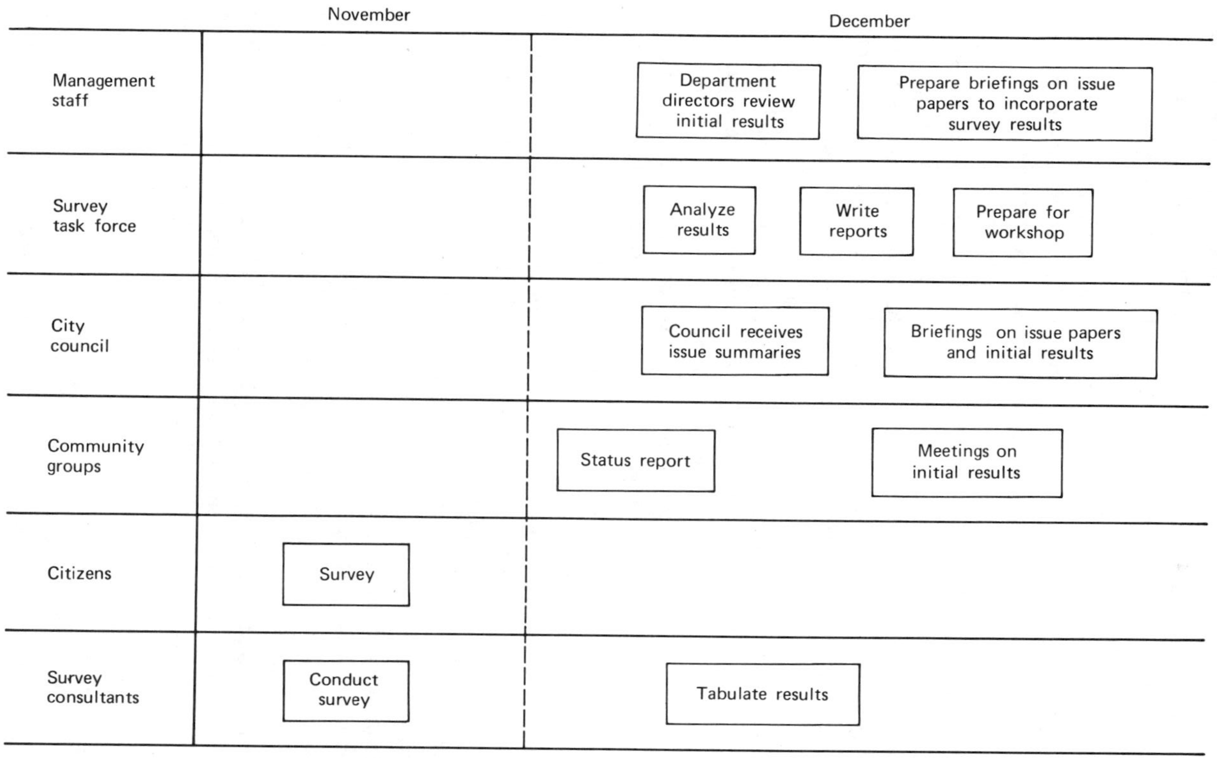

Figure C.7. Phase 3: Issue testing.

The initial results of the survey were released to the city manager and department directors on December 6, 1974; this was a Friday, so the results could be incorporated into the council briefings that began the following Monday. The city council received booklets with summaries of the issue papers, similar to those the management group had received prior to the October Asilomar session. The council received the three new issue papers prepared after Asilomar: the subjects were tennis, city disaster preparedness, and emergency communications. Three day-long city council briefing sessions were held the second week of December. At these meetings, department directors and some of the management group presented the issues as defined in the issue papers. The presentations emphasized options the city council could choose to address the issues. At the end of the briefings, the project manager presented the initial survey results and the plans for action on the results. Those plans included a town workshop and citizen task forces.

Community groups were involved through a status report and through personal contact. All 80 community groups that were involved in the community outreach phase of the project were contacted again to arrange a briefing session of the survey results in January. Several additional groups were also contacted. Besides the survey consultants, citizens, management staff, and city council, a new group became involved during the issue testing phase of the project: The Citizen Survey Task Force was formed to analyze the results, prepare reports, and prepare for the town workshop. The task force team consisted of the project manager, the community relations program manager, a public works employee (draftsperson), a recreation assistant, a public safety analyst, a public safety program manager, and a librarian. The public safety analyst on the task force prepared results and initial interpretations of results; the community relations program manager and the project manager prepared the report to citizens on the results; the draftsperson made charts, posters, and other visual aids to display the results; the recreation assistant was in charge of facility preparation for the workshop; and the librarian contacted community groups.

With the survey conducted, the results tabulated and analyzed, and reports written, the issue testing phase of the project was completed. Management staff, city council, community groups, and citizens were now ready for the final stage of the process.

Phase 4: Issue Action

The last phase of the project was using the information gathered in the previous phases to recommend changes in city services. This six-month phase, issue action, is depicted in Figure C.8. The tasks of this phase were to (1) inform people of survey results, (2) train workshop participants, (3) encourage workshop attendance, (4) hold a town workshop, (5) meet in task forces, and (6) recommend action to the city council.

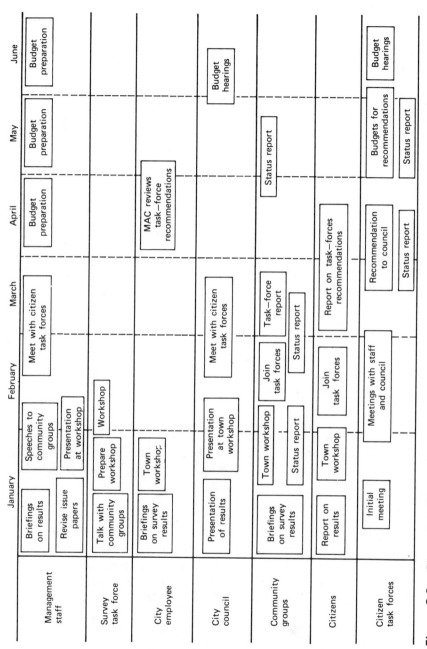

Figure C.8. Phase 4: Issue action.

The first task of this phase was to get the survey results to all the groups. The first announcement of the results was made at the regular city council meeting on January 7, 1975. The oral report on initial results did not include cross-tabulations. After the report on results, the mayor announced the council's plans for working with the results: a town workshop on Saturday, January 18, 1975, followed by citizen task forces to recommend programs to the city council.

Citizens at large were told of the survey results through a report mailed to every resident (see Figure C.9). The same week that the council heard the results and the mayor announced plans for working with the results, reports to citizens arrived in each household in the city. Press conferences were held with news media so there would be adequate news coverage of the results. A sample of an article relating to the project is shown in Figure C.10. In addition, several local radio stations interviewed the project staff regarding the survey process, the results, and plans for the workshop.

The same week the council and citizens heard survey results, the management group heard the results. On January 8, the management group met for an afternoon session to get results and prepare for briefing others on those results. Each manager saw copies of the citizen survey for the first time, got booklets containing the cross-tabulations and analysis of results, had the opportunity to discuss results, and was briefed on the next phase of the project.

The management group, in turn, held meetings with all city employees to discuss survey results. These meetings were scheduled during the two weeks prior to the workshop. Managers met with employees in small groups to discuss results, implications for departmental operations, and plans for the workshop and citizen task forces.

Members of the management group contacted community groups as well as employees. Community groups were first told of the survey results and workshop plans through these personal meetings. The survey task force and members of the management staff also went to 17 meetings of community groups scheduled between January 7th and 17th. Groups with no regularly scheduled meeting during that time were invited to an evening briefing session on January 9. That night there were 70 people representing 52 groups. The interest in survey results at this meeting was high. Each representative saw the survey for the first time, received a copy, and had an opportunity to discuss results and process with the project manager. The project manager also explained the process for using the results and recommending changes in city services. Representatives were encouraged to tell other members of their group about the results, the workshop, and the task forces.

After informing interested groups, the second task of the issue action phase was to train workshop participants. The initial briefing of the management staff and subsequent sessions with employees and community groups constituted the basic workshop training for the management staff. The preparation and revision

NOTE Your participation in the following meetings will give the city the direction it seeks:

DATE	LOCATION	PUBLIC MEETING
January 14 8 p.m.	City Council Chambers	Public Hearing — Program & Project budget suggestions
January 18 10 a.m.	**Community Center**	**Workshops on survey results "New Directions for Sunnyvale"**
January 31	Location and time to be announced at the workshop	Begin citizen task forces

Members of the City Council
Charley C. Allen, Mayor
Etta S. Albert   Donald E. Koreski
Gilbert R. Gunn   Donald S. Logan
Charles H. Hefferlin   Harold C. Shields

BULK RATE
POSTAGE
PAID
Sunnyvale,
California
94088
Permit No. 112

New Directions for Sunnyvale

Step 1 Citizen Survey

Figure C.9.   Report to citizens on survey results.

R The esults

On this page are the preliminary results of the citizen survey. All percentages you see are percentages of the total sample of 653. These are initial results. Not all of the questions are included because there was not time enough to prepare a full report before January.

None of the responses are analyzed by geographical area, age, sex, income, housing type, or any of the other demographic data collected. More of this information and other results and analysis will be available at the January 18th workshop.

Open Space

The term "open space" meant many things to many people. In Sunnyvale, the definitions most frequently given are:

Parks and playgrounds	54%
Undeveloped land	33%
Orchards	30%
Empty lots, no buildings	20%
Agricultural land	10%

(the total is greater than 100% because of multiple responses)

37% of the people in Sunnyvale are very interested, 37% are somewhat interested, and 25% are not very interested in the issue of open space.

Public Transit

Citizens rate public transit as follows. 6%, very satisfactory; 18%, somewhat satisfactory; 42%, not very satisfactory; 33%, no opinion.

67% of the people think it is very important to have public transit in Sunnyvale; 16% think it's somewhat important, 10% think it's not very important, and 7% have no opinion.

Public Safety

35% of the people feel very safe walking alone in their neighborhood at night; 45% feel reasonably safe; 18% feel not safe.

Citizens also ranked how important the enforcement of the following six kinds of laws is to them. The areas are, ranking in importance: 55%, Juvenile delinquency control, including vandalism; 19%, Traffic laws; 11%, Laws against using marijuana; 8%, Laws against bad checks and stolen credit cards; 5%, Bicycle rules and regulations; 3%, Leash laws (dog and cat).

New Services

Here is a list of possible **new services** the City could provide. Citizens chose the **one** they would most like the city to provide and the **one** they would least like the city to provide.

	% Most Like	% Least Like
Increase Job Opportunity	19	2
Major Redevelopment Project for Downtown Area	9	22
Providing Housing for People with Low and Moderate Incomes	17	7
Settling Tenant-Landlord Disputes	2	27
A Program to Inspect the Conditions of a House or Apt. or Townhouse and Require It to Meet Health, Safety and Housing Codes Before Someone Moves In.	8	4
Provide Emergency Medical Service (Paramedic Rescue Teams Sent to Places Where There is a Medical Emergency)	36	1
Provide a Central Information and Referral Service	4	15
Provide Child Care	4	22

Citizen Participation

61% of the people feel they could have a say about the way the City Government is running things if they wanted to (6% had no opinion).

61% of the people say they are willing to work on a task force or citizens committee to improve some of the conditions they are concerned about (7% had no opinion).

General City Appearance

For each of these services, citizens rate the job the City is doing as very satisfactory, somewhat satisfactory, or not very satisfactory, and whether they feel the service is very important, somewhat important and not very important

SATISFACTORY % IMPORTANT

	Very	Somewhat	Not	No Opinion	Very	Somewhat	Not	No Opinion
Landscaping of the sides and middle strips of major streets		40	10	2		31		1
Lighting on neighborhood streets		31	18	3	85	12		1
Conditions of streets	52	36	10	2	80	17		1
Neighborhood cleanliness (garbage or litter)	57	28	13	2	90	8		1

Parks & Recreation

The following is a rating of the effectiveness of neighborhood parks in meeting people's needs and whether the item is important.

	SATISFACTORY %				IMPORTANT			
	Very	Somewhat	Not Very	No Opinion	Very	Somewhat	Not Very	No Opinion
The facilities in the park ball fields, play ground equipment, picnic tables, etc	61	20	7	12	64	23	11	2
Maintenance of park grounds	74	17	2	7	74	19	4	2
Feeling of personal safety while in the park	51	28	11	10	86	8	4	3
Directed activities (arts and craft classes, organized ball games, dramatics, carnivals)	47	19	6	28	52	28	14	6
Undirected activities (picnics, kits, walks, tennis)	45	27	8	20	54	28	13	5

Library

For each of the following items, please rate the effectiveness of the Sunnyvale Library in meeting your and your family's needs as very satisfactory, somewhat satisfactory or not satisfactory. Please also tell me whether the item is very important to you, somewhat important or not very important.

	SATISFACTORY %				IMPORTANT			
	Very	Somewhat	Not Very	No Opinion	Very	Somewhat	Not Very	No Opinion
Research (patents, business, students, etc.)	44	18	2	37	61	18	14	8
Leisure reading (fiction, magazines)	54	16	1	29	51	29	13	7
California and local history	33	19	2	46	41	29	19	11
Bookmobile (mobile branch library)	28	14	4	53	47	19	22	12
Children's library	45	12	1	42	67	10	13	10
Seminars (special classes on various subjects)	16	16	3	65	32	29	22	17
Audio-visual services: films, tapes, art prints, etc.	21	16	3	60	38	29	19	15
Ease of getting to library	58	16	8	18	62	22	9	7
Hours library is open	55	16	3	26	63	21	8	9
Library has the books you want	49	20	5	27	73	14	6	8

Other Services

	SATISFACTORY %				IMPORTANT			
	Very	Somewhat	Not Very	No Opinion	Very	Somewhat	Not Very	No Opinion
Water services	82	13	4	1	95	5	0	0
Sewer services	83	12	3	3	95	4	1	0
Garbage collection services	73	18	9	1	96	3	0	0
Planning and zoning	28	35	20	17	78	13	3	6
Informational reports to citizens from city hall (including Recreation/Activities Guide, class schedule, newsletters, etc.)	58	21	13	8	65	25	9	2
Helpfulness of City employees	45	26	8	20	82	13	1	4

Citizen survey results to guide city's future

The first glimpse of what may become the new face of government in Sunnyvale will come Tuesday with the release of the results of the city's first scientific survey of residents.

The $14,000 poll was conducted by the Field Research Corporation of San Francisco during November and early December and included personal interviews with 600 Sunnyvale residents selected through scientific procedures which attempt to guarantee that the sample represents a cross-section of the city's population.

Sunnyvale's officials had been gearing up for the poll for the past two years in hopes that it will inaugurate a new era in the city—an era in which services for residents become the main part of government activity, rather than the provision of the basic building blocks of the physical city.

According to City Manager John Dever, those building blocks—streets, gutters, storm pipes, civic buildings—have nearly all been built. His budget message earlier this year noted that 1974 "marks the turning of the corner to full maturity that has been a community goal for the past 22 years."

The citizens survey is the key in helping decide which path the city will take now that it has turned the corner.

Are residents most interested in getting an efficient rapid transit system? Is child care a crying need for a large sector of the population? How concerned are residents about the city's lack of identity and what are they willing to do about it?

Questions such as these have been posed to the sample of residents who were interviewed for the poll. Their answers were cross-tabulated and then summarized by the city staff.

This voluminous stack of information will be relayed to the City Council Tuesday. But it will be only the first step in determining the kinds of programs the city will launch during the next few years.

Most management personnel working for the city have drafted "issue papers" dealing with their particular fields in an attempt to define their view of the direction which the city government should head.

These, too, will be presented to the council.

Dever said the survey and issue papers "should sharpen the decision-making process for the City Council, as well as clearly outlining the difficult choices among the many competing needs which are restricted by financial limitations."

After receiving the survey results and issue papers, it will be up to the council members to decide how they want to respond to the needs and desires expressed by the people who were polled.

City officials acknowledge that they have been searching for innovative ways to involve as many citizens as possible in implementing programs which the council reads as being the key ones pointed out by the survey.

The method which currently seems to be most likely is the creation of "task forces" of residents and officials who would delve into specific issues, such as child care, traffic or open space.

The stage at which such task forces would enter the decision-making process is unclear.

The council will not be tied in a direct way to following the courses indicated in the survey results. However, the results will be adding a quantitative element into the political picture which has not existed before. To buck a trend which has shown up clearly in the survey would now be clearly a way of acting contrary to the expressed wishes of a segment of the city's population.

Figure C.10. Report on survey from the Sunnyvale *Valley Journal*, January 3, 1975.

of the issue papers and discussion of issues at Asilomar had given the managers a comprehensive understanding of the issues.

Their training prior to the workshop focused on incorporating citizen survey results and practicing the verbal delivery of the information. Each manager was assigned to a specific workshop session and was expected to be knowledgeable on that topic. If managers were not making the actual presentation, they acted as reserves, ready to lead small-group discusions with citizens. The week before the workshop, the council received revised issue papers that incorporated survey results. Each council member was asked to chair one or two workshop sessions. The council met with management staff assigned to their workshop sessions to review the schedule, ask questions, develop a format for the meeting, and review the issue papers and survey results.

Once the groups were informed and the participants trained, the next task was to encourage workshop attendance. To encourage participation, the city provided transportation to the community center from all park sites and a free lunch the day of the workshop. Efforts to get citizens to come to the workshop included (1) the report to citizens sent to homes, (2) personal invitations addressed to 800 community leaders, (3) telephone calls just before the workshop, (4) posters in the community, (5) fliers sent home with schoolchildren, and (6) news articles describing the workshop.

Community groups were urged to attend during their informational meetings on survey results. The mayor and council also used the personal invitations to invite members of community groups. City employees were invited to attend in the survey briefing sessions held with their supervisors and through the employee news bulletin. Posters were displayed in city hall, the library, and the community center to remind everyone of the workshop's date, place, time, and purpose. With all this preparation, the town workshop called "New Directions for Sunnyvale" began.

On Saturday, January 18, 550 people met at the community center to hear results, discuss issues, and plan new directions for the city. They began the day in the gym with the mayor's welcome and a brief review of the six-month project. The vice-president of Field Research Corporation, the consultants for the survey, then explained the survey techniques. He explained the concept of a random sampling procedure, the interviewing methods, cross-tabulations, and his confidence in the results. He invited anyone with questions regarding the survey technique to meet with him in a separate workshop session.

After the opening session, the people went to various rooms in the community center to discuss the survey results, the status of city services, and options for the future. In the morning, five workshop sessions met to discuss public safety, child care, housing, waste treatment, and transportation. A council member opened each session and introduced the city staff present. The assigned member of the management staff (usually the same person who had prepared the issue paper) presented the issue and the survey results. Speakers used many visual aids in their presentations, and written reports were available. Booklets of survey results, including cross-tabulations and analyses were available in each session. Booklets were printed by issue area, so people interested in only one topic (e.g., child care) could get the total responses for that topic only. In addition, copies of the total questionnaire and overall percent responses were available in the workshop session.

The formats of the sessions varied according to the number of people in the session, the nature of the topic, and the preference of the speakers. Large sessions (100–200 people) on, for example, transportation and emergency medical services, were primarily presentations with question-and-answer sessions. Smaller sessions (e.g., a child care session of 40 people) began with a presentation and then broke into four small groups to discuss issues. The management staff in each session took minutes of the session. Citizens were free to attend more than one morning session, and several did.

At the end of each session, citizens were encouraged to sign up for task forces to work on the issues and recommend action. At noon, workshop participants went back to the gym for a fried chicken lunch and more talk. Council members and city staff discussed issues and concerns with citizens. Chairs were arranged in circles of 10 to encourage discussions. An information booth was staffed the entire day to give directions to the sessions, provide copies of all printed reports and questionnaires, answer questions, and sign people up for task forces.

After lunch, five more sessions—on recreation, citizen participation, open space, library, and economic development—were held. These sessions were conducted in the same manner as the morning sessions. Attendance in the afternoon was about the same as in the morning. Most people who came in the morning stayed all day. At the end of the day, 250 people had signed up to work on the 10 task forces. The topics of the 10 task forces corresponded to the 10 workshop sessions of the day. The council member and speaker assigned to a particular workshop session was also assigned to the corresponding task force.

After the workshop, the next task of the issue action phase of the project was to meet in the task forces. All task-force meetings were public meetings. Any citizen could join a task force at any time and receive personal notice and minutes of all task-force meetings. Each week a schedule of task-force meetings was published in the newspaper and was posted in city hall, the library, and the community center.

During February and March, there were 94 separate task-force meetings. Citizens asked questions, made field trips, researched specific proposals, examined the city budget, talked with experts, searched for ways to pay for each proposal, and prepared reports on their research and recommendations.

The child care task force provides a typical example of the task-force process. There were approximately 45 people attending the first task-force meeting at the community center, most of whom had been in the Saturday workshop session two weeks before. About 15 had been in the day care interest groups that were involved in the project the summer before the issue research phase. About 10 were day care professionals, directors and teachers in day care centers, or advisers in county day care programs. The remaining 20 were interested citizens, some with small children, others without.

After opening remarks by the council member and city staff, the group decided to break into three working subcommittees. Each subcommittee selected its own chairperson and set the date and purpose of its next meeting. The group decided that each subcommittee would meet weekly during the six-week period allotted to the task forces. Each subcommittee would prepare a report on its findings and recommendations to bring to the entire child care task force. The task force as a whole would prepare the final report and recommendations to the city council. A staff member met with each of the subcommittees. Members wrote the minutes of the meetings, and the staff member had them typed and sent to each member of the task force the week of the meeting.

The child care task-force members made a comprehensive list of existing day care centers in Sunnyvale and the type and cost of the care provided. They also talked with representatives of a neighboring city, Palo Alto, that had begun work in child care. They reviewed state licensing requirements and regulations for federal Community Development Block Grant funds, developed sample budgets, and heard reports on new program ideas, centers lacking sufficient funds, and ways to raise city money. In the final task-force meeting with the council member, the task force prioritized its recommendations and proposed implementation over a three-year period. The costs of the recommendations were computed, and the task force recommended ways to pay those costs. The final recommendation to the city council, submitted in March, was as follows:

During fiscal year 1975–76:

1. That the city fund a child care center with Community Development Block Grant Funds, according to the guidelines established by the task force.
2. That the city designate a nonprofit corporation to implement and coordinate the task force recommendations and hire a mobilizer to administer disbursement of money and develop community support for child care.

During fiscal year 1976–77:

3. That the city review for funding the following child care programs in priority order:
   a. Support for existing nonprofit child care programs.
   b. A combination day care home—preschool program.
   c. An extended day care program.
   d. An infant-toddler program.
   e. A sick child care program.
   f. A part-time child care program.

Funding:

1. The child care center will be funded by the $50,000 from the federal Community Development Block Grant funds.
2. The $29,050 for the mobilizer's salary and office expenses will be funded by a 0.1 of 1 percent increase in the utility user's tax.

The final task of the issue action phase was for all task forces to recommend actions to the city council. Each recommendation had a cost computed and a revenue source identified. All recommentations were presented publicly at a city council meeting. Summaries of all the task-force recommendations were printed in a report to citizens mailed to every household in Sunnyvale (see Figure C.11).

In March all 10 task forces presented their recommendations and reports to the city council. The recommendations and a description of the entire "New Directions" project were printed in a separate booklet and were made available to interested citizens and community groups. Final reports and recommendations were mailed to every citizen who had signed up for a task force or had asked for information regarding the task force.

Once the council heard the recommendations and citizens received information regarding them, the city staff began to analyze the recommendations for inclusion in the budgeting process. The managers prepared a separate program budget for every recommendation of every task force. These budgets were included as a separate section of the regular Resource Allocation Plan. Copies of this entire section were mailed to every task-force member, all community groups, and anyone else requesting it. A schedule of budget hearings was sent with the budget sections.

During the city council budget hearings, citizens had the opportunity to discuss recommendations and revenue sources. At these hearings, city staff presented the task-force recommendations and alternative ways of accomplishing them. The city council, after studying recommendations and alternatives, amended the budget to include changes in existing programs and new programs and services.

The year-long "New Directions" project used a variety of methods to involve groups in the city's decision-making process. Citizens, the city council, and city staff were involved through briefings, training sessions, public meetings, group discussions, written reports, surveys, and task forces. The project explored the range of existing and potential city services. These groups, through their involvement, developed new directions for Sunnyvale.

PART II: THE RESULTS

The "New Directions" project has had a lasting impact on the city. The specific results include adjustments in existing programs, new programs, and the continuation of citizen involvement in the goal setting and budget development process. Each task-force recommendation was considered in the regular budget-

CITY MEETINGS

(All meetings listed begin at 8:00 p.m.)

DAY	LOCATION	PUBLIC MEETING
Tuesdays	CITY COUNCIL CHAMBERS	City Council Meeting
2nd and 4th Wednesdays	CITY COUNCIL CHAMBERS	Parks & Recreation Commission
2nd and 4th Mondays	CITY COUNCIL CHAMBERS	Planning Commission
3rd Monday	LIBRARY	Library Board

Members of the City Council

Charley C. Allen, Mayor

Etta S. Albert	Donald E. Koreski
Gilbert R. Gunn	Donald S. Logan
Charles H. Hefferlin	Harold C. Shields

BULK RATE
POSTAGE
P A I D
Sunnyvale,
California
94088
Permit No. 112

March 1975

Figure C.11. Report that was mailed to citizens of task force recommendations.

New Directions for Sunnyvale

Step 2 - The Recommendations

Introduction

The City of Sunnyvale is making a unique effort to involve citizens in the decision making process of its government. Sunnyvale has asked the entire comunity to help plan for the complicated needs of the future. Over 1000 people participated in the initial phase of this process, contributing ideas, suggestions and opinions in the design of a citizen survey. In November, an independent opinion sampling firm conducted a scientific community-wide survey involving 653 Sunnyvale citizens. The results of this survey reflect the concerns and goals of the entire community.

Every citizen in the city was invited to a workshop January 18 to learn more about the survey results. Over 500 citizens attended the all-day workshop to discuss public safety, child care, housing, waste treatment, transportation, recreation, citizen participation, open space, library and economic development. Background and financial information were also presented to citizens at the workshop sessions. At the end of the day 250 people had signed up to work on ten citizen task forces.

From January to March these task forces met at a total of 94 separate meetings. Citizens asked questions, made field trips, researched specific proposals, examined the city budget, talked with experts, searched for ways to pay for each proposal and prepared their recommendations. On March 11 all task force recommendations were presented to the City Council for consideration in the preparation of the city's budget for the next fiscal year.

Complete task force proposals are available at the Sunnyvale Public Library, 665 W. Olive and the City Clerk's office in City Hall, 456 W. Olive. The City Council needs to hear the opinions of all Sunnyvale citizens. If you were unable to join a citizen task force, write or talk to city council members about your opinions.

The following report is a summary of the recommendations of the citizen task forces.

Citizen Participation and Information Recommendations

COMMUNITY INFORMATION BOARDS — City Council should explore implementing weather-proof, vandal-proof community information bulletin boards in neighborhood shopping centers. Representatives of the Citizen Participation Task Force, Merchant Association representatives and shopping center proprietors would work with City Staff on this research.

INFORMATION/REFERRAL — The City should fund an information/referral position at Sunnyvale Community Services. (Estimated salary cost: $9,000).

A phone line on the City switchboard should be established directly to Community Services for information/referral purposes.

Develop a system of channeling after hours requests for information through the reference desk of the Sunnyvale Library using a written form or a tape recorder.

FUNDING — Community Development Block Grant funding of the information/referral position should be investigated.

NEIGHBORHOOD REPRESENTATIVES — That a Council of Neighborhood Representatives be established by an election process to establish a two-way communication between City Hall and neighborhoods. The Council of Neighborhood Representatives would help City Council learn the needs and concerns of neighborhoods. It would also provide the mechanism for disseminating all pertinent city information to neighborhoods.

Representatives on the Council of Neighborhood Representatives should be elected annually from 12-16 areas of the city based generally on population. Each representative would be required to hold a minimum of two town hall meetings annually in their neighborhoods.

The City Government should hold a minimum of three briefings for the Council of Neighborhood Representatives annually. In addition, the representatives should receive council agendas, and can request specific background material from the agenda that pertains to their neighborhood.

Child Care Recommendations

During the fiscal year 1975-76, the Child Care Task Force recommends funding a child care center with money from the Community Development Block Grant ($50,000), according to guidelines established by the Task Force. In addition, City Council is asked to designate a non-profit corporation to implement and coordinate Task Force recommendations. The position of a city-funded "Mobilizer" is recommended to administer disbursement of money and develop community support for child care. The Task Force suggests that the $29,050 for the Mobilizer's salary and office expenses can be funded by a .1 of 1% increase in the utility users tax.

City funding of child care programs during the fiscal year 1976-77 are listed in priority order by the Task Force: (1) support for existing non-profit child care program; (2) combination day care home/preschool program; (3) an extended day care program; (4) an infant/toddler program; (5) a sick child care program; (6) a part-time child care program.

Economic Development Recommendations

CENTRAL CORE REDEVELOPMENT — Recognizing that "downtown Sunnyvale" is in danger of deteriorating, the Economic Development Task Force recomends that the City Council act as the Redevelopment Agency for Sunnyvale. The Task Force requests immediate action to set the boundaries of the survey area as described in the Larry Smith & Co. report and schedule public hearings as necessary to adopt a redevelopment plan for the Sunnyvale downtown area. A total service area for Sunnyvale citizens is needed to provide better facilities and merchandise within a short distance, advises the task force.

INDUSTRIAL DEVELOPMENT — The Economic Development Task Force recommends that the present committed industrial land be developed to its maximum taxable base. Furthermore, permits for mobile home parks in industrially zoned areas should no longer be issued. Present regulations for industrial development should be reviewed, according to the Task Force, to keep Sunnyvale competitive with surrounding cities. Continued citizen involvement is recommended by the Task Force, including an advisory board of professional people to review industrial architecture and landscaping.

Housing Recommendations

The Housing Task Force recommends that a study group be formed to work with city staff to study in depth the affirmative action housing program. The responsibilities of this study group would be to: procure and coordinate data about local housing needs; study methods of procuring low and moderate income housing; provide housing information; and work with the County Housing Authority on leased housing and rent supplements.

Emergency Medical Services Recommendations

* Training of Public Safety Officers should be upgraded to Emergency Medical Technician I level within a three year period.

* The City should maintain the current level of ambulance service.

* Give Public Safety Officers the option of becoming paramedics at the end of the three years.

* Be prepared when El Camino Hospital is ready to implement paramedic services.

* The city paramedic system should consist of three paramedic teams.

Library Recommendations

The Library Task Force recomends enlarging the Library building by approximately 13,500 square feet to provide needed space for reading and research, an audio-visual program and additional space for books. This expansion would cost approximately $985,000.00, which could be funded through a bond issue if necessary. Another concern of the task force is that the book collection be kept up to date and large enough for patrons.

Open Space Recommendations

As shown by the recent open space bond election and the citizens' survey, there is prompt need for open space acquisition in Sunnyvale. Open space sites should be preserved where needed most, considering population of the area, location and accessibility of existing open space and imminence of development. Surplused school sites and privately held parcels should be given equal consideration to achieve equitable distribution of open space throughout the community.

The Task Force advocates fee-title acquisition, long term lease or lease-purchase arrangements, as well as cooperative purchase with another public agency.

FUNDING — (1) Property tax override election for a specific period. (2) Federal and state open space funds. (3) Revenue sharing and Community Development block grant funds. (4) Sale of Mountain Park to public agency. (5) General obligation bond. (6) Active support of state legislation which would allow school districts to lease sites for appropriate long-term community use. (7) Mandatory dedication of open space or payment in lieu of dedication.

Public Safety Recommendations

PUBLIC INFORMATION AND INVOLVEMENT — New lines of communication should be opened between Public Safety and the community. A bilingual position of Public Relations Assistant should be established.

COMMUNITY SAFETY — The Task Force recommends the addition of four sworn officers around the clock to Patrol Division (18 new personnel). This increase is to be covered by a 1½% public utility tax.

JUVENILE DELINQUENCY - Promote community-wide youth seminars directed toward gaining more knowledge about the causes of juvenile problems. Provide for the continuing study of juvenile problems by a citizen task force involving the youth of the community.

Recreation Recommendations

CHILDREN AND YOUTH —
* Programs should assure equal opportunities for sexes.
* A Community Center - type facility should be developed on the north side, possibly funded through a block grant; $600,000 for acquisition and $150,000 for operation.
* Year-round youth employment service, administered by a full-time staff member. Cost estimated at $40,000 per year for administrative assistant, offices, part-time secretarial services, telephone, etc.
* Establish citywide youth advisory board to evaluate programs and services. Estimated cost: $1500 for printing, staff time and miscellaneous.
* Provide shelter for patio area at Orchard Gardens Park. Estimated cost: $10,000 for capital expenditure.

SPORTS, AQUATICS AND TENNIS —
* Tennis facilities should be expanded to complete Phase I and Phase II of the Las Palmas Tennis Center, hire a professional at the Tennis Center, and install backboards and wind screens at all tennis facilities. Phase I is presently budgeted from Revenue Sharing funds in the amount of $671,563. Phase II will cost an estimated $400,000 and would have to be provided from a future bond program. Salary for the tennis pro is estimated at $6000 the first two years. Backboards and wind screens would cost $2000 per court x six courts for a total of $12,000.
* Expand the Gymnastics and Open Gym programs. The cost for expanding the programs is estimated at $20,140, but would be offset by revenue.
* Acquire multiple purpose open space recreation use areas for various sports activities. Funding: future bond issues.

ADULT AND CULTURAL —
* Develop a comprehensive performing and fine arts program. Estimated cost: $9250 which would be offset by revenue from performances and public programs.
* Provide budgetary support of $7500 to the development of the Historical Museum of the Sunnyvale Historical Society and Museum Association.
* Examine the Parks and Recreation Department activity fee structure (costs and facility rental) with aim of reducing current costs to Sunnyvale residents.

GOLF —
* Resident and non-resident green fees should be established with higher non-resident fees. The additional income from non-residents, estimated at $30,000 per year, could help offset the senior citizen and student rate.
* A special rate for students and senior citizens who are residents of Sunnyvale should be established.
* Sunken Gardens Golf Course should establish an 18-hole green fee at the following suggested rates for weekends and holidays:
  Residents — $2.50 for 9 holes, $4.00 for 18 holes;
  Non-Residents — $3.00 for 9 holes and $5.00 for 18 holes.
  The suggested weekday rate is:
  Residents — $2.00 for 9 holes, $3.50 for 18 holes;
  Non-Residents — $2.50 for 9 holes, $4.50 for 18 holes.

Transportation Recommendations

To improve the current transit system, the Transportation Task Force recommends an immediate survey of origins and destinations to find out were people live and where they want to travel.

Sunnyvale's supplemental transit service for the elderly and handicapped should be continued under the current private ownership arrangement with the taxi company. If, however, the Santa Clara County Transit District acquires the taxi company, City Council should demand the same level of service from the District.

City Council should recommend to the District that future busses be purchased with diesel power instead of propane. This would allow greater flexibility of equipment at more competitive prices.

City Council should recommend to the District diversion of dial-a-ride busses to heavily traveled commuter routes from 6:00-8:30 a.m. and 4:00-6:00 p.m. From 8:30 a.m. to 4:30 p.m., these busses should be utilized in a regularly scheduled route to connect neighborhoods with downtown shopping centers and other activity centers as well as the existing inner-city arterial system.

FUNDING — If the County Transit District demonstrates it can make efficient use of its existing equipment and resources and develops a satisfactory system expansion program, the City Council should consider supporting additional funding measures.

Waste Treatment Recommendations

RECYCLING CENTERS — The Task Force sets a goal to salvage maximum amounts of materials from solid wastes by a series of recycling centers. A model recycling center is recommended for Fremont High School, to be operated by the Fremont High School Ecology Club. Based on the experiences at the Fremont High School Recycling Center, several similar recycling centers should be established at other schools, churches, shopping centers, etc. City cost is estimated at $370 to set up the Fremont High School Center and at $170 for each additional recycling center.

BOTTLE BILL — The City should actively promote legislation at the State level to require returnable bottles in California as the State of Oregon has required.

WATER QUALITY — In the case of a severe earthquake, many serious main breaks could occur in the water distribution system. Power to the submersible pumps in the City's water wells could be interrupted. The Task Force recommends provision of automatic shutoff of valves at the major tanks to save water in emergencies. Estimated cost of valves: $147,500. Additionally, one permanent and one portable generator should be provided to generate electricity in case the commercial source fails. Estimated cost of generators is $138,500.

FUNDING — Finance the generators by an increase in water rates, 1.1% over four years or 2.2% over two years. The valves could be financed by increasing the water rates by approximately 0.6%.

SOURCE SEPARATION OF SOLID WASTES — The Task Force recomends establishment of an ad hoc committee to study the possibility of a source separation program for Sunnyvale. This committee should have approximately a six month deadline to prepare a report for consideration at the next budget hearings.

ing process, and most were implemented in some form. Some recommendations resulted in shifts of emphasis in a program's goals and the allocation of recources to meet those goals. Others resulted in entirely new programs. Once the council made the budget decisions, task-force members and other interested citizens were notified of these results.

Existing programs were adjusted to incorporate survey results and task-force recommendations. For example, park and recreation expanded programs for the performing arts and fine arts and for teenagers. In public safety, nine additional public safety officers were allocated to the existing programs.

An example of a new program is the neighborhood center that was developed at a surplus school site in a relatively isolated section of the city. The need for better city services in this neighborhood had been shown in citizen survey data. The center houses extension library services, expanded recreation programs, and special public safety services. Librarians provide all services available at the main library, a recreation coordinator designs recreation programs specifically suited to community needs, and a public safety officer walks the beat, gets to know the community, and works on special problems. All these services are in addition to the regular city services to the area.

Community Development Block Grant funds were used to implement child care task-force recommendations. The demographics from the survey identified census tracts with the greatest child care needs and helped determine the final location for the new facility.

Other new programs include a recycling center at a high school and a completely new department—the Department of Employment Development, which was created to train and employ residents. Additional new programs were slated as ballot measures because of the expense involved in implementing the recommendations. Voters have the opportunity to tax themselves for open-space land acquisition and emergency medical services.

The city council financed actions through available funds (some federal money was used) and by changing the taxes. The council imposed a 1 percent utility user's tax, a new construction tax, and a prorated business license tax. They lowered the property tax from $1.31 to $1.18 per $100 assessed valuation. The intention of the council was to pay for these new programs while at the same time shifting the tax burden away from individual property owners and toward business and industry. This is a new direction for Sunnyvale.

EMPLOYEE SURVEY AND REACTIONS TO IT

THE SURVEY

The second phase of the Total Performance Measurement (TPM) project was that of employee attitude measurement. The employee has a great deal of effect on the services an organization delivers—positive or negative. He or she can slow down work or speed it up, create a good public image or a bad one. The employee, more than any other single factor, affects the effectiveness and efficiency of an organization. The use of employee attitudes as a measure of performance was new and, as such, received a lot of attention throughout the TPM project. To define measures and initiate reporting systems is a multiyear process that Sunnyvale began several years ago. The focus on employee attitudes for this particular project was to add a new dimension to existing performance measures and begin to integrate all three measures—citizen satisfaction, employee attitudes, and productivity data.

Management's Involvement

The city manager's interest in and commitment to the project was clear from the outset. Department directors were carefully briefed on the project's concept, purpose, and plans at the initial stages of the project. At a two-day management retreat, all 50 program managers (from first-line supervisors to the city manager) discussed the project and its implications fully before data collection began. The management group's understanding of and commitment to the project was a key factor to its success. This commitment was crucial to gain credibility with employees and insure that action would be taken.

Regular project status reports were published in the employee newsletter and posted on employee bulletin boards to communicate management's commitment to the project. The city manager and project coordinator discussed all phases of the project with a standing employee committee, the Manager's Advisory Council (MAC). Program managers discussed the two-day training session, the project's purpose, and employee concerns with their staffs.

Training for managers was an important element of the TPM process in Sunnyvale. The entire management group of 50 attended two important training sessions during the process. Managers were interested in discussing the project informally to express their concerns and ask questions about the concept. The amount of time, resources, and energy necessary to successfully complete the project required substantial commitment from the chief executive and the total management group.

Employee Involvement

Fourteen groups of employees, representing all departments and major job classifications, met with the consultant who was to administer the employee survey. He explained the project and its purpose and listened to employee concerns about the organization. Employees involved in these interviews discussed them freely with their co-workers, which heightened interest in the project.

MAC, a standing committee of 20 employees representing each department and each shift within a department, also met with the consultant during the initial phase of the project. Throughout the project, MAC members received all the information about the project, advised the city manager on the best ways to involve employees, and related ideas and concerns of their co-workers. The discussions with MAC were a valuable source of employee reactions and suggestions for improvement in the process.

Despite these efforts to inform and involve employees, managers later felt that employees did not have a clear understanding of the entire process at the time the employees took the survey. The time delay (four months) between initial employee interviews and questionnaire administration probably hindered that understanding. In addition, information was usually written and not discussed, which made it more difficult to answer questions and get ideas from employees.

All employees were involved with the construction of the questionnaire. The administration of this questionnaire affected the way employees answered the questions and, later, how much credibility employees gave to the results.

Productivity Measurement

Before the employee questionnaire was administered, improvements were made in Sunnyvale's method of measuring productivity. The first change was to begin to measure program *output*, rather than each individual activity leading to that output. For example, in the recreation program, rather than measuring participants served, the measurement became participant hours provided—which more accurately measures accomplishments, or outputs. The second change was to weight productivity against work hours. Previously, production units included all program activities, but did not include any measure of work hours. The third change was to express unit costs and total program costs in constant dollars (modified by the San Francisco Bay Area Consumer Price Index), as well as actual dollars. In the past, costs were expressed in actual dollars only, which did not take inflation into account.

The productivity measurement changes have improved Sunnyvale's Planning, Programming, Budgeting System. After the productivity data were gathered, the overall productivity trend and dollar costs were computed for the city. As shown in Figure C.12, productivity in Sunnyvale has increased at an average annual rate of 4.3 percent, saving the city an estimated $3 million over the last three years.

Employee Survey Results

The city received computer printouts of part of the employee survey results for (1) each work unit, (2) divisions of the two largest departments, and (3) all eight departments. The city also received two master books with *all* questions coded by either occupation or organization.

In addition to written results, consultants verbally presented overall city results to the management group and related them to productivity measures and citizen satisfaction. The city received a copy of the charts used in the oral presentation and made copies available to employees.

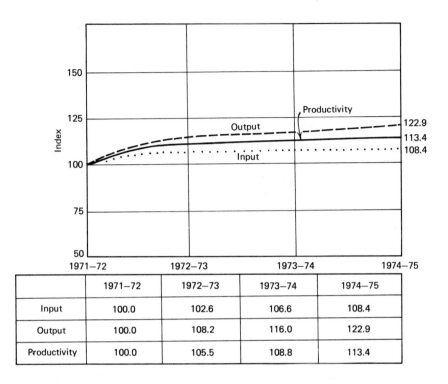

	1971–72	1972–73	1973–74	1974–75
Input	100.0	102.6	106.6	108.4
Output	100.0	108.2	116.0	122.9
Productivity	100.0	105.5	108.8	113.4

Productivity Savings

	1971–72	1972–73	1973–74	1974–75
Labor cost (including benefits)	$7,291,603.72	$8,209,625.86	$8,938,126.67	$10,023,842.17
Staff hours	1070483.3	1113629.4	1139964.9	1193728.3
Productivity increase (over base period)	0	5.5%	8.0%	12.4%
Savings	0	$ 451,529.42	$ 715,050.13	$ 1,242,956.42
Inflated savings	0	$ 512,133.70	$ 761,528.38	$ 1,242,956.42
Total dollar savings				$ 2,516,618.50
Work-hour savings		61249.6	91197.2	148,022.3
Total work-hour savings				300,469.1

SUNNYVALE PERFORMANCE DATE: Productivity trends
DEPARTMENT: Total, city
SURVEY CODE:

Figure C.12.   Productivity trends and savings in Sunnyvale.

Each employee received a copy of the partial survey results for his or her work unit, which included answers to questions on (1) the organization in general, (2) job and work load, (3) effectiveness, (4) earnings, (5) advancement, (6) recognition and performance, (7) communications and grievances, (8) management, and (9) immediate supervision (see Figure C.13).

The survey results for each work unit and department were the basis for group discussions and the development of work unit action plans. The only part of the survey results reported in work-unit printouts (about half the 140 questions on the survey) were those relating to standard questions used with other organization in other parts of the country. The value of the questionnaire would have increased if results had been reported for questions specific to Sunnyvale.

Productivity Data and Citizen Satisfaction Data

The other two types of data for TPM—productivity and citizen satisfaction data—were not discussed as much as the employee attitude data because they were familiar to the organization. The productivity data did, however, help put the attitude data into perspective in the individual work units.

The citizen survey used in this project was designed and conducted in November 1974 for a purpose different from that of the TPM "customer attitude survey." The November 1974 citizen survey specifically avoided a user survey design; it was designed for assessing goals of the city. Because the design and purpose was different, only a few questions could be used for the TPM project. Those few questions used were reported in the oral presentation, but were not fully integrated into the analysis.

An example of a question that appeared on both the citizen survey and the employee questionnaire concerned employee helpfulness and cooperation with citizens.

EMPLOYEE QUESTIONNAIRE
"In general, how would you rate the courtesy and cooperation in dealing with citizens?"

Very Good	Good	So-So	Poor	Very Poor
40%	49%	11%	1%	0

CITIZEN SURVEY
"How would you rate your satisfaction with the helpfulness of city employees?"

Very Satisfied	Somewhat Satisfied	Not Very Satisfied	No Opinion
45%	26%	8%	20%

	NUMBER VALID ANSWERS	1	2	RESPONSE CATEGORIES 3 4 5 6 7 8 9						MEAN	RANK	INVALID

/THESE ITEMS ARE ABOUT COMMUNICATIONS/GRIEVANCE C/_

PERCENT

QUEST 024-- ALL IN ALL, HOW WOULD YOU RATE SUNNYVALE ON COMMUNICATING TO EMPLOYEES ABOUT MATTERS THAT AFFECT THEM?
1-VERY GOOD 2-GOOD 3-SO-SO 4-POOR 5-VERY POOR 6-NO IDEA

	NUMBER VALID	1	2	3	4	5	MEAN	RANK	INVALID
MANAGERS	53	11	40	25	13	11	2.74	0/0	0
PARKS AND RECREATION DEPT-MANAGERS	12	0	25	58	17	0	2.92	2/3	0
REGULAR EMPLOYEES	428	5	20	29	24	21	3.36	0/0	5
PARKS AND RECREATION DEPT-EMPLOYEES	83	6	30	31	8	24	3.15	4/9	5
TEMPORARY EMPLOYEES	73	11	19	20	23	21	3.25	0/0	1
PARKS AND RECREATION DEPT-TEMPORARY	30	13	17	27	37	13	3.20	2/3	0

QUEST 062--DO YOU AGREE-DISAGREE: ENOUGH NOTIFICATION IS USUALLY GIVEN TO EMPLOYEES BEFORE CHANGES ARE MADE IN PROGRAMS, POLICIES
1-STRONG AGREE 2-AGREE 3-NEITHER 4-DISAGREE 5-STRONG DISAGREE

	NUMBER VALID	1	2	3	4	5	MEAN	RANK	INVALID
MANAGERS	53	6	30	17	40	8	3.13	0/0	0
PARKS AND RECREATION DEPT-MANAGERS	12	8	25	8	42	17	3.33	2/3	0
REGULAR EMPLOYEES	431	5	29	17	34	16	3.27	0/0	2
PARKS AND RECREATION DEPT-EMPLOYEES	83	7	35	18	29	11	3.01	4/9	0
TEMPORARY EMPLOYEES	74	4	32	18	27	19	3.24	0/0	0
PARKS AND RECREATION-TEMPORARY	30	3	30	7	37	23	3.47	3/3	0

QUEST 025--ALL IN ALL, HOW WOULD YOU RATE SUNNYVALE ON LISTENING TO EMPLOYEES (THEIR IDEAS FOR IMPROVEMENTS, ETC.)?
1-VERY GOOD 2-GOOD 3-SO-SO 4-POOR 5-VERY POOR 6-NO IDEA

	NUMBER VALID	1	2	3	4	5	MEAN	RANK	INVALID
MANAGERS	53	17	34	34	9	6	2.53	0/0	0
PARKS AND RECREATION DEPT-MANAGERS	12	17	25	50	8	0	2.50	2/3	0
REGULAR EMPLOYEES	427	4	19	33	22	22	3.37	0/0	6
PARKS AND RECREATION DEPT-EMPLOYEES	83	6	22	35	14	23	3.27	4/9	0
TEMPORARY EMPLOYEES	73	10	21	34	22	14	3.10	0/0	1
PARKS AND RECREATION-TEMPORARY	30	13	20	30	30	7	2.97	2/3	0

QUEST 042--DO YOU AGREE-DISAGREE: EMPLOYEES CAN USUALLY GET A FAIR HEARING FOR THEIR COMPLAINTS
1-STRONG AGREE 2-AGREE 3-NEITHER 4-DISAGREE 5 STRONG AGREE

	NUMBER VALID	1	2	3	4	5	MEAN	RANK	INVALID
MANAGERS	53	23	51	15	9	2	2.17	0/0	0
PARKS AND RECREATION DEPT-MANAGERS	12	25	50	17	8	0	2.08	2/3	0
REGULAR EMPLOYEES	429	5	27	26	30	11	3.14	0/0	4
PARKS AND RECREATION DEPT-EMPLOYEES	83	8	36	18	23	14	2.99	3/9	0
TEMPORARY EMPLOYEES	74	4	32	31	23	9	3.01	0/0	0
PARKS AND RECREATION DEPT-TEMPORARY	30	3	37	30	27	3	2.90	2/3	0

Figure C.13. A sample computer printout from the Total Performance Measurement Employee Survey. This printout shows the results of the employee survey in tabulation form. The question is stated with the various types of responses that were available to the person taking the survey. *Column 1* indicates the number of valid answers by individuals who responded. *Column 2* represents a percentage of the individuals who responded according to the choices. All questions had 5 or 6 choices: very good, good, so so, poor, very poor, and no idea. Under column 2 the percentage shown represents what percentage of the people taking the survey responded with "very good" or "strongly agree," and so on. These responses are represented in percentages, and do not indicate how many actually responded in that manner. *Column 3* represents the mean of the responses. *Column 4* represents the rank that is the order of the various units within a grouping. *Column 5* gives the number of invalid responses.

485

In the work-unit meetings, attention focused on employee attitude data rather than citizen satisfaction or productivity data. Citizen satisfaction data did not exist for all units, so they could not be used. Managers were generally more interested in productivity data than were employees, although some employees were more interested after the survey than previously.

Action Plan Development

Employee participation in developing written action plan of recommendations for change was crucial to the success of this project. Employees and their supervisors held over 200 meetings during a 30-day period following the survey to discuss issues and develop recommendations. One of the most valuable aspects of the TPM project was getting employees and supervisors talking with each other about problems. Such extensive employee participation was an innovation in itself. Many work units felt that the discussions were useful and should be continued regularly, and they included this recommendation in their action plans.

The unit action plan provided a positive focus for discussion. Employees received a written format as a guideline for submitting their recommendations. In the action plan, employees first stated their goals (i.e., problems stated positively or strengths to maintain). Next, they listed their recommended actions with a timetable, if appropriate. The level of responsibility (unit, department, or city) for the action was then stated, along with any recommendations for methods to evaluate the actions taken (see Figure C.14).

During the action-plan development, management facilitators, when requested, worked with several work units in departments other than their own to make discussion easier. The idea of using facilitators for this project originated with MAC. Some employees said they felt uncomfortable with the idea of disccusing the survey results with their immediate supervisors; others did not. The option of using a facilitator, either at the initial meeting or at subsequent meetings, was the group's response to a potential problem.

Facilitators served as a planning committee to advise the project coordinator on the needs and attitudes of those in the employee meetings. Facilitators also advised the project coordinator on the entire employee survey process, helped design action-plan formats, and assisted in the evaluation of the project.

Work-unit action plans were passed on to department directors and then intact to the city manager. The department directors also prepared department action plans based on suggestions from work-unit plans (see Figure C.15). The departmental plans included goals, employees' recommended actions, departmental analysis and recommendations, and a schedule for implementation. Some actions were taken immediately following this process. In the Department of Park and Recreation, for example, a work-unit recommendation was that the director hold quarterly meetings with each work unit; this was initiated.

WORK UNIT: *Parks and Recreation Management* ACTION PLAN SUMMARY FOR: *Department of Parks and Recreation*

Goal (Problems Stated Positively/ Strengths To Maintain)	Action (Specific Recommendations with Time Frames When Appropriate)	Responsibility (Unit, Dept., City)	Evaluation
More advance notice be given on special projects as well as a number of other projects passed down from the city manager, Department of Administration, and Finance Department	Whenever possible, projects should be planned on an annual basis so that the department can plan work accordingly. When last-minute projects must be done, more consideration should be given to the problems within the Parks and Recreation Department relative to work load because of the number of seasonal problems, such as summer preparation, special recreation programs being offered, etc.	City manager, Departments of Finance and Administration	Continuous
Try to increase the efficiency and smooth the operations of the Parks and Recreation Department.	That the city try to establish a yearly calendar of projects and activities that will require additional time of the operating departments.	City manager	July 1
	That the city annually review upcoming special projects and prepare a calendar for all departments. Examples would be budget deadlines, issue paper projects, employee survey projects, citizen survey.		

Figure C.14. Work-Unit Action plan format.

DEPARTMENT OF PARKS AND RECREATION: ACTION PLAN

OBJECTIVE: *Improve Communications*

Goal	Subject Area	Proposed by	Proposed Department Action	Schedule
1. Make both full-time and part-time recreation personnel aware of goals and objectives of the department as well as other matters affecting them.	Concerned employees wish to be more aware of what is going on in the department. This includes changes that will be made, programs that will be implemented, capital construction, as well as other changes. These individuals have face-to-face contact with the public, and it would be beneficial for them to be aware of plans for the department.	Sports, N. Playgrounds and Teens, S. Playgrounds and Teens, Comm. Center, P & R Management, Rec. Assistants, Building Maintenance, Golf Course, Street Trees, Clerical, S. Park Maintenance	Department director will meet with all work units at least 4 times a year. This can be done at a specially arranged meeting or at a regular staff meeting. Director to visit all park sites on an informal basis at least 2 times a year.	Immediately
2. That policies, procedures, and other information affecting employees be made available to them on a regular and continuous basis.	Employees would like to be better informed on programs operated by the department and the city, as well as be aware of changing policies by personnel and finance.	Sports, N. Playgrounds and Teens, Comm. Center, P & R Management, Street Trees, S. Park Maintenance	The city manager's office and Department of Administration and Finance provide a system of keeping employees better informed regarding matters affecting them. Expand information in paychecks, newsletter.	July 1976

| 3. Increase management's awareness and appreciation of programs offered by the Recreation Division. | That the city manager as well as the city council visit programs and functions of the Recreation Division on a more regular basis, some of these visits to be on an informal basis where staff could communicate with them on a one-to-one basis. | Comm. Center, P & R Management | The department director will inform the city manager of specific programs. | Immediately |
| 4. More feedback be given to all personnel within the department. | Employees, in general, feel that they would like more feedback relative to programs and activities they are responsible for that are done well. At the same time they are interested in knowing what corrective action should be taken in a more formal, regular, ongoing basis. | Sports, P & R Management, Golf Course | The department director, recreation supervisors, and city manager should commend employees verbally as well as in writing for outstanding efforts. | Immediately |

Figure C.15. Department action plan.

Actions called for by the Department of Park and Recreation, that were outside its control were referred to the appropriate other city department for action. Suggestions affecting the entire organization (like revising the oral boards for job interviews) were referred to the city manager for action. Suggestions in the area of employee committees (like adding part-time employees to committees) were referred to those committees for discussion. All negotiable items (e.g., wages and benefits) were referred to the meet-and-confer sessions scheduled to be held the following year.

All recommendations were analyzed and approved or disapproved. If approved, actions were scheduled for implementation and evaluation; if disapproved, employees were given an explanation as to why no action would be taken. The city manager met with each work unit to discuss action plans and his disposition on citywide recommendations. Department directors sent memorandums to appropriate persons instructing them of action that needed to be taken as a result of action programs that they felt were appropriate. These actions were also indicated on the departmental action programs (see Figure C.16).

For the next 12 months, each department prepared bimonthly reports indicating which of the recommended actions had been implemented or evaluated. The city manager reviewed the reports to see what had been accomplished and if the desired effect had been achieved. Copies of each department's reports were posted in that department so employees could monitor the progress of their suggestions throughout the year. Every other month progress reports were sent to all employees by each department director. Outstanding achievements were posted in the biweekly employee newsletter. Figure C.17 is an example of one page of the bimonthly report.

Efforts to improve each work unit as well as overall department improvement began with the initial employee interviews and continued for a year following the project. The work-unit planning discussions was also continued, which generated new action plans for future work unit and departmental improvement. The TPM project has made managers more aware of employee concerns (e.g., communication) and employees more aware of managers' concerns (e.g., productivity). Managers and employees are more aware of how their concerns affect the organization. These and other benefits occurred even before managers and employees developed action plans.

After hearing the results of the employee interviews, the city manager initiated a committee of managers and temporary employees to analyze benefits for temporary employees; the personnel office began the process of eliminating "junior" from employee titles, and all managers held briefing sessions with their employees. The Recreation Division established five additional full-time positions.

During the initial gathering of productivity data, the city changed its method of measuring productivity in the budget. These changes improved Sunnyvale's Planning, Programming, and Budgeting System and will be ongoing.

CITY OF SUNNYVALE
CALIFORNIA
May 27, 1976

To: Recreation Supervisors

From: Director of Parks and Recreation

Subject: Employee Survey--Action Goal #6, Increase Organizational
Effectiveness

One of the action goals was for each of you to establish
goals and objectives for each work site or each person
in charge of a work site. This would be the basis upon
which to evaluate them at the end of a program or other
specific time period, as determined by you and them.
This project could get too entailed so it would be my
suggestion that we establish 8 to 10 specific goals and
objectives at each area that could be incorporated into
the leader's evaluation. I would suggest you experiment
with this process and we will evaluate it at the end of
the summer.

John G. Williams
Director of Parks & Recreation

JGW/dh

GP-816

Figure C.16.   Memorandum for action as called for by departmental action plan.

CITY OF SUNNYVALE
CALIFORNIA
July 21, 1977

	City Manager
	Assistant City Manager
To:	All Parks and Recreation Department Employees
From:	Director of Parks and Recreation
Subject:	Status Report of TPM

Following is an update of the TPM Project on actions taken during the past 6 months. Anyone having specific questions regarding any of the actions may feel free to contact me directly.

Number of departmental actions	48
Number of actions initiated to date	48
Number of actions completed/continuing	42
Number of actions not complete	6

IMPROVE HUMAN RELATIONS AND SUPERVISORY PRACTICES

Goal 1. Improve supervisory practices in working with employees.

Status: During the month of May I conducted a Supervisors' Training Program with several Parks Division Supervisors. In addition, a second session was held for all management personnel on Effective Discipline Procedures, to follow up the session offered at the Asilomar Conference. The job rotation of 2 supervisors in the department gave a broader insight into department procedures and appeared to improve departmental relationships. Several supervisors have signed up for a Supervisors and Management Training Session during the month of July.

Goal 2. Supervisors to be better informed of specific work activities performed by employees.

Status: Supervisors have been encouraged to spend more time becoming familiar with the specific activities and assignments of employees. I have checked on a number of occasions and specific times are being scheduled for meetings to accomplish this goal.

IMPROVE COMMUNICATIONS

Goal 1. Make full time and part time Recreation personnel aware of goals and objectives of the department as well as other matters affecting them.

Status: As Director I have continued to meet with Recreation units to keep them posted on activities and projects within the department. A Teamwork Workshop was offered to all Recreation personnel during the month of November. A second Teamwork Workshop was offered during the month of April. Bob Wilson and I have completed meeting with all Park Division personnel at a lunch meeting to answer specific questions and review status of department projects and operations. We are starting a second round of meeting with the Parks crews, at coffee, with the same intention.

Figure C.17.   Sample of bimonthly report to employees.

Sunnyvale's employee survey project improved city services and provides useful information to other organizations interested in TPM. The city learned that (1) employee attitudes do affect performance, (2) competent management and high productivity (in terms of quality and quantity) are welcomed by employees, and (3) performance is a combination of many diverse elements. Performance measurement needs to be comprehensive if it is to be a viable management tool in a changing organization.

After the department action plans are reviewed and the project is discussed at the end of the first (1977) year, the city will be able to assess the impact of the recommendations on the organization's performance. The need for readministering any part or all of the survey to selected groups can be determined at that time. The impact of the TPM process in Sunnyvale's organizational performance will be reported in the 1978 issue of *Productivity Programs in the Federal Government,* an annual report to the President and the Congress published by the Joint Financial Management Improvement Program.

REACTIONS TO EMPLOYEE SURVEY

The general, reaction to the TPM project was favorable; it was a reasonable addition to the work of the City of Sunnyvale, done in a style familiar to the organization. As the survey data showed, management and employees view Sunnyvale as an innovative governmental organization and are accustomed to trying new ideas, the project's link to productivity improvement also related to the ongoing Planning, Programming, Budgeting System and the performance auditing procedures. The citizen survey component was no surprise since it consisted solely of the citizen survey done in November 1974. The process of meeting in work groups to solve problems was familiar to managers and to some employees. The purpose and process of the project were generally compatible with City of Sunnyvale employee expectations.

Citizens and unions were essentially uninvolved in the project; unionized employees participated in the process, but union leadership was not officially involved in the project. The news media reported the project to citizens at the initial release of survey and productivity data. The only other public discussion of the project was when the city council approved the expenditure of funds and the acceptance of the federal grant for the project at their regular public meeting.

The reaction of managers and employees involved in the project is summarized in the following discussion of the five stages of the project.

Phase 1: Initial Orientation, and Interviews (August 1975)

The initial orientation involved the consultants, the city manager, all eight department directors, and the project coordinator. The manager's interest and commitment to the project was clear from the outset. Department directors asked about the employee survey; some expressed reservations about raising employee expectations they might not be able to fulfill. From other questions asked at the meeting, it seemed that the method of integrating citizen survey, employee survey and productivity data was the least clear of the concepts explained.

Directors were cooperative in supplying productivity data requested, even when it meant reviewing records for data not regularly reported. Managers viewed refinement of productivity data as a way to improve the existing Planning, Programming, Budgeting System.

The first contact employees had with the project was during the group interviews with the consultant. Employees were very interested in the interviews and willing to talk candidly about their perception of their work environment. Initially, both employees and managers were interested in the project and saw its potential benefits.

Phase 2: Management Training and Employee Orientation (October 1975)

The momentum of the initial contact with the city was regenerated when the consultant firm returned with the results of the initial interviews. At the management workshop in Asilomar, managers spent two days reviewing the interview results and the project's concept, objectives, and timetable. Managers recommended changes in the process, notably the inclusion of some temporary employees in the survey process. Managers also recommended immediate action on some citywide employee complaints (e.g., elimination of "junior" titles) and initiated a committee to explore the more complicated issue of benefits for temporary employees.

Besides citywide issues, managers also took action on some departmental concerns. Managers in departments receiving the most criticism began corrective action immediately. For example, managers in the library began weekly meetings to discuss problems and work toward solutions. In all departments, managers met with employees after the Asilomar session to discuss the project and the concerns expressed in employee interviews and the management workshop.

MAC, the representative group of employees, discussed issues with the city manager and recommended the best ways to involve employees in the TPM project. MAC became the employee advisory committee for the entire project. The reaction at this stage of the project was again one of interest, anticipation of benefits, and willingness to take corrective action.

Phase 3: Questionnaire Administration (January 1976)

Members of MAC reported a high interest in the employee survey, which was verified by a 97 percent response rate. Many employees also wrote detailed comments to the survey questions.

From the later work in employee groups, facilitators thought that employees had not understood the TPM concept and the specific purpose of the survey at the time the questionnaire was administered. Even though managers had briefed employees in October, much had been forgotten by January.

Phase 4: Feedback of Results and Management Training (March 1976)

To prepare the employees for using the TPM data, the project coordinator held individual briefing sessions with each department director and MAC. In these meetings, managers and employees scheduled and developed the guidelines for the initial meetings in work units (employees and their immediate supervisor). Detailed descriptions of the project and how the data was going to be used were published in the biweekly employee newsletter and posted on employee bulletin boards.

At the suggestion of employees, a group of facilitators (managers from other departments who would meet with work units to facilitate discussion) were trained in conducting the initial meetings with employees and supervisors. The training for the entire management group began with the consultant firm presenting the results of the employee survey and productivity analysis one afternoon. The following day, managers and consultants met for training on interpreting and using the survey and productivity results and meeting with employees.

Managers felt that there was too much time between questionnaire administration and the feedback of results. The discussions and resource material from the Asilomar workshop had to be reviewed prior to the training session to achieve continuity. Despite the lag time, managers were very interested in employee survey results and productivity information and carefully analyzed their departments' data. There was a lot of material presented that could be introduced only at the training session. Some managers thought that more training spread over the time between survey administration and receiving of the results would have better prepared them for the employee meetings.

Phase 5: Employee Meetings (April 1976)

The general reaction to the employee meetings on survey results and productivity information was that this phase of the project was crucial: Getting to this point was what the project was all about. The development of action plans was the culmination of all the data collection and training. Employees and managers worked together to develop responsible suggestions for improvement. The organizational climate during the month of meetings was one of cooperative activity, anticipation, and in some cases uneasiness.

Specific comments by facilitators illustrate the general reaction to this phase of the project.

"Given the right environment, people will honestly talk about problems. Fairly sensitive topics have been openly discussed and I've also heard some brand new ideas in these sessions."

"They [employees] know exactly what they're angry about and they can articulate their problems very clearly, regardless of the level of their sophistication."

"Employees at first were a little afraid to meet with the supervisor because the group had not discussed issues together for a long time."

"At first, there was a lot of skepticism expressed about the commitment of the city manager, but they [employees] seemed impressed with the manager's making it clear that there was a lot of time, money, and commitment in the project and that he wanted something to come out of it."

"They [employees] feel very confident that their ideas are going to be looked at because managment has made them feel confident."

"One concern of the crews was 'where to get the time to go to all these meetings when my work is stacking up.'"

"Some supervisors were really unprepared for criticism. They didn't know about all these problems in the [work] unit. It's hard to take all that at once. As a facilitator, I asked the supervisor to prepare a reaction to questions regarding supervision to discuss at the next meeting. That seemed to ease the confrontation."

"In some cases, rapport with supervisor was a major plus. Their [employees'] immediate supervisor is their pal, the one that's trying to take care of them against these odd decisions that are coming at them from Mount Olympus."

"Some employees tried to direct everything toward meet-and-confer items. We told them they could discuss whatever they wanted to but that no changes could be made on those items until negotiation."

"In general, I thought employees were extremely responsible and ethical about the survey. They worked hard. Oh, some of the temporaries who haven't been here long and were mad about benefits just marked everything as really bad, but in the discussions I think they realized there were other things they liked or disliked. But something needs to be done with the temporaries or I lose my credibility as a department director."

"The need for this type of analysis on an ongoing basis is definitely clear. It delivers a clear blow for good management practice and against bureaucratic entrenchment."

"Overall, the groups that I had the opportunity to meet with, including my own division, felt that the process was a very valuable one and hope that they have the opportunity for future inputs."

"A great deal has already been accomplished in the area of departmental communications. From this standpoint alone, the process was worth the time and effort put into it. The employees welcomed the opportunity to discuss their problems in an objective manner with their supervisors."

"Employees are now waiting to see what happens from the department and the city."

PRODUCTIVITY MEASUREMENT

The third component of the Total Performance Measurement (TPM) process involved the selection and utilization of various productivity measurements and the establishment of criteria and/or standards against which to compare performance, goals, and standards; the latter is known as performance auditing. Productivity measurements assist the manager with decisions to be made in the future. The city of Sunnyvale has been involved in performance and service-quality measurement for several years. With the addition of citizen evaluation and needs assessment, along with data on employee attitudes and needs, a new dimension was added to productivity measurement that would affect both the efficiency and the effectiveness of the services delivered.

Productivity measures can also be useful in helping the manager determine the relationship of organizational inputs, or resources, and use of these inputs to the outputs that might be produced. Therefore productivity measurements serve two important functions: (1) They allow managers to gauge work unit performance against an absolute standard and (2) provide measurements to show managers the relationship between the expenditure of resources and the services that are created.

As an example of the first function, a park maintenance department may establish a set of work procedures that represent the ideal standard of acceptable performance expected of its employees. It is important to recognize that the TPM system calls for employee involvement in the development of work standards. They should not be seen as being rigid or inflexible; rather, they should be mutually determined.

The second function involves the determination of work units, program costs, and the cost of other intangibles. For the manager to make effective decisions, she/he must know the actual costs of each function or operation within her/his department. Knowledge of this type of data presents the manager with the opportunity to make decisions based on comparisons between activities based on cost. By breaking down the work of the city and departments into comparable units, the manager is able to look at these units with respect to cost and relate this to a number of other factors, including the number of participants served (quantitity) and/or the quality of their experience. Typically, this type of approach is thought of as a benefit analysis. It is important to note that productivity measurements must be quantifiable in terms of the goals and objectives of the city or department. This means that a city must be able to define exactly what it is trying to do and then relate it to a numerical scale that allows measurement.

Performance auditing places a new premium on economy of resources, innovation, and information. It examines what processes should be followed in setting and meeting standards.

PERFORMANCE AUDIT DEFINED

Performance auditing as defined in the 1972 *Standards for Audit of Governmental Organizations, Programs, Activities and Functions* contains the following elements:[1]

1. *Financial and legal compliance*—determines
    a. whether financial operations are properly conducted
    b. Whether the financial reports of an audited entity are presented fairly, and
    c. whether the entity has complied with applicable laws and regulations.
2. *Economy and efficiency*
    a. determines whether the entity is managing or utilizing its resources (personnel, property, space, etc.) in an economical and efficient manner and
    b. identifies the causes of any inefficiencies or uneconomical practices (including inadequacies in management information systems, administrative procedures, or organizational structure).
3. *Program results*—determines
    a. whether the desired results or benefits are being achieved,
    b. whether the objectives established by the legislature or other authorizing body are being met, and
    c. whether the agency has considered alternatives that might yield desired results at a lower cost.

SUNNYVALE'S INVOLVEMENT

There were three reasons why Sunnyvale tried the performance audit: (1) to pretest national standards for local government, (2) to better define goals and measure progress toward meeting these goals, and (3) to improve the performance, productivity, and quality of municipal services.

As to the first reason, Sunnyvale decided to experiment with performance auditing to test the standards proposed by the General Accounting Office (GAO) in *Standards for Audit*. Sunnyvale had worked with the International City Management Association (ICMA) in examining national standards and their implications for federal-city relationships, intracity comparisons, and accountability to citizens. When ICMA and GAO decided to run pilot projects in several cities, Sunnyvale saw a way to test the standards and develop a workable way of applying them.

---

[1] *Standards for Audit of Governmental Organizations, Programs, Activities and Functions*; By the Comptroller General of the United States; U.S. General Accounting Office, 1972, Washington, D.C. p. 2.

As to the second reason, Sunnyvale saw performance auditing as an essential step in a goals-setting process. Goals and effectiveness measures are prerequisites for performance auditing.

As to the third reason, setting meaningful, measurable objectives is a basic element of improving the performance, productivity, and quality of municipal services. Measuring productivity is not the same as improving it, but it is a necessary first step.

Sunnyvale is accustomed to financial and legal audits; they are an inherent part of municipal operation. Sunnyvale's project was built on seven years' experience with computer-based management information systems and a comprehensive, operational Program, Planning, Budgeting System. Since 1970 Sunnyvale has also worked to define and measure economy and efficiency. Sunnyvale has an eight-year program budget with unit costs, quality goals (effectiveness measures), and a production plan determined for each program.

Sunnyvale's weakest suit of the three necessary for performance auditing was measuring program results, the other two being financial compliance and economic efficiency. The impact of governmental services on the community is not known. The clientele for services is not clearly indentified. Goals are frequently not measured or measurable. Performance auditing focuses on these problems.

Sunnyvale has benefited from the project and the audit guide. Goals are better defined, effectiveness measures make more sense, and information systems are sharper. Many areas needing more information and better or different sources of information are identified. The methodology is useful and is being used.

Quantifiable goals for each department were established as a result of the performance audit program in the Public Safety Department and were an official part of the city council's resources allocation plan for 1975–76. Program managers worked together to improve goals that were incorporated into the resource allocation plan for fiscal year 1976–77. Progress toward meeting those goals is monitored and entered in the Electronic Data Processing (EDP) information system and staff audits of performance every 28 days. Managers review progress toward meeting goals with the employees they supervise. The performance audit methodology is being used for management and control.

Sunnyvale realized that the determination of goals is crucial to performance auditing. To augment the goal-setting process by involving citizens, the performance audit project was linked to a citizen survey project. The citizen survey covered all city services and was designed to get citizen opinion of the quality and importance of city services. It also tested service options so that people could state their goals for new services.

The performance audit concept has also changed the employee evaluation. An employee achievement plan followed by an employee plan audit is the basis for evaluating employee performance. Program goals are discussed in terms of the individual employee's responsibility in meeting them. The employee and supervisor work together to formulate the employee audit plan, as well as modify existing ones. During the next few years, Sunnyvale hopes to further refine a performance audit system.

REACTIONS AND ASSESSMENTS

Performance auditing requires careful thinking. It is not so much a check on the past as a way of planning for the future. It is more analysis than audit and, as such, requires examinations of alternatives and options. Sunnyvale's experience shows that performance auditing is still in the pioneering phase. Few norms exist for city services, and much training is needed in the goal-setting process. Sunnyvale is exploring the relationship of performance auditing to flexibility in policy analysis. Once goals are committed to paper, they must still be responsive to changing conditions.

Even at the developmental stage, however, performance auditing is useful. The process helps to refine existing goals and effectiveness measures and to develop new ones. Performance auditing is a good basis for resource allocation. It defines responsibilities so that the budget is a stronger planning and control document. It also identifies strengths and weaknesses in the information system. The concept and methodology of performance auditing is sound. Performance auditing is one way to determine productivity, innovation, and impact. Performance auditing is not an extra frill tacked on to a governmental operation; it involves the substance of the organization.

But much remains to be done, particularly in the development of standards. It will take more training of personnel, better information systems, and improved goal-setting processes to fully utilize performance auditing. The next steps Sunnyvale is taking are in that direction.

DATA INTEGRATION

The final step in the Total Performance Measurement process is the total integration of all data into a unified , comprehensive system of management. Citizen survey information, employee survey information, and performance measurement data are combined in order to target areas that need to be changed or adjusted. It is at this point that the manager makes decisions and redirects or rechannels the work of the organization. With the data provided, the system gives the manager the opportunity to make corrective actions and thereby increase the organization's effectiveness.

Figure C.18 depicts the process of integration in a systems framework. As indicated in the diagram, the first step is the diagnosis of problems and needs within the organization through utilization of the three components of performance measurement.

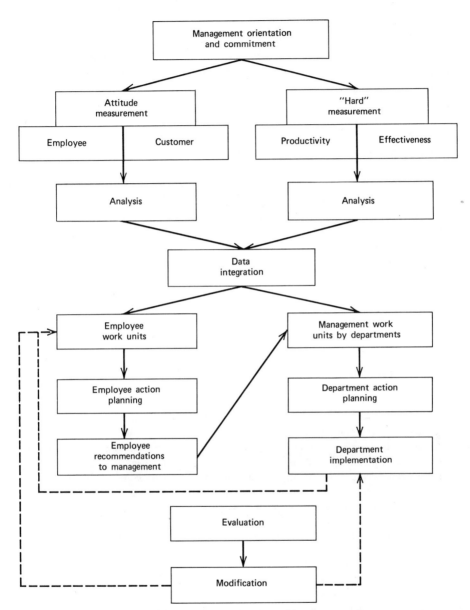

Figure C.18. Total performance measurement and implementation.

The next step is to identify solutions to these problems and/or ways of meeting employee and citizen needs. There are two sets of solutions that can be utilized to solve organizational problems. The first set of solutions are known as "structural solutions." These involve such actions as changing the organizational structure, redesigning work loads and jobs, and improving the physical setting within which individuals work. The second set of solutions deal directly with individuals and are known as "human solutions." Opportunities to increase productivity might focus on the training and development of staff, better selection and placement methods, and the creation of a work environment that allows for employee motivation.

The third step in the process is the measurement of performance results. And, lastly, this total systems approach includes a feedback mechanism that allows the process to recycle itself on a continuous basis; that is, performance is measured, problems are identified, solutions are sought, and performance is remeasured. In this way, the organization is able to continuously measure changes in the needs and attitudes of employees and citizens.

SUMMARY

Sunnyvale has benefited from the Total Performance Measurement (TPM) project. The experience has provided the following lessons:

1. The concept of multiple performance measures is useful in improving existing measurement systems and developing new ones.
2. A focus for the project is necessary to make it manageable. That focus can be a particular measure (e.g., productivity data, citizen satisfaction data, or employee attitude data) or a selected activity for which all three measures will be developed.
3. The amount of time, resources, and energy necessary to successfully complete the project requires substantial commitment from the chief executive and the entire management group. That commitment needs to be demonstrated to employees.
4. Employee involvement in the TPM process increases the potential benefits to the organization and is facilitated by an ongoing communication process between managers and employees.
5. Clarity in survey administration increases the credibility of survey results.
6. The quality and completeness of the survey results affect the scope of subsequent discussions and the credibility of the process.
7. Differences in the types of data, familiarity of data by employees, and time frame for the collection of data affect their use.
8. Continuous training including all managers and as many employees as feasible, increases the benefits of TPM.
9. Facilitators can make group discussions easier and can assist in designing and evaluating employee meetings.
10. Employee meetings are the source of organizational improvements; employee involvement in the analysis of survey results is possible and better fits with the "bottom-up"

approach described in the TPM process; and employee meetings are more beneficial when focused on action plans.

11. Action plans are clearer and more beneficial when they incorporate goals, recommended actions, responsibility, and methods for evaluation. Progress on implementing action plan needs to be monitored and reported to employees.

12. Successful project management requires clear organizational objectives, plans for project development, implementation and evaluation, and an on-site coordinator in charge of the project.

Sunnyvale's pilot project improved city services and provided useful information to other governmental organizations interested in TPM. Perhaps the greatest lessons of the TPM project are the following: (1) Employee attitudes *do* affect performance. (2) Competent management and high productivity (in terms of quantity and quality) are *welcomed* by employees. (3) Performance is a combination of many diverse elements; performance measurement needs to be more comprehensive if it is to be a viable management tool in improving governmental services.

Appendix D
Organizing a Leisure
Service: "Art in the Park,"
A Case Study

This appendix traces the organization and implementation of a leisure service activity—"Art in the Park"—from its initial stages of development to its completion. The period covered runs from January 1972 until June 1972. Organized under the auspices of the Wooster (Ohio) Park and Recreation Department, this activity combined the efforts and resources of the department with a community service group, the Welcome Wagon Club. The initial stimulus for the program emerged in January; an effort to expand the department's summer activities, particularly in the area of special events. In addition, the department was concerned with providing opportunities for family-oriented recreation, structured in such a manner as to be easily accessible to the family as a whole.

The undertaking was viewed by the staff of the department as one that would require considerable assistance from voluntary human resources. Therefore it was decided to approach a community service club to cosponsor the event. The assistance of the Welcome Wagon Club was solicited in late January, and a meeting was arranged with their Ways and Means Committee to discuss the project in early February. A general agreement was reached between the department and the Welcome Wagon Club that the department would essentially be responsible for all costs incurred in the organization and implementation of the project and would provide physical facilities. The Welcome Wagon Club would assume all responsibility for organizing, promoting, and implementing the activity under the direction and with the approval of the Director of Parks and Recreation. An excerpt from the minutes of the Ways and Means Committee, February 10, follows:

A. Art in the Park approved as the Ways and Means project for six months.
B. Park and date were not agreed on.
C. Three committees were organized.
   1. Artists' entries and demonstrations.
   2. Publicity and entertainment.
   3. Refreshments.

D. It was recommended that we have a children's workshop.
E. It was recommended that we have a children's art exhibit.
F. Artist entry fee was discussed, but not agreed on. The original sum mentioned was $10.
G. It was decided to limit the show to fine art.
   1. To avoid competition with the Arts and Crafts Show and
   2. To avoid "junk," as the show will not be prejudged
H. It was decided to allow demonstrations of arts and crafts, the demonstrators being allowed to sell also.
I. It was decided to have a bake sale (later vetoed).
J. It was agreed to have entertainment.
K. It was decided not to have a raffle (later agreed on).

One week later, the Ways and Means Committee's management group for "Art in the Park" met with the director of Parks and Recreation to delineate the specifics of the activity. It was decided that the activity would take place at Christmas Run Park, on the bank of a lovely pond surrounded by hillsides and trees, from 11:00 A.M. to 6:00 P.M., on June 11, 1972. The park was selected because it was located in the center of the community, easily accessible to major transportation throughfares. Further, it was chosen because of its close proximity to the churches located in its community. Because this activity was planned for a Sunday, it was thought that it would be convenient for people leaving church to go directly to the event. A price for artist's entry was set, as was an admission fee. The admission fee was set at $.25 and was established as a donation, rather than a requirement for admission. Artist entry fees were also kept low as a method of encouraging artists to participate in this first-time event. It was also proposed that a logo be designed to coordinate the event's promotional activities. In addition, the events that were to take place on the day of the activity were finalized at about this same time. It was decided that there would be an art exhibit, craft demonstrations, entertainment, food and beverages, a raffle, a children's art exhibit selected competitively from area schools. Committees were formed to organize and implement these activities, including the following: artists' entries, admission, artist assistance, publicity, play-area supervision, children's exhibit, children's workshop, entertainment, physical/set-up, refreshments, parking, and craft demonstrations.

On March 13, the project was presented by the Director of Parks and Recreation to the Parks and Recreation Board for its approval. The goal of the program was to provide an opportunity for professional and amateur artists to exhibit and sell their artwork and to offer an enjoyable afternoon for area citizens. The event was enthusiastically received by the board and unanimously accepted, along with other projected summer activities.

Early in April a card file was established on the area artists, through researching art associations, craft associations, and personal contact with known indi-

ART IN THE PARK

Purpose: To provide an opportunity for professional and amateur artists of Wayne and adjoining counties to exhibit and sell their artwork and to offer an enjoyable afternoon for area citizens.

Place: Christmas Run (City) Park, located on Blessing Avenue in Wooster.

Date: Sunday, June 11, 1972, 11:00 A.M. to 6:00 P.M.

Alternate: Sunday, June 18, 1972, 11:00 A.M. to 6:00 P.M.

Fee: General exhibitor fee is $4.00,
Student exhibitor fee is $2.00
    (no commission).

Exhibits: Spaces will be available to exhibit the following:
All hanging paintings or drawings, water colors, collages, etc.
Sculpture.
(All work must be original.)

Regulations: Regulations regarding set-up schedule, hanging, price tags, and so on, will be included in an information bulletin that will be sent to all enrolled artists.
There will be no prejudging.

Liability: The Welcome Wagon Club and the Wooster Parks and Recreation Department will not be responsible for loss, theft, or damage to the artworks exhibited.

Entry Deadline: May 26, 1972.

Registration: Send the completed attached entry form, with check or money order made payable to *Welcome Wagon,* to:

Mrs. Joseph Biafore
"Art in the Park"
550 Morgan
Wooster, Ohio 44691

Information: For additional information call: 262-6155

Figure D.1.

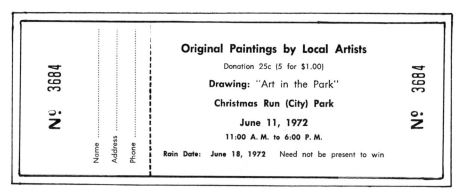

Figure D.2.   Raffle ticket—"Art in the Park."

vidual artists. A general bulletin describing the event, including an entry form, was then sent to all artists listed in the card file. The information contained in this mailing is found in Figure D.1. At this time, raffle tickets and fliers were printed for distribution (Figure D.2 and D.3). The raffle was conceived as a method of drawing more attention to the activity throughout the community. The paintings for the raffle were donated by two leading area artists. Fliers were produced and distributed while selling the raffle tickets and were also distributed later in schools, through community groups, and were placed in grocery bags at all leading supermarkets in the area.

In addition, other promotional activities were begun in the media. CATV, a cable television station in Wooster, was contacted, and future spots concerning the activity were arranged. WWST radio station was also approached, and it agreed to pretape several promotional spots to run on the station beginning about two weeks prior to the onset of the activity. Lastly, the *Wooster Daily Record*, the one local area newspaper, was asked to do a series on area artists whose work would be appearing in the art show and entertainers who would be performing. The *Record* was most obliging and dispatched reporters to cover these stories. Toward the middle of April, a letter was sent to all community groups announcing "Art in the Park" (see Figure D.4).

Also this month, the Welcome Wagon Club, during its regularly scheduled meeting, briefed the larger club membership about the event, organized the group into work groups, distributed raffle tickets and fliers to be, in turn, distributed by the members. The appropriate members and chairperson began contacting local entertainment groups and artisans who would be willing to demonstrate their crafts. These individuals were approached with the request that they donate their time and talents for a worthy community activity.

May was an extremely busy month. Many promotional activities were implemented. A schedule was established to speak at area service clubs to promote the

EXHIBITION AND SALE OF FINE ART:

Christmas Run (City) Park
Blessing Ave., Wooster
Sun , June 11, 1972
11 A.M. – 6 P.M.

Drawing
Bake Sale
Box Lunches
Entertainment
Children's Exhibit
Children's Workshop
Craft Demonstrations

Sponsored by
The Welcome Wagon Club
and
The Wooster Parks and Recreation Department

Donation 25¢
(Children free)

Raindate: June 18

Figure D.3. Flier—"Art in the Park."

Figure 9.

CITY OF WOOSTER · DEPARTMENT OF PARKS AND RECREATION
400 HILLSIDE DRIVE · WOOSTER, OHIO 44691 · (216)345-7400

August 17, 1972

Dear Friend:

June 11, the Welcome Wagon Club of Wooster and the Wooster Parks and Recreation Department will sponsor an exciting event: "Art in the Park." This project, a first for Wooster, will focus on the exhibition and sale of fine art in Christmas Run (City) Park.

In that this is a new event in our community, we would appreciate an opportunity to visit your group in May, and give a brief synopsis of the activities that will be offered. This presentation would not consume more than a few minutes of your meeting time.

Promotion for this event will include a drawing June 11, whereby selected participants will receive paintings by well known area artists. Tickets for this drawing will be sold (a donation to the Welcome Wagon Club) by Welcome Wagon members prior to "Art in the Park." If agreeable to your group, our representative would like to offer these tickets for sale to your membership.

"Art in the Park" is a stimulating project, which we believe will excite the enthusiasm and support of your members.

Sincerely,

Susan Edginton

Susan Edginton
Welcome Wagon Club
Ways and Means Co-Chairman

R.S.V.P.: 262-4306

STAFF

CHRISTOPHER EDGINTON	ROBERT LANG	CLARENCE MOSHER	MARGARET POLLOCK
Director of *Parks and Recreation*	*Superintendent* *of Recreation*	*Superintendent* *of Parks*	*Program Supervisor* *of Senior Citizens*

Figure D.4.   Letter sent to announce "Art in the Park."

event, distribute fliers, sell raffle tickets, and showing the donated paintings. The *Wooster Daily Record* ran its first article concerning the event on Saturday, May 6.

She'll Display Paintings, Sculpture

Mrs. Hulswitt Is One of Artists Participating in Art in the Park

Newcomer, Mrs. C. E. (Norma) Hulswitt, will be displaying works of sculpture and paintings at the Art In The Park show on June 11. This artist moved here from Parma only six weeks ago.

She was an evening student at Cleveland Institute of Art for several years and studied with Bob Backston and David Giogi. Mrs. Hulswitt is a member of Studio West, a group of Cleveland artists which meet weekly for life drawing. The group will exhibit during the month of June at the Center Gallery in Parmatown Shopping Center.

This artist is currently exhibiting paintings and sculpture at the Baycrafter spring show at Higbee's in Cleveland. The show ends May 26.

In the past few years Mrs. Hulswitt has done water colors on location in Lakeside, the Virgin Islands and industrial areas of Cleveland. In addition, she has done farms and old houses in the outskirts of the Cleveland area.

She works in water colors, acrylics, oils, and sculpture materials such as concrete, clay, plaster, wood, plastics, and soapstone.

As a hobby Mrs. Hulswitt does rock polishing and collects rocks whenever she is travelling.

Welcome Wagon Club is sponsor of the show which will be open from 11 A.M.–6 P.M. in Christmas Run Park. The public is invited to attend.[1]

On May 9 the Welcome Wagon held its regularly scheduled meeting. Fliers and raffle tickets were redistributed to the membership. The sign-up sheet was again passed around to solicit assistance for the various functions on the day of the event. Approximately 80 individuals from the Welcome Wagon Club volunteered to assist in the implementation of this activity. The planned activity was broad enough in scope to necessitate the use of this many volunteers.

During the next week, posters were printed professionally and distributed to area merchants and schools for window or counter display. Large billboards were also prepared; they were ultimately placed in two key locations in the city, where they would have the greatest impact (Figure D.5). The entertainment was finalized during this time period—six groups, ranging from country and western to gospel jazz to rock, donated their services. Persons willing to provide all-day craft demonstrations were also finalized at this time, including individuals

[1] *Wooster Daily Record*, Wooster, Ohio, May 1972.

Figure D.5.   Billboard—"Art in the Park."

involved in woodworking, jewelry making, and pottery making. Two feature stories concerning one of the entertainment groups and one of the craftsmen appeared in the *Daily Record.*

Country Swingers Will Perform at Art in the Park

R. D. Stahl and the Country Swingers will provide country and western music at Art in the Park on Sunday. Most of the eleven-member group are native Woosterians, and four of the members have been associated with the group for over 25 years.

The Country Swingers frequently entertain at local gatherings. They have performed at the Wayne County Fairgrounds, various area schools and, as members of the "Country and Western Music Association of America," they periodically perform at Huntsinger Park in Mansfield. Most recently, the group appeared in Canal Fulton.

PLAYED OVER FORTY YEARS

Richard (Rich) Stahl plays violin and mandolin with the group. He has been playing these instruments for more than 40 years. Bill Drouhard, who plays lead guitar, has also had much experience in music; he has played for 25 years. Paul Suttle, 30, has played the banjo since he was ten years old. Sally and Wendell Haven are a husband

and wife team within the group. Wendell plays bass guitar and Sally plays guitar and sings. A family trio includes J. Douglas Mossir and his sons. Mr. Morris plays guitar and sings. His sons Todd, age 7, and Curt, aged 10, play guitar and mandolin, respectively. Other group members are Donald Gain, on guitar; Vendall Morris, a singer with the group, and Clem Bratcher, who sings and plays guitar.

ONE OF SIX GROUPS

The Country Swingers group is one of six groups which will be performing on Sunday at Art in the Park, Christmas Run (City) Park. Also featured will be The Gospel Chorus, directed by Mrs. Darwin Saunders; John Schmidt of the Green Tin; Rasheva; Kitty, Bud, and Barry, and the 20-voice Chippewa Valley Chapter Chorus.

Art in the Park, to be held from 11 A.M.–6 P.M., will include fine arts exhibits, arts and crafts demonstrations, as well as children's exhibit and workshop. It is cosponsored by Welcome Wagon Club and Wooster Department of Parks and Recreation. The event is open to the public.[2]

College Student Designs Wedding Rings Tim McCreigth's Work Will be Among Crafts Displayed at Art Show in Park

by Marrlys Victor

The wedding rings blessed today at the altar for the wedding of Kathy Vincent and John Ferris were originals designed for them by College of Wooster student, Tim McCreight.

The designs cast in the silver bands by Tim represent the couple's feelings about each other and the world in which they live. In one panel is the mandla, a type of cross which Tim says is "a Christian symbol of God's radiating love."

In another panel are the figures of a man and woman clasping hands with a child between them. This represents the couple's work with handicapped children. John is a speech therapist at Apple Creek State Institute and Kathy is in special education classes.

DEPICTS ECOLOGY CONCERN

The panel with a bird, fish and tree depicts their concern for ecology. The symbols of the anchor of hope and the tree of life are combined in one design and the marriage symbol, intertwined rings with a cross and candles is in another. Tim used dental instruments to carve designs in the wax model.

Tim, who says, "I made our wedding rings," is a self-taught silver craftsman and a sculpture major. As a freshman he decided to try working in silver and sent for $20 worth of equipment. His workshop was a table at the end of his bed.

Before long he was teaching classes at Lowery Center Craft Center and became

---

[2] *Wooster Daily Record*, Wooster, Ohio, May 1972.

Chairman of the Center. He has quit this now that is combining 40 hours of craft work with a full college schedule.

He has made rings for six or eight couples and did those for himself and his wife last year after he was given some amethysts. Then he says, "Friends wanted some like mine. I made them and they stopped back eight or nine months later. They looked horrible to me and I asked them to let me remake them." The couple was very satisfied with the originals but consented to let Tim redo the pair.

ORIGINAL WORK

Tim doesn't confine himself to any one type of jewelry. He does original necklaces, pendants, earrings or whatever anyone requests. There are no duplicates. Some of his pieces are constructed using silver or gold wire or sheets of metal. "Most people start this way," he notes. Other pieces are cast. "This involves molten metal," he explains, "and is a much more complicated process. Rings are made this way."

This craftsman has his shop, a very neat one, in an upstairs room in the couple's home at 217 College Avenue. His wife, Jay, was a student in his first class, "one of the more promising ones." Her interest didn't continue and she "won't come near the workshop," he laughs. Jay is a sociology major and, like Tim, a junior this year. She works in a local retail store.

Tim says that "silver was always a hobby," that he is creating items 40 hours a week and selling in local shops.

His work will be among crafts (one in each medium) demonstrated at "Art in the Park" which will be held Sunday, June 11. Other crafts demonstrated will be candle making, sculpturing, charcoal sketching, weaving and leather tooling. This is in addition to paintings by area artists, which will be a feature of the day. Wooster Parks and Recreation Department and Welcome Wagon Club will sponsor the festival from 11 A.M.–6 P.M. in Christmas Run Park. The public is invited.[3]

During the last days of May, the final arrangements for equipment (e.g., stage, PA system, and snow fencing on which to hang pictures) were made, as was the actual plan for set-up. Radio spots were recorded and began appearing on the local station. A final mailing to area artists was made. Arrangements were made to have the cover of the brochure for the activity printed (see Figure D.6). This was done free of charge at the Wayne County Vocational School. During this period of time, a Parks and Recreation Department summer brochure was distributed to over 4000 homes, with the following insert:

ART IN THE PARK

Be sure and look forward to the first annual outdoor exhibit co-sponsored by the Parks and Recreation Department and Welcome Wagon Club at Christmas Run Park, Sunday, June 11, 11:00 A.M.–6:00 P.M. Details concerning entry and other information will be available through the Daily Record and the Administrative Offices of the Parks and Recreation Department.

[3] *Wooster Daily Record*, Wooster, Ohio, May 1972.

Figure D.6. Brochure cover—"Art in the Park."

514

Three newspaper articles also appeared during this time, two more feature articles on artists and one article featuring the summer weekend activities of the Parks and Recreation Department.

Seventeen Year Old to Exhibit in Art in Park Show

by Kim Watkins

At 17 Mark Monahan will be the youngest exhibitor at the Art in the Park show in Christmas Run Park, Sunday, June 11. But young though he may be, Mark is no neophyte in the field of art.

As a child he was fond of doing pencil drawings. In 1967, encouraged by his mother and some neighbors, he joined an adult art class taught by Gertrude Ward at the Wooster YMCA. He still studies with Mrs. Ward who, together with instructors at school, has given him his formal training. In 1971 he exhibited five of his works at the Wayne County Fair and came away with five ribbons—four blues and a red.

Laughs Mark, "My mother thought the one thing that got the red ribbon was a little gloomy. It was a spring scene with a stormy sky, and it wasn't one of her favorites. But it sold."

Mark prefers working in acrylics, a plastics-based paint, rather than in oils, and uses slate, wood or Masonite in preference to canvas.

"I like to work in acrylics," he explains, "because it dries faster. To most people this fast drying is a drawback because it is difficult to blend colors—oil is much easier to blend. I guess I just like to be different."

His favorite subjects are landscapes and buildings, particularly old structures. In March the cover of a *Daily Record* supplement carried a color reproduction of one of his favorites, an acrylic on slate of Wooster's Todd house.

"My ideas come from the outside. I look around and see what there is—and I enjoy being outside when I work," he notes.

Mark, who also occasionally illustrates his own poetry, averages three to four hours a day for several days to complete a work. He will include 18 originals in the June 11 exhibit.

INTERESTED IN ANTIQUES

Another of Mark's interests is antiques—furniture, glassware, bottles. He has thought of going into the business of restoring antique furniture and is currently working on redoing 10 panels of an old organ for a couple who were in art class with him. He uses acrylics in renovating the original painted designing. "I'm going by the light outline where it remains and using my own imagination to fill in the colors and the details," he explains.

SOLD OVER 20 PIECES

The young artist has already sold over 20 of his works, the proceeds from which go to buy art supplies.

"I do some Italian manuscript style lettering," he adds, "but I do very, very few portraits. Only one amounted to anything but it's something I will do more of. Now it's hard for me. I've done some sculpture, too, but I find it hard to work on a surface that isn't flat."

Several months ago he began to work in pen and water color, and he is scheduled to do some sketching during the June 11th art show which will be open from 11 A.M.– 6 P.M.

With an art career in mind Mark, who is a junior at Triway High School, hopes to attend Columbus Institute of Art. He is the son of Mr. and Mrs. Laurence Monahan, 207 Valley View Drive, Wooster.[4]

Will Exhibit "New Things" as Well as Traditional Work
Fran Grande to be Among Artists at "Art in the Park"

by Kim Watkins

"I'm at the point in my work," says Wooster artist Fran Grande, "that I'm experimenting with new things." Miss Grande will exhibit some of these "new things" together with some of her more traditional work at the Art in the Park show to be held at Christmas Run (City Park), Wooster, Sunday, June 11, from 11 A.M.–6 P.M.

The young artist began her serious study in the field when she was just in fifth grade. One of her teachers at St. Mary's School spotted her talent and recommended that she enroll for summer school art classes to be held at the local high school.

BROAD ART PROGRAM

During the session, taught by Harry Hetman, she was exposed to a broad art program including work in block printing, ceramics and color experiments.

"I still have a notebook Mr. Hetman had us make listing everything we were doing. And I think I remember each day's activity because it was so exciting to me," she recalls.

During her high school years she also studied under the direction of Mrs. Joan Carpenter and William Spratley. It was Mrs. Carpenter who suggested that she take an art course at the College of Wooster.

With the help of Donald MacKenzie of the College's art department she enrolled in a drawing course taught by Sybil Gould during her senior year in high school. When she attended the College of Wooster, she continued her work with Miss Gould and also studied oil painting under the tutelage of George Olson.

---

[4] *Wooster Daily Record*, Wooster, Ohio, May 1972.

STUDIED IN ITALY

In the summer of 1970 a group of six students from the College spent four weeks studying the Italian language and culture in Perugia, halfway between Florence and Rome. There she also studied Etruscan art history with Emmanuella Fabricotti at the Universita Italiana per Stranieri de Pergula.

Miss Grande prefers drawing and sketching in charcoal and in pen and ink but also works in oils and acrylics. Recently she began embroidery on leather.

MORE MANEUVERABLE

"Embroidery," she explains, is basically like needlework and crewel, but I feel that it is more maneuverable. It's like painting a picture." At the moment she is working on an embroidered leather vest she hopes to exhibit.

She will include at least six paintings, two matted drawings and some of her embroidery in the June show.

"I LIKE PEOPLE"

"I'm a figure person basically—I like people—but I will be showing only one figure this time. All the rest are landscapes," she pointed out. Although this exhibit will be her first, she has sold a number of her works.

In addition to her other art work, she has done some commercial drawings for advertising for The Cherry Tree and has considered the possibility of a career in the field.

Miss Grande is the daughter of Mr. and Mrs. Francis A. Grande, 745 Pittsburgh Avenue, Wooster.

(Approximately 45 area artists will display their work at the show. Wooster artists Robert Carafelli, Gertrude Ward and Krista Roche have each donated a painting which will be awarded to visitors to the show).[5]

Summer Weekends Have Filled Schedule Here

The weekends will be filled with fun as the Wooster Parks and Recreation Department holds a special event almost every weekend during the summer.

Art in the Park will kick off the season June 11 at Christmas Run Park, co-sponsored by the Welcome Wagon Club and the Parks and Recreation Department. It will entail an all day exhibition of fine art and craft making. Mayor Roy Stype will serve as honorary head official on June 17, as "Stype's Stampede" is held at Christmas Run Park, the first country run of the year at 1 P.M.

The Great Balloon Race will be the big event for the first weekend of the 1972 Playground Program. Each child will receive a helium filled balloon and a card with his name on it to attach to the balloon, and at a given signal all balloons will be

[5] *Wooster Daily Record*, Wooster, Ohio, May 1972.

released. The person whose card is returned from the greatest distance will receive a prize.

The first annual Ted Evans Golf Classic will be June 25 at the College of Wooster golf course, entry blanks available at the Department of Parks and Recreation or the College golf course. Entry fee is $8.

OTHER FUN

A bike hike will highlight the weekend of July 1, as the police escorted group starts at Christmas Run park and travels completely around the City. The hike starts at 8 A.M.

Hall of Fame day will be July 29 when the Department will sponsor a trip to the Pro Football Hall of Fame. Buses will leave Freedlander Park at 11 A.M. and will return by 6 P.M. Fee is $3 for adults and $2.25 for children 13 and under.

The AAU Swim and Diving Meet will be the weekend of August 5.

The first annual table tennis tournament will be Saturday, August 12, at the Freedlander Park and entry fee is 50 cents. A water carnival at Christmas Run Park pool will close out the summer August 26.

Further information and registration for all programs is provided by the Parks and Recreation Department at the Freedlander Park offices.[6]

The final ten days prior to "Art in the Park" constituted a period of consolidation and coordination of the processes and people involved in the event. Some of the activities that took place during this period can be viewed through a portion of the Welcome Wagon schedule for organizing the activity.

By June 8:

1. Distribute fliers to area grocery stores.
2. Staple brochures together.
3. Collect children's artwork from the schools.
4. Remind all entertainers of the event, date, and time.
5. Begin making name tags for workers and name tags and place cards for artists.
6. Mimeograph artist's suggestion form.
7. Contact all Welcome Wagon members for support and to confirm work area and time schedule.
8. Make raffle-ticket box.

On June 10:

1. Prepare food area.
2. Buy food.
3. Put up snow-fence boundaries.
4. Put up stage for entertainment.
5. Install PA system for entertainment.

[6] *Wooster Daily Record*, Wooster, Ohio, May 1972.

6. Remove stumps for parking.
7. Transplant billboard at Reed Park to Christmas Run Park.
8. Organize Children's Workshop materials and blow up balloons.

Immediately prior to the activity, a number of promotional activities were undertaken. Perhaps one of the most effective was the distribution of fliers on the day before the event to all major area grocery stores. These fliers were placed in grocery bags by the store packers. In addition, television interviews were conducted, in which members of the Welcome Wagon Club and the Parks and Recreation Department discussed the activity and displayed the pictures to be given away at the show. A final article prior to the event was published in a special Saturday supplement—"Right Around Home"—the day before the event.

Outdoor Art Gallery in Christmas Run Park

by Chris Smith

Christmas Run Park will take on the look of an outdoor art gallery Saturday.

The Wooster Parks and Recreation Department and the Welcome Wagon Club are sponsoring the first annual "Art in the Park" from 11 A.M. to 6 P.M.

More than 600 works by some 50 area artists will be displayed on circles of snow fence near the park's pond. Many pieces will be sold.

The artwork includes oil and acrylic paintings, water colors, pen and ink drawings, batiks, lithographs, photographs, pastels, hangings and sculpture. Art by grade school children will also be on display.

A workshop where children can color and create collages will be directed by Pam Lang.

Artists will be working on sketches and paintings in the park, and Gertrude Ward will be available to sketch patrons.

A number of crafts will be demonstrated—candle making, tin work, jewelry making, wood working, weaving, macrame, stoneware, and pottery. Many of these items also will be for sale.

Music will accompany art in the park.

Among those performing will be Kitty, Bud and Barry, R. D. Stahl and the Country Swingers, John Schmidt, the Gospel Chorus from the Second Baptist Church, the Chippewa Valley Chapter Chorus (a barber shop group) and Rasheva.

Five artworks will be given away, including an oil painting donated by Gertrude Ward, two Robert Carafelli pen and ink drawings, and two water colors by Krista Roche.

Soft drinks, hot dogs, popcorn, and box lunches will be available. Picnic tables will be available.

Rita Biafore, one of the project's coordinators, said they are extremely pleased with the number of artists exhibiting.

"Besides local artists we've received entries from as far away as Painesville, Lakewood, and Bucyrus," Mrs. Biafore said. "While some art shows pick exhibitors, we opened the show to anyone who wanted to display their work.

Susan Edginton, another co-ordinator, said proceeds will go to Welcome Wagon and the Parks and Recreation Department.[7]

The day of the event, Welcome Wagon hostesses awaited the artists with coffee and donuts, name tags, and assistants to help the artists carry their works to the park and hang them. There were approximately 50 artists and over 600 pieces of work exhibited.

In addition to the art exhibit itself, there was a potpourri of other activities that were occuring simultaneously. Entertainment was provided every hour, on the hour, and received enthusiastic response. The children's art exhibit and workshop, called the "Tot Spot," was an extremely popular area. The children's exhibit attracted many parents and other relatives to view their children's work. The Tot Spot provided children with an opportunity to create their own world of art in pastels, crayon, or collage.

The craftsmen were demonstrating their respective skills during the course of the afternoon, and many artists chose to work on the spot—sketching, painting, and so on—which created a spontaneous festive atmosphere.

The *Daily Record* printed two follow-up stories on the activity the following day.

Over Four Thousand View Art in the Park

by Gene Schromen

They were "strolling through the park one day." Not in the merry month of May, but on a June day about which poets write. The strollers included over 4,000 men, women, and children.

These people visiting Christmas Run Park Sunday were truly strolling, for it was necessary to stroll to get the full benefit of Art in the Park, sponsored by City of Wooster's Department of Parks and Recreation and the Welcome Wagon club.

52 EXHIBITS

Fourty-six artists, both professional and amateur, from Wayne and adjoining counties exhibited their work, with many of them sketching through the show which lasted from 11 A.M.–6 P.M. Half a dozen crafts were displayed with demonstrations being given by some. Crafts included weaving and macrame, woodworking, pottery, candlemaking, stoneware, and silversmithing.

Over 500 paintings were exhibited, with snow fences snaking through the area beyond the pond to provide hanging space for the art work. Art media ranged from oils, watercolors, and pastels to charcoal. There were ink drawings, batik, acrylics on wood, slate and stone, polymer, oil in barnsiding, and lithographs.

Artists ranged from teenagers to older folks. One 14-year-old girl teamed up with

[7] *Wooster Daily Record*, Wooster, Ohio, May 1972.

her father to display paintings. One exhibitor is a member of Sunnyside Club and another is a resident of College Hills Retirement Village.

TOT SPOT

Added attraction at the show was a Tot Spot, a workshop for children where they could create their own "masterpieces" on the spot. Another feature geared to children was an exhibition of art work (approximately 78 pictures) done by children in the Wooster elementary schools. Art work by two children in each of the grades in the local schools had been chosen and placed on exhibit.

MUSICAL ENTERTAINMENT

During the afternoon entertainment was provided by five groups, including Kitty, Bud and Barry; R. D. Stahl and the Country Swingers; the Gospel Chorus; the Chippewa Valley Chapter Chorus; and Rasheva.

Paintings donated by Gertrude Ward, Krista Roche, and Robert Carafelli were awarded to Donna Bradford, Reed Tittle, Marla Franks, Pat Wanat and R. S. Wenger.

Food was available at the pavilion and picnic tables around the pond provided eating space.

Chairmen for Art in the Park included Chris Edginton, Director of Wooster Department of Parks and Recreation; Mrs. Joseph Biafore, Mrs. John Streeter, Mrs. Robert Lang, Mrs. Charles Bates, and Mrs. Susan Edington of Welcome Wagon Club. Mrs. Norman Swenson served as consultant.

Purpose of the exhibit was to provide artists an opportunity to exhibit and sell their art work, and to offer an enjoyable afternoon for area citizens.

The "first" for Wooster proved to have appeal for both artists and spectators.[8]

Wooster's Art in the Park Show is Successful

Sunday's Art in the Park, brainchild of Welcome Wagon and Wooster City Department of Parks and Recreation, succeeded in doing what it set out to do. It provided an opportunity for artists to exhibit and sell their art work and it offered an enjoyable afternoon for area residents.

Not only did the event provide individuals an opportunity to view painting in various media, see artists at work and watch demonstrations by craftsmen, but it provided features of interest to children.

More than 4,000 persons attended the event. Fifty-two persons had exhibits. Numerous musical groups performed.

Both the department and the club should be commended for the smooth-running venture—a first in the city. May we hope that the enthusiasm expressed by artists and viewers will give the sponsors the incentive to make Art in the Park an annual event.[9]

---

[8] *Wooster Daily Record*, Wooster, Ohio, June 1972.
[9] *Wooster Daily Record*, Wooster, Ohio, June 1972.

Following the event, thank-you letters were sent to each of the individuals who donated their time in the area of entertainment and craft demonstrations, the artists who donated paintings for the raffle, and all the participating artists. Also, an extensive evaluation of the program was conducted, including the review of written evaluations requested of all artists participating.

"Art in the Park" is basically an example of how to mount a large-scale activity with almost certain success by availing the Parks and Recreation Department of media support and the services of community groups. Although this activity is broad in scope, the principles that provide its backbone are applicable to any level of endeavor and for any type of activity. For example, the media in this community were most cooperative in promoting other activities of varying scope, and other community groups were enlisted to provide the organization and workers for various Parks and Recreation activities on a smaller scale (e.g., the annual Easter egg hunt).

Author Index

Subject Index